THE OXFORD ENCYCLOPEDIA OF

ECONOMIC HISTORY

THE OXFORD ENCYCLOPEDIA
OF
ECONOMIC
HISTORY

Joel Mokyr

Editor in Chief

VOLUME 5

Spices and Spice Trade

—

Zoos and Other Animal Parks

Index

OXFORD
UNIVERSITY PRESS
2003

OXFORD

UNIVERSITY PRESS

Oxford New York

Auckland   Bangkok   Buenos Aires   Cape Town   Chennai
Dar es Salaam   Delhi   Hong Kong   Istanbul   Karachi   Kolkata
Kuala Lumpur   Madrid   Melbourne   Mexico City   Mumbai   Nairobi
São Paulo   Shanghai   Taipei   Tokyo   Toronto

Copyright © 2003 by Oxford University Press, Inc.

Published by Oxford University Press, Inc.
198 Madison Avenue, New York, New York 10016
www. oup.com

Oxford is a registered trademark of Oxford University Press

Library of Congress Cataloging-in-Publication Data

The Oxford encyclopedia of economic history / Joel Mokyr, editor in chief.
p. cm.
Includes bibliographical references and index.
ISBN 0-19-510507-9 (set)
ISBN 0-19-517090-3 (v. 1: alk. paper)
ISBN 0-19-517091-1 (v. 2: alk. paper)
ISBN 0-19-517092-X (v. 3: alk. paper)
ISBN 0-19-517093-8 (v. 4: alk. paper)
ISBN 0-19-517094-6 (v. 5: alk. paper)
1. Economic history–Encyclopedias. I. Title: Encyclopedia of
economic history. II. Mokyr, Joel. III. Oxford University Press.
HC15 .O94 2003
330'.03–dc21

2003008992

1 3 5 7 9 8 6 4 2
Printed in the United States of America
on acid-free paper

Common Abbreviations Used in This Work

AD	*anno Domini*, in the year of the Lord
ASEAN	Association of Southeast Asian Nations
b.	born
BCE	before the common era (= BC)
c.	*circa*, about, approximately
CE	common era (= AD)
CEO	chief executive officer
cf.	*confer*, compare
d.	died; penny (pl., pence)
diss.	dissertation
EC	European Community
ed.	editor (pl., eds), edition
EEC	European Economic Community
EU	European Union
f.	and following (pl., ff.)
FAO	Food and Agriculture Organization
FDI	foreign direct investment
fl.	*floruit*, flourished
FTA	free trade area
GATT	General Agreement on Tariffs and Trade
GDP	gross domestic product
GNP	gross national product
G-10	Group of Ten industrialized countries
IMF	International Monetary Fund
ISI	import-substitution industrialization
l.	line (pl., ll.)
LDC	less developed country (pl., LDCs)
MDC	more developed country (pl., MDCs)
MFN	most-favored nation
MITI	Ministry of International Trade and Industry (Japan)
MNC	multinational company (pl., MNCs)
n.	note
NAFTA	North American Free Trade Association
NBER	National Bureau of Economic Research
n.d.	no date
NGO	nongovernmental organization
no.	number
n.p.	no place
n.s.	new series
OECD	Organization for Economic Cooperation and Development
OEEC	Organization for European Economic Cooperation
OPEC	Organization of Petroleum Exporting Countries
p.	page (pl., pp.)
pt.	part
r.	reigned
R&D	research and development
rev.	revised
s.	shilling
SEC	Securities and Exchange Commission (United States)
ser.	series
supp.	supplement
UNESCO	United Nations Educational, Scientific, and Cultural Organization
UNRRA	United Nations Relief and Rehabilitation Administration
USD	U.S. dollar(s)
USSR	Union of Soviet Socialist Republics
vol.	volume (pl., vols.)
WHO	World Health Organization
WIPO	World Intellectual Property Organization

THE OXFORD ENCYCLOPEDIA OF
ECONOMIC HISTORY

S

(CONTINUED)

SPICES AND SPICE TRADE. The import of Asian spices into Europe in the early modern period was not only a major economic enterprise but also the preeminent "glamour" trade of the time. These spices were mostly used as medicine and to flavor food. Different spices were believed to cure disorders of the stomach, the intestines, the head, and the chest, and were also used to aid digestion. The ages-old use of spices expanded in an increasingly prosperous Europe in the fourteenth and fifteenth centuries. A fifteenth-century cookbook recommended the cooking of pork with cloves, mace, dried currants, almonds, and sugar. Spices also had a mundane but necessary role in European cooking. Most cattle were slaughtered in the autumn, since there was little feed available during the winter. Their meat was then salted or smoked to preserve it, but it deteriorated rapidly. Spices, especially pepper, were widely used to disguise the semiputrid smell and keep the meat palatable through the winter. As meat consumption increased in a more prosperous Europe, so did the demand for pepper.

The principal spices imported from Asia into Europe included pepper, cinnamon, cloves, and nutmeg and its derivative mace. Pepper far outranked all other spices as a trade item and a product in everyday use. Around 1500 the main production area for pepper (*Piper nigrum*) was Malabar on the southwest coast of India, with other areas in Siam (now Thailand), the great island of Sumatra, and the Sunda island. Cinnamon (*Cinnamomum verum* or *Cinnamomum zeylancium*) came only from Sri Lanka, growing in a strip twenty to fifty miles wide and two hundred miles long from Chilaw to Walawe on the west coast of the island. Clove, the dried, unopened flower of a tropical evergreen tree growing 12 to 15 meters high, belongs to the myrtle family and botanically is variously called *Syzgium aromaticum* or *Eugenia caryophyllus*. It grew in islands such as Amboyna, Ternate, Tidore, and Ceram in the group of islands collectively known as the Moluccas (or spice islands) in the eastern extremity of the Indonesian archipelago. The nutmeg tree, grown only in the six small Banda islands in the Moluccas, is called *Myristica fragrens Houtt* or *Myristica fragrens*, and provides two products. Its fruit has an outer fleshy layer; then a bright red lacelike covering, which is mace; then a hard shell; and inside this the kernel,

which is the nutmeg. The trees are usually four to ten meters high. In response to pressures generated by European attempts at monopsonizing these spices, production areas for some of them changed noticeably over the sixteenth and the seventeenth centuries. Portuguese control over Malabar resulted in pepper production in other areas, notably to the north in Kanara and also in western Sumatra. There were also attempts to move cinnamon production out of Sri Lanka. Late in the seventeenth century, the Portuguese, having lost nearly all their share of the spice trade to the Dutch, tried to cultivate spices in Brazil instead; in 1678 the king told the viceroy in Goa to send plants such as pepper, clove, cinnamon, nutmeg, and ginger from India to other Portuguese areas, especially Brazil. These efforts continued through the eighteenth century but with little success.

Prior to the arrival of the Portuguese in the Indian Ocean at the end of the fifteenth century, a well-established network of spice trading covered different segments of the ocean. The focal supply point for the Indonesian spices was the port city of Malacca, where they were taken by local traders. The extensive trade to China was handled almost exclusively by Chinese merchants and that to the west by a host of traders, many of them Muslims from a wide range of homelands. The dominant group seems to have been that from Gujarat. The usual route was to transport the spices to Calicut, whence they were taken either north to Gujarat and the markets of northern India or across the Arabian Sea to west Asian ports such as Aden, Mocha, and Hormuz, and from there were distributed all over the Middle East. The margin of profit generally appears to have been quite high. Early in the sixteenth century, traders reportedly made 400 percent profit taking pepper from Malacca to China. In Calicut mace cost twelve or fifteen times the cost of production in the Banda islands, and nutmeg thirty times.

Some of the spices reaching the Middle East found their way to Europe via the Mediterranean, by way of either the Red Sea or the Persian Gulf. The Red Sea route terminated at the Egyptian port of Alexandria on the southern coast of the Mediterranean and involved only a small stretch of overland transportation, whereas the Persian Gulf route made use of the Tigris or the Eupharates rivers and a fair

amount of caravan transportation across Iraq and the Syrian desert. Important among the Mediterranean destination ports on this route were Tripoli (in Syria) and Beirut, with this traffic handled exclusively by merchants from the Middle East. At the Mediterranean ports, the spices were bought mainly by merchants from Venice and Genoa. Although both routes had been in use for centuries, the relative amount of traffic on either at any time depended partly on political circumstances. During the eighth and the ninth centuries the Persian Gulf route was the dominant one, but the decline of the Abbasid caliphate and the rise of the Fatimids in Egypt tilted the balance from the eleventh century onward significantly in favor of the Red Sea route. This period also witnessed a substantial increase in the volume of Euro-Asian trade in spices. Evidence from the end of the fourteenth century and early years of the fifteenth century suggests that the volume of the Alexandria trade was considerably larger (nearly double on average) than that via Beirut. However, since the latter handled the expensive spices much more than the former, the difference between the two ports was not great.

The arrival via the Cape of Good Hope of three Portuguese ships under the charge of Vasco da Gama at Calicut on 20 May 1498 marked the inauguration of a new era in the history of Euro-Asian trade in spices. As the Portuguese had discovered the Cape route, they promptly exercised the right to its exclusive use. But the attempt to monopolize the Euro-Asian spice trade required the total exclusion of the merchants from Calicut, Cambay, and other Asian ports from the Red Sea and the Persian Gulf, through the use of the *cartaz* system. Hormuz, at the entrance to the Persian Gulf, was captured in 1515; the failure to capture Aden was made up for by the dispatch each season from Goa of a fleet to lie off the entrance to the Red Sea. Raids on departing fleets at Calicut were common, and the result was practically a ruination of the spice trade with the Persian Gulf and the Red Sea. It was reported as early as 1504 that the Venetian galleys calling there found no spices at either Alexandria or Beirut.

The dislocation in the spice trade proved only temporary. By the second decade of the sixteenth century, cracks had already begun to appear in the Portuguese system. A key element in the situation was the financial priorities and compulsions of the Estado da India. Given the rather precarious state of the finances of this body, it was imperative that no opportunity be missed to tax Asian shipping by making it call and pay duties at Portuguese-controlled

◀ SPICE TRADE. *Commerce of Spices at the Molucca Islands*, watercolor by Guillaume Le Testu (c. 1509–1572). From *Cosmographie Universelle*, 1555, folio 32v. (Service Historique de l'Armée de Terre, Vincennes, France/Giraudon/Art Resource, NY)

ports. Hormuz was one such strategically located port, through which substantial quantities of pepper and other spices passed. In the second half of the sixteenth century, the Red Sea spice trade also began to revive. The Estado simply lacked the resources in men and ships to sustain an effective blockade of the Red Sea year after year. C. R. Boxer has even suggested that the volume of Acheh pepper reaching Jeddah at the end of the sixteenth century was larger than what the Portuguese were taking to Lisbon by the Cape route.

In the Portuguese imports of Asian spices into Lisbon, pepper predominated throughout the sixteenth century and the early part of the seventeenth. The volume of cloves, nutmeg, mace, and ginger that the Portuguese carried to Europe was indeed small. Only Sri Lankan cinnamon assumed some importance in the second half of the sixteenth century in these imports. An overwhelming bulk of the pepper was procured on the southwest coast of India, the only other source tapped being the port city of Malacca. In India, the procurement was begun at Calicut on the Malabar coast; but it was soon found expedient to shift the center of pepper procurement to Cochin, where the more cooperative Mappila and the Syrian Christian merchants were used as brokers and intermediaries. With the aid of the dependent *raja* of Cochin, the Portuguese tried to establish a monopsony in pepper there. However, the *raja* had no real control over the areas where pepper was grown or over the routes used for its transportation; so the monopsony never really worked. In the second half of the sixteenth century, in addition to Cochin, Kollam, and marginally Cannanore on the Malabar coast, the Estado also increasingly procured pepper on the Kanara coast. Data for the period 1612 to 1634 suggest that Kanara provided roughly two-thirds of the total Indian supplies compared to Malabar's one-third.

When the Dutch and English East India companies mounted their successful challenge of the Portuguese monopoly of the Cape route at the beginning of the seventeenth century, two major developments marked the Euro-Asian spice trade. One was the collapse of the land-cum-water routes carrying spices to the southern coast of the Mediterranean, and the other a quantum jump in the volume and the value of the Euro-Asian seaborne trade in spices. Initially at least the principal interest of both the English and the Dutch in Asia was the procurement of pepper and other spices for the European market. The first two English voyages were directed at Bantam in Java, where a factory was established in 1602. From 1613, Sumatra became the chief supplier of pepper to the English company. The Dutch had a larger resource base than the English and aggressively pursued the procurement of monopsonistic privileges in the Moluccan spices. Between 1605 and 1609, the Dutch company managed to wrest from the authorities in Amboyna and Ternate agreements obliging the producers to supply their cloves exclusively to it. A similar agreement was concluded in 1605 with the Banda group of islands for the procurement of nutmeg and mace. The latter agreement was renewed after the conquest of the islands by the Dutch company in 1621. The aggressive policies of the Dutch inevitably brought them into conflict with the English. Hostilities erupted in 1618, and the English emerged distinctly the worse of the two. The London agreement of 1619 provided for an English share of one-third in the trade of the spice islands and one-half in the pepper trade of Java, so long as the English paid one-third of the cost of maintaining the Dutch garrisons in the area. However, because of both continuing Dutch hostility and a shortage of English resources, the arrangement did not quite work. Henceforth, the English procured pepper mainly at Bantam and cloves at Makassar, where they were smuggled in large quantities, by both the merchants from Makassar and those operating from many of the Malayan ports. From 1643 onward, the Dutch managed to contain the amounts smuggled; but only after conquering Makassar, in 1669, did the Dutch finally gain an unqualified monopsony in cloves.

The Dutch East India Company's procurement of spices in the Moluccas and Sri Lanka was marked by utter ruthlessness, involving intense exploitation of the producers. In order to contain smuggling by controlling output, the Dutch periodically engaged in a large-scale extirpations of nutmeg and clove trees. The abysmally low prices paid for the spices, combined with an absolute monopoly (except in the case of pepper) in the European market as well as the rest of Asia, made the Dutch trade in spices such as cloves, nutmeg, mace, and cinnamon a source of unprecedentedly high rates of gross profit, often exceeding 1,000 percent and sometimes reaching 4,000 percent. It should, therefore, come as no surprise that in 1619 to 1621, spices accounted for as much as 74 percent of the total value of Dutch imports into Europe. By the middle of the century, this figure was still as high as 68 percent. By the end of the seventeenth century, however, this figure had fallen to 23 percent and by 1778 to 1780 to 12 percent. This decline should be interpreted rather carefully, for in absolute terms there hardly was a decrease. Indeed, the invoice value of the imported spices was higher in the last triennium than in the first. The steep decline in percentage terms basically reflected the enormously larger share of Indian textiles and raw silk in the fast-growing total import bill. The continuing key role of monopoly spices as a generator of revenue for the Dutch company can best be captured by noting that in 1778 to 1780, against a share of a mere 3 percent in the invoice value, the share of these spice in the total sales proceeds in Amsterdam was as much as 24 percent.

By making available to the company a staple item of trade in demand all over Asia and entailing an extraordinarily high rate of return, the spice monopoly also played a major role in facilitating and promoting the large and highly profitable participation by the Dutch East India Company in intra-Asian trade in the seventeenth and the eighteenth centuries. Take the example of Mughal India. The company's factory at Agra, with its concentration of the Mughal Court and the aristocracy, was a major outlet for spices such as cloves, nutmeg, and mace. As they are luxury consumption goods, one would ordinarily expect the price elasticity of demand for these spices to have been reasonably high; but the demand for spices in India was inelastic over a very broad price range. The reason evidently was that although the richer strata of Muslim society with a fondness for spiced food were willing to pay extremely high prices for the coveted spices, most other sections of the community found them beyond their reach even with any sharp declines in the price. It thus was optimal for the company to peg the prices at extremely high levels with a view to generating the maximum possible monopoly revenue from these spices.

In today's world, easy and cheap availability has by and large ended the mystique once associated with spices, which have become routine and humble culinary accessories. Yet their story in the early modern period has a drama all its own. A study of the spice trade in many ways encapsulates the early modern European presence in Asia. The Dutch East India Company policies in the spice islands can perhaps be viewed as an early example of the ugly face of colonialism.

[*See also* Salt and Salt Making.]

BIBLIOGRAPHY

Bassett, D. K. "The 'Amboyna Massacre' of 1623." *Journal of Southeast Asian History* 1 (1960), 1–19.

Boxer, Charles R. "A Note on Portuguese Reactions to the Revival of the Red Sea Spice Trade and the Rise of Atjeh." *Journal of Southeast Asian History* 10 (1969), 415–428.

Boyajian, James C. *Portuguese Trade in Asia under the Habsburgs, 1580–1640*. Baltimore, 1993.

Chaudhuri, Kirti N. *The Trading World of Asia and the English East India Company, 1660–1760*. Cambridge, 1978.

Das Gupta, Ashin, and Pearson, Michael N., eds. *India and the Indian Ocean, 1500–1800*. Calcutta, 1987.

Disney, Anthony R. *Twilight of the Pepper Empire: Portuguese Trade in Southwest India in the Early Seventeenth Century*. Cambridge, Mass., 1978.

Glamann, Kristof. *Dutch-Asiatic Trade, 1620–1740*. Copenhagen and The Hague, 1958.

Hieatt, Constance B., and Sharon Butler. *Pleyn Delit: Medieval Cookery for Modern Cooks*. Toronto, 1976.

Kieniewicz, Jan. "The Portuguese Factory and Trade in Pepper in Malabar during the Sixteenth Century." *The Indian Economic and Social History Review* 6 (1969), 61–84.

Lane, Frederic C. "The Mediterranean Spice Trade: Further Evidence on its Revival in the Sixteenth Century." *American Historical Review* XLV (1939–1940), 581–590.

Masselman, George. *The Cradle of Colonialism*. New Haven, Conn., 1963.

Pearson, Michael N., ed. *Spices in the Indian Ocean World*, vol. 11 in the series *An Expanding World, The European Impact on World History 1450–1800*. Brookfield, Vt. 1996.

Prakash, Om. *European Commercial Enterprise in Pre-Colonial India*, vol. 2.5 in the series *New Cambridge History of India*. Cambridge, 1998.

Prakash, Om. "Restrictive Trading Regimes: VOC and the Asian Spice Trade in the Seventeenth Century." In *Emporia, Commodities and Entrepreneurs in Asian Maritime Trade ca. 1400–1750*, edited by R. Ptak and D. Rothermund, pp. 107–126. Stuttgart, 1991.

Steensgaard, Niels. *The Asian Trade Revolution of the Seventeenth Century: The East India Companies and the Decline of the Caravan Trade*. Chicago, 1974.

Wake, C. H. H. "The Changing Pattern of Europe's Pepper and Spice Imports, ca. 1400–1700." *Journal of European Economic History* 8 (1979), 361–403.

OM PRAKASH

SPORTS AND SPORT INDUSTRY. The origins of most sports are shrouded in the uncertain mists of history. Anthropologists know that the Olympic Games date back to at least 776 BCE, representing the oldest known form of organized sport. The only sport with a known date of origin is basketball, invented by James Naismith in the fall of 1891 in Springfield, Massachusetts.

In general, sports followed a similar pattern in their development. They began as childhood games, evolved into accepted leisure time activities for adults, and then became industries employing professional athletes. At each juncture their roles and acceptance in society expanded across age groups and income classes. Sports today are enjoyed on two levels, as a participatory activity and as a spectator sport, competing with many other forms of entertainment for leisure expenditures.

The Olympic Games were originally a five-day festival with religious connections. The ancient Olympics ended in 391 CE, when a decree issued by the Roman emperor Theodosius I prohibited all pagan worship, which included the Olympic Games. The games were reborn on the initiative of Baron Pierre de Coubertin in Athens in 1896.

Leisure Activities. The acceptance of sports by adults has its roots in two distinct classes, the wealthy and the working class. The wealthy began participating in sports as leisure activities, of which tennis, lawn bowling, and golf are the earliest known examples. The wealthy also were drawn to spectator sports early on, for example, horse racing, on which wagers could be placed. Boxing matches and wrestling, pitting humans instead of animals against one another, were another form of early spectator sports popular among the upper classes. These latter sports were derivations of the early gladiator matches in the ancient Roman Empire.

The working class was also drawn to sport, in some cases for the wagering excitement, in others for the ability to participate in a form of leisure physical activity. Workers gathered to play their games, often representing town, company, or church teams. The pride of winning the contest was represented by a trophy or cash prize put up by the participants. As the stakes grew, so did the degree to which teams were willing to go to win the contests. Professional team sports have roots in these early town contests.

The first professional athletes were individuals hired by teams bent on gaining an advantage in the match with a rival. The use of an individual or two eventually led to whole teams paid to perform. As the best players were gathered together, the level of play was elevated. Once the athletes began to earn a salary, the teams needed a method of recouping the costs of these salaries, and the admission charge was born. The demand for the product resulted from the better quality of play exhibited by the professional players.

Sports that have succeeded commercially are widely recognized as businesses in the entertainment industry. The growth of professional sports in an economy is a function of economic development. As wealth and leisure time grow, so does demand for sports as a consumption good.

As spectator sports increased in popularity, complementary markets evolved. Cricket fields in nineteenth-century England were often sponsored by hotels that provided the advertising for the match, which in turn generated business for the lodging and pub. Brewers were also early ancillary participants in sporting matches, providing liquid refreshments for patrons. Governments recognized the revenue potential of sports as well. As early as the eighteenth century English brewers who provided ale for cricket matches and horse races received tax breaks.

A symbiotic relationship evolved between newspapers and sports. As newspapers proliferated in the eighteenth century, sports matches were reported more frequently. The reporting of sports events was a way to entice the lower classes to read papers. In postbellum America increasing literacy and leisure time brought the American public to newsprint as never before.

Sometimes an ancillary group benefits so much from sports that it creates a league as a marketing vehicle for its own product. In 1946 a group of American arena owners seeking tenants formed a professional basketball league, the Basketball Association of America (BAA), to compete with the existing National Basketball League (NBL). The two leagues competed to sign the best players, driving up salaries and decreasing profits, until they ultimately merged, forming the National Basketball Association (NBA) in 1949. To an extent seldom appreciated by sports historians, the all-England cricket tour of 1859 was a vision of America's sports future. It revealed for the first time organized team sports' vast potential as a vehicle of mass entertainment. The English team played to sellout crowds across the United States. The tour also revealed the emerging association between organized team sports and civic pride, the best example being the team's hastily arranged final match at Rochester. In an eerily modern scenario Rochester officials appropriated public funds to upgrade the city's cricket ground to entice the English team to town. The mayor claimed the money was well spent to show that Rochester was no less a community than places like New York and Philadelphia.

Amateur versus Professional. Tension between amateur and professional athletes was a prominent problem in twentieth-century sports. In individual sports, such as golf and tennis, the distinction between amateur and professional was sometimes not clear. The Olympic Games are the most famous example of amateur athletics, and they were the last major sporting event to openly allow professional athletes to participate. The nineteenth-century British aristocracy, not the ancient Greeks, invented the concept of athletic amateurism. The aristocracy was interested in promoting amateur status for athletes as a means of preventing the rougher, lower-class participants from competing in the same games.

While professional athletes were officially banned from Olympic competitions, the distinction between amateur and professional was somewhat arbitrary. Athletes were allowed sponsorships to cover their training costs but could not earn salaries for their performances. This loophole was often exploited, most notably by athletes from Soviet bloc countries. They often held state jobs while they trained in their sports full-time. This conflict was officially put to rest at the International Olympic Committee (IOC) conference in 1981, when the ban on professionals was eliminated. At that same conference the IOC voted to allow American television networks to dictate the scheduling of certain events in return for higher rights fees. It was a watershed year for the Olympics, as the IOC tacitly admitted that the games were as much a business as an athletic spectacle.

The struggle between amateur and professional athletes has its origins in the nineteenth century, when the presence of professional athletes began to emerge. In some sports it ended quickly and gave way to professionals at the highest levels. This was most apparent in team sports, where professional leagues featured entire rosters of paid players, while amateur leagues, separate in organization and competitors, survived on a lesser, more often local scale.

In the early days of tennis and golf, professionals were distinct from amateurs in that they earned their livings from the game. Their primary source of income was as a club pro, since few professional tournaments existed. It

was not until 1968 that professionals were first allowed to play in the major tennis tournaments. Wimbledon was the first major tournament to invite professionals to compete against amateurs. The other major tournaments immediately followed suit, and the positive market reaction to the higher caliber of play soon led to a series of tournaments for professionals. In golf the professional tournaments came earlier, though the prize money was not significant enough for more than a few of the best players to earn a living as a touring professional.

Television played a major role in promoting golf and tennis tournaments around the world, paying sponsorship fees that increased the size of the purse and thus attracted more and better players. The sale of sponsorships for individual tournaments further increased the cash prizes and increased the level of play and fan interest, leading to further increases in sponsorship and television money in an upward spiral that continues into the twenty-first century.

Boxing is an example of an individual sport that attracted professionals at an early stage. The earliest boxing matches featured Roman slaves and ended with the death of the loser. Primarily for this reason, boxing disappeared from the public view for nearly two millennia before it regained popularity in England and its colonies in the late eighteenth century. Early boxing matches were popular as a means of wagering. In the United States these matches often pitted slaves against each other, with hefty wagers on the outcome. Because of its brutality, boxing quickly was outlawed in most countries and in all states of the United States. It also fell off in popularity among spectators when allegations of match fixing cropped up.

Boxing regained its popularity in the late nineteenth century. John L. Sullivan, credited with saving the sport and boosting its global popularity, became the first individual athlete to tour and exhibit his skills. English cricket teams pioneered the athletic team tour, but Sullivan was the first individual to do so. His tour was significant for many other reasons as well. While the concept of touring was popularized by vaudeville acts and politicians, Sullivan toured longer and covered a greater area than anyone had before. He blazed the endorsement trail for modern-day athletes as well, earning endorsement deals and making vaudeville appearances as well as opening a popular saloon that banked on his name.

Athletic endorsements grew in size and stature as television exposure increased the visibility of athletes. In some cases, athletes earned more from endorsements than from their sports. In 1990 Jennifer Capriati, a 14-year-old American, received $5 million in endorsement contracts before playing her first professional match. The golfer Tiger Woods took endorsements to a whole new level when he signed deals with Nike and American Express upon turning professional in 1996. The endorsements were multiyear, hundred-million-dollar deals, greatly eclipsing any amount of money he could possibly earn actually playing golf over his lifetime.

Sponsorships, another source of revenue for sports, date back to 1887, when the French magazine *Vélocipède* sponsored the first automobile sporting event. Kodak was a sponsor at the first modern Olympic games in 1896. The most recent role of sponsors has been in the purchase of the naming rights for public arenas and stadiums.

Sports Broadcasts. Television has been the greatest force in shaping sports in the last half of the twentieth century. The financial success of sports is based on exposure on television. The most successful professional team sports in the world generate more money from television rights fees than they do from live attendance. Golf and tennis owe their large purses to the growth of television fees in the last two decades. The less-successful professional sports have improved their status greatly with television packages but are still not on the same par as the aforementioned sports.

The tradition of Hockey Night in Canada began on radio in 1935. The Canadian Broadcasting Company began doing weekly television broadcasts in the 1950s. For years either the Montreal or the Toronto team was televised every Saturday night during the season. When the two teams met in the 1959 Stanley Cup, the television ratings set an all-time high in Canada. Hockey's status in the United States can be summed up in its television history. The first national television contract in the United States was not arranged until 1994 on the fledgling Fox Network.

Sports dominate the all-time top-rated television programs in the United States, and the National Football League (NFL) dominates television sports with twenty-two Super Bowls and the 1981 National Football Conference (NFC) championship game among the top fifty most popular broadcasts. Super Bowl broadcasts hold four of the top ten and ten of the top twenty spots. Sports hold five of the top ten spots, including the women's figure skating finals at the 1994 Winter Olympics along with the Super Bowls.

The most popular sporting event in the world is the World Cup soccer tournament, an international soccer championship held every four years and, like the Olympics, staged each time in a different country. More people watch the World Cup than any other sporting event. It was inaugurated in Uruguay in 1930 as more of the world's best players became professionals and a true championship match could not be played in the Olympics, where the international championship had been staged previously.

Television has not always had a positive impact on sports. While television created a vast audience for sports in the 1950s, it drastically reduced attendance in small towns for minor league ball clubs and local boxing clubs, leading to their dissolution. By 1959 television did not need boxing anymore and, moving on to other forms of entertainment, cut back on boxing telecasts. By this time, however, overexposure had seriously damaged the sport. The arrival of Cassius Clay, now Muhammad Ali, on the scene in the early 1960s gave a much-needed boost to a sport that had lost its allure. Ali resurrected boxing in the twentieth century much as Sullivan had in the previous century.

In 1970 the NFL began its Monday Night Football broadcasts. This meant that the NFL was broadcast on all three national networks, risking the same overexposure that had killed boxing. The league was willing to take this risk for rights fees totaling more than $150 million over three years. Television rights fees became the primary source of revenue, displacing live attendance.

Leagues. Sports leagues have all evolved in a monopoly framework, seeking to control the competition, the consumer base, and the labor pool with varying degrees of success. In team sports the owners formed cartels. Organizers of individual sports, like tennis and golf, attempted to control the tournaments, while boxing was monopolized in the 1940s by the mob, which controlled the television rights and the heavyweight championship fights. Without fail the most financially successful sports leagues have been cartels that thrived on the back of exploited labor and monopolized geographic areas for teams. In the United States competing leagues arose to cash in on the monopoly profits in football, hockey, basketball, and baseball, and in every case they were either bankrupted or merged into the established league. As a result, despite a century of monopoly profits, each of these sports still enjoys monopoly status.

In other parts of the world, though sports are at least as popular, this format has not been as apparent. In Europe football leagues are divided into divisions, with the worst teams in each division dropping down a rung and the best moving up to the next division at the end of each season. These divisions are primarily organized on a scale of city size and revenue-generating ability. The top division teams are in major metropolitan areas, while the bottom division teams are in smaller towns and older stadiums. The lower division teams generate less revenue and hence pay lower salaries and attract lesser talent. For the most part teams in the lower leagues survive by developing players and selling them to teams in the higher leagues, where the players can generate greater marginal revenues.

Labor markets for players have evolved similarly across leagues and national boundaries. In all team sports the original labor pool was exploited because the league, as a cartel, was a monopsonistic employer. The standard player contract in professional sports leagues had a form of reserve clause, which the teams and leagues instituted under the guise that it was required to keep teams balanced, games competitive, and the league viable. In the name of preservation, the team owners exercised monopsonistic control over athletes, exploiting their labor for monopoly profits. Players were signed to contracts that bound them to the signing team indefinitely. The team had the right to renew the player's contract each year, restricting the player's ability to bargain and thus depressing wages.

Players began to level the playing field in the 1970s through a series of legal victories and the growing strength of their unions. As a result of the rapid increase in the strength of player unions, the Major League Baseball Players Association is considered one of the strongest labor unions in the world. Other gains that improved the lot of players included the method by which they were signed to their first professional contracts. In North American team sports, teams were assigned exclusive rights to bargain with newly eligible players. In football and basketball, players were prohibited from the league until they had completed their college eligibility. This created a serious problem for those talented athletes who were not academically inclined. Players won the relaxation of this restriction in the courts. Now the most talented athletes are signed out of high school or leave their college teams early to pursue the wealth in the professional leagues.

In all cases players eventually won the right to bargain freely with other teams, thus dramatically increasing their wages. Through a series of strikes, which hit every major sport at one time or another, players have won the right to bargain with competing teams for contract terms, substantial pension increases, and a host of lesser concessions. The result has been a dramatic increase in the compensation earned by professional athletes.

To date no original league has failed. Indeed professional soccer in Europe; baseball in Asia, South America, and North America; and hockey, tennis, and basketball in Europe and North America have thrived. The popularity of the sport, the quality of competition at the highest level, the vast amounts of television and sponsorship dollars, and the monopoly status of leagues have generated revenues sufficient to guarantee large paychecks for athletes and profits for owners. The last quarter century in American sports, however, has been marred by labor unrest between athletes and owners. This conflict has centered around the method of splitting the revenues and has led to work stoppages in all four major team sports.

Women in Sports. The role of women in sports has grown over time. Although there were female competitors in the Olympics as early as 1900, the IOC did not regard their presence as official until 1912, when women's swimming events were sanctioned. Until 1960 they were prohib-ited from running distances in excess of two hundred meters.

Arguably the greatest impact on women's sports came in the person of Babe Didrickson Zaharias, the first female superstar athlete. She excelled at everything she did, from collegiate track star to 1932 Olympic track and field champion to golf professional. Shortly after achieving her Olympic triumphs, she hit the vaudeville circuit, displaying her incredible athletic talents to admiring audiences across the country and promoting the idea that women could also be athletes. When she eventually turned to golf, she was responsible for the growth and early survival of the Ladies Professional Golf Association.

Team sports have not been as successful for women. A women's World Cup was inaugurated in 2000, but female athletes played to a much smaller audience than did males. In the United States professional women's baseball and basketball leagues have failed, including the All American Girls Professional Baseball League during World War II and the recent collapse of one of two competing professional basketball leagues. The second, the Women's National Basketball League (WNBA), survives on subsidies from the NBA.

Women have enjoyed their greatest financial success in individual sports, such as tennis, golf, and figure skating. The 1994 women's Olympic figure skating finals is the only sport other than football to crack the top fifty television shows in United States. Women's professional tennis got a boost in 1973, when Bobby Riggs challenged Billie Jean King to a match and lost. The gimmick attracted a huge television audience and captured a new audience for tennis. As tennis began to appear regularly on television, prize money increased, as did sponsorships.

Recognition has not led to financial equality, however. As the purses grew, so did the disparity between prizes for men and women. Gladys Heldman, founder of *World Tennis* magazine, led the revolt of women who split away from mixed tournaments and in 1970 started their own tour, originally sponsored by Virginia Slims. The women's tours in both golf and tennis still pay significantly less than their male counterparts.

The current status of sports is decried by many as having become too commercialized. However, sports have been commercial enterprises since the nineteenth century. The only real change is the reporting of the financial dealings. As players gained the right to negotiate with competitors, their salaries increased dramatically, and financial news about sports began to creep into the news along with the reporting of the games on the field.

Despite all of the attention sports receive from the media, they are a minor portion of the economy. Numerous studies of the economic impact of professional sports all come to the same conclusion: the attention they receive is grossly disproportionate to their economic importance.

BIBLIOGRAPHY

Bankes, Christina, ed. *Chronicle of the Olympics 1896–1996*. New York, 1996.

Bowen, Roland. *Cricket: A History of Its Growth and Development throughout the World*. London, 1970.

Burke, Robert F. *Never Just a Game: Players, Owners, and American Baseball to 1920*. Chapel Hill, N.C., 1994.

Burke, Robert F. *Much More Than a Game: Players, Owners, and American Baseball since 1921*. Chapel Hill, N.C., 2001.

Collins, Bud, and Zander Hollander, eds. *Bud Collins' Modern Encyclopedia of Tennis*. Detroit, 1994.

Grimsley, Will. *Golf: Its History, People and Events*. Englewood Cliffs, N.J., 1966.

Hollander, Zander, ed. *The Modern Encyclopedia of Basketball*. Garden City, N.Y., 1979.

McClellan, Keith. *The Sunday Game: At the Dawn of Professional Football*. Akron, Ohio, 1998.

Melville, Tom. *The Tented Field: A History of Cricket in America*. Bowling Green, Ohio, 1998.

Sammons, Jeffrey T. *Beyond the Ring: The Role of Boxing in American Society*. Urbana, 1988.

Wagg, Stephen. *The Football World*. Sussex, U.K., 1984.

MICHAEL J. HAUPERT

SRI LANKA. The recorded history of Sri Lanka (formerly Ceylon) and its economy dates back to around the third Century BCE. A civilization developed in the dry zone, which though sometimes disrupted by internal conflict and wars with invaders from south India, flourished for over a millenium. Centered first around the capital of Anuradhapura (first to tenth centuries CE) and then Polonnaruwa (c. eleventh to twelfth centuries CE), this was an agricultural economy based on a vast and intricate system of artificial reservoirs (tanks) and canals. A flourishing economy was strengthened by domestic and international trade. Gems, pearls, elephants, and ivory were exported, while horses, precious metals, wines, and earthenware products were the main imports. Located in the middle of the trade routes from Arabia to East Asia, and in close proximity to India, Sri Lanka was an international market. The port of Mahatitta on the northwestern coast served as a center of entrepôt trade. Persian traders were found in Anuradhapura, while Pliny (23–79 CE) records the arrival of ambassadors from Lanka at the court of the Roman emperor Claudius (r. 41–54 CE). The Chinese traveler Fa-hsien (399–414 CE), who resided in Anuradhapura around the beginning of the fifth century CE, recorded complex socioeconomic conditions in Anuradhapura. Mercantile settlements existed outside Anuradhapura. Archaeological finds of various Eastern and Western coins evidence the existence of a monetized economy. Records of grain banks have also been found, where deposits of paddy (rice) earned 50 percent interest and other grains 25 percent.

Foreign trade was undertaken directly by the state as an important source of revenue, particularly in the twelfth century. A special department was established by the king to control the pearl banks, gem mines, and lands producing exportable commodities.

Continuous onslaughts by South Indian invaders in the thirteenth century caused the collapse of the dry zone civilization and economy. The Sinhala people drifted to the wet zone in the west, southwest, and the central hills, while a Tamil kingdom emerged in the north. The irrigation works fell into disuse. The regional kingdoms possessed neither the social nor the economic sophistication of the former kingdoms. Domestic trade continued at a lower level, while international trade was generally limited to India, though expeditionary fleets from China made their presence felt at least on two occasions in the early part of the fifteenth century.

Advent of the Europeans. The economic structure of Sri Lanka was based primarily on subsistence agriculture when the Portuguese first arrived on the island in 1505 CE. Drawn by a desire to control East-West commerce and the highly lucrative export of cinnamon from Sri Lanka, the Portuguese gradually took control of the country's entire southwestern and northern coastal area. By the first quarter of the seventeenth century, only the Kandyan kingdom, with its power base in the central hills, remained independent. Control of the seas around the island enabled the Portuguese to maintain a monopoly of the export of precious cinnamon. However, the expanding mercantile interests of the Dutch, operating through the Vereenidge Oost-Indische Compagnie (Dutch East India Company, VOC), threatened Portuguese control and, with the assistance of the Sinhala king in Kandy, ended Portuguese power by 1660. The Dutch extended the monopoly on international trade to almost all imports and exports. Although cinnamon commanded extremely high prices both in Europe and the East, at a negligible cost to the Dutch East India Company in Sri Lanka, virtually none of the benefits of the exports accrued to the exporting country—an extreme case of colonial exploitation. The Kandyan kingdom itself was economically underdeveloped. Subsistence agriculture predominated, and economic activity was more nonmonetary. Wealth was represented mainly by land and its produce. Payment for services was often in kind or by the grant of lands for service, particularly by the king.

British Influence. Political developments in Europe affected Sri Lanka. The expansion of the activities of the British East India Company led to competition with the Dutch East India Company, and by the end of the eighteenth century, Great Britain had established a presence in Sri Lanka. With the Peace of Amiens in 1802, Dutch territories in Sri Lanka were taken over by the British.

Following the ceding of the Kandyan kingdom to the British in 1815, the entire country became a part of the British Empire.

The nineteenth century saw a major economic transformation. Beginning as a subsistence economy, it ended the century as a dual economy, dominated by plantation agriculture. A network of roads and railways helped develop these plantations. The economic importance of cinnamon diminished rapidly in the first quarter of the century, and by mid-century, coffee was preeminent. Large-scale coffee plantations were developed with the sale of crown land. Seasonal demand for labor was met by inflows from south India. Although the coffee industry was destroyed by a leaf fungus in the 1870s, tea, rubber, and coconut had become adequate replacements by the end of the century. Little had been done to develop the neglected irrigation schemes and the expansion of the plantations reduced the forest area available for "slash and burn" cultivation.

Considerable economic growth was achieved in the first half of the twentieth century, mainly in the plantation sector. The expansion of tea plantations led to a permanent inflow of labor from south India. Exports of tea, rubber, and coconuts accounted for about 90 percent of export earnings (60 percent from tea) and more than half of government revenue when independence was obtained in 1948. Imports were mainly food items. The population nearly doubled during this period. Initial steps were taken to improve peasant agriculture, through the settlement of colonists in the dry zone, accompanied by restoration of some irrigation works in this area. There was, however, very little development of an industrial base.

Independence and After. The half-century after independence can broadly be separated into three segments. The first decade was a period of free-market policies. Commercial crops provided export earnings. Significant investments were made in domestic agriculture, welfare expenditure was high, and the financial sector was limited. The next two decades were characterized by centralized, inward-looking planning, with widespread state intervention in economic activity. Rapid industrialization was attempted through state-owned enterprises, while the bulk of the plantations were brought under state control. State-dominated financial entities were in operation. Economic liberalization began in 1977 with a move to free-market policies and an opening of the economy to international market forces. State intervention in economic activity declined significantly, while the financial sector developed, and a fundamental change occurred in the structure of the economy. The dependence on agricultural exports was greatly reduced with the emergence of industrial exports, mainly garments.

At the beginning of the twenty-first century, Sri Lanka had an open, market-oriented economy with a Human Development Index far in excess of countries with comparable levels of income.

[*See also* Great Britain, *subentry on* British Empire.]

BIBLIOGRAPHY

Central Bank. *Economic Progress of Independent Sri Lanka*. Colombo, 1998.

De Silva, Chandra Richard. *Sri Lanka: A History*. Delhi, reprint 1992.

De Silva, Kingsley M. *A History of Sri Lanka*. Delhi, 1981.

Karunatilake, H. N. S. *Economic Development in Ceylon*. New York, 1971.

Knox, Robert. *An Historical Relation of the Island of Ceylon*, rev., enlgd. 2d ed., 2 vols., edited by J. H. O. Paulusz Dehiwala, Sri Lanka, 1989.

Siriweera, W. I. *History of Sri Lanka*. Colombo, 2002.

Siriweera, W. I. *A Study of the Economic History of Pre-Modern Sri Lanka*. Delhi, 1994.

Snodgrass, Donald R. *Ceylon: An Export Economy in Transition*. Homewood, Ill., 1966.

University of Peradeniya. *History of Ceylon*. Vol. 1 (Parts 1 & 2). Colombo, 1959.

University of Peradeniya. *History of Ceylon*. Vol. 3. Colombo, 1973.

University of Peradeniya. *History of Sri Lanka*. Vol. 2. Dehiwala, Sri Lanka, 1995.

P. W. R. B. A. U. HERAT

STABILIZATION POLICIES. Demand management has usually been defined as fiscal and monetary action designed to affect total nominal expenditure in an economy in order to iron out unwelcome fluctuations in output and employment. Such policies would presumably be unnecessary in a perfectly competitive, self-stabilizing, economy or in a perfectly planned central economy. Experience has shown, however, that perfect central planning is utopian, while modern capitalist economies are subject to significant nominal rigidities. These in turn imply that rapid returns to equilibrium following shocks are highly unlikely to occur, particularly so in the labor market.

The recognition of the importance of stabilization policies goes back to Keynes's *General Theory*, whose "fundamental practical message [is] that a private enterprise economy . . . *needs* to be stabilized, *can* be stabilized, and therefore *should* be stabilized by appropriate monetary and fiscal policies" (Modigliani, 1977, p. 1). Hence, demand management acquired respectability only after World War II. Through the nineteenth and the first half of the twentieth centuries, government intervention in the economy was widespread but seldom took on a purposeful stabilization role; what macroeconomic policy there was, was usually subject to some simple rules of conduct. Policy activism to control demand spread across the industrialized world after 1945, only to retreat again in the 1980s and 1990s in the light of its perceived failures.

The Nineteenth Century. In the nineteenth century and until 1913, governments in Europe, Japan, or in the so-called European offshoots—the United States, Argentina, the Dominions (Canada, Australia, New Zealand, South Africa)—did not feel responsible for ensuring high levels of activity or employment. They intervened frequently and their polices had widespread micro- and macroeconomic effects, but these were designed to promote certain industries, to build infrastructures, to ensure a defense capability, and so on. Macroeconomic policy was based on a simple rule-based framework: monetary policy should follow the gold standard's so-called "rules of the game," thereby ensuring external equilibrium and convertibility, while fiscal policy should aim at balanced budgets, thereby convincing the private sector of the soundness of public management. In practice, the rules of the game were often broken and governments were not always able to stick to balanced budgets. Yet these exceptions to the rules were not seen as having significant macroeconomic consequences since there was a strong belief in the capacity of the economy to ensure a virtually continuous full-employment equilibrium (though the term was not, of course, used at the time).

And it is true that the nineteenth century economy was almost certainly a good deal more flexible than its twentieth century counterpart. Trade unions were much weaker and markets were, probably, more competitive than they have since become. Indeed, there is evidence suggesting that, in the United States at least, wage and price rigidities were a good deal more widespread after World War II than they had been from 1890 to 1930. In addition, the large agricultural sectors of the time, particularly in continental Europe and in Japan, played a much more effective shock absorption role in periods of urban unemployment than they do today.

Cycles and crises were there, of course, but these were seen more as financial and price cycles than as output cycles, sparked by fluctuations in construction activity, by technological breakthroughs, by gold discoveries, or by sudden financial panics. Given the beliefs of the time, policies to deal with these cycles were seen as unnecessary; and given the economic structures of the time, the need for them may not have been overwhelming.

The Interwar Years. World War I and its aftermath significantly altered this picture. Nominal rigidities increased as trade union power strengthened and the process of industrial concentration, begun at the turn of the century, gradually diminished the competitiveness of product markets. At the same time, the spread of universal suffrage put a much greater onus on governments to deliver not only the beginnings of social protection, but also high levels of employment. The policy responses to this new world were, however, totally inadequate. In the 1920s, governments harked back to the gold standard and to balanced budgets. With the Great Depression of the 1930s, the certainties of an older era disappeared, but their place was taken by ad hoc responses, many with counterproductive outcomes and none illuminated by a consistent theoretical framework.

A widespread perverse reaction to external shocks came in the form of protectionism; a similarly widespread reaction to domestic shocks came in the form of restrictive fiscal (and sometimes even monetary) measures. Thus, policy almost certainly provided the initial destabilizing impulse for the Great Depression in the United States. And similarly deflationary policies in the early 1930s in Germany added to the recession of the time.

As depression continued, countries gradually moved away from the orthodoxy of the time and groped for alternative solutions. A textbook written in the late 1930s (Laufenberg, 1938) provides some evidence as to the views of the time on how business cycle fluctuations could be dampened. Recommended measures include such obvious policies as tax cuts and public works; beggar-thy-neighbor responses, such as depreciation; and quirkier remedies such as price controls and capacity reductions. Public works were, indeed, one widespread response (for example, in Nazi Germany, but also in France, Italy, Denmark). Expansionary fiscal policies and budget deficits were adopted in Japan and Sweden. Cheap money, and competitive depreciations, came in Great Britain and Japan. More direct intervention boosted the purchasing power of French workers, saved large chunks of Italy's corporate sector from bankruptcy, or sustained incomes and employment through the U.S. New Deal policies.

It is in this confused world that Keynes beamed his message that fiscal policies should be designed to balance the economy and not the budget and that monetary policies should be used primarily to ensure domestic rather than external goals. And the message was eagerly seized by a new generation of economists and policymakers. Even during the war, work at the League of Nations in particular set forth a virtual blueprint for what was to be the postwar domestic and international policy framework.

The "Golden Age." A good deal of that framework found its way into the Bretton Woods institutions that regulated international trade and payments through the "Golden Age" and beyond. Incorporation of the Keynesian aim of high employment into domestic policymaking took longer. The United Kingdom and the United States did so relatively early and fairly explicitly, the first in drafting the 1944 White Paper on Employment Policy, the second in passing the 1946 Employment Act; similar commitments were made by some smaller European economies (the Netherlands, Norway, Sweden). Elsewhere in Europe (and in Japan), the priority was not so much cyclical stabilization as reconstruction and rapid growth. Policies were thus targeted more on stimulating investment (Germany or Japan), developing the southern part of the country (Italy), or even framing overall industrial expansion through indicative planning (France).

Despite these differences, the experience of the 1950s suggests that there was in fact a relatively similar policy stance almost everywhere. Most countries refrained from widespread discretionary action, but virtually all engaged in accommodating the needs of rapidly growing economies. Counter cyclical fiscal policy was hardly needed, given the absence of pronounced fluctuations (though some was taken in the United States in 1958), while monetary policy was generally supportive of expansion. Even that paragon of financial virtue and anti-inflationary credibility, the Bundesbank, allowed Germany's money supply to grow at well above two-digit annual rates through the 1950s and the 1960s.

Discretionary policies came in the 1960s. Economists became increasingly convinced that cycles could be tamed and turned to fine tuning aggregate demand. Countries that had previously shunned demand management now actively used fiscal policies to dampen slowdowns (for example, Japan in 1965, Germany in 1967, or France on several occasions during the decade). And international organizations approved of such action—the Organization for Economic Cooperation and Development (OECD), for instance, published a report by a panel of experts recommending discretionary fiscal intervention to stabilize the economy. By the early 1970s, active demand management had become the new orthodoxy. Thus, the mild slowdown of 1971 produced a concerted expansionary push in all the major economies that led to the unsustainable boom of 1972–1973.

In addition, other instruments were added to the standard monetary and fiscal tools. Several countries experimented with wage and price policies to deal with inflationary pressures (the United States, the United Kingdom, France), and some of these experiments took the form of direct controls; others interfered with credit allocation (France and Japan already since the 1950s, Italy in the 1960s and thereafter). And, at least in Europe, the spreading of welfare provisions attempted to replicate some features of macroeconomic stabilization at the microeconomic level—unemployment, health and pension benefits, as well as legislation protecting employment, were all instruments that aimed at smoothing individual life-cycle fluctuations.

Finally, an attempt was also made to extend discretionary policy action from the domestic to the international arena. The idea of international economic policy coordination, implicit in the Bretton Woods framework, became explicit after the breakdown of the fixed exchange rate system and saw probably its most ambitious formulation at the time of the Bonn 1978 summit of the major economies. Detailed plans were drawn up at the time for U.S. action to reduce domestic oil demand and for German and Japanese expansionary action on the fiscal front.

The 1980s and 1990s. Yet, by 1978, the world already appeared to be retreating from policy interventionism, a retreat that continued in the next two decades. For one thing, the oil price shocks of the period created a dilemma for stabilization policies since they were both deflationary in quantities and inflationary in prices. If policymakers privileged the fight against inflation, they suffered from high unemployment; if they followed the opposite course, they were hit by rising prices and depreciating currencies. Much more importantly, an intellectual revolution had earlier begun to put in doubt the effectiveness and relevance of demand management itself. For one thing, it was claimed that too little was known about the size of lags and multipliers for fine tuning to have its desired timely effects. For another, the view that a trade-off existed between unemployment and inflation gave way to the vertical Phillips curve idea put forward by Friedman. If unemployment could no longer be changed by demand manipulations, other than in the short run, much better for policy not to interfere with the day-to-day workings of the economy.

This withdrawal from demand management was, however, more apparent in the rhetoric of policy announcements than in the practice of policy action. Through the 1980s and much of the 1990s, governments still used fiscal and monetary instruments to affect aggregate demand. What changed was that their intervention was no longer designed to stabilize output, but to reduce inflation (or, in the west European case in the later 1990s, to meet the restrictive public finance conditions set by the Maastricht Treaty for Monetary Union).

By the beginning of the twenty-first century, however, western Europe at least seems to have moved one further step away from policy activism. While monetary policy retained a good deal of discretion in the United States, as did fiscal policy in Japan, both the Eurozone and the United Kingdom adopted policy rules for their Central Banks and Ministries of Finance. Inflation had to be contained to some low figure and budgets had to be broadly balanced, if not year by year, then through the cycle—a return, in some ways at least, to the orthodoxy of the nineteenth century.

Effectiveness. When assessing the effectiveness of demand management policies, two main questions arise: Can such policies affect the level of aggregate demand? If so, can they also stabilize the level of output?

On the first issue, there is a well-known literature that disputes the effectiveness of policy activism. In its moderate form, this literature argues that expansionary fiscal policies will be almost wholly crowded out by interest-rate-induced offsetting changes in expenditure, while expansionary monetary policies will lead to eventual inflation. In its radical new classical formulation, policy impotence is even more pronounced. Fiscal activism can have no effects in a world of rational and forward-looking households, while monetary policy leads to virtually immediate and complete price responses. Only unannounced measures that take the private sector by surprise could conceivably have some temporary impact.

Looking back at the history of the last half of the twentieth century, such views seem to fly in the face of virtually all the available empirical evidence. Changes in macroeconomic policies affected economies throughout this period. James Tobin's judgment on U.S. experience in the 1970s that "The major turns in [the economy's] direction conformed to the desires and intentions of the managers of aggregate demand" (Tobin, 1980, p. 21) could be repeated for many other countries. Thus, Great Britain's stop-go developments in the 1960s clearly responded to policy changes; Germany's 1968–1969 or 1978–1979 recoveries were engineered by the authorities, as were Italy's recessions of 1964–1965 or 1992–1993; the generalized boom of the early 1970s or slowdown of the early 1980s were both powerfully helped by policies.

The weights of the two major policy instruments have changed through the period, but neither was ever impotent. In the Golden Age world of fixed exchange rates, fiscal policy mattered more and crowding-out was minor (deficits were small or non-existent and monetary policy was, in any case, accommodating). The move to floating weakened fiscal policy effectiveness, along Mundell-Fleming lines, and this process was reinforced in some countries by the liberalization of domestic financial markets, since this reduced the liquidity constraints that faced households. But, by the same token, these changes reinforced the power of monetary policies.

Much more controversial is the issue as to whether policies were successful in stabilizing activity. This was not always an official aim. External constraints in the Bretton Woods era were often a more important consideration than the wish to reduce fluctuations (indeed, in Japan cycles in these years were probably policy induced). And the 1980s, in particular, saw concerted efforts not to smooth the cycle but to reduce inflation. Yet, there were also many episodes in which governments attempted to avoid recessions or excessive booms.

The empirical evidence on this issue is mixed. Numerous country studies have tried to show that well-meaning attempts at stabilization turned out, in fact, to be destabilizing. Other studies point in the opposite direction. Two major comparative works carried out at the OECD for the Golden Age period suggest that fiscal policies were, on the whole, stabilizing in most of the countries surveyed and so were probably monetary policies, at least in the short run. Few of these various findings, however, command universal acceptance. For those to whom government interference in the economy is basically suspect, neither qualitative nor econometric evidence on some particular episode, will ever be sufficient to establish that macroeconomic discretion can improve on spontaneous market outcomes. And similarly, for those who believe that market economies are prone to bouts of instability, empirical evidence on some failures of intervention will not dampen a basic enthusiasm for countercyclical action.

A broader, if more tentative, way of assessing success or failure is to compare periods in which policy activism was present with earlier periods when it was not. Comparisons of this kind on the whole suggest that the postwar era was much more stable than the 1870–1913 years, let alone to the two interwar decades. This greater stability could, of course, have been due to structural changes on the output side, to variations in demand composition, to different behavior on labor or capital markets, to the effects of international trade, or even to better statistics. Yet, attempts to allow for such factors often tend, if anything, to reinforce the original conclusion of much greater post-1950 stability (see, for instance, Boltho, 1989).

Almost by default, the most plausible explanation for such an improvement lies in the major change in policy activism described in the historical sections above. Even if discretionary policies, and particularly fine tuning, may have had disappointing or, at times, even perverse results, postwar policy activism may still have had an overall favorable stabilizing influence through the operation of two alternative channels. First, and rather obviously, the greater post-1950 presence of social welfare programs and the greater incidence of progressive taxation, have powerfully strengthened the workings of automatic stabilizers. These must have smoothed income and employment fluctuations.

Second, the knowledge that governments in the Golden Age were more actively committed to countercyclical policies, may well have influenced the behavior of the private sector in a stabilizing direction. In total contrast to the idea that only unanticipated government action can affect the economy, this view would hold that it was precisely the announcement that policies would be framed so as to dampen the cycle, that convinced the private sector that fluctuations would be less severe and made it act accordingly (see, for instance, Baily, 1978). What mattered, in other words, was not so much the impact of a particular tax, expenditure, or interest rate decision, but the general feeling of confidence that governments would try to, and succeed in, controlling the business cycle.

Such ideas are unfashionable today. The old view that economies are basically self-stabilizing has regained momentum. It is unlikely that many observers adhere to the make-believe world in which unemployment fluctuations result from the optimizing decisions of rational individuals subject to unobservable, unmeasurable, and implausible productivity shocks. Yet scepticism about the power of governments to control cycles led many countries, particularly in Europe, to return to simple policy rules. The experience of the United States in the 1990s (a prolonged expansion almost fine tuned by monetary policy) goes against this view; Japanese experience in the same decade (a prolonged stagnation despite expansionary policies) may reinforce it. Either way, demand management policy is in intellectual retreat. Yet one major component of the Keynesian message—the need for automatic stabilizers, and hence the acceptance of at least temporary budget deficits—has become an intrinsic part of any modern economy.

[*See also* Business Cycles *and* Great Depression.]

BIBLIOGRAPHY

Ackley, Gardner, and Hiromitsu Ishi. "Fiscal, Monetary, and Related Policies." In *Asia's New Giant*, edited by Hugh Patrick and Henry Rosovsky. Washington, D.C., 1976. A discussion of Japan's experience.

Arndt, Heinz W. *The Economic Lessons of the Nineteen-Thirties*. Oxford, 1944. An early survey of the cyclical experience of the pre–World War II era.

Baily, Martin N. "Stabilization Policy and Private Economic Behavior." *Brookings Papers on Economic Activity* 1 (1978), 19–59.

Bispham, John, and Andrea Boltho. "Demand Management." In *The European Economy: Growth and Crisis*, edited by Andrea Boltho. Oxford, 1982. A discussion of Europe's experience.

Boltho, Andrea. "Did Policy Activism Work?" *European Economic Review* 33.9 (1989), 1709–1726.

Friedman, Milton. "A Monetary and Fiscal Framework for Economic Stability." *American Economic Review* 38.3 (1948), 245–264. First presents the case against discretionary action.

Friedman, Milton. "The Role of Monetary Policy." *American Economic Review* 58.1 (1968), 1–17. A very influential article that strengthens the case against discretionary action by postulating a vertical Phillips curve.

Gordon, Robert J. "Postwar Macroeconomics: The Evolution of Events and Ideas." In *The American Economy in Transition*, edited by Martin Feldstein. Chicago, 1980. A discussion of the U.S. experience.

Hansen, Bent. "Fiscal Policy in Seven Countries, 1955–1965." OECD Report. Paris, 1969. Presents estimates for the countercyclical role of policy.

Heller, Walter, et al. "Fiscal Policy for a Balanced Economy: Experience, Problems, and Prospects." OECD Report. Paris, 1968. An official report broadly in favor of policy activism.

Keynes, John Maynard. *The General Theory of Employment, Interest, and Money*. London, 1936. The seminal work that provided the theoretical underpinning for demand-management policies.

Laufenberg, Henry. *L'intervention de l'état en matière économique*. Paris, 1938.

League of Nations. *The Transition from War to Peace Economy*. Geneva, 1943. A further attempt to put into practice Keynesian ideas.

League of Nations. *Economic Stability in the Postwar World*. Geneva, 1945. One of the first attempts at putting into practice the new Keynesian ideas.

Lewis, W. Arthur. *Growth and Fluctuations, 1870–1913*. London, 1978. A survey of the cyclical experience of the pre–World War II era.

Modigliani, Franco. "The Monetarist Controversy or, Should We Forsake Stabilization Policies?" *American Economic Review* 67.2 (1977), 1–19.

"The Role of Monetary Policy in Demand Management." OECD Report on Monetary Policy. Paris, 1975. A further official report broadly in favor of policy activism.

Tobin, James. "Stabilization Policy Ten Years After." *Brookings Papers on Economic Activity* 1 (1980), 19–89.

ANDREA BOLTHO

STAPLE MARKETS AND ENTREPÔTS. Although the term *staple market* is not in favor, the term *entrepôt* is still in common usage; it currently means a "place where goods are stored, free of duty, for export to another country." In the past, the terms *entrepôt* and *staple market* were interchangeable, and their use was not restricted to duty-free storage; they usually denoted a place to which relatively large quantities of a particular merchandise were brought and stored before being exported or distributed in the hinterland. Storage is an essential function of a staple market and, although of uncertain origin, *staple* is often traced back to the Middle Dutch word (fourteenth century) *stapel*, meaning pile or heap.

Following Eli F. Heckscher (*Mercantilism*, London and New York, 1994, vol. 2, pp. 53–79), three categories of staple markets may be distinguished: marts, staple towns, and national staples. The establishment of marts is associated with times—such as the Middle Ages in Europe—when authorities could not or would not protect the life and belongings of strangers. In those days, merchants with a common background or a common interest often tried to reduce the risk of doing business by associating themselves in voluntary organizations, creating commercial centers abroad. These organizations of wholesale merchants (Hanse or Hansa, as they are called in Northern Europe) not only offered protection but also were effective in obtaining privileges from local rulers or from the sovereign in the host country. So the medieval Hanseatic League—a federation of free German cities and towns that sought to protect their ongoing position in European trade—acquired extensive exemptions from English customs, a large degree of autonomy, and a share in municipal authority in London. The Hanseatic League prospered until the sixteenth century.

The staple was originally a voluntary organization of English merchants, when in 1313 the English king realized their potential abroad and ordered that all English wool be brought to one place, which simplified the enforcement of trade regulations and the collection of customs dues. His power to establish the woolstaple in, or withdraw it from, a particular town or country also served as a foreign-policy instrument.

The need for merchants to cooperate, thus reducing the risk of doing business, and to establish commercial centers abroad matched a policy adopted by many local governments to further the interests of their citizens (but not necessarily all of them), by turning their cities and towns into staple markets. For this reason, urban magistrates were eager to attract foreign merchants, and they were usually willing to accept the conditions for the establishment of a staple or *Kontor*. There were also other, more aggressive, means to promote local interests. A place could be made a staple town by preventing goods from passing through it. In the eleventh century, cities in northern Italy adopted this policy from Byzantium; from Italy, the practice spread throughout Europe.

A city usually needed a charter granting it the right to force merchants to come there and put their merchandise on sale. Such was the situation in the German city of Cologne (Köln), where, beginning in the thirteenth century, goods moving in either direction on the Rhine River had to be unloaded there and offered for sale, even if their final destination was to be elsewhere. This staple right led to needless expenses for unloading and transshipments. The purpose was to appropriate the largest possible share of the river trade at the expense of other centers. Forcing goods to enter the city, however, was usually only one aspect of the staple policy. Many urban governments also tried to transfer business from the hands of strangers into those of their fellow citizens. Foreign merchants in a city were therefore often forced to do business exclusively with native dealers, which prevented them from trading with other strangers who were met there. In addition, they were not allowed to engage in retail trade, and their stay in town was often limited in time (the duration of annual fairs, for example). All the rules were implemented to benefit the local economy—specifically its traders, brokers, shippers, and carriers—at the expense of outsiders.

The staple town served as a model for countries that tried to force international trade through their national staple markets at the expense of—or with the deliberate purpose of causing damage to—other nations. In Europe, the medieval colonial powers of Portugal and Spain were the first to develop a policy aimed at turning their countries into staple markets in intercontinental trade; their colonial trade was a monopoly of the Crown. In Portugal, all trade with the colonies had to be conducted through the Casa da India in Lisbon, where the spices from Asia were sold. In Spain, the Crown delegated its monopoly in colonial trade to a guildlike organization, the Casa de Contrataciòn, controlled by royal officials. Its establishment in

1503 in Seville made the city the entrepôt for Spain's trade with the Americas, which remained so until the Casa was transferred to Cádiz in 1680. In a similar fashion, the Dutch East India Company was established in 1602, having been granted by the Dutch government a monopoly on all Dutch trade with Asia. It ordered that all ships were to return to *patria* (the homeland), thereby making Holland an important staple market for pepper, spices, and Asian commodities in general. In England, the Navigation Act of 1651/1660 and the Staple Act of 1663 completed the legislative basis of a national staple policy that was aimed at making the country the entrepôt for all colonial produce and for all foreign commodities that were destined for the British colonies.

Staple markets do not solely result from economic policy but reflect the organization of the premodern market. In his work on capitalism, Werner Sombart (1924) associated the system of annual fairs and mobile merchants, typical for much trade in marts and staple towns, with the limited extent of trade. Only when or where the volume of trade was sufficiently large could the old trading system, based on fairs, develop into a new organizational framework, in which merchants (and their merchandise) no longer moved from fair to fair but stayed at home, kept large stocks, and conducted business throughout the year. Even in that case, according to Sombart, all premodern trade had to be *Lokohandel*: trade conducted in actual (staple) marketplaces, where the merchandise was present, and buyers and sellers met one another.

Others have elaborated on Sombart's work and have suggested that *Lokohandel* and the staple markets became integrated into a larger European or even global hierarchy of markets. Thus, T. P. van der Kooy (*Hollands stapelmarkt en haar verval*, Amsterdam, 1931) blended Sombart's work with views derived from the marginal utility school in economics. He argued that the structure of trade would necessarily have to be hierarchic, with the surpluses of local markets being sent to regional markets, those of regional markets to national markets, and so on. At the top of this hierarchical system of markets was the central, or world, staple market that regulated the world's production and consumption. There, the surpluses of all the other markets were redistributed and prices were set. According to vander Kooy, this central organization of international trade only disappeared when, during the course of the nineteenth century, a growing and more stable demand accompanied by major changes in shipping (scheduled services and steam-powered ships) and communications (telegraph) made staple markets obsolete.

Neither Sombart's assumption that all premodern trade necessarily had to be conducted in actual marketplaces nor van der Kooy's view of the hierarchical structure of the market system with a single world staple market at the top is sufficiently supported by facts. Sale by sample, for example, is known to have existed from medieval times onward, and for most products a clear hierarchy of markets cannot be established. Consequently the great staple cities of their time—Antwerp, Amsterdam, and London—attracted large volumes of merchandise not because the premodern economy needed a single center to store and distribute the surpluses of world trade but (1) because they served as gateways for well-developed hinterlands and (2) because of economies of scale in broader markets and the market services (credit, insurance, information, and shipping) that were available.

These "modern" characteristics made premodern staple markets prone to the problem of all wholesale trade: elimination. As in modern markets, the wholesale trade in entrepôts and staple markets was based on intermediation, which was bound to disappear when the benefits of buying and selling in intermediate markets no longer outweighed the additional costs for transport and storage. In many branches of trade, direct links between producers and consumers were established long before the age of steam-powered ships and telegraphs. Only when trade was backed up by staple rights, political force, or geographical imperatives were staple markets secure.

[See also Fairs and Hanseatic League.]

BIBLIOGRAPHY

Braudel, Fernand. *Civilization and Capitalism, 15th–18th Century*, vol. 3, *The Perspective of the World*. London, 1985.

Glamann, Kristof. "The Changing Patterns of Trade." In *The Cambridge Economic History of Europe*, vol. 5, *The Economic Organization of Early Modern Europe*, edited by E. E. Rich and C. H. Wilson, pp. 185–289. Cambridge, 1977.

Klein, Peter W., and Jan Willem Veluwenkamp. "The Role of the Entrepreneur in the Economic Expansion of the Dutch Republic." In *The Dutch Economy in the Golden Age*, edited by Karel Davids and Leo Noordegraaf, pp. 27–53. Amsterdam, 1993.

Postan, Michael. "The Trade of Medieval Europe: The North." In *The Cambridge Economic History of Europe*, vol. 2, *Trade and Industry in the Middle Ages*, edited by M. Postan and E. E. Rich, pp. 119–256. Cambridge, 1952.

Schumpeter, Joseph A. *History of Economic Analysis*, edited by Elizabeth Boody Schumpeter. London, 1972. Note especially Part 2, chapter 7.

Sombart, Werner. *Der moderne Kapitalismus: Historisch-systematische Darstellung des gesamteuropäischen Wirtschaftslebens von seinen Anfängen bis zur Gegenwart*, vol. 2. Munich, 1924. Note especially chapters 31 and 38.

CLÉ LESGER

STATE FARMS. Ownership of land has often been nominally in the hands of the sovereign government. In some countries at certain points in time, the state has taken a more direct role in farming. The most pervasive form of this was in the Soviet Union, where a large group of farmers was forced to work on state farms directly under the control of government officials.

State control over agriculture in the USSR began in late 1917, after the revolution, when decrees banning the private ownership of land were enacted and peasant land committees were formed to take over management of private farms. This process was completed by mid-1918, with authority for these collective farming units, or *kolkhozes*, decentralized at the village level. Centralized authority over these soviets was gradually increased in the next few years, but it was not until the early 1920s that the central government gained full control over them.

The Soviet state farms, *sovkhozes*, were begun in early 1919 as the state directly took over the larger privately held farms. The declared aims were to raise agricultural productivity and output, create the conditions for a transfer to communist agriculture, and establish farms where new agricultural methods could be tested.

In 1928, with the onset of a poor grain harvest, Joseph Stalin shifted the priorities of Soviet agriculture. As *sovkhozes* were more productive than the communal *kolkhozes* and turned over more of their output to central planners than did collective farms, Stalin expanded the state farm system at the expense of the *kolkhozes*. Up until the end of communism in the USSR in 1989, *sovkhozes* continued to be formed from the collective farms, becoming more important (in terms of area sown) in 1970.

The management of a farm was rigidly controlled. The manager was required to obtain state permission for any change of land use (for example, from pasture to plow land) and was forced to use specified agronomic methods of growing and harvesting the crop, even if such methods were unsuitable for that area or crop. Managers were told what to produce, and they had no control over the prices they received for their produce and limited control over how they allocated funds within the farm. The early decades of state farming were generally disappointing, with low productivity growth and failure to generate large agricultural surpluses. State farms required an inflow of resources to keep functioning, rather than providing the government with a valuable asset.

Incentive structures, including the right of members of state farms to consume the harvest surplus above the amount required to be given to the state, were introduced in the 1960s. The main problem with state farms has been the incentive problem. Individual workers' productivity is usually difficult to measure, so wages are based on average productivity. This gives individuals incentives to shirk, as their actions have negligible effect on the total output. However, when all workers shirk, productivity falls dramatically and has to be induced by some method. The Soviet method of inducing productivity was the threat of imprisonment or deportation to a worse location.

The breakup of the USSR in the early 1990s brought a program whereby state farms voted as to whether to remain state owned or to privatize. About seven thousand farms chose to remain state owned, while nine thousand chose to privatize. Government subsidies to state farms increased during the 1990s as input prices rose to free market levels.

State intervention in agriculture in China began in the early 1950s. Land was redistributed among poor and landless peasants, and peasants were encouraged to share their labor with each other in times of need. In 1955 producers' cooperatives were formed to pool land use (although ownership remained private) and to try to achieve economies of scale. While this process evolved quickly, in 1956 and 1957, before it was complete, the farms were reorganized into collective farms, which were larger in size than cooperatives and abolished private land ownership. In 1958 these were amalgamated into communes, which coordinated industry and education as well as agriculture. Private plots of land were abolished in the communes. Because of the drop in productivity, in 1959 a decentralization of agriculture began with production units of 100 to 350 families, rather than the 5,000 to 8,000 families of the communes, and a return of the private farm plots. Policy became gradually more liberal over the decades, with the advent of private markets for farm products in the 1980s and long-term rental contracts for land, typically around fifteen years, begun in the 1990s.

When the communists took over Cuba in 1959, they began state farms there. The large private estates not divided up for use by peasant farmers but instead were given over to government management as state farms. Around half the arable land became state farmland in 1959, and the state continued to take over more farmland. Consequently by the late 1980s the state had approximately four-fifths of the land, output, and agricultural labor force. Over time they have gained much local autonomy, with some incentives for individual workers to improve productivity, such as individual plots for workers. As is expected in a system with a lack of incentives, state farms had a lower productivity than private farms, with private farms producing around 40 percent of the total agricultural output from only 20 percent of the land. The collapse of the Soviet Union in 1989 created a huge problem for Cuba, which had been used to importing food and petroleum at subsidized rates. Forced to dissolve the state farm system in 1993, the state encouraged workers to farm cooperatively. Free farm markets, allowed in 1994, decreased food supply problems and eased the heavy flow of subsidies the government gave to state farms.

While many African nations have experimented with state involvement in agriculture, Ethiopia instigated the largest state-run farm program in 1975. All land was nationalized to be farmed by all who wanted to operate it. Peasant organizations were formed at a small-scale level, but the preexisting large-scale commercial farms were turned into state farms. Although distribution of farm income was to be based on the quality and quantity of work, there was also a lower bound of the amount needed to maintain a reasonable lifestyle. State farms never accounted for more than 5 percent of the cultivated area. With the removal from power of the Marxist regime, state farms were auctioned off to private individuals in 2000 and 2001.

BIBLIOGRAPHY

Atkinson, Dorothy. *The End of the Russian Land Commune, 1905–1930.* Stanford, Calif. 1983.

Dobrovolsky, Alexander. *Economic Administration and Labor Productivity on a Soviet State Farm.* East European Fund, Mimeographed Series No. 63. New York, 1954.

Ghai, Dharam, Cristóbal Kay, and Peter Peek. *Labour and Development in Rural Cuba.* New York, 1988.

Gregory, Paul, and Robert Stuart. *Soviet Economic Structure and Performance.* New York, 1990.

Karcz, Jerzy F. *The Economics of Communist Agriculture.* Edited by Arthur W. Wright. Bloomington, Ind., 1979.

Medvedev, Zhores A. *Soviet Agriculture.* New York, 1987.

"Privatisation Puts 357 Million Dollars into State Coffers." <http://allafrica.com>.

Saich, Tony. *Governance and Politics of China.* New York, 2001.

Stuart, Robert C., ed. *The Soviet Rural Economy.* Totowa, N.J., 1983.

Walker, Kenneth R. *Planning in Chinese Agriculture.* London, 1965.

LYNDON MOORE

STEELMAKING. Steel is an alloy of iron and carbon, often containing various small percentages of other metals (nickel, chromium, manganese, etc.), which create the many varieties. Before the introduction of the Bessmer process (c. 1860), steel was produced in small quantities, either by reintroducing a small precentage of carbon into iron or, less frequently, by removing the excess of carbon from cast iron. The first possibility offered various methods—for example, cementation or carburization (cabonization): charcoal was added to iron ore to give, by smelting, a "natural steel" or, more frequently, pieces of wrought iron were put together with charcoal into small converting furnaces to give an "artificial steel."

Long before Europe, metalworkers in China, India, and parts of the Middle East were mastering a high-quality production of iron and steel. In China, steelmaking was far more advanced than in Europe, and the technique of cofusion was well developed: low and high carbon scraps of iron were mixed together in a furnace. In India, another method of carburization gave a high quality of steel, called "wootz steel": the Indian steelmakers mixed, in a crucible, iron ores and pieces of a special wood and/or green leaves. China had been first to produce cast iron, in the fifth century BCE, and Chinese smiths had produced steel in quantity, by cofusion, at least since the fifth century CE. A Chinese document, the *Pei Chi Shu* of the early sixth century CE, mentioned this technique, which was later described in the *Pên Tshao Thu Ching*, compiled in 1070 CE: "By mixing and uniting the raw [cast iron] and the soft [wrought iron] for making the edges and points of sabers and swords; this is called steel." The Chinese had also invented the coal refining that produced coke in blast furnaces as early as the thirteenth century CE, while in Europe such a technique appeared in England only in 1709. From 1000 to 1200 CE, the Chinese iron and steel industry was settled in large plants, with hundreds of workers at Cixian in the south of Hebei Province, in Shandong Province, and in the north of Jiangsu Province. These ironworks not only produced armaments and tools for the state but also pieces of iron and steel for agricultural tools.

In India, the steelmakers of Konasamundram and Dimdurti in Hyderabad produced the renowned "wootz steel" beginning in the fifth century CE. This was a raw material employed to forge Damascus blades (for swords and scimitars) in the workshops of Damascus (Syria), Isfahan (Persia), and in South India.

In Europe, although luxury steel blades had been forged by early medieval Celts, Germans, Scandinavians, and Slavs, they were never to the scale and quality of the Chinese and Indian craftsmen. European metallurgy had become stagnant after the fall of the Roman Empire; European steelmaking would be linked to the Renaissance technological advance of pig iron production, when mid-fourteenth-century blast furnaces using charcoal and refinery furnaces produced the first pig iron. Thereafter in Europe, the wrought iron production stage (an indirect method of iron production) was ignored, and wrought iron was obtained through the "direct method" in Catalan, Corsican, Styrian, or Norman works. A mix of iron ore and charcoal was heated in a small furnace under regular ventilation, by bellows, to obtain a ball of iron paste ready to hammer. The direct method had been inherited from the Gallo-Roman smiths of late antiquity. In the Early Middle Ages, ironsmiths became itinerants who traveled from one domain to another to produce small pieces, as needed, for agricultural tools and to forge costly pieces of armament. In the Alpine region, Early Christian monks—Cistercians and Carthusians—played an important role in regenerating industry and propagating metallurgy in Styria, Carinthia, Lombardy, and Piedmont, as well as in the French Dauphiné region during the twelfth century. At that time, heavy waterwheels began to be used as mill wheels, to activate bellows and hammers. Metallurgy, which had become a nomadic activity, then became a sedentary one—located along streams in the forest (for the supply of charcoal). In the Venetian Republic, the ironmasters of the Brescia-Bergamo region not only produced steel by the cementa-

tion method, they forged luxury pieces of armament. As early as the thirteenth century, they also managed to produce a kind of cast iron by the indirect method (known by Chinese masters before the first century CE). In the Dauphiné region of France, furnaces gave a "steeled" iron that was produced using manganese iron ores. From the Early Middle Ages onward, steel production by the cementation method was the speciality of Styria and Carinthia, where the renowned "German steel" was first made to forge luxury swords and armor.

A technological breakthrough was reached in Europe in the mid-fourteenth century, in the region between the Meuse and Rhine rivers, with the discovery of the indirect method of wrought iron production, called the "Walloon method." With a blast furnace using a heavy bellows that was activated by water wheels, the temperature could reach the point of fusion (1,535° Celsius), and pig iron flowed out of the crucible. Cast iron was soon being molded to make cooking pots and pans, firebacks, gun barrels, and cannonballs. Blooms of pig iron were also reheated in small furnaces that were fueled by charcoal (refineries), to produce iron that was decarbonized by hammering and thereby transformed into forgeable pieces of wrought iron. The indirect method and the use of blast furnaces (Ger., *Flussofen*) instead of traditional Catalan or Styrian bloomery furnaces (Ger., *Stuckofen*) were only slowly diffused into Europe during the sixteenth century. At that time, some of the most important metallurgical regions in the Alps and, above all, in the Basque country continued to use the direct method. In 1545, the Basques of Biscay (Vizcaya) and Guipúzcoa had more than three hundred metal furnaces, most then in the hands of merchant-entrepreneurs from Bilbao (Spain), who developed an international trade of iron and steel production. Forges of the County of Foix or Nivern (France) and the Alpine Brescian and Styrian works also maintained the direct technique and continued to produce a high quality of steel by the cementation method.

Beginning in the Ardennes region of France, blast furnaces and refinery forges spread throughout the country during the fifteenth century. The adoption of the blast furnace transformed steelmaking. Pieces of pig iron could be decarbonized through a process of successive melting, hammering, and reheating. Around 1530, the first hydraulic hammers to produce steel bars appeared at Rives in the Dauphiné (maybe from German Westphalia). From the "Pays de Bray" they reached England, where the first blast furnace was built in 1495 in the Weald. From there, the indirect method was diffused during the late sixteenth century, to reach the Dean Forest, West Midlands, Yorkshire, and South Wales by the early seventeenth. The Belgian region of Liège was at that time a major centre of iron and steel production, and its trade was stimulated by the economic power of Antwerp. In the late 1570s, some iron-masters of Liège succeeded in adapting the rolling-slitting mill, to produce iron sticks for nailmakers. Since 1568, however, the economic chaos resulting from civil war had deeply affected Liège's industry; to survive, Liège's iron-masters reoriented their trade toward Amsterdam, Lux-embourg, and the Rhineland. Within this context, the Liège merchants and entrepreneurs played a leading role in the transfer of technology to the Basque country and to Sweden. In 1612, the Belgian Louis de Geer set up blast furnaces and forges to produce pieces of artillery for the Swedish Crown. He also recruited Walloon (Belgian) skilled workers, and from 1615 to 1640 at least 300 fami-lies emigrated to Sweden. Raised to the Swedish peerage in 1627, de Geer is regarded as the founder of the Swedish iron industry located in the Uppland. In theory, the Wal-loon method would have been able to produce steel by de-carbonizing cast iron, but it seemed too difficult to control the process, so the cementation method was still pre-ferred.

From the sixteenth century until the late eighteenth, the usual ironworks included a blast furnace that used char-coal, with an output of 1,200 to 2,000 kilograms/day, and power was supplied by vertical water wheels. Because of the huge quantities of charcoal needed (3 tons of charcoal for 1 ton of pig iron) the furnaces were still situated in or near the forests, which often created great difficulties for transport. The capacity of the forests to produce fuel limit-ed the number of ironworks, while the whole industry also dependend on the weather—with freezing temperatures limiting the use of the water wheels. The output of pig iron and wrought iron, and of steel, remained low until the mid-eighteenth century, although it is hard to give esti-mates. According to Stefan Kurowski (see Braudel 1981), European iron production only reached 150,000 tons/year in 1540, 180,000 tons/year around 1700, and 600,000 tons/year in 1790. The main products remained armaments and luxury blades, a speciality of such places as Toledo, Bres-cia, Milan, Graz, Cologne, Solingen, Regensburg, Nordlin-gen, Nuremberg, Saint-Etienne, and Liège.

During the Renaissance, Vanoccio Biringuccio describ-ed in *Della pirotechnia* (1540) a reverberatory furnace. Us-ing it, some Italian masters reached very high tempera-tures and produced good quality wrought iron and steel. Their method was close to the puddling process that was invented in the late 1700s. The Swedish metallurgist T. O. Bergmann had discovered the influence of carbon content on the hardness of steel in the early 1700s, while in France, René A. F. de Réaumur in his *Art de convertir le fer forgé en acier* (Paris, 1722) presented his examination of the vari-ous qualities of steel then known and invented the first methods of metallography. Yet during the first half of the eighteenth century, European steel was still produced by

the cementation process. In England, smiths of Newcastle upon Tyne imported Swedish iron bars to produce first "blister steel" by cementation, then by further heat treat-ment and forging, the shear steel required for cutlery.

The output of European pig iron—the raw material for producing wrought iron and steel—remained a bottleneck because of small capacity blast furnaces, high costs of charcoal, and irregular water power. A major step forward was realized in England in 1709 when Abraham Darby managed to use coked coal as a fuel in his furnace at Coal-brookdale in Shropshire. For a long time, however, the pig iron produced with coke offered poor quality in compari-son with pig iron produced with charcoal. Moreover, to convert coked pig iron into wrought iron was very expen-sive because of the presence of unwanted silicon in coked iron. Not until 1760 did Darby's son succeed in producing cheap cast iron, by remelting the pig iron in a foundry fur-nace to remove the silicon.

At first, coke was produced in the same way as charcoal, by burning crude coal in stacks, but soon closed ovens shaped like beehives were adopted to increase productivi-ty. By the end of the 1700s, coke had largely replaced char-coal in the most important British ironworks, particularly in Scottish and Welsh blast furnaces. The capacity of blast furnaces was increased through the replacement of old-fashioned bellows by new waterpower-blowing cylinders, invented around 1760 by John Smeaton. During the late 1700s, French, Walloon, and German metallurgists be-came increasingly anxious about British production, and the discovery of the secrets of coked pig iron became a ma-jor issue. Iron produced using coke was not the only prob-lem to solve; the process of turning pig iron into wrought iron remained a major bottleneck. In England, the Wood brothers pioneered the so-called potting process, using crucibles to heat pig iron—however, the solution was to adapt the reverberatory furnaces. In 1784, Henry Cort suc-cessfully invented the puddling process of pig iron into a coal-burning reverberatory furnace, and he also trans-formed the bloomings obtained into bars and sheets by us-ing rolling mills. Combining the puddling process with rolling heated metal was known, on the Continent, as *forge à l'anglaise* at the beginning of the 1800s. Cort's process be-came a major component of the Industrial Revolution, be-cause with it, small forges were transformed into large ironworks—the *fabriques de fer*—in which tons of metal plates, rails, and bars were increasingly produced.

The breakthrough in steel production was made by the English clockmaker Benjamin Huntsman (1704–1776) who started his investigation at Doncaster in Lincolnshire and continued, after 1740, at Sheffield. In order to produce a homogeneous steel, he smelted it at a very high temp-erature, in sealed claycrucibles, with some charcoal and crushed glass as the chemical reagent. Around 1750,

STEELMAKING. *Forging the Shaft: A Welding Heat,* painting by John L. Weir, 1877. (Metropolitan Museum of Art, New York)

Hunstman managed to produce crucible steel, but only in small quantities and at a high cost. By 1787, at least six ironworks at Sheffield were employing his crucible process. The success of Sheffield steel stimulated other initiatives across Europe. In Switzerland, J. C. Fisher of Schaffhausen managed not only to rediscover Huntsman's method in but also invented copper-steel and nickel-steel alloys. In 1802, the Poncelet brothers succeeded in producing fine crucible steel in Liège, using iron ore from the Pyrénées.

At the same time, progress was being made on the theoretical front, with the research of C. A. Vandermonde, C. L. Berthollet, and G. Monge ("Mémoire sur le fer," *Mémoires de l'Académie Royale des Sciences,* Paris, 1786, pp. 132–200). They stated that the steel produced by the cementation process was iron, reduced as far as was possible, then combined with a proportion of charcoal, which was itself a form of carbon.

[*See also* Bessemer Process; Metallurgic Industry; *and* Siemens-Martin Process.]

BIBLIOGRAPHY

Barraclough, K. C., *Steelmaking before Bessemer.* 2 vols. London, 1984.
Braudel, Fernand. *Civilization and Capitalism 15th–18th Century,* vol. 1, *The Structures of Everyday Life: The Limits of the Possible.* London, 1981.
Braunstein, Philippe. "Innovations in Mining and Metal Production in Europe in the Late Middle Age." *Journal of European Economic History* 12 (1983), 573–591.
Kellenbenz, Herman. *Schwerpunkte der Eisengewinnung und Eisenverarbeitung in Europa, 1500–1650.* Cologne, 1974.
Leboutter, R. "La métallurgie dans la région liégeoise du XVe siècle à l'aube du XIXe siècle." In *Wandlungen der Eisenindustrie vom 16. Jahrhundert bis 1960. Mutations de la sidérurgie du XVIe siècle à 1960,* edited by Hans-Walter Herrmann and Paul Wynants, pp. 57–183. Facultés Universitaires Notre-Dame de la Paix, Colloques Meuse-Moselle, Namur, 1997.
Mokyr, Joel. *The Lever of Riches: Technological Creativity and Economic Progress.* Oxford, 1990.
Needham, Joseph. *The Development of Iron and Steel Technology in China.* London, 1958.
Schubert, H. R. *History of the British Iron and Steel Industry from c. 450 B.C. to A.D. 1775.* London, 1957.
Sprandel, Rolf. *Das Eisengewerbe im Mittelalter.* Stuttgart, 1968.
Woronoff, Denis. *Histoire de l'industrie en France du XVIe siècle à nos jours.* Paris, 1994.

RENÉ LEBOUTTE

STEPHENSON FAMILY. British engineer George Stephenson (1781–1848) was falsely hailed by Samuel Smiles, a nineteenth-century biographer, as the inventor of the locomotive; but he and his only son, Robert (1803–1859), were responsible for several major advances in railway technology.

The British Industrial Revolution began in a prerailway environment with Britain possessing the world's best road and water transport systems. Advances in steam-engine and iron-making technology during that revolution set the stage for the railway, which supported all later industrialization. After Richard Trevithick developed the high-pressure steam engine in 1804, he and a handful of others began to experiment with locomotives. George Stephenson, a self-taught steam-engine mechanic, was located advantageously: the south Durham area was rich in coal but poorly served by water transport. Inspired by the locomotives of others, he built and sold several to local collieries.

The Stockton and Darlington Railway was originally planned for horse traction; but after parliamentary approval was obtained, key investors became impressed with both Stephenson and the locomotive. Stephenson was hired as chief engineer, and resurveyed the line to follow a flatter route. Although he achieved the first use of locomotives on a public railway when it opened in 1825, stationary engines or horses were used on steeper gradients until 1834.

Stephenson recognized the need to advance locomotive and rail design in concert. He hired capable assistants, including his son, and likely was often credited with their innovations. He developed the steam blast, which increased draft by channeling exhaust steam through the chimney. He replaced complex systems of gearing by directly powering the wheels. With ironmaster William Losh, he developed stronger rails and a system of pistons on axles to support the engine, significantly reducing rail damage.

His relationship with Losh, who also built his locomotives, ended when Stephenson recognized the superiority of wrought iron rails. Leading investors in the Stockhon and Darlington joined the Stephensons in forming the Robert Stephenson and Company locomotive works. Management of this firm often suffered as both Stephensons ventured far afield to work for other railways. There was also conflict between father and son. The firm was often late in fulfilling orders, and its earliest locomotives frequently broke down.

The Liverpool and Manchester Railway, the first railway to rely exclusively on locomotives when it opened in 1830, had hired George Stephenson as surveyor. When in 1829 it held a competition for best locomotive, the Stephensons' *Rocket* was victorious. This award firmly established them as leading railway experts, and they were involved in some capacity in most British railways and many foreign projects. Their 4'8.5" gauge became standard in much of the world, and their locomotives were employed worldwide. However, they were as guilty as other engineers of the cost overruns that plagued British railways; and they were slow to recognize the advantages of resting rails on wooden ties rather than concrete blocks.

Robert Stephenson was much better educated than his father, attending Edinburgh University for a term. He would excel in bridge construction. He used James Nas-myth's steam hammer to drive the foundations for a six-arch iron bridge over the Tyne, and conceived a much-copied tubular design for the Britannia Bridge over the Menai Strait.

BIBLIOGRAPHY

Carlson, Robert E. *The Liverpool and Manchester Railway Project.* Newton Abbot, 1969.

Davies, Hunter. *George Stephenson: A Biographical Study of the Father of the Railways.* London, 1975.

Kirby, Maurice W. *The Origins of Railway Enterprise: The Stockton and Darlington Railway, 1821–1863.* Cambridge, 1993.

Rolt, L. T. C. *George and Robert Stephenson: The Railway Revolution.* London, 1960.

Vaughan, Adrian. *Railwaymen, Politics, and Money: The Great Age of Railways in Britain.* London, 1997. Downplays the role of George Stephenson as inventor, but recognizes his entrepreneurial role and praises Robert Stephenson's engineering.

RICK SZOSTAK

STINNES, HUGO (1870–1924), German industrialist.

The Stinnes family began its association with coal and shipping in the early nineteenth century. Mathias Stinnes, Hugo's grandfather, established his company in Mülheim in 1808 and began shipping coal in 1810. During the nineteenth century, Mathias was able to expand his export and import business throughout the Ruhr district and especially along the Rhine River. Mathias's son (who was Hugo Stinnes's uncle, Mathias Jr.) expanded the operations, as did Hugo's father, Herman Hugo Stinnes, until his death in 1887.

In 1893, Hugo Stinnes, then just twenty-three, founded the Hugo Stinnes GmbH, enabling him to consolidate his family's growing interests in shipping and mining. Soon after the creation of the Rhine-Westphalian Coal Syndicate and the Rhine Coal and Shipping Company (established in 1903), the entire Ruhr district's production, distribution, and pricing of coal was controlled. Stinnes moved quickly to integrate forward into steel production, as well as electricity, gas, and water utilities. In 1901, he had founded the German-Luxembourg Mining and Smelting Company (referred to often as "Deutsch-Lux"), which quickly became an important producer with factories in Bochum, Dortmund, Mulheim, Emden, and Differingen (in Luxembourg), along with mines all along the Ruhr basin. Stinnes's shipping interests turned this vertically integrated nexus of production into a major export and domestic supplier.

Not content to be merely involved in coal extraction, iron and steel production, and shipping, Stinnes expanded into utilities, shipbuilding, and the machine construction industries. Stinnes shepherded the Rhein-Westfalian Electric Company into the electric provider for all of the Rhein-Westfalian industrial area, thereby vastly expanding electricity production and distribution. Stinnes achieved

HUGO STINNES. (Underwood & Underwood, New York/Prints and Photographs Division, Library of Congress)

this expan sion partially by making sure that municipalities (Essen, Solingen, etc.) owned shares in the company, as well as individuals. By the outbreak of World War I in 1914, this was the largest electric company in all Germany. While expanding into electricity, Stinnes was also extending into shipbuilding in Bremen and Hamburg. The Hugo Stinnes Shipping Company made possible the Hugo Stinnes Corporation for Shipping and Overseas Trade, established in 1917, in preparation for Germany's assumed victory and annexation of new territories—but that was not to be. During the war, Stinnes continued to integrate vertically and horizontally, moving into the production of trucks and airplanes by the end of 1917. He was a major war materials producer and had restructured his holdings in anticipation of German victory. With Germany's defeat in 1918, however, Stinnes had to restructure. With Germany's loss of the Lorraine region to France, the Deutsch-Lux lost some important coal and iron-ore fields, as well as connections with its iron and steel production in Luxembourg.

While rebuilding and extending his industrial empire, Stinnes fought against the growing socialism in Germany and became a member of the parliament (Reichstag) under the German People's Party (Deutchenationale Volkpartei). He strongly pursued policies of free-market operation and thought that the structure and success of his own enterprises would form a guiding example for German business and policy. He argued late in 1918 that concessions would have to be made to labor so that Germany could quickly expand without having to deal with labor unrest and shortages. In November 1918, the last month of the war, various industrial organizations and labor signed the Stinnes-Legien Agreement, giving labor, among other things, an eight-hour day, the recognition of unions, and mandatory collective bargaining.

Stinnes then expanded his operations to regain complete control over extraction, production, and distribution. In addition to his industrial pursuits, Stinnes acquired many newspapers, among them the *Deutsche Allgemeine Zeitung*. In 1920, along with Albert Vögler and Emil Kirdorf, Stinnes put together and jointly controlled the Rhine–Elbe Union, thus recreating the vertical structure from mining, to iron and steel production, to finished goods production that he had had before the war. Stinnes further pursued this process with connections to the Siemens Corporation, creating the Seimens-Rhine-Elbe-Schuckert Union. This expansion moved Stinnes's interests out of Rhine-Westphalia into other areas of Germany. His domestic expansion was concurrent with his increased international interests; Stinnes eventually had interests in firms in Austria, Switzerland, the Balkans, Russia, and Argentina.

By the time of his death in 1924, Stinnes had, by force of will and negotiation, created a gigantic vertical and horizontal trust that existed not so much from financial manipulation but from agreements and joint operations. After his death, the entire structure quickly fell apart; his death marked the end of an era. He did not live to see either the Locarno agreements or the revitalization of the German Ruhr industry. His legacy is often treated as one of errant trustification during Germany's postwar hyperinflation—but he is the transitional figure who went from the creation of combinations and associations to the full mergers that resulted in the giant enterprises of the interwar era. Even though the Stinnes concerns had financial difficulties and the Siemans-Rhien-Elbe-Schuckert Union drifted apart, his son was able to save the German-Luxembourg firm, with help from American investors, joining in the 1926 formation of the huge United Steel Works (Vereinigte Stahlwerke).

BIBLIOGRAPHY

Brinckmeyer, Hermann. *Hugo Stinnes*. New York, 1921. A bit of an apologist for Stinnes but a good source for his personal history and industrial combinations.

Feldman, Gerald. *The Great Disorder: Politics, Economics, and Society in the German Inflation, 1914–1924*. New York, 1993. A majesterial account of the German inflation with a detailed account of Stinnes's economic and political influence; see especially chapter 6 for an account of Stinnes's influence and combine building.

Feldman, Gerald. *Hugo Stinnes: Biographie eines Industriellen, 1870–1914*. Munich, 1998.

Wulf, Peter. *Hugo Stinnes: Wirtschaft und Politik, 1918–1924*. Stuttgart, 1979. In German. Excellent source of the literature on Stinnes. Wulf has also written on Stinnes's ownership of the *Deutsche Allegmine Zeitung* and his breakdown of cooperation with Bremen and Hamburg shipbuilders.

DANIEL BARBEZAT

STOCK MARKETS. Modern financial scholarship has followed two broad approaches in comprehending stock market function. One school has studied these markets primarily from an efficiency perspective. A vibrant theoretical research tradition first pioneered by Franco Modigliani and Merton Miller evaluated hypothetical perfect markets with no transaction costs and frictionless transfers of information. A second line of inquiry, the trail blazed by Thomas H. Meckling and Michael Jensen, has focused on the problematic asymmetric distribution of information between enterprise insiders and external investors. A central question for this latter school has been how risks associated with informational asymmetries have affected contracting between investors and their corporate agents.

This essay assesses stock market evolution by blending notions of market efficiency and agency with intellectual constructs from institutional economics. The focus is the interdependent array of institutions and organizations that drive stock market dynamics. According to Douglass North, institutions in this context are the formal and informal rules of the game that guide the action of financial market participants; organizations, on the other hand, are formal groups performing specialized stock market functions. Moreover, organizations and their controlling institutions incorporate knowledge of past experience. Through a process of path-dependent learning, institutions embed knowledge of earlier practices that have proven to be successful or unsuccessful in effectively ordering finance. It was a process of change that often was also reactive to exogenous developments in the economic, social, and technological realms.

Stock Market Origins. Modern stock markets trace their origins to anonymous markets for public debt that emerged in European centers during the late seventeenth century, particularly London. In fact, the term *stock* was the shortened form for *loan stock* or *debt*. Although there were some traces of primitive financial market dealing in the Middle Ages, mostly involving partnerships between literate craftsmen and magnates with surplus resources, this did not foster stock market development until much later. Instead, the new markets for public debt initially were most effective in assuaging the pressing financing problems of nascent nation states. From the state's perspective, such markets were advantageous because they facilitated the efficient concentration of large amounts of capital. The continuous liquidity afforded by these markets enabled governments to avoid the daunting problem of paying back both principal and interest simultaneously at maturity, a requirement that had impaired the finances of many medieval regimes. One spectacular example of this was the default in 1339 of King Edward III of England in payment of loans to his Florentine bankers during the Hundred Years' War. Broad, anonymous markets were also attractive to investors because they provided liquidity that facilitated the readjustment of private portfolios. Moreover, in these imperfect markets, debt contracts contained information about rate, principal, and term that gave investors a means for evaluating their worth. Risk perceptions could also be further reduced by hypothecating revenues from particular taxes or lotteries. And property rights were increasingly protected by the evolution of commercial law and judicial systems.

Debt was generally preferred over equity by investors, even with the rise of large trading entities in Europe's nascent stock markets. The few companies that successfully marketed equity were usually great enterprises enjoying state-granted monopolies, for example, for foreign trade with particular regions. A barrier to broad public equity ownership was the insufficiency of timely and accurate information to form reliable estimates of future profits. In this regard, public investors were at a disadvantage vis-à-vis corporate insiders. Not surprisingly, the share owners of one of the most successful enterprises of this period, the British East India Company, were insiders, as were the great merchants who distributed its imports to various European markets or their political allies at court or in Parliament.

The problem of asymmetric information in equity investing was also demonstrated in two great speculative bubbles about 1719–1720—the South Sea Company in London and John Law's Company of the western part of Paris. In both instances, the exchange of stock in state-sanctioned trade monopolies for public debt was perceived as an effective palliative for improving the health of governmental finances. But a serious mispricing of corporate equity resulted because of the inherent problem of forecasting future financial results and opportunistic manipulation of market prices by insiders. The combined impact of a subsequent currency collapse and the demise of the Company of the West seriously inhibited the growth of securities markets in France. Similarly, the failure of the South Sea Company led to the enactment of restrictive legislation in Great Britain, making it difficult for nearly a century to raise capital through the formation of joint-stock companies without specific Parliamentary sanction.

Effects of the Transportation Revolution. Stock market development accelerated during the transportation revolution of the nineteenth century and the financing requirements of great canal and railroad systems. Besides

London, Amsterdam, and Paris, the pressing financing requirements of national transportation sectors enlivened financial dealing in such emergent centers as Brussels, Frankfurt, Milan, New York, and a host of other centers. But as in the case of the great trading companies, serious informational asymmetries induced early rail promoters to rely heavily on bond finance while retaining substantial equity ownership. However, this began to change in the 1840s with the rise of preferred stock investment in British rails.

British corporations were restricted in the amount of debt they might issue in relationship to equity. The issuance of preferred stock satisfied state financing mandates but without diluting the ownership interests of common shareowners. Moreover, preferred stock found acceptance because it was endowed with bondlike attributes that were familiar to contemporary investors. They had, for example, prespecified dividend rates, liquidation values, and procedures defining how issues might be retired, such as through the use of sinking funds. From the issuers' perspective, the main advantage of preferred stock was that it reduced fixed interest charges and the potential dangers of insolvency. This latter feature made preferred stock a major source of refinancing railroads in the United States after the great bankruptcies of the 1870s and 1890s.

Moreover, the asymmetries that had inhibited public investment in railroads gradually diminished because of the rise of new information sources. A growing knowledge base about the industry provided an analytical focus for estimating the future contours of railroad finance both in Europe and the United States. Prominent members of the rising new profession of economics increasingly wrote about various aspects of railroad economics and governance. Periodicals appeared that monitored developments in railroad operations and finance. The appearance of extensive governmental statistical series further informed investors about railroad economic performance and potential. In the United States, for example, the Interstate Commerce Commission (ICC) launched its *Statistics of Railways of the United States* in 1886 to provide a wealth of information about all aspects of railroad functioning.

During the late nineteenth and early twentieth centuries, stock markets further expanded in Europe and the United States because of the rise of giant industrial enterprises. Unlike the railroads, industrial enterprises tended to finance their activities much more from retained earnings than from bonded debt. In fact, ownership interest often remained narrowly concentrated in some of the largest U.S. companies—for example, Dupont, Standard Oil, Carnegie Steel, and Ford Motor Company—until well into the twentieth century. With the shift to broader public ownership, preferred stocks (stocks that have a fixed dividend payment and seniority in pay out over common stock) were initially popular among investors both because of their debtlike features, which made them easier to evaluate than ordinary equity, and previous experience with these securities in railroad finance. Moreover, the problem of asymmetric information in equity valuation was addressed in a manner similar to that experienced by the railroads. Industry was studied both by professional economists and through a growing specialized periodical literature.

In Great Britain, successive Companies Acts since the mid-nineteenth century mandated greater financial disclosure and eventually the filing of statements certified by professional accountants annually with the Registrar of Companies. Although U.S. industry initially was not required to prepare standardized reports for government, except in the case of regulated industries, many corporations voluntarily sought to diminish investor risk perceptions by engaging public accountants to certify their annual financial statements. Risk perceptions were further educed through the passage of protective legislation.

During the 1920s, in the United States the focus was primarily on the state level, where so-called "blue sky" laws sought to prevent fraud in the floatation of new securities issues. The focus shifted to the federal level after the advent of the New Deal administration in 1933. The Securities Acts of 1933 and 1934 established a federal regulatory agency, the Securities and Exchange Commission, to monitor the issuance and trading of investment securities. These laws mandated transparency of corporate affairs through filings of financial statements and other types of disclosures. They also protected investors by providing legal redress for losses due to agent malfeasance.

Global Stock Markets. Significant cultural and politico-economic differences have contributed to the development of global stock markets. The type of system that emphasizes transparency and professional responsibility that has flourished in both the United States and United Kingdom differs from the predominant patterns in continental Europe and Asia. British and U.S. financial institutions evolved in societies with strong traditions of individualism and free market competition. In the more tightly ordered societies of continental Europe and Asia, on the other hand, economic affairs were more commonly governed by informal coalitions of governmental, banking, and industrial interests.

Giant banking institutions or postal savings systems play a far more significant role in concentrating savings than in the financial markets. They have frequently served as the model for many of the recently emergent stock markets in Asia, such as those in Indonesia, Korea, Taiwan, and Thailand. In Germany, for example, the *Hausbanks* had until recent years typically maintained large investment holdings in their nation's largest business enterprises. Agency risk was diminished in these cases through the transparency of borrower affairs made possible by monitoring performed by banks' professional agents or *Treuhander* who are stationed permanently at client businesses. Only recently has the German government adopted policies to abandon the *Hausbank* system in favor of the more open Anglo-American form of finance. Foremost in this regard are special tax advantages allowed to banks in disposing of their holdings of client company equity.

In Japan, on the other hand, lead banks form closely knit alliances with industrial, financial, and transportation enterprises through complex cross-shareholding arrangements. The lead bank, serving as the primary source of capital to the elements within the group or *keiretsu*, exercises control through its powers of approving annual operating budgets. This system, however, is in the process of reform. The problem is that the value of many banks' equity stakes have been seriously diminished by prolonged stock market decline in the 1990s. The loss of portfolio value is so threatening to the viability of the Japanese banking that alternatives to the traditional *keiretsu* structure may well be embraced.

While significant international differences still prevail, other factors have contributed to the convergence of global stock market governance. Progress has been achieved in harmonizing global financial reporting standards through the efforts of the International Accounting Standards Committee. Besides supporting international accounting standardization, international bodies, such as the United Nations and the European Union, have actively supported the better global coordination of stock market regulation and oversight. Greater international integration has also been facilitated by new technologies, particularly the development of the Internet. This latter modality makes it easier for investors worldwide to monitor activity on a host of national stock markets. It also provides the potential for traded companies to provide continuous disclosure about their financial and operating activities.

Factors Contributing to Stock Market Evolution. Besides these general historical patterns, other factors have contributed to stock market evolution. Abiding concerns about the risk of loss due to the poor performance of a particular security or the overall risk of the market affected the development of financial institutions and theory in two ways. First, drawing on the example of older commodity markets, options and later futures contracts were created to transfer either the systemic risk of the market or that of particular shares. The option contract incorporated a discount rate for calculating the net present value of a right to buy or sell a security at a future date. Much of the trading of shares in the eighteenth-century Amsterdam markets, for example, took the form of options because it avoided the cumbersome transfer procedures required of equity contracts.

Although the use of options had a long history, it was a practice first rigorously addressed in financial theory as part of the extension of the optimal pricing model defined by John Linter and William F. Sharpe in the 1960s. In 1973, Fisher Black and Myron Scholes first propounded their Nobel Prize–winning model for efficient option pricing. That same year, the Chicago Board of Options Exchange was formed to trade share options and was soon followed by similar initiatives on the American, Pacific, Philadelphia, and New York Stock Exchanges. Both options and futures contracts were soon offered for the S&P 500, the Value Line Index, NASDAQ, and the New York Stock Exchange Index.

A second mechanism for risk diffusion that facilitated stock market growth involved the development of a better understanding of how to structure efficient portfolios. Historically, access to contracts with differing legal or temporal attributes enabled investors to minimize losses due to the credit risk of particular investments or to capitalize on changes in the economic environment. Investors in eighteenth-century London could allocate their wealth through both long- and short-dated debt contracts as well as the equity of state-sanctioned monopolies. Later in the later nineteenth and early twentieth century, both unit trusts and mutual funds in Great Britain and the United States emerged whose diversified portfolios afforded protection against the credit risk of particular holdings. One variation of this practice was the so-called "balanced fund," composed of equal weighting of bonds and equities. The negative price covariances of these two classes of securities at different stages in the business cycle insured against total loss of capital due to market fluctuations. By the 1950s and 1960s, the pragmatic rules followed by practitioners were evaluated and formulized in theory by Harry Markowitz, John Lintner, William F. Sharpe, and other academic researchers.

Another prerequisite for stock market flourishing was the prevalence of a stable social order conducive to exploitation of economic opportunity. Excessive social flux raised perceptions of risk among investors. This inhibited the making of long-term capital commitments by raising transaction costs through high-risk premium demands. The achievement of such environmental stability was dependent on many elements. One aspect of this is the maintenance of political tranquility. The New York market, for example, first became a haven for flight capital in 1848 when simultaneous social uprising disturbed the political tranquility of several major European states. Another was the existence of a judicial system that is effective in protecting property rights and fairly enforces commercial law. The system of law ideally should allow the efficient international flow of capital, labor, or goods. Yet another aspect would be the establishment of a sound currency regime to preserve the purchasing power of the cash flows that affect the value of financial securities. This latter goal usually involves the creation of a central bank with responsibility for defining monetary policy to assure price stability, full utilization of resources, and maintaining balance in external accounts. In addition, such institutions also served as creditors of last resort during financial panics. In England, the establishment of a central bank occurred in the closing decades of the seventeenth century while in the United States a central bank did not emerge until 1913.

Professional knowledge was also crucial to effective stock market regulation. This was best reflected in the similar experience of the British and American markets. Securities markets required regulation that protected investor interests by promoting competency, probity, and transparency in financial dealing while avoiding efforts to control prices or market competition. Transactional efficiency in securities markets was dependent on the effective interaction of many professional groups. Markets relied on accountants, auditors, investment bankers, brokers, engineers, underwriters, and other classes of specialists. Risk perceptions declined when investors believed that their interests were protected by legal sanctions, enabling them to recover losses due to agent incompetence or dishonesty.

Government regulation undermined stock market growth when it interfered with the operation of market forces. Rules that distorted the unfettered transfer of goods, capital, and labor undermined the efficient allocation of economic resources. In the United States, restrictions on competitive practices have generally occurred at the periphery of the securities markets. The ICC (Interstate Commerce Commission), for example, offset the benefits that derived from its mandatory disclosure regime by its strong control over interstate competition and rail rate setting. The overall effect of these actions was to lower the returns to finance capital by distorting the distribution of scarce resources.

Although stock market dynamism was very responsive to innovation in either technology or management, novel developments often had their own asymmetries that created serious security pricing problems. The precise effects of particular innovations on enterprise cash flows frequently were difficult to assess. In their price-search function, stock market participants at times seriously misappraised the future benefits of change and its impacts on corporate cash flows. Historically, this was manifest in aggressive bidding for securities, which seemed excessive when more information about the actual potentials of an innovation later became available. Efficient pricing of new enterprises was a path-dependent process. Witness, for example, the costly learning that occurred in the early valuations of the

South Sea Company in 1720, or RCA in the 1920s, or the dotcoms of the 1990s. Although each development was recognized as an important change, market participants initially were unable to assign an accurate valuation to the securities of these companies. It was only after the passage of time that sufficient learning could take place about the economic potentials of each enterprise to support a more reasonable estimation of value.

[*See also* Business Cycles; Financial Panics and Crashes; *and* Great Depression.]

BIBLIOGRAPHY

CONTEMPORARY FINANCIAL THEORY

Bernstein, Peter L. *Capital Ideas: The Improbable Origins of Modern Wall Street*. New York, 1992.

Black, Fisher, and Myron Scholes. "The Pricing of Options and Corporate Liabilities." *Journal of Political Economy* 31 (May–June 1973), 637–659.

Fama, Eugene F., and Michael C. Jensen. "Agency Problems and Residual Claims." *Journal of Law and Economics* 26 (1983), 327–349.

Lintner, John. "Security Prices, Risk, and Maximum Gain from Diversification." *Journal of Finance* 20 (1965): 587–615.

Markowitz, Harry. "Portfolio Selection." *Journal of Finance* 7 (March 1952), 57–91.

Meckling, William H., and Michael C. Jensen. "Theory of the Firm: Managerial Behavior, Agency Costs, and Ownership Structure." *Journal of Financial Economics* 3 (1976), 305–370.

Modigliani, Franco, and Merton H. Miller. "The Cost of Capital, Corporate Finance, and the Theory of the Firm." *American Economic Review* 48 (June 1958), 261–297.

Sharpe, W. F. "A Simplified Model for Portfolio Analysis." *Management Science* 10 (January 1963), 277–293.

EVOLUTIONARY ANALYSIS IN ECONOMICS

Nelson, Richard, and Sidney Winter. *An Evolutionary Theory of Economic Change*. Cambridge, Mass., 1982.

North, Douglass C. *Institutions, Institutional Change, and Economic Performance*. New York, 1990.

BROAD PATTERNS OF FINANCIAL MARKET EVOLUTION

Baskin, Jonathan Barron. "The Development of Corporate Financial Markets in Britain and the United States, 1600–1914: Overcoming Asymmetric Information." *Business History Review* 62 (Summer 1988), 199–237.

Dickson, P. G. M. *The Financial Revolution in England: A Study of the Development of Public Credit, 1688–1756*. New York, 1967.

Kindleberger, Charles P. *A Financial History of Western Europe*. 2d ed. New York, 1993.

Neal, Larry. *The Rise of Financial Capitalism: International Capital Markets in the Age of Reason*. New York, 1990.

Smith, George David, and Richard Sylla. *The Transformation of Financial Capitalism: An Essay on the History of American Capital Markets*. Cambridge, Mass., 1993.

PARTICULAR STOCK MARKET HISTORIES

Attard, Bernard. "Making a Market. The Jobbers of the London Stock Exchange, 1800–1986." *Financial History Review* 7 (April 2000), 5–24.

Morgan, E. Victor, and W. A. Thomas. *The London Stock Exchange: Its History and Functions*. 2d ed. New York, 1969.

Sobel, Robert. *The Big Board: A History of the New York Stock Exchange*. New York, 1965.

Thomas, W. A. *Provincial Stock Exchanges*. London, 1973.

Thomas, W. A. *The Big Bang*. Deddington, U.K., 1986.

CORPORATE GOVERNANCE AND MARKET REGULATION

Parrish, Michael E. *Securities Market Regulation and the New Deal*. New Haven, 1970.

Sakakibara, Eisake, and Robert Allan Feldman. "The Japanese Financial System in Comparative Perspective." In *Japanese Capital Markets: Analysis and Characteristics of Equity, Debt, and Financial Futures Markets*, edited by Edwin J. Elton and Martin J. Gruber, pp. 27–54. New York, 1990.

Seligman, Joel. *The Transformation of Wall Street: A History of the Securities and Exchange Commission and Modern Corporate Finance*. Rev. ed. Boston, 1995.

Walter, Ingo. *The Battle of the Systems: Control of Enterprises and the Global Economy*. Kiel, Germany, 1993.

SPECIAL COMPLEMENTARY TOPICS

Baskin, Jonathan Barron, and Paul J. Miranti, Jr. *A History of Corporate Finance*. New York, 1997.

Carosso, Vincent P. *Investment Banking in America: A History*. Cambridge, Mass., 1970.

Carosso, Vincent P. *The Morgans, Private International Bankers, 1854–1913*. Cambridge, Mass., 1987.

Chancellor, Edward. *Devil Take the Hindmost: A History of Financial Specualtion*. New York, 1999.

Kindleberger, Charles P. *Manias, Panics, and Crashes: A History of Financial Crises*. Rev. ed., New York, 1989.

Strouse, Jean. *Morgan: American Financier*. New York, 1999.

Wilkins, Mira. *A History of Foreign Investment in the United States to 1914*. Cambridge, Mass., 1989.

PAUL J. MIRANTI

SUDAN [This entry contains three subentries, on the economic history of western, central, and eastern Sudan.]

Western Sudan

The Sudan is a zone of land to the south of the Sahara (not to be confused with Sudan, the country to the south of Egypt). The term came from Arabic, *bilad es Sudan* ("the land of the blacks"). The Western Sudan became important to the Arab world and Europe as a source of gold. It was the site of sub-Saharan Africa's first urban communities, with early development of long-distance trade, and a series of imperial states that were centered on the middle Niger Valley: Ghana, Mali, and Songhai. Early interpretations of the region's history were focused on gold and the imperial states, but archaeological work has established that cities and long-distance trade existed before the gold trade. Consequently, more attention now focuses on the region's ethnic and social diversity and on dynamics of internal change. The region, today, is poor.

Annual rainfall increases from north to south, but the rainfall is not dependable, the topsoils are thin, and the land's harshness is moderated by only three rivers that flow off the mountains of Guinea's Futa Jallon. Of these, the most import is the Niger, which splits into several channels within the so-called Inner Delta, as it moves north into the southern Sahara before turning south to seek its outlet in the Gulf of Guinea. The Sahara was in prehistoric times much wetter than it is today, and crocodiles and hippopotami lived where today only camels and goats roam, herded by pastoralists. Cattle first moved into this area about 5000 BCE; thereafter, some of the indigenous hunter-gathers became nomadic pastoralists. Some became fishermen, living by the shores of large lakes (today oases or depressions), where a fishing culture permitted a more sedentary existence. Near the lakes, women began the selective gathering of plants, then began farming about 3000 BCE. The existence of specialized groups of fishermen, farmers, and herders remains one of the region's characteristics of this region.

The most important early population centers in the region to be studied by archeologists, Dia and Jenne (Djenne), had emerged late in the first millennium BCE, on the edge of the Niger's Inner Delta. Clusters of specialized communities were found there, and metalsmiths were found to be working iron in the western Sudan by the third century BCE. Eventually, an endogomous caste system emerged, which included smiths, leather workers, and *griot*s (musicians and keepers of tradition). Although documentable only from the fourteenth century CE, castes probably emerged earlier; caste taboos permitted isolation of their magical powers, while also allowing each group to maintain a monopoly of its craft and to pass on its skills selectively.

The gradual drying of the Sahara region began about 2000 BCE. The peoples living on Saharan grasslands moved to the north or south, also leaving islands of settlement in the desert oases. Although there had always been some crossing of the Sahara, the desiccation isolated the Sudan from the ancient Near East just as the civilization of ancient Egypt began its time of glory. While a farming and trading community emerged on the fringe of the Nile Delta, desiccation produced another at the desert edge; there, declining resources and increasing population led to increased conflict and the emergence of small states. South of the Sahara, that process was also shaped by the interaction—both via trade and conflict—between nomads and agriculturalists. The nomads needed grain and cloth, the farmers needed salt and animals. The small sub-Saharan states provided the framework within which larger overarching states developed. Toward the end of the first century BCE, the use of camels (from Central Asia) was begun on the northern fringes of the Sahara. The herding and riding of camels made possible new patterns of pastoralism in that desert and facilitated trade across it.

Ghana probably emerged between the second and fourth centuries BCE. Kumbi Saleh, thought by many to be the first capital of Ghana, is in an area that could not provide food or water for an urban population today. In the late 600s CE, the Islamic conquest of North Africa stimulated trade there; the Arabization of the local Berbers sent literate Muslims across the Sahara, attracted by gold, which had probably been filtering across the Sahara for centuries. The gold trade was part of a larger commerce between North Africa, the Sahara, and the Sahel; gold and gold products found their way north while northern products went south (including books, beads, precious stones, cloth, and metalwares). The gold was mined in eastern Senegal, western Mali, and northern Guinea. Ghana seems to have been an "umbrella" kingdom, one that maintained a loose hegemony over several other states; it had a large cavalry force, which guaranteed the security of trade routes. Ghana was not, however, the only kingdom to emerge along the desert's edge. Arab chroniclers tell of Takrur and Silla in the Senegal River Valley and Gao in the bend of the Niger River. Less is known about those states, though all are in areas where rivers flow through dry grasslands, so they were probably the destinations for nomadic migrations.

Islam attracted many converts; the Arab chroniclers record the conversions of the rulers of the states of Takrur, Ghana, and Gao in the eleventh century. Islam then provided literate specialists for those states and a unifying ideology. Long-distance traders then became attracted to Islam's universal moral code, to the idea of one God, and especially to the existence of a common commercial law practiced throughout the Islamic world. Islam also facilitated bonds with the various Muslim communities. When traders became a distinct social group is not documented, but long-distance trade brought salt, copper, beads, and precious stones to sub-Saharan market, cities as early as the first millennium CE. Specialized trading communities existed long before the collapse of Ghana in the thirteenth century, which created a struggle for succession that was won by the Mali of Sundiata Keita. Mali was to the south of Ghana, and it extended its authority west to the mouth of the Gambia River, where salt and forest products could be bought and sent east to Gao. Soninke traders (known as *juula*), claiming Ghanaian origins, spread out within that empire and developed links with the Hausa, then they opened trade with the rich goldfields of the lower Volta region. With the fall of Ghana, the major trans-Saharan traders shifted their southern terminus first to Awdagust and then to Timbuktu. A river trade route was developed between Timbuktu and Jenne (Djenne), to provide food that could not be grown around Timbuktu. Jenne was the point at which trade goods were moved from canoe to donkey for trade into the rain-forest zone. The *juula* had created commercial cities (markets) along their major trade routes; often they were twin cities, like Kumbi Saleh, where a Muslim market town coexisted with a warrior community.

Tales of the gold of Mali attracted the Portuguese who were sailing down the coast in the 1400s. They soon founded settlements at Arguin on the Mauritanian coast and at El Mina ("the mine") near the Akan gold areas of present-day Ghana, and they traded for gold in all the rivers in between. The competition for the products of West Africa then redirected some trade to the Atlantic shore and set up a competition between Saharan (Gulf of Guinea to the Mediterranean) and Atlantic traders. Though gold remained the most important export of the Akan areas, the slave trade (originally within Africa and to the Near East) speedily took precedence elsewhere on the coast (to Europe and the New World).

In 1464, the Songhai empire began its expansion in the bend of the Niger; it soon took over much of the former Malian empire. Songhai, in turn, was defeated by Morocco in 1591. Although the Moroccan soldiers in Songhai became a military elite (known as the arma), they were never able to create a new empire. The Western Sudan then broke into its constituent ethnic and political units, many of them quite small. When some new political centers emerged, they were to the south and were linked to the European slave trade. In the late 1600s, Europe's increased demand for sugar production in the West Indies led to the rise of West African militaristic states that were capable of providing slaves; Segou and Kaarta emerged in western Mali; Futa Jallon in Guinea; and Asante in southern Ghana. Asante was located in the rain forest, yet most of its slaves came from its northern tributaries and, therefore, were mainly from the savanna (grasslands).

Crucial to that, slave trade was the relationship between warriors and traders. Warriors captured slaves that traders marketed—in exchange for cloth, weapons, and metal goods. The warriors were hard-drinking, often pagan, and hedonistic, but proud of their courage and generosity; the traders were Muslims, often frugal and austere, but interested in accumulation. Each used many of the slaves they handled. At the peak of the trade, in the late 1700s, there were probably as many slaves kept as exported. The warriors recruited some of the captured boys as soldiers, kept some of the women as wives and concubines, and often depended on slave communities for their food. The merchants used some of the slaves to feed their families, thus freeing themselves for trading expeditions; some of their slaves also worked as porters, while some of the women were kept as concubines. The effect of that slave trade on other economic activities is hard to measure, but ongoing warfare and raiding threatened many forms of commerce and economic activities, whereas the presence of slave labor stimulated others. Cloth became the most important import, but even so the local textile industry grew. On the

MALI. A Tuareg family outside their desert shelter, Timbuktu, 1992. (© Betty Press/Woodfin Camp and Associates, New York)

northern bank of the Senegal River, the Muslims used slaves in the forest areas to produce gums and to grow kola nuts. From 1700, the kola trade increased steadily, from the middle Volta to northern Nigeria. In many areas, smelting declined with the import of iron, but the production of iron goods continued and increased.

European and American abolition of slavery destroyed most of the export slave trade, though it did not die out until almost 1900. Slaves were instead kept in Africa and redirected to producing goods for the European markets, particularly West African palm oil and peanuts. There was also an expansion of kola nut, gum, and textile production, then late in the 1800s, cotton, coffee, and rubber. Local warfare was stimulated by the continuing demand for slaves, by new weapons, and by Muslims in the Western Sudan who wanted to create societies ruled only by Islamic law. Some *jihads* (Islamic "holy wars") originated in resistance to the effects of the export slave trade, but all the new West African states ended up protecting their own people by enslaving others.

With European colonial rule (France, Britain, Italy, Spain), the Western Sudan was largely marginalized. It produced few exports that justified the expensive trip to the coast. Only Senegal remained important; its coastal towns were the base from which the French built their African empire. Dakar was the capital of French West Africa and its most important port. Senegalese peanuts (for peanut oil) were, for most of the twentieth century, the most important export from French Africa. Gambia was also a peanut exporter. The biggest development project in the interior, Mali's Niger Project, involved the growing of cotton plants in irrigated fields—but it was poorly conceived and inefficiently managed. Despite that, a traditional economy has remained very productive in Mali. Although Mali's exports of both cotton and gold foundered on the willingness of local artisans to pay higher prices than French exporters, the result was that the local jewelry and textile industries continued to produce a competitive product. Mali's major commodity export during the Colonial era was, therefore, peanuts. Guinea was even poorer than Mali; after a brief period, when its rubber exports boomed, it relied on tropical crops, like bananas. The once powerful Futa Jallon became particularly poor and overpopulated.

The Western Sudan's most important export was its people. *Juula* traders moved into petty commerce in French Equatorial Africa and, later, Congo. Soninke sailors worked for the French navy and became the first African migrants to Europe. Other Soninkes became transporters in Ivory Coast or teachers in Gabon. Turkas from Burkina Faso, Bambaras from Mali, and Fulbes from Guinea migrated to work in Senegal's peanut fields. Particularly important in the cocoa fields of Ghana and Ivory Coast were members of the Mossi.

Independence from European colonialism opened opportunities. Guinea's rich bauxite mines went into production shortly before independence, but they eventually supported one of the most inefficient of the socialist governments in Africa. From 1968 to 1983, the Western Sudan suffered serious droughts. Senegal and Gambia remained primarily peanut producers, but they also developed a tourist industry. Dakar became a center of light industry and an exporter of fish and phosphates. In Mali, the world price of peanuts no longer justified the transport costs; instead, Mali exported cotton, grown not in irrigated fields, but in the country's southern rain-fed areas. During the 1990s, new resources in Mali were invested in mining.

BIBLIOGRAPHY

Barry, Boubacar. *Senegambia and the Atlantic Slave Trade*. Cambridge, 1998.

Bovill, E. W. *The Golden Trade of the Moors*. 2d ed. Oxford, 1970.

Brooks, George. *Landlords and Strangers: Ecology, Society and Trade in Western Africa, 1000–1630*. Boulder, 1993.

Curtin, Philip. *Economic Change in Precolonial Africa: Senegambia in the Era of the Slave Trade*. Madison, Wisc., 1975.

Mauny, Raymond. *Tableau géographique de l'Ouest Africain au Moyen Age*. Dakar, 1961.

McDougall, Ann. "The View from Audagust: War, Trade and Social Change in the Southwestern Sahara, from the Eighth to the Fifteenth Century." *Journal of African History* 26 (1985), 1–31.

McIntosh, Roderick. *The Peoples of the Middle Niger: The Island of Gold*. Oxford, 1998.

Manchuelle, François. *Willing Migrants*. Athens, Ohio, 1998.

Meillassoux, Claude, ed. *Development of Indigenous Trade and Markets in West Africa*. Oxford, 1971.

Roberts, Richard. *Warriors, Merchants and Slaves: The State and the Economy in the Middle Niger Valley, 1700–1914*. Stanford, Calif., 1987.

Roberts, Richard. *Two Worlds of Cotton: Colonialism and the Regional Economy in the French Soudan, 1800–1946*. Portsmouth, N.H., 1996.

Tamari, Tal. "The Development of Caste Systems in West Africa." *Journal of African History* 32 (1991), 221–250.

Webb, James. *Desert Frontier: Ecological and Economic Change along the Western Sahel, 1600–1850*. Madison, Wisc., 1995.

MARTIN A. KLEIN

Central Sudan

Central Sudan encompasses a large area of West Africa, extending from the bend of the Niger River eastward across Lake Chad, northward to the Air Massif in the southern Sahara, and southward to the Niger-Benue confluence, encompassing most of modern northern Nigeria, Niger, and Chad. Before the twentieth century, a number of powerful African states arose in the region and developed a monetized economy long before the arrival of European trade. Until colonial conquest, the region's economy responded to a different set of imperatives than that of the economies of the southern forest zone of West Africa, which were tied much earlier to the Atlantic world.

Interecological Trade. The economy of central Sudan was based on the movement of people and goods in "corridors" that crossed different ecological zones. These ecological zones produced different kinds of goods, which could then be traded. In average years, farmers would have more than they could eat or use, and trade was possible between regions that produced different things. Most items/goods served local or regional demands, such as agricultural goods, and therefore moved short distances. However, these islands of economic power were linked together by long-distance and regional trading networks. Long-distance trade was generally carried out in specific products in response to specific market demands and was especially responsive to ecological variations in demand and production. Because of the high transport costs associated with the movement of goods across West Africa, this trade tended to be centered on luxury goods, such as kola nuts, gold dust, salt, and slaves. However, in many cases bulky goods, including agricultural products, traveled long distances by taking advantage of nomadic transhumance cycles.

Until the seventeenth century, the majority of West African economic activity was centered in the desert-savanna region rather than in the coastal zone. The "desert-side" sector was an engine of economic growth that linked North Africa, communities in the Sahara, states of the savanna, and the forest region in a system of exchange and production. In this sector, products of the Sahara and Sahel were traded for products of the savanna and forest zone. For example, the savanna zone traded agricultural surplus with the desert-side sector for livestock and salt. Every year, Tuareg caravans came from the Sahara to markets in central Sudan loaded with salt, which would be exchanged for millet, textiles, and slaves. The desert-side sector was divided into specialized zones of production. Production was located in specific areas, as were resources, which therefore structured the way the West African economy evolved.

The use of cowrie shells and gold or silver coins as currency gradually connected the economy of central Sudan. Cowries facilitated trade and exchange and were normally used within a single market, rather than carried from one market to another. Most cowries came from the Maldives via North Africa or the middle Niger. The cowrie zone expanded throughout the precolonial period. It first developed in the upper and middle Niger Valley during the medieval period and gradually spread eastward into central Sudan, reaching Hausaland by the 1570s. In the nineteenth century, cowries traded by Europeans on the coast found their way into the interior via major trade routes as the savanna and coastal cowrie zones met. The increased supply then led to inflation.

States and the Economy to 1600. It was long thought that trans-Saharan trade stimulated the formation of states and economies in the region. However, urbanization, economic specialization, and regional trade predated the expansion of long-distance trade. Indeed, long-distance trade tapped into preexisting networks. The advent of camel-borne trade (c. 400 CE) between North Africa and central Sudan did encourage further economic growth. The societies of the savanna zone traded leather, cattle, and cloth southward for ivory and gold, which was then traded across the desert via Berber camel caravans for salt, metals, and luxury goods. North African merchants exchanged West African products with European merchants, linking central Sudan with the rest of the world. The trans-Saharan slave trade was also initiated, which produced as many slaves as did the transatlantic slave trade, only over a much longer period of time. Larger state systems came with burgeoning trade and production. Initially, states arose in the western Sudan (e.g., Ghana, Mali, and Songhai). Songhai influenced the economic development and growth of central Sudan, as trade passed from Songhai through Hausaland to Bornu. The *Wangara*, a group of traders based in Songhai who shared an occupational identity, helped to integrate central Sudan into the broader savanna economy.

In central Sudan, a regional economy developed that was centered on the state of Kanem and its successor, Bornu. Kanem and Bornu sat astride key trade routes. They were founded northwest of Lake Chad around 900 CE by groups of nomadic pastoralists. Kanem tapped trade routes northward into Tunisia and Libya, northeast into the Nile valley, and southward into the forest zone of modern Nigeria. Kanem also gained control of salt deposits at Bilma in the Sahara. Kanem exported slaves, garnered through trade and warfare, as well as ivory and foodstuffs. Gradual urbanization occurred, and a state capital was founded in the eleventh century at Njimi. Eventually, the gradual desiccation of the Sahara and political infighting led to Kanem's decline.

By the fourteenth century, the Saifawa dynasty relocated their state to Bornu around Lake Chad. The reinvented empire prospered. Bornu developed extensive trade routes, and after the first permanent capital was founded at Birnin Gazargamo at the end of the fifteenth century, it dominated trans-Saharan trade and salt production. Firearms imported from North Africa increased the strength of the Bornu military. A Bornu-Hausa regional economy emerged in the middle of the fifteenth century as merchants traded salt and horses to the Hausa city-states for gold and textiles, thereby linking both Hausaland and Bornu with the trade and production of Songhai.

Rise of the Hausa States and the Sokoto Caliphate.
By the 1450s, some Hausa towns became centers of economic activity, while the Tuareg formed a political confederation based around the city of Agadez that dominated the Sahelian side of the trans-Saharan trade and invested in savanna-based agriculture. With the collapse of Songhai in 1591, West Africa's economic center shifted eastward toward central Sudan. It was only after the fall of Songhai

and the gradual shift of the locus of trans-Saharan trade that the regional economy in this part of central Sudan took off. Numerous cities in Hausaland became important agricultural centers by farming new crops of bulrush millet, pepper, and sorghum. This led to population growth and further market demand for foodstuffs. The growth of agricultural production also encouraged economic specialization, as increasing numbers of people entered into specialized craft or livestock production.

Kano, Katsina, and Gobir were important centers for trans-Saharan trade and manufacturing, especially cloth dyeing and leatherworking. The Hausa states raided for slaves extensively in the regions to the south because slaves were used in both production and trade. They also traded for gold with the Akan. Long-distance trade promoted the development of trading diasporas, as traders assumed ethnic identities that were tied to their role in long-distance trade. Hausa traders were effective in creating and maintaining these kinds of trading diasporas. This facilitated trade because Hausa merchants had assured places to stop and relationships of trust with one another, and could extend credit within and beyond Hausaland.

Usman dan Fodio's holy war that swept through the region between 1804 and 1808 had a tremendous impact on economic history. Before 1804, each Hausa state operated independently. Afterward, Hausaland was united as the Sokoto Caliphate. The creation of the caliphate stimulated the production of commodities destined for the regional economy and long-distance trading networks. The desert-side sector expanded in scope, while agricultural and craft production increased as economic sectors were integrated. Slave-based agricultural production became a central facet of the economy, which stimulated extensive slave raiding and trade. The slave-based "plantation sector" produced cotton and foodstuffs for local consumption and export.

Gradually, the grain and textile belts of the central caliphate became tied to areas of grain and cotton production. A unified state secured trade and created safer conditions for commerce by building fortified settlements in key areas and by encouraging Fulani nomadic pastoralists to become sedentary. The reinvigorated religion of Islam solidified the economy of central Sudan by strengthening connections and credit between merchants. Kano was the economic center of the caliphate. It served as the southern terminus of the trans-Saharan trade, as an entrepôt for regional trade (kola trade to Asante, natron to Bornu, and trade with the Yoruba states to the south), and as a center for local trade. As Kano's share of the trans-Saharan trade increased, Bornu's declined, leading to an economic downturn in Bornu.

From Colonialism to Neocolonialism. Colonialism reoriented the trade and production from the desert-side sector to the coastal zone as internally based trade and production declined. The region became tied to the world economy as a producer of raw materials. Colonial economic policies were designed to extract surplus from African economies as cheaply as possible. European firms purchased the primary goods produced by Africans and set the terms of exchange Africans received for their goods. This system sowed the seeds for the economic underdevelopment of central Sudan. Although the amount of external trade increased from the precolonial period, Africans did not reap the benefits of economic expansion.

The British, French, and Germans conquered most of central Sudan by 1903. Most of the Sokoto caliphate and Hausaland were incorporated into the British Empire, initially as the Protectorate of Northern Nigeria. The goal of every colonial power was to make colonies pay for their own governance. Frederick Lugard and other British officials initiated a new system of taxation, with the hope that this would force Africans to produce commodities. African farmers sold their crops on the British-controlled market for cash, known as *cash cropping*. This income was then taxed by the British to help pay for their administration. The British thereby received the raw materials they wanted and forced Africans to pay for the costs of colonial rule.

The region had a long history of peasant production. This pattern continued in the colonial period. Cash crops produced by Africans became a vital part of the colonial economy. Capitalism and colonialism initially had limited success in transforming the societies and economies of central Sudan. African social and economic forms showed flexibility and dynamism, and for a period they survived the entire process described above. A "hybrid" society took shape that was partly peasant and partly capitalist. Although African farmers were often viewed as "backward," they were partly responsible for the success of cash-crop farming. Africans were not passive victims of colonialism; they adapted their precolonial structures in innovative ways to take advantage of opportunities presented to them. For example, the British initially hoped to encourage cotton cultivation in northern Nigeria by building a railway to Kano, which arrived in 1911. Although British officials tried to get farmers to produce cotton for the railway, farmers started to produce and sell groundnuts as word swept through the region that prices were good. African *choices* started the great groundnut boom, in defiance of British desires and expectations.

One of the main results of cash cropping and wage labor was to increase the social and economic disparities between Africans and to increase their vulnerability to price fluctuations that were determined in markets located outside Africa. When prices were good, some Africans benefited. But when prices dropped, many more suffered. For example, the Great Depression struck Africans hard because the prices they received for their commodities dropped dramatically. Cash-cropping regions tended to draw labor from noncash-cropping regions, thereby initiating cycles of labor migration. Precolonial methods of coping with famine were also undermined by the spread of capitalist relations of production. This decrease in food security was exacerbated by the reduction of food-crop production. Little remained of the interdependent economic system of the precolonial central Sudan. For example, the French attempted to restrict the movement of people and livestock for administrative reasons. This policy undermined precolonial agricultural techniques and safeguards that had previously been able to respond to changes in ecology and the environment at the desert edge.

The profit gained from these enterprises was not reinvested in central Sudan. The infrastructural improvements made by the British and French were directed toward improving communication and transportation networks, rather than developing self-sufficient African economies. Local craft industries were undermined as imports from the industrial world took their place. Europeans also controlled the finance and banking sectors, which effectively shut most Africans out of large-scale marketing and trade.

The desert-side sector withered as colonial policies encouraged a reorientation of trade southward. Conflict between the French and the Tuareg undermined the salt trade, and the movement of goods toward the coast meant that the trans-Saharan trade also collapsed. The economy of the French regions of central Sudan declined in contrast to some growth in British-controlled areas. The French pursued more limited economic goals than did the British, and they invested even less than the British in infrastructure, transport, and development. These policies marginalized the French-controlled regions of central Sudan. The British-dominated areas benefited from access to the wealth of southern Nigeria. Thus, while the entire region was faced with the pressures of conforming to a colonial economy, the French-controlled regions of Niger and Chad did much worse in the long run than did British-controlled northern Nigeria.

After the independence of Nigeria, Niger, and Chad in the 1960s, the economy was further undermined. Economic activity occurred largely within national boundaries or was differentially directed toward world markets. Much of this activity remained focused on primary production, although each nation attempted to build an industrial base and promote agricultural diversification through direct government intervention. Nigeria was the most successful because it had access to oil revenue. As the population in parts of the region climbed and as cities grew larger, food production actually declined in favor of other primary products and forms of wage labor. The economic situation of the 1960s was largely favorable. As prices for primary products fell, however, the balance of payments also moved against African states, initiating a cycle of debt.

During the 1970s, uranium production bolstered the performance of Niger's economy. When uranium prices fell in the 1980s, however, the economy stagnated. Nigeria faced similar problems when oil revenue dropped in the 1980s. Each state tried to close its open economy by instituting partial or total price controls, currency restrictions, and government subsidies. These policies failed, given each nation's dependence on external markets and capital. Economic hardships were compounded by sahelian droughts between 1968 and 1974 and 1982 and 1984. By the 1980s, each state was in economic crisis. Both the World Bank and the International Monetary Fund tried to revive the economies of Nigeria, Chad, and Niger. Unfortunately, these organizations adopted market-driven, top-down strategies that resulted in cuts to social services and government programs without boosting rural production or industrial development.

BIBLIOGRAPHY

Austen, Ralph. *African Economic History*. London and Portsmouth, N.H., 1987.

Baier, Stephen. *An Economic History of Central Niger*, Oxford, 1980.

Brenner, Louis. *The Shehus of Kukawa: A History of the al-Kanemi Dynasty of Bornu*. Oxford, 1973.

Charlick, Robert B. *Niger: Personal Rule and Survival in the Sahel*. Boulder, 1991.

Cordell, Dennis. *Dar al-Kuti and the Last Years of the Trans-Saharan Slave Trade*. Madison, Wis., 1985.

Falola, Toyin. *The History of Nigeria*. Westport, Conn., 1999.

Hogendorn, Jan S. *Nigerian Groundnut Exports: Origins and Early Developments*. Zaria, Ethiopia, and Ibadan, Nigeria, 1978.

Hopkins, A. G. *An Economic History of West Africa*. New York, 1973.

Johnson, Marion. "The Cowrie Currencies of West Africa, Part I." *Journal of African History* 9.1 (1970), 17–49.

Johnson, Marion. "The Cowrie Currencies of West Africa, Part II." *Journal of African History* 9.3 (1970), 331–353.

Last, Murray. "Reform in West Africa: the *Jihad* Movements of the Nineteenth Century." In *History of West Africa*, edited by J. F. A. Ajayi and Michael Crowder, pp. 1–47. London, 1985.

Lovejoy, Paul E. "Plantations in the Economy of the Sokoto Caliphate." *Journal of African History* 19.3 (1978), 341–368.

Lovejoy, Paul E. "The Characteristics of Plantations in the Nineteenth-Century Sokoto Caliphate." *American Historical Review* 84.5 (1979), 1267–1292.

Lovejoy, Paul E. *Salt of the Desert Sun: A History of Salt Production and Trade in the Central Sudan*. Cambridge, 1986.

Lovejoy, Paul E., and Stephen Baier. "The Desert-Side Economy of the Central Sudan." *International Journal of African Historical Studies* 8.4 (1975), 551–581.

Mahadi, Abdullahi. "The Aftermath of the *Jihad* in the Central Sudan as a Major Factor in the Volume of the Trans-Saharan Slave Trade in the Nineteenth Century." *Slavery and Abolition* 9 (1988), 111–127.

Phillips, Anne. *The Enigma of Colonialism: British Policy in West Africa*. London, 1989.

Watts, Michael. *Silent Violence: Food, Famine, and Peasantry in Northern Nigeria*. Berkeley, 1983.

SEAN STILWELL

Eastern Sudan

From the Gebel Marra range in the west, across the Nile River, to the Red Sea in the east, and south from the Sahara to the northern limits of Africa's equatorial forests, Sudan's eastern region has long relied on hunting, gathering, herding, farming, and fishing as economic activities. In the north, along the Sahara's edge, pastoralists still engage in camel herding, while those in the south tend herds of cattle. Across the broad savanna, hoe farmers still cultivate sorghum and millet along the rivers, the seasonal riverbeds, and on the uplands. The Gebel Marra range divides the Lake Chad basin to the west from the Nile River basin to the east. The Bahr al-Ghazal, a major tributary of the White Nile, flows eastward to join that river, which emerges from the marches of the Sudd in southern Sudan. The White Nile joins the Blue Nile at modern-day Khartoum, before flowing farther northward toward Dongola and the south of Egypt. In its annual flooding, the Nile provides rich alluvial soil; it is also an effective means of transport, and has supplied fish throughout the long history of eastern Sudan.

Overlaying the basic subsistence activities are the commercial and political life of the region. Trade first developed there through the exchange of small surpluses that were produced by subsistence farmers, pastoralists, hunters, and fishers. Regional trade also developed across ecological zones and in such minerals as salt, copper, and gold. Long-distance trade from the region utilized the Nile Valley or the Red Sea, went across the Sahara and, to a lesser extent, into the sub-Saharan forest. The region's political life has involved the creation of small polities as well as five great cycles of empire building—during the eras of ancient Egypt, Hellenism, early Islam, later Islam, and modern times. The states and empires greatly affected the economic life of the region, as rulers sought to control labor, land, manufacturing, mining, trade, and taxation.

For the earliest cultures in eastern Sudan, the best evidence comes from the Nile Valley region known as Nubia. Archaeological evidence indicates that Paleolithic (Stone Age) cultures existed there, using stone tools for hunting on the savanna; later, during the Mesolithic, there was fishing from the Nile and the collecting of wild grains. Until then, the communities usually had fewer than twenty individuals. Even later, about 6000 BCE, Neolithic peoples near modern Khartoum used pottery and had domesticated sheep, goats, and cattle; the evidence for grain cultivation there really begins about 4000 to 3200 BCE, when wheat, barley, peas, and lentils were farmed.

Ancient Egyptian Era: 3200 BCE–350 BCE. Both written and other archaeological material show considerable interaction between Old Kingdom Egypt and Nubia. During Egypt's empire building, Egyptian influences expanded southward along the Nile, so the southern boundaries of a succession of Nubian polities also shifted southward. New Nubian settlement patterns and economic activities began, with towns formed as political centers and trading posts. Trade with Egypt increased to include such export items as slaves, animals, forest products, and minerals. During Egypt's Old Kingdom era, copper from a source far to the west of the Nile was smelted at Buhena, south of the Second Cataract of the Nile. Gold from Nubian mines along the Allaqi River supplied Egypt during Middle Kingdom times and then in New Kingdom times.

Late in New Kingdom times, the kings of Napata in Nubia conquered Egypt—they then installed themselves as Egyptian pharaohs from 751 to 635 BCE. Napatan society consisted of three classes: a small ruling elite, a large peasantry, and an urban middle class of merchants and artisans. Several economic factors were basic to Napata's political strength. First was the *shaduf*—a counterweighted, human-powered, water-lifting device—that was introduced from Egypt; it greatly facilitated irrigation and thus increased agricultural production along the Nile. Second was a new overland route between Napata and Debba, carrying trade by donkey and increasing both towns' prosperity. Third was control of the gold mines that came to the Napatan kings.

Greco-Roman Times, the Hellenistic Era: 350 BCE–600 CE. The city of Meroë was begun during Napatan times, some 200 kilometers (300 miles) south of Napata, between the Fifth and the Sixth Cataract of the Nile River. Part of its hinterland was the Butana steppe, whose many streams favored both cultivation of drought-resistant millet and cattle pastoralism; this mixed economy bolstered Meroë's urban prosperity, trade, and industry. The Meroitic iron industry is known from the evidence of huge slag heaps. Much of the iron was used to make tools, weapons, ornaments, and hardware items. Meroë was at the center of a number of trade routes, including the Bayuda Road from Meroë to Napata; the road to Abyssinia; and the road to Suakin on the Red Sea. In addition, south of Meroë, the Nile was readily navigable. Another trade route by passed the Nile and four cataracts and went directly to Egypt, while passing near goldfields along a tributary of the Allaqi River (in the first century CE, this route grew in importance, as newly introduced camels became the preferred carriers of the desert trade). The Meroitic ruling elite controlled much of the best farmland as manors, but the ability of millet to thrive on the rainlands, away from the Nile, ensured that a large part of the population could find land to farm; they could then exchange their grain for the animal products of local pastoralists.

Following Alexander the Great's conquest of Egypt in 332 BCE, Hellenistic influences went south via the Nile and from Red Sea ports. Later, in the first century CE, Roman activities in Upper Egypt (the South) furthered Meroë's southern focus. By the third century CE, Nubian agriculture benefited greatly from the introduction of a new irrigation device, the *saqiya*. It uses an animal-powered, wooden, horizontal-geared wheel to move a vertical wheel on an axle, with a second vertical wheel that lifts a rope chain and a series of pottery buckets; these raise water from a well below to fill a trough that leads to irrigation channels. The *saqiya* was able to lift water higher and more efficiently than the *shaduf* and so greatly increased Nubia's arable land. One result was an increase in trade from Egypt. Bronze, glass, and ceramic items were exchanged for Nubian foodstuffs and some southern trade goods. As the Roman occupation of Egypt impoverished Napata's trade partners, this prosperity declined. Nomads quickly learned the commercial and military uses of the camel in the rainlands and the desert so that they could profit by carrying, or even disrupting, the caravan trade. To the east in Abyssinia, a rival state, Axum, rose. By the fourth century CE, Meroë's power was ended.

Between the fourth and sixth centuries CE, Christianity was introduced from both Roman Egypt and Christian Axum—and it soon became the dominant religion. By the sixth century CE, three Christian Nubian kingdoms had formed: Nobatia in the north, Makuria in the middle, and Alodia in the south. Economically, Christian Nubia probably resembled Christian Abyssinia. Crops and domesticated animals, then including the pig, were raised by peasants. The building of walled forts and monasteries suggests the possibility of a manorial system, but little clear evidence supports this supposition—and there is little evidence on taxation. The monasteries were largely self-sufficient; they produced food, pottery, and wine for their own needs, and sent any surplus to market.

Early Islamic Era: 600–1500 CE. In the name of the Prophet Muhammad, Muslim armies moved up the Nile after conquering Egypt in 641. The Muslims were generally successful across all of North Africa, but in attacking the kingdom of Makuria, they were defeated and a treaty (known as *baqt*) regulated diplomatic and economic relations between them and Makuria. Although the treaty's text is highly suspect—owing to progressive elaborations and anachronisms—it included an annual exchange of slaves from the south for such provisions as foodstuffs, wines, and cloth from Egypt.

From the seventh to the thirteenth century, the Christian hold was eroded in northern Nubia and the lands between the Nile and the Red Sea. That weakening began with Muslim rulers in Egypt exerting control over gold mines and other mining in the lands of the nomadic Beja. Muslims also infiltrated Nobatia; by the ninth century, they were landholders there and used that foothold as a base for trade upstream. Muslim economic and commercial practices soon

EASTERN SUDAN. Bean fields, thorn trees, wheat crops, and straw at the edge of the Nile River, near Khartoum, Sudan, 1959. (Eliot Elisofon/Eliot Elisofon Photographic Archives/National Museum of African Art, Smithsonian Institution, Washington, D.C.)

dominated in the northern zone of Makuria, even as Muslims were forbidden access to the southern zone. By 1174, a Muslim official with the title of *kanz al-dawla* was placed over the northern Muslim province of Makuria. Alodia underwent a similar infiltration and by the twelfth century, the kingdom began to decay. Repeated Muslim attacks from Egypt led to the fall of Makuria in 1276; by the fourteenth century, the old Makurian kingdom was gone, and its population subjected to sale as slaves. Pastoral peoples gradually escaped from the control of the Christian kingdoms as they also converted to Islam.

Later Islamic Era: 1500–1900 CE. Islamic kingdoms came to dominate eastern Sudan, not only Sinnar on the Nile but the Tunjur Empire, which had two successor states—Dar Fur, on the eastern side of Gebel Marra, and Wadai to its west. By the seventeenth century, Dar Fur and Sinnar were well-established. Each had a powerful central government that relied on cavalry for military dominance of the plains, controlled the best agricultural lands through written sultanic land grants, collected taxes from peasant farmers, sought to control camel pastoralists to

the north and cattle herders to the south, permitted slave raids on non-Muslim peoples to the south, and regulated the trans-Saharan trade routes north to Egypt (which had become part of the Ottoman Empire). Dar Fur struggled for dominance—first with Wadai to the west, then with Sinnar over the vast area of Kordofan, which was between Dar Fur and the Nile. Merchants in both Sinnar and Dar Fur sought to escape close regulation of their commercial activities and to bolster their own economic power, mainly by gaining control of agricultural lands.

An invasion from Egypt in 1820 brought an end to Sinnar. Egypt's systematic exploitation of Sinnar's resources led to emigration, particularly from Dongola. The exiles fled south along the Nile, to the frontiers of Abyssinia (Ethiopia), and west to Kordofan, Dar Fur, and Wadai. They bolstered the long-distance trading networks and opposed the further extension of Egyptian power in eastern Sudan, yet they benefited from the increased trans-Saharan trade in slaves, ivory, ostrich feathers, and gum arabic. From 1820 to 1880, the volume of trans-Saharan slave trading from eastern Sudan to Egypt has been estimated at

360,000 people. Dar Fur was overthrown in 1874 by al-Zubayr, the leading slave-and-ivory trader operating in the non-Muslim territories to its south. Resentment against the harsh regime along the Nile, and against Egypt's attempts (as British economic and moral influence increased there from the 1850s) to eliminate the slave trade, led many merchants, including slave traders, to support the Mahdist revolt of 1882 to 1898. The Mahdi, a charismatic Muslim leader, and his successor emulated the political and economic practices of the early Muslim caliphate; the Mahdist state was the first government to bring almost the entire area of modern Sudan under its control.

Modern Era: 1900 to 2000. In 1898, the Mahdist regime was defeated by the British and replaced by the Anglo-Egyptian Condominium Agreement of 1899, a British colonial regime that soon expanded its control from Egypt to the south and over all the Sudan (as it was then known). A modern infrastructure, including railroads, roads, telegraphs, and ports was then built by British engineers. Much of the effort was for the benefit of the colonial regime, which had planned to develop cotton production on the Gezira irrigation scheme—an agricultural project established in 1926, of which a third grew cotton, with profits to go toward social development. (When costs rose and cotton prices dropped, increasing debt led to international loans.) Early in World War II, in June 1940, Italy declared war and Italian troops from Abyssinia took Sudanese frontier towns. Although the British were outnumbered, they and the Sudanese Defence Force prevailed. Sudan gained its independence from Britain in 1956; the new government continued parliamentary rule and many policies of the colonial regime. Soon, however, there was civil war between Sudan's Muslim North and the non-Muslim South over cultural and politico-economic issues, such as the proper role of Islam in Sudan and the insufficient resources devoted to the improvement of the South. Since the 1960s, civil war has drained the central government finances and prevented the achievement of Sudan's agricultural potential; it has devastated the economy of the South, where the fighting has taken place, and has blocked the full development of sizable oilfields. Since the 1970s, drought and warfare have contributed to serious famines, to foreign funding from Libya and Iraq, and to the reappearance of instances of slavery. The civil wars have sought to deal with the underlying problem—how to build unity in a multiethnic and multireligious country.

BIBLIOGRAPHY

Adams, William Y. *Nubia: Corridor to Africa*. Princeton, 1977. A thorough study of Nubia; its changing contexts, from ancient to modern times.

Austen, Ralph. "The Mediterranean Islamic Slave Trade out of Africa: A Tentative Census." *In The Human Commodity: Perspectives on the trans-Saharan Slave Trade*, edited by Elizabeth Savage, pp. 214–248. London, 1992.

Burr, J. Millard, and Robert O. Collins. *Requiem for the Sudan: War, Drought, and Disaster Relief on the Nile*. Boulder, 1995.

Ewald, Janet J. *Soldiers, Traders and Slaves: State Formation and Economic Transformation in the Greater Nile Valley, 1700–1885*. Madison, Wisc., 1990.

Holt, P. M., and M. W. Daly. *The History of the Sudan: From the Coming of Islam to the Present Day*. Boulder, 1979. A general introduction to Sudanese history.

Kapteijns, Lidwien. *Mahdist Faith and Sudanic Tradition: A History of the Masalit Sultanate, 1870–1930*. London, 1985.

La Rue, George Michael. "The Export Trade of Dar Fur, ca. 1785–1875." In *Figuring African Trade*, edited by G. Liesegang, H. Pasch, and A. Jones. Berlin, 1986.

Lesch, Ann. M. "Sudan." In *Encyclopedia of the Modern Middle East*, edited by Reeva Simon, Philip Mattar, and Richard W. Bulliet, pp. 1691–1696. New York, 1996.

Niblock, Tim. *Class and Power in Sudan: The Dynamics of Sudanese Politics, 1898–1985*. London, 1987.

O'Fahey, R. S. *State and Society in Dar Fur*. London, 1980.

Shinnie, P. L. *Ancient Nubia*. London, 1996.

Spaulding, Jay. *The Heroic Age in Sinnar*. East Lansing, Mich., 1985.

Spaulding, Jay. "Precolonial Islam in the Eastern Sudan." In *The History of Islam in Africa*, edited by Nehemia Levtzion and Randall L. Pouwels, pp. 117–129. Athens, Oh., 2000.

GEORGE MICHAEL LaRUE

SUEZ CANAL. The Suez Canal was projected in the 1850s, when world trade expanded faster than in any other decade of the nineteenth century. The promoter was Ferdinand de Lesseps (1805–1894), who had been vice consul in Cairo (1832–1837), during the inauguration in 1835 of the overland route through Egypt to India. The ship canal was excavated by local labor and French dredgers between 1859 and 1869. A sea-level waterway free from locks throughout the ninety-eight miles of its length, it links the Mediterranean to the Red Sea. The first commercial vessels to use the new route were steamships laden with cotton from India, although neither steamships nor Indian cotton had been significant in world trade in the 1850s. During the 1880s, the canal became an important highway of commerce at the expense of the Cape route. For some eighty-seven years (1880–1967), the canal continued to fulfill that function. However, it is misleading to suggest that the opening of the canal ushered in a new era in the economic development of Asia. That process was geared primarily to intra-Asian trade rather than to trade with the West. In any case, world trade expanded much faster before 1869 than after. Exports from Asia increased fourfold faster between 1860 and 1870 than they did between 1870 and 1880, while India attained its all-time peak share in world trade during the year 1865. The canal nevertheless carried westward such exports as tea from China, raw cotton from Bombay, rice from Rangoon, wheat from Karachi, tin and rubber from Malaya, and from 1908, soya from Manchuria. In return, Europe shipped to the East manufactures, especially textiles, machinery, railway plant, cement, fertilizer, kerosene, and petrol. Those products remained in aggregate less in volume but higher in value than the northbound cargoes.

Two world wars drastically reduced shipping tonnage, by 58 percent (1913–1917) and by 69 percent (1939–1942). The world economic depression of 1929–1932, however, affected traffic less than other sectors of the world economy because a new trade had emerged in the export of oil from the Persian Gulf. The northbound flow of crude oil began from Iran in 1912 and was supplemented by oil from Saudi Arabia in 1939 and from Kuwait in 1951, when the Anglo-Iranian Oil Company was nationalized. Tanker tonnage became predominant during 1948, and Greek shipowners became leading clients of the canal company, using flags of convenience from 1949.

The construction of the canal through a desert led to the establishment of five new towns, Port Said (1859), Ismailia (1862), Port Ibrahim (1870), Port Tewfik (1882), and Port Fuad (1926), all named after members of the ruling dynasty. The old town of Suez, two miles west of the waterway, became the frontier town between east and west under the influence of Rudyard Kipling's "Mandalay" (1890). The canal was linked to the Nile Delta by the Sweetwater Canal (which reached Ismailia and Suez in 1863 and was extended to Port Said in 1893) and the railway (which reached Ismailia and Suez in 1868 and was extended to Port Said in 1904). The British occupation of Egypt, dating from 1882, was ended and full Egyptian independence was established by means of the abolition in 1949 of the Mixed Courts created in 1876, the republican revolution of 1952, the evacuation of British troops (1954–1956) and the nationalization (26 July 1956) of the canal company. The Suez crisis of 1956 has been the subject of numerous political histories, but its economic significance has never received the attention it deserves. The waterway was closed for five months (1 November 1956–8 April 1957). The great oil companies decided to develop the oil resources of Libya, Algeria, and Nigeria in order to reduce their dependence upon the Suez route. The new producers required five years to develop their capacity. As their output came onstream in1961, the share of the canal in the oil trade of the world began to decline from the peak of 27 percent in 1960 to 7 percent in 1986 and 1 percent in 1999. Its share in total world trade shrank from 15 percent in 1960 to 5.9 percent in 1999, or to the level of 1920, since dry cargo failed to compensate for the loss of the oil trade. The Suez Canal Company, created in 1858, was transformed in 1957 into a French corporation and was renamed the Compagnie Financière de Suez. It became the leading financial company of France and until 1992 never reported a loss during 135 years of existence.

The closure of the canal for eight years (6 June 1967–5 June 1975) after the Six Day War diverted traffic once more to the Cape route and stimulated a boom in the construction of super tankers. The Asian-Pacific world became the source of the largest traffic to the reopened canal. Dry cargo, however, was increasingly diverted after 1984 to multimodal transport services via new land bridges between Asia and the West. After 1986, container traffic surpassed tanker tonnage to become the principal source of revenue to the Suez Canal Authority, created in 1956. Among the users of the canal, the British flag was surpassed in 1965 by that of Liberia, which in turn ceded primacy in 1995 to that of Panama. The influence of the canal helped to transform one of the most introverted societies in the world into one of the most dependent upon the outer world.

BIBLIOGRAPHY

Adams, John. "A Statistical Test of the Impact of the Suez Canal on the Growth of India's Trade." *Indian Economic and Social History Review* 8 (1971), 229–240.

Farnie, Douglas A. *East and West of Suez: The Suez Canal in History, 1854–1956.* Oxford, 1969.

Farnie, Douglas A. "Transportation Strategies of Oil Companies and Tanker Operators in Relation to the Suez Canal, 1929–1989." EU1 Colloquium Paper IUE 122/93 (Col. 19), European Networks (XIXth–XXth Centuries). New Approaches to the Formation of a Transnational System (Air, Land, and Sea). Florence, 1993.

Farnie, Douglas A. "Les stratégies de transport des compagnies pétrolières et des armateurs et le Canal de Suez, 1929–1989." In *Les réseaux européens transnationaux XIX–XX siècles: Quels enjeux?*, edited by Michèle Merger, Albert Carreras, and Andrea Giuntini, pp. 385–395. Nantes, France, 1995.

Julien, H. C. *Le Trafic du Canal de Suez: Conjuncture économique et prévisions.* Paris, 1933.

DOUGLAS A. FARNIE

SUGAR (sucrose) has become an everyday, relatively cheap product in the developed world. Yet for much of its history, it was a luxury. It is found in many plants but is commercially derived from two: cane, a type of (tropical) grass, and beet (*Beta vulgaris*), a temperate root crop. This distinctive phenomenon has had a profound influence on sugar's economic history since the early nineteenth century.

Early History. Cane was known in New Guinea from circa 8000 BCE, but the origins of sugar extraction are less clear. The first certain written account of sugar making dates from circa 500 CE, though much earlier records (in Sanskrit texts c. 350 BCE) refer to sweetened foods using cane derivatives. Sugar was probably introduced in Europe by Arab invaders in the eighth century. Productive centers developed in the eastern Mediterranean, Sicily, and North Africa. In the fourteenth and fifteenth centuries, the main European center of cane-sugar production shifted to the Atlantic island possessions of Spain and Portugal. Slave labor (initially alongside free workers) had been used from the outset, and this was extended to similar colonies across the Atlantic. (Columbus took cane to the Spanish Caribbean on his second voyage in 1493.) Slavery was thus associated with cane-sugar plantations until its abolition in the nineteenth century. Curtin (1990) has shown how African-American slaves outnumbered settlers of European origin in sixteenth-century Latin America.

Crude sugar, extracted by crushing the cane with some mechanical device and concentrating the juices, was shipped to European centers for refining and sale. The pattern remained largely unaltered for two centuries. Growth in demand was met by extending plantations, rather than major technological advances. After British, Dutch, and French colonists took Caribbean and Latin American possessions in the seventeenth century, British refineries soon came to occupy a leading position and provide the major market. Sugar growing was established also in colonies in the East Indies and the Pacific as well as in imperial China. The latter is now thought to have been on a significantly larger scale than suggested in the classic work by Deerr (1949–1950).

Modern Techniques and Markets. In the nineteenth century, some real competition developed with the production of sugar from beet, stimulated by the decline in cane-sugar imports during the Napoleonic wars. For the first time, sugar was produced on a large scale in temperate regions, especially in France, Germany, the Habsburg Empire, the Russian Empire (Poland and Ukraine), and in parts of the United States; the market hegemony of cane producers was challenged. Sugar beet provided a cash crop and a valuable part of a rotation at a time when grain prices were falling. The extraction and refining of sugar also played a big part in industrial development in central Europe. Indeed, its role in this region has been compared with that played by cotton textiles in the British Industrial Revolution. Buoyant demand and secure profits from protected markets stimulated investment and innovation. Major technological developments increased the level of extraction of sugar from beet. Many of these developments were later adapted to cane-sugar processing.

By the last quarter of the nineteenth century, most of the sugar consumed in Europe was derived from beet. Production began to outstrip demand, the excess being exported at a loss, or "dumped." Great Britain, which maintained a policy of free trade, provided the major market for beet sugar despite the long-established production capability within its empire. After several abortive attempts, an international agreement to eliminate subsidized exports was signed in 1902. Yet despite this rapid expansion of production, sugar remained a luxury for most of the century, reaching popular consumption only in Great Britain and the United States; the latter became the largest import market in the 1880s. As well as a sweetener in coffee, chocolate, and tea, sugar was also used in manufacturing jam, confectionery, candy, and carbonated drinks.

Between World War I and World War II, production doubled, the increase being mostly of cane (from Cuba and Java especially). But sugar beet was grown more widely in Europe (including Great Britain) as well. Once again, there was a tendency to overproduce, which greatly aggravated the impact of international economic depression at the end of the 1920s. The international market was compromised as colonial powers (Great Britain, France, the Netherlands, Japan) gave preferential market access to sugar produced within their empires. A further agreement was signed in 1937 effectively to establish an international cartel. In the years following World War II, global production continued to grow at a rate faster than international trade volumes. Countries became more self-sufficient, and "trade" was further regulated. The International Sugar Agreement of 1953 set a pattern for later years (similar agreements followed in 1958, 1968, 1977, and 1984) in securing market shares at guaranteed prices. The "free" market accounted for only half of world trade in the 1960s and has continued to fall in subsequent years. Sugar producers, therefore, depended on markets secured by agreement, as in the United States, the British Commonwealth, or the European Union (though this was effectively self-sufficient by 1976). Cuba, for instance, had exported most of its product to the United States after 1898 but, following the 1959 revolution, became reliant on exports to the USSR and other east European economies, establishing a formal agreement in 1964.

Trade agreements became more important for producers as world "market" prices reached an all-time low in the 1980s. Many national markets are protected by tariffs, however. In advanced countries like the United States, this has provided a favorable environment for competing alternatives to sugar, like high-fructose corn syrup and synthetics, which are widely used in manufacturing and as low-calorie sweeteners.

BIBLIOGRAPHY

Abbott, George. *Sugar*. London and New York, 1990.
Albert, Bill, and Adrian Graves, eds. *Crisis and Change in the International Sugar Economy, 1860–1914*. Norwich, U.K., 1984.
Albert, Bill, and Adrian Graves, eds. *The World Sugar Economy in War and Depression*. London, 1988.
Chalmin, Phillipe. *The Making of a Sugar Giant: Tate and Lyle, 1859–1989*. Chur, Switzerland, 1990.
Curtin, Philip D. *The Rise and Fall of the Plantation Complex: Essays in Atlantic History*. Cambridge, 1990.
Deerr, Noel. *The History of Sugar*. 2 vols. London, 1949–1950.
Galloway, J. H. *The Sugar Cane Industry: An Historical Geography from its Origins to 1914*. Cambridge, 1989.
Mazumdar, Sucheta. *Sugar and Society in China*. Cambridge, Mass., 1998.
Mintz, Sidney. *Sweetness and Power: The Place of Sugar in Modern History*. New York, 1985.
Munting, Roger, and Tamas Szmrecsanyi, eds. *Competing for the Sugar Bowl*. Saint Katharinen, Germany, 2000.

Timoshenko, Vladimir, and B. C. Swerling. *The Worlds' Sugar: Progress and Policy.* Stanford, Calif., 1957.

ROGER MUNTING

SUMPTUARY LEGISLATION. Sumptuary legislation regulates the acquisition and the consumption or use of goods, especially clothing, food, and beverages. The Roman state regularly issued such laws, as have governments throughout the ages, and many still do. In Western history, however, the period between about 1300 and 1700 was exceptional in this regard. So abundant was the legislation in this period, in both absolute and relative terms, that scholars working in Western languages have devoted most of their energy to this extraordinary episode, implicitly taking these laws and the impulses that fueled them as paradigmatic.

Although occasional sumptuary laws appeared during the early and High Middle Ages, it was only around 1300 that political authorities began a systematic effort to restrict expenditures of this kind. From that date until the 1700s, kings, dukes, cities, bishops, popes, and universities alike mounted a virtual crusade to prescribe dress, limit expenditures on public display, and control consumption of food and alcohol. During the eighteenth century, however, the regulations were allowed to lapse. Most efforts at enforcement thereafter were abandoned with such finality that subsequent ages have lost memory of them, regarding these rules as quintessentially archaic features of premodern culture, even mistakenly labeling the practice "medieval" although the legislation was typical only of the last centuries of that period and extended well into the next.

Scholars seeking to account for this history have often looked no further than the legislation itself, where the rule makers often explained themselves, variously emphasizing moral, social, or economic imperatives. Because luxury was itself a danger, as many ordinances intoned, a mark of pride and an incitement to sin, it was incumbent upon the good ruler to curtail excessive expenditures and to compel citizens to control their appetites and repress the urge to display their wealth. Rulers thus restricted expenditures for the drink for a wedding supper, permitted only a limited number of guests at a funeral, or constrained a noble from buying more than two gowns trimmed in fur. Other rules, especially those concerning dress, stressed the relationship between consumption and the social order. Arguing that the cut of a costume, the materials from which it was made, the decorations it bore, even its color, marked—indeed, determined—social place, these regulations used costume to define social hierarchy, demarcate social classes, and distinguish the legitimate from the marginal members of society. A nobleman could, for example, wear ermine and his wife silk and rubies although merchants were permitted only fox and their wives just woolens and pearls. Prostitutes were to mark their status by wearing a particular color, often red, while Jews were required to display another, frequently yellow. In the same breath, many documents warned against "extravagance" in general, linking lavish spending with economic ruin, equating sobriety in dress and demeanor with economic prudence, or attributing economic woes to injudicious outlays on imported goods.

Although never denying that these were indeed the express objectives of the legislators, scholars have more recently delved deeper, focusing attention on the sociopolitical and cultural features of the age that made associations of this kind possible: why, for example, it would have seemed necessary or possible to establish social rank by means of expenditures of this kind; what vision of appropriate social order was implicit in the regulations; why luxury was so roundly condemned at a time when rulers were themselves spending ever more on luxury goods; why only certain kinds of expenditures were the object of regulation; why some people were signaled out by the regulations; why consumption spending was regarded as economically "wasteful."

Careful research on the specific content of the regulations, their timing, and their issuers, combined with close attention to the socioeconomic, political, and cultural upheavals that defined the period, have exposed patterns that help address many of these questions. Some scholars have argued that the radical redistribution of wealth following the Black Death and a new anxiety about the fragility of life and about God's anger toward man that accompanied this disaster together fueled the regulatory impulse. Others have investigated variations in the legislation's content from the fourteenth to the fifteenth and then on to the sixteenth century, or with a shift from urban issuer to royal, or with regard to Italy or Germany rather than, say, England. In general, scholars have noted that the earliest legislation contained rather general admonitions about the moral dangers of all kinds of luxury spending, whereas later regulations tended to focus more on dress than on funerals or weddings, using dress both to demarcate a rigid social order and to protect local industries. Another visible pattern concerns gender. Much legislation concerning dress sought to identify and preserve gender difference, defining what kind of clothing was appropriately male or female; other laws, particular in Italian cities, targeted women's dress, charging that women's unbridled lust for finery was the source of civic and moral disorder.

Subsequently, scholars have begun to formulate more general explanations. Although rejecting or profoundly nuancing interpretations that characterized these rules as futile attempts to control passions for consumption newly unleashed by commerce, scholars nevertheless have acknowledged that the legislation must be understood as an expression of cultural unease about the meaning of the movable wealth that exploded in this age. This argument sees sumptuary legislation as a discourse about the good society and the things that threaten it. As such, the laws marked an important step in the evolution of the modern state, defining it as an institution responsible for the public good and legitimated by its capacity to nurture this good. In some scholars' work, the legislation is also seen as a discourse about the self, a self that exists only through a representation that is profoundly, almost exclusively, material. Accordingly, the explosion of legislation in this period, especially about dress, marked a transitional moment in Western culture, a moment when it was not yet possible to imagine a fully interiorized self but during which the tools for constructing the exterior self were too varied to manage. In this interpretation, the issue of gender is key, for the self, these scholars have pointed out, can be imagined only as a gendered self. Finally, it has been suggested that the regulatory impulse so exuberantly on display in these centuries has not, in fact, entirely expired in the West; instead it has shifted from public displays of material goods to control of the body. Today Western governments do not tell people what to wear or how much to spend on their weddings or funerals, but they seek to control alcohol consumption and the use of drugs and tobacco, prescribe seat belts and motorcycle helmets, promote good nutrition, and in general celebrate the sound body and mind, all in an energetic effort to "govern" the civic whole.

BIBLIOGRAPHY
Baldwin, Frances E. *Sumptuary Legislation and Personal Regulation in England*. Baltimore, 1926.
Brundage, James A. "Sumptuary Laws and Prostitution in Late Medieval Italy." *Journal of Medieval History* 13 (1987), 343–356.
Bulst, Neithard. "Zum Problem städtischer und territorialer Kleider-, Aufwands- und Luxusgesetzbegung in Deutschland (13–Mitte 16. Jahrhundert)." In *Renaissance du pouvoir et genèse de l'état*, edited by André Gouron and Albert Rigaudière, pp. 29–57. Montpellier, 1988.
Bulst, Neithard. "Feste und Feiern unter Auflagen: mittelalterliche Tauf- und Begräbnisordnungen in Deutschland und Frankreich." In *Feste und Feiern im Mittelalter: Paderbonner Symposium des Mediävistenverbandes*, edited by Detlef Altenburg et al., pp. 39–51. Sigmaringen, 1991.
Hughes, Diane Owen. "Sumptuary Laws and Social Relations in Renaissance Italy." In *Disputes and Settlements*, edited by John Bossy, pp. 69–99. Cambridge, 1983.
Hughes, Diane Owen, "Distinguishing Signs: Ear-rings, Jews and Franciscan Rhetoric in the Italian Renaissance City." *Past and Present* 112 (1986), 3–60.
Hunt, Alan. *Governance of the Consuming Passions: A History of Sumptuary Law*. New York, 1996.
Hunt, Alan. "The Governance of Consumption: Sumptuary Laws and Shifting Forms of Regulation." *Economy and Society* 25.3 (1996), 410–428.
Kraemer-Raine, Pierre. *Le luxe et les lois somptuaires au Moyen Age*. Paris, 1920.
Rainy, Ronald. "Dressing Down the Dressed-up: Reproving Feminine Attire in Renaissance Florence." In *Renaissance Society and Culture*, edited by John Monfasani and Ronald G. Musto, pp. 217–237. New York, 1991.

MARTHA HOWELL

SWEDEN. *See* Nordic Countries.

SWIDDEN AGRICULTURE. Swidden agriculture is arguably the most primitive system of cultivation. It differs from most other traditional agricultural systems in the length of the period of rest (fallow) between two cultivation cycles, which can last longer than thirty years. In other words, the cropping ratio (the ratio of actually cultivated land to total land in use) does not exceed 0:10–0:12, while in settled agricultural systems it exceeds 0:50. During this period of rest, the land is left untouched, and thus it can recover its natural vegetation. At the start of the cultivation cycle, the vegetation is cut and burned (the system is also known as slash-and burn-agriculture). This is not only the most efficient way to dispose of the material: it also increases the amount of nitrogen and other fertilizing materials in the soil. The land is cultivated for some years until it is exhausted and abandoned to restart the cycle somewhere else.

The peculiar features of swidden agriculture have three important implications: first, the new fields are full of rocks and tree stumps, and clearing them is long and tiresome work. It may be not worth doing in a field that will be abandoned in a short time. This makes using a plow difficult, as the tool can be easily damaged. This may account, at least partially, for the prevalence of hoeing instead of plowing to break the ground, which is a well-known feature of traditional agriculture south of the Sahara (with the exception of Ethiopia). This is not, however, the only reason. In fact, the widespread diffusion of the tsetse fly in many areas makes cattle raising impossible. Second, if new fields are far away from the old ones (as it is usually the case), the cost of commuting daily from the village may be quite high. It is thus necessary to move the whole village; and, therefore, swidden agriculture is also known as "shifting cultivation". This continuous mobility has profound implications on the way of living, as well as on social and political organization. Third, swidden agriculture is incompatible with Western-type individual (or household) property rights on land. Re-establishing them (i.e., resurveying the land, setting precise boundaries, and recording them) at every change of location would be very expensive, while in swidden agriculture there is no technical need for clearly defined field boundaries. On top of this, clearing is almost necessarily a cooperative undertaking, and thus the property rights belong to the village or to the tribe. These

Swidden Agriculture. Forests being cleared in Kendawangan, Indonesia, 1998. (© Mike Yamashita/ Woodfin Camp and Associates, New York)

"rights" cannot refer solely to the land under cultivation at any moment in time, but also have to cover the area under rest. In the nineteenth century, Western colonial administrators tended to neglect this basic fact and to behave as though most of the African land was not utilized and thus "up for grabs". On the other hand, in swidden agriculture the rights on labor—the scarce resource—are quite clearly defined: the product belongs to the household. It may have to pay taxes.

This basic scheme can be enriched with several variants. First, the length of the periods of cultivation and of rest could vary, and thus the cropping ratio could vary from 0:01 (i.e., one year of cultivation and ninety-nine of rest) to 0:10–0:15 (i.e., three years of cultivation and thirty of rest). Beyond the latter figure, shifting cultivation evolves in a somewhat different system, variously called "recurrent cultivation," "rotational bush fallow," and so on. The cropping ratio depends on population density and on environmental factors, such as the quality of the soil, the location, and the amount of rainfall. They determine the type of vegetation that can grow during the period of rest—tropical rain forest in wetter areas, and grass of different height in drier ones (known as savanna)—and the speed of its growth. As a rule, tropical forest takes a longer time to grow, and thus the overall cycle is usually longer than in savanna areas. However, this rule has a lot of exceptions, as in some savanna areas the soil is so poor that it needs a lot of time to recover. Second, the techniques are indeed primitive, but there some (slightly) less-primitive versions.

For instance, the cultivators may enhance the fertility of the soil by increasing the amount of ashes beyond the amount provided by the natural vegetation. They can bring additional combustible material (brushwood, grass) to the designed fields and burn it on site (the citemene system) or burn it elsewhere and bring only the ashes. They may reduce the dispersion of fertilizing material from ashes by burying them in the ground. Finally, they can spread household refuse or whatever manure they have on the fields (compound cultivation). Manure is, however, usually reserved for garden plots, which usually surround the village and supply vegetables. Finally, the crop mix differs. Clearly, swidden agriculture is largely a subsistence system, and in most cases there are no markets at all for agricultural products. In theory, it is not incompatible with the production of cash crops for export, and there are some instances of it. However, the shifting of location and the small amount of product greatly would increase the transaction costs. The main subsistence crop varies according to the environment and the available labor input. For instance, in nineteenth-century and early-twentieth-century Africa, the staple foods were plantains, cassava, and sorghum in forest areas and millet, cassava or sometimes maize (itself a new entry) in the savanna. Each of them needs a different labor input and provides different amounts of calories per unit of land.

In spite of its technical backwardness, swidden agriculture does not necessarily provide a very low standard of living. The yields depend on the soil and environment, but they can be quite high. The hourly labor productivity can be quite high as well, if conditions are favorable. However, the number of hours of labor is low and concentrated in short periods of time. Therefore, the yearly income is usually quite low. The productivity is used to increase leisure instead of the consumption of goods. The consumption of leisure is quite unbalanced by gender: in most cases, males have to clear the land and perform some particularly heavy tasks, but cultivation is mainly a female occupation.

Clearly, swidden agriculture is viable only when land is very abundant and population density (or carrying capacity) is very low. A denser population can be sustained, reducing the length of rest, introducing regular rotations, and, above all, intensifying the cultivation—working more carefully, planting two different crops (with different life cycles) on the same fields (which reduces risk of poor harvest and erosion, a serious problem in the tropics), maybe shifting to plow cultivation. But this process of intensification changes the very nature of swidden agriculture. There are, as mentioned, intermediate stages, but in the long run, it is necessary to find radically different ways to restore fertility, such as integration with cattle raising, whose manure allows fallow to reduce to one year every other or every two years, or irrigation, as water brings fertilizing materials. These methods were adopted in Europe and China many millennia ago. Swidden agriculture has remained in use since the nineteenth and twentieth centuries in some areas of South America, Southeast Asia (e.g., Malaya, Thailand, Myanmar), and above all in sub-Saharan Africa, where the tropical environment and the diffusion of the tsetse fly have prevented the diffusion of cattle-raising. In the last decades of the twentieth century, also in Africa, swidden agriculture has almost completely disappeared or has changed beyond recognition. The process has been accelerated by the availability of artificial fertilizers, which offer a powerful alternative way of restoring fertility. Swidden agriculture is now almost a curiosity of the past.

BIBLIOGRAPHY
Allan, William. *The African Husbandman*. London, 1965. A "classic" general description of swidden agriculture.
Anthony, Kenneth R., Bruce F. Johnston, William O. Jones, and Victor C. Uchendu. *Agricultural Change in Tropical Africa*. Ithaca and London, 1987. An empirical analysis of the process of intensification in the last fifty years.
Boserup, Ester. *The Conditions of Agricultural Growth: The Economics of Agrarian Change under Population Pressure*. Chicago, 1966. The classic book on population growth and intensification.
Feeny, David. *The Political Economy of Productivity: Thai Agricultural Development, 1880–1975*. Vancouver, 1982. Includes a discussion of intensification in Thailand.
Harris, David. *The Origins and Spread of Agriculture and Pastoralism in Eurasia*. Washington, D.C., 1996. A description of the early development of swidden agriculture.
Miracle, Marvin P. *Agriculture in the Congo Basin: Tradition and Change in African Rural Economies*. Madison, Wis., 1967. The first systematic attempt to describe agricultural change in the long run in a core of swidden agriculture.
Morgan, W. B. "Peasant Agriculture in Tropical Africa." In *Environment and Land Use in Africa*, edited by M. F. Thomas and G. W. Whittington, pp. 241–272. London, 1969. Another general overview of the system.

GIOVANNI FEDERICO

SWITZERLAND *[This entry contains two subentries, on the economic history of Switzerland before and after 1815.]*

Switzerland before 1815

The Swiss Celts, the foremost tribe being the Helvetii, succumbed to Roman domination in the second half of the first century BCE. The early Roman military posts of Noviodunum (Nyon) at the lake of Geneva and Augusta Raurica (Augst) in northwestern Switzerland became prosperous cities featuring all amenities of Roman life, including amphitheaters and public baths. Retired Roman soldiers, who had received land grants, colonized the Swiss plateau, establishing luxurious country estates. Under Roman overlordship, the acculturated Helvetii founded a new capital, Aventicum (Avanches), which became an important administrative center. The Romans built the first efficient network of roads in Swiss history. The Great Saint Bernhard Pass in western Switzerland linked Italy with Gaul, and the passes across the Rhaetian Alps in eastern Switzerland provided the shortest route to the German frontier.

At the end of the Roman era, the Alamanni invaded Switzerland from the north, the Burgundians entered from the west, and the Langobards settled on the southern slopes of the Alps. During the fourth and fifth centuries, the Roman population withdrew to western Switzerland and along the trade routes toward Italy, into the Alps. The invading Alamanni maintained their cultural identity, whereas the Burgundians and Langobards became romanized. This settlement accounts for the four national languages of modern Switzerland: German is spoken in the Alamanni region in northern Switzerland, and Latin vernaculars—French, Italian, and Romantsch—took hold in the Roman sanctuaries in western Switzerland, the south, and the Alps. Christianity, which had spread to Switzerland in Roman times, suffered a setback during the Alamannic invasion. In the seventh and eighth centuries, Irish monks were instrumental in rechristianizing northern Switzerland.

The severe social and economic retrogression that followed the fall of the West Roman Empire lasted until Carolingian times (751–843) and beyond. By the tenth century, upper Italy and Flanders had emerged as the main economic areas of Europe. Merchants from these regions crossed the Great Saint Bernhard Pass in western Switzerland (and the Mont Cenis farther to the south) to meet at fairs in the Champagne in northeastern France. Around 1200 the opening of the Saint Gotthard Pass in central Switzerland provided a new route from Italy to Germany. From the tenth century to the thirteenth century Europe enjoyed a period of prosperity and population growth. In Switzerland many cities and villages were founded, including Fribourg (1157), Berne (1191), and Lucerne (after 1200). Food production kept pace with population growth because of land clearing, improved methods of cultivation (three-year crop rotation), and favorable climatic conditions that allowed for the planting of cereals and even vines in the Alps. Population growth and improved agricultural productivity increased the price of land relative to labor. This enriched the nobility whose main revenue source was land tenure and feudal bondage of serfs. At the same time, cheap labor provided the economic conditions for the rise of medieval monasticism. Important Swiss abbeys included Saint Gall in northeastern Switzerland and Saint Maurice at the Great Saint Bernhard route.

The Holy Roman Empire, despite its name essentially Germany, succeeded the Carolingian empire in central Europe. The new empire had a strongly decentralized structure with powerful duchies and a weak emperor, appointed from the ducal families by a small group of electors. In 1231 the valley of Uri at the northern approach to the Saint Gotthard Pass gained imperial autonomy, making it directly subordinate to the emperor. In 1240 the neighboring valley of Schwyz achieved the same status. In 1291 Uri, Schwyz, and Unterwalden concluded a treaty, the so-called Bundesbrief (*pacte fédéral, patto federale, patg federal*), which is commonly regarded as the original federal charter of Switzerland, although it was not the first agreement among the three valleys. The treaty provided for law and order in central Switzerland at a time when imperial rule was weak. The signatories also agreed on military assistance against ducal encroachments upon their autonomy within the empire. During the fourteenth century the Swiss league repeatedly clashed with the Habsburgs, who tried to consolidate their possessions in central Europe. In 1386 the Swiss decisively defeated the Habsburg nobility in the battle of Sempach.

The Swiss league prevailed against the Habsburgs to a large extent because of the severe European crisis from about 1350 to about 1450. The Black Death struck for the first time in central Europe in 1348. It is more than pure coincidence that Zürich, Glarus, Zug, and Berne all joined the Swiss league shortly afterward, between 1351 and 1353. During the European crisis the population fell from about 800,000 to 600,000 inhabitants, within the confines of modern Switzerland. The population decline reduced

the price of land relative to labor, reversing the situation that had existed during the High Middle Ages. Falling revenues from land tenure and feudal bondage accounted for the economic and political decline of the local nobility, which had been associated with the Habsburgs. Many of the surviving populace moved to the cities, taking advantage of rising wages and cheap urban real estate. In the cities, political power shifted from the nobility to trade guilds, opening the door for associations with the Swiss league. Switzerland also benefited from an eastward shift of European trade during the Hundred Years' War between England and France (1337–1453). The Swiss plateau became an important thoroughfare for trade from the Rhone valley in southern France to the Hanseatic cities in northern Germany and the Baltic. Much of the commerce that had been transacted at the Champagne fairs moved to Geneva in western Switzerland, as well as to Frankfurt and Besançon. During the fifteenth century the Swiss league expanded aggressively as new members joined it, and military conquests became subordinate territories.

From the sixteenth century to the eighteenth century Switzerland experienced a period of political and economic stagnation. In the cities a new aristocracy emerged whose interests matched those of the medieval nobility, drawing income from land tenure and feudal bondage. In the Alps the democratic tradition of open-air assemblies coexisted with the influence of leading families and the church. Switzerland remained a loose association of independent states that jealously guarded their petty interests until the nineteenth century. Conflicts between states sometimes degenerated into outright civil wars. The guild system and state protectionism interfered with trade and economic development.

In the sixteenth century, Switzerland harbored two Protestant reformers: Zwingli in Zürich and Calvin in Geneva. Calvinism spread to the west—France, the Netherlands, and Great Britain—and to eastern Europe. The Reformation succeeded in Swiss cities, where it was supported by the aristocratic elite; hence, it did not lead to a liberalization of the oppressive guild system or to the abandonment of city prerogatives in the countryside. Switzerland had the good fortune to stay out of the Thirty Years' War between Protestants and Catholics that devastated Germany (1618–1648), although the war spilled over into the Grisons, a close ally of the Swiss confederation. The Tagsatzung, an assembly of state representatives, successfully adopted a neutral stance that was necessitated by animosity between Protestant and Catholic Swiss states. Bonjour (1965–1976) attributes the evolution of Swiss neutrality to divergent state interests.

The Swiss population rose from about one million inhabitants in 1600 to 1.7 million in 1800. Before the Industrial Revolution the largest Swiss cities were Geneva and Basle with around 10,000 people each. Demographic data exhibit strong fluctuations, reflecting economic conditions and the ravages of infectious diseases. The Black Death periodically continued to afflict Switzerland until the seventeenth century. From the sixteenth century on, agriculture achieved some productivity gains through specialization—animal husbandry in the Alps and cereals and wine production on the fertile Swiss plateau. Home weaving and spinning supplemented rural income, in particular in northeastern Switzerland. Still, the scourge of famines, caused by harvest failures or created by trade barriers and wars, did not disappear until the Industrial Revolution. As economic prospects were poor at home, a large number of Swiss served as mercenaries, often on opposing sides, in European wars until the nineteenth century. Foreign powers, especially the king of France, paid vast sums to state governments for the right to enlist Swiss troops.

From the seventeenth century to the early eighteenth century, an influx of Huguenots (French Protestants) sparked a cultural and economic revival in western Switzerland. In the Protestant Swiss states the population was receptive to the ideas of the French Enlightenment, which provided for a set of values conducive to economic development. Geneva became a world center for printing cotton fabric. The printing process was organized along industrial principles in factories that employed hundreds of workers. Raw cotton fabric was either imported from India or woven in preindustrial conditions in home workshops in northeastern Switzerland. Watchmaker's shops spread in the Jura mountains along the Swiss-French border where there were no trade guilds. The nascent industrialization accounted for a growing income gap between Protestant states on the Swiss plateau and Catholic Alpine states, setting the scene for political conflict in the nineteenth century. The French Revolution heightened political aspirations in the economically advanced Swiss states. In 1798 in many places the population welcomed invading French troops as liberators from oppressive aristocratic regimes. Under Napoleon's tutelage Switzerland abolished aristocratic privileges and trade guilds, states and subordinate territories became cantons with equal rights, and a unified national economic and currency area was established. In 1815 the restoration of the old order by the Congress of Vienna led to a temporary setback although the cantonal structure survived.

BIBLIOGRAPHY

Bergier, Jean-François. *Histoire économique de la Suisse; Die Wirtschaftsgeschichte der Schweiz; Storia economica della Svizzera.* Lausanne, 1984; Zürich, 1990; Lugano, 1999.

Bonjour, Edgar. *Geschichte der Schweizerischen Neutralität.* 9 vols. Basel, 1965–1976. The main source on Swiss neutrality; written before the current controversy on Swiss foreign policy during World War II.

Dictionnaire Historique de la Suisse; Historisches Lexikon der Schweiz; Dizionario Storico della Svizzera. Forthcoming. Since 1998, articles can be viewed on the Internet at <http://www.dhs.ch>.

Handbuch der Schweizer Geschichte. vols. 1 and 2, 2d ed. Zürich, 1980. The standard source on the political evolution of Switzerland; includes an extensive bibliography.

Head, Randolph C. *Early Modern Democracy in the Grisons: Social Order and Political Language in a Swiss Mountain Canton, 1470–1620.* Cambridge, 1995.

King, James C., and Vogler, Werner, eds. *The Culture of the Abbey of St. Gall.* Stuttgart and Zürich, 1991. A cultural history of a center of European monasticism.

Nouvelle histoire de la Suisse et des Suisses; Geschichte der Schweiz und der Schweizer; Storia nuova della Svizzera e degli Svizzeri. Lausanne, 1998; Basel, 1986; Bellinzona, 1983. A comprehensive account of Swiss history stressing cultural, political, economic, and demographic aspects of history; includes an extensive bibliography.

Pfister, Ulrich. "Proto-Industrialization in Switzerland." In *European Proto-industrialization,* edited by Sheilagh C. Ogilvie, and Markus Cerman, pp. 137–154. Cambridge, 1996.

Weber, Ernst Juerg. "'Imaginary' or 'Real' Moneys of Account in Medieval Europe? An Econometric Analysis of the Basle Pound, 1365–1429." *Explorations in Economic History* 33 (1996), 479–495.

E. Juerg Weber

Switzerland after 1815

In 1798 revolutionary France invaded Switzerland and put an end to the old order. After half a century of struggle and turmoil, the advocates of a modern political system based on the principles of the sovereignty of the people, the separation of powers, and civil liberties succeeded in establishing the federal constitution of 1848, amalgamating the formerly sovereign cantons in a confederation and thus laying the foundation for modern Switzerland. Intercantonal customs duties were abolished; the various cantonal currencies and weights and measures were replaced by the Swiss franc and the metric system, respectively. This did not argue a total economic unification of the Swiss market. Up to 1882 every canton retained its specific business law, and the National Bank, with its allotted function as the central bank of Switzerland, was only instituted in 1907.

The construction of railways set in with some delay but was advanced vigorously as soon as the constitution furnished the necessary legal framework. The opening of the Gotthard Railway (1882) with then the longest tunnel (fifteen kilometers) all but completed the main Swiss railway network.

The federal authorities subscribed to an economic policy of strict nonintervention. Demands of a sociopolitical order were late to be heard and still later to become politically effective with enactment of the first Federal Factory Law (1877), Compulsory Health Insurance and Industrial Injuries Insurance (1912), and the Social Security Statute (1948).

Under pressure of necessity rather than from choice, Switzerland in matters of foreign trade policy has at all

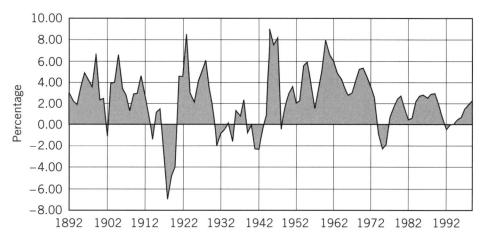

FIGURE 1. Growth rates of real GDP (3-year moving averages). SOURCE: Ritzmann-Blickenstorfer, 1996, p. 866; Bundesamt für Statistik, ed., *Statistiches Jahrbuch der Schweiz,* Zürich, 1995–2002.

times been committed to the doctrine of free trade. For Switzerland, landlocked and suffering from a shortage of natural resources, external trade increasingly became a vital necessity. Furthermore the small size of the country forbade any indulgence in tariff wars. In the second half of the nineteenth century, the sum total of Swiss exports amounted to about one-third of GDP. It dropped to a mere 10 percent during the crises of the 1930s and rose to about one-quarter after World War II.

Nineteenth Century. Until 1885 the textile and the watch and clock making industries were the principal industries in Switzerland. They exported more than 90 percent of their production.

The first comprehensive Swiss census (1798) yielded a total population of 1.65 million, which doubled to 3.3 million by 1900. Throughout the nineteenth century marriages and birthrates were still closely connected with long-term economic fluctuations. Migration movements reacted even more promptly to cyclical factors. In periods of economic upswing, there was a noticeable increase of internal migration to industrial areas and to cities, whereas in times of crisis, emigration to foreign countries was clearly predominant. Statistics demonstrate that between 1800 and 1888, a surplus of 332,600 people emigrated to foreign countries as compared with immigrations from abroad. After 1888 the traditionally negative migration balance turned into its opposite, an epoch-marking turning point in Swiss history. As early as 1914 some 15 percent of the resident population was foreign-born. That percentage far exceeded the respective resident populations of all other European countries.

The emergence of an international agrarian commodities market brought down the grain prices, while at the same time, the various industries offered higher wages. As a result, Swiss farmers gradually gave up the production of cereals, switching to animal husbandry and dairy farming, both of which were laborsaving and better adapted to the climatic-topographical conditions of the country.

In addition to the traditional cheese production, the food-processing industry appeared on the market, without which the expansion of dairy farming would have been unthinkable. The new industry absorbed the overflow of milk, processing it mainly into condensed milk and chocolate. The finished products found a ready market abroad. Thus in Vevey, on the border of Lake Geneva, Henri Nestlé started in 1867 his production of baby food, adding in 1878 the production of condensed milk and a little later the production of chocolate. His initially modest enterprise has developed into one of the most important foodstuff manufacturing firms worldwide.

The worldwide economic crisis of 1873 particularly affected the important watch and clock making industry. That industry had supplied some two-thirds of the sum total of clocks and watches reaching the international market, but by 1877 exports to the United States alone had diminished by some 80 percent. Not before the conversion of the customary production in small ateliers to a mechanized output had taken place did the Swiss trade in clocks and watches regain its former predominant position on the international market.

Broadly speaking the 1873 depression amounted to a period of restructure of the old, established industries. The following upswing, however, which set in after 1885 and led to a considerable and prolonged economic growth that lasted with only short interruptions up to the beginning of World War I, was owed to the "new" industries, the chemical and engineering industries. As early as the first half of the nineteenth century, some metalworking and machine

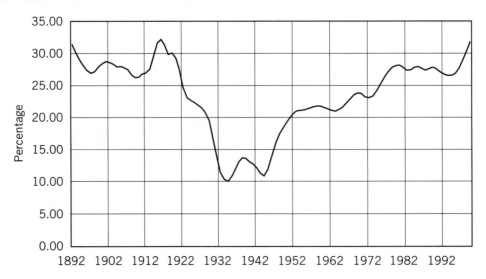

FIGURE 2. Exports (in percentage of GDP; 3-year moving averages). SOURCE: Ritzmann-Blickenstorfer, 1996, p. 866; Bundesamt für Statistik, ed., *Statistiches Jahrbuch der Schweiz*, Zürich, 1995–2002.

factories had developed from the repair workshops of the textile industries. But only after 1885 did the engineering industries advance to their position as a leading sector, particularly in the field of electrical engineering. Engineering works, such as the Maschinenfabrik Oerlikon (established 1876) or Brown, Boveri & Company (1891), were instrumental in developing new technologies in the fields of electric traction and long-distance transmission of energy.

The chemical industry, including CIBA (1884), Sandoz (1886), and Hoffmann–La Roche (1894), all located in Basel, produced aniline dyes for the textile industries as well as pharmaceuticals and held an important share of the international market. Swiss output in 1895, compared by value, amounted to almost one-fifth of German production and just about equaled the total output of all other countries combined.

Nevertheless until the outbreak of World War I and because of the enormous boom experienced by stitch work, the textile industries remained the most important employers and retained the most important exports in terms of value and quantities. High-quality lacework from Saint Gall was exported worldwide, particularly to the United States. Owing to the vagaries of fashion trends, however, the demand for embroidery work collapsed almost entirely after World War I.

By 1910 the sometime agrarian state had turned into a fully industrialized nation. The former portion of the population that was agricultural, approximately two-thirds, had dwindled to only slightly more than one-fourth, while those employed in the secondary sector had risen from one-fourth of the population to a little less than half. From 1888 onward, the number of factory hands had greatly increased, but the third sector scored the most substantial growth. Insignificant in 1800, the services sector registered 12 percent in 1870 and in 1910 as much as 23 percent of the total of employed persons. These data reflect the improvement of the public health and educational systems, the expansion of public administration and civil service, and the growth of specialized enterprise in a society increasingly based on the division of labor. The importance of the tourist industry is often underestimated. Tourism experienced its heyday during the belle epoque around 1900. The gross product of the tourist trade in 1912 added up to 175 million francs, just about matching that of the metal and machine industries (183 million francs) and almost doubling that of the watch and clock making industry (94.5 million francs).

Whereas the "old" textile and watch and clock making industries were mostly situated in rural districts, the "new" industries were dependent on optimum traffic routes and the best possible channels of communication. The same holds true for all kinds of service industries. These new requirements led to an explosive urbanization of Switzerland after 1888. In 1850 less than 10 percent of the population was recorded as living in cities (that is, communities with ten thousand or more inhabitants). By 1910 the urban population had grown to more than one-fourth of the total Swiss population or some one million people. Zürich in 1894 was first to attain more than 100,000 inhabitants and therefore metropolitan status. By 1910 it was matched by Basel and Geneva.

The rapid pace of transformation, combined with an almost total absence of social policy, led to severe social conflicts. The 1880s witnessed the birth of a new labor movement that was increasingly aggressive. Switzerland was shaken by a veritable chain of strikes, the provisional peak of which was reached by way of one million strike days in 1907. In an attempt to overcome the profound social crisis, the authorities, conjuring up a common historical past, in 1891 laid down 1 August as the Swiss national holiday, arguing somewhat speciously that this was the day of the foundation of the Swiss nation six hundred years before (in 1291). Furthermore rural Switzerland was promoted as the genuine representation of the country, ironically when the rural population was plainly becoming a minority. Thus the National Exhibition of 1896 in Geneva displayed a *village suisse*, featuring veritable cows veritably browsing in front of Alpine scenery constructed of wood and painted canvas. This image of Switzerland as a "nation of shepherds and peasants," successfully marketed by the Swiss tourist trade to the present day, proved a powerful myth and a most efficient means of self-identification almost to the end of the twentieth century.

The Twentieth Century. Neutral Switzerland escaped World War I. Some export firms realized fat profits, while the living standards of large sections of the population perceptibly deteriorated and real wages decreased by 20 to 25 percent. Eventually the social crisis culminated in the general strike of November 1918.

The disruption of nations, social order, and economic systems, combined with the relative stability of the Swiss currency and the proverbial discretion of Swiss financial institutions, made Switzerland by 1918 a safe haven for foreign moneys. To a much higher degree than the legendary but by no means unique Swiss banking secrecy, this comparative safety of funds has been instrumental in the extraordinary international success of Swiss banking and insurance businesses up to this day.

On the whole Swiss economic development between the world wars approximately matched the international pattern with a serious postwar crisis (1921–1922), followed by the short-lived prosperity of the Golden Twenties, and then the worldwide depression, manifested in Switzerland only in 1931 but lasting longer there than elsewhere. A currency devaluation by 30 percent (November 1936) eventually enabled Switzerland to catch up with the international market.

The country made progress on the level of social differences, seemingly irreconcilable in the years following 1918. There was a cautious, gradual rapprochement between leftists and rightists enhanced by the threat of German Nazism. In 1937 trade unions and employers' organizations of the metal and engineering industries agreed on a "peace pact" that was subsequently adopted by numerous other industrial branches and that led to the virtual disappearance of strikes in Switzerland.

Unlike in 1914, Switzerland survived World War II (1939–1945) as a unified nation without any social problems worth mentioning. Economically speaking it collaborated to a large extent with Nazi Germany. It had in fact hardly any alternative after the capitulation of France

MODERN SWITZERLAND. Counting cash receipts from all over the world at the Pictet Bank, Geneva, 1986. (© Jacques Chenet/Woodfin Camp and Associates, New York)

TABLE 1. *Population and Work Force*

			PERSONS GAINFULLY EMPLOYED SECTORS (PERCENTAGES)			
YEAR	POPULATION (MILLIONS)	GROWTH RATE PERCENTAGES	TOTAL (MILLIONS) PER ANNUM	PRIMARY	SECONDARY	TERTIARY
1800	1.666		[0.76]	[66.0]	[26.0]	[8.0]
1850	2.393	0.73	[1.08]	[57.0]	[32.0]	[10.00]
1860	2.510	0.48	—	—	—	—
1870	2.655	0.56	—	—	—	—
1880	2.832	0.65	—	—	—	—
1888	2.918	0.37	1.305	37.44	41.62	20.94
1900	3.315	1.07	1.555	30.97	44.89	24.14
1910	3.753	1.25	1.783	26.76	45.49	27.75
1920	3.880	0.33	1.872	25.79	43.82	30.39
1930	4.066	0.47	1.943	21.28	44.26	34.46
1941	4.266	0.44	1.992	20.83	43.56	35.61
1950	4.715	1.12	2.156	16.49	46.59	36.92
1960	5.429	1.42	2.515	11.61	50.7	37.69
1970	6.270	1.45	2.996	7.7	48.24	44.06
1980	6.366	0.15	3.054	7.1	39.5	53.4
1990	6.751	0.59	3.813	4.2	31.0	64.7
2000	7.204	0.65	3.873	4.6	26.7	68.6

Data in brackets are estimates.
SOURCE: Kneschaurek, Francesco, "Wandlungen in der schweizerischen Industriestruktur seit 1800," in *Ein Jahrhundert schweizerischer Wirtschaftsentwicklung*, edited by Schweizerische Gesellschaft für Statistik und Volkswirtschaft, Bern, 1964, p. 139. *Statistisches Jahrbuch der Schweiz*, edited by Bundesamt für Statistik, Bern, 1872–1990, Zürich, 1995–2002.

(June 1940). Switzerland supplied Germany with war materials, granted one billion francs in loans, and functioned as a center of transactions for gold and foreign currency. Not before the 1990s did a violent controversy arise as to whether this policy, highly successful as a means to maintain territorial integrity, was also justifiable morally.

In the war-worn Europe of 1945, Switzerland's intact infrastructures and production centers provided an excellent starting position. More than doubling its GNP per head, the country enjoyed a period of sustained economic growth between 1950 and 1974. In the 1960s however, the first growth problems appeared. Reckless dealings with (cheap) energy and the available space caused environmental problems, and inflation rates rose to 10 percent per annum. In addition a general social discomposure, caused by sudden change, was manifested in the troublous youth movement of 1968 and in a growing xenophobia nourished by the abrupt accretion of the quota of foreigners living and working in Switzerland (17 percent of the population).

The crisis of 1974 lasted for a relatively short time, since the threatening oversupply of labor was predominantly exported by way of dismissing foreign workers and sending them back home. Throughout the 1980s economic performance remained uneven and sluggish, the rate of

growth of GNP per head averaging 1.1 percent between 1976 and 1990 as compared to 3.1 percent between 1950 and 1974. The renewed depression of the 1990s proved much more serious. For the first time since 1936, unemployment reached a peak of over 5 percent.

The so-called "electronic revolution" and the transition to a postindustrial society entailed enormous problems of readjustment in Switzerland as elsewhere. The share of employed persons in the secondary sector, 50 percent in 1960, shrank to a mere 25 percent by 2000. Some onetime world-famous Swiss enterprises of the engineering and electrical industries disappeared from the market. The chemical industry underwent a number of mergers, and Novartis thereby emerged as one of the giants of the chemical industries worldwide. (In 1970 Ciba and Geigy merged to create Ciba-Geigy, which merged in 1996 with Sandoz to create Novartis.)

Growth within some branches of the services sector, such as banking and retail businesses, was equally connected with considerable amalgamations. Out of the original five big commercial banks, only the Union Bank of Switzerland and Crédit Suisse remain as "global players."

Structural problems also piled up within the realm of social policy. In 1900 every woman still gave birth to 3.8 children on an average, but this fertility rate, with the exception of the baby boom years (1941–1964), has been sinking steadily to today's index of about 1.6. Combined with a steadily rising life expectancy, this fertility decline threatens serious problems with respect to the financing of old-age pensions.

In the course of the nineteenth century the original policy of strict nonintervention gradually gave way to the conviction that active state control is imperative in certain areas of economic life, such as legislating working conditions (prohibition of child labor in 1877), supporting exposed branches (for example, subventioning agricultural enterprises), or assuming desirable entrepreneurial functions (for example, the nationalization of the railways in 1902). Despite the lack of any constitutional foundations before 1947, when the so-called "economy articles" were adopted by popular vote, state intervention multiplied during the world wars and the crisis-afflicted 1920s and 1930s.

Until the 1990s the turn toward neo-liberalism met with little response in Switzerland. Even then it was complied with partially and hesitantly, as the voters' distrust of privatization of well-established and reliable public institutions remained considerable.

Economically Switzerland after 1945 easily adapted to the West while, referring to its neutrality, persistently rejecting any political alliances. During the Cold War, Switzerland succeeded in plausibly passing for a "special case" in between the power blocs. Even when, after the breakdown of the Soviet Union, a repositioning within the international community of states became of paramount importance, it took yet a further decade for Swiss citizens to agree to the opening up of their foreign policy. The relationship between Switzerland and the European Union was at last settled in 2001 by means of bilateral treaties, and Swiss accession to the United Nations was resolved by vote in 2002.

While it remains difficult to quantify, the living standard has undoubtedly risen in the course of the last two centuries. One of the indications thereof is the steadily rising life expectancy. Amounting to just under 40 years in 1850, to 50.6 years in 1910, and to 62.7 years in 1941, it was 76.7 years for men and 82.8 years for women in 1999. The real wages of workers trebled between 1910 and 1970, gradually permitting expenditures in addition to purely elementary needs. The share of income that average working-class families were in a position to spend for holidays, traveling, or cultural events amounted to merely 6 percent around 1921 and to 23.2 percent in 1971. The main accretion of real wages fell within the boom years of the 1950s and 1960s and remained sluggish after the crisis of 1974. On an international level and in terms of the per capita product, Switzerland numbers among the most prosperous countries worldwide.

[*See also* Chemical Industries *and* Clock Making and Time Measurement.]

BIBLIOGRAPHY

Bairoch, Paul, and Martin Körner, eds. *Die Schweiz in der Weltwirtschaft.* Zürich, 1990. A collection of essays on Switzerland with respect to the world economy. Especially notable is an article by David S. Landes, "Swatch! Ou l'horlogerie suisse dans le contexte international."

Bérgier, Jean-François. *Histoire économique de la Suisse.* Lausanne, Switzerland, 1984. A general survey from the late Middle Ages arranged thematically, stressing the continuities rather than disruptions among the several periods.

Busset, Thomas, et al., eds. *Chemie in der Schweiz: Geschichte der Forschung und der Industrie.* Basel, 1997. A collection of essays on the Swiss chemical industry, its research and development.

Cassis, Youssef, and Jakob Tanner. "Finance and Financiers in Switzerland, 1880–1960." In *Finance and Financiers in European History, 1880–1960,* edited by Youssef Cassis, pp. 293–316. Cambridge, 1991.

Craig, Gordon. *The Triumph of Liberalism: Zurich in the Golden Age, 1830–1869.* New York, 1986. One of the rare books in English on Swiss economic history. Economic development is seen in the broader context of political and cultural history; spirited but not always reliable in details.

Fritzsche, Bruno, ed. *Historischer Strukturatlas der Schweiz: Die Entstehung der modernen Schweiz.* Baden, Switzerland, 2001. Some three hundred maps visualize, on a regional basis, the demographic and economic development in conjunction with the emergence of the new transportation and communication networks. Explanatory texts in German.

Fritzsche, Bruno. "Industrial Revolution in Switzerland." In *The Industrial Revolution in National Context, Europe and the USA,* edited by Mikulas Teich and Roy Porter, pp. 126–148. Cambridge, 1996.

Gruner, Erich. *Arbeiterschaft und Wirtschaft in der Schweiz, 1880–1914.* 3 vols. Zürich, 1987–1988. The most exhaustive material on political, social, and economic structures and relations during the crucial years of 1880–1914.

Müller, Margrit. "Coping with Barriers to Trade: Internationalisation Strategies of Swiss Firms in the Interwar Period. "In *Transnational Companies, Nineteenth–Twentieth Centuries,* edited by Hubert Bonin et al. Paris, 2002.

Ritzmann-Blickenstorfer, Heiner, ed. *Historische Statistik der Schweiz.* Zürich, 1996. More than one thousand tightly packed pages of historical statistics; introductory texts in German, French, and English; and an extensive bibliography.

Schröter, Harm G. "Swiss Multinational Enterprise in Historical Perspective." In *The Rise of Multinationals in Continental Europe,* edited by G. Jones and H. G. Schröter. Aldershot, U.K., 1993.

Siegenthaler, Hansjörg. "Die Schweiz 1815–1914." *In Handbuch der europäischen Wirtschafts- und Sozialgeschichte,* vol. 5, edited by Wolfram Fischer, pp. 443–473. Stuttgart, 1985. A condensed analysis based on economic theory.

Siegenthaler, Hansjörg. "Die Schweiz 1914–1984." In *Handbuch der europäischen Wirtschafts- und Sozialgeschichte,* vol. 6, edited by Wolfram Fischer, pp. 482–512. Stuttgart, 1985. A condensed analysis based on economic theory.

BRUNO FRITZSCHE

SWOPE, GERARD (1872–1957), American corporate executive whose life coincided with major changes in U.S. society, including assertive unionism and government activism during and after the Great Depression of the 1930s; the United States becoming a global economic power; and the electricity revolution that transformed American industry, commerce, communications, transportation, and society.

Born in Saint Louis, Missouri, he was seven years old when Thomas Alva Edison invented the electric light bulb. Swope graduated from the Massachusetts Institute of Technology (MIT) in 1895, the year that Niagara Falls generated its first hydroelectric power. Electrical technology required knowledgeable salespeople to get customers to purchase capital-intensive systems, and Swope excelled at this. He became the domestic and international sales manager for the equipment-manufacturing subsidiary of the American Telegraph and Telephone Company (AT&T) by 1910 and the second president of the thirty-year-old General Electric Company (GE) in 1922.

Private and off-putting, Swope was a power broker of American corporate and political life. He did not like cocktail parties, but he was the right man to get complicated jobs done. Privacy came, in part, from his unusual background, one then rare in corporate America: Swope was a child of Reform Judaism who had met and married his wife, Mary Hill, while both were resident volunteers at Jane Addams's Hull House in Chicago, the first social-welfare settlement house in the United States.

During the 1920s, Swope built GE into a symbol of progress, by steadily expanding the company into electrical consumer goods for both homes and businesses. In labor relations, GE developed the employer-based policy of Welfare Capitalism as a substitute for either strikes or state-sponsored programs in a country where large companies, weak unions, and small government created a decentralized, partial, and employment-based welfare state.

The Great Depression gave Swope distinctive scope. Locked in Republican minimal-government mindsets, most corporate leaders had no solutions for catastrophe. In 1931, Swope proposed a nationalized version of Welfare Capitalism, to be overseen by industrial trade associations, in order to stabilize wages and prices and end "free-rider" behavior. The "Swope Plan" was central to the drafting of the National Industrial Recovery Act of 1933 (NIRA). In 1933, Swope was recruited by New Deal Democrats as the first president of the Business Council, an elite advisory body of corporate leaders. Castigated as "tame millionaires," the Business Council during and after Swope's leadership played the politics of "Yes, but . . ." rather than "No." This allowed him and other like-minded business leaders to influence the formulation and implementation of important reform programs, such as social security (in fact, Swope worked on the advisory panels that created the Social Security Act of 1935). Instead of denying, conspiracy theorizing, or blaming political messengers for bad

GERARD SWOPE. (Royden Dixon/Prints and Photographs Division, Library of Congress)

news, Swope concentrated on crafting solutions for Depression-era problems. His practical accommodation—not the angry whine of most businesspeople of the period—helped preserve American capitalism.

Today, the Business Council and its organizational siblings, the Business Roundtable and the Committee for Economic Development, exist as forums for policy debate and contact with government in those many circumstances when government is asked to be a financier, investor, subsidizer, guarantor, lawgiver, regulator, or international trade promoter of last resort. Instead of ascribing messianic qualities to marketplace competition, entrepreneurs, or corporations, Swope understood that societies are also part of capitalist equations.

BIBLIOGRAPHY

Case, Josephine Young, and Everett Needham Case. *Owen D. Young and American Enterprise: A Biography*. Boston, 1982.

Frederick, George, ed. *The Swope Plan: Details, Criticisms, Analysis*. New York, 1931.

Jacoby, Sanford. *Modern Manors: Welfare Capitalism since the New Deal*. Princeton, 1997.

Kahn, E. J. *The World of [Herbert Bayard] Swope*. New York, 1965.

Loth, David. *Swope of G.E.* New York, 1958.

McQuaid, Kim. *Big Business and Presidential Power: From Roosevelt to Reagan*. New York, 1982.

KIM MCQUAID

SYNTHETIC FIBERS INDUSTRY. Synthetic fibers and human-made plastics are the two most important applications of polymer chemistry. Polymers are large chains of simpler molecules (monomers) strung together by chemical bonds. Natural fibers, such as cotton, wool, and silk, are also polymers.

When Hermann Staudinger, a prominent German chemist, and others clarified the nature of polymers in the 1920s, chemists tried to develop substitutes for naturally occurring fibers using wholly human-made materials or, as a famous advertisement put it, from "coal, air, and water," although these fibers are better described as being from petroleum, oil, and water. Within little more than a decade, the three major synthetic fibers—nylon, polyester, and acrylic—were introduced, and a fourth, polypropylene, followed in the 1950s. Since polypropylene is mainly used as a plastic material and its use as a fiber is chiefly for floor covering, this essay focuses on rayon, nylon, polyester, and acrylic.

Synthetic fibers have had a huge impact and have pervaded modern life in so many ways that they are taken for granted. Yet in the mid-twentieth century, women rioted in the streets of San Francisco to get nylon stockings. The worldwide production of raw cotton, by far the most important natural fiber, barely doubled between 1960 and 1999. The production of wool, the natural fiber next in importance to cotton, barely increased (although it increased by about 50 percent by 1980). Also between 1960 and 1999, the total production of synthetic fibers increased almost thirtyfold. In the year 2000, the total production of human-made fiber was reported at a little over 31 million metric tons and that of synthetic fiber at 21 million metric tons. In the same year, polyester accounted for 60 percent of the total production of synthetics, followed by nylon (13 percent), polypropylene (9 percent), acrylic (8 percent), and cellulosic fibers, chiefly rayon (8 percent). The impact of synthetic fibers has been, ironically enough, far greater on the poorer rather than the richer nations. In the 1980s and 1990s, production of synthetic fibers increasingly shifted to the populous developing countries in Asia, away from the developed countries but also away from Eastern Europe.

At the beginning of the 1950s, nylon was the dominant synthetic fiber. The global output of nylon in 1959 was 421,000 metric tons, of which all but 71,000 metric tons was in the United States and Western Europe. By contrast, the combined output of all synthetic fibers in 1959 was just under 700,000 metric tons. Over time, polyester has grown in importance and accounts for about 60 percent of the total production of synthetic fiber.

The global output of polyester fiber grew from 105,000 metric tons in 1959 to over 17.5 million metric tons in 1999, a more than 177-fold increase. By comparison, the production of nylon increased from 421,000 metric tons to about 4 million metric tons over the same time period, a less than tenfold increase. Over the same period, acrylic production increased twenty-five–fold.

The vast bulk of the increase in polyester production in fact took place in the 1990s in the Asian countries, especially China, Taiwan, South Korea (each of which produces more polyester than the United States), and India. As late as 1975, the total Asian production (excluding Japan) was less than 350,000 metric tons. By 1980, however, this had nearly tripled, and it increased nearly 400 percent to just over 4 million metric tons in 1990. Over the 1990s, production tripled once again to over 12.5 million metric tons. By contrast, polyester fiber production in the United States and Western Europe combined increased from 89,000 metric tons to nearly 1 million metric tons in 1975 and more than doubled to 2.5 million metric tons by 1990, with the United States and Western Europe producing 1.4 million metric tons and 1.1 million metric tons respectively. Subsequently, production increased in the United States to 1.7 million metric tons but declined in Western Europe to just under 950,000 metric tons in 1999.

Acrylic and nylon do not show such a marked dominance of the Asian countries. Indeed, nylon production is still relatively heavily concentrated in Western Europe and especially in the United States. In 1999, together they produced 50 percent of the worldwide nylon fiber output of just over 3.9 million metric tons and accounted for just over 25 percent of the worldwide acrylic output.

Innovation. The slowly developing scientific understanding of polymers in the 1930s was crucial for starting the polymer industry, and the growth and success of synthetic fibers depended heavily on innovations on a number of fronts. Before a new polymer could become a fiber, it had to be drawn, spun, or woven into fabric, dyed, and finished. At each stage, existing techniques had to be modified to adapt to the new polymer, and in many cases, entirely new techniques and equipment developed. For instance, the major synthetic fibers tend to repel water and thus were difficult to dye using dyes employed for cotton or wool. The solutions to these problems included blending with other fibers, introducing small amounts of other materials during production to produce "copolymers," and producing new types of dyes.

Synthetic fibers compete both with natural fibers as well as with each other. Their success depends crucially upon access to cheap inputs. New processes for producing these inputs cheaply, in large volumes and at the required levels of purity, have played an important role in the success of synthetic fibers. These new processes required considerable chemical engineering skills along with advances in chemical catalysis and in refining technology. In recent years, innovations have focused on the physical form (rather than the chemical composition), producing microfibers or very fine fibers for all the major synthetics, which yield a silky yet durable fabric.

At the firm level, perhaps the most significant challenge in the commercialization of a new fiber was in developing the market. This involved, among other things, deciding upon the most profitable market for a fiber that had only been produced in a lab, with little guarantee about how the fiber would behave as a fabric. The specific market targeted would determine which properties of the fiber to develop. Whereas nylon was quickly adopted in the women's hosiery market, the applications of polyester and acrylic developed through the slow and costly process of trial and error with little guidance from science.

Thus, the growth of synthetic fibers owes not only to those chemical firms that discovered ways to synthesize the long molecular chains that became the fiber but also to the firms that discovered ways of processing these chains and especially to those that discovered new ways of producing the key chemical intermediates and the basic petrochemical building blocks for those intermediates. That said, it is difficult not to single out one firm, DuPont, for its role in discovering, developing, and commercializing major synthetic fibers.

Rayon: "Artificial Silk." Silk's high cost made it one of the first targets (along with rubber) for substitution by synthetic polymers. The earliest silk substitute, rayon, was developed in the late nineteenth century and early twentieth century, and a number of European researchers and firms made substantial contributions to its development. Although strictly speaking rayon was not a synthetic fiber since it was produced from cellulose (derived from wood and cotton), experience with rayon helped firms such as DuPont greatly in developing synthetic fibers.

In 1900, the total European production of rayon was 2 million pounds, and it rose to 15 million pounds in 1910. During this time, the United States was a large importer of rayon. Courtaulds, a well-established British silk-weaving firm, was the first to establish rayon production in the United States in 1911 through a subsidiary called the American Viscose Company. In the 1920s, a new form of rayon fiber, called acetate rayon or acetate, was introduced. Acetate was far less flammable than other types of rayon.

Rayon was a formidable technological accomplishment. However, since rayon was made from cellulose, it tended to weaken upon absorbing water. Further, rayon was difficult to dye, and most varieties of rayon tended to be stiff and coarse, more like horsehair than silk. A number of minor and major innovations, detailed in David A. Hounshell and John K. Smith, *Science and Corporate Strategy* (1988, pp. 161–182), were vital for the growing use of rayon. In a pattern that became common to the true synthetic fibers that followed, the growth of rayon was a slow process, as rayon producers gradually improved the strength and dyeability, learned to make finer yarn, and improved other qualities of the fiber that broadened its use from ribbons to stockings and socks and to the larger markets of women's dresses.

Rayon has decreased in importance over time, as new synthetic fibers have been developed. Yet despite its many shortcomings, rayon still is used in applications where its absorbency is valuable, such as cigarette filters and diapers, and it is blended with other fibers to impart a silky, luxurious feel. Despite the stiff competition from a variety of synthetic fibers commercialized around or shortly after World War II, the worldwide production of rayon rose to a peak of about 4 million metric tons in 1965, slowly but steadily falling to a little over 2.1 million metric tons in 1999. The fall has been sharp in the developed countries. Production in Western Europe, Japan, and the United States in 1999 fell to less than half of what it was in 1960. However, production in the developing countries of Asia rose steadily from negligible levels to a point at which China and India are among the largest producers of the fiber; together with other Asian countries (excluding Japan), they account for more than 50 percent of the worldwide production of rayon.

Nylon. DuPont, an American chemical firm, entered rayon production using technology licensed from France, hoping to capitalize on its long experience with nitrocellulose explosives. The profitable experience with rayon induced management to support fundamental research, including research in polymer science. As a part of this initiative, DuPont in 1928 hired Wallace H. Carothers, then a chemistry instructor at Harvard University. Carothers made fundamental contributions to polymer science, providing important empirical support for Staudinger's theories about the nature of polymers, and in 1931 published a famous paper in which he described condensation polymerization.

In addition, Carothers's group made two discoveries of immense economic importance. In April 1930, the group discovered the first synthetic rubber, which DuPont commercialized as neoprene, and the group discovered the technique of "cold drawing" a fiber to increase its strength. A key step in the discovery of neoprene was Carothers's insight that the formation of large chains (required for natural rubber) was inhibited by the formation of water during the polymerization reaction. This led to the development of new methods and equipment to remove water that were of great value in the next discovery, nylon, in 1934.

Nylon is a polyamide, a long chain formed by reacting adipic acid and hexamethylene diamine. Both of these molecules have six carbon atoms; consequently, the resulting polymer is also called nylon 6,6. Initially used for parachutes, tow ropes, and other wartime materials, nylon's fine yet strong, silky fibers made it an obvious and popular substitute for silk in women's hosiery, the initial market

SYNTHETIC FIBERS. Preparing rayon thread at the Denomah Mills, Taftville, Connecticut, 1940. (Jack Delano/Prints and Photographs Division, Library of Congress)

DuPont targeted when commercial production started in 1940. Nylon heralded the start of the synthetic fiber era and earned enormous profits for DuPont over the next four or five decades. In addition to hosiery and intimate apparel, nylon is widely used in ropes and cord, sleeping bags, and when blended with other fibers, in athletic apparel and swimwear.

Nylon underscored the potential for other synthetic fibers. DuPont controlled nylon, thanks in part to a broad patent filed by Carothers that reflected the enormous scientific research he had done to investigate the suitability of different types of polymers for synthetic fibers. Yet as broad as Carothers's patent was, it left two important gaps.

The first gap enabled Paul Schlack, a prominent German chemist working for IG Farben, the dominant German chemical firm between the two world wars, to develop a polyamide fiber quite similar to nylon. Schlack had worked on condensation polymers starting in 1928, before

Carothers, and appears to have been aware of the potential of polyamides as synthetic fibers. However, the IG Farben management was dissuaded from supporting this line of research by the fall in the price of cotton in 1928–1929 and by the need to protect the firm's investments in rayon. DuPont's 1937 patent jolted Schlack into resuming his research on polyamide fibers.

Caprolactam is a ring-shaped molecule with six carbon atoms and with an amino group at one end of the ring and an acid group at the other. Contrary to what was asserted in Carothers's patent, Schlack succeeded in polymerizing caprolactam in January 1938. The resulting polymer, perlon, closely resembled nylon. (Perlon is also known as nylon 6 to distinguish it from DuPont's nylon 6,6.) DuPont and IG Farben cross-licensed each other in 1939, although each focused on developing its own innovation. Both types of nylon became commercially popular, although DuPont tended to control access to its technology.

At the end of World War II, the Allied governments published the IG Farben process for nylon 6 and made it publicly available to all as a part of the war reparations. This made nylon 6 especially attractive to Holland, Italy, Japan, and Eastern European countries. Also, a number of processes for caprolactam were developed between 1945 and 1965, not only by BASF (a leading German firm and constituent of IG Farben) but also by firms such as DSM (Netherlands), Allied Chemical (U.S.), and Toyo Rayon (now Toray) from Japan.

Polyester Terepthalate: The Miracle Fiber. Carothers also overlooked the potential of another polymer, polyester, which had been synthesized in his own lab. Carothers incorrectly believed, based on his experience with aliphatic (straight chain) polyesters, that all polyesters had low melting points and were easily hydrolyzed and therefore were unsuitable for textile fibers. In 1939, two English industrial chemists, T. J. Whinfield and J. T. Dickson, working for the Calico Printers Association, a textile industry trade group, discovered that the polymer polyester, formed by reacting terepthalic acid (a ring-shaped molecule) and ethylene glycol, could be drawn into fibers with good properties.

Calico Printers sold the patent to the leading British chemical company, Imperial Chemical Industries (ICI). After World War II, ICI licensed DuPont. Though ICI had the basic patent, DuPont had more experience with synthetic fibers and consequently led the development of polyester fiber. Polyester fibers were strong, shrink- and wrinkle-resistant, easily washed, and quick drying. However, they were difficult to dye, limiting their use for apparel. Although some attempt was made to target polyester as a wool substitute, DuPont was developing acrylic fibers for that market. Initially, therefore, polyester was promoted for tire cord. However, the experiment failed, and fifteen years passed before polyester tire cord became popular.

Along with dyeing problems, polyester as textile yarn posed a number of other problems, including the buildup of static charge during processing and the tendency of fabrics woven from polyester to pile—to develop little balls of fabric on the surface. After considerable development effort, polyester fibers found widespread uses in shirts, suits, and knitted garments, typically when blended with other fibers, such as cotton, rayon, and wool. Usually textile firms were the innovators in developing new types of blended material. Not only did blends have better dyeability, washability, and so on, blending also increased the productivity of textile machinery, because the addition of polyester thread greatly strengthened cotton fibers, making it possible to run textile machinery at much higher speeds. In addition to apparel, polyester fibers are used for drapery, carpets, sheets and pillow cases, seatbelts, and fillers for pillows and furniture.

Competition from DuPont and an inability to invest on a large enough scale to exploit the full potential of the invention led ICI to license its technology to a number of other firms, including Hoechst and Glanzoff in Germany, Toyo Rayon in Japan, and Celanese in the United States. Although this provided considerable revenue for ICI, it also increased competition in the market, and coupled with the open licensing of the key intermediates for polyester (see below), it meant that entry barriers into polyester were sharply reduced. As new processes were developed for the key inputs and costs and prices dropped, new applications and markets were found, and the total production for polyester eventually far surpassed that for nylon or acrylic. The low prices greatly benefited consumers and enhanced demand, but competition was so severe that even some of the pioneers could not survive. In 1997, ICI sold its polyester business as a part of an extensive restructuring.

Acrylic. The third major synthetic fiber, acrylic, is a polymer made from acrylonitrile (with a small percentage of some other molecules called copolymers). Hermann Mark, a chemist at IG Farben, invented and patented the polymer in 1929, but IG Farben did not vigorously develop it. DuPont, in contrast, was systematically targeting various natural fibers. In 1941, Ray Houtz at DuPont discovered how to spin polyacrylonitrile into a fiber using methods similar to those used for rayon, a technique called "dry spinning." This fiber could be drawn to produce a fine silk-like fiber that resisted acid and decay from sunlight and bacteria.

If left undrawn and "crimped," the acrylic fiber possessed many of the properties of wool. A number of difficulties had to be solved before acrylic could successfully compete with wool. Acrylic fiber was especially difficult to dye, and acrylic fabric did not stand up well to use. Eventually these problems were addressed by developing new types of dyes and by producing a mixed polymer consisting of 94 percent acrylonitrile and 6 percent methyl acrylate, which DuPont first commercialized in the 1950s and which became popular for blended wool and worsted fabric. Over time, other blends found uses such as fleece linings and fluffy toys.

Again DuPont's scientific expertise in polymers and its experience in discovering and developing synthetic fibers were vital to its success. Also, DuPont was greatly helped by its strong links with textile producers and makers of textile machinery, its strong balance sheet, and its diversified chemical operations that provided the building blocks for acrylic polymer.

Since the basic patents on acrylic polymers had long expired, a number of firms quickly entered the market. The global production of acrylic fibers grew steadily until the late 1970s from 109,000 metric tons in 1959 to 2.083 million metric tons in 1980. During in the 1980s, total production increased only slightly overall, with a marked decline of over 30 percent in U.S. production and a noticeable increase in production in Asian countries.

Other Synthetic Fibers. Other than nylon, polyester, and acrylic, only polypropylene fibers have succeeded in attaining a substantial market share, that for nonapparel applications, such as floor covering. From negligible levels in 1960, the production of olefin fibers (mainly polypropylene fibers) increased to 355,000 metric tons in 1970 and to over 4.6 million metric tons by 1999. In addition, specialty fibers, designed for applications that prize attributes such as strength (aramid) or elasticity (spandex), have succeeded in establishing market niches. The major synthetic fibers themselves are likely to be blended with other fibers. Indeed, polyester blended with cotton turned out to have far greater success in material for shirts than pure polyester. Blending not only provided properties users wanted, in some cases it was also easier to dye and process blended yarns. That no new fiber has been commercialized in the last half-century or so testifies to the tremendous versatility of the existing fibers. It also speaks to the cost and difficulty of developing a synthetic fiber.

The Innovation System of Synthetic Fibers. The successful commercialization of synthetic fibers involved innovations up and down the value chain, not merely the discovery of how to synthesize the polymer. The polymer had to be drawn and spun into a fiber, dyed, and ultimately woven into fabric. The properties of these polymers depend in subtle ways on how the polymer is drawn or spun into a fiber, not only on its chemical composition. For instance, if drawn in a specific way, polyester fibers resist water and, if crimped, acquire the resiliency of wool. Moreover, by exposing polyester fabric to heat, the fabric becomes wrinkle resistant. All of these properties and more are naturally affected by blending with other fibers in ways that are difficult to predict in advance, although polymer scientists have made a great deal of progress in linking the physical properties of the fiber to that of the fabric.

Spinning Technology. Little of the technology required for nylon existed even five years before its commercial introduction. In addition to developing the chemical processes, DuPont had to develop new fiber spinning technology. Existing technology had been developed for rayon, which did not melt and was spun in solution. Although this method was applicable to acrylic fiber, DuPont had to develop a new technology for nylon wherein the solid polymer was melted and then extruded through small openings in a metal plate to form fibers upon cooling. This melt-spinning technology proved applicable to polyester fiber as well.

New Processes for Intermediates and Inputs. To successfully compete with natural fibers, such as cotton, silk, and wool, synthetic fibers had to be produced cheaply.

This required cheap inputs and large-scale production to realize the economies of scale well known in the modern chemical industry. Both posed challenges. At the time these new fibers were first synthesized, many of the inputs were mere laboratory curiosities and were not commercially available. Typically innovators like DuPont used the most obvious and frequently inefficient processes to produce these inputs. Sensing the opportunity, others developed more elegant and efficient processes. Once developed, these new processes were offered for license. The availability of processes for inputs and intermediates promoted entry into the markets for polyester, acrylic, and even nylon and contributed to the rapid diffusion of their production to countries in Asia and Eastern Europe.

This is exemplified by the case of polyester. Of the two main intermediates used for polyester, ethylene glycol and terepthalic acid, only the former was a well-known compound. It was used as an antifreeze, among other things. However, though ethylene glycol was commercially available, it was produced by an inefficient process of reacting ethylene (a basic petrochemical) with chlorine. This method, in practice since World War I, was inefficient and environmentally unfriendly. In 1933, E. Lefort of France developed a method of directly oxidizing ethylene with oxygen using a silver catalyst, and Union Carbide commercialized this technology in North America. In 1953, Inspired by Lefort's process, Scientific Design, a start-up firm focused on developing new chemical processes, developed a process for ethylene oxide that used air instead of oxygen. Royal Dutch Shell, a large Anglo-Dutch oil firm, followed closely and developed an oxygen-based process. Since ethylene oxide is easily converted to ethylene glycol, these processes were of great significance for ICI and other producers of polyester. In a significant break from the past, both Shell and Scientific Design actively competed to license their technologies to producers the world over. By the mid 1990s, Shell's technology accounted for 40 percent of the global polyethylene capacity, followed by Scientific Design with 30 percent and Union Carbide with 15 percent. As is the case with the other chemical processes, the cost of producing ethylene oxide decreased steadily over the next three or four decades as the scale of production more than doubled and yields increased by 50 percent.

Scientific Design also developed a novel process for producing terepthalic acid, which DuPont and ICI (the two main producers of polyester) had hitherto produced by directly oxidizing para-xylene, a by-product from coal distillation and later from refining. The existing process was inefficient and polluting, and para-xylene itself was not readily available. Beginning in late 1947, UOP, a firm specializing in developing new refining technology, pioneered methods of producing aromatic compounds—ring-shaped compounds of carbon and hydrogen, such as benzene, toluene, and xylene—from petroleum feedstock using a platinum catalyst. Institut Français du Pétrole (IFP), a French research organization, and Phillips Petroleum, a U.S. oil firm, also made significant contributions to developing new technologies for producing and extracting aromatic compounds from refinery by-products. It is said that this new technology enabled one refinery to produce more of these aromatic compounds than the total production from coal tar during World War II. As firms specializing in technology development rather than manufacturing, UOP and IFP widely licensed their technology.

Complementing the advances in para-xylene technology, Scientific Design in 1953 pioneered a process for directly oxidizing para-xylene to produce terepthalic acid of high purity. Although DuPont stuck to its existing methods for producing terepthalic acid, Amoco (then Standard Oil of India) licensed the process from Scientific Design and entered into the production of purified terepthalic acid, selling its output to polyester fiber producers. Amoco also significantly improved the Scientific Design process. Outside the United States, Scientific Design widely licensed the technology to ICI and Mitsui Petrochemicals, a Japanese company, among others.

Diffusion. The widespread licensing of synthetic fiber technology and of the technology for producing the major inputs contributed greatly to the shift in the synthetic fiber industry away from the United States and other developed countries to the developing countries, especially in Asia. The ready availability of technology reduced the profitability of synthetic fiber producers in developed countries to the point where many had to exit, as exemplified by the decision by ICI to leave polyester production. Although the large Western firms set up production capacity around the world, the diffusion of the industry to Asia has been by investments made by Asian firms. For the most part, the technology for producing key inputs and for producing synthetic fibers is available for license. In addition to specialized engineering firms, a number of chemical producers also offer their technology for sale. For instance, the available data show that between 1986 and 1996 specialized engineering firms provided technology for over three-quarters of the synthetic fiber plants. Although this share is undoubtedly an overestimate because of the manner in which the data were collected, it nonetheless points to an important factor that helped the growth of synthetic fiber production in developing regions.

BIBLIOGRAPHY

Achilladelis, Basil. "A Study in Technological History: The Manufacture of Perlon (Nylon 6) and Caprolactam by IG Farbenindustrie." *Chemistry and Industry* (1970), 1549–1554, 1584–1588, 1608–1611. Technical description of the development of nylon 6 by Paul Schlack.

Arora, Ashish, and Alfonso Gambardella. "Evolution of Industry Structure in the Chemical Industry." In *Chemicals and Long Term Growth*, edited by A. Arora, R. Landau, and N. Rosenberg. New York, 1998. Describes the role of technology licensing in promoting market competition and the spread of the chemical industry to developing countries.

Coleman, Donald C. *Courtaulds: An Economic and Social History.* Vol. 2. Oxford, 1969. Rayon industry.

Fiber Organon. Vols. 60–71. Fiber Economic Bureau Inc., 1989–2000. Basic data source for the synthetic fiber industry. Available from www.fibersource.com.

Goldenberg, David I. *The U.S. Man-Made Fiber Industry: Its Structure and Organization since 1948.* Westport, Conn., 1992.

Hollander, Samuel. *The Sources of Increased Efficiency: A Study of DuPont Rayon Plants.* Cambridge, Mass., 1965. Describes the various major and minor process innovations that increased productivity in rayon production.

Hounshell, David A. "The Making of the Synthetic Fiber Industry in the United States." Unpublished manuscript. Pittsburgh, Pa. A masterful history of the role of DuPont in the synthetic fiber industry and of the many challenges involved in making a polymer into a successful textile fiber.

Hounshell, David A., and John K. Smith. *Science and Corporate Strategy.* Cambridge, 1988.

Landau, Ralph. "The Process of Innovation in the Chemical Industry." In *Chemicals and Long Term Growth*, edited by A. Arora, R. Landau, and N. Rosenberg. New York, 1998. Describes the process innovations in the key chemical intermediates for polyester and polypropylene.

Markham, Jesse. *Competition in the Rayon Industry.* Cambridge, Mass., 1952. On the rayon industry.

McMillan, Frank M. *The Chain Straighteners.* London, 1979. Excellent nontechnical introduction to polymer science and to the discovery and development of polypropylene.

Reader, William J. *Imperial Chemical Industries: A History.* Vols. 1–2. Oxford, 1970–1975. History of ICI; describes ICI's role in developing polyester and in the synthetic fiber industry more generally.

Remsberg, Charles, and H. Higden. *Ideas for Rent: The UOP Story.* Des Plains, Ill., 1994. History of UOP; describes UOP's role in developing innovative processes for basic petrochemicals used to produce synthetic fibers.

Spitz, Peter H. *Petrochemicals: The Rise of an Industry.* New York, 1988. Brief histories of the development of the major synthetic fibers and a good nontechnical introduction to the basic technologies involved.

Textile Oraganon. Vols. 32–59. Fiber Economic Bureau Inc., 1961–1988. Basic data source for the synthetic fiber industry.

Tisdell, Clement A., and P. W. McDonald. *Economics of Fibre Markets: A Global View of the Interdependence between Man-Made Fibres, Wool, and Cotton.* Oxford and New York, 1979.

ASHISH ARORA AND RALPH LANDAU

SYRIA. *See* Levant.

T

TABOOS. Taboos can be seen as constraints in the allocation of actions that can transform into a general principle encompassing other resources and their distribution over time as they are built up in societies. The selective channeling of resources to roles by taboos thus structures exchange through determining significant properties and characteristics of relational networks. Perhaps the earliest taboo is seen today in mass or dance: one must not speak out of step or step out of line. Synchronicity in ritual becomes an ordered progression in exchange. As modeled in *Sync* (2003) by the mathematician Steven Strogatz, initial offerings differ from reciprocations, whether in kind or quantity, as with interest-bearing loans. Another early taboo is that on incest, which effects a dispersion of kinship ties and thereby weaves together larger social units through a process of generalized exchange described by the sociologist Peter Bearman in "Generalized Exchange" (1997).

Taboos also generate guidance for the flow of goods between tribes during ceremonial occasions for large-scale exchange. Three levels of taboo can be discerned within the exchange system of the Hageners of the New Guinea highlands. In *The Rope of Moka* (1971), the anthropologist Andrew Strathern documents a complex exchange system revolving around a system of capital accumulation. Taboos enforce a sequential return on an initial gift and designate the correct gift, as weighed against the first with adjustments made for the time spent between exchanges. One may return with an *anmbile kng* (tongue pigs), if paying out when receiving, or with a *kng mbukl-øl* (pigs on the back of), if much time elapses. These exchanges resolve intertribal conflict. In the midst of warfare, public exclamations initiate the transformation of conflict into exchange by reminding participants of their crosscutting marriage ties, implicitly invoking a well-articulated prohibition against nonreciprocity to fathers of wives—and to a lesser degree brothers-in-law and cousins of wives—enforced through spells and marital separation. Even in peace the men must scramble to extend their credit and exchange network in order to meet the demands of their (multiple) wives' families. In concert, the ban on incest, manifest in exogamy, and the father-in-law–brother-in-law–cousin taboo combine to push individuals to overcome existing production limitations and support a thriving economy, reducing social and financial uncertainty for individual participants.

Taboos thus can indirectly funnel the ambitious into the accumulation of capital through complex credit networks laced through an entire society, even a tribal one. But the outcomes can feed back into further taboo. A taboo on usury plagued the merchants of western Europe well into the sixteenth century. By one telling, the usury laws hampered capitalist expansion for centuries, exemplifying an irrationality external to the ideal functioning of the modern marketplace. Remove the teleology from the argument and it is apparent that this one prohibition profoundly affected the contents of economic transactions for centuries, with the most immediate effects in the shipping and trade industries. Likewise the sociologist Vivianna Zelizer has demonstrated in *Markets and Morals* (1977), that, while marine and fire insurance offerings proliferated after the American Civil War, a taboo on quantitative valuations of human life constricted the growth of life insurance firms until late in the century. Earlier in that same century slavery had been the predominant example of quantitative valuations of human life. As the economist Douglass North asserts in *Institutions, Institutional Change, and Economic Performance* (1990), the end of slavery actually threatened the stability of a large portion of the world economy at the time, forcing a reorganization of the cotton, sugar, and coffee industries. It was anathema, not economics, that brought about the end of slavery.

It is common for taboos restricting intersocietal trade to delimit the boundaries of economic systems, and gradations in the volume of interchange demarcate a scale of status reaching from friends into strangers and foes. The anthropologist Marcel Mauss's *The Gift* records multiple examples of the principle that exchange with enemies or unacceptable others is taboo and fraught with danger. The Dutch, English, and Portuguese conferred degrees of civilization (within their own value systems) to societies they encountered according to levels of complexity in trade, credit, and financial institutions. Thus the Mughals were to be held in a little bit of awe by sixteenth-century and seventeenth-century adventurers, whereas the Caribs and Arawaks were pressed into slavery or for the most part eradicated. Reciprocal exchange tends to be limited to those groups or gods deemed human, humane, or civilized, which has the invidious byproduct of assigning subhuman status to groups with radically different systems of social organization. Both usury laws and the institutions of slavery were bound up with boundary regulation: between Africans and Europeans in one case, Catholics and Jews in another, and the scarcity in the United States now of Cuban cigars in yet another case.

International trade separates out the "us" from the "them" through the imposition of customs, duties, and embargoes. Taboos can be manipulated by vested interests for political ends (for example, American trade with Cuba or the Arab boycott against Israel), social ones (prohibitions against narcotics or genetically modified agricultural products), or even aesthetic ones (bans on billboards and franchise restaurants in some communities). The same processes of division and regulation, in which taboos entailing restrictions are replicated, multiplied, and further embedded, occur across qualitatively diverse social divisions. Thorstein Veblen constructed *The Theory of the Leisure Class* (1899, 1965) around the recognition of a taboo on labor. Compliance with the taboo is signaled through leisure and conspicuous consumption, which takes multiple outward forms ranging from the potlatch to the lifestyle of a Des Esseintes, J.-K. Huysmans' quintessential decadent, or a North American housewife. This compliance creates systems of aesthetics, couture, and living standards. All of these use sensibility to separate out and organize people into hierarchical forms as classes and status groups. Value and social standing are doled out inversely to the amount of real labor involved in jobs. And as the division of labor increases, ever finer gradients are established. Those that must resort to labor for personal subsistence are assigned lowest status. Since paid labor is one of the few means by which one may maintain and improve one's living conditions, only a few lucky families are able to elevate their positions except around a working life. The result, as seen by Veblen, is increasing rigidity in stratification systems that were triggered by taboo in the first place. Impacts of taboos inescapably mark all economic systems.

[See also Usury.]

BIBLIOGRAPHY

Bearman, Peter. "Generalized Exchange." *American Journal of Sociology* 102.5 (1997), 1383–1415.

Mauss, Marcel. *The Gift: The Form and Reason for Exchange in Archaic Societies*. Translated by W. D. Halls. New York, 1990.

North, Douglass C. *Institutions, Institutional Change, and Economic Performance*. Cambridge, 1990.

Strathern, Andrew. *The Rope of Moka: Big-Men and Ceremonial Exchange in Mount Hagen, New Guinea*. Cambridge, 1971.

Strogatz, Steven. *Sync: The Emerging Science of Spontaneous Order*. New York, 2003.

Veblen, Thorstein. *The Writings of Thorstein Veblen: The Theory of the Leisure Class* (1899). Reprint, New York, 1965.

Zelizer, Vivianna. "Markets and Morals: The Development of Life Insurance in the United States." Ph.D. diss. Columbia University, 1997.

HARRISON WHITE AND EMILY ERIKSON

TAIWAN. A small island economy of only thirty-six thousand square kilometers, Taiwan has relatively little in the way of natural resources. From the early seventeenth century to 1895, Taiwan was ruled first by the Dutch (1624–1662), then by the Cheng regime (1662–1683), and then by the Ching empire (1683–1895). Taiwan became a colony of Japan in 1895, and it has been ruled by the Nationalist government since 1945.

From Dutch Rule to the Ching Regime. In the early seventeenth century, the Dutch East India Company came to the East to trade with China, finally settling in southern Taiwan in 1624. During this time, there were some Chinese and Japanese living on the coast, but the island was inhabited mainly by aborigines, who were engaged in fishing, hunting, and trading. The Dutch soon realized that Taiwan's deer hide and sugar were profitable traded goods. In 1633–1660, Taiwan's annual export of deer hide averaged 71,915 pieces.

In February 1662, Cheng Ch'eng-kung (Koxinga) defeated the Dutch and became the new ruler of Taiwan. The Cheng regime was succeeded by the Ching in 1683, and Taiwan's role as an entrepôt for Chinese foreign trade changed immediately. Foreign trade now was through Amoy instead of Taiwan. For most of the Ching, Taiwan was only a small part of the Chinese economy. There were reports that rice and sugar were exported to China, but no reliable data are available for detailed analysis. In 1862, Taiwan was opened for international trade, and the trade again brought opportunity for development. The most valuable export at this time was tea, followed by sugar. The total export to gross domestic product (GDP) ratio in the late 1890s was about 15 percent. The most important import was opium, which sometimes amounted to more than 50 percent of total imports. As a result of continued

TABLE 1. *Change in Life Expectancy*

		1906	1921	1926–1930	1936–1940	1956
Taiwan:	male	27.7	34.5	38.8	41.1	60.2
	female	29.0	38.6	43.1	45.7	64.2
China:	male	—	—	24.6	—	46.1
	female	—	—	23.7	—	48.1

SOURCE: Taiwan: Barclay (1954), p. 154; Chen (1979), p. 165; *Statistical Abstract of Taiwan Province, Republic of China, 1946–1967*, pp. 66–68 (1971). China: Banister (1987), pp. 6, 116.

TAIWAN. Street scene, 1983. (© Chuck Fishman/Woodfin Camp and Associates, New York)

immigration from China, Taiwan's population and cultivated land area increased greatly during the Ching.

Taiwan under Japanese Rule. Taiwan was ceded to Japan in 1895. Under the Japanese government, a traditional and backward agricultural economy was transformed into a modern economy. The important first step of Japanese reform was infrastructure construction. A big project that built a railway connecting Keelung and Kaoshiung was finished in 1907. Upon completion of the railway, the transportation system on the western coast changed immediately. Export products were first transported to either Keelung or Kaoshiung by railway, and then shipped by large steamships. (See Ho, 1978, for a detailed survey on Taiwan's development during the Japanese era.)

Another important institutional change was a land-tenure reform initiated in 1898. During Ching rule, most of the land was owned by two kinds of owners, an absentee landlord and a resident landowner. A high proportion of land was not registered, and landowners did not pay taxes.

In the land reform, all lands were registered, the absentee landlords were obliged to exchange their rights for interest-bearing bonds, and the resident landowners were guaranteed title to their property. The land reform clarified property rights, enhanced government tax revenues, and made it easier for Japanese firms to purchase large amounts of land in Taiwan.

The colonial government established the Bank of Taiwan in 1899, and an efficient financial market was formed. The purpose of all the reforms was to provide a good environment for investment, and to attract big Japanese firms to Taiwan. They turned out to be very successful. In the 1900s, several big Japanese sugar companies were established in Taiwan, and the value of sugar production quickly exceeded that of tea. In the mid-1920s, a new breed of rice, called Ponlai, was developed. From then on, Ponlai rice and sugar were the two primary exports.

Between 1905 and 1940, Taiwan's per capita GDP annual growth was about 1.9 percent. As shown in Table 1, life expectancy for Taiwanese males was 27.7 years in 1906, and it increased to 41.1 years in 1936–1940. Life expectancy for Chinese males in 1926–1930 was only 24.6 years, which was lower than the Taiwanese figure for 1906. The Japanese government also emphasized primary education of the Taiwanese. In 1917, some 13 percent of the school-age (six to fourteen years) Taiwanese children were in school, and that number increased to 71 percent in 1943. (For an evaluation of the colonial government's education policy, see Tsurumi, 1984.)

The Nationalist Government. At the end of World War II, Taiwan was transferred to China. The Nationalist government confiscated all the Japanese properties, and almost all Japanese private enterprises were converted into public enterprises. The policy was a manifestation of the full-scale economic control to be imposed on Taiwan later by the Nationalist government. As a result of the government intervention, hyperinflation occurred in 1945–1949. (See Wu, 1997, for a discussion on the economic-control policies and the hyperinflation episode of 1945–1949.)

The Nationalist government retreated from the mainland to Taipei in December 1949, and tension across the Taiwan Strait escalated. The fate of Taiwan was permanently changed when the Korean War broke out on 25 June 1950. The U.S. government immediately decided to give economic and military aid to Taiwan, which secured Taiwan's future. In the early 1950s, U.S. aid helped to balance the budget deficit and stop the hyperinflation. Starting in the mid-1950s, the focus of the aid program gradually changed to development. Besides financing investment projects, the U.S. aid program encouraged deregulation and promoted the notion of the market mechanism. For example, U.S. aid financed 74 percent of all domestic investment in infrastructure (Jacoby, 1966, pp. 34, 129–149, and 176). It has been generally recognized that the deregulation of the late 1950s was crucial for Taiwan's later growth.

The Nationalist government carried out a land reform in 1949–1953. The reform induced wealth redistribution because landowners were forced to sell their land at a price below the market level. Tenants benefited from the reform. It has been argued that the redistribution effect of the land reform was one of the reasons why, up to the early 1980s, Taiwan's income distribution improved with rapid growth. (See, e.g., Kuo et al., 1981.)

Between 1960 and 1999, Taiwan's average per capita real GDP growth was 6.2 percent, among the highest in the world. Rapid economic growth was accompanied by dramatic change in the economic structure. The ratio of value-added of agriculture to GDP declined from 32.3 percent in 1951 to 2.1 percent in 2000. The ratio of industry increased from 21.3 percent in 1951 to 45.5 percent in 1981, and then decreased to 32.4 percent in 2000. More important, economic growth improves well-being. As shown in Table 1, life expectancy for Taiwanese males in 1956 was 60.2 years and for females 64.2 years. In 1999, it had been extended to 72.6 years and 78.3 years, respectively.

Several interpretations have been proposed to explain why Taiwan's growth rate has been so high. Some emphasize that export-orientation and human capital accumulation are important. Others have proposed that the market-oriented and competitive environment is the key. To many economists this remains an open question.

[*See also* China *and* Japan, *subentry on* Japanese Empire.]

BIBLIOGRAPHY
Banister, Judith. *China's Changing Population*. Stanford, Calif., 1987.
Barclay, George W. *Colonial Development and Population in Taiwan*. Princeton, 1954.
Chen, Shao-hsing. "Social Change and Demographic Change in Taiwan." In *Social Change and Demographic Change in Taiwan*, edited by Shao-hsing Chen, pp. 93–177. Taipei, 1979.
Ho, Samuel P. S. *Economic Development of Taiwan, 1860–1970*. New Haven, 1978.
Jacoby, Neil. *U.S. Aid to Taiwan*. New York, 1966.
Kuo, Shirley W. Y., Gustav Ranis, and John C. H. Fei. *The Taiwan Success Story*. Boulder, 1981.
Provincial Government of Taiwan. *Statistical Abstract of Taiwan Province, Republic of China, 1946–1967*. Taipei, 1971.
Tsurumi, E. Patricia. "Colonial Education in Korea and Taiwan." In *The Japanese Colonial Empire, 1895–1945*, edited by Ramon H. Myers and Mark R. Peattie. Princeton, 1984.
Wu, Tsong-Min. "The Nationalist Government's Economic Policies Regarding Taiwan: 1945–1949." *Taiwan Economic Review* 25.4 (1997), 521–554.

Tsong-Min Wu

TANZANIA. *See* East Africa.

TARIFFS. *See* Commercial Policy, *subentry on* Tariffs.

TAWNEY, R. H. (1880–1962). English economic historian.

Richard Tawney was born in Calcutta. After studying at Oxford, he established himself there as a teacher to the Workers Educational Association from 1908 to 1914. Tawney taught political economy at Glasgow University from 1906 to 1908. After marrying Annette Jeanie, sister of Lord Beveridge, in 1909, the couple settled in Manchester. At Manchester University, the pioneer economic historian George Unwin became Tawney's mentor. Among his colleges were T. S. Ashton and A. P. Wadsworth. As a soldier in World War I, Tawney was wounded in action at Fricourt in France in 1916 and was sent home as a convalescent. In 1917, he became a lecturer in economic history at the London School of Economics (LSE) and remained there until 1949. Tawney became reader in 1923 and professor in 1931. He also became an honorary fellow at Peterhouse, Cambridge, and in many other universities. At LSE he founded the Economic History Society in 1926 and also became the coeditor (with Ephraim Lipson) of *Economic History Review* from 1927 to 1934.

Besides being a pioneer economic historian, Tawney is best characterized as a moral socialist with Christian overtones. As a young man, he was under the influence of William Morris (1834–1896) and John Ruskin (1819–1900). In 1906, he joined the Fabian Society and in 1909, the Independent Labour Party. His morally based socialism, which he developed in *The Acquisitive Society* (1920)—his "socialist bible" according to himself—and *Equality* (1931), made him critical of Soviet communism and set him against old comrades, such as Sidney and Beatrice Webb and Harold Laski. In the early 1930s, he visited China and wrote *Land and Labour in China* (1932), a remarkable study on the land issue that even may have influenced Mao Tse-tung.

As a social and economic historian, Tawney gained recognition early on with *The Agrarian Problem in the Sixteenth Century* (1912). It was an innovative work, depicting the effects of the Tudor enclosure movement. His dark picture of rural England during the sixteenth century was without a doubt colored by his radical views regarding contemporary matters, such as the early-nineteenth-century poor law reform. His pioneer study on this epoch was followed up in *Tudor Economic Documents* (1924), which he coedited with Eileen Power.

Perhaps his most famous work was *Religion and the Rise of Capitalism* (1926). More than just an English sequel to Weber's famous thesis, it provides a broad picture of sixteenth-century religious, moral, and political ideas linked to social and economic change. Another famous contribution to scholarly discussion was his article "The Rise of the Gentry" for *Economic History Review* (1941). Tawney's last book, the less-well-known *Business and Politics under*

James I: Lionel Cranfield as Merchant and Minister (1958), was his tour de force in which he mixed political history with economic history and history of ideas.

As a scholarly writer, Tawney is characterized by his literary style, a keen interest for detail, and a great ability to synthesize. Much of what he wrote was colored by his moral and political views in favor of the poor, the workers, and the landless.

BIBLIOGRAPHY

Collini, Stefan. *Public Moralists: Political Thought and Intellectual Life in Britain, 1850–1930.* London, 1991.

Dahrendorf, Ralf. *A History of the London School of Economics and Political Science, 1895–1995.* Oxford, 1995.

Harris, José. *William Beveridge: A Biography.* Oxford, 1977.

Ormrod, David. "R. H. Tawney and the Origins of Capitalism." *History Workshop* 18 (1984), 138–159.

Tawney, Richard H. *The Agrarian Problem in the Sixteenth Century.* London, 1912.

Tawney, Richard H. *The Aquisitive Society.* London, 1920.

Tawney, Richard H. *Religion and the Rise of Capitalism: A Historical Study.* London, 1926.

Tawney, Richard H. *Equality.* London, 1931.

Tawney, Richard H. *Land and Labour in China.* London, 1932.

Tawney, Richard H. *The Attack and Other Papers.* London, 1953.

Terrill, Ross R. H., *Tawney and His Times.* London, 1974.

Winter, J. M. Introduction to *History and Society: Essays by R. H. Tawney.* London, 1978.

LARS MAGNUSSON

TAXATION *[This entry contains two subentries, on taxation and public revenue and on local taxation.]*

Taxation and Public Revenue

Benjamin Franklin wrote, "In this world nothing can be said to be certain, except death and taxes." A better pairing would have been war and taxes, since war has been a primary impetus for changes in taxes and other forms of government revenue.

Whether religious or secular, ruling groups needing revenue have resorted either to the output of their own property or that of the surrounding population. Since land was the preeminent asset for much of human history, governments created various methods to extract resources from landowners. The ingenuity of rulers in finding new revenue sources was matched by that of the taxed in finding ways to avoid or reduce their burdens.

Whatever the form of public revenue, especially taxation, all governments need to assess the cost and benefits of any policy. Adam Smith listed four maxims regarding taxation in Book V of *An Inquiry into the Nature and Causes of the Wealth of Nations*: Taxes should be proportionate to ability to pay; taxes should be certain and not arbitrary; taxes should be levied at a time or manner in which it is convenient for the taxpayer to pay it; and taxes should be set up to both take out and to keep out of the pockets of the people as little as possible, over and above what it brings into the treasury. Or, more simply put, the maxim is: equity, certainty, convenience, and efficiency.

Many governments have found that balancing equity and efficiency is a difficult process. French rulers prior to the revolution enforced a tax on salt. Since salt was relatively price insensitive, the tax created little inefficiency and did not greatly erode the tax base. However, the general populace considered the tax obnoxious and inequitable. When the United States government placed a tax on luxury boats during the late 1980s, sales of U.S.-made luxury boats plummeted, creating much inefficiency and greatly eroding the tax base.

The poll tax, or capitation, exemplifies the clash between equity and efficiency. The tax is a fixed amount per head and is thus nondistortionary in that it does not affect any marginal trade-offs, so that the tax is efficient. However, people with smaller incomes or wealth are disproportionately taxed, so that the poll tax is usually seen as inequitable.

The convenience of collecting taxes and other public revenue has varied greatly throughout history. Customs duties were attractive because they were easily collected at the ports and, in some cases, difficult to evade. Occasionally, a government found itself expending more resources in collection than it actually collected. Governments must consider the potential for legal tax avoidance and illegal tax evasion. Land was and is a popular tax base because of the difficulty in avoiding the taxes.

Basic Forms of Public Revenue. Governments derive revenue from taxes, ownership of productive resources, sales of monopoly power, impressing goods and services, lotteries, and the creation of money. To correct revenue shortfalls, governments borrow funds on a short-term or long-term basis.

Income and property taxes are direct taxes. Governments can easily tax the value of land, although establishing the value can be difficult. Most governments tax interest income, dividend income, and capital gains on equities, bonds, or other assets, including those bequeathed in the form of estate taxes, inheritance taxes, gift taxes, and outright confiscation.

Indirect taxes consist primarily of taxes on commercial transactions. Sales taxes can be general or selective; sales taxes that are selectively placed on specified items are known as excise taxes. Sales taxes can be *ad valorem* (a percentage of the price or value of the commodity) or specific (levied on the basis of physical measures). To tax services, such as legal services or business transactions, governments resort to stamp taxes, whereby such transactions require a government stamp for which a fee is charged.

Governments owning land and minerals reap revenues by charging severance taxes (taxing the extraction of natural resources), grazing fees, recreation and park entry fees, and other charges (such as fishing and hunting licenses). Similarly, governments charge for their services via license fees (marriage, business, drivers', and automobile licenses are common) and building permits. Governments sell vanity rights such as nobility titles. Governments sell monopoly rights via franchise fees. Because of the government's superior ability to coerce individuals, many governments have compelled its residents to provide labor or sell their output at below-market wages.

Lotteries appeal to governments and citizens alike. Organizing and running lotteries is not difficult. Since citizens voluntarily play, this method of raising revenue is popular. However, lotteries are susceptible to corruption, whether actual or perceived.

Since most governments have some control, if not outright monopolization, of the money supply, the temptation to tax and to earn seigniorage via inflation is chronic. Profligate governments are particularly susceptible to inflation's charms, including the Confederate States of America (1861–1865), Weimar Germany (1922–1923), and Kuomintang China (1940s).

Public Revenue and Taxes throughout History. Public revenue and taxes have played a role throughout civilization.

Ancient societies. Small hunter-gatherer groups did not have governments to support (nor services to receive). Such groups might have made sacrifices to deities, perhaps for a successful hunt, and such sacrifices might have been the forerunner to public revenue and taxation. The evolution of farming communities, often beset with large cooperative projects such as irrigation, and the creation of more sophisticated social organizations, often characterized by a hierarchy, generated the need for public revenues. In some cases, contributions were voluntary, such as the Middle Eastern *zakat* (obligatory almsgiving). Whether the need was for labor and material for large-scale projects, for defense, or for religious sacrifice to satisfy deities, religious leaders or secular rulers demanded resources.

The earliest rulers may have been self-sufficient, with extensive landholdings or ownership of mines, saltworks, stone quarries, or other productive assets. Other rulers monopolized foreign trade or gained wealth through raiding and war. Religious leaders and temples also owned productive resources. At some point, though, the rulers and priests either needed additional resources or sought to use their power to compel neighboring people to support and contribute to temples and imperial households. Rulers and priests gave protection from invaders, granted trade privileges in some cases, built public works such as irrigation systems and viaducts, and appeased the gods.

The earliest taxes were paid in-kind, since there was no money. Cattle, grain, and wool were common in-kind produce. Given the rudimentary transportation network facing most governments, spoilage and pilferage (not to mention avoidance) was inevitable. Decentralization of collection points might have alleviated the transportation difficulty but created two countervailing problems: a greater area to defend and provincial officials or tax farmers to collect taxes. Although rulers could employ tax collectors, such employment created a principal-agent situation and its attendant problem of monitoring: Would the agents (collectors) diligently and honestly collect and deliver the tax revenue?

Even with the invention of money, in-kind payments continued to exist, especially in agrarian societies. The use of money forced citizens to enter the labor market, such as Zulus in southern Africa, with their cattle-based economy, under British rule. In-kind and money payments required record keeping, measurements, and conversion rates. Whether or not government officials invented writing and numbers, such officials were certainly among the earliest users.

In tribal societies, all able-bodied men provided labor for group projects. With a hierarchical society, many rulers and priests also demanded some sort of corvée, or compulsory labor, aside from the in-kind and money contributions. Such compulsory work created a dependable source of labor (if the ruler could solve the evasion problem) and military force, reduced uncertainty and helped maintain control, and allowed subjects to demonstrate their personal loyalty to the ruler.

Land was the major form of wealth in most ancient societies and therefore became the main tax base, whether from its produce or the wealth it generated. Rulers also used land to reward subjects for faithful behavior, transforming land acreage into a marketable commodity. Mesopotamian kings maintained their armies by land grants. Many ancient societies had both secular and religious leaders. Since religious leaders held much land, some secular rulers began to tax temple holdings.

In Egypt and Mesopotamia, the temple and government were synonymous. Thus, voluntary contributions to the temple initially sufficed. In return, the temple provided insurance against famines. Eventually, the contributions became mandatory tithes. The Egyptians also used a poll tax, and people too poor to pay the poll tax provided labor instead. The Babylonians created a centralized government that used local administrators. Local merchants and bankers collected the taxes and were forerunners of tax farmers. Other rulers employed royal collectors.

In ancient China, there were no priests, so the secular rulers did not face the duality found in Western societies. The rulers created a decentralized system of tax administrators; to mitigate the monitoring problem, rulers used their relatives as the administrators. During the Zhou

TAXATION IN ANCIENT TIMES. Payment of tributes and taxes. Roman bas-relief of a funeral stele from Noviomagus (Nijmegen, Netherlands), second to third century BCE. (Rheinisches Landesmuseum, Trier, Germany/Foto Marburg/Art Resource, NY)

dynasty (900–800 BCE), the chamberlain evolved into a civil administrator who collected taxes and supervised the royal domain. After 771 BCE, the centralized government dissipated, and feudal princes ruled the provinces, creating a tradition of independent provincial administration.

In ancient India, a *gopa* (local official) collected taxes from several local villages. The gopa was just the first of a line of officials, which included district officers, central government auditors, and the king's principal minister of finance (*samaharta*). The samaharta's duties included collecting taxes, formulating financial policy, and overseeing the state finances. Ancient rulers also collected tolls, customs duties, and special taxes to commemorate state occasions. In addition, sovereigns frequently confiscated an heirless man's property upon his death. Because most ancient societies did not create a large surplus above subsistence, rulers had to be careful not to overtax their subjects. As the holder of surplus, a ruler also had to be prepared to dole out supplies in the case of a famine.

Roman Empire. Roman citizens, like Greek citizens before them, considered direct taxes humiliating and paid them only in times of emergency. On occasion, the direct taxes, the *tributum* (a property tax), would be repaid once the emergency ended. Instead, Roman rulers relied upon indirect taxes, such as customs duties (*portoria*), rents from public land (the *ager publicus*), and taxes upon con-

quered territories (often a fixed amount, *vectigalis stipendiarium*, or a tenth of the produce, the *decumae*). The Romans also confiscated large amounts of war booty and tribute from conquests. War captives and people unable to pay the various taxes became slaves. The slaves provided labor, and the taxation of manumission of slaves (at 5 percent) provided revenue for the government. To enforce compliance, Roman law held family members and neighbors responsible for a person's failure to pay the required taxes or to provided sufficient labor.

Customs duties included tolls for crossing rivers and bridges. Since the empire was subdivided into many customs areas, officials repeatedly collected customs duties as the goods crossed administrative borders; the customs duties, a seemingly moderate 2.5 percent levy, accumulated rapidly and raised the final selling price considerably.

The Roman Republic used tax farmers to collect some of the taxes. Prospective tax farmers bid for the right to collect taxes. The *publicani*, people from the Equestrian class (ranking below the ruling senators), possessed the necessary capital (often in the form of partnerships or limited companies, or *societates*) to become tax farmers. Since the rulers received the winning bids in advance of the collection, the tax farmers essentially provided a loan to the rulers. Thereafter, the *publicani* collected the taxes, often goods-in-kind, which they sold on the open market.

TAXATION. *The Tax Collector*, painting by Paul de Vos (1596–1678). (Galleria Sabauda, Turin, Italy/Alinari/Art Resource, NY)

Because the *publicani* held large amounts of produce, they could influence the price to their advantage. Eventually, the Roman Empire, beginning with Augustus, replaced the tax farmers with government officials.

Augustus (d. 14 CE) reorganized the Roman tax system. He raised revenues from government mines, sold state property, and encouraged cultivation. He established a civil service to handle tax collection, hoping to curb the abuses and to increase the government's share. Land continued to be taxed, via the *stipendiaria* or the *tributaria* (a proportional property tax). The direct *tributum* tax was eventually levied against all land outside Italy. Augustus also created new indirect taxes, including a 5 percent inheritance tax (*vicesima herediatium*), a 1 percent sales tax on public auction (*centesima rerum venalium*), and a 4 percent tax on the sale of slaves (*vicesima quinta venalium mancipiorum*). The inheritance tax affected citizens, but there were exemptions for near relatives and poor persons. Although the inheritance tax was unpopular among the citizenry, Augustus threatened to substitute a direct tax in its place. The citizenry chose the less obnoxious inheritance tax. To increase their revenue from these taxes, subsequent emperors conferred citizenship to people in conquered territories. The sales tax, modest as it might appear, often served as a second tax on estates. With the death of a citizen, his property was sold and taxed at auction.

Aside from funding the army, some Roman emperors spent large sums on lavish living, ostentatious building proj-

ects, and other profligacy. Caligula (d. 41 CE) was among the most notorious spendthrifts. To maintain lavish spending, subsequent rulers resorted to new and more onerous taxes and confiscation. Unfortunately, these rulers were unable to halt the ongoing inflation that plagued the Roman Empire, due partly to faltering productivity (which, in turn, was a result of heavy-handed government taxation and military policies) but more to the continuing debasement of Roman coinage. Diocletian (r. 284–305 CE) relied primarily upon the *capitatio* (poll tax) and *jugatio* (tax on landed property). He rationalized the system by sending out swarms of officials to measure the land and to take a census. Large landholders were responsible not only for their own taxes but those of their tenants. The resulting liability impoverished or discouraged many landholders, further reducing productivity. The already thin line between free man and slave narrowed.

Medieval and early modern Europe. The medieval era witnessed surprising growth in the breadth and sophistication of instruments for generating public revenue. Indirect taxes began to displace direct taxes. Rulers enlisted professional civil officials to collect taxes and to provide fiscal information, which was useful when negotiating with representative bodies. Rulers created new forms of government debt, and eventually markets developed to trade these new instruments.

Certainly, the era did not start auspiciously. With the collapse of the Roman Empire in western Europe, large-scale government lapsed. The growing number of landless people sought sustenance from the remaining landowners. In essence, in return for their labor, these people received food, shelter, and protection; the lord augmented his revenue through his monopolization of various services. The evolving system of feudalism rested upon local relationships with mutual obligations. Throughout the medieval era, rulers gradually controlled larger areas and more people. Changing military technology requiring specialized training and ever more expensive equipment raised military expenditures.

As agricultural productivity increased, landless workers collected in towns and cities. Rulers encouraged the growth of towns and facilitated trade by issuing sound currency and by offering protection and enforcement of laws. As commercial transactions increased and were concentrated in fairs, rulers taxed them. By the late thirteenth century, English kings levied customs duties on wool exports. Such revenue, often collected by bankers who served as tax farmers, enabled these kings to borrow on a relatively stable tax base. Other rulers imposed sales taxes, gabelles, on goods and services. Medieval rulers sometimes taxed the extensive wealth of the church.

To avoid conflict with the wealthier subjects, rulers levied regressive taxes. Wealthy merchants and landowners often served as tax farmers and lenders. Rulers often exchanged favors, business and political, for loans. On other occasions, Flemish and English rulers issued tallies of receipt for purchases—in essence, short-term forced loans without interest. Lending to rulers was a risky venture, because some rulers on occasion repudiated their loans, arrested lenders and confiscated their property on trumped-up charges, or repaid loans with debased currency. French kings Philip the Fair (d. 1314) and John the Good (d. 1364) excelled at the latter policy, presumably earning their monikers for characteristics other than fiscal probity. Rulers occasionally used the threat of currency debasement to entice payment of tallages in return for a pledge to maintain a sound currency. Still, the rates of interest were high enough to entice potential lenders; and even if the interest rate was low, the lender might get trade concessions or control of a lucrative tax farm. In other cases, lenders might receive nobility. Twelfth-century Italian cities pioneered a permanent funded debt.

The resort to tax farming meant a surer but smaller yield from taxes, making it more difficult to sustain and redeem loans. Rulers who repudiated or stopped paying interest on loans found this to be a temporary palliative, for subsequent lenders often demanded even higher rates of interest. Therefore, impecunious rulers found themselves pawning royal jewels, mortgaging property, and engaging in other dire measures to satisfy lenders.

Philip II of France (Philip Augustus; d. 1223) was one of the most successful medieval rulers. He inherited a France partially occupied by English kings. Philip confiscated King Johns' English possessions in northern France by declaring them to be forfeit; and he also confiscated vacant fiefs and lands belonging to heirless nobles. Philip temporarily enlisted the Templars to maintain his treasury, but he later created a civil service based on merit, with salaried bailiffs responsible for the administration of his growing kingdom. The bailiffs successfully collected the revenue from town charters, fees on foreign merchants, and other sources. Philip's wealth grew steadily, and he died as one of medieval Europe's wealthiest rulers. His legacy provided future French kings with a sounder revenue system than that enjoyed by their English rivals. Later, medieval French kings imposed the taille, a fixed charge on every French person without exemptions. By 1600, the taille comprised a large proportion of royal revenues.

The chief achievement of medieval governments was the creation of new systems for incurring and sustaining long-term financial obligations—though not specifically debts—while avoiding the church's prohibition on usury. From Carolingian times, landowners had occasionally bequeathed land to monasteries, stipulating that the donor and his or her heirs were to receive an annual usufruct in the form of a *census* (or *cens*). From the early to mid-thirteenth century, urban governments in northern France

and the adjacent Low Countries issued a revised form of this contract, the rente, similar to the modern annuity, by which they sold the right to a fixed annual payment, which was usually financed from excise taxes levied on consumption of "products of the land": bread, beer, wine, cheese, meat, textiles, etc. Such *rentes* were either for one lifetime or for several (i.e., transferable to children and grandchildren as heritable *rentes*). While some thirteenth-century theologians were concerned that *rentes* were an evasion of the usury doctrine, Pope Innocent IV decreed (about 1251) that they were not loans but sales contracts that were fully licit so long as the annual payments were tied to products of the land.

Sometimes civic governments, after finding that such annual payments became onerous, asserted the right to redeem the *rentes*. While some creditors objected to such redemptions because of an expected decrease in annual incomes, others sought the right to reclaim at least part of their forfeited capital by selling their rente claims to third parties. But secondary markets offering full negotiability were slow to develop, a limitation that undoubtedly hindered the full development of this form of urban financing. These *rentes* did not fully displace conventional loans but offered an often useful alternative. The practice spread throughout Flanders, the Low Countries, and Germany during the fourteenth and fifteenth centuries. Indeed, the major principalities, if not kingdoms, in these regions also came to adopt this form of state finance.

In the Mediterranean south, Catalan towns had also resorted to similar *rentes*, known as *censals* (heritable) or *violaris* (lifetime) during the fourteenth century. In 1489, Ferdinand (Aragon) and Isabella (Castile) issued them as *juros de heredad* to finance their war with Granada, which led to Spanish unification (1492). Their son Charles (1517–1556; Holy Roman Emperor from 1519) made them the foundation for the royal finances of Habsburg Spain. Under his rule, the Habsburg Netherlands—though drawing on the precedents of Flemish urban finance—also made the sales of such *rentes* an integral part of national finance. In Spain, his son Philip II (1556–1598), though sometimes defaulting on his loans, nevertheless ensured that his government met its annual payment obligations on the *juros*, which became a favored international investment instrument, especially because they were fully negotiable.

From as early as Spanish unification in 1492, Spain's voyages of exploration and conquest had elevated the country to the forefront of world powers. These conquests provided Spanish rulers with labor and precious metals. The Spanish kings demanded the *quinto real* (royal fifth) of all of the bullion imported, as well as other taxes on the imports. Had the Spanish kings been content with this literal gold mine, Spain's economy might have reaped long-term benefits. However, they pursued aggrandizement via wars of conquest, so that their expenditures escalated faster than the inflow of precious metals. The taxes on precious metals comprised only one-fourth of total revenue in most years. Spain already had the *alcabala*, a general sales tax initiated during the fourteenth century. Since these metals and bullion receipts provided insufficient revenue to support Spain's chronic wars, the kings heavily taxed the population. The large landholders and church lands were exempt from direct taxation, which meant that the poorer people had to bear the tax burdens in the forms of internal tariffs and tolls on commerce. The crown offered patents of nobility to wealthy merchants, in effect, a one-time payment by the merchant for a long-term tax exemption. Kings Charles and Philip II borrowed large sums from private financiers such as the Fugger family. The interest payments eventually consumed the majority of the crown's yearly revenue, and the kings responded by suspending interest payments or by converting the debts into *juros*. Spain's military adventures failed to redress its fiscal woes, and its military and economic power waned.

Early modern France, the Habsburg Low Countries, and England. Sixteenth-century French kings had also resorted increasingly to the issue of *rentes* but did not succeed then in making them fully negotiable. Indeed, in the early sixteenth century, most debt instruments lacked perfect negotiability. Surprisingly, the evolution of such negotiablity had begun in fifteenth-century England, specifically with bills of exchange, a contract that the Italians had originated in the late thirteenth century to effect payments in foreign cities without shipping bullion. This greatly reduced transaction costs due to the risks of piracy, highway robbery, and confiscations, especially when most states came to ban bullion exports. But such bills lacked not only negotiability—they were almost always held to maturity—but also, as informal unnotarized documents, protected in most courts. In late-medieval England, however, Parliament empowered civic courts to bypass common law and utilize the international law merchant. In 1436, the Mayor's Court of London did so (in *Burton* v. *Davy*) for the first time in Europe, providing full protection for third-party bearers of bills of exchange to sue the payer for full payment and costs. That provided precedents for civic courts in Lübeck (1499 and 1502) and then in Antwerp (1506) and Bruges (1527) to award similar protection to creditors of both bills of exchange and bills obligatory (promissory notes). Those legal decisions in turn provided the foundations for the States General of the Habsburg Netherlands to issue Europe's first truly national legislation, between 1537 and 1541, that provided complete protection for the property rights of creditors in all such bills and thus the conditions necessary for full-fledged negotiability. This legislation also made interest legal up to 12 percent, thus

implicitly permitting discounting, an essential ingredient of genuine negotiability. Such legal protection spurred on the use of bearer bills (though discounting itself was still slow to spread). During the sixteenth-century, south German banking houses, in particular the Fuggers, traded both *juros* and *renten* on the Antwerp *Beurs* (bourse), developing this secondary market to make Antwerp the financial capital of Europe, until the Revolt of the Netherlands (1566–1648) caused that market to shift to Amsterdam in the north (Holland).

Early modern Netherlands. The Netherlands looms large in the history of public revenue and taxation. After the Revolt of the Netherlands against Spanish Habsburg rule in 1566 or, more particularly, after the 1576 Union of Utrecht, which led to the creation of the independent Republic of the United Provinces (the seven northern provinces), the Dutch established a public revenue system that eighteenth-century England would emulate. Previously in the Habsburg Netherlands, the emperor had largely depended upon subsidies (taxes) granted by the then seventeen provinces. Each province was responsible for a share of the annual tax and of the extraordinary tax (*beden*). The provinces then apportioned their share of the annual tax among the cities and towns. Since the central government had no direct tax revenue, its ability to borrow was limited. In 1542, the emperor sought to increase tax revenue and bolster his ability to borrow by levying a 10 percent tax on income from real property and excise taxes on beer, wine, and woolen cloth. In return for accepting these new taxes, Holland gained the right to control the collection and disbursement of its tax revenues. The province used its new-found tax revenue to retire some of its debt and to create trust in its *renten*. The 1542 policy had the perverse effect of boosting the provinces' financial strength, while the central government continued to rely upon shaky deficit finance and subsidies from Spain.

The northern provinces, particularly Holland and Zealand, grew financially strong enough to succeed in their revolt, although the lengthy struggle severely tested their finances. At times, the provinces suspended annual payments on their *renten* while raising tax rates (perhaps fourfold on a real per capita basis). The populace accepted this increased burden, partly because it was self-imposed.

Although the Union of Utrecht stipulated that tax revenues be levied at the same rate throughout the provinces, the idea proved unworkable. The provinces resorted, with minor adjustment for Zealand's economic deterioration, to the old Hapsburg imperial quota system. The central government attempted to meet naval expenditures via excise taxes, but commerce avoided the taxes via smuggling; the individual provinces had little incentive to suppress smuggling. In a sense, the new Dutch central government was worse off than the Habsburg emperor, since revenue from crown domain now reverted to the provinces. Thus, the provinces continued to maintain a weak central government. Eventually, Holland dominated the assumption of the provinces' collective debts and the formulation of fiscal policy.

Ironically, the provinces began to levy their own excise taxes, and Holland took the lead with its *gemene middelen*. Excise taxes, which included stamp taxes, provided the foundation of Holland's public revenue. Tax farmers, who were typically small operators, unable to exert much political power, collected specific excise taxes. From the government's perspective, excise taxes were flexible, easily expanded, and predictable because of tax farming. Tax farmers also deflected the population's anger at paying taxes. Conversely, the excise taxes were regarded as regressive and somewhat avoidable and required enforcement. Holland later introduced exemptions and sliding scales, and evidence suggests that these efforts mitigated the regressive nature of the excise taxes. To reduce the losses from tax avoidance, the province taxed consumers on an assumed level of consumption (rising with the higher occupational level or wealth of the taxpayer).

The provinces also used property taxes, collecting taxes on land rents and house rental values, and direct taxes, including an inheritance tax (*collaterale successie*). During emergencies, the provinces enacted direct capital levies, essentially forced loans, on wealthier citizens. Local taxes included tolls and levies to support infrastructure. Thus, the Dutch experienced a breadth and depth of taxes unique in Europe. Holland's tax revenues tripled from 1588 to 1628, and real per capita tax burdens jumped during the last thirty years of the seventeenth century. Even after the Peace of Utrecht, the real per capita tax burden did not abate because of the economic stagnation of the eighteenth century. Holland appeared to have nearly exhausted the tax-paying capacity of its citizens by the eighteenth century.

The provinces issued three forms of debt instruments: *obligatien* (promissory notes), *losrenten* (redeemable annuities), and *lijfrenten* (lifetime annuities). These were initially widely held. Johan de Witt pioneered the application of probability theory to *lijfrenten* to demonstrate that such instruments should be age adjusted. Dutch creditworthiness was such that by 1640 Holland could convert its *losrenten* and reduce both interest rates and debt-service expenses.

For much of the seventeenth century, strong economic growth and years of peace enabled the Netherlands to maintain a stable and enviable public creditworthiness. The renewal of warfare in the 1670s and stagnating economic conditions contributed to the gradual erosion of Dutch credit. The introduction of a gambling or lottery element to the *losrenten* reflected the growing crisis. Purchasers of a *losrenten* entered a lottery whereby fifteen per-

cent of them would win a life annuity. Such lotteries recurred in the eighteenth century. But these tactics could not reverse the failing credit, and in 1713, the government suspended payments for nine months.

Most of the eighteenth century was in some way an unraveling of what the Dutch had accomplished in the previous century. A stagnant economy and rising debts triggered sales of state property, introduction of a graduated income tax, and forced loans. Naturally, these policies proved unpopular and triggered riots, usually in the form of attacks on those convenient targets: tax farmers. The Fourth Anglo-Dutch War in 1780 provided one final fiscal crisis before the invasion of French Revolutionary armies and the fall of the Dutch Republic in 1795.

France and Great Britain.   Meanwhile during the mid-seventeenth century, Jean-Baptiste Colbert, France's capable first minister for Louis XIV, succeeded in improving the administration of taxes. He compelled tax farmers to return some of their gains and repudiated some of the outstanding bonds. While members of the wealthier class suffered from these policies, the general populace applauded them. He eliminated some loopholes in the tax system by verifying claims of nobility, and he attempted to make taxes less oppressive. These endeavors brought in more revenue from the existing tax system; but France still retained a much more unwieldy system of collectors compared with England, which instituted a system of well-trained, supervised corps of collections, which reduced smuggling and corruption.

Colbert also recognized potential gains from economic warfare. To combat England's and Holland's growing economic strength, he hoped to enhance France's ability to export goods. He established customs tariffs in 1664, and then greatly increased the rates in 1667, particularly with regard to English and Dutch manufactured goods. In the monetary arena, he succeeded in stabilizing the value of France's silver coinage.

The French monarchy had authority over spending, but the Parlement de Paris controlled taxation. The Parlement was loath to raise taxes, except temporarily during wartime. France exempted land owned by the church and the nobility from taxation, leaving a reduced tax base to bear higher tax rates. In contrast, the British Parliament gradually assumed control of taxation, borrowing, and expenditure.

Both the French and English governments, however, fundamentally depended upon public borrowing to finance their wars. To facilitate borrowing, both nations drew upon the tools developed during the previous centuries. The English eventually relied more upon perpetual annuities to finance their long-term debt than did the French. Both governments devised a variation of life annuities: tontines. Under a tontine, a group of subscribers advanced money to the government. Subsequently, the government made annual payments to the group, with the surviving group members sharing the proceeds. The government's obligation ended with the death of the last member of the subscribing group. English officials priced the tontines close to an actuarially sound level, while French officials provided generous rates of return to their subscribers. Thus, the tontines brought in much more revenue in France than in England, although the tontines never comprised a major proportion of French government borrowing. Some historians deduced that French officials were not as competent in calculating the actuarially sound values for their tontines, but the American economist David Weir (1989) suggests that the generous terms for tontine subscribers were a political sop to the urban middle-class subscribers who did not enjoy exemptions from other taxes.

The generosity of the French tontine system eventually tempted French officials to terminate or repudiate existing tontines. In 1770, Controller General Terray froze tontine payments at 1769 levels and began converting them to life annuities. The conversion process left subscribers worse off and eroded their faith in the Crown. In contrast, although the British government paid close to actuarially sound returns, that government did not repudiate its debt even though the policy meant significantly higher rates of taxation than in France.

A French default on its debt shortly after 1780 caused the French government to begin some reforms, including raising taxes and cutting nonwar expenditures. Finance minister Jacques Necker also attempted to use a tax-smoothing policy (accumulating surpluses and reducing the debt during peace). His attempt at fiscal restraint helped lower interest rates. But the policy was vulnerable to contemporary exigencies, and later finance ministers were unable to control expenditures, leading to chronic deficits and growing debts. While short-term borrowing allayed the fiscal crisis temporarily, the more permanent solutions of raising taxes or defaulting sparked intense debate. Holders of government debt, the rentiers, competed with taxpayers to curry favor from the Parlement. However, Parlement shifted responsibility to the Crown. The Crown recognized that another default would not only create discontent among the rentiers and raise future interest rates, but it would also strike a severe blow to its prestige. The finance minister Charles-Alexandre de Calonne formulated the *subvention territoriale*, a tax-in-kind on all landed income with no exemptions. Unfortunately, even the removal of the exemption for clergy and nobility would have failed to add enough revenue to balance the budget, so an increased tax rate was also needed. His plan was defeated, and a series of increasingly desperate fiscal and monetary policies culminated in severe inflation during

the mid-1790s. The financial chaos was a factor in the overthrow of the monarchy.

The Revolutionary government could not find attractive solutions and opted to embark on a series of territorial conquests, but the victories were insufficient to balance the budget or to stem the inflationary pressures. The Revolutionary Convention implemented price controls in 1793; however, the controls not only failed to alleviate the inflationary pressure but angered the public. The controls did temporarily increase the convention's gains from seigniorage. By late 1795, the convention's gains from seigniorage dwindled, and it promised to halt the printing press, even holding a public burning of plates and printing equipment. In early 1796, the convention introduced a new currency, the *mandats territoriaux*, but it succumbed to the temptation to overissue the new currency. By 1797, the directory passed the "bankruptcy of two-thirds," effectively repudiating much of the debt. Rentiers, wearied by constant wrangling over payment, and other citizens, who practiced widespread tax evasion, accepted the repudiation.

After Napoleon seized power, tax collections began to recover. Because of the repudiation, interest payments were significantly lower. He imposed direct taxes and indirect taxes, and his military conquests reaped revenue (although these conquests required large sums). Relative to the old system, Napoleon held the advantage of exerting power over both taxation and expenditure.

Early modern England and modern Great Britain. During the late seventeenth century, England had also adopted much of the Dutch financial system but only after the Dutch Prince of Orange became King William III of England, after the Glorious Revolution of 1688. Then from 1693, England established a permanently funded national debt based on the sale of fully negotiable and ultimately perpetual annuities, which were originally issued for thirty-two or ninety-nine years or for the lifetime of the holder. When governments reserved the right to redeem annuities, they could redeem them to exploit favorable changes in interest rates or avoid having to redeem bonds at inconvenient junctures. In this sense, the creation of long-term debt instruments represented a boon for government finance. Subsequently, from 1749 to 1752, Chancellor of the Exchequer Pelham effected his famous "conversion" of all outstanding issues of annuities, some paying 5 or 6 percent, into the consolidated stock of the nation, popularly known as consols, paying 3.5 percent (and 3.0 percent after 1756). But to do so, he had to promise not to redeem them for thirty years (and they were not, until 1888, when they were converted into 2.75 percent and then into 2.5 percent consols).

To support the burgeoning permanent public debt, Parliament had long relied upon indirect taxes such as customs duties, excise and stamp taxes, and direct taxes on manifestations of wealth and income. The English taxes were usually levied uniformly, unlike those of France and the Netherlands. British citizens disliked direct taxes, viewing them as a threat to liberty, and they only acquiesced to an income tax during the Napoleonic Wars because of Pitt's promise that the tax would be rescinded when peace returned. After some debate, the tax was indeed abolished in 1816. The burden of the excise tax pressed heavily upon the poorer classes, spurring unrest and occasional riot. Excise taxes and customs duties became the most important revenue sources during the eighteenth century, while land taxes receded in importance.

Although the British economy had grown throughout the eighteenth century, economic downturns reduced the amount of excise taxes and customs duties. Wars also reduced revenue from customs. Still, this system enabled Great Britain to maintain higher tax and debt ratios to gross national product (GNP) than France did. The British government often ran debt burdens that consumed 40 percent or more of state income. Since the French kings had periodically defaulted on their debts while the British government was scrupulous in meeting interest payments, British creditworthiness was higher and its debt service was lower. Finally, the Bank of England, established in 1694–1697 as an integral mechanism in the establishment of the permanently funded national debt, was a superior institution for marketing securities, whether long-term annuities or short-term treasury bills.

The British public revenue system's strength certainly contributed to the nation's victory over Napoleon in 1815. Although Parliament did not have direct control over the money supply, it did authorize the Bank of England to suspend the convertibility of paper currency into gold (in 1797). During the ensuing credit expansion for the duration of the Napoleonic wars, British prices roughly doubled; but since it was not hyperinflation, such financial policies did no serious harm to the government's credibility. Parliament's ability to repeatedly borrow rested upon its ability to generate enough tax revenue to meet its interest obligations. Because customs duties and excise taxes were nearing their limits, the imposition of an income tax during the Napoleonic Wars sustained this policy of borrowing. Great Britain emerged from the Napoleonic Wars with a debt equal to two years of its national income. However, the large debt burden did not prevent growth over the next century, although it might have slowed growth.

After defeating Napoleon, the British government moved toward free trade, which it finally achieved in the late 1840s. The dwindling tariffs and duties meant that the government needed to find other revenue sources. Indeed, as a preparatory step to the introduction of free trade, the Peel ministry of 1842 reintroduced the income tax, at 7d per pound sterling (2.92 percent), which subsequently increased with the introduction of free trade in 1846. During the late nineteenth century, an articulate group of British thinkers, including George Bernard Shaw and Sidney and Beatrice Webb, advocated a single tax on land, but their efforts were futile.

Early modern Prussia and its evolution into modern Germany. In marked contrast to Spain, the Netherlands, and England, the Hohenzollern dynasty lacked other overseas colonial possessions. The dynasty's careful management of its land, mines, and iron foundries provided half of the government's total revenue. It also granted monopoly rights to industry and enacted protective tariffs. The government efficiently collected taxes while carefully conserving its revenues. As the Prussian army gained a formidable reputation, the government received subsidies from allies. Frederick the Great husbanded his armies as well as he did his financial resources, as he rarely embarked on any overly ambitious campaigns. Thus, Prussia was, until the Napoleonic era, one of the better-managed European powers.

After the Napoleonic era, the Germanic states gradually coalesced into a formidable military power. The stunning victories over France in the Franco-Prussian War (1870–1871) resulted in a 5-billion-franc indemnity upon France and the acquisition of the rich provinces of Alsace-Lorraine. The German Empire featured an absolute monarch, a representative parliament, and a democratic electorate. The kaiser could theoretically trump the parliament and impose his will. The princes of the various states making up the German Empire maintained power through the Federal Council. Finally, the democratically elected Reichstag articulated the desires of the masses.

German government spending existed on three levels: the Reich, the federal states, and local. An income tax qualification for suffrage at the federal state level disenfranchised poorer Germans. The federal governments reflected the interests of wealthier Germans by pursuing conservative fiscal policies. The Reich featured more universal suffrage and often leaned toward more liberal policies. Each level of government had its sources of revenue. The Reich had tariffs, postal and telegraphic services, stamp duties, consumption taxes, and other minor taxes. In the decade prior to 1914, the Reich received most of its revenue from tariffs and taxes on consumption. The federal states retained the power to enact direct taxes, while the local governments relied upon property taxes and revenue from public utilities. Since the Reich was not allowed to borrow except for extraordinary circumstances, federal and local governments were required to make up any shortfall via matricular contributions. The federal governments jealously guarded their monopoly on direct taxes. The wealthier Germans disliked direct taxes, but given the limited suffrage at the federal level, at least they could control any such tax.

Since Bismarck was constrained from increasing the imperial tax base via direct taxes, he rescinded the existing free trade policy and levied tariffs. The tariffs both protected German industry and agriculture and created a large revenue for the Reich. The Reich's other main sources of revenue came from indirect taxes upon alcohol and tobacco consumption. These taxes were so successful that Parliament passed the Franckenstein Clause in 1879 that capped the Reich's take; any tax revenue above 130 million marks had to be shared with the federal governments. Thus, matricular contributions became a permanent feature of German government finance, but the flow of tax revenue from the Reich to the federal states eventually reversed.

Germany's military buildup triggered growing government debts at all levels. The Reichstag was unwilling to increase indirect taxes and tariffs because these taxes bore hardest upon the poorest Germans. Wealthier Germans stymied popular support for allowing the Reich to usurp the right to levy direct taxes. The Reich's growing deficit could, theoretically, be remedied by matricular contributions, but these entailed greater taxation at the federal and local levels. By 1913, German governments were hamstrung by fiscal constraints, and only a large *Wehrbeitrag* in 1914 greatly increased Reich revenue as war began.

In the aftermath of Germany's loss in World War I, the victorious Allies imposed massive reparations, equal to two years' worth of German national income. In 1920, the British economist John Maynard Keynes warned of the potentially dire effects of the reparations. The nascent Weimar government ultimately resorted to inflation. Although the hyperinflation in Weimar Germany may not have been the worst inflationary episode in history, it was one of the most fateful. During 1922 and 1923, prices increased an average of over 300 percent per month and triggered political discord that eventually toppled the Weimar regime and replaced it with the Nazi regime under Adolf Hitler.

Indeed, the Weimar regime's hyperinflation was one of seven twentieth-century hyperinflationary episodes examined by economist Philip Cagan. He found that the regimes collected less than 10 percent of normal national income. Since hyperinflation often resulted in reduced real national incomes as the prices became useless as signals and as people attempted to evade the inflation tax, the policy was particularly deleterious in the long run. In addition, hyperinflation reduced the real value of other taxes collected, so further recourse to the printing press became almost a necessity.

The United States of America. The British colonists sought independence from Great Britain largely because of taxation and land access issues. The slogan "No taxation without representation" remains an icon for Americans.

From the British perspective, the first half of the slogan was the real issue. Indeed, subsequent democratically representative American governments would find that their constituents were not always fond of "taxation with representation."

Although there had been long-standing British taxes upon the colonists, the Seven Years' War with France severely strained the Crown's budget. The Crown enacted several laws designed to further colonial defense, including assuming responsibility of "Indian" affairs, a currency act, a Sugar Act protecting West Indian interests, and the Stamp Tax. The colonists reduced their imports of taxed goods and protested the Stamp Tax.

The British government probably did not unduly tax the colonists. Lance Davis and Robert Huttenback (1982) believe that the colonists were lightly taxed relative to Europeans. Another economist, Gary Walton (1971), calculated that the gross cost of British protection and regulation was about 1 percent of annual income in the 1770s; conversely, the British Crown poured resources into the colonies, so the colonists were more likely net beneficiaries of largesse. Indeed, Adam Smith (1981, p. 616) wrote that colonies were frequently a costly endeavor for a government.

The rebellious colonists quickly discovered how difficult it was to finance warfare. The nascent Continental government had no existing nonmilitary expenditures to reduce. Its ability to tax was puny, and its ability to borrow was questionable. Congress printed paper money (Continentals), creating inflation and economic chaos, as well as the priceless epithet "Not worth a Continental." However, the issuance of paper money generated purchasing power, albeit inefficiently, for the new government. Ultimately, Congress confiscated supplies.

Americans found that the Articles of Confederation were ineffective, especially since the individual states retained the power to tax. The Constitution granted the national government, under Article I, Sections 8 and 10, the power to tax, borrow, create money, and regulate commerce.

Colonial governments in America relied upon property taxes. After independence, the states jealously defended their priority with regard to property taxes and dissuaded the federal government from usurping the tax. The property tax proved popular, as it was progressive and not easily evaded. During the Great Depression, many states supplemented their property tax revenue with retail sales tax revenue. Lotteries had been popular in early American history, but after allegations of corruption tainted the Louisiana state lottery, most states stopped using them. Since 1960, many states have reintroduced lotteries.

The federal government relied primarily upon customs duties. Until the Civil War, revenue from land sales and the customs duties proved sufficient for the government to acquire new territory, provide national defense and some internal improvements, maintain other basic government programs, and pay interest on and reduce the national debt (including the states' debts assumed at the time of confederation). Indeed, Alexander Hamilton (the first Secretary of the Treasury) successfully established the country's credibility in the international lending market; the nascent country did not default on the interest on its debts.

The federal government earned revenue from land sales, particularly from new acquisitions. Conversely, the costs of surveying, administering the sale, and defending the property offset some of the new revenue. The land sales usually accounted for 5 to 10 percent of total federal receipts but occasionally comprised more than 40 percent.

During the Civil War, the federal government issued bonds, made greenbacks legal tender, and implemented a variety of taxes, including a modest income tax. The federal government avoided a ruinous inflation (prices roughly doubled during the war) that might have deranged the economy.

The federal government's achievements contrasted sharply with those of the Confederate government. Southerners proved resistant to widespread taxes, although there was agitation for taxing wealthy citizens. Confederate bonds fluctuated greatly during the war, especially in response to battlefield successes and failures. Southerners relied upon inflation. Prices increased by 2,800 percent during the war, exerting punitive taxes upon soldiers and their families (the nominal pay for soldiers barely doubled) and discouraging trade. Indeed, the Davis administration eventually resorted to impressing goods.

Although the federal government enacted modest corporate and income taxes, Congress rescinded them shortly after the war. Popular support for both forms of taxes grew during the Populist era, as farmers and workers hoped to shift the burden of taxation upon the wealthy. In 1894, Congress resurrected the income tax. However, the Supreme Court ruled the tax unconstitutional in *Pollock* v. *Farmers' Loan & Trust Company*, thereby forcing Congress to pass the Sixteenth Amendment in 1913. Woodrow Wilson pressed for increased tax rates and a broader tax base, so that by 1920, the top marginal rates were more than 70 percent. From 1902 until the 1920s, the income tax replaced the tariff in importance and comprised 50 percent of federal revenue by the 1920s. The emphasis on income and corporate taxes sets the United States apart from most of the industrialized world.

Treasury Secretary Andrew Mellon recognized that many wealthy Americans in the early 1920s avoided the federal income tax by investing in tax-exempt bonds rather than private bonds and equities. Thus, he successfully lobbied for a reduction of the marginal tax rate. His policies generated increased tax revenue while reducing the tax load on lower-income Americans.

Congress restored a permanent corporate tax in 1909. The tax equaled 7.1 percent of gross domestic product (GDP) in 1943 but receded to about one-third of its importance by the 1990s. Most of the decrease resulted from the falling proportion of corporate profits relative to output.

The exigencies of the Great Depression and World War II forced the federal government to raise taxes and to increase borrowing. Despite the vastly larger expenditures, the policies, along with wage and price controls, succeeded in limiting price increases to a doubling. The national debt increased to greater than the yearly national output, but it gradually dwindled in the postwar era.

After the war, the federal government retrenched, but Cold War military expenditures kept spending as a whole from falling to prewar levels. Marginal tax rates on income reached as high as 90 percent during the 1950s, but Congress cut these rates during the Kennedy and Reagan administrations, dropping the highest federal income tax rate to 28 percent. Subsequent legislation raised the top marginal rate to 39.6 percent.

The federal government enacted payroll taxes to fund Social Security and Medicare programs. Employers and employees shared the legal incidence of these taxes, although many economists believe that the employees ultimately bore most of the actual burden. For many Americans, the payroll tax surpassed the income tax and became the largest tax.

The federal government received moderate amounts of revenue from leasing its lands for grazing, oil exploration, and other productive purposes. In some cases, the fees appeared to be set below hypothetical market prices. Although these programs brought in billions of dollars of revenue, the moneys comprised a small proportion of the overall revenue.

Throughout much of the postwar era, the federal government ran budget deficits. The national debt grew during the 1980s and 1990s but, relative to national output, did not match the level of the immediate postwar period.

Middle East. Several Islamic governments had enacted poll taxes (*jizya*) from the seventh century. These taxes were levied upon non-Muslims, although there were exemptions for women, children, and disabled or unemployed men. Recognizing the discriminatory nature of the tax, the Ottoman Empire finally abolished it in 1855.

The Ottoman Land Code of 1858 also sought to modernize the government's revenue collection. Previously, the Ottoman state relied upon taxes on agricultural lands, the *timar* system. The government granted land to military officers who collected the land tax and maintained military forces. The land tax system was replaced by a tax farming policy (*iltizam*). Individuals bid for the right to collect taxes. The taxes were split proportionally according to the winning bid. The individual winning the right held it for life and could even bequeath it. During the 1840s, the Ottoman government wanted to increase cultivation of existing lands and abandoned land, so the agricultural tax was reduced from 50 percent to 10 percent. The land code replaced the tax farming system. The new system allowed individuals to own the land and then pay taxes, whereas previously the state owned the land and leased it to peasants, and the tax farmers collected the taxes. The new system succeeded in raising the revenue collected from agricultural taxes.

Japan. With the "opening" of Japan in the 1840s, the Japanese government sought to modernize. After an initial bout of inflation, the government levied a land tax based on the potential productivity of the land. The land tax comprised the majority of government revenues up to 1900. Because the tax was levied on potential productivity, it brought in a steady revenue as well as encouraged owners to use the land. In addition, the government created tariff protection for its nascent manufacturing sector.

After World War II, Japan adopted a new tax system based upon recommendations by the American Shoup Mission. The Japanese adopted direct taxation in the form of personal and corporate income taxes. Because a greater proportion of smaller businesses in Japan are incorporated compared with similar-sized American counterparts, the corporate income tax comprises a larger proportion of the overall Japanese tax revenue (almost 30 percent). In 1988, to alleviate the reliance upon direct taxes, the government created a 3 percent consumption tax, but this tax brought in less than 10 percent of the total revenue. The government also abolished existing commodity taxes on automobiles and consumer electronic products. Even with the consumption tax, direct taxes, including an inheritance tax, continued to provide 70 percent of the overall government revenue in 1991. Local governments relied upon a combination of resident taxes (placed upon individuals and corporations) and fixed-asset taxes on real property.

Taxation in the Modern Industrialized World. Of the countries involved in the Organization for Economic Cooperation and Development (OECD), government (federal, state, and local) tax revenues averaged almost 39 percent of GDP in 1993. Japan and the United States had relatively low tax shares (about 29–30 percent), while Sweden had a relatively high tax share (almost 50 percent). The United States and Japan rely more on income and corporate income taxes than do the other members of the OECD, which rely more on consumption taxes.

European governments replaced the cascade type or turnover tax with the value-added tax. Under the turnover tax, the government collected sales tax on the value at each stage of production and distribution. Products with many stages of production and distribution were at a disadvantage compared with those with only a few stages. The more modern and widespread value-added tax removed this distortion by taxing only the incremental change in value at each stage of production and distribution. With the unification of the European market, European governments have reduced tariffs that served both as vehicles for revenue and protection of specific industries.

While some governments provided food and poor relief in the past, social programs burgeoned during the twentieth century. Growing productivity increased the surplus above subsistence in many countries, and governments could feasibly weave social safety nets to ameliorate economic insecurity. Unemployment insurance, retirement funds, and health care were only the most prominent programs. Given the aging populations in most of the OECD countries, the viability of social programs, especially retirement and medical, may be the biggest political problem of the twenty-first century. Increasing social insurance taxes runs the risk of discouraging younger workers.

[*See also* Government Borrowing; Inflation Tax; *and* Lotteries.]

BIBLIOGRAPHY

Adams, Charles. *For Good and Evil: The Impact of Taxes on the Course of Civilization*. London, 1993. Adams provides a witty look at taxes and disgruntled citizens. He has a definite point of view, but he presents it in an entertaining fashion.

Ball, Douglas. *Financial Failure and Confederate Defeat*. Urbana, 1991. Given the Confederate government's need for haste in the face of a federal onslaught, that government faced unenviable choices. Ball sorts out the various policies and identifies why the Jefferson Davis administration ended up relying upon inflation and confiscation.

Brewer, John. *The Sinews of Power*. Cambridge, 1988. Brewer contrasts British and French policies for raising revenue between the Glorious Revolution and France's revolution.

Brownlee, W. Elliott. *Federal Taxation in America: A Short History*. Cambridge, 1996. Brownlee explains why the United States federal government eventually relied more on direct taxes than most other industrialized countries.

Cagan, Phillip. "The Monetary Dynamics of Hyperinflation." In *Studies in the Quantity Theory of Money*, edited by M. Friedman, pp. 25–117. Cagan combines theory and history in an oft-cited work on monetary policy gone awry.

Cameron, Rondo. *A Concise Economic History of the World: From Paleolithic Times to the Present*. New York, 1989. Cameron provides a general survey of economic development with discussion of taxation and public revenue policies.

Davis, Lance, and Robert Huttenback. "The Cost of Empire." In *Explorations in the New Economic History: Essays in Honor of Douglass C. North*, edited by Richard Sutch, Roger Ransom, and Gary Walton, pp. 41–69. New York, 1982. Davis and Huttenback examine the costs of maintaining the North American colonies.

Levi, Margaret. *Of Rule and Revenue*. Berkeley, 1988. Levi places taxation policy within a "Theory of Predatory Rule," whereby transaction costs, rates of time preference, and other economic theory combine to explain why various forms of taxation are chosen over other forms.

Marshall, Alfred. *Principles of Economics*. 8th ed. London, 1979. Marshall formalizes many economic principles and provides a sophisticated analysis of taxes and their incidences.

Munro, John. "The Late-Medieval Origins of the Modern Financial Revolution: Overcoming Impediments from Church and State." *The International History Review* 25.2 (June 2003).

O'Brien, Patrick. "The Political Economy of British Taxation, 1600–1815." *Economic History Review* 41.1 (1988), 1–32. O'Brien provides a quantitative examination of British taxation sources.

Slemrod, Joel. "The Economics of Taxing the Rich." In *Does Atlas Shrug?*, edited by Joel Slemrod, pp. 3–28. New York, 2000. Slemrod and several other leading tax economists describe the latest trends in public finance theory.

Smiley, Gene, and Richard Keehn. "Federal Personal Income Tax Policy in the 1920s." *Journal of Economic History* 55.2 (1995), 283–303. The authors examine U.S. Treasury Secretary Andrew Mellon's campaign to reduce marginal income tax rates and increase revenue from the tax. Unlike Art Laffer in the late 1970s, Mellon had empirical reasons to support his tax cut.

Smith, Adam. *An Inquiry into the Nature and Causes of the Wealth of Nations*. Indianapolis, 1981. Smith's book is an essential first stop to understanding public revenue throughout history, as well as a wealth of information regarding economic principles and the value and cost of maintaining colonies.

Stigler, George. "Bernard Shaw, Sidney Webb, and the Theory of Fabian Socialism." In *Essays in the History of Economics*, pp. 268–286. Chicago, 1965. Stigler depicts British liberals' infatuation with a single (land) tax as cleverly as Bernard Shaw.

Tracy, James D. "Taxation and State Debt." In *Handbook of European History, 1400–1600: Late Middle Ages, Renaissance, and Reformation*, edited by Thomas A. Brady, Heiko A. Oberman, and James D. Tracy, pp. 563–584. Leiden and New York, 1994–1995. Tracy provides a wide-ranging overview of late medieval financial policies.

Vries, Jan de, and Ad van der Woude. *The First Modern Economy: Success, Failure, and Perseverance of the Dutch Economy, 1500–1815*. Cambridge, 1997. The authors provide a detailed examination of the Dutch economy from the late medieval period to the end of the Napoleonic War.

Walton, Gary. "The New Economic History and the Burdens of the Navigation Acts." *Economic History Review* 24.4 (1971), 533–542. Walton assesses the burdens of the Navigation Acts upon the British colonies.

Webber, Carolyn, and Aaron Wildavsky. *A History of Taxation and Expenditure in the Western World*. New York, 1986. This book provides a thorough examination of taxation and public revenue throughout Western history.

Weir, David. "Tontines, Public Finance, and Revolution in France and England, 1688–1789." *Journal of Economic History* 49.1 (1989), 95–124. Weir provides an excellent analysis of the role of tontines in British and French financing.

White, Eugene. "The French Revolution and the Politics of Government Finance, 1770–1815." *Journal of Economic History* 55.2 (1995), 227–255. White examines the French system of public revenue and compares it with the British system.

DAVID G. SURDAM

Local Taxation

Local taxation provides revenue for counties, cities, towns, and villages, whereas central taxation provides revenues to states, republics, nations, and federations. Early forms of local public finance, in feudal and monarchical models, were much like that of the city-state of Athens, which derived most of its revenue from rents on public lands and profits from the city's mines. It also collected fees for services, fines for infractions, and duties from importers, aliens, and slaves; but generally these early forms of local public finance avoided direct taxes on citizens, except during times of war.

Modern governments are characterized by a spectrum of taxation authority between central and local governments. Highly centralized forms rely on a national government to raise and control the bulk of tax revenues while limiting the types and amounts of taxes available to local governments. Historically, much of continental Europe, Africa, and South America would be characterized as centralized. Federations are decentralized into national, state, and local levels, each with its duties and revenue sources, although responsibility is often shared and revenue redistributed from one level to another. There can even be substantive differences within a federation; in the United States, for example, local governments in many Northern states have more autonomy than state governments in Southern states, where state governments have a more dominant role over the taxing authority of local governments. An additional complication is the independent governmental unit that provides a specific service, but whose taxing authority can overlap the jurisdictions of several local governments.

Nations such as the United States, Canada, and Australia offer examples of fiscal federalism, where government is based on national and state constitutions as well as the rules incorporating local government units, which specify the rights, duties, and taxing authority of national, state, and local governments. A major advantage of fiscal federalism is that government services can be assigned to the appropriate level. For example, the national government would be in charge of international diplomacy, state governments would be assigned the task of regulating inland water systems, and local governments would be assigned the responsibility for organizing fire-protection services. Federalism allows for the decentralization of government with the goal of matching the provision of public services with the preferences of the local community. It also allows for migration, free trade, and a common set of legal and economic institutions over a large geographic area and thus optimizes productivity. This freedom of movement constrains local governments in their ability to tax and offer services because high taxes will cause individuals and businesses to emigrate to low-tax governments, and overly generous public services will encourage immigration of low-income individuals and nonresidents who take advantage of the services at the expense of the local taxpayers.

A theoretically ideal government is based on the Tiebout hypothesis, where local governments obtain tax and fee revenues from the local population in return for government services. Efficiency in the type, amount, and provision of government services is based on the notion that people can better affect the electoral process, express their interests, and monitor their representatives in local government than in centralized government. The Tiebout hypothesis asserts that if citizens are highly dissatisfied with local taxes or services, they can "vote with their feet" and move to a local government that better suites their tastes for taxes and services. Direct democracy, the threat of taxpayer and business emigration, and even taxpayer revolts can force local governments to behave properly, like firms in competitive markets, by keeping taxes and the costs of government in line with the services provided. In the Tiebout hypothesis, local governments that are small in size compete with one another. This condition ensures that local governments provide efficient, low-cost services and prevents them from behaving like monopolists. Statistical studies seem to indicate that there are few economies of scale in the provision of most traditional public goods by local government.

Local government has always played an important role in the United States, but until recently economic historians have largely neglected the role of local taxation. This neglect may stem in part from the fact that local government and its taxes were based on the constraints of the Tiebout hypothesis, at least until the twentieth century. In the colonial period, local government played an important role in everything from economic development to military defense, but in terms of revenues it was more dependent on fees, fines, and drafting labor than on direct taxation such as property and poll taxes. After the American Revolution and the adoption of the Constitution, the federal government assumed authority over customs duties and monetary affairs; but state governments were the dominant level of government before the Civil War, with financing based heavily on the general property taxes (land, improvements, personal property, slaves, etc.) and debt.

After the war, local governments (and their political patronage machines) became the dominant level of government as Republican policy promoted industrialization and urbanization over agrarian interests. It was during this period that local governments undertook the production of services previously provided by the private sector, such as garbage collection and education; greatly expanded other services, such as police protection; and took on roles in such new areas as public utilities and transportation. Also local governments then came to dominate American public finance, and local taxes were based very heavily on property taxes.

A third major phase in American fiscal history began during the Great Depression, when the burden of property taxes led to the formation of taxpayer organizations across the country. With Prohibition, cities lost tax and license revenues associated with alcohol sales, and they became almost entirely dependent on property taxes to pay for growing expenditures. Taxpayers complained about the heavy burden of the property tax, the unfairness of property tax rates, and the arbitrariness of assessing property values. Tax rates were reduced and tax-limitation laws were enacted across the country until 1933, when the lost revenues could be replaced with alcohol taxes when alcohol consumption was again legal. The property tax thus had important political ramifications in the adoption of the Twenty-first Amendment to the Constitution, repealing Prohibition, and in the presidential election of 1932. The property tax also had important political ramifications in igniting a series of tax revolts in the 1970s that culminated in the passage of Proposition 13 in California, and more recently in a series of court decisions that declared unconstitutional the property tax and education-funding systems in several states.

Local governments have continued to grow in terms of tax revenues, but their funding has experienced a relative decline compared to the massive revenue increases of the federal government. Since the Great Depression, state and federal governments have greatly increased their grants to local governments. This outside funding helps local governments overcome the constraints of the Tiebout hypothesis and spend more on subsidies, welfare programs, and other urban problems. Many states and cities adopted sales taxes during the period between the Great Depression and the 1960s, and local sales taxes have become more important for counties and municipalities, now accounting for over 60 percent of non–property tax revenues with the remainder coming from income, license, and other taxes. Once popular during the Colonial era, state-run lotteries have made a resurgence in the United States and Europe since the 1960s as a means of increasing the general fund and targeted educational budgets. Thus, property taxes have become less important in funding all forms of state and local governments in the United States except for townships and school districts.

There is still much debate about the incidence, efficiency, and fairness of the property tax. The incidence of a tax refers to who ultimately bears the economic burden of the tax rather than who actually pays the tax bill. For example, a landlord pays the property taxes, but the tax incidence is shared with the tenant if the value of the property falls and rents increase. The efficiency of property taxes is often questioned because high property taxes can discourage home ownership and property development, but this disadvantage is largely offset by the tax advantages of home ownership and by the fact that alternative taxes can create even greater inefficiencies than property taxes cause. The burden of the property tax is generally proportional to income and considered to be roughly equivalent to the benefits that citizens derive from local government services over their lifetime. Secondary sources of local taxation include the sales tax, excise taxes, license fees, and income taxes. These taxes have tended to remain small when citizens can easily avoid high rates by traveling or moving to nearby low-tax governments. High tax rates tend to be highly inefficient because they distort economic decision making. The economic burden of sales and excise taxes fall especially heavily on low-income workers, whereas income taxes tend to be roughly proportional to income.

The property tax continues to play a dominant role in local public finance in federal governments such as those of Australia, Canada, and the United States and in nonfederated countries such as Ireland, the Netherlands, New Zealand, and the United Kingdom. From the government's view, property-tax revenues are relatively stable over the business cycle and provide an autonomous revenue source that increases the independence of local government. From the citizens' perspective, the property tax provides clear information about the cost of government services and helps them to influence the level of taxation and services. Although there is still debate over the incidence, efficiency, and equity of the property tax, economists have found that it provides a clear and direct signal to citizens concerning the costs of government, and it makes possible small local governments that are competitive and can efficiently address the demands of their citizens.

BIBLIOGRAPHY

Beito, David T. *Taxpayers in Revolt: Tax Resistance during the Great Depression*. Chapel Hill, N.C., 1989.
Cannan, Edwin. *History of Local Rates in England*. 2d ed. London, 1912.
DiLorenzo, Thomas J., and James T. Bennett. *Underground Government: The Off-Budget Public Sector*. Washington, D.C., 1983. Analysis of how local governments have avoided restraints on spending with various off-budget measures.
Ely, Richard T. *Taxation in American States and Cities*. New York, 1888.
Fisher, Glenn W. *The Worst Tax? A History of the Property Tax in America*. Lawrence, Kans. 1996. Shows the evolution of property taxation from England to the 1990s with special reference to Kansas. The author argues that the property tax helps ensure citizens' control over their government and prevents centralization and government inefficiency.
Holcombe, Randall G., and Donald J. Lacombe. "The Growth of Local Government in the United States from 1820 to 1870." *Journal of Economic History* (March 2001), 184–189.
Howe, Edward T., and Donald J. Reeb. "The Historical Evolution of State and Local Tax Systems." *Social Science Quarterly* 78.1 (March 1997), 109–121.
King, David, ed. *Local Government Economics in Theory and Practice*. New York, 1992. An international sampling of public-finance issues affecting local government.
Legler, John B., Richard Sylla, and John J. Wallis. "U.S. City Finances and the Growth of Government, 1850–1902." *Journal of Economic History* 48.2 (June 1988), 347–356.
Monkkonen, Eric. *The Local State: Public Money and American Cities*. Palo Alto, Calif., 1995.
Oates, Wallace E. *Fiscal Federalism*. New York, 1972.
O'Sullivan, Arthur, Terri A. Sexton, and Steven M. Sheffrin. *Property Taxes and Tax Revolts: The Legacy of Proposition 13*. New York, 1995.
Owens, Jeffrey, and Giorgio Panella. *Local Government in International Perspective*. Amsterdam, 1991.
Raimondo, Henry J. *Economics of State and Local Government*. New York, 1992.
Sylla, Richard. "Long-Term Trends in State and Local Finance: Sources and Uses of Funds in North Carolina, 1800–1977." In *Long-Term Factors in American Economic Growth*, edited by Stanley L. Engerman and Robert E. Gallman, pp. 819–862. Chicago, 1986.
Thornton, Mark, and Chetley Weise. "The Success of the Great Depression Tax Revolts." *Journal of Libertarian Studies* 15.3 (summer 2001), 95–105.
Wallis, John Joseph. "American Government Finance in the Long Run: 1790–1990." *Journal of Economic Perspectives* 14.1 (winter 2000), 61–82. Quantitative assessment of federal, state, and local taxation and indebtedness.

MARK THORNTON

TAX FARMING. Tax administration can be structured in many different ways. In the tax farming option, the tax farmer pays the ruler a fixed amount (often determined by auction) for the right to collect a certain tax in a defined area. Anything the tax farmer collects above the purchase price is his or her profit, and if the tax farmer collects less, he or she takes the loss. Unlike bureaucratic state administration, in which principals pay agents a fixed sum and use monitoring and sanctioning to insure compliance, in tax farming the agent is made the residual claimant (that is, the actor that bears the risks and gets the net profits or takes the loss from the activity) and thus has a direct interest in adequate performance. Control is still necessary in this case, since agents must be prevented from collecting too much tax and thus harming the tax base.

When direct control of agents is not possible or too costly, rulers use tax farming to give agents stronger incentives to collect taxes. In short, principals choose to make their agents residual claimants when low control capacities make hierarchical control less efficient (that is, result in lower net revenue). The main structural factors that affect rulers' control capacities are the level of development of technologies of control (communications, transportation, record keeping), the size of the country, and the nature of the tax. The lack of developed communications and transportation technology explains why tax farming was used in most premodern states.

There are two additional reasons for the widespread use of tax farming in premodern states. First, it provides predictable revenue, since the farmers pay a fixed sum every year. Second, tax farming was used to provide loans to the state. All tax farming arrangements are short-term loans. The tax farmers pay the ruler a fixed sum of money first and then collect the taxes. Since tax farmers had to be wealthy individuals with liquid assets, rulers often got long-term loans from them as well. In the absence of a state bank, rulers' need for credit often made them dependent on tax farmers, which in some cases explains the persistence of this tax system.

Tax farming was used extensively in premodern empires. The Romans began using tax farming around the third century BCE. It was used for both direct and indirect taxes in the republic and was retained for indirect taxes throughout the empire. Tax farming had always been used on some state lands in the Ottoman Empire, but its use spread rapidly from the 1580s onward. It was employed until the bureaucratizing reforms of the 1840s.

In early modern Europe tax farming was generally used for indirect taxes (sales, customs, excise) but not for direct taxes (land, hearth, poll). In France indirect taxes were usually farmed from the thirteenth century until the Revolution, with the exception of a few short periods for certain taxes. Direct taxes were farmed only in the thirteenth century and between 1643 and 1661. In England tax farming was the dominant mode of collection for indirect taxes (customs were the main type), but bureaucratic state administration was sometimes used. Direct taxes were never farmed during the period of English absolutism (1485–1640). The situation in the Netherlands was similar to the English case. Both tax farming and bureaucratic state administration were used to collect indirect taxes, but the former was used in most areas most of the time. Spain used tax farming for most taxes (although it relied primarily on indirect taxes) throughout the early modern period.

There was a strong tendency in both empires and states for tax farms to centralize over time. Tax farms in republican Rome were initially small and were controlled by local tax farmers. One of the main changes in tax farming in the late republic was that the farms increased substantially in size. The vast number of small tax farms in France were consolidated over time, eventually combining to form one large organization. The process began in the sixteenth century and culminated when the general farms brought all of them together in 1723. The consolidation of tax farms began later in England, but the relative simplicity of the English fiscal system allowed it to conclude more quickly. Most of the major customs revenues were brought together in the great farm of the customs in 1604. The silk customs were included in the great farm in 1621; in 1632 the petty farms of the currants, sweet wines, and French wines were merged; and in 1640 the great and petty tax farms were consolidated. No such consolidation took place in the Dutch Republic. In Holland multiple farm ownership was rare among the hundreds of separate tax farms until the abolition of the system in 1747.

The consolidation of tax farms increased efficiency by facilitating economies of scale and reducing transaction costs. However, it had two other consequences that led to the decline of tax farming: rulers feared their increasing dependence on large tax farming corporations, and tax farmers developed many efficient collection techniques, which lowered the costs of shifting to state administration. When state administration took over for tax farms in England, they used all of the innovations made by the tax farmers, including the instruction manual for officials. Ironically tax farming made state administration efficient enough to collect indirect taxes.

The main virtue of tax farming—the strong incentives it provided to collect as much revenue as possible—also contributed to its decline. Most taxpayers hated tax farmers, and for this reason the system did not survive the democratizing revolutions in England (1640–1688) and France (1789). Tax farmers were attacked by the revolutionaries in both countries. In fact the building housing the tax farmers was attacked prior to the Bastille at the beginning of the French Revolution.

[*See also* Taxation, *subentry on* Taxation and Public Revenue.]

BIBLIOGRAPHY

Ashton, Richard. *The Crown and the Money Market, 1603–40*. Oxford, 1960. Discusses tax farming in Stuart England, focusing on the role of tax farmers in providing loans to the state.

Brewer, John. *The Sinews of Power*. London, 1989. Outlines the causes of the end of tax farming in England and its replacement by state bureaucracy.

Kiser, Edgar. "Markets and Hierarchies in Early Modern Tax Systems: A Principal-Agent Analysis." *Politics and Society* 22.3 (1994), 284–315. Comparative analysis of tax farming in early modern Europe, concentrating on the difference between direct and indirect taxes.

Levi, Margaret. *Of Rule and Revenue*. Berkeley, 1988. Argues that the dependence of the state on tax farmers explains its persistence in republican Rome.

Matthews, George. *The Royal General Farms in Eighteenth Century France*. New York, 1958. Detailed account of the organization of centralized tax farming in France.

Salzman, Ariel. "An Ancien Regime Revisited: Privatization and Political Economy in the Eighteenth Century Ottoman Empire." *Politics and Society* 21.4 (1993), 393–423. Analyzes different types of tax farming used in the Ottoman Empire.

Weber, Max. *The Agrarian Sociology of Ancient Civilizations* (1909). London, Reprint, 1976. Argues that variations in discount rates of rulers explain the rise and decline of tax farming in Rome.

EDGAR KISER

TAYLOR, FREDERICK WINSLOW

TAYLOR, FREDERICK WINSLOW (1856–1915), engineer, management theorist, and creator of scientific management.

Born into a wealthy Philadelphia family, Taylor demonstrated an aptitude for science, mathematics, and mechanical innovation at an early age. Starting at the Midvale Steel Company in 1874, he rose rapidly as a production manager and engineer. He also obtained a mechanical engineering degree from Stevens Institute of Technology, awarded in 1883. These early experiences—which provided many of the anecdotes and "object lessons" featured in his books and articles—exposed him to contemporary factory operations and an emerging movement to improve and rationalize those operations.

In the l880s the factory system was still relatively new and managerial practices were mostly ad hoc responses to mechanization. To young engineers such as Taylor, they reflected haphazard responses to immediate problems rather than an approach based on systematic investigation and analysis. Taylor and others began to look critically at contemporary practices and devise new methods. Historians have labeled the results of their work "systematic management." By l889, when Taylor left Midvale, he was one of the most vigorous and enthusiastic proponents of systematic management. His specific contributions included a piece-rate plan and stopwatch time studies, which identified and timed individual features of operations or jobs in order to eliminate wasteful activities.

As an industrial executive (1890–1893) and consultant (1893–1901), Taylor extended his studies of machinery and managerial procedures. His work for the Bethlehem Iron Company (1898–1901), where he was given substantial leeway to introduce his methods, was particularly productive. By the time he left Bethlehem, Taylor believed he had a comprehensive plan that would enable any factory to operate more efficiently and profitably. This plan, later known as "scientific management," was a synthesis of contemporary systematic management and Taylor's distinctive contributions such as time study.

For the last decade and a half of his life, Taylor devoted himself to publicizing his managerial innovations. He attracted a group of able assistants and disciples, including H. L. Gantt and Frank B. Gilbreth, who installed the Taylor system in industrial establishments, and Morris L. Cooke, an adept publicist. Cooke helped Taylor write a popular account of his ideas, *The Principles of Scientific Management* (1911), which became a best-selling book and an influential guide to the new management. Yet Taylor's life was troubled. He was ill-equipped temperamentally for his new role and made many enemies. A celebrated conflict with the leaders of the American Federation of Labor temporarily slowed the diffusion of scientific management and caused him much embarrassment. By 1915, these controversies, a hectic travel schedule, and illness (probably diabetes) had taken a substantial physical toll. Taylor succumbed to pneumonia after a strenuous lecture trip.

In the decade after his death, Taylor's critique of unsystematic management and his managerial techniques (though not his entire system) spread widely in the United States, Europe, and Japan. His central underlying idea—that systematic study and reorganization could improve the effectiveness of any activity—attracted an even larger audience. By the 1930s, Taylor's name was associated with virtually any endeavor that promised to improve the efficiency of an individual, group, or institution.

BIBLIOGRAPHY
Kanigel, Robert. *The One Best Way: Frederick W. Taylor and the Enigma of Efficiency*. New York, l997. A readable, comprehensive biography.
Nadworny, Milton J. *Scientific Management and the Unions, 1900–1932*. Cambridge, l955. The great controversy of Taylor's later years.
Nelson, Daniel. *Frederick W. Taylor and the Rise of Scientific Management*. Madison, Wis., 1980. Taylor's career as a manager and theorist.
Taylor, Frederick W. *Scientific Management*. New York, l947. A collection of Taylor's major publications.

DANIEL NELSON

TEA (*Camellia* or *Thea sinensis*), a white-flowered evergreen plant, originally grown in Asia to provide the leaves—which are picked, dried, sometimes flavored, and processed—both for local use and international trade. The tea plants, bushes, and shrubs are grown on plantations, and the leaves are used with boiling water to make a drink. The origins and date of the discovery of tea are uncertain. One theory is that ancient Asian peoples who lived in the mountainous forests of what became the border of Assam and Myanmar (Burma) found that the leaves made a refreshing drink. Tea was perhaps also eaten as a vegetable, chewed, pickled and/or sniffed like snuff in this area, as it still is today in parts of Southeast Asia. Several thousand years ago, the knowledge of tea spread to China, where it was first prized as a medicine and as a drink that helped in meditation and concentration. Tea was grown for commercial production by the Chinese and introduced into Japan in the eighth century CE (but remained as a medicinal herb in monastery gardens). It was reintroduced in the twelfth century and considered of great medical and spiritual importance in the Zen form of Buddhism. In Japan's growing acceptance of Buddhism, it became the center of Japanese cultural life—influencing religion, aesthetics, social and political customs, and the economy; the Japanese even perfected a tea ceremony. By the sixteenth century, tea was established as the national drink of half the world's population. Tea was marketed through brokers as green, black (fermented), or oolong (semifermented); it is graded by leaf size into orange, pekoe, or souchong.

Tea was first mentioned in European sources in 1559, and Ukers (1935) provides a good general survey of its introduction into Europe and England. The first tea cargoes are believed to have been shipped into Amsterdam in 1610 by the Dutch East India Company. It was first served to the public in England in 1657, in taverns and inns, in a manner similar to beer. It was very expensive at first, a luxury, served in coffee houses until the early eighteenth century. By 1710, about half the tradesmen who shipped and left

TEA. Women picking tea at an estate in the Himalayas, India, between 1890 and 1923. (Frank and Frances Carpenter Collection/Prints and Photographs Division, Library of Congress)

inventories in London had silver and porcelain tea equipment. The consumption of tea grew immensely from 1720 to 1730, when a direct trade link between Europe and Cathay (China) was established. Some suggested figures for the growth of imports into England are as follows (as expressed in weight by the pound, roughly half a kilo): 4,713 in 1678; 370,323 in 1725; 65 million in 1775; almost 24 million in 1801. By the end of the eighteenth century in England, various estimates suggest that each citizen in England may have been drinking up to two cups of tea per day, on average. It was not a drink confined to the rich; considerable evidence shows that ordinary people and even the poor drank large quantities of tea. England, and for a time America, were the main Western consumers of tea; on the Continent coffee and other drinks were preferred.

The economic and other effects of the tea trade with China on Western civilization were enormous. Tea stimulated ongoing trade with China. It led to the European development of fine ceramics and porcelain and altered social habits. It may also have had some effect on health in Europe. When tea was first introduced there, various physicians experimented with what was considered a medicinal herb; they found that it seemed to contain properties that, for example, delayed putrefaction in frogs' legs. Their 1600s research has been confirmed, since polyphenols in

tea—closely related to the antiseptic phenol used by British surgeon Joseph Lister in 1867 to sterilize hospitals—may be a very important antibacterial agent. The slight astringency comes from the antibacterial tannins. Researchers have argued that the dramatic fall in the mortality rate in England from 1740 onward, credited as being a necessary precondition for urbanization and the Industrial Revolution (and which has hitherto never been explained), may have been one of the effects of the explosion of tea drinking (replacing Dutch gin for many who became teetotalers).

Tea drinking and the tea trade was expanded in the nineteenth century. The British developed tea plantations in Assam (India) and on the island of Ceylon (present-day Sri Lanka) in the mid-nineteenth century. This had a considerable effect on the local populations, who were often moved to supply labor. Tea drinking was encouraged in Europe and the European colonies to provide markets for the product. In the early twentieth century, the general population of India began to drink tea on a large scale, and this also affected their health, social customs, and trading patterns during the British Empire and since independence in 1947.

The Asian tea plant, which has a mild form of caffeine (theine), and the antibacterial polyphenol, has become (after water) the source of the most widely drunk substance.

It has stimulated trade, encouraged crafts, in particular pottery, enhanced ritual and religion, become a central social institution in much of Asia and the United Kingdom, enslaved and employed hundreds of thousands of plantation workers, and possibly helped provide the populations that began the Industrial Revolution.

BIBLIOGRAPHY

Forrest, Denys. *Tea for the British: The Social and Economic History of a Famous Trade*. London, 1973.

Forrest, Denys. *The World Tea Trade: A Survey of the Production, Distribution and Consumption of Tea*. Cambridge, 1985.

Goodwin, Jason. *The Gunpowder Gardens: Travels through India and China in Search of Tea*. New York, 1993.

Macfarlane, Alan. *The Savage Wars of Peace: England, Japan and the Malthusian Trap*. Oxford, 1997. See chapter 8.

Marks, V. "Physiological and Clinical Effects of Tea." In *Tea: Cultivation and Consumption*, edited by K. C. Willson and M. N. Clifford. London, 1992.

Okakura, Kakuzo. *The Book of Tea*. Tokyo, 1991.

Stagg, Geoffrey V., and Millin, David J. "The Nutritional and Therapeutic Value of Tea: A Review." *Journal of Science, Food and Agriculture* 26 (1975).

Ukers, William H. *All About Tea*. New York, 1935.

ALAN MACFARLANE

TEACHING PROFESSION. It is widely accepted that there exists a direct relationship between the quality of the teaching force and the quality of schools. A common assumption is that improved payment can help recruit and retain better teachers, thereby leading to improvement in the quality of schools. How did teacher compensation and salary develop over time, and what might be the impact of these developments on the quality of teachers and teaching? The literature presents conflicting views concerning this question. Thus, Figlio (1997), on the one hand, finds a significant positive relationship between teacher salaries and quality measured by undergraduate college selectivity and subject matter expertise. On the other hand, Ballou and Podgursky (1995) show that across the board raises in teacher salaries produce only modest improvement in attracting more able teachers. Such raises tend to encourage teachers to stay longer in their position and lowers the probability of hiring new teachers with high ability.

Southwick and Gill (1997) argue that the use of a unified salary for secondary school teachers whose pay is based solely on the years of schooling and teaching experience results in adverse selection in the market for teachers. We start with a comparison of public expenditure on education and salaries of teachers in several countries in different geographical areas.

Table 1 shows great gaps in expenditure in percentage of gross domestic product (GDP) and in teacher salaries between different countries. High state expenditure on education as a percentage of GDP does not necessarily correlate with high teacher salaries, as can be seen in the table.

TABLE 1. *Teacher Salaries: An International Comparison*

STATE	TOTAL EDUCATION SPENDING AS A PERCENTAGE OF GDP, 1997[1]	AVERAGE TEACHER SALARY * IN ELEMENTARY SCHOOLS IN PPPs, 1999[2]	AVERAGE SALARY IN THE NATIONAL ECONOMY[3]	RATIO OF AVERAGE TEACHER SALARY TO AVERAGE SALARY IN THE NATIONAL ECONOMY (%)
Canada	6.9	31,168	25,348	123
Finland	6.4	24,799	27,119	91
France	6.6	26,599	21,588	123
Israel	9.1	13,792	18,439	74
South Korea	7.4	39,411	16,476	239
Spain	6.2	28,614	15,498	184
Sweden	8.5	24,364	27,828	87
United States	7.2	34,705	36,072	96

GDP = gross domestic product

PPPs = purchasing power parity

* Salaries are calculated in American dollars.

[1] State of Israel, Central Bureau of Statistics. *The National Education Spending in 1997–1999*. Tel-Aviv, 2001, table 4.

[2] SOURCES: Israeli Federation of Teachers. *Your Rights.* 2000. (The salary table, in Israeli new Shekels, is updated to 1 January 1999.)

Organization for Economic Cooperation and Development. *Education at a Glance: OECD Indicators 2001.* Paris, 2001, table D1.

[3] Data were taken from each state's statistical report and are not calculated in PPPs. In Canada, a weighted average of men's and women's salaries was calculated, according to their percent of the labor force (ages fifteen to sixty-four).

TABLE 2. *Estimated Average Salaries of Teachers and Selected Other College Graduates (U.S.)*

	1962	1970	1980	1990	1994
Teacher	$5,512	$8,635	$16,100	$31,347	$35,764
Accountant	7,416	10,686	21,299	35,489	39,815
Attorney	11,844	16,884	33,034	59,087	71,328
Computer systems analyst	NA	NA	NA	47,958	55,998
Engineer	10,248	14,695	28,486	49,365	56,191
Assistant professor, public university (1964)	7,700	10,800	17,800	32,730	37,220
RATIO OF OTHER OCCUPATIONS TO TEACHERS					
Accountant	1.34	1.24	1.32	1.13	1.11
Attorney	2.15	1.96	2.05	1.88	1.99
Computer systems analyst	NA	NA	NA	1.53	1.57
Engineer	1.86	1.70	1.77	1.57	1.57
Assistant professor, public university (1966)	1.28	1.25	1.11	1.04	1.04

NA = not available
SOURCE: Based on data from Nelson, F. H., and K. Schneider. *Survey and Analysis of Salary Trends, 1995.* Washington, D.C., 1995. Appears in: Odden, A., and C. Kelley. *Paying Teachers for What They Know and Do.* Thousand Oaks, Calif., 1996, p. 8.

Sometimes the percentage of overall expenditure assigned to teachers' salaries is relatively small. For example, in Israel, only 56 percent of the education budget goes to teacher salaries. The impact of salaries on recruitment and retention will be discussed further on. An important point concerns the ratio between teacher salaries and the mean income in the economy. This ratio has bearing on the professional status of teachers and the attractiveness of the occupation. From this point of view, South Korea represents the highest and Israel the lowest status of teaching.

Table 2 shows estimated average salaries of teachers and selected other college graduates. This table, taken from Odden and Kelly (1996), shows that teachers are generally paid less than many other workers with similar levels of education and training.

What meaning can be ascribed to these differences? How do they arise? What is the significance of salaries and compensation schemes in teachers' work and the status of teachers? How do cultural and local differences express themselves in teacher compensation? These are some of the questions and issues dealt with in this article.

Compensation for Teachers' Work. In the 1800s, before salary schedules were adopted, a major portion of teacher compensation in the United States consisted of free board provided in the homes of students' parents. In those times, teaching was not considered a career, and in most areas married women were prohibited from teaching. As the organization of schools changed and the number of graded schools grew, teacher education demands increased and licensing procedures were adopted. The boarding system of compensating teachers was gradually replaced in the early 1900s by a grade or position-based salary schedule. The gradual decline in the number of one-room schoolhouses and the expansion of graded schools, with students placed into classrooms by age and ability, brought about a minimum salary level with a graded compensation schedule. Teachers were paid based on their years of experience, gender, race, and the grade level that they taught. School administrators could introduce a subjective measure of merit into teachers' salaries. In 1897, the Chicago Teachers Federation was formed to raise "the standard of the teaching profession for securing for teachers conditions essential to the best professional service" (Tyack, 1974, p. 260).

As a result of the efforts of this and other associations of teachers, a single salary schedule for teachers was introduced. All classroom teachers were paid on the same scale, regardless of gender, race, grade level taught, or family status of the teacher. Pay level was determined by a teacher's years of experience and level of academic preparation. By 1950, 97 percent of all schools in the United States had adopted the single salary schedule. Guided by the slogan "Equal pay for equal work," which was demanded by an assertive female workforce, "the single salary schedule addressed two important teacher needs: equity and objectivity" (Odden and Kelly, 1996, p. 30). Despite these advantages, the single salary scheme had its critics. Single salary pay does not provide incentives for teachers to improve their skills, and it does not take into consideration differences in competency and performance. As far back as 1867, the superintendent of the Adams County, Pennsylvania, schools, Aaron Sheely, argued that paying all teachers the same salary "offers a premium to mediocrity if not to positive ignorance and incompetency. Inducements should always be held out to teachers to duly qualify themselves for their work" (English, 1992, p. 6). The National Commission on Excellence in education report, titled *A Nation at Risk* (1983), recommended that teachers salaries be "professionally competitive, market sensitive and performance-based" (p. 30).

In the 1980s, performance-based compensation schemes, such as merit pay and career ladders, were started. According to Odden and Kelly (1996), a variety of merit pay programs have been tried across the United States with limited success. Studies of such programs have identified some inherent weaknesses (see, e.g., Murnane and Cohen, 1986).

Although merit pay is intended to reward excellence in teaching, it is difficult to define "excellent" or "best." Another compensation plan, career ladders, were an attempt to overcome the flat career structure of teaching and to introduce categories of promotion, such as apprentice, professional or master teacher, based on peer and supervisor performance evaluations. Teachers are paid according to their position on the rungs of the ladder. Jacobson (1995), who investigated modes of monetary incentives for teachers' work, came to the conclusion that "while it is not clear whether monetary incentives affect the quality of teacher performance, taken together, the studies do indicate that monetary incentives have a significant influence on the way teachers behave in the educational labor market" (p. 32).

Deferred salary leave plans allow teachers to voluntarily defer part of their salary for several years to fund a year's leave of absence. More time rather than more money seems to be what some teachers want. Israel is the only country in which a sabbatical every seventh year, with up to two-thirds of salary, is part of the general compensation scheme for all teachers.

Teacher Salaries and Compensation Schemes in Geographical and Cultural Contexts. Despite differences between countries and regions, total public educational expenditure in the past two decades has been phenomenal. It increased by 75 percent as a ratio of national income in developing countries, and by about 50 percent in developed countries. In all educational systems, public educational expenditure is dominated by personnel costs, especially teacher salaries. This fact makes teacher compensation the dominant factor to be considered in planning educational endeavors and reforms. Because of the salary increases in the pay structure of teachers associated with seniority, there is a built-in tendency for teacher costs to rise over time. This is true for developed as well as developing countries. Still, the price of teachers relative to the average worker's productivity has fallen in many low-income countries, especially in sub-Saharan Africa. In Egypt, teachers are among the lowest status group in the professional hierarchy, and, despite an increase in 1993–1994 teachers' salaries, are failing to keep up with the increasing cost of living. According to a report by the Organisation for Economic Cooperation and Development (2001), there are various ways of managing teacher development. In the words of this report, "each education system is a working system, which to a greater or lesser degree has satisfied the requirements of its society" (p. 13).

Trade-offs are made between the level of teacher salaries, the size of classes, and the number of teaching hours required of teachers. For example, in Chile, the Philippines, and Thailand, comparatively high salaries for primary teachers are compensated by a high number of teaching hours or large classes. In Indonesia, low salaries and a high teaching load are partially compensated by smaller classes. There are exceptions, like Uruguay, with small primary classes, a low teaching load, and high salaries.

It is especially difficult to recruit and retain teachers in rural areas, and many education systems have developed rural incentives, such as wage premiums, subsidized housing, and special in-service training. McEwan (1999) analyzed rural teacher recruitment based on the economic theory of compensating "wage differentials." The assumption is that teachers value both pecuniary and nonpecuniary aspects of their work and are willing to trade off one against the other to achieve higher levels of job satisfaction.

Argentina, for example, offers rural teachers up to 80 percent bonus on their base salary. Egypt seniority requirements are reduced by two to four years, and teachers get longer vacations, as well as travel allowances. Colombia offers rural teachers special training, and Mexico has reduced rent housing or special housing for rural teachers. Iraq maintains free housing for its rural teachers.

Tsang (2000) summed up the economic analysis of teacher supply in the following way: "[T]eachers are a key ingredient of educational production and an adequate supply of skilled teachers is a prominent policy concern in many countries. The economic factors affecting teacher supply are teachers' salaries and working conditions relative to those in other occupations, and the costs of teacher preparation relative to those for other occupations" (p. 140).

Private and Public Teaching Contexts: An International Comparison. There exists great diversity across societies concerning the division of the responsibility for education between the private and the public sector. James

TEACHER. Classroom in Chuka Boys Secondary School, Chuka, Kenya, 1992. (© Betty Press/ Woodfin Camp and Associates, New York)

(1987) suggested a theoretical model, which explains those differences on the basis of excessive and heterogeneous demand due to religious and linguistic differences, and by the supply of nonprofit entrepreneurship in society. According to James, excess demand is more likely to be the cause for a private sector in developing countries, and differentiated demand the source for a private sector in industrial societies. Teacher salaries in private and public sectors vary. Merit pay is used in a large number of private schools, where the percentage of teachers with merit pay rose from 20.9 percent in 1987 to 38.1 percent in 1993. During that time, the percentage of teachers with merit pay in public schools rose from 13.6 to 14.7 percent. There are also differences in the way schools link compensation to performance. In public school, this happens often as a one-time cash bonus, whereas private schools are more likely to build the increase into teachers' base salary.

The Role of Unions in Teacher Compensation. Teachers' unions are a common feature of the labor market in developed countries. Their major role is collective bargaining for their members, concerning salaries and the structure of teachers' work, such as the weekly number of teaching hours. In the United States, unionized teachers have higher salaries and more influence on instructional policies than non-unionized teachers. Zwerling and Thomason (1995) estimated that a 10 percent increase in the state density of teachers' unions increases the highest teacher salaries by 2.6 percent and the lowest by 0.2 per-

cent. There is a strong inverse relationship between the use of merit pay and the degree of union influence. Ballou (2001) concluded that the incidence of merit pay plans, their size and survival, are greater the less influence teachers' unions have. Peltzman (1996) claimed that growing teacher unionization and a shift of responsibility to state governments from 1971 to 1991 adversely affected the performance of college-bound public school students, those who did not go to college, those in the lower ranks of achievement, and black students. Despite these cautionary voices, it is important to note the positive impact of unionization on equity issues.

Equity Issues. The profession of teaching over the years has seen some progress, from arbitrating discriminatory practices of teacher compensation to establishing a more equitable state of remuneration. Over time, teaching in many countries has been transformed from being largely men's work to women's work. Data from England, for example, show clearly the feminization of teaching. In 1870, men outnumbered women slightly; by 1910, women outnumbered men by over three to one, and by 1930, four to one (Bergen, 1982). Similar patterns can be shown for the United States. In both countries, there existed a significant salary difference, with women earning about half to two-thirds of the salary for male teachers. Apple (1986), in a chapter titled "Teaching and Women's Work," analyzed the historical context of the control of teaching and curricula in the light of its relationship to gender and class divisions.

He argued that elementary school teaching became "women's work" because men left the occupation: "For many men the opportunity cost was too great to stay in teaching" (p. 62).

Men who stay in education are to be found in higher status and higher paying positions. Because teaching, especially in elementary schools, is generally not well paid, women teachers in the past did not stay passive and started unified action to improve their economic well-being, leading to salary increases and finally to equal pay for male and female teachers.

Fultz (1995) studied the salary discrimination of African American teachers in the South between 1890 and 1940 and found that meager salaries for black teachers were one of the most pervasive aspects of the African-American educational experience during that period. In the 1940s, the legal campaign of the National Association for the Advancement of Colored People forced southern school boards in the United States to abolish separate and unequal salary schedules for black and white teachers.

The Role of Pay as a Motivator in Teaching. Adequate pay is critical in attracting and retaining qualified teachers, but a complex set of factors is influencing motivation to become and stay a teacher. Odden and Kelly (1996) argued that salaries and compensations are important. Low relative salaries are associated with a decline in the quality of people attracted to teaching and loss of teachers to other occupations. Higher relative salaries have the opposite effect. These findings have policy implications for the retention of teachers. New ideas for teacher compensation have to be tried. "New compensation components should not be viewed as motivators by themselves, but rather as part of an overall set of education system strategies designed as a whole to advance teacher expertise and to educate students to high standards. The new pay structures—competitive salary levels, competency-based pay, and group performance awards—reinforce the larger systemic bundle of overall goals and motivational strategies" (Odden and Kelly, 1996, p. 75).

A Look Forward. Teacher compensation constitutes the largest portion of education budgets; therefore, it is of utmost importance to find effective and appropriate ways of paying teachers. The process of changing teacher compensation has to be viewed in the context of enhancing the profession as a whole. According to Odden and Kelly (1996), three aspects of teacher professionalization are relevant to a discussion of teacher compensation:

- A new concept of teaching as a highly complex and multifaceted activity aiming at high achievement for all students
- Creation of detailed records of practice that can be used to describe and assess practice relevant to external criteria

- Development of assessment modes for beginning and expert teachers that indicate their level of teaching relative to carefully selected external criteria

New strategies of teacher compensation that match these effects to professionalism in teaching will have to be devised and implemented.

BIBLIOGRAPHY

Apple, M. W. *Teachers and Texts.* New York and London, 1986.
Ballou, D. "Pay for Performance in Public and Private Schools." *Economics of Education Review* 20 (1986), 51–61.
Ballou, D. and M. Podgursky. "Recruiting Smarter Teachers." *Journal of Human Resources* 30.2 (1995), 326–338.
Bergen, B. "Only a Schoolmaster: Gender, Class and the Effort to Professionalize Elementary Teaching in England, 1870–1910." *History of Education Quarterly* 22.1 (1982), 1–21.
English, F. "History and Critical Issues of Educational Compensation Systems." In *Teacher Compensation and Motivation*, edited by L. Frase, pp. 3–25. Lancaster, Pa., 1992.
Figlio, D. N. "Teacher Salaries and Teacher Quality." *Economics Letters* 55.2 (1997), 267–271.
Fultz, M. "African-American Teachers in the South, 1890–1940: Growth, Feminization and Salary Discrimination." *Teachers College Record* 96.3 (1995), 544–568.
Guthrie, J. W. "School Finance: Fifty Years of Expansion." *Future of Children* 7.3 (1997), 24–38.
Jacobson, S. L. "Monetary Incentives and the Reform of Teacher Compensation: A Persistent Organizational Dilemma." *International Journal of Educational Reform* 4.1 (1995), 29–39.
Jacobson, S., and S. Kennedy. "Deferred Salary Leaves for Teachers." *Canadian Administrator* 31.3 (1991), 1–11.
James. E. "The Public/Private Division of Responsibility for Education: An International Comparison." *Economics of Educational Review* 6.1 (1987), 1–14.
McEwan, P. J. "Recruitment of Rural Teachers in Developing Countries: An Economic Analysis." *Teaching and Teacher Education* 15 (1999), 849–859.
Murnane, R. I, and D. K. Cohen. "Merit Pay and the Evaluation Problem: Why Most Merit Pay Plans Fail and Few Survive." *Harvard Educational Review* 56 (1986), 1–11.
National Commission on Excellence in Education. *A Nation at Risk: The Imperative for Education Reform.* Washington, D.C., 1983.
Odden, A., and C. Kelly. *Paying Teachers for What They Know and Do.* Thousand Oaks, Calif., 1996.
Organisation for Economic Cooperation and Development. UNESCO Institute for Statistics, World Education Indicators Program. *Teachers for Tomorrow's Schools: Analysis of the World Education Indicators, Executive Summary.* Paris, 2001.
Peltzman, S. "Political Economy of Public Education: Noncollege-bound Students." *Journal of Law and Economics* 39.1 (1996), 73–120.
Protsik, J. *History of Teacher Pay and Incentive Reforms.* Paper presented at the Conference on Teachers Compensation Consortium for Policy Research in Education, Washington, D.C., 2–4 November 1994.
Schultz, P. T. *Accounting for Public Expenditures on Education: An International Panel Study* (Yale Economic Growth Center Discussion Paper 742). New Haven, 1995.
Sharpes, D. K. "Incentive Pay and the Promotion of Teaching Proficiencies." *The Clearing House* 60 (1987), 406–408.
Southwick, L., and I. S. Gill. "Unified Salary Schedule and Student SAT Scores: Adverse Effects of Adverse Selection in the Market for

Secondary School Teachers." *Economics of Education Review* 16.2 (1997), 143–153.

Tsang, M. C. "Cost Analysis for Educational Policy Making: A Review of Cost Studies in Education in Developing Countries." *Review of Educational Research* 58.2 (1988), 181–230.

Tsang, M. C. "The Economics of Resourcing of Education." In *The Routledge International Companion to Education*, edited by B. Moon, S. Brown, and M. Ben-Peretz, pp. 128–152. London and New York, 2000.

Tyack, D. B. *The One Best System: A History of American Urban Education*. Cambridge, Mass., 1974.

Zwerling, H L., and T. Thomason. "Collective Bargaining and the Determinants of Teachers' Salaries." *Journal of Labor Research* 16.4 (1995), 467–484.

MIRIAM BEN-PERETZ

TECHNOLOGY. Of all the many contributions of social sciences to the study of technology, economic history can reasonably claim to have made one of the greatest. This exceptional achievement has, rather surprisingly, been little observed by economic historians themselves but is evident from perusing the bibliographies of standard textbooks in "innovation studies" (e.g., Freeman and Soete, 1997). Such a contribution to understanding goes far beyond that of, say, economists, who in principle draw a sharp dividing line between phenomena they treat as endogenous and those they consider exogenous, with technology lying predominantly in the latter category.

Technology should be regarded as more than the aggregate of manufactured products and the processes that produce them. These artifacts, which are what are often popularly categorized as technology, in practice depend upon broad and deep knowledge bases for their conception and production. Such knowledge bases may be codified into symbols that can be readily circulated, such as printed manuals or lines of software code, but very often are tacit and unexpressed—possibly inexpressible—in any depicted form. Knowledge of this kind cannot be reduced to information, such as often found in economists' treatments of technology; such knowledge has to be learned, through learning processes that remain only partially understood. A common if mundane example is learning the process of riding a bicycle—no amount of printed instruction on how to ride will enable most people to hop on a bicycle for the first time and confidently pedal off. Such knowledge is instead accumulated, often only after long periods of trial and error, and often involving a succession of willing but ultimately unsuccessful pioneers. This represents the *-ology* part of the word *technology*. Economic history provides countless examples of the painful process of gestation of major new technologies in this fashion.

By analogy, technical change is sometimes contrasted with technological change, as reflecting a change in practice without any change in the underlying knowledge base.

For example, a firm may adopt a technique that is new to the firm but not new to the country in which it is located. Generally, however, such distinctions are glossed over.

The above distinctions between endogeneity and exogeneity and between knowledge and information help distinguish the contributions of economic historians from economists, even though the boundary is frequently blurred in practice. On the other side is another blurred boundary, between economic historians and historians of technology. The latter tend to accentuate invention processes, while the former generally pay more attention to innovation, commercialization, and diffusion of technologies. The obvious reason for this distinction is that economic historians tend to be interested primarily in the economic impact of technological change, especially the impact on economic growth. Historians of technology tend to put more emphasis on intellectual advance and heroic pioneering.

Differing perspectives converge to a degree in the recent contributions of the so-called evolutionary economics school, drawing on earlier works of nonorthodox economics thinking, and especially the work of Joseph Schumpeter. A separate tradition in economic history also hinted at the case for considering technological evolution alongside social evolution (Usher, 1954). To keep the discussion within bounds, this entry focuses almost exclusively on the contributions of economic historians.

Evolution of Technology. Technology generally is considered to be a phenomenon of the modern world. To many people, technology consists of artifacts that have changed within their lifetimes, probably because encountering these involves individuals in a process of relearning. However, ancient and medieval historians have shown that technological change has a long history of impact on societies. All artifacts within our compass have at some stage involved some relearning, and it is easy to underestimate the impact of a plethora of advances such as the horse collar, which in medieval times allowed a horse team to pull much heavier weights than the yoke that it replaced (Mokyr, 1990a; White, 1962). As the work of scholars such as Usher has showed, technological change is coterminous with human history, even though its pace may have accelerated in the last quarter-millennium.

Historians have nevertheless been anxious to promote the view that technological change has clustered in certain periods, which they refer to as industrial revolutions. The first and most celebrated of these revolutions originated in Britain in the second half of the eighteenth century. (This has not prevented a minority of historians from arguing that a technological revolution surrounded the adoption of the water wheel in medieval times, even if its initial impact arose primarily in the processing of agricultural products, especially grain milling.) According to some scholars, the first Industrial Revolution was unusual not just because the changes of this period affected a wider band of industrial activities, since even at this time the initial effects were mostly confined to a narrow list of sectors (especially textiles), sometimes referred to as "leading sectors" (Rostow, 1960). In this view, what distinguished the first Industrial Revolution was that technological change became cumulative. Whereas previous breakthroughs like the undershot water wheel comprised a big step forward followed by a long period over which they were absorbed into regular productive activity, the breakthroughs of the Industrial Revolution of the late eighteenth century led to a succession of further advances, which in turn triggered still further advances. The countless number of innovations were not necessarily of individual importance on the scale of the water wheel, but their cumulative impact was, in the end, of dramatic significance. As the philosopher A. N. Whitehead expressed it, industrialization brought with it the "invention of the method of invention." Earlier changes involved a period of disequilibrium followed by a return to some kind of equilibrium as the technological change was absorbed, but now there was no return to equilibrium—instead, a systemic change took hold in which entrepreneurs had to suppose that any improvement they adopted might soon be eclipsed by another superior one.

Related to this is a commonly drawn contrast between radical technological change and incremental technological change. Historians have been drawn to the eye-catching "radical" changes like the invention of the steam engine or the computer, but more careful analysis has stressed that the longer-term buildup of "anonymous" or "incremental" changes may have just as large a cumulative effect (Landes, 1969). In any event, it is not usually appropriate to imply that these are alternatives—they interact sequentially, as argued below.

In regard to the pattern of technological evolution that followed the first Industrial Revolution, one view familiar to economic historians maintains that there were a small number of further leaps forward, which can also be referred to as industrial revolutions. Specifically, there was a second Industrial Revolution in the second half of the nineteenth century, beginning with the adoption of new processes for making steel, and moving on to innovations in such fields as chemicals, electricity, and transportation. In a similar vein, a third Industrial Revolution may have been taking place in the second half of the twentieth century, built around information and communications technologies, biotechnology, advanced materials, and the like.

One particular perspective on the notion of great leaps forward is to envisage them as part of a process described by some evolutionary biologists as "punctuated equilibria" (Mokyr, 1990b), periods of turmoil followed by a gradual settling down into existence in conditions brought about by the new technological paradigms. There are two potential problems with this view, both of which can probably be accommodated. One is that there may never be any return to equilibrium after the "punctuation," as already implied. The second is that the changes may not appear revolutionary at first—often, they occur in traditional lines of activity in a more evolutionary way, as if incremental, and only slowly take on properly revolutionary characteristics permeating industry and society at large.

An alternative view, influenced rather than advanced by economic historians, contends that major technological changes arise more frequently than implied by the industrial revolution approach. Noteworthy here is the "long-wave" school (Freeman and Louçã, 2001), which makes use of the concept of long waves of forty to sixty years' duration. In this perspective, the various technological advances that comprise the aforementioned industrial revolutions are unpicked and clustered at approximately half-century rather than full-century intervals. This arguably provides a more consistent way of describing the technological changes themselves, viewed from an engineering standpoint. However, the approach also has two potential drawbacks. The first is that the chronology is perhaps too irregular to be summarized into half-century cycles; the second is that the wider interactions with economic and social change are less pervasive than they are under the "industrial revolutions" perspective. A compromise is to argue that the units of analysis differ—the long-wave view is especially (although not exclusively) focused on the technological patterns, while the industrial revolutions view focuses on industrial patterns more broadly.

A popular thesis in the literature on management of innovation is that innovation pursues a life cycle. In particular, the "product life cycle" hypothesis contends that a new product begins by being produced by a rapidly proliferating number of producers in a profusion of models (Utterback and Abernathy, 1975). Over time, the product standardizes and one or more dominant designs emerge, like the Boeing 707 design for jet aircraft. From the industrial revolutions perspective, the seemingly consistent factor over time is the early emergence of major innovations in process rather than product. The initial phases of industrial revolutions tend to be characterized by major new processes to produce existing goods. Thus, the first Industrial Revolution brought steam power and machinery as process innovations to bear upon already widely purchased products, such as clothing. The second Industrial Revolution brought new processes such as chemical and electricity production, and the third brought processes to enable the development of information and communications technologies and biotechnology. The changes in products, such as the appearance of the automobile, came at a later stage in the progress of these industrial revolutions. Thus, in a longer-term historical context and with a different focus, the pattern appears predominantly one of proceeding from process to product innovation, in direct opposition to the product life cycle hypothesis.

In historical practice, technologies do not follow a life cycle in the way that products are supposed to; instead, technologies are accumulated. The appearance of a new technology does not necessarily drive out an old one. Chemical means of producing textiles (artificial fibers) supplement rather than replace mechanical means (for natural fibers). Particular products often incorporate the new technologies by adding them to the means of production, rather than by simply replacing them. Over time, products come to incorporate a greater range of technologies, even though consumers may not be much aware of this fact. Modern food processing, the result of evolution from a very old industry, involves technological innovations from such fields as pharmaceuticals, biotechnology, smart materials (for packaging), computing, advanced instrumentation, and machinery. Industries, including those often regarded as low tech, thus augment their range of production technologies. Products in this sense become more complex, even though their outward appearance may not look radically different. The contrary notion of creative destruction, as argued by Schumpeter to describe the evolution of markets, applies more at the level of products than of technologies—undoubtedly consumers face a choice between clothing made from natural fibers and that from synthetic fibers. Technologies are, on the other hand, often better described as following paths of creative accumulation rather than creative destruction.

Sources of Technology. According to what is often called the linear model of technology, technology originates in scientific discoveries, which become embodied in technical inventions, then become commercialized and widely diffused, resulting finally in promoting economic growth. This chain reaction is thought of as quasi-automatic in the linear model and has been a powerful stimulant over many decades for government intervention to boost scientific research.

The inherent plausibility of at least some kind of chain reaction has attracted economic historians to espouse similar views. Each of the major industrial revolutions has appeared to be preceded by or associated with breakthroughs in basic science. In the case of the first Industrial Revolution, it has been widely observed that a "scientific revolution" had occurred a century earlier. Although there were many other forerunners of the first Industrial Revolution (in agriculture, trade and commerce, property rights, and finance), many historians have been inspired to connect the first Industrial Revolution causally to the seventeenth-century scientific revolution. The problem is

to pin down what the causal relationship actually was, if any. The direct relationships in terms of fields of scientific inquiry as opposed to technological endeavor do not suggest many overlaps, although some authors claim to find them (e.g., Jacob, 1997). Nor was Britain particularly conspicuous as a leader in science. The most convincing arguments for a causal connection are twofold. One is that there was an artifactual link through scientific instruments, which could be adopted in industry or at least could provide the inspiration and practical framework for industrial instrumentation. A second and probably more powerful link was through changes in modes of thought: the seventeenth-century scientific revolution implied a shift toward investigation through experimentation, and this inspired some eighteenth-century engineers to conduct technological experiments of their own, albeit in different fields.

Science was more definitively involved in the second Industrial Revolution, though even by the late nineteenth century it might be said that science was responding to technological advance as much as technology was responding to scientific advance. Breakthroughs such as that by Bessemer in steel were published in scientific journals but were largely the result of practical tinkering. Even closer interactions between science and technology, for instance in recent biotechnology, may be witnessed in the so-called third industrial revolution, yet even now the causal interlinkages between science and technology are complex and probably mutual. The linear model is not as dead as some have pronounced it to be, but it remains far from being an adequate explanation of technological change by itself.

The obvious alternative explanation advanced in innovation studies is "demand-pull," as opposed to "science-push," as encapsulated in the well-known aphorism "Necessity is the mother of invention." Empirical studies in the 1960s and early 1970s appeared to confirm the view that innovations were overwhelmingly market-led. At the same time, Schmookler (1966) provided evidence from economic history of the powerful role of demand-pull, by showing how fluctuations in patents in some key American industries of the late nineteenth and early twentieth centuries followed rather than preceded fluctuations in demand (measured by investment, output, etc.). This appeared to be valid in the short term as well as over longer waves.

Schmookler's own evidence and arguments, however, also indicated some role for science-push. Moreover, the nature of demand-pull was left unexplained in much of this work, if we leave Schmookler's more analytical work aside. It was difficult to relate observed changes in technology to economists' notions of shifts in the demand curve. However, it is conceivable that a more dynamic notion of demand-pull than can be derived from economic theory

WINDMILL. Drawing by Théodore Rousseau (1812–1867), France. (Prints and Photographs Division, Library of Congress)

might restore some role for demand in accounting for industrialization. In the innovation studies literature today, the most popular thesis is probably the "coupling" model—science-push and demand-pull both play a part, but there can be long and varying lags between scientific breakthroughs and industrial innovation, whereas demand operates more immediately.

Institutional incentives to generate innovation have attracted much attention from economic historians as well as practical policymakers. Patents help to measure technological change, as in Schmookler's work, but are more importantly seen as stimuli to foster such change. Studies for both the United Kingdom and United States indicate a rising "invention industry" in the nineteenth century, spurred by the prospects of the licensing of patents. In the twentieth century, the role of the individual inventor was largely usurped by large corporations, which have established legal departments to handle repeated patenting. Innovation has grown most rapidly within these large companies because of the importance of tacit knowledge and of knowledge specificity.

Directions of Technology. A popular argument that historians have been eager to embellish is that technological change can be regarded as being induced by biases in particular directions, especially toward labor saving. It is important to be careful about defining what a labor-saving (or other) bias comprises. Various plausible definitions have been offered, but they essentially emphasize that it is relative rather than absolute labor-saving that matters. The great majority of innovations save at least some labor relative to the value of output; that is, they raise labor productivity, but not necessarily through saving more labor than through other factors. In a relative sense, an innovation that saves some labor but more capital (such as land) is relatively labor-using, not labor-saving.

Within this definition, there remains a widespread feeling that the U.S. economy of the nineteenth and twentieth centuries saved labor, to a greater extent than, say, the U.K. economy, for the reason that labor was scarce and/or costly in the United States. The intellectual base of this supposition was explored by Habakkuk (1962), and it continues to be referred to as the Habakkuk hypothesis. In actuality, Habakkuk was very guarded about making any assertions, and his work is ultimately inconclusive. In truth, it is extremely difficult to make a logical theoretical argument for the seemingly self-evident proposition that scarce and/or expensive labor should induce a labor-saving bias in technology. The propositions that continue to draw most respect, perhaps, are two: one that complementarities between greater capital and land availability encouraged greater labor-saving in the United States; and second, that there were greater technological opportunities at the labor-saving end of the technological spectrum, as mechanization progressed (the latter probably was Habakkuk's overall verdict).

Even in Britain, however, anxieties about scarcities of particular kinds of labor could act as what Rosenberg

(1976) called a focusing device for technological change. The best-attested case during the first Industrial Revolution was the invention of the self-acting mule for cotton spinning, where the inventor, Richard Roberts, was funded by Lancashire cotton manufacturers to break the power of the expensive and scarce mule spinners.

A somewhat overlapping literature considers the American system of manufactures that developed during the nineteenth and early twentieth centuries (Hounshell, 1984; Rosenberg, 1969). From the early years of the nineteenth century, some branches of U.S. manufacturing established principles of interchangeable parts and standardization, e.g., in guns, clocks, and sewing machines. These developments came to fruition in mass production and the assembly line. One consequence was doing away with specialist skilled labor to design and incorporate different components into a product: as Henry Ford expressed it, on the assembly line there were no "fitters." However the product could then be designed in only a limited number of ways, so once the product was standardized (as per the product life cycle view), it was open to challenge from superior designs.

Others have seen the advantage of standardization and mass production less in terms of labor-saving and more in terms of savings in time (Henry Ford also stressed this point). The business historian Alfred Chandler (1977) has underlined the economies of speed obtainable from such methods. These time-saving aspects of technical change allow a different means for bringing back demand factors into accounting for technological change—instead of the impact of demand on product quality, this emphasis is on impact on process quality (von Tunzelmann, 1995).

While for the United States in the nineteenth century there seems to be a plausible case that both labor and capital were scarce relative to vast empty lands—as reflected in the massive inflows of both labor and capital from the Old World in the second half of the century—in other countries, different scarcities acted as focusing devices for technological change. In Germany, shortages of natural resources are thought to have promulgated a search for synthetic resources (e.g., synthetic rubber) and helped underpin the expansion of the German chemical industry. In Japan, severe shortages of land gave a land-saving impetus to changes in agriculture. A high man-to-land ratio in Japan led to an emphasis on biological innovations such as fertilizers, which raised land productivity; whereas in the United States over the same period, a low man-to-land ratio placed the emphasis on labor-saving mechanical innovations such as the combine harvester and the tractor (Hayami and Ruttan, 1971).

Technology Diffusion. An orientation to the most pressing economic needs would be expected to facilitate the more rapid diffusion of an invention. Diffusion processes have, however, been studied largely independently of innovation processes, and by a whole range of social scientists often independently of one another (for a good synthesis, see Rogers, 1995). The most common approach is to take an innovation, usually a product innovation, as an accepted fact and then graph its uptake.

Two patterns dominate the literature. One is the exponential model, which describes a rapid early surge that steadily tapers off. Such models are most often encountered in the marketing literature and tend to be associated with minor changes in product. The other, and more frequent case in economic history, is the S-shaped path, which can be produced by a range of mathematical functions, of which the logistic curve is the most commonly estimated because of its ease of computation. With the S-shaped curve, an innovation is slow to take off at first, but once it passes a barrier at say 5 to 10 percent of final impact, diffusion speeds up as adopters jump on the bandwagon. For a logistic curve, the maximum rate of diffusion is attained at 50 percent of the final ceiling level. Then those who will eventually adopt but have not yet done so will begin to be outnumbered by those who have already adopted, so the diffusion rate slows down, and in due course asymptotically approaches the final ceiling.

Although many curves of this kind have been successfully fitted, considerable doubts have been raised about whether this adequately describes typical diffusion processes. The model is often described as being of an "epidemic" kind, in which the "contamination" consists of the new technology attacking an initially expanding and then contracting number of possible victims. The usual presumption is that adopters are initially ignorant and await the spread of information telling them of the virtues of the new technique. This, however, leaves the knowledge accumulation aspect out of the account. A number of models therefore try to incorporate more plausible learning mechanisms. This leads to the view now widely accepted among innovation studies experts that innovation and diffusion are not readily separable into distinct phases but in practice tend to be interlinked through multiple feedbacks.

A further implication of this view is to modify earlier findings that profitability is the main driving force behind diffusion processes. The evolutionary school holds that although profitability may be closely correlated with diffusion processes, it is not necessarily exogenous to them, rather, the profitability is itself generated by the induced effects on both the supply side (newer forms of the technology, new capital and skill resources, etc.) and the demand side.

Other economic historians have successfully developed models to explain the evolution of demand. David (1975) used the threshold model to contend that different potential adopters may be in different situations regarding the profitability they would individually derive from adoption. David pointed to the adoption of mechanical reaping in agriculture in the American Midwest, where farms had to be large to warrant paying the capital cost of purchasing a mechanical rather than a hand reaper.

Recent work has focused on the spread of new technologies to very different types of users. The usual examples here are radical process technologies, such as the steam engine or the computer. These so-called general purpose technologies (GPTs) provide spillover by being adopted outside their initial niche (the "leading sector") into a broad range of application sectors; for example, the steam engine going from mining to textile manufacturing, other manufacturing, and transportation. As with the chain-linked interaction of innovation and diffusion, however, one should not assume that the extension from one use to the next is going to be costless. Considerable adaptation to the new use (e.g., from the fuel-using to the fuel-saving steam engine in passing from coal mining to manufacturing, from the low-pressure to the high-pressure engine in proceeding from manufacturing to transportation) is often necessary for commercial success.

Similar arguments arrayed across regions and countries rather than across economic sectors have generated an enormous literature on technology transfer. The term is used in two rather different ways—first, to describe commercialization processes of taking technology out of the laboratory and into industry, in line with the linear model, and second, to describe geographic dispersion. Like diffusion processes within a particular region or country, this is often regarded as imitation and the source of spillover externalities. As with the cross-sectoral imitations, the reality is often far from costless. Recent emphasis has been placed on the very different abilities of different countries to benefit from such spillovers, depending on their social capability (Abramovitz, 1986).

Impacts of Technology. Ultimately, the economic purpose of both innovation and imitation in technology is to engender economic growth. Studies by economists using neoclassical production functions hugely boosted the respect for technology through finding that apparently most recorded growth came from this source rather than conventionally measured factor inputs, such as capital. Abramovitz (1956), however, emphasized that the "residual" unexplained by capital accumulation was a collection of many different elements of which technological change was only one—the residual was a "measure of our ignorance."

Growth accounting approaches thus tried to break down the residual, referred to as total factor productivity (TFP), into its components. Although the motivation was justifiable, one should be wary of the results. Many assumptions, some reasonable, others scarcely defensible, were needed to crack open the residual. There is in any case a more general and less widely recognized problem. The contribution of technology may in some respects be larger than its TFP. For instance, in East Asian economies in the 1980s and 1990s, technology and technology policy probably worked as much through recruiting capital and labor into industry as through raising TFP. The neoclassical assumption that technology is exogenous breaks down at this point.

Economists tend to regard divergences between radical technological change and productivity growth as paradoxical, as in by the celebrated "Solow paradox" that the rapid spread of computers from the 1970s coexisted with a productivity slowdown. To an economic historian, this does not appear so paradoxical. None of the three industrial revolutions was a period of especially rapid productivity growth. Following the GPT model, industrialization was a time to sow; the time to reap came late, as the technologies diffused into whole new areas of application. This was true for machinery in the first Industrial Revolution and for electricity in the second.

This illustrates how misleading inferences can be drawn from taking technological change to be exogenous. The literature on innovation at large has benefited extensively from the broader perspectives in which economic historians have drawn together evolution, sources, directions, diffusion, and impacts of technology. Theoretical perspectives remain fluid; an understanding of the relationships between technology and economic growth remains rather primitive. The economic historian will continue to be a key figure in illuminating this crucial topic.

(*See also* Habakkuk Hypothesis; Industrial Revolution; Patents; *and* Social Savings.)

BIBLIOGRAPHY

Abramovitz, M. "Resource and Output Trends in the United States Since 1870." *American Economic Review* 46, (1956), 5–23.

Abramovitz, M. "Catching Up, Forging Ahead, and Falling Behind." *Journal of Economic History*, 46(1986), 385–406.

Chandler, Alfred D. Jr. *The Visible Hand: The Managerial Revolution in American Business*. Cambridge, Mass., 1977.

David, P. *Technical Choice, Innovation and Economic Growth: Essays on American and British Experience in the Nineteenth Century*. New York, 1975.

Freeman, C., and F. Louçã. *As Time Goes By: From the Industrial Revolutions to the Information Revolution*. Oxford, 2001.

Freeman, C., and L. Soete. *The Economics of Industrial Innovation*. 3d ed. London, 1997.

Habakkuk, H. J. *American and British Technology in the Nineteenth Century: The Search for Labour-Saving Inventions*. Cambridge, 1962.

Hayami, Y., and V. W. Ruttan. *Agricultural Development: An International Perspective*. Baltimore, 1971.

Hounshell, D. A. *From the American System to Mass Production, 1800–1932: The Development of Manufacturing Technology in the United States*. Baltimore, 1984.

Jacob, M. *Scientific Culture and the Making of the Industrial West*. Oxford and New York, 1997.

Landes, D. S. *The Unbound Prometheus: Technological Change and Industrial Development in Western Europe from 1750 to the Present.* Cambridge, 1969.

Mokyr, J. *The Lever of Riches: Technological Creativity and Economic Progress.* New York, 1990a.

Mokyr, J. "Punctuated Equilibria and Technological Progress." *American Economic Review, Papers Proceedings* 80 (1990b), 350–354.

Rogers, E. M. *Diffusion of Innovations.* 4th ed. New York, 1995.

Rosenberg, N., ed. *The American System of Manufactures.* Edinburgh, 1969.

Rosenberg, N. *Perspectives on Technology.* Cambridge, 1976.

Rostow, W. W. *The Stages of Economic Growth: A Non-Communist Manifesto.* Cambridge, 1960.

Schmookler, J. *Invention and Economic Growth.* Cambridge, Mass., 1966.

Usher, A. P. *A History of Mechanical Inventions.* Rev. ed. Cambridge, Mass., 1954.

Utterback, J. M., and W. J. Abernathy. "A Dynamic Model of Process and Product Innovation." *Omega* 3 (1975), 639–656.

Von Tunzelmann, G. N. *Technology and Industrial Progress: The Foundations of Economic Growth.* Aldershot, U.K., 1995.

White, L. *Medieval Technology and Social Change.* Oxford, 1962.

NICK VON TUNZELMANN

TELEGRAPH. The search for ways in which time-sensitive information could be communicated faster than the fastest person could run, or the fastest horse could travel, has preoccupied mankind for millennia. Coded signals can and have been sent through all manner of ingenious methods—using sound over short distances and light over longer. Optical systems have exploited smoke signals, mirrors, beacons, and, in systems reaching their apotheosis early in the first half of the nineteenth century, semaphores.

Optical Telegraphy. Claude Chappe's (1763–1805) optical telegraph, first implemented in 1793, consisted of stations located at high points on mountains, specially constructed towers, and church belfries. Each station was manned by two operators with telescopes aimed in opposite directions and topped by an assemblage of three arms connected to each other, along with brass wires, pulleys, and rods to controls below, such that each arm could be rotated freely through a common vertical plane. Each of the arms could appear in any of eight orientations 45 degrees separate. The Chappe semaphore used a basic transmission code of ninety-eight elements, meaning that each signal communicated approximately 6.5 bits ($\log_2 98$) of information.

During the height of the Napoleonic Wars, Chappe telegraphs extended into French-controlled territory in Italy, Germany, and the Low Countries, but it was after the coming of peace in 1815 that the system reached its fullest extension, albeit within national boundaries. At its peak, semaphore lines, most radiating from Paris, extended over 5,000 kilometers (3,100 miles) of French territory. Under good conditions, a message could be sent from Paris to Marseilles in an hour and a half.

The Chappe system was by no means the only optical technology, but it was the most successful. During the Napoleonic Wars, for example, the six-shutter Murray telegraph connected London with Portsmouth, but the system fell into disuse with the coming of peace. In the United States, visual semaphores were common in commercial cities such as San Francisco and New York, where they announced the impending arrival of merchant ships, their location today memorialized in such place names as Telegraph Hill. The Chappe system, however, had proven capability over long distances, a point attested to by the proposal before the U.S. Congress in 1837 to build an optical line along the coast from New York to New Orleans using it. The proposal was vigorously opposed by Samuel F. B. Morse (1791–1872), a professor of painting and sculpture from New York, who had recently patented and was then lobbying Congress to support a different technology.

Optical telegraphs had obvious deficiencies in the areas of both reliability and bandwidth. Transmission using the French system could be and was disrupted by fog, rain, and heat inversion, and was never successfully pursued at night. Optical telegraphy has today been almost completely supplanted, with the exception of specialized application such as naval signaling. Nevertheless, the principle of sending information using relay stations connected by lines of sight persists on land in the network of microwave dishes situated on top of tall hills or towers.

Electromagnetic Telegraphs. The eighteenth century witnessed a variety of experiments employing static electricity to move information across distance. Pith balls corresponding to individual letters could be displaced by static electricity sent over wires, or an electrical current could induce a chemical reaction in liquid, producing gas bubbles. But static electricity is high voltage and low amperage and is subject to severe drop-offs in signal strength, particularly under conditions of atmospheric disturbance.

The electromagnetic telegraph built on early-nineteenth-century scientific and technological advances in the production, storage, and use of electricity. The invention of the battery by Alessandro Volta (1745–1827) in 1800 provided an important foundation for new telegraph technology by offering a reliable source of low-voltage, high-amperage electricity. It now became technically possible to transmit signals less subject to degradation over distances. The Wheatstone telegraph, developed in England, made use of the principle discovered by Hans Christian Ørsted (1777–1851) in 1820 that an electric current could deflect a magnetic needle, while the Morse telegraph used current to drive an electromagnet, a device recently perfected by Michael Farraday (1791–1867) and Joseph Henry (1797–1878).

Morse's magnet originally attracted a needle that made marks on a piece of paper traveling underneath it. He eventually replaced this with a sounder, with the decoding of the sounds into letters done directly by the telegraph operator. In 1843, Morse wrangled $30,000 from the U.S. Congress, built a line from Baltimore to Washington, D.C., and transmitted on 24 May 1844 the famous first message, "What hath God Wrought?"

The development of the telegraph network was extraordinarily rapid after this demonstration, with industry consolidation under the leadership of Western Union. The first transcontinental telegraph line opened in 1861, eight years before the completion of the transcontinental railroads. Although a poorly insulated cable had operated for three months in 1858, the transatlantic connection was not permanently established until 1866. The International Telegraph Union was established in 1865 to facilitate telegraphic communication among nations.

In addition to advances in insulation technology, subsequent improvements included duplex (messages sent in both directions along one wire), quadruplex, and multiplex systems, to which Thomas A. Edison contributed. Each dramatically increased bandwidth over given wires. Morse code, expanded in 1851 as International Morse Code to include diacriticals, survives to this day, although the Telex and TWX systems of the mid-twentieth century used the 5-bit Baudot code (from which the modern term *baud*). ASCII, the 7-bit American Standard Code for Information Interchange, was introduced in 1966 and underlies twenty-first-century e-mail, fax, and Internet communication.

Economic Impacts. Aside from its use by households to transmit personal greetings or family news, the telegraph had impacts in two major areas: military and diplomatic command and control, and the commercial transmission of high-value, time-sensitive information. In England and the continent, the former impacts dominated; for example, the technology greatly enhanced the global reach of the British Empire.

Commercial uses were most highly developed in the United States. In 1848, the Associated Press was formed as a means whereby newspapers could share telegraphic expenses. The intensity of the demand for time-sensitive information is reflected in the operation prior to the Atlantic cable of a system whereby carrier pigeons flew information from westbound ships docking in Newfoundland to Maine, where it was fed into telegraph lines that carried it to New York and the rest of the country. Other key uses were in financial markets and in logistical command and control in large business enterprises. The latter began with the railroad sector, extended to wholesale and retail distribution, and, eventually, to select manufacturing industries.

The railroad and the telegraph lived a symbiotic relationship, with lines strung along previously acquired railroad right-of-way. The telegraph was critical for keeping trains from colliding. The telegraph operator in the town's station was able to service other customers during periods

TELEGRAPH. General operations department, Western Union, 1875. (C. K. Bill/Prints and Photographs Division, Library of Congress)

in which the logistical needs of transportation did not require his attention.

In wholesale distribution, the telegraph, in conjunction with the railroad, enabled the development of two revolutionary institutions, the mail-order house and the department store. In both instances, the key to financial success was high rates of stockturn just as it is today in the retailing success stories of the early twenty-first century.

In manufacturing, the twin technologies revolutionized the commanding heights of the sector, underlying Andrew Carnegie's success in steel, John D. Rockefeller's with Standard Oil, and James B. Duke's in cigarettes. The telegraph, in conjunction with icing stations and refrigerated rail cars, enabled the distribution of fresh meat and vegetables from California and America's heartland to eastern cities from a remarkably early period.

The telegraph's use in financial markets was perhaps the most remarkable. Two entirely separate systems enabled million-share trading days on the New York Stock Exchange as early as 1886 and led to consolidation and a sharp drop in the number of exchanges in the United States. One system, the stock ticker (a technology to which Edison also contributed), was a broadcast technology transmitting a record of all completed trades. The second was a set of dedicated point-to-point private wires for transmitting customers' orders from retail brokerages to the floor of the exchange and confirmation of execution in the reverse direction.

The telegraph represented the first manifestation of an important new wave of technical innovation, one that, on balance, saved capital rather than labor. Everything else being equal, capital-saving innovations will tend to reduce the output to capital ratio, a measure of capital productivity. Capital productivity rises when an innovation permits a larger flow volume of output to be reaped from a given capital stock. For fixed capital, this generally means managing the resource so as to increase its average utilization rate. For inventories, it means increasing the rate of turnover, so that a given inventory stock supports a larger volume of sales or production.

The telegraph facilitated both of these efficiencies, particularly in the United States, where, along with the railroad, it provided the preconditions for what Alfred Chandler (1977) called modern business enterprise. A relatively modest investment of about $50 million to $150 million in a telegraph network, for example, enabled most of the U.S. rail system to be single tracked, yet avoid expensive and deadly collisions. The alternative of double tracking would have entailed additional expenditures of about $1 billion in 1890, in 1890 prices. A single-tracked system uses its rails and roadbed more intensively and can be understood as an innovation that increased utilization rates.

These technological innovations need to be understood in context. The late nineteenth century, the heyday of the construction, extension, and consolidation of the telegraph network in the United States, continued to be dominated by labor-saving innovation, most powerfully the railroad itself, with its prodigious appetite for financial and physical capital. Most of the improvement in labor productivity between 1870 and 1891 came about as the result of capital deepening (rise in the capital to labor ratio). Indeed, capital productivity declined, a pattern similar to that prevailing between 1972 and 1997. But, especially between 1913 and 1964, a very different pattern is evident, with capital productivity soaring in the context of very high multifactor productivity growth.

These mid-century developments represented the coming to fruition of nineteenth-century investments in new information technologies: the telegraph and subsequently the telephone, in conjunction with the delayed impact of electrification on the organization of American manufacturing. It remains to be seen whether investments in new information systems in the past few decades will usher in a second era of rapidly increasing capital productivity.

BIBLIOGRAPHY

Belloc, Alexis. *La télégraphie historique, depuis les temps les plus reculés jusqu'à nos jours*. Paris, 1888.

Chandler, Alfred. *The Visible Hand: The Managerial Revolution in American Business*. Cambridge, Mass., 1977.

DuBoff, Richard. "Business Demand and the Development of the Telegraph in the United States, 1844–1860." *Business History Review* 54 (1980), 457–479.

Fahie, John J. *A History of Electric Telegraphy, to the Year 1837, Chiefly Compiled from Original Sources, and Hitherto Unpublished Documents*. London, 1884.

Field, Alexander J. "Modern Business Enterprise as a Capital-Saving Innovation." *Journal of Economic History* 47 (June 1987), 473–485.

Field, Alexander J. "The Magnetic Telegraph, Price and Quantity Data, and the New Management of Capital." *Journal of Economic History* 52 (June 1992), 401–413.

Field, Alexander J. "French Optical Telegraphy, 1793–1855: Hardware, Software, Administration." *Technology and Culture* 35 (April 1994), 315–347.

Field, Alexander J. "The Telegraphic Transmission of Financial Asset Prices and Orders to Trade: Implications for Economic Growth." *Research in Economic History* 18 (1998), 145–184.

Gordon, Robert J. "U.S. Economic Growth since 1870: One Big Wave?" *American Economic Review Papers and Proceedings* 89 (1999), 123–128.

Headrick, Daniel R. *The Tools of Empire: Technology and European Imperialism in the Nineteenth Century*. New York, 1981.

Headrick, Daniel R. *The Invisible Weapon: Telecommunications and International Politics*. New York, 1991.

Shannon, Claude E. "A Mathematical Theory of Communication." *Bell System Technical Journal* 27 (1948): 327–333, 623–656.

Thompson, Robert Luther. *Wiring a Continent*. Princeton, 1947.

U.S. House of Representatives. *Telegraphs for the United States: Letter from the Secretary of the Treasury Transmitting a Report upon the Subject of a System of Telegraphs for the United States*. 25th Congress, 2d session, 1837, House doc. 15.

Wilson, Geoffrey. *The Old Telegraphs*. London, 1976.

ALEXANDER J. FIELD

TELEPHONE INDUSTRY. Americans Alexander Graham Bell and Elisha Gray filed competing patents for telephony on 14 February 1876. Independently, they had realized that electrical waves moving down a telegraph wire were analogous to sound waves moving through air. Since sound comprised a spectrum of frequencies, or tones, the electrical wave also could comprise a spectrum of frequencies. Each frequency might carry an independent message, and capacity would be limited only by the number of distinguishable sound frequencies. Although they were not the first men to experiment with voice communication— Phillip Reis proposed the first electric telephone in 1861— the approach taken by Bell and Gray became the technological basis for the development of the modern telephone. In his patent application, Bell laid out a design that called for a transmitter and a receiver, each of which was equipped with an electromagnet with one of its poles near a diaphragm. The human voice would vibrate the diaphragm sufficiently to generate an electric current in the magnet. This current then would flow through a wire and cause the receiver's diaphragm to move with a similar

TELEPHONE. Using a Bell telephone. From Robert Brown's *Science for All*, London, c. 1880. (Image Select/Art Resource, NY)

vibration, thereby reproducing sound. Bell went on to say that the transmitter would vary the resistance in a circuit in accordance with the voice; that is, it would be a variable-resistance transmitter, which was also Gray's core idea.

Bell and his backers prevailed in subsequent disputes, but in 1881 they bought out Gray's Western Electric Company to ensure a stable manufacturing source for their rapidly growing company. Telegraph giant Western Union, which had invested in Western Electric, had declined to buy the key telephone patents in 1876, probably because the telephone's limited transmission range (about twenty to thirty miles) meant that the new technology offered no challenge to Western Union's intracity, long-distance monopoly. Moreover, Western Union was then fighting off a hostile takeover bid. Western Union reconsidered and launched a competing telephone service with the assistance of Thomas Edison, which substantially strained Bell's financial resources in its early days. The two companies reached a compromise in 1879, which allowed Bell to enter the long-distance market but preserved Western Union's monopoly over the transmission of financial data—the ticker tape.

Western Union's initial assessment was not far off the mark, and the telephone was first deployed in the United States and Europe in the late 1870s as a series of small, local networks. Bell and his backers had expected to license the technology and profit from the royalties. Unable to raise sufficient capital, the company incrementally moved toward a model of regional service companies in which a franchise licensed the technology and built a local monopoly. Deployment of long-distance service in the 1880s revealed a rather alarming degree of technological incompatibilities among the franchises, and the company embarked on a program of corporate integration in which Bell interests achieved control over the local monopolies, which were knit together into a technologically compatible, hierarchical structure of regional operating companies. The Bell system, or American Telephone and Telegraph (later simply AT&T), comprising integrated local and long-distance service together with research (Bell Labs) and manufacturing (Western Electric), dominated U.S. telephone service until the U.S. Supreme Court ordered its break-up in 1982. It was then the world's largest corporation, and, since 1913, had evolved into a publicly regulated private monopoly. At least until 1930, it also dominated technological development. Other important corporate equipment manufacturers were ITT, which was prominent in Spain and in Latin America; Siemens & Halske, which made significant investments in northern Italy as well as in Germany; and Ericsson.

The American public/private model was, for the most part, exceptional. Like the postal service and telegraphy, which were understood to have military and strategic value, telephony was integrated into most nations' communications infrastructures in what became known as the integrated post office/telegraph/telephone (PTT) model. (There were periods of private ownership in France and Italy, but the fledgling systems of village networks were nationalized in 1889 in France and in 1907 in Italy.) Typically, a service provider—or incumbent—functioned under a government license with monopoly control.

Interest in telephony had spread rapidly in the 1870s in Europe because it fulfilled imperial goals as well as the needs of the industrializing nations for rapid communications and efficient markets. Franco-Italian rivalries in northern Africa contributed to the expansion of the communications systems, first along the coast and then inland, to the benefit of the central government and the business community.

Similarly in Australia, telephone service to the outback was introduced via the existing postal service network to which telegraph connections already had been established. In the authoritarian postcolonial Latin American nations, concessions were granted to private firms, first for telegraphy in the 1850s and 1860s and then for telephony in the 1870s and 1880s, so that private capital supported a state-centered system in which telephony remained limited and subordinate to telegraphy.

The U.S. federal government was weak compared with European and Latin American states and had declined to purchase rights to the telegraph in the mid-1840s, thus establishing a relatively open environment where commercial and economic concerns predominated. In the more urbanized areas of the United States (and Europe), the growing cities provided favorable demographic conditions, even given the limited transmission range of the early technology. From a technical point of view, there were three principal challenges associated with scaling up the system: signal attenuation, which limited transmission range; design of the switchboard, which limited the number of calls an exchange could handle; and line capacity.

As conceived by Bell himself, telephony was a point-to-point service. Switching, that is, managing the linkage of incoming and outgoing subscriber lines at a central office, developed from the earlier local (or district) telegraph concept and was pioneered by several licensees in 1877. This set of interconnections became known as an exchange, and Bell, as of February 1878, began to encourage its franchisers to organize exchanges. Integration of long-distance service into the local monopolies and development of the decentralized/hierarchical structure led to a period of experimentation in pricing, whether flat-rate or metered (or toll), and a period of technological experimentation in switchboard design, which today would be understood as a problem of combinatorics and human factors.

The switchboard design issue eventually was resolved in 1897 with the introduction of a hierarchical system design that called for a series of boards specialized for incoming or outgoing calls and then interconnected by a series of

transfers. Whereas a small town might be served by a single exchange, cities, which constituted Bell's target community, were served by a series of local exchanges, more or less at the neighborhood level, which were interconnected by trunk lines. Critical to the success of the system was introduction of stable electrical power and the common battery design, which embedded a single source of power into an integrated design.

The core issue, whether organizational or technical, concerned integration: the extent to which local service could be integrated into long-distance service. Since the plant (lines, exchanges, offices, etc.) was integral to the long-distance connections, a pricing policy on "separations" was articulated. Local service within a geographically defined region was at a flat rate and eventually was regulated at the state level; long distance was metered, based on the length of the call and the destination; after 1934, it was subject to regulation by the U.S. Federal Communications Commission. Based on a complex series of formulas, rates for long-distance calls factored in the value of the local plant. Regulators tended to favor maintaining low local rates in support of a policy of universal access. Because long-distance costs fell rapidly in the United States after World War II as a result of improved technology, long-distance rates ended up cross-subsidizing low local rates, so that on the eve of deregulation, U.S. local rates were artificially low and long-distance rates artificially high. Given mandatory interconnection at the local level, required since the early twentieth century, there was room for price competition in long-distance services, which was successfully exploited by MCI in the post–World War II decades.

It had not been entirely clear that an integrated local/long-distance service was necessary; but physicist Hammond Hayes of American Bell (a precursor to AT&T), who had overseen the development of the switchboard system, resisted proposals to establish concurrent local/long-distance systems. He launched a research program in the 1880s on overcoming signal attenuation, the source of limitation in transmission range. In addition to the goal of building an integrated system, the program signified the emerging integration of science-based engineering research into the corporate culture, which became embodied in the corporate lab, a hallmark of AT&T as well as of other technologically intensive corporations such as Westinghouse and General Electric.

The technical problem was solved in two major steps: the development of the loading coil, based on research by Bell engineer George Campbell and Columbia University's Michael Pupin; and the development of amplifiers, based on John Ambrose Fleming's diode and Lee de Forest's triode, as refined by Harold Arnold. Attenuation, or reduction in the strength of the signal, depended on signal frequency, and some frequencies were absorbed more than others. One solution was to use large-gauge copper wire, which had high conductivity and low resistance; but it was prohibitively expensive. Independently, Campbell and Pupin realized that by spacing out iron along the line, they could take advantage of a phenomenon known as inductance, which had the effect of increasing current and decreasing signal attenuation.

Deployed after 1899, loading coils—coils of wire around iron cores—increased transmission ranges in open-air lines (as opposed to the buried lines characteristic of urban environments) from eight hundred to seventeen hundred miles. Pupin sold the American rights to his design to AT&T but sold the European rights to Siemens & Halske, who developed it independently. Danish telegraph engineer Emil Krarup came up with yet another method of increasing self-inductance. By the eve of World War I, traffic had been opened on a 1,350-kilometer line linking Berlin and Milan, and Germany had begun to look into the possibility of improved communications between Berlin and Bucharest with a view toward Constantinople and the eastern Mediterranean.

Transmission range remained a limiting factor, particularly in the United States, where transcontinental connections became an explicit business objective for AT&T after 1908 when the company was reorganized by J. P. Morgan. Since 1893, when the key patents expired, the Bell system had been engaged in intense competition with newly formed telephone companies, the so-called independents. AT&T had focused on the urban centers and business clients, leaving swaths of the country unserved, a gap neatly filled by the independents. The most consistently successful independents tended to start out as small local companies that were gradually tied together into multi-exchange systems. Typically, telephone companies that were marginally successful in a single small town became profitable when connected to larger, neighboring centers, thus tapping into the highly lucrative short-distance toll (or nonlocal) service. These companies did not offer significant long-distance service, and their subscribers at the turn of the century did not appear to care. At the turn of the twentieth century, independents controlled more of the U.S. national market for local telephone service, where the vast bulk of the traffic was carried, than Bell did.

Theodore Vail, who had been with AT&T in the 1880s and was brought back by Morgan in 1908, embraced a vision of integrated local/long-distance service of national scope under the aegis of a single corporation—his original definition of "universal service"—and not the welter of competing technological standards, services, and competitors that he faced. He embarked on a program of mergers and acquisitions accompanied by a conciliatory approach to state and federal regulatory authorities intended to qui-

et protests over antitrust that had begun to surface, as well as the research program that resulted in increased line capacity—carrier circuits—and transcontinental telephone service, which relied on Arnold's refinement of de Forest's audion to amplify the signal.

The audion was essentially a vacuum tube that contained three elements: a filament that emitted electrons when heated, a positively charged metal plate that attracted the electrons, and a negatively charged grid in between that could control the electron current as it passed. A signal applied to the grid modulated the electron current and resulted in an amplified signal in the plate circuit. Initial experiments indicated that the audion could not sustain stable signals at the high voltages required for effective application to telephony. Arnold's design employed a high-vacuum, oxide-coated filament, a more precisely placed grid, and a new grid circuit. This "high vacuum thermionic tube," or vacuum tube, for short, provided the pivotal technology for the transcontinental line and, unexpectedly, put AT&T in a key position for the development of radio in the 1920s.

Within the company, Vail articulated an ethos of service and of superior technical achievement, which could pose a contradiction. For example, the company proved reluctant to deploy automatic switching, preferring the "human touch" of human operators; but AT&T also used its technological superiority as a way of barring interconnection between local, independent telephone service and its long-distance network. Complaints from the International Independent Telephone Association mounted, and in 1910 the U.S. Department of Justice filed suit against AT&T under the Sherman Antitrust Act after the telephone giant announced plans to acquire a 30 percent share in Western Union as well as yet another merger with another regional independent. In the first of a series of negotiated settlements and compromises, AT&T vice president Nathan Kingsbury signed a consent decree in 1913 with the Justice Department in which the company agreed to sell its holdings in Western Union, to cease acquiring independent companies without prior approval from the Justice Department, and to permit interconnection with independents provided that they met AT&T's technical specifications.

On the eve of World War I, competition between AT&T and the independents had pushed telephone diffusion to one telephone per fifty-seven inhabitants in the United States. Outside of Scandinavia (where Sweden reported one telephone per seventy inhabitants), teledensity in Europe was lower, even in Germany and England, where the strategic business value of telephony was recognized. Both the French and the Germans found their communications systems inadequate during the war, and the Germans embarked on a massive construction effort in an attempt to establish links between the eastern and western fronts. By the end of the war, the U.S. Signals Corps had made substantial improvements to the French systems, which were returned to French control in 1919. In the continental United States, there is some evidence that the buildup for the war extended the domestic infrastructure into still-underserved rural areas in which new air bases and training areas were rapidly constructed.

During the war, the U.S. government briefly nationalized the telephone system, but control reverted to AT&T, which embarked on another round of mergers and acquisitions. The 1920s were prosperous in the United States, and telephone service again expanded. However, subscribership declined in the 1930s, particularly in rural areas, owing in part to the substitution effects of the automobile. Canadian rural telephone service appears to have recovered more rapidly than U.S. service.

Worldwide, teledensity increased after World War II. The United States reached 90 percent penetration at the household level in 1970, the result of mandatory interconnection with remaining independent companies after 1924, universal service requirements, and a program of rural electrification in the 1930s and 1940s. Latin American nations conformed to the European PTT model in the immediate postwar period, although this did not mean nationalizing the equipment suppliers directly. By 1985, France, the United Kingdom, and the Federal Republic of Germany had reached comparable penetration levels. The 1995 data showed teledensity to be highest in the developed world (681 per thousand population in Sweden) and lowest in the poor and relatively isolated regions (0.8 per thousand population in the Democratic Republic of the Congo).

Microwave transmission technologies as well as satellite-based communications systems offer fast, global connectivity, but access remains uneven. Since 1996, deregulation of domestic telephone service and opening of local markets to competition have a global trade issue that has become intertwined with the deployment of packet-switched technologies—the Internet. Whereas a future of rapid, global communications systems fundamental to the information economy seems clear, the specifics of how that will be achieved, and for whom, are not.

[*See also* Information and Communication Technology.]

BIBLIOGRAPHY

Baur, Cyntha. "The Foundations of Telegraphy and Telephony in Latin America." *Journal of Communication* 44 (Autumn 1994), 9–25.

Bertho-Lavenir, Catherine. "The Telephone in France: National Characteristics and International Influences." In *The Development of Large Technical Systems*, edited by Renate Mayntz and Thomas P. Hughes, pp. 155–177. Frankfurt am Main, 1988. Overview of the development of the French PTT with information on teledensity.

Brittain, James E. "The Introduction of the Loading Coil: George A. Campbell and Michael I. Pupin." *Technology and Culture* 11 (January 1970), 36–58.

Chandler, Alfred Dupont, Jr. *The Visible Hand; The Managerial Revolution in American Business*. Cambridge, Mass., 1977. Classic study of the development of the American corporation in the mid-nineteenth century, including discussions of communications, transportation, and finance.

"Communications." In *Britannica Book of the Year, 1999*, pp. 832–837. Chicago, 1999. Statistics at the national level of communications media and services available to citizens; includes a detailed note on sources, data consistency, and other sources for similar information.

Du Boff, Richard B. "The Telegraph in Nineteenth-Century America: Technology and Monopoly." *Comparative Studies in Society and History* 26 (October 1984), 571–586. Looks at the rise of the Western Union monopoly.

Fagen, M. D. ed., *A History of Engineering and Science in the Bell System: National Service in War and Peace (1925–1975)*. Murray Hill, N.J., 1975.

Fagen, M. D., ed. *A History of Science and Engineering in the Bell System: The Early Years (1875–1925)*. Murray Hill, N.J., 1975. Standard work on technologies within the Bell System, including radio, radar, electronics, and so on, as well as telephony.

Fischer, Claude S. *America Calling: A Social History of the Telephone to 1940*. Berkeley, 1992. Social-constructivist view into the history of telephony.

Galambos, Louis. "Looking for the Boundaries of Technology Determinism: A Brief History of the U.S. Telephone System." In *The Development of Large Technical Systems*, edited by Renate Mayntz and Thomas P. Hughes, pp. 134–153. Frankfurt am Main, 1988. Excellent synopsis of U.S. development.

Garnet, Robert W. *The Telephone Enterprise: The Evolution of the Bell System's Horizontal Structure, 1876–1909*. Baltimore, 1985. One of several historical studies (see the Temin, Smith, and Wasserman entries) investigating the origins of the Bell system.

Hoddeson, Lillian. "The Emergence of Basic Research in the Bell Telephone System, 1875–1915." *Technology and Culture* 21 (1981), 512–544.

Hughes, Thomas P. *American Genesis: A Century of Innovation and Technological Enthusiasm, 1879–1970*. New York, 1989. Covers a number of technologies and is particularly strong the emerging relationship between public/private sector R&D.

Israel, Paul B. *From Machine Shop to Industrial Laboratory: Telegraphy and the Changing Context of American Invention, 1830–1920*. Baltimore, 1992. Recent definitive study of the development of telegraphy.

Kragh, Helge. "Telephone Technology and Its Interactions with Science and the Military, ca. 1900–1930." *Boston Studies in the Philosophy of Science* 180 (1996), 37–67. Concise discussion of development of telephony in Europe, based on original sources in French and German.

Langdale, John V. "The Growth of Long-Distance Telephony in the Bell System: 1875–1907." *Journal of Historical Geography* 4 (1978), 145–159. Articulates the argument, since challenged, that long-distance telephony was criical to the emergence of the Bell system in the United States.

Lipartito, Kenneth. *The Bell System and Regional Business; the Telephone in the South, 1877–1920*. Baltimore, 1989. Prize-winning study that examines the tension between local telephone systems and a long-distance, national system.

Mueller, Milton. "The Telephone War: Interconnection, Competition and Monopoly in the Making of Universal Telephone Service, 1894–1920." Ph.D. diss., University of Pennsylvania, 1989. Includes an excellent discussion of the development of the switchboard.

Pool, Ithiel de Sola. *Technologies without Boundaries: On Telecommunications in a Global Age*, edited by Eli M. Noam. Cambridge, Mass., 1990. Anthology of several significant studies.

Raines, Rebecca Robbins. *Getting the Message Through: A Branch History of the U.S. Army Signal Corps*. Army Historical Series. Washington, D.C., 1996. Basic source on communications systems in the U.S. Army; especially useful for the World War I period.

Reich, Leonard S. *The Making of American Industrial Research: Science and Business at GE and Bell, 1876–1926*. Cambridge, 1985. Covers development of the corporate lab and the rise of the technologically intensive industries.

Smith, George David. *The Anatomy of a Business Strategy: Bell, Western Electric, and the Origins of the American Telephone Industry*. Baltimore, 1985.

Tarr, Joel A., with Thomas Finholt and David Goodman. "The City and the Telegraph, Urban Communications in the Pre-telephone Era." *Journal of Urban History* 14 (November 1987), 38–80. Looks at early attempts to devise switching technologies and communications in the local market.

Temin, Peter, with Louis Galambos. *The Fall of the Bell System; A Study in Prices and Politics*. Cambridge, 1987. Definitive historical study of deregulation; includes unprecedented access to AT&T executives as well as to the archival materials.

Thomas, Frank. "The Politics of Growth," In *The Development of Large Technical Systems*, edited by Renate Mayntz and Thomas P. Hughes, pp. 179–214. Frankfurt am Main, 1988. Overview of the development of the German PTT with information on teledensity.

Wasserman, Neil H. *From Invention to Innovation: Long Distance Telephone Transmission at the Turn of the Century*. Baltimore, 1985.

AMY FRIEDLANDER

TENANT FARMING. Tenant farming is nearly as old as the private ownership of property. Indeed, it may precede individual ownership, as it first appears to have emerged after communal systems of ownership were broken up into leases to individuals, as happened in England and Rome. The essence of tenancy is straightforward. The "tenant" is the cultivator of the land but not the owner. In return for the right to use the land, the tenant owes a rent. Tenancy can be said to have numerous origins because it was not always directly implanted from somewhere else but appears to have arisen independently at various locales. Certain forms of tenancy emerged from a breakdown of slavery (in the Roman Empire and the Americas). Sometimes tenancy was the result of conquest. For example, the Athenians rented conquered land to their former owners. For most of northern Europe, tenancy emerged from feudalism. Elsewhere in the world (for example in South Africa, India, and most of the Americas) tenancy was often implanted by European colonists, both before and after slavery. Most forms of tenancy emerged in Europe following feudalism. Under feudalism, all users of land (except for the sovereign) were essentially tenants, though their rights and obligations varied considerably, from the "tenants in chief," who were the de facto owners, to the serfs, who could be considered part slave and part tenant.

The Black Death (c. 1347–1352) represents a watershed in the emergence of what we would consider tenancy today. Prior to the Black Death, most serfs, who owed the lord labor dues as well as other obligations, could be considered "customary tenants." After the Black Death, as labor became scarce, tenants received more legal rights. In England, copyhold tenure emerged. Copyhold tenants possessed a copy of the terms of their lease with the lord of the manor. This copy made their rights more secure than those of customary tenants. In some parts of England, copyhold tenure could be passed on to one's heirs.

In France, tenancy emerged later than in England, and it took different forms in the north and south. In the north, peasants secured leases to land on large estates. The leases typically extended for years (odd years up to ninety-nine) and some leases were hereditary. The arrangements in Flanders were similar to those in northern France. In southern France, *métayage* (a form of sharecropping) arose. Like sharecropping in the southern United States several centuries later, *métayage* has been blamed for low productivity and the poverty of the peasants. In the United States sharecropping differs from share tenancy, but in Europe authors frequently use the terms interchangeably. Italy had sharecropping, share tenancy, and fixed rent contracts. In Spain, share arrangements, *rabassa morta*, prevailed in vineyards from at least the mid-seventeenth century until the twentieth century.

The security of tenancy varies with the length of the contract. Under "tenancy at will" (known as *precarium* under Roman law), either party could terminate the contract at any time. Over time, this form of contract lost favor because of its negative impact on productivity. The cultivator has little interest in investing in the productivity of the crop if he is uncertain that he will be able to reap the reward. Particularly for annual crops such as wheat, corn, and cotton, annual contracts are common, though they are often continued for many years if the terms and results remain satisfactory to both parties. When crops are perennials (for example, from vineyards), care of the vines or trees is important to the owner and longer term contracts are generally the norm.

In most developed agricultural systems, tenancy confers legal rights to the tenant. In return for the rights to access the land, use the land to produce crops, and lay claim to the output, the tenant owes the owner of the land (government, crown, corporation or individual) rent. In contrast, the right to access the land of wage workers or sharecroppers is at the discretion of the landowner. Wage workers and sharecroppers do not have a direct claim to the output. They are either owed a wage (per day, month, or year) or a share of the output as compensation for their labor. The legal distinction can be important because of possible debts of the worker for loans over the crop year. Rents can be in cash or in kind, and fixed or a share. Share tenants owe the landlord a share of the output or of the proceeds from the output. Fixed-rent tenants owe the landlord an ex-ante specified amount of cash or crop.

If cash is the form of payment, the tenant is a fixed-cash rent tenant. If crop is the form of payment, the tenant is a standing renter or cash crop renter. Cash crop renting was quite common in some times and places. For example, cash crop renters accounted for two-thirds of the tenants in the rice regions of China in the early 1930s. The term *standing renter* is not used universally, but was the common appellation in the U.S. South in the late-nineteenth and early- to mid-twentieth centuries.

In addition to the legal distinctions, there are *de facto* distinctions between sharecroppers and share tenants. Typically, a sharecropper only supplies labor to the production process, whereas a share tenant generally supplies capital in the form of work stock or other assets. For example, he might own the vines, as in *rabassa morta*. In compensation for supplying part of the capital the share tenant receives a greater share than a sharecropper, making his work incentive more "high powered."

To produce output the owners of land have several options: (1) work the land themselves with family labor; (2) hire wage workers or sharecroppers; or (3) lease the land to a tenant under a fixed or share arrangement. These legal or customary distinctions have important economic implications regarding the distribution of risk between landlords and those who work the land (wage workers, sharecroppers, and tenants) and incentives for labor effort. Frequently, economists have developed mono-causal theoretical models, basing them on either risk or incentives alone, as the explanation for contract choice. I argue that both landlords and labor take into account both risk and incentives, but the magnitude of the importance of risk and incentives varies over time, across regions, across crops, and across individuals. Farming is a risky business. It could rain too much, rain too little, or rain at the wrong times. Frost can destroy a crop, as can hail, tornadoes, or insects. In short, there are myriad ways in which output can fluctuate. We refer to the deviations from expected output as yield risk. As if yield risk were not enough to make a farmer lose sleep at night there is price risk. Prices can vary over the year (interseasonal price variation) as well as across years. Deviations from expected prices are known as price risk.

If a landowner relies on family or outside wage workers, he assumes all the risks from fluctuations in output or prices. Conversely, the wage workers assume no risk, provided the landowner is wealthy enough to pay them if crops fail completely. Sharecroppers and share tenants bear risk proportional to their share of the crop. Cash tenants bear all the risk associated with prices and yields, provided there is no explicit or implicit escape clause in times of disaster. Standing renters bear all the risk associated with yields, but share the price risk with the landlord. The perceived price and yield risks and the preferences between landlords and prospective tenant are factors in the selection of the type of tenant contract. Numerous scholars have argued that share contracts are chosen (in part) to distribute risk across tenants and landlords.

Two of the essential differences across contracts (e.g., wage, share, or fixed rent) are the incentive they give workers to stint on their labor effort and the incentive for landlords to monitor workers. Given that yields can fluctuate for a number of reasons, it is generally not possible to judge labor effort by measuring output. The incentive to monitor by landlords and the incentive for workers to reduce labor effort vary with the residual claimancy of the owner. Residual claimancy is the contracted right of one party to the residual output after all other contractually obligated inputs have been paid. (In a firm we call it the right to the profits.) It is not only labor effort in the fields that needs to be monitored. Landlords and others have an incentive to monitor the use of all assets that they bring to the production process, though labor-monitoring costs can be considered a residual to the monitoring of the other assets. If a single farmer supplies all inputs to the production process, all costs of stinting or abuse are internalized, so monitoring costs disappear. We presume that it is impossible to shirk on one's own time. (In the language of an economist one is simply making a labor/leisure trade-off.)

Consider the following simplified production process for cotton. Output is a function of land (quantity and quality), physical capital (a mule/horse or tractor), human capital of the farm owner and operator, and labor effort. We assume that the market for inputs is competitive and endowments vary across farmers; that is, some farmers have land and mules. These farmers are looking to hire laborers, some of whom have farm experience and mules and are searching for land. How do suppliers and demanders of inputs match up? (Often and in many places the competitive conditions described here did not hold. Nevertheless, it is a useful analytical benchmark because the degree of monopoly power generally affects the economic returns to the landlords and laborers more than the contractual form.)

As an example, suppose a resident farm owner with considerable farming experience and a mule is looking for a laborer. He is willing to supply all the inputs except for labor. Given his endowment, what would the best match be? He would search for a laborer who has no capital and little farming experience. In this way, he would get the best return on his human and physical capital. In this situation, the farmer has an incentive to be in the fields to monitor his physical capital (the mule in particular) to prevent its depreciation, and to furnish directions (human capital). Given the presence of the landlord for these reasons, the marginal cost of monitoring labor effort is low; there are economies of scope across monitoring.

TENANT FARMING. A farmer and his children at a cotton farm near Anniston, Alabama, 1936. (Dorothea Lange/Prints and Photographs Division, Library of Congress)

When workers are endowed with more physical or human capital, the landlord cannot benefit from such economies of scope. As a result, the direct costs of monitoring the labor effort of these workers is greater than for workers with less capital. In order to reduce the costs of monitoring better endowed workers, landlords will negotiate tenant contracts, which increase the work incentive of labor. Tenant contracts can be seen as a means for landlords to reduce their monitoring costs compared to what they would be if they hired sharecroppers or wage workers. Tenant contracts, along with monitoring, are not the sole means of providing incentives for work. The prospect of contract renewal may encourage effort, as might social norms—"an honest day's work for an honest day's pay."

Tenancy has frequently been villainized, but given its persistence over time and across space it most likely does allocate risk and provide incentives for labor effort. Why, then, has it been denounced? Some naïve economists argued that share contracts are inefficient. The question is, inefficient compared to what? The alleged inefficiency arose from share tenants who didn't work hard enough; tenants would stop working when the portion of the marginal product that they received (e.g., two-thirds of the additional product) was equal to the value of their leisure.

For an efficient amount of effort the total marginal product should be equal to the opportunity cost of labor, or leisure.

Several arguments can be made to counter the claim of inefficiency. First, given that share tenancy and sharecropping have been used independently by different cultures across centuries, it is highly unlikely that so many people could have persistently settled on a contract for which there was a superior alternative. Most likely one did not exist. Fixed contracts, although they get the labor/leisure trade-off correct, cost tenants greater risk. Although wage contracts give the landowner the incentive to contract for the appropriate amount of labor, they require far more monitoring than contracts for share tenants. Share contracts are only inferior to some yet-to-be-discovered utopian contract—not a good criterion for claiming inefficiency. Additionally, laborers may voluntarily work harder in an effort to compete against other tenants for a renewal of their contracts. Landlords can also reduce the otherwise inefficient amount of labor expended by stipulating a certain amount of effort, such as from dawn to dusk during cotton-picking season, or by directly monitoring the labor.

A more compelling case against tenancy can be made on the grounds of equity rather than efficiency. Whether it is fair for some people to be able to live off the work effort of others simply because they own land depends in large part on cultural norms. For centuries (one example is the Middle Ages) one's ultimate position in life was more or less predetermined at birth by the occupation of the father. If your father was a tenant, you were likely to become a tenant or a tenant's wife. If your father was a butcher, baker, or candlestick maker, you would probably follow the same occupation. As long as this rule was perceived as legitimate, no social unrest accompanied high levels of tenancy. Social unrest over the issue of tenancy arose only when it was possible to act on it.

Birth did not determine occupational status as rigidly with the settlement and development by Europeans of what is now the United States and Canada. The abundance of land allowed tenancy to be seen as the penultimate rung of the agricultural ladder, on the way to becoming an owner. (Lack of tenurial mobility typified most of the rest of the world—specifically, South America, Asia, and Africa.) In Canada and the United States, whether one ultimately became an owner was perceived as being the result of a mixture of good luck and hard work. The agricultural ladder went from wage worker to sharecropper (in the U.S. South), to tenant (share or fixed), and ultimately to owner. Many owners took this route. Even black workers had a reasonable (given the discriminatory laws and norms in place) chance of ascending the ladder to ownership. For example, in the southern United States in 1880, 25 percent of black farm operators (owners, tenants, sharecroppers) owned the land that they operated. In the North the likelihood of ascending was greater. But there were times when social commentators perceived of tenanancy as the last step. Moreover, there was a worry that previous landowners were falling into tenancy as the result of foreclosures.

Tenancy reform in the United States first became a plank of the political platform with the Populists in the late nineteenth century. Over time, as land became scarcer (the late nineteenth century witnessed the "closing of the American frontier"), land prices increased and it seemed to become even more difficult to become an owner. This view has merit; there is some evidence that the average age of attaining ownership status was increasing over time. However, part of the increase was the result of males spending a longer time in school or in outside employment. The time spent in farming before becoming a landowner may not have changed much, but we do not have evidence one way or the other before the 1920 Census of Agriculture. The Populists also complained that land speculators were driving up the price of land, although there is little evidence to support this view. No one owned enough land to influence prices.

The pleas for reform in the United States waned as the agricultural sector boomed after the recession of the 1890s, only to resurface with the increase in farm failures in the 1920s and 1930s. Coincident with the rise in farm failures was an increase in the percentage of farms operated by tenants. One interpretation of the increase in tenancy was that the United States was becoming a land of absentee owners. Though plausible, this would be a mistaken view. The increase in tenancy was mostly driven by a decline in wage workers rather than by absentee ownership. A good rule of thumb is that bankers make bad farmers. When a bank forecloses, it tries to sell the farm as quickly as possible. A foreclosure typically results in a former tenant becoming an owner. For the most part the informed observers of the times (e.g., agricultural economists in the Department of Agriculture and academia) were not alarmed, but the Roosevelt administration in mid-thirties made tenancy part of its reform efforts through the Farm Security Administration.

The reforms centered on the South. The movement for reform started with the premise that the majority of tenants (sharecroppers and tenants) in the South are poor, that their poverty is the result of tenancy. This is akin to "shooting the messenger." It was true that tenants in the South were poor, but the poverty stemmed more from the lack of civil rights for blacks and the low levels of schooling for both black and white tenants, leaving them with few off-farm opportunities. The reform efforts never amounted to much because they ran into opposition from the southern elite. With the advent of World War II, the pleas for reform dissipated as soon as the farm sector boomed in the 1940s. Besides, the administration in Washington had more pressing concerns. Farm tenancy is still prevalent in the Midwest, but it is no longer of political concern because tenancy no longer indicates a low social status. Indeed, many tenants are as wealthy as landowners and many owners lease in some land as well as farming their own.

Though land reform and tenant reform are no longer political issues in the United States, they are burning issues in other regions of the world (particularly Mexico and South and Central America) and have been into the twenty-first century. The lack of tenurial mobility has kept alive movements to redistribute land.

[*See also* Agricultural Rents; Sharecropping; *and* Tenant Right.]

BIBLIOGRAPHY

Ackerberg, D. A., and M. Botticini. "The Choice of Agrarian Contracts in Early Renaissance Tuscany: Risk Sharing, Moral Hazard, or Capital Market Imperfections?" *Explorations in Economic History* Forthcoming.

Allen, D. W., and D. Lueck. "The Role of Risk in Contract Choice." *Journal of Law, Economics, and Organization* 15.3 (October 1999), 704–736.

Allen, D. W., and D. Lueck. "The Nature of the Farm." *Journal of Law and Economics* 41.2 (October 1998), 343–386.

Allen, D. W., and D. Lueck. "Contract Choice in Modern Agriculture: Cropshare Versus Cash Rent." *Journal of Law and Economics* 35 (October 1992), 397–426.

Alston, Lee J. "Tenure Choice in Southern Agriculture, 1930–1960." *Explorations in Economic History* 18 (1981), 211–232.

Alston, Lee J., Samar Datta, and Jeffrey B. Nugent. "Tenancy Choice in a Competitive Framework with Transactions Costs." *Journal of Political Economy* 92 (1984), 1121–1133.

Alston, Lee J., and Joseph P. Ferrie. "Paternalism in Agricultural Contracts in the U.S. South: Implications for the Growth of the Welfare State." *American Economic Review* 83 (1993), 852–876.

Alston, Lee J., and Joseph P. Ferrie. *Paternalism and the American Welfare State: Economics, Politics, and Institutions in the U.S. South, 1865–1965.* Cambridge, 1999.

Alston, Lee J., and Robert Higgs. "Contractual Mix in Southern Agriculture since the Civil War: Facts, Hypotheses and Tests." *Journal of Economic History* 42 (1982), 327–353.

Alston, Lee J., and Kyle D. Kauffman. "Agricultural Chutes and Ladders: New Estimates of Sharecroppers and 'True Tenants' in the South, 1900–1920." *Journal of Economic History* 57 (1997), 464–575.

Alston, Lee J., and Kyle D. Kauffman. "Up, Down, and Off the Agricultural Ladder: New Evidence and Implications of Agricultural Mobility for Blacks in the Postbellum South." *Agricultural History* 72 (1998), 263–279.

Alston, Lee J., Gary D. Libecap, and Bernardo Mueller. *Titles, Conflict and Land Use: The Development of Property Rights and Land Reform on the Brazilian Amazon Frontier.* Ann Arbor, 1999.

Atack, Jeremy. "Tenants and Yeoman in the Nineteenth Century." *Agricultural History* 62 (1988), 6–232.

Atack, Jeremy. "The Agricultural Ladder Revisited: A New Look at an Old Question with Some Data for 1860." *Agricultural History* 63 (1989), 1–25.

Black, John D., and R. H. Allen. "The Growth of Farm Tenancy in the United States." *The Quarterly Journal of Economics* 51 (1937), 393–425.

Bloch, M. *French Rural History.* Berkeley, 1970.

Botticini, Maristella. "Agrarian Contracts in 1427 Tuscany." In *Land, Labor, and Tenure: The Institutional Arrangements of Conflict and Cooperation in Comparative Perspective*, edited by F. Galassi, K. Kauffman, and J. Liebowitz, pp. 31–40. Seville, 1998.

Brandt, Karl. "Fallacious Census Terminology and Its Consequences in Agriculture." *Social Research: An International Quarterly of Political and Social Science* 5 (1938), 19–36.

Buck, John Lossing. *Land Utilization in China: A Study of 16,786 Farms in 168 Localities, and 38,256 Farm Families in Twenty-two Provinces in China, 1929–1933.* New York, 1964.

Carmona, Juan, and James Simpson. "The 'Rabassa Morta' in Catalan Viticulture: The Rise and Decline of a Long-Term Sharecropping Contract, 1670–1920s." *Journal of Economic History* 59 (June 1999), 290–315.

Cohen, J. S., and F. L. Galassi. "Sharecropping and Productivity: Feudal Residues in Italian Agriculture, 1911." *Economic History Review* 43 (1990), 646–656.

Epstein, S. R. "Moral Hazard and Risk Sharing in Late Medieval Tuscany." *Rivista di Storia Economica* 11 (1994), 131–137.

Eswaran, Mukesh, and Ashok Kotwal. "A Theory of Contractual Structure in Agriculture." *American Economic Review* 75 (1985), 352–367.

Galassi, F. L. "Moral Hazard and Asset Specificity in the Renaissance: The Economics of Sharecropping in 1427 Florence." *Advances in Agricultural Economic History* 1 (2000), 177–206.

Goldenweiser, E. A., and Leon E. Truesdell. "Farm Tenancy in the United States." *Census Monograph IV.* Washington D.C., 1924.

Gray, L. C., Charles L. Stewart, Howard A. Turner, J. T. Sanders, and W. J. Spillman. "Farm Ownership and Tenancy." U.S. Department of Agriculture, *Yearbook, 1923*, pp. 507–600. Washington D.C., 1924.

Higgs, Robert. "Race, Tenure and Resource Allocation in Southern Agriculture, 1910." *Journal of Economic History* 33 (1973), 149–169.

Higgs, Robert. "Patterns of Farm Rental in the Georgia Cotton Belt." *Journal of Economic History* 34 (1974), 468–482.

Hibbard, Benjamin H. "Tenancy in the Southern States." *Quarterly Journal of Economics* 27 (1913), 482–496.

Hoffman, P. "The Economic Theory of Sharecropping in Early Modern France." *Journal of Economic History* 44 (1984), 309–319.

Hopcroft, Rosemary L. *Regions, Institutions, and Agrarian Change in European History.* Ann Arbor, 1999.

Jones, P. J. "From Manor to Mezzadria." In *Florentine Studies*, edited by Nicolai Rubinstein, pp. 193–241. Evanston, Ill., 1968.

Jones, P. J. "Medieval Agrarian Society in Its Prime: Italy." In *The Cambridge Economic History of Europe*, vol. I, edited by M. M. Postan and H. J. Habakkuk, pp. 340–430. Cambridge, 1964.

Otsuka, K., H. Chuma, and Y. Hayami. "Land and Labor Contracts in Agrarian Economies: Theories and Facts." *Journal of Economic Literature* 30 (1992), 1965–2018.

Reid, Joseph D., Jr. "Sharecropping as an Understandable Market Response: The Post-Bellum South." *Journal of Economic History* 33 (1973), 106–130.

Reid, Joseph D., Jr. "Sharecropping in History and Theory." *Agricultural History* 49 (1975), 426–440.

Schuler, E. A. "Social Status and Farm Tenure—Attitudes and Social Conditions of Corn Belt and Cotton Belt Farmers." U.S. Department of Agriculture, The Farm Security Administration, and the Bureau of Agricultural Economics Cooperation. *Social Research Report No. IV.* Washington, D.C., 1938.

Shlomowitz, Ralph. "The Origins of Southern Sharecropping." *Agricultural History* 53 (1979), 557–575.

Woodman, Harold D. *New South: New Law.* Baton Rouge, 1995.

Woofter, Thomas J. *Landlord and Tenant on the Cotton Plantation.* Washington, D.C., 1936.

Wright, Gavin. *Old South, New South: Revolutions in the Southern Economy since the Civil War.* New York, 1986.

LEE J. ALSTON

TENANT RIGHT, in its broadest sense, might be said to include any tenurial rights enjoyed by the tenant in addition to those specified in the rental agreement with the landlord. These rights were sanctioned by custom and usage and could exist under both feudal and market forms of economy. Such extracontractual claims might include the right of a son or close relative to succeed the father on the landholding, as seems to have been the case with Scottish kindly tenure. Or they might include the right to charge compensation from an incoming tenant for capital outlays where the fruits of that investment had not been exhausted, as was allowed on many English estates. Because these rights were specific to an individual estate or locality, there was a bewildering variety of practice. Naturally, the scope and content of these social and institutional arrangements also varied over time, in response to changing economic, demographic, political, or security circumstances. Tenant right practices, and the understandings that underpinned them, therefore defy classification except at a microhistorical level.

There can be few societies, though, in which tenant right came to assume the importance, economically and politically speaking, that it did in Ireland. While there is no fixed definition of the custom, a common thread is that it referred to the right of an outgoing tenant to sell his occupation rights to an incoming tenant, as happened in Ulster and, to a less-marked degree, in other parts of Ireland during the eighteenth and nineteenth centuries. The sums of money involved were substantial, ranging from the equivalent of a few years' rent before the Great Potato Famine of the 1840s, to a figure of ten or more times the annual farm rent by the later nineteenth century. The origins of the custom seem to date back to the late seventeenth century and may have been influenced by the earlier English border custom that had been carried over by settlers from that frontier region to Ulster—hence, the synonymous term, *Ulster custom*.

But there is an anomaly here. As it was the landlord and not the tenant who owned the land, what was there to sell? One is driven to the conclusion that many Irish landlords— popular accounts of predatory Irish landlordism notwithstanding—did not charge the full Ricardian or competitive rent. Otherwise, there would have been nothing to sell. More formally, the tenant right payment might be viewed from an economic perspective as the present value of the difference between the future competitive rent stream and the actual rent stream, both suitably discounted for risk, uncertainty, and time preference. Still, why should landlords tolerate such an apparent infringement of their property rights? More recent interpretations suggest that tenant right could be part of a rational strategy of estate management. The landlord had first claim on any debts, primarily rent arrears, owed to the estate; and these were deducted from the sum paid for the tenant right. In effect, the landlord sacrificed a potentially higher rent for the greater ease and certainty of securing the rental income.

By the end of the nineteenth century, tenant right was well on the way to being extinguished. This was due to a massive program of agrarian reform that transferred the ownership of the farmland of Ireland to the sitting tenants. But it was prolonged public and political controversies surrounding tenant right that prepared the way for these more far-reaching changes.

[*See also* Ireland.]

BIBLIOGRAPHY

Devine, Thomas M. *The Transformation of Rural Scotland: Social Change and the Agrarian Economy, 1660–1815*. Edinburgh, 1994. Valuable on Scottish tenurial practices.

Dowling, Martin W. *Tenant Right and Agrarian Society in Ulster, 1600–1870*. Dublin, Ireland, 1999. The most comprehensive account of the origins, meaning, and significance of Irish tenant right.

Guinnane, Timothy W., and Ronald I. Miller. "Bonds without Bondsmen: Tenant-Right in Nineteenth-Century Ireland." *Journal of Economic History* 56.2 (1996), 113–142. A challenging re-interpretation of the economics of tenant right.

Solow, Barbara L. *The Land Question and the Irish Economy, 1870–1903*. Cambridge, 1971. The pioneering analytical account of the "peculiar institution" of Ulster custom.

LIAM KENNEDY

TEXTILES. The acquisition of textiles, primarily for clothing, but also for many other domestic and industrial uses, has been a challenge that all societies historically have faced. Textiles have been, and still are, an essential of life. They provide warmth, comfort, and protection. They have long been necessary in many industries; for example, agriculture, transport, and printing. Textiles fulfill many other roles and functions in societies—cultural, symbolic, religious, status, occupational, authority, safety and health. They also have broad connections to other economic and social activities.

Thus all societies have been confronted with the problem of supplying their textile needs. Some have solved the problem by imports. Over the course of history textiles have been by far the most important traded manufacture. But most societies have sought the means to produce textiles themselves, have experimented with the manipulation of fibers, and have learned to produce textiles. Experimentation, which continues to this day, has produced a remarkable range of techniques and products. Technological and product development has been progressive from earliest societies, although many techniques and products have also been discarded over time.

Societies have attempted to use many vegetable and animal fibers. In the last century, man-made or artificial fibers have been a focus of textile development and often a solution to changing textile needs. Vegetable fibers include many types of grasses and plants. Three in particular have provided qualities that facilitated both ease of working and the creation of final products that accorded with the needs of societies: flax, hemp, and cotton. Other vegetable fibers have served vital specific functions.

Spinners and weavers across many societies have experimented with the hair and fur (there is no real technical difference except for length) of many animals. A remarkable range of animal fibers have been converted into textiles, including the hair of many varieties of goats, camels, rabbits, horses, and other creatures. Of these, the fleece of the sheep, a most versatile animal, offers the greatest advantages in production, processing, and the creation of final products. The filament produced by silk worms, although more difficult to process, has also provided an important fiber for many societies and for trade.

TEXTILES. Rolls of British woolen cloth being readied for world distribution, London, 1962. (*New York World-Telegram* and the *Sun* Newspaper Photograph Collection/Prints and Photographs Division, Library of Congress)

In the quest for textiles, societies have, historically, had to meet a series of challenges. The first has been the acquisition of appropriate fibers for their needs. All the major fibers have been developed to produce a huge variety of qualities and attributes appropriate for different methods of processing and for different end uses. Creating those qualities has been a continual task. In some instances the challenge has taken place within the context of alternative market demands, not least, for example, in the often conflicting requirements of the sheep farmer for meat and wool. During the long process of industrialization, within which textiles were so often at the forefront, the range and complexity of the textile fibers demanded and supplied grew hugely. Varieties of wool, cotton, flax, and silk multiplied, as did the number of minor fibers used in the broad textile trade. Rising world populations and increasing wealth in many societies extended textile demand and put pressure on raw material supplies. Solutions had to be found through the opening up of new supplies and the use of new fibers. In more modern times the great developments in raw material supply have been the provision of raw cotton by the American South, the extension of wool growing to the southern hemisphere, the reuse of fibers, and the development of artificial fibers.

Raw cotton production in the American South took off from the late eighteenth century on, and was the major contributor to the ability of the textile industry to clothe a rapidly expanding population in the developing world at a price it could afford. One of the greatest challenges the textile industry has ever faced was to process that increased supply efficiently. The impact on the subsequent clothing costs of societies, and on other textiles, had far-reaching ramifications. Cotton spread across other countries, adding both quantity and variety of fiber quality to world cotton supply.

The qualities of the wool fiber ensured continued demand for it in spite of the challenge from the much cheaper cotton. The wool textile industry was faced with the need to constrain its costs to compete with cotton, in a context of rising demand for its limited raw material supplies. The demand for wool encouraged countries of the Southern Hemisphere, notably Australia, New Zealand, and Argentina, to farm sheep. The wool they provided allowed the further growth of wool textile production from the nineteenth century on. The discovery of the means of reclaiming and reprocessing already used wool fibers, at the same period, added a most important additional source of raw material. Improvements in the ability to combine cotton and wool in textile manufacture gave a further boost to the industry, and an additional important source of raw material was acquired later in the nineteenth century through the skin-wool trade—the ability to claim wool from the skins of sheep slaughtered for meat.

The creation of man-made fibers was initially aimed at replicating the qualities of natural fibers and at improving supply and reducing price. They were evolved partly through the adaptation of by-products of other industries, but more generally through dedicated research and development, which before long produced fibers and filaments with new qualities. These innovations had a profound influence on all the textile industries over the past century and they continue to do so. They have both substituted for and complemented natural fibers. But the natural fibers that were found, many centuries ago, to provide the best qualities for production, processing, and use all survive as significant components of the modern textile industry. No major new natural fibers have been added to the repertoire of raw materials of textile manufacturers, although adaptation in the production and use of those fibers remains a continuous process.

Historians have typically put textiles into a few main categories—cotton, wool, linen, silk, and manmade—but the history of the development of textiles should be painted with a broader brush. The association between different textile fibers, their processing, and their products has been close. Textile producers combine different fibers during processing to help overcome technical problems of production and to provide products with particular qualities, but finding the right combinations has been a struggle. Different fibers have shared in the experimentation of new production methods. Solutions for one fiber have often been adapted and adopted for others. Similarities of plant and processes, of financial and commercial requirements, and of labor skills, and the process of combining textile fibers in production require the historian to consider textiles as a generic industry, even though the components may have separate problems and experiences.

The second challenge in the creation of textiles has been to work the various fibers into forms that enable them to be processed. In both manual and machine processing the textile fiber has to withstand the stresses put upon it. To this end fibers have undergone careful selection and improvement, different fibers are selected for different production methods, and the fibers undergo an initial preparatory processing. The relationship between textile fiber and production process has not been all one way, however. Fibers have been refined in relation to the processes that they had to undergo. Processes are continually adapted according to the properties of the fiber and the purposes for which it is destined. Some prepared textile fibers are suitable for immediate end uses—in pack-ings and stuffings, for example—but most are destined for further manipulation.

Processing the prepared fiber into a form suitable for its final purpose has been a continual challenge throughout the history of the textile industries. Mainly, but not entirely, processing consists of creating a yarn through the twisting and drawing out of fibers. At this point it may be used or processed further, most often for weaving or knitting into a fabric. An alternative means of creating a fabric has been the felting and matting of fibers. Finally the fabric, however produced, has to be finished according to the exigencies of the market. Finishing includes adding color, if that has not been done at the fiber preparation or spinning stage, and creating fullness, strength, and an appropriate surface finish.

The final stage, the final challenge, is to convert the textile product into its end use. That conversion—for example, into clothing, furniture, or household and industrial fabrics—is generally considered an inherent part of the textile industry. But textile products are used in many different ways in a multitude of other industries.

[*See also* Clothing Trades; Cotton; Cotton Industry; Fashion Industry; Linen Industry; Sheep and Goats; Silk Industry; *and* Wool Industry.]

BIBLIOGRAPHY

Chapman, S. D. *The Cotton Industry in the Industrial Revolution.* Basingstoke, U.K., 1972.

Cole, Arthur Harrison. *The American Wool Manufacture.* 2 vols. Cambridge, Mass., 1926.

English, W. *The Textile Industry.* London, 1969.

Farnie, D. A. *The English Cotton Industry and the World Market, 1815–1896.* Oxford, 1979.

Goodman, J., and K. Honeyman, *Gainful Pursuits: The Making of Industrial Europe, 1600–1914.* London, 1988.

Graham Clark, W. A. *Manufacture of Woolen, Worsted, and Shoddy in France and England and Jute in Scotland.* Washington, D.C., 1909.

Jenkins, D. T., ed. *The Industrial Revolution*, vol. 8, *The Textile Industries.* Oxford, 1994.

Jenkins, D. T., and K. G. Ponting. *The British Wool Textile Industry 1770–1914.* London, 1982.

Kerridge, Eric. *Textile Manufactures in Early Modern England.* Manchester, 1985.

Murphy, W. S. *The Textile Industries.* London, 1910.

Textile Institute. *Textile Terms and Definitions.* 6th ed. Manchester, 1970.

Wadsworth, A. P., and J. de L. Mann. *The Cotton Trade and Industrial Lancashire, 1600–1780.* Manchester, 1931.

DAVID JENKINS

THAILAND. Thailand is a country of many peoples. The original inhabitants were the Mon and Khmer, the Tai peoples who migrated from southern China into modern Laos, Burma, and Thailand between the seventh and thirteenth centuries, and more recently, Chinese and Indians have arrived.

The modern geographical area of Thailand was inhabited by hunter-gatherers up until ten to twenty thousand years ago, when the inhabitants began to engage in settled agriculture and to domesticate animals, such as the chicken. Bronze smelting arrived in the region around five thousand years ago and iron working about three thousand years ago. The region then was sparsely settled in comparison with China and India.

The Tai people were inhabitants of the lowland valleys of southern China, and they engaged in wet rice cultivation. The expansion of Chinese power in the early centuries CE saw the beginnings of Tai migration to the south and west. They were involved in raising cattle, fishing, and weaving cloth and implements as well as growing rice. They lived in villages that were grouped into a larger unit, the *müang*, based on both physical and personal relationships among villages.

A different group of people, whom the Tai used as slaves and menial laborers, lived in the hills and generally held the status of vassals of the Tai. The Tai gradually moved away from the Chinese and Vietnamese peoples toward the river valleys south and west and steadily increased in population. The Nan-chao Empire in southern China flourished in the eighth and ninth centuries. Maintaining contact with India across the northern part of modern Thailand, the empire brought a flow of trade goods and ideas, such as the spread of the Buddhist faith among the Tai. At this time, Thailand had no centralized government, and power remained with local chiefs and within the *müang*. In this paternalistic society, chiefs provided security and material rewards, such as food, while the villagers provided labor and respected the chief. The chief nominally owned and controlled the land, although in practice individual families claimed and farmed their own plots.

Empires and Monarchs. The empire of Angkor rose in importance in the early ninth century and swiftly expanded from Cambodia to encompass most of modern Thailand. Governors were established in the provinces with the assistance of a military garrison, administrative officials, and a highway network. By the eleventh or twelfth century, the Tai had mostly finished their migration into modern Thailand and Laos. By settling on the lowland plains of the fertile Chaophraya Valley, they were able to generate enough of a food surplus to form cities and an urban population. The strong Buddhism within the Tai people apparently enabled them to assimilate the other lowland people in the Chaophraya Valley into the Tai culture rather than the other way around.

In the thirteenth century, small Tai states formed on the western edge of the Angkorian Empire and generally pushed back Khmer influence. The northern Tai state of Lan Na become predominant under King Mangrai, who in 1292 founded the city of Chiang Mai, which has remained the regional capital. Another state, Sukhothai, on the edge of the plains near the beginning of the hill country of northern Thailand, also rose to prominence. Sukhothai enjoyed an agricultural surplus, a well-developed textiles industry, and a high degree of personal freedom under the ruler. During this period, the written form of the Thai language developed. The silkworm industry and mulberry cultivation became popular, and silk was exported into Angkor. The Tai kingdoms began sending diplomats on overseas missions and engaging in foreign trade with China and India both overland and by sea.

In 1351, the empire of Ayudhya, based in the river port city of the same name, began to rise in importance. The empire expanded under a highly centralized system of manpower requisition in which each freeman was obliged to serve the king for six months of every year either as a laborer or in the army. Such a system stood in contrast to the traditional relationships whereby freemen gave service to personal patrons while ignoring state boundaries. It was also possible for a freeman to sell himself and his family into bondage. He retained his civil rights and was paid a sum of money for which he gave up his labor services for a period of time. This gave Ayudhya an advantage over its neighbors, as it could call on a large supply of labor in times of need. Control of distant provinces and important administrative posts was usually given to relatives of the king to maintain loyalty. In the fifteenth century, King Borommatrailokanat implemented a great codification of laws, both civilian and military, and divided the bureaucracy into functional areas. Education for priests and laymen was mainly in the hands of monasteries during premodern times, while women were educated at home.

In the fifteenth century, Malacca was founded as a trading entrepôt through which Ayudhya exported rice and imported luxuries and cloth from India. The king maintained a monopoly on international trade, which, with the flowering of Indian commerce upon the arrival of Europeans on its shores in the sixteenth century, increased the wealth and power of the ruling, urban class at the expense of the rural populace. The first Europeans in Thailand, the Portuguese, derived commercial treaties with Ayudhya and supplied it with guns and ammunition. The seaborne trade shifted the focus of Southeast Asian societies seaward and encouraged internal migration to these parts.

A comprehensive military invasion from Burma in 1558 initiated the looting of major Tai cities that continued until 1569, when Ayudhya was sacked and large sections of the country were depopulated. The period immediately after this was one of rebuilding international trade with Portugal, the Spanish-controlled Philippines, and Japan and the building of new commercial relations with the Dutch and the English, who established trading posts at Ayudhya. Thailand mainly exported rice, hides, spices, and tropical woods in return for cloth, luxury goods, firearms, and silver. The threat of internal rebellion and many irregular successions to the throne prompted Ayudhya to hire skilled foreigners for key administrative posts, those whose loyalties were not with any one court faction. The kingdom of Lan Na, under the control of Burma, did not fare so well in those years as its residents were subject to heavy taxes, frequent conscriptions into the army, and often resettlement into Burma proper.

In the early eighteenth century, a strong Thailand successfully invaded and exacted tribute from Cambodia, and its exports of rice to China boomed. However, this economic success led to problems, for many farmers evaded the compulsory labor service to the king or paid off their service with commodities in lieu of work. As a result, the king had difficulty raising labor in times of need, such as the prolonged Burmese invasion of the 1760s. Ayudhya was captured and pillaged in 1767 with great loss of life and property, and the survivors were forced into slavery in Burma.

Nevertheless, recovery was swift. A new capital was founded at Thonburi (opposite modern Bangkok) six months after the sack of Ayudhya, and a new kingdom began. In 1774, Lan Na rebelled against Burma and went over to the Thailand side, prompting a raid from Burma and the depopulation of Chiang Mai, which remained deserted for some years afterward. A new king in 1782 moved the capital across the river to Bangkok and began construction of new palaces and canals. Merchants and traders moved there soon after. The island of Penang was ceded to the East India Company in 1785 to gain an ally against Burma, and Chiang Mai and western Lan Na were resettled to protect against future invasions. A modernization of the legal code was completed in 1805. To protect against manpower shortages, freemen were tattooed with details of their town of residence and immediate master, which enabled the king to maintain his power at the expense of regional nobles. Raids into Burma were carried out from northern Thailand to capture villagers and resettle them in Thailand. The early nineteenth century saw the largest geographical expanse of Thailand, including modern Thailand, Cambodia, Laos, and parts of northern Malaysia. The central states, full parts of the empire, provided tax revenue and manpower, while the outer periphery often remained quasi-independent, only paying tribute to Bangkok.

A treaty signed with Great Britain in 1826 defined the boundary between Thailand and British-controlled Burma, set up a framework to resolve disputes, and reduced trade taxes on foreign merchants. This reduction in trade barriers expanded Thailand's foreign trade, especially with Singapore in the midcentury. In the 1830s and 1840s, the country undertook a mass resettlement of Laotian villagers from the east side of the Mekong River to the western side, closer to central Thailand on the Khorat Plateau. British pressure through the nineteenth century forced Thailand in 1855 to further reduce trade taxes, to remove state export monopolies, and to permit foreigners to own land and be subject to foreign courts if charged with any crime while in Thailand. Trade expanded further on steam-powered vessels, which brought steam-powered industry to Thailand in the second half of the century.

Toward the end of the nineteenth century, Thailand, under pressure from the French in the east, ceded Cambodia and then Laos over a period of forty years. Early in the twentieth century, Britain took northern Malaysia from Thailand along with the rights to construct and finance the railway between Bangkok and Singapore. In contrast with many other developing countries at the time, Thailand, rightly afraid of giving away too much power to European interests, did not enter into foreign loans but was forced to devote more expenditure to the military to ward off future European encroachment on its territory.

Modern Era. In a reform of the governance of Thai provinces in 1893, governors were appointed by merit rather than by birth, and the power of the regional elite rapidly declined. Governors were given wider powers, courts were overhauled, the educational system was expanded, and the police force was revamped. This enabled state revenues to double over a period of years and brought security to the countryside. With the movement to a fully cash economy, compulsory labor service was abolished in 1905, although universal military conscription partly took its place. The population inside the current boundaries of Thailand rose from fewer than four million people before 1700 to six or seven million in 1900, when it began to grow rapidly.

An increase in the price of rice in the late nineteenth century spurred a 50 percent increase in the land area devoted to its cultivation and a tenfold increase in exports in fifty years. The elimination of compulsory labor facilitated this growth, as villagers worked in the area most economically productive for them. Also at this time, a large-scale immigration of Chinese people occurred. Settling mainly around Bangkok, their share of the population increased to around 10 percent at the end of the century. The Chinese provided the labor force for the industrialization of the country, building its canals, railways, buildings, and industrial plants.

During World War I, Thailand took the side of the Allies, which enabled it to send representatives to the peace conferences and to gain the power to demand the full sovereignty of Thai courts over foreigners and the right to set their own tariffs by the mid-1920s. Volatility in the rice price in the same decade put much pressure on the current account, in turn forcing a large budget deficit, partly caused by excessive spending by the monarch. The Great

THAILAND. Shopkeepers at the floating market in Damnoen Saduak, near Bangkok, 1999. (© A. Ramey/Woodfin Camp and Associates, New York)

Depression hit Thailand hard. Depressed demand for Thai commodity exports forced increased taxes on the middle class. A military coup in 1932 ended the absolute monarchy. Thailand went off the gold standard the same year, which stimulated exports and boosted the economy out of recession. In the 1930s, the new government increased spending on education fourfold, which paid large dividends in future decades as literacy increased markedly.

The Thai economy boomed in the 1950s as the primary exports of rice, rubber, and tin were in high demand during the Korean War and a manufacturing industry began to develop. Thailand entered into a military alliance with the United States, which became a major source of military and development aid. Education was again expanded in the late 1950s, and universities were brought to regional centers. A liberal promotion of free trade and foreign investment again drove the economy forward during the 1960s. The quickly growing population was less than fifteen million before World War II but reached thirty-four million by 1970. A lack of immigration from China and assimilation into the Thai culture has meant that racial problems have become less important. In the 1970s, the economy switched focus away from agricultural, forestry, and mining sectors toward manufacturing and tourist services.

In the 1980s and the early 1990s, the remarkable growth in the secondary and tertiary sectors continued, and living standards rose across the country. The first to suffer from the currency crises that swept Southeast Asia in the late 1990s, Thailand experienced a two-year recession.

BIBLIOGRAPHY

Chakrabongse, Prince Chula. *Lords of Life: A History of the Kings of Thailand*. London, 1960.

Girling, John L. S. *Thailand: Society and Politics*. London, 1981.

Insor, D. *Thailand: A Political, Social, and Economic Analysis*. New York, 1963.

Jacobs, Norman. *Modernization without Development: Thailand as an Asian Case Study*. New York, 1971.

Kasetsiri, Charnvit. *The Rise of Ayudhya: A History of Thailand in the Fourteenth and Fifteenth Centuries*. Kuala Lumpur, Malaysia, 1976.

Neuchterlein, Donald E. *Thailand and the Struggle for Southeast Asia*. Ithaca, N.Y., 1965.

Silcock, T. H. *Thailand: Social and Economic Studies in Development*. Canberra, 1967.

Smith, Ronald Bishop. *Thailand; or, The History of the Thais from 1569 A.D. to 1824 A.D.* Bethesda, Md., 1967.

Terwiel, Barend J. *A History of Modern Thailand*. Saint Lucia, Queensland, Australia, 1983.

Thomlinson, Ralph. *Thailand's Population: Facts, Trends, Problems, and Policies*. Bangkok, Thailand, 1971.

Wood, W. A. R. *A History of Thailand*. Chiang Mai, Thailand, 1924.

Wyatt, David K. *Thailand: A Short History*. New Haven and London, 1982.

LYNDON MOORE

THEATER ARTS. Throughout human history, theater has been widely practiced as an amateur pursuit—in community rituals, in religious observations, or as a pastime for the love of it; but in many cultures it has evolved into a profession, sometimes commercialized and recently fully industrialized. The two systems may be mutually supportive, as in the ancient Athenian Dionysia, where selected *choregoi* (wealthy patrons) each paid a chorus of local citizens to practice songs and dances parttime in preparation for being joined by professionals who were paid by the state and traveled from festival to festival performing the speaking roles. Whether a mass event involving tens of thousands of people, such as the Greek festivals, or a strictly private enactment for an exclusive audience, such as the Lord Chamberlain's Men performing *Twelfth Night* at court for Queen Elizabeth I, theater is defined by the presence of spectators for a live presentation involving narrative and role play by actors. These lines may be blurred, functions may be exchanged during the course of a performance, and the presentation may be of any scale; but these are the indispensable elements. Besides what is typically thought of as theater—the presentation of a spoken dramatic play, fully memorized and with accompanying costuming, appropriate scenic elements, and "heightened" reality requiring a suspension of disbelief by audience and actors—the term also encompasses pageantry, processionals, some spiritual possession rites, and a range of genres, from dance through opera, that mix and hybridize endlessly. It is a truly protean practice, sometimes aspiring to art, existing to represent the entire spectrum of human experience through mimetic embodiment.

Social and Economic Considerations. The civic manifestations of theater are varied: the Athenian contests in the fifth century BCE; royal and mayoral entries and inaugurations since the Middle Ages; *landjuweel* festivals sprouting out of Renaissance chambers of rhetoric in the Low Countries; and in the twentieth century, state-subsidized national and local theaters, performing arts centers, and civic centers celebrated from Seoul to Sydney, Accra to Ottawa, and Wuppertal to Washington, D.C. All are of a piece with a vital festival circuit that has sprung up globally since 1945, emulating Avignon and Edinburgh, encompassing the gamut of work from highbrow to irreverent, elite to avant-garde, establishment to student, and drawing in tourist revenue and cultural capital in kind with Olympic games, trade fairs, and sport franchises. In socialist Europe, almost all theaters were nationalized in the twentieth century.

For-profit theater has existed since the Middle Ages, with itinerant troupes migrating throughout Europe as jongleurs, troubadours, and meistersingers. They played at inns, barns, markets, and fairs, and usually their audience's payment was voluntary. Some of these troupes evolved in the sixteenth and seventeenth centuries into more permanent companies, playing in the *corrales* of Madrid, the Bankside playhouses of London, and the Théâtre du Marais in Paris. The trend is traceable interna-tionally through what became known as *commedia dell'-arte troupes* (literally "theaters of the profession," which specialized in improvised comedy)—originating in Italy and spreading their traditions and stock characters to France, Spain, England, and German-speaking portions of Europe; deeply influencing Molière, Lope de Vega, and Jonson; spawning the puppet stalwarts Hanswurst and Punch; inspiring the British harlequinade and pantomime; and influencing twentieth-century actor training and politically explicit theater worldwide. *Commedia dell'-arte traditions* often were rejected in the eighteenth century in favor of a literary theater (the tradition of commedia erudite), usually not for profit, aspiring to produce the works of poets in vernaculars, and leading to German ducal theaters (e.g., Weimar and Saxe-Meiningen), Scandinavian royal theaters (e.g., Drottningholm and Kongelige Teater) and later national theaters. In France, Molière's Troupe de Roy—blending comic improvising traditions with Frenchified ballet and comedy, and elevating the result to serious art—evolved into the Comédie-Française, a national theater in existence since 1680.

Whether as a civic or a commercial entity, the appropriateness of producing theater has often been contested in the West. Plato objected to the inability of mimesis to project truth, and Tertullian regarded shows as pleasures that draw people away from God and propagate vice. Following Philip Stubbes's opinion that plays are "sucked out of the Devills teates to nourish us in ydolatire, hethenrie, and sinne," public theater was banned by Puritans during the English Interregnum; and several New England colonies passed statutes against it, lumping acting with gambling, thieving, and harlotry. (The frequency with which such statutes appeared might indicate the infrequency with which they were observed.) Other arts gained acceptance much more readily and thoroughly than the theater. Music was enshrined as a mode of worship, architecture heralded the might of individuals and states alike, and painting was venerated as the mark of confident and prosperous nations: all found powerful patrons among the clergy, statesmen, royalty, and burghers. The theater thrived when it found a patron, famously under James I and Charles I and even more so under Louis XIV; but more often troupes scuttled from town to town seeking dispensation from magistrates or seeking to evade legal detection altogether. This was one form of state control over the theatrical marketplace, and censorship of scripts was another. The concept that the theater warranted respect on a par with the other arts was explored by Goethe at Weimar in the late eighteenth century, and the idea that it could be useful to the state was an implicit part of French policy for almost a century after the Revolution, as well as British deregulation through the 1843 Theaters Act; but there was rarely official sanction of Adam Smith's view that it was the

THEATER. Interior of the Theater an der Wien, site of the first performance of Ludwig van Beethoven's only opera, *Fidelio*, in 1809. Watercolor, 1825. (Historisches Museum der Stadt Wien, Vienna/Erich Lessing/Art Resource, NY)

state's duty to create and sustain institutions such as theaters, profitable or otherwise. Even William Archer, the champion of an international modernist style, did not dare argue for a state-financed national theater in laissez-faire Great Britain at the outset of the twentieth century. The conviction that theater should necessarily be supported by the public purse did not gain wide endorsement until the founding of national arts councils in the wake of World War II, first in Britain then in Canada, Australia, and elsewhere. The U.S. National Endowment for the Arts, under constant attack from the political heirs of Tertullian and Stubbes, compares extremely unfavorably in its support of an entire nation of artists when its budget is put alongside that of a modest-sized western German city.

Although many theaters now subsist on a combination of civic, regional, and federal grants (either tax subsidies or lottery profits), it is now considered impossible for all but the most commercial theaters to meet all the expenses of a unionized workforce through grants and box office revenue alone. From the 1980s, under the influence of Reaganite and Thatcherite agendas, additional corporate and foundation sponsorship has become the norm in national, regional, and civic theaters. Increasingly, too, theaters are forming alliances to coproduce shows, sharing the costs of design, development, and rehearsal and having successive runs in the allied venues. The purely commercial tier—most of what is called Broadway in New York and the West End in London—is made feasible by patient but usually disappointed investors hoping for long runs, national tours, and international transplants. This commercial theater trades quite explicitly on "star" talent for box office allure, often giving well-known cinema actors the chance to ply their skills in a rewarding way than in films but at salaries that are a fraction of what film companies can pay. By these means, Britain has achieved a theatrical trade surplus in excess of its steel industry.

Below both the commercial and the large subsidized theaters exists a huge array of companies known variously as fringe, off-off-Broadway, or storefront, often catering to a less risk-averse consumer than the larger theaters do, in small venues at significantly lower ticket costs. These theaters typically operate on a combination of below–union scale wages and volunteerism offset by modest box office returns and small project-based grants.

Industrial Organization: Employment. Much of theater history is marked by voluntary participation, through either social involvement in rites of passage, seasonal celebrations, or transfers of power. Thus, an Objibwa shaman's induction into the Grand Medicine Society, a Staffordshire maid's impersonation of Queen of the May, and a Kwakiutl chief's potlatch have much in common with the coronation celebrations of Tsar Nicholas II. Throughout medieval Europe, glaziers, shipwrights, bakers, and mercers annually staged the biblical stories, coordinated as cycles (mystery plays) or biographies of Christ (Passion plays). The reward for participation in all such cases is purely social.

Among professionals, there are two traditional varieties of artists: those tied to a particular company or patron, such as the *sociétaires* of the Comédie-Française, and freelancers, such as Charlotte Cushman or Ira Aldridge, nineteenth-century stars who toured Europe playing principal roles in established companies. Nowadays, most artists work under contract for a particular show or period of time; but dance companies tend to specify long periods of employment, because of the nature of the repertoire.

Since the late eighteenth century, much of this kind of labor has been brokered by theatrical agents. Originally based in "houses of call," which out-of-work performers frequented to find what was available, thus providing a service to employers and employees alike, agents now are gatekeepers of the profession. Newcomers find it increasingly difficult to get auditions without an agent, and agents take care of the increasingly legalistic aspects of negotiating contracts. During the nineteenth century, agents served chiefly the lower ranks of the dramatic profession and the music hall (vaudeville in America, *café chantant* in France) where labor was easily expendable and laborers were largely interchangeable. Now, having the services of an agent is a mark of stature—not necessarily success but potentiality, desirability, and marketability.

When Adam Smith noted in *The Wealth of Nations* that the performer "puts a price upon his loss of *caste*," he meant that the source of performers' ability to demand high wages was the prejudice that decried the exercise of performers' talents "as a sort of public prostitution." The ability to demand high wages is a fairly recent phenomenon, and even so very selectively applied. When William Shakespeare, writer but also actor in the Lord Chamberlain's Men, bought the elegant New Place in Stratford-upon-Avon and invested in malt, he did so from his profits as a shareholding actor and writer in Burbage's company. Shareholding's cousin, the "commonwealth" system, was usually the resort of actors abandoned on the road by an insolvent manager, and an indication of instability in organization rather than communitarian goals. Since the Renaissance, players usually have been waged under contract. In the stock system that prevailed until the mid-nineteenth century, contracts were generally for a season (a year or less). Some performers commanded high salaries commensurate with their ability to draw spectators. Although rates of reward could be high, most performers earned subsistence wages when the inevitable periods of seasonal unemployment and expenses of their trade were factored in. According to Equity statistics, modern actors can expect to work on average three weeks out of the year; the rest of their time is spent "resting," that is, working in another trade. In this market, any actor whose living is earned entirely from the theater is considered a great success.

Since the mid-eighteenth century, actors have organized collectively for self-help, mutual help, and savings purposes to insure themselves against the exigencies of fragile employment, ill-health, and other hardships. In the nineteenth century, Masonic lodges catered to a wide socioeconomic spectrum within the profession, but served only men whose families benefited only if the Mason died. Meanwhile, theater companies organized their own, relatively egalitarian, friendly societies, granting sick pay, medical costs, superannuation, and survivors' pensions. In England, these societies first served specific theaters (the first being the Covent Garden Theatrical Fund in 1765, modeled on French precursors) or circuits (such as the York circuit fund, from 1815 on); but subsequent Victorian funds were industrywide (the Royal General Theatrical Fund, founded in 1839, and the Dramatic, Equestrian and Musical Sick Fund of 1855), in part in recognition of the growing unlikelihood that a career would be spent in a single company. In the 1880s and 1890s, numerous purely charitable funds were founded by leading performers for the relief of those fallen on hard times, without membership requirements. The Theatrical Ladies Guild (1891) was the earliest in Britain dedicated exclusively to women and children, recognizing a wide range of needs: medical expenses, food, decent clothing in which to appear presentable while seeking work, and the necessities of newborns. In the absence of social welfare, this aid could be a lifesaver.

Actors' employment was so tied to personal relationships with employers that they were loath to stand collectively; and because they usually aspired to being managers, they sympathized with their employers. In Britain, music hall and variety artists, whose labor was more depersonalized than that of stage actors, held a widespread strike in 1908. Their work was perceived separately from that of dramatic actors, who did not manage to establish their trade union, Actors' Equity of Great Britain, until 1929, long after the French, Germans, Danes, and Americans did so. In the United States, actors in the Yiddish theater were the first to organize, as the Hebrew Actors' Union (1899). The Actors' Society of 1896 led in 1913 to the Actors' Equity Association, which became an affiliate of the American Federation of Labor (AFL) in 1919 when it struck, swelling its membership from twenty-seven hundred to fourteen thousand. Closed shops followed in 1924, and mandated employer contributions to pensions began in 1960. The unions have been instrumental in enforcing wage scales, payment for rehearsals, backstage safety, and standardized contracts.

Stage hands organized earlier than performers. In England, their pay went to "bosses," who distributed it among the male laborers in a department. Thus, Victorian payrolls typically show a single entry for the "Master carpenter and assistants," "Propertyman and assistants," or "Gas engineer," rather than an entry for each laborer. This system gave the workers an edge as organized blocs. In 1866, scene shifters at thirteen theaters all over London struck for a sixpence per night increase, seeking parity with Covent Garden's scene shifters, who earned two shillings a night, the same wage the Standard Theater in the East End paid to the fly, stage, and cellar-level bosses. The strike was broken, and twenty-nine operatives at the Princess's were fired. In 1890, kick-started by the dock strike the year before, twelve carpenters at the Adelphi Theater approached their boss for a wage increase and were summarily dismissed. This incident directly resulted in the formation of a trade union, now known as the National Association of Theatrical, Television, and Kine [Cinematic] Employees. Theater managers found it all too easy to stamp out collectivization, and an industrywide union was the only solution, with the traditional women's department, the wardrobe, the last to be successfully recruited. An affiliated American union was founded in 1893, joining with a Canadian counterpart in 1898 to become the International Alliance of Theatrical Stage Employees. The IATSE houses are all closed shops; whether a theater is unionized depends on the size of the house and the strength of the local.

Technological Considerations: Aesthetics. Theater celebrates the visual and aural labors of actors and musicians, encouraging the invisibility of stage hands' and technicians' labor whenever possible. Exceptions exist among certain ancient puppetry forms—the manipulators of *bunraku* in Japan or *wayang kulit* in Indonesia are fully visible to spectators—as well as modern-day anti-illusionist choices such as scene and property changes on open stages. For the most part, when scenic spectacle has been part of an aesthetic, its effect has been achieved in part through the seeming erasure of the mechanisms of movement or change and the invisibility of human operators. The *deus ex machina* (god in the machine) of the Greek stage is impressive only because the actor-as-god moves through the auspices of an unattributable means, though the technician knows it to be wood and levers. Likewise, Baroque deities and cherubim floating amid canvas and pigment clouds are entrancing in part because the platforms, ropes, and pulleys suspending them are obscured, and the sweating laborers are hidden behind the scenes.

Hand labor was the dynamo equally for Greeks' *ekkyklema* (rolled platforms for displaying tableaux) and medieval mansion stages (which, as pageant wagons, became portable). Perspective painting techniques, reintroduced to the theater through Serlio's commentaries on Vitruvius's *De Architectura* (1537–1551), created an illusion of depth, cohesion, and proportion, and revolutionized stages and staging. In Japan the Noh stage and in Europe the public stages adopted a platform and perfunctory architectural frontage, but stages for the display of perspective scenery became normative in European private theaters. First explored by Scamozzi in the theater at Sabbioneta in 1588, this vista scenery, enhanced by the chariot-and-pole mechanics of Torelli from the 1640s on, pioneered the practice that prevailed for three centuries. Italian technology was exported throughout Europe by artists such as the Bibienas, who first made their mark with the Teatro Farnese in the 1680s. They designed intricate systems consisting of multiple pairs of side flats (canvas stretched on frames) coordinated with overhead borders and back panels on drops. All the pieces connected to slots, ropes, and pulleys, and could be moved simultaneously from under and behind the stage, in full view of the audience but apparently without human agency. The success of this technology lay in the unification of architectural expertise, mechanical engineering, and painterly knowledge in a single designer. A nautical protocol prevailed in shifting from one scene to another: codes of whistles signaled operators when to pull a rope or shift a counterweight, a direct adoption of sailors' work with the hemp rigging and canvas sail on wooden ships. From the mid-seventeenth century on, perspective scenery also became ubiquitous in public theaters.

Although the systems for moving the canvas scenery had been so simplified by the end of the eighteenth century that sometimes they could be operated by a single individual at a crank, more complex forms of illusion were being introduced that sustained demands for laborers. Practicable scenery—the castle rampart, the Oedipus Tower, the bridge—that could be walked upon, fallen from, and dangled over, involved greater three-dimensionality in engineering, and in the nineteenth century considerably more sculptural plasticity, than mere trompe l'oeil painting. It also required legions of carpenters to move it quickly on and off the stage during performances. The nineteenth-century stage was a warren of pieces that were trucked in at stage level, emerged through trap doors, and dropped down from the flies. All this required extensive hand labor, sometimes hundreds of men, coordinated by a stage manager. Only with hydraulics, elevator stages, and electric-powered revolves, first introduced to Germany and the United States at the turn of the twentieth century, did this demand for labor abate.

The theater never adopted steam power to move even the heaviest scenery; the noise of the engines and byproducts of combustion would have marred the performances' audibility and visibility. Although steam as a vaporous decorative element was used at Munich in about 1880, it was notoriously difficult to control and disperse. Except in the largest theaters and in opera houses, electricity has not been extensively incorporated into shifting; instead, the costs of labor in the twentieth century encouraged a minimalist aesthetic, first expressed in the revival of the bare stage, then widely incorporated into thrust arrangements with the audience on three sides of the playing space. This concept tends to reduce scenery to a few pieces of furniture and almost eliminates the costs of building as well as shifting it; successive locales are facilitated by the imagination rather than the carpenter. Alternately, the postmodern aesthetic allows for the simultaneous presentation of multiple locales, differentiated by lighting, platforms, and usage. Thus, the economy of a single-set design can be accomplished; sometimes costly to build, it requires little labor during the run of a show.

Although the theater can dispense with scenery entirely—an open or "found" playing space surrounded by the audience is common in many cultures, from Yoruba rituals to aboriginal storytelling to the "environmental staging" of the 1960s and after—the theater is almost unthinkable without illumination. Outdoors, sunshine is adequate, but there have been relatively few traditions of daytime performance. Moonlight must be augmented, as in the all-night *kathakali* of Kerala. Indoors, even in the daytime, artificial lighting is needed. The Renaissance theater used smoky torches, but candles and oil lamps remained the preferred means until early in the nineteenth century, as chandeliers over the stage, sconces on balconies, battens behind side flats, and "floats" at the forestage illuminated the various areas. Legions of children trimmed the wicks and replaced the fuel throughout performances. Candlelight could be colored through using glass media, though with great compromises to intensity. Mobile light, simulating the movement of a celestial object, could be indicated but not well simulated, even with the addition of reflectors.

The introduction of gaslight to England and America in 1816–1817 revolutionized stage lighting, considerably increasing flexibility of location, special effects, and intensity. Stinking tallow and spermicetti were banished in favor of odoriferous coal gas, which emitted a great deal of heat and presented an enormous fire hazard but burned bright and white and could be controlled throughout the theater by a single operator. Wonderful effects of chiaroscuro could be achieved by an engineer's twist of a stopcock. When filled with beeswax—or, worse, the infinitely more economical dripping, reeking tallow—chandeliers were difficult to access during performances. When these devices were replaced by gas, the auditoriums and deep stage areas alike were illuminated as never before. The Paris Opéra of 1857 included twenty-eight miles of gas piping supplying 960 jets. The entire depth and breadth of a stage became usable, but intense illumination of the performer's face remained troublesome except at the extreme front of the stage, and even so shadows still were not thoroughly eliminated.

The 1837 introduction of limelight, a technology originally developed for lighthouses, to theaters allowed use of an intense focused beam that registered even through the brightest gas effect. Mounted in the flies and manipulated by a chemist who ignited jets of hydrogen and oxygen over a piece of quicklime, limelight was used as a mobile "spotlight" to follow stars or create special effects, such as moonbeams or dream "shafts."

The second revolution in lighting began in 1881, with the introduction of incandescent electric fixtures at the Savoy Theater in London. They presented considerably diminished fire risk, were manipulable, could be easily colored by using glass or films, remained comparatively cool, were completely odorless, and could be hung and directed so as to illuminate actors' faces from all angles anywhere on stage. Subsequent innovations in electric lighting have concentrated on focusing the light, the control of individual rather than "ganged" instruments, and, most recently, dynamism, as automated fixtures in every instrument allow for infinite resettings programmed into a central computer. There is no longer a question of adequate or even well-directed light; designers can determine mood through light utilization as never before. The work of choosing, hanging, focusing, and programming lighting instruments has become increasingly specialized with these new technologies, and the job of running the lighting board has become more art than science.

Chemical flash powders have been deployed since the Middle Ages to authenticate dragons and hell mouths. Everything from sulfur to fireworks has been ignited in indoor theaters to augment battles, royal fêtes, conflagrations, and disasters of every kind. Pyrotechnists were employed for centuries until fire marshals clamped down on their use in the twentieth century, and such special effects were relegated to electric lighting and projections. Sound effects—thunder rolls, metal sheets, pounding cannon balls, and so on—have been used for atmospheric purposes since the Greeks, but until recently were not considered an employment specialty. With the introduction of reel-to-reel tape in the 1950s, recorded effects could be reliably arranged and cued for the first time. More recently, the introduction of economical CD-ROM technology has encouraged the utilization of full-fledged soundscapes; and gone are the days of technically proficient electricians at a tape machine. Sound designers often have backgrounds in the recording industry or musical composition, and with MIDI (Musical Instrument Digital Interface) controls can send cues from one computer to dozens of devices with unprecedented agency over the level, length, source, and mixture of sound. This is an emerging area of stage technology, and in the United States the United Scenic Artists Union, which embraces other elements of design, has not yet claimed sound although IATSE has a branch in New York.

Costs and Feasibility. The costs of technology escalated in the Renaissance, but with the adoption of courtly scenic traditions by public theaters in the Baroque period it became necessary to increase the size of auditoriums in order to finance the spectacles. The scenery was standardized: stock settings for palaces, forests, streets, and cottages were reusable in countless plays. The late-nineteenth-century theater hit the apogee of spectacle; long before naturalism's reconstructive aesthetic was consolidated by David Belasco, the stage thrilled with torrential waterfalls, full-rigged ships rocking on fulcrums, ice floes, sinking watercraft, and remounted naval triumphs, to name just a few of the aquatic standards. From the 1860s on, the stock repertoire system was almost entirely superseded by long runs in every genre except grand opera. From then on, scenery was specially designed for a particular production, tied to a particular play, and not readily transferred. It could be warehoused and then remounted or sold, but it could not be reutilized by the same management in recognizable form. The scenery thus significantly increased the costs of the research and development phase of production, which were recoverable only if a long run was achieved.

Long runs significantly altered the staffing and financing of dramatic theaters. In order to offset some of the risk of investing, theaters increasingly relied on out-sourced manufacturing, contracting out scene building instead of maintaining scenic shops and carpenters or painting bays and scene painters. The expense of costuming lesser players generally had been borne by theaters' wardrobe departments, with principal actors usually supplying their own costumes. Still, this necessitated a costuming workforce of many dozens in a theater such as Drury Lane, where a premium was put on spectacle: during the 1812–1813 season, 54,697 yards of cloth and 8,462 dozen buttons were brought to the theater to be stitched by hand with 362 pounds of thread. Increasingly, from the mid-nineteenth century on, costumes and props were rented from specialty suppliers rather than fabricated and stored by theaters themselves. The variety of historically accurate equipment, furniture, wigs, footwear, and gowns available for rent in most European capitals was mind-boggling. Workers once retained on theater payrolls—armorers in the metal trades; property makers in whitesmithing, paper-making, and upholstery; painters combining expertise as colorists with the skill of illusionists; boot- and shoemakers in the bespoke leather trades; seamsters and tailors in clothing fabrication; carpenters and joiners representing the building trades; and peruquiers in wig making—all joined the bill posters, printers, publishers, iron mongers, basket workers, silver and gold leaf appliers, glaziers, mer-

cers, and fancy-goods suppliers of all descriptions who had long been contracting with theaters on a custom basis. The tradition of contracting workout still prevails in commercial theater, is ubiquitous in opera outside major capitals, but is less so in regional and civic theaters, which tend to be more self-sufficient with their use of technicians and artisans.

Safety. Large gatherings have presented dangers to public safety throughout history. Tacitus described how the gladiatorial amphitheater at Fidena, five miles from Rome, built by Atilius solely "for sordid gain" in 27 CE, "failed both to lay the foundation in solid ground and to secure the fastenings of the wooden structure above" (*Annals* IV). It collapsed inward, and maimed or crushed tens of thousands of spectators. The age of gaslight marks the period of greatest risk from fire. Not including panics or structural collapses, which both remained prevalent causes of death, Sachs and Woodrow give a low-ball estimate of 9,335 human lives lost in fires in the century prior to 1896 (*Modern Opera Houses and Theaters, London, 1896–1898*).

Choquet's figures show a high loss of life in 1830s (800 deaths occurring in the 1836 Saint Petersburg fire out of a total of 813 that decade) and great mortality in the decade of the 1840s (1,670 deaths in the 1845 fire in Canton and 200 in the fire at Quebec the following year), rivaled by the 1870s (600 deaths in Tientsin, 283 in Brooklyn, and 110 in Sacramento). The infamous 1881 fire at the Ringtheater in Vienna, where 386 perished—some from effects of fire and others from stabbing and strangulation—in the same year that electricity was introduced to the Savoy made Europeans sit up and take notice. Choquet's death count from 1800 to 1885 is 5,374 from a total of 665 fires, or 62.5 deaths per year, with an average of 8 deaths per fire (Strathclyde Regional Archives MP 18.498).

The conflagrations culminated in 1903 with the tragic deaths of 600—mostly children—at the Iroquois Theater in Chicago. British authorities had implemented regular inspections in 1855 and enforced more stringent safety codes beginning in 1890, but it was the Iroquois Theater fire that spawned the most exacting regulations, strangling Chicago's theater industry until 1970.

Theaters were insurable, but only at great expense, and rarely at their full value. In Britain, owners of the real estate were usually not the operators; so the British insisted that lessees insure only the fabric of the building and not the stock or fixtures within it. Although insurance added considerably to the cost of doing business, fire was to be expected. In 346 fires traced by Sachs and Woodrow, the average longevity of the theaters was eighteen years. Nine percent of theaters burned before they were a year old, 21 percent burned between the second and fifth years, and 19 percent were destroyed between the sixth and tenth years. Asbestos safety curtains were effective only when the proscenium wall was fireproofed with steel, insistence up-on clear aisles was helpful only when the exit doors were made to swing outward, and the containment of fire was lifesaving only when spectators did not stampede in panic. Even after theaters out-sourced much of their manufacturing, they could not banish combustibles; paint thinners and sawdust were inevitably nearby, and performers themselves—clad in gauze frocks in perilous proximity to open gas jets—regularly went up in flames. The adoption of electricity, periodically upgraded to facilitate greater equipment loads, was met with the constant vigilance of civic authorities, curtailing incidents of fire. In many Western nations, theaters are under double surveillance, by fire marshals and by the workers' unions.

Management and Entrepreneurship. Among professional theaters, the classic form of managerial organization is family-based. Among the Gelosis, Ichikawa Danjūrōs, and Kembles, multiple generations have held sway in some of the most important European companies. Britain pioneered public ownership, in the stock issues of many so-called theaters royal, beginning with Edinburgh in 1767. Perhaps this is why entertainment was an early and prevalent exploiter of relaxed limited-liability laws in the mid-nineteenth century. Hundreds of theaters and music halls all over Britain were funded this way. A few became extraordinarily large: Registered in 1899 with joint capital of £1,650,000, based on ten separate companies with fourteen music halls, Moss' Empires had grown to £2,086,000 by 1906, with the addition of other properties funded by public stock issues. With twenty houses in 1900, and thirty-five in 1906, it grew rapidly into the largest theater enterprise in the world, and approximately the forty-fourth largest industrial enterprise in Great Britain, ranked by market value of capital. By 1912, Moss' Empires formed a cartel with other chains to control well over one hundred of the most important music halls. With the demise of music hall and revue as viable forms, the company still exists as a major force in London's dramatic marketplace.

In the United States, the Shuberts hybridized the family business with the modern corporation. Originally, three brothers managed properties nationwide out of New York, with limited forays abroad. They were a family business in that most of the capital came from within the partnership, yet a corporation in fact, with $700,000 shares in S. S. & Lee Shubert Inc. bolstering a total of $2,285,799 assets in stock, real estate, cash, and other holdings by 1910. This was a highly stable business, even with the death of the partners, surviving to the present day as the Shubert Organization, which still owns theaters all over America including at least sixteen on Broadway. Enterprises such as the recently failed Livent, producer of *Showboat* and *Ragtime*, also have concentrated artistic autonomy with the founder but raised capital from the stock market rather than a coterie of private investors. Livent's development of exclusive bookings in theaters in Toronto, New York, Chicago, and Vancouver parallels the Shuberts' origin in 1900.

The structure of private limited-liability companies is replicated, in part, within civic theaters through the introduction of boards of directors—prominent community members rather than stockholders—who oversee the financial operations and authorize artistic choices that may be merely suggested by the professional artists. In commercial theaters, the common pattern is for producers to rent from theater owners, just as has been the custom since the boom in permanent public playhouses began in the late seventeenth century. The smallest companies may have boards of directors more closely allied to the artistic talent than boards of the larger companies; the small companies have less to manage and less to lose.

Despite the success of new rival media—recorded sound, film, television, and software—theater continues to survive, and in many markets to thrive. In some respects, the form enjoys greater cultural capital—in both its commercial and its civic manifestations—than it has held since rulers embraced it in the Renaissance. "Liveness," while entailing inefficiencies of labor and expense, carries a cachet and an appeal that sustain theater's competitive edge even in the digital age, even as it increasingly explores new hybridities with such media.

[*See also* Music Industry.]

BIBLIOGRAPHY

Archer, William, and Granville Barker. *Scheme and Estimates for a National Theater*. New York, 1908. A detailed plan for noncommercial theater, in a revised edition that includes the authors' reactions to criticism.

Bailey, Peter. *Music Hall: The Business of Pleasure*. Milton Keynes, 1986.

Baker, Robert Osborne. "The International Alliance of Theatrical Stage Employees and Moving Picture Machine Operators of the United States and Canada." Ph.D. diss., University of Kansas, 1933. The only comprehensive study of stagehands' unionization.

Baumol, William T., and William G. Bowen. *Performing Arts: The Economic Dilemma*. New York, 1966. The classic study of U.S. market forces coinciding with the establishment of the National Endowments.

Bernheim, Alfred L. *The Business of the Theater: An Economic History of the American Theater, 1750–1932* (1932). Reprint, New York, 1964. Unsurpassed as a study of Jacksonian-era American theater and the competition offered by early cinema.

Bolton, Edward. *Culture Wars: Documents from the Recent Controversies in the Arts*. New York, 1992.

Crowhurst, Andrew. "Big Men and Big Business: The Transition From 'Caterers' to 'Magnates' in British Music-Hall Entrepreneurship, 1850–1914." *Nineteenth Century Theater* 25.1 (1997), 33–59.

Davis, Tracy C. "Theatrical Charity and Self-Help for Women Performers." *Theater Notebook* 41.3 (1987), 114–128.

Davis, Tracy C. *The Economics of the British Stage, 1800–1914*. Cambridge, 2000.

Harris, John S. *Government Patronage of the Arts in Great Britain*. London and Chicago, 1970.

Hemmings, Frederick W. J. *The Theatre Industry in Nineteenth-Century France*. Cambridge, 1993.

Hemmings, Frederick W. J. *Theatre and the State in France, 1760–1905*. Cambridge, 1994.

Izenour, George C. *Theatre Technology*. 2d ed. New Haven, 1996.

Kershaw, Baz. "Discouraging Democracy: British Theater and Economics, 1979–1999." *Theatre Journal* 51 (1999), 267–283.

Leinwand, Theodore B. *Theatre, Finance and Society in Early Modern England*. Cambridge, 1999.

Looseley, David L. *The Politics of Fun: Cultural Policy and Debate in Contemporary France*. Oxford, 1995.

Macleod, Joseph. *The Actor's Right to Act*. London, 1981. Discusses the formation of American and British Actors' Equity trade unions.

Marquis, Alice Goldfarb. *Art Lessons: Learning from the Rise and Fall of Public Arts Funding*. New York, 1995.

Milhous, Judith, Gabriella Dideriksen, and Robert D. Hume. *Italian Opera in Late Eighteenth-Century London*, vol. 2, *The Pantheon Opera and Its Aftermath, 1790–1795*. Oxford, 2000.

Rosselli, John. *The Opera Industry in Italy from Cimarosa to Verdi: The Role of the Impresario*. Cambridge, 1984.

Tenney, John. "In the Trenches: The Syndicate–Shubert Theatrical War." *The Passing Show: Newsletter of the Shubert Archive* 21.2 (1998), 2–18.

Wilson, Peter. *The Athenian Institution of the Khoregia*. Cambridge, 2000.

TRACY C. DAVIS

THREE-FIELD SYSTEM. *See* Crop Rotation.

THYSSEN, AUGUST (1842–1926), German entrepreneur and steel industrialist.

After his death, international newspapers regularly commented that Thyssen was the great "Americanizer" and "trustmaker" among German industrialists. Among the wealthiest men in Germany, Thyssen was dubbed by *The New York Times*, the "Rockefeller of the Ruhr." In 1925, Thyssen had to decide whether to submerge his family enterprise into the new German steel trust, Vereinigte Stahlwerke (VSt, United Steel Works), which was modeled on U.S. Steel. (At the time, VSt became the second-largest corporation in Germany behind IG Farben, as well as the second-largest steel corporation in the world behind U.S. Steel.) VSt would be either the crowning achievement of Thyssen's long career or the end of one of Germany's most successful privately held enterprises. August Thyssen died just weeks after the founding of VSt. His two heirs, Fritz Thyssen and Heinrich Thyssen-Bornemisza, could not agree about joining VSt, so Heinrich Thyssen-Bornemisza remained independent, but Fritz Thyssen brought his part of the inheritance into VSt.

The Thyssen-Konzern, several legally independent firms acting as a single enterprise, became one of Germany's largest industrial complexes, rivaled only by Siemens or Krupp. Like many German firms, this enterprise was built on aggressive exporting, a strong producer orientation, the commercialization of new science-based technologies, and an increasing tendency to scale combined with a commitment to vertical integration and product scope.

In 1871, the year of German unification, Thyssen had founded his first steel venture, Thyssen & Co., in Mülheim (Ruhr), a rolling mill that manufactured strip steel, sheets, plates, and pipes. Alone, it became one of Germany's largest pipe and tube producers, and it acted as the financial holding of the Thyssen-Konzern before 1914. Thyssen & Co. included a machine-engineering department that eventually manufactured entire rolling mills, steam engines, and water-pumping equipment, largely as an in-house contractor for other Thyssen ventures. After 1900, it commercialized the high-powered gas engine, which generated electricity for lighting and driving steel works, blew compressed air into blast furnaces and steel converters to improve the quality of the steel, and delivered excess electricity to regional electric companies. Thyssen led the world in the application and development of regeneration economies—the recycling of waste gas energies from steelmaking operations, to drive these powerful gas engines and turbines. In 1911, this department became the Thyssen & Co. Machine Company (Maschinenfabrik Thyssen & Co. AG) to "conquer the domestic and world market." It soon played a crucial role in developing the distinctive "German" path of corporate and technological development that stressed the recycling of "waste" material, including by-products from coking and steelmaking operations. It also epitomized the many German companies that integrated research and development (R&D) facilities into their business organizations; this combination of theoretical science, applied research, and commercialization is combined in the German term *Verwissenschaftlichung*, the "scientific professionalization" of production.

In the 1890s, Thyssen & Co. ventured into gas and water supply because public works proved inadequate. Thyssen's gas and waterworks became the largest long-distance supplier in Europe, the first of its kind. Its growth conveniently helped maintain a steady demand for pipes and pumping equipment. In 1921, Thyssen formed the Gasgesellschaft mbH, Hamborn, the direct legal predecessor of Thyssengas GmbH. Thyssen's fame, however, came from his activities as a coal magnate and steel industrialist. In the late 1880s, to head off the threat of cartels in affecting coal and intermediate supplies, he purchased all the shares of the Gewerkschaft Deutscher Kaiser (GDK, the legal predecessor of Thyssen AG or Thyssen-Krupp AG). He transformed the GDK into a fully integrated coal-mining and steel firm built near Duisburg, the largest inland harbor in Europe. By 1913, Thyssen's GDK was the sixth-largest industrial firm in Germany. Thyssen also established a number of other ventures before World War I: a large ironmaking

AUGUST THYSSEN. "Germany's Rockefeller" on his eightieth birthday, 1922. (Underwood & Underwood/Prints and Photographs Division, Library of Congress)

operation for specialty pig iron; a strip steel, wire, and pipe plant; an innovative mineshaft construction company; and limestone mining operations. He also acquired some specialty steel goods manufacturers, had financial stakes in various iron-ore fields across Europe, and moved forward into shipping and distribution. In 1912, he had begun building the most modern, the most "American" steel plant on the continent, in Alsace-Lorraine, the Stahlwerke Thyssen AG. After Germany's loss in World War I, France was awarded this firm.

August Thyssen, one of Germany's most powerful industrialists, had a reputation for ruthless and relentless expansion. (His favorite saying was: "If I rest, I rust.") Unlike the American steel magnate Andrew Carnegie's rhetorical sympathy for the ordinary worker, Thyssen gained a reputation as a hard-driving hardliner regarding labor. In fact, Thyssen was respected and feared rather than revered or loved—and his firms became hotbeds of labor unrest after World War I.

While other German steel combines grew through merger and acquisition, Thyssen managed to create a relatively balanced, vertically integrated Konzern through his own efforts. Despite his public disparagement of cartel inefficiency, Thyssen was a ubiquitous, uncomfortable, but leading presence in German cartels. Thyssen's expansion had rested entirely on private means, and he remained suspicious about issuing equity that might lead to "speculation," limit his "freedom," or jeopardize family control. Thyssen reinvested most of his profits. He did borrow from banks, but the banks never achieved much leverage over him. Thyssen played the banks against one another in his own interests and became notorious for his unconventional financial methods. The constant tension between maintaining family ownership while sustaining rapid expansion, innovation, and competitiveness characterized his strategy.

Although Thyssen gained a reputation as a pioneer of vertical integration, his pioneering achievement lay in the management of these vertically integrated, diversified firms. Unlike other German steel companies, which incorporated their core operations into one large legally unified firm, Thyssen formed a *Konzern*—a multisubsidiary structure of legally independent but affiliated firms that acted as a "single enterprise." In its formal structure, it most resembled a Japanese zaibatsu, in which a family or single powerful entrepreneur managed. Unlike zaibatsu, it did not command the market share and remained largely committed to related product areas. Despite his reputation as an autocrat, this decentralized structure required strong-willed, independent leadership personalities, and Thyssen had a sense for discovering young talented managers and placing them in positions of responsibility. All his executives felt that he genuinely listened to their advice.

Although August Thyssen exemplified the classic family-oriented entrepreneur, he built one of the most sophisticated, modern managerial hierarchies. He established a series of formal corporate offices that administratively bound the legally separate companies into a systematic whole. He developed an early version of the multidivisional structure, or M-form, similar to Mitsui, Mitsubishi, DuPont, General Motors, Siemens, or IG Farben. Ironically, Thyssen's obsession with family control, which made capital scarce, contributed to this development.

[*See also* Zaibatsu.]

BIBLIOGRAPHY

Arnst, Paul. *August Thyssen und Sein Werk*. Leipzig, 1925.
Augustine, Dolores. *Patricians and Parvenus: Wealth and High Society in Wilhelmine Germany*. Oxford, 1994.
Baumann, Carl-Friedrich. *Schloß Landsberg und Thyssen*, edited by Thyssen Aktiengesellschaft and August Thyssen-Stiftung Schloß Landsberg. Duisburg, 1993.
Fear, Jeffrey. "August Thyssen and German Steel." In *Creating Modern Capitalism: How Entrepreneurs, Companies, and Countries Triumphed*

in Three Industrial Revolutions, edited by Thomas K. McCraw, pp. 183–226. Cambridge, Mass., 1997.

Treue, Wilhelm. *Die Feuer Verlöschen Nie: August Thyssen-Hütte 1890–1926*, vol. 1. Düsseldorf, 1966.

Uebbing, Helmut. *Wege und Wegmarken: 100 Jahre Thyssen 1891–1991*, edited by A. G. Thyssen, Berlin, 1991.

JEFFREY FEAR

TIMBER AND LOGGING INDUSTRY. From antiquity to the present, economic power has depended on possessing fleets of cargo ships and, for their security, naval vessels. Until the two ironclads the *Merrimack* and the *Monitor* faced off near the Virginia coast in 1862, almost every ship that had ever sailed was built from wood. Hence, over the millennia, societies regarded wood as vital and access to forests essential. Timber playing such a major role in societal survival and prosperity gave rise to large-scale logging at a very early date.

Early History. Records show a major forestry industry emerging in the early third millennium BCE. With wood native to Egypt never growing large enough to build ships of sufficient size capable of carrying on international commerce or doing battle, Egyptian pharaohs early on realized that their power depended on finding and controlling accessible forested regions in foreign lands. They therefore took control of heavily forested Phoenicia sometime before 2600 BCE. A hieroglyph from the period clearly shows the relationship between two nations, depicting an Egyptian overseeing much smaller Phoenicians either felling cedars with axes and ropes or bowing. Documents from this period confirm Egyptian exploitation of Phoenician woodlands. Egypt's power over this land waxed and waned with its own political fortunes.

Farther east, in what is known as the Fertile Crescent, dominant rulers of various city-states and dynasties raised expeditions to conquer the "cedar mountain" for its timber. The cedar mountain had no fixed location. The only certainty to its whereabouts was that the cedar mountain always existed somewhere in the hills and mountains of the Euphrates, Tigris, and Karun watersheds. For Enannatum, an early ruler of Lagash (a major city-state in Mesopotamia), the cedar mountain existed in the hills just east of the lower Tigris. He overthrew the ruler of this area to acquire its timberlands. After nearby forests such as this one became depleted of large trees, later rulers in the region such as Sargon and Naram-Sin placed the cedar mountain northwest of the Fertile Crescent in present-day Turkey. Their troops conquered the indigenous people who lived in these mountains for access to timber growing there. To secure a continual flow of large wood, Naram-Sin slew the king of Ebla, who ruled over the routes to this well-timbered area. Timber-felling parties rafted the fallen logs down the river courses that passed through the various city-states adjacent to the Persian Gulf. Mesopotamian rulers also traded for timber as far east as the west coast of India. They used much of the wood to build cargo ships on whose decks a variety of imports enriched the Fertile Crescent.

By the end of the third millennium BCE, Near Eastern kingdoms seemed to have focused their attention on Crete for timber. A Cretan hieroglyphic seal dated to around the beginning of the second millennium BCE, showing a ship with five tree signs, one tree singled out and four in a cluster, suggests commerce in timber between Crete and the outside world at this time. The inclusion of a boat could refer to the use of wood for its construction or to the means of exporting the wood. Trade between the Mediterranean island and the Near East apparently injected enough new wealth into the local economy to transform fairly swiftly a minor island into one of the most powerful states in the Mediterranean.

As the Athenians and the Persians fought for hegemony over the Greek peninsula in the fifth century BCE, both sides realized the importance of controlling accessible timber resources for outfitting their own navy as well as denying the other the same capability. For this reason, the timber-rich and very accessible Strymon valley bordering Thrace and Macedonia became the focal point of Persian and Athenian interest. The Persians, for example, expelled the indigenous Greek population from the area and kept it off limits to even their most loyal Greeks allies. Athens's wooden warships defeated the Persians at Salamis and drove the Persians from the Greek peninsula. Over the next century, Athenian control of the seas made the Greek city-state preeminent in the Mediterranean. To secure their hold, though, required a large and reliable source of timber. The Athenians therefore colonized Amphipolis, which controlled access to the Strymon valley. When the Athenian forces lost Amphipolis in the Peloponnesian Wars, they tried attacking Sicily to wrest control of Italy and Sicily's immense forests. With the failure of that military venture, the desperate Athenians established a monopoly on timber supplies from Macedonia, eventually constructing the hulls there and then towing them to Athens. Other Greek city-states envying Athenian wealth and power schemed to wrest control of Macedonian timberlands from Athens. Eventually, under a strong monarch, Philip, father of Alexander, the Macedonians took control of its own timberlands and soon became the most powerful state in Greece.

The Romans, too, recognized the importance of wood for shipbuilding. Cicero explained that "we cut trees to build ships, which sail in all directions to bring all the needs of life." In earlier times, the Romans built most of their ships around Pisa and then exploited the Ligurian woods. In later days they found supplies in France and North Africa.

TIMBER INDUSTRY. Logs of hardwood being loaded onto barges for export, Sarawak, Malaysia, 1992. (© Kal Muller/Woodfin Camp and Associates, New York)

European Timber Trade. Wood remained plentiful in one Italian region: the territory that later became the Venetian Republic. The great need for wood by Venice's Muslim neighbors in the southern Mediterranean and their willingness to pay dearly for it stimulated the growth of Venice's shipping industry, which came to rule the eastern Mediterranean, and provided the Venetian Republic with large amounts of gold to buy luxury goods from the East and sell them to European markets. The profits from this trade made Venice the richest European state of the Renaissance. To maintain supremacy at sea from generation to generation, the Venetians consolidated their production of warships in one location they called the Arsenal (Arabic for "house of construction") and began, in the thirteenth century CE, to restrict the commerce and felling of oak near riverbanks to guarantee a secure supply of timber for the Republic. But no sanctions proved strong enough to stop competing interests—farmers who wished the land cleared for crops versus industrialists who needed the oak for fuel—from deforesting the timber on which the shipbuilders depended.

By the 1600s, lack of wood in nearby forests sent the local Venetian shipbuilding industry into decline. In contrast, Holland had easy access to huge tracts of timber along the Rhine, Meuse, and Moselle rivers as well as the Baltic, allowing the treeless nation to build great fleets for the lucrative Far East and transatlantic trade. France and Great Britain likewise took advantage of their proximity to these forests and also built large fleets to profit from the mercantile opportunities offered by the opening of these great oceanic highways. The general scarcity of timber in the southern Mediterranean restricted the Venetians from building ships of great size and entering these lucrative overseas markets.

Unfettered access to the Baltic demonstrates the significance the timber trade played in the fate of nations. A member of the British Parliament remarked that if the Dutch fleet closed the sea to the British, "We can neither defend ourselves nor employ ourselves."

Fortunes in America. Fortunately, timber growing in the British colonies in America provided the English with an alternative. Especially valued were the large trees that could mast the Royal Navy. Just how valued these became to England can be seen in the diaries of Samuel Pepys, whose job it was to outfit the English Navy. In the midst of the Second Dutch War, ships carrying masting timber from America were long overdue. When they finally arrived, Pepys regarded it as "a blessing, mighty unexpected and without which, we must have failed." Although England tried through various acts of Parliament to preserve old-growth white pines in New England for masting its huge battleships, American settlers saw turning large trees, including those the English wished to conserve, into lumber and selling them on the international market as a profitable way to obtain the necessary startup capital for farming. Traders using ships built from American timber and usually sailing from Boston traded staves in the Canary Islands and Madeira for wine, then exchanged the wine in England for finished goods, which they then transported back to the colonies and sold.

American traders also used lumber to initiate what became known as the "Evil Triangle." The wood went down to the "Sugar Islands"—(those in the West Indies) to build and maintain sugar mills. There the traders exchanged the timber for rum, which they took to Africa to trade for slaves, bringing back to the West Indies more African slaves and trading the human cargo for molasses, which in Boston they distilled into rum to trade with the Native Americans for pelts, which brought great profit on the world market. Through the timber trade, New England became the most dynamic part of America. The New England timber trade also forced the colonists into conflict with the Native Americans, who correctly saw the destruction of the woods as the end to their way of life, as well as with the British, who viewed the cutting down of timber preserved for the Royal Navy as a threat to its power throughout the world.

Independence gave the Americans control over the vast forestlands that spread from the East all the way to the Mississippi. Tench Coxe, a close friend of Thomas Jefferson and James Madison, better understood than his more famous contemporaries what this great supply meant for the development of the nation. Coxe observed that "no country, so well accommodated with navigation, and adapted to commerce and manufactures, possesses as great a treasure" of wood and timber. In Coxe's analysis, America's bountiful supply of timber and its vast river system that gave the nation easy access to these great forests would provide the young country with an immense and unequaled store on which to build from, giving the United States a distinct commercial advantage over its industrial rivals in Europe. The crucial role wood played in the United States' phenomenal growth between the founding of the Republic and the Civil War proved Coxe's assessment prophetic.

The plethora of waterways and trees in the newly acquired lands west of the Allegheny Mountains proved a boon to lumberjacks and farmers. Pine logs from the great timber regions of Minnesota and Wisconsin were floated from tributaries of the Mississippi into the main river. Timber rafts headed for sale in New Orleans filled the Mississippi. Wooden boats and ships opened the old American west (lands east of the Mississippi River, north of the Ohio River, and west of the Allegheny Mountains) to settlement. How else could farmers in places like Ohio, Indiana, and Illinois expect to move their goods to distant markets except by navigation? At first, western farmers floated their products down the Ohio and Mississippi rivers by wooden flatboats. The flatboat suffered a major and insurmount-

able flaw: it could only sail with the current. The development of the keelboat initially solved the problem. Steamboats, though, built from the timber growing near the rivers on which they navigated, beat out all the competition. A round-trip voyage from Pittsburgh to New Orleans by flatboat took more than a year as the flatboatmen had to make the return trip by foot. The same trip took six or seven months by keelboat, while the steamboat made the journey in a little more than three weeks. Steamboats were lauded by mid-nineteenth-century pundits as the most important technological development to have occurred in the United States because they "contributed more than any other single cause to advance the prosperity of the west," opening up markets for the millions settling in the region and feeding the entire nation.

Changing Economics. The clash in 1862 between the two ironclad ships the *Merrimack* and the *Monitor* immediately made wooden warships obsolete, and wood lost its geopolitical significance. Likewise, around the same time period, railroads diminished the importance of riverboats. Ironically, when wood declined from a vital resource to a mere consumer product, the demand for wood, and the timber industry's ability to provide, skyrocketed. The steam engine followed by the internal combustion engine revolutionized access to the forest and transport of forest products to consumers. Until the late nineteenth century, the timber industry depended on man or animal power for transport. Except under special circumstances where wood could be skidded over snowy terrain, the economics of physically hauling timber overland kept lumberjacks confined to working no more than 15 miles (24 kilometers) from a navigable waterway where the timber could be cheaply and easily floated or carried by ship. Trees growing beyond remained untouched. But the railroad and later tractors or trucks opened up the most remote woodlands to the logging industry. Axes and saws, used to fell trees from earliest times until the nineteenth century, gave way in the twentieth century to mechanical devices ranging from the chain saw to mobile machinery that can fell and process logs on site, changing logging from a labor-intensive to a capital-intensive industry as well as radically stepping up the tempo of tree cutting. The ever-growing demand for construction material and pulp for paper products has provided timber and logging concerns with the means for financing the industrialization of forestry.

Rain forests have been particularly affected by industrial forestry over the last half century. The demand for exotic woods by those in wealthier nations has driven the logging industry in these regions. Loggers cull the preferred hardwoods from the other trees in the forest. To gain access to these trees and to haul the logs overland for export, they build roads. The roads provide entry for the increasing number of landless masses to the forests. Once there, they burn down what is left and cultivate what they can. When the land inevitably gives out, they move deeper into the forests and continue to practice slash-and-burn agriculture. In this fashion, more and more luxuriant growth turns barren.

[*See also* Forests and Deforestation; Wood as Fuel; *and* Woodworking Industry.]

BIBLIOGRAPHY

Drushka, Ken, and Hun Konttinen. *Tracks in the Forest.* Helsinki, 1997.
Myers, N. "The Present Status and Future Prospects of Tropical Moist Forests." *Environmental Conservation* 7.2 (1980), 101–114.
Perlin, John. *A Forest Journey: The Role of Wood in the Development of Civilization.* New York, 1989.
Richards, J., and R. Tucker, eds. *World Deforestation in the Twentieth Century.* Durham, 1988.

JOHN PERLIN

TIMBUKTU. Timbuktu is situated at the interface of desert and water. The city, which evolved from a nomadic encampment of the Tuareg, about the year 1100 CE, is at the desert's southern limit, a few kilometers from the Niger, where the town of Kabara serves as its river port. During its early centuries, its salt trade and handcraft industries attracted settlers—merchants and their families and then Muslim scholars from such Saharan oases as Walata, Touat, Ghadames, the Fezzan, and the southern reaches of Morocco.

Ghadames traders played an important role in Timbuktu trade from the fifteenth to the nineteenth century. Ghadames was a gateway to Tripoli on the Mediterranean Sea, to routes leading to Egypt, and to trade connections with Kano for trade between Hausaland and the Niger Bend. Touat was another trade entrepôt, with routes radiating out to Fez, Algiers, and Tunis in the north, to Gao, Agades, and Katsina in the south. The Jewish merchants of Touat had a major role in trade before they were banned in the late 1400s; they had trade networks of their own that extended into many areas of the Mediterranean world, not least the Ottoman Empire and the Iberian Peninsula. Timbuktu also attracted migrants from such sub-Saharan cities as Djenné and Diakha (both close to the southern end of the Inland Delta of the Niger).

Situated at a strategic point for the exchange of Saharan–North African goods as well as tropical African goods, Timbuktu became a major center of commercial exchange. Slabs of rock salt came from the Saharan salt pans of Taghaza, and later Taoudeni. There were North African products, such as cloth, brass bowls, weaponry, books, and horses. By the sixteenth century, some European manufactured goods reached Timbuktu via the trans-Saharan trade, in particular cloth. There are today Arabic

TIMBUKTU. Tuaregs congregate in the city's walled marketplace, 1961. (*New York World-Telegram* and the *Sun* Newspaper Photograph Collection/Prints and Photographs Division, Library of Congress)

manuscripts from the 1500s copied in Timbuktu on paper that originated in the mills of northern France, Germany, or Italy—according to their watermarks.

At the heart of Timbuktu's economy until the late 1500s, was the gold trade. From that, Timbuktu gained its fabled reputation in North Africa and Europe. The boom period began in the 1300s, when merchants from Djenné opened a route southward to the periphery of the forest zone, to what is now the Republic of Ghana. The gold, largely in the form of gold dust, was brought to Djenné overland, traded to Timbuktu by river, and there traded to Saharan and North African merchants, in exchange for rock salt but also all manner of other goods in trans-Saharan commerce.

The gold trade probably reached its peak during the 1500s, stimulating a desire among Moroccan rulers to control it directly. Thinking that Timbuktu was the gold's source, they undertook the conquest of the city and of the Songhai Empire, of which it was a part in 1591. While that alone might have diminished Timbuktu's gold trade, the Portuguese were then establishing trading posts around the West African coast to syphon off the gold. At about the same time the Spanish conquest of much of Central and South America took finished gold products in quantity from the Native Americans and shipped them to Spain.

The slave trade remained significant to Timbuktu's commerce into the 1800s. The chief exportation route from Timbuktu was to Touat; there, the slaves could be traded to North African locations, usually Morocco, where a black slave militia had been created after its conquest of Timbuktu in 1591. In the late 1600s, the Alawid Sultan Isma'il pressed into military service at least fifty thousand (some estimates put the number as high as 250,000) black slaves and former slaves. Further evidence for the trade comes from correspondence sent in 1615 by some scholars of Touat to the Timbuktu scholar Ahmad Baba, asking which of the slaves traded there were lawful to be owned according to Islamic law. The response classified slaves ethnically and religiously (only non-Muslims could legitimately be enslaved); the slaves known to Timbuktu were from a wide variety of ethnic groups living in much of what is now Burkina Faso, northern Ghana and Togo, and as far away as northern Nigeria and the kingdom of Benin.

The 1600s and 1700s are generally considered centuries of economic downturn for Timbuktu; that was not necessarily so, although the Middle Niger region was not as politically stable as it had been in the 1500s under Songhai rule. By the late 1700s, Morocco was opened to active trade with Europe through its port of Mogador (or Essaouira), established for that purpose. Gold was no longer a major item in trans-Saharan trade, but items wanted in Europe—gum arabic, ostrich feathers, and ivory—were, and one of the sources of such items was Timbuktu.

Tunisia's abolition of slavery in 1846 and France's abolition of slavery in their colony of Algeria in 1848 reduced the scale of the trade; then France's occupation of Timbuktu in 1894 ended the slave trade there. The colonial rule of French West Africa dramatically changed the trade routes; after talk of a trans-Saharan railroad, the chief pathway for Middle Niger–region trade was through the upper Niger and the Senegal River Valley or through such coastal gateways in Senegal as Saint Louis and, later, Dakar. The trade in rock salt continued and exists, though in reduced volume, to this day.

Timbuktu's economy depended on its role as an entrepôt for trans-Saharan commerce, which was much reduced in the 1900s. Its main trading activities under colonial rule and since independence in 1960 have been with nomadic tribes and such small southern Sahara towns as Araouane and Bou Djebeha. Timbuktu is a distribution point for imported goods that reach it by boat or truck from Mali's capital, Bamako, and for grain cultivated in the Inland Delta of the Niger, to its southwest. In the 1970s, a drought and famine devastated the agrarian economy. Tourism has begun to stimulate Timbuktu's economy, and Mali's government is encouraging tourism for the city and for the national economy.

BIBLIOGRAPHY

Barth, Heinrich. *Travels and Discoveries in North and Central Africa* New York, 1857–1859. Reprinted in London, 1965. Barth spent six months in Timbuktu in 1853.
Bovill, E. W. *The Golden Trade of the Moors.* Princeton, 1995.
Dubois, Felix. *Timbuctoo the Mysterious,* translated from French by Diana White. London, 1897.
Haidara, Isma'l Dadi. *Les Juifs de Tombouctou.* Bamako, Mali, 1999.
Hunwick, John O. "Islamic Financial Institutions: Theoretical Structures and Some of Their Practical Applications in Sub-Saharan Africa." In *Currencies, Credit and Culture: African Financial Institutions in Historical Perspective,* edited by Endre Stiansen and Jane Guyer, pp. 72–99. Uppsala, Sweden, 1999.
Hunwick, John O. *Timbuktu and the Songhay Empire.* Leiden, 1999.
Miner, Horace. *The Primitive City of Timbuctoo.* Rev. ed. New York, 1965.
Webb, James L. *Desert Frontier: Ecological and Economic Change along the Western Sahel, 1600–1850.* Madison, Wis., 1995.

JOHN HUNWICK

TIMOR. *See* Portugal, *subentry on* Portuguese Empire.

TITHE. The tithe was a 10 percent tax levied by the medieval church on most kinds of personal income; it was the church's principal source of revenue. It furnished basic support for the clergy, paid for church buildings, their upkeep and contents, and also financed poor relief, care for the sick, and other social services.

A command to pay one-tenth of the annual increase in livestock and agricultural harvests to the temple priesthood appears in the Torah and became a staple feature of Jewish law. Early Christian teachers seem to have been ambivalent about this obligation, which they associated with the formalism of Pharisaic Judaism; but Saint Paul, among others, clearly expected that Christians would contribute to the support of poor and distressed members of their community.

The payment of annual tithes apparently remained primarily a moral obligation during the early centuries of Christian history, but beginning in the sixth century church authorities began to impose sanctions on those who failed to contribute. Every Christian, at least in principle, was thus obliged to pay tithes on virtually every type of income—even pirates in the North Sea paid tithes on their spoils. By the eighth century kings had also begun to help collect the tithe in various parts of western Europe. As secular rulers became involved in collecting tithes, however, they also commenced to appropriate part, and sometimes all, of the resulting revenue for their own purposes. Ecclesiastical income consequently diminished, so that resources, not only for the maintenance of churches and the clergy, but also for poor relief, began to dry up.

In reaction against this state of affairs, the leaders of the eleventh-century church reform movement demanded that secular authorities abandon their hold on tithe revenues. In 1050 Pope Leo IX denounced laymen who retained any part of the tithe that they helped to collect. Despite a series of reiterated prohibitions, churchmen found it impossible to reclaim total control of tithe payments. In 1215 the Fourth Lateran Council adopted a compromise solution that reserved a major part of tithe collections for church purposes, but permitted temporal authorities to reserve a small portion for their own use. Even after this concession, however, church authorities had to struggle continually to make good their claims.

Rules for the collection and distribution of tithes were extremely complex. This inevitably gave rise to numerous disputes and a huge volume of litigation. Overt resistance to the tithe was relatively uncommon: few people flatly refused to pay, but cheating and fraud were commonplace. The difficulties of collection eventually became so troublesome that during the late Middle Ages, especially in Italy, communities began to pay their clergy salaries in lieu of tithe income, so that priests became increasingly dependent on municipal governments.

The tithe nonetheless survived in many places until recent times. In England, for example, the last vestiges of tithe obligations on real property finally vanished in 1977, although Ireland had abolished them in 1871 and Scotland in 1925.

BIBLIOGRAPHY

Boyd, Catherine E. *Tithes and Parishes in Medieval Italy: The Historical Roots of a Modern Problem.* Ithaca, N.Y., 1952.

Constable, Giles. *Monastic Tithes from Their Origins to the Twelfth Century*, vol. 10, *Cambridge Studies in Medieval Life and Thought*, new series. Cambridge, 1964.

Constable, Giles. "Resistance to Tithes in the Middle Ages." *Journal of Ecclesiastical History* 13 (1962), 172–185.

Gilchrist, John. *The Church and Economic Activity in the Middle Ages.* London, 1969.

Tierney, Brian. *Medieval Poor Law: A Sketch of Canonical Theory and Its Application in England.* Berkeley and Los Angeles, 1959.

JAMES A. BRUNDAGE

TOBACCO. Tobacco, a plant growing wild in many sections of South and North America, and smoked by the indigenous population, was encountered by the early Spanish explorers, who brought it back to Europe for their personal use. By the late sixteenth century, it was known to botanists in most countries of western Europe but used by only limited circles of the population in ports and other large towns, particularly sailors and the more raffish sections of the urban populace. In the seventeenth century, however, its use spread to the interior of western and central Europe, a dispersion very likely facilitated by the movement of armies in the Thirty Years' War. At first its use was prohibited in several jurisdictions but these bans were progressively lifted. The last major territory closed to tobacco was Muscovy, but Peter the Great—about the time of his trip to the West in 1697—legalized it there too. In the eighteenth century, although pipe smoking remained quantitatively the most important form of consumption, snuff became the most fashionable form. In this mode its use spread among women who could take snuff in polite society.

In the early nineteenth century, cigar use became conspicuous among the prosperous in many European countries. The cigar's introduction is reported to have been facilitated in England by the young officers who were introduced to it when serving in Spain during the peninsula campaign. In the late nineteenth century, cigarettes became the most fashionable mode of tobacco consumption, starting in Russia and spreading to the West. Pipe smoking, of course, continued to be popular, and men employed in factories, mines, or warehouses, where fire was prohibited, continued to use chewing tobacco and oral snuff. As far as can be determined, per capita consumption, where permitted, was well under one pound per head in the seventeenth century and rose only slowly by the end of the eighteenth century to about 1.5 pounds per head in Britain and one pound in France. This slow upward trend continued during the nineteenth and twentieth centuries, and after World War II, consumption reached 3 pounds per head in France, 4 to 6 pounds per head in the Netherlands, Belgium, Denmark, and Canada, and 7.5 pounds in the United States.

TOBACCO. Women harvest tobacco leaves, Java, Indonesia, 1985. (© Kal Muller/Woodfin Camp and Associates, New York)

From the seventeenth century onward, Europe's state treasuries took a major interest in the spread of tobacco use. France established its state tobacco monopoly in 1674, which was followed by similar policies in Spain, Portugal, Russia, Sweden, and many German and Italian states. In Britain, Ireland, the northern Netherlands, and the major Hanseatic ports, the trade was left in private hands but was subject to heavy taxation. In England this was at least 100 percent of prime cost in the last seventeenth century, over 200 percent by 1759, and progressively higher in later centuries. In France, the tobacco monopoly was abolished during the French Revolution but reestablished by Napoleon; it had produced about 7 percent of total state revenues on the eve of the Revolution, while in contemporary Spain tobacco's share reached at least 25 percent of state revenues.

The initial area of commercial cultivation in the Americas was in the province of Bariñas in modern Venezuela. From there the Spanish carried the commercial cultivation to Cuba, Mexico, and elsewhere in their American empire. Simultaneously it was introduced into Brazil (also under the Spanish crown before 1640), particularly in the modern provinces of Bahia and Maranhão. Brazilian tobacco was to be an important item in the West African slave trade as well as in the North American fur trade. From the Spanish and Portuguese colonies, the commercial cultivation of tobacco spread quickly to the English and French islands in the West Indies. Although a variety of tobacco (*Nicotiana rustica*) was well known to the in-

digenous population of North America, the introduction of the West Indian variety (*Nicotiana tabacum*) provided the basis for the successful commercial production in the English colonies of Virginia and Maryland. By the end of the seventeenth century, the Chesapeake region was quantitatively the most important source of Europe's tobacco. In the Spanish, Portuguese, and French colonies tobacco had at first usually been spun into long ropes or cords wound into rolls.

The English growers in the Chesapeake preferred to dry their tobacco leaf in sheds and pack the dried leaf tightly into hogsheads (large barrels). Leaf so processed was convenient for snuff manufacturers. By the end of the seventeenth century about two-thirds of the tobacco shipped to England was reexported; by the 1770s, England and Scotland reexported nearly 85 percent. Leaf or roll tobacco could be converted to snuff by hand, but in Britain and the United Provinces (Canada), this conversion was commonly done in wind or watermills. The coarsely ground snuff was then sold to retailers, often called snuffmen, who added the scents desired by their retail customers.

In the eighteenth century, additional areas of cultivation developed in the Rhineland, the Low Countries, Ukraine, and around Salonika in the Ottoman Empire. In the nineteenth century, cultivation spread from the Chesapeake to other parts of the United States, particularly North Carolina and Kentucky, while European colonists introduced it into Rhodesia (now part of Zambia and Zimbabwe) and elsewhere in Africa. The development of machinery to make cigarettes encouraged the emergence of very large tobacco companies in nonmonopolized areas. They were often pioneers in intensive and aggressive advertising. Only at the end of the twentieth century did a powerful anti-tobacco movement develop that was able to obtain legislation restricting such advertisements.

BIBLIOGRAPHY

Arents, George. *Tobacco: Its History Illustrated by the Books, Manuscripts, and Engravings in the Library of George Arents, Jr.* 4 vols. New York, 1937–1952.

Goodman, Jordan, Paul E. Lovejoy, and Andrew Sherratt. *Consuming Habits: Drugs in History and Anthropology.* London and New York, 1995.

Gray, Lewis Cecil. *History of Agriculture in the Southern United States to 1860.* 2 vols. New York, 1941.

Price, Jacob M. *Tobacco in Atlantic Trade: The Chesapeake, London, and Glasgow, 1675–1775.* Brookfield, Vt., 1995.

Price, Jacob M. *Overseas Trade And Traders: Essays on Some Commercial, Financial, and Political Challenges Facing British Atlantic Merchants, 1600–1775.* Brookfield, Vt., 1996. Includes a chronological list of all the author's articles from 1954 to 1996.

Rogozinski, Jan. *Smokeless Tobacco in the Western World, 1500–1950.* New York, 1990.

Vigié, Marc et Muriel. *L'herbe à Nicot: Amateurs de tabac, fermiers généraux et contrebandiers sous l'ancien régime.* Paris, 1989.

JACOB M. PRICE

TOBACCO INDUSTRY. To the extent that a formal tobacco manufacturing industry existed at all in Europe before about 1750, it was almost entirely under the control of governments. The importance of tobacco as a source of tax revenue, and the ensuing need to prevent smuggling of the product, meant that nearly all European states prohibited tobacco growing, and most farmed out the monopoly right to produce tobacco goods to corporations via a system of concessions. The factories of these corporations handled four separate products: powdered snuff; cut tobacco for smoking; and two types of rolled tobacco, soft for chewing or smoking and hard for grating into snuff. However, such large-scale factory-based tobacco production in Europe during the eighteenth century was designed more with a view to regulating trade than with facilitating value-enhancing manufacturing or product development.

In the United Kingdom, however, where the state did not directly control manufacturing, after 1750, a group of small-scale tobacco manufacturers developed to process leaf imported from the plantations of Virginia and Maryland. The fashion for taking snuff that emerged from the mid-eighteenth century in Europe enabled certain leading firms to develop more sophisticated products that were sold using their own brand names. Moreover, during the nineteenth century, the United Kingdom's leading tobacco firms witnessed a significant degree of mechanization, and by the 1880s relatively highly capitalized companies, such as the Bristol firm of W. D. & H. O. Wills, had been able to gain a significant share of the national market for their branded products.

Until the mid-twentieth century, consumption patterns remained culturally specific and a decline in popularity of smokeless tobacco after 1800 across much of Europe (apart from Scandinavia) was not mirrored in the United States, where chewing (plug) tobacco—the ubiquitous "quid"—and the spittoon remained preeminent. Entirely different methods of smoking tobacco existed elsewhere: the hookah in the Middle East, the bidi in India, tobacco wrapped in corn silk in Brazil. This preponderance of consumption methods was reflected in the diverse range of leaf types and curing methods that were to be found internationally. From the 1880s, however, all this began to change.

The catalyst for change was the cigarette, a type of tobacco product that before 1850 was practically unknown. According to Goodman (1993) the habit of smoking tobacco wrapped in fine paper—the "papelate"—first seems to have been practiced in Spain during the seventeenth century. The birth of the modern cigarette, however, was largely the result of two North American innovations during the second half of the nineteenth century: the development of "bright" tobacco and the invention of a machine that could automate the process of rolling cigarettes.

Many of the handmade cigarettes that were produced in Europe during the mid-nineteenth century by the French tobacco monopoly and later by English firms featured leaf grown in parts of the Ottoman Empire. Early cigarettes were thus generally thought of as being Turkish in origin. However, the accidental discovery in America (1839) of a new method of curing the strains of tobacco grown in Virginia and Carolina using hot air (flue-cured) produced a bright-yellow leaf that was extremely well suited for use in cigarettes. What can be considered as the modern American cigarette was launched by the New York firm of F. S. Kinney in 1872 when it introduced to the market a handmade product that used a blend of Turkish and flue-cured bright tobacco under the brand name "Sweet Caporal." Other firms soon followed Kinney's lead, including the Virginia-based enterprise of Allen & Ginter, which used flavored Burley tobacco grown in Kentucky to replace the costly imported Turkish tobacco in its brands. By 1880 sales of cigarettes in the United States reached 500 million per annum, and Allen & Ginter emerged as the leading manufacturer in this rapidly growing segment of the tobacco industry that was dominated by a handful of firms.

The main impediment to further expansion of the industry after 1880 lay in the fact that cigarette-making constituted a labor-intensive, handicraft activity that required a huge workforce comprised mainly of young girls. In March 1881 the American engineer James A. Bonsack patented the most successful of a number of cigarette-rolling machines that were developed in response to this obvious bottleneck. In England, Bonsack granted an exclusive license for his invention to the Wills firm, whose "Woodbine" brand quickly emerged as the market leader. In the United States, the issue of licensing the machine was more complex, but the firm that displayed a willingness to push ahead most quickly, W. Duke & Sons of Durham, North Carolina, was able to reap the principal benefits from mechanization. Led by an astute and ruthless business tycoon, James Buchanan (Buck) Duke, the firm thrust full-steam ahead in the production of machine-made brands of cigarettes. Using a mixture of price cutting, advertising, and corporate acquisition, by 1890 Duke's firm was strong enough to browbeat the other four leading U.S. cigarette manufacturers into forming a joint venture under the identity of the American Tobacco Company (ATC), capitalized at $25 million.

For two decades ATC provided the American economy with one of its leading examples of what Alfred Chandler in his book *Scale and Scope* (Cambridge, Mass., 1990) has termed the modern industrial enterprise. Within the United States, ATC extended its control into the markets for snuff, plug, smoking tobacco, and small cigars, while abroad the company developed export markets in Canada, Central America, Europe, Australia, and the Far East, supported in some cases with local production facilities. When, in September 1901, ATC acquired control of the Liverpool cigarette manufacturer Ogden, Duke found himself confronting the massed ranks of the United Kingdom's tobacco industry as a group—thirteen leading firms pooled their resources, under the strategic leadership of Wills, to form the Imperial Tobacco Company (ITC) in a bid to thwart the American raider. After a conflict lasting twelve months, and which spread to markets as far apart as Japan, Australia, and the West Indies, the two giant concerns called a truce and settled the affair by a remarkable act of international economic collaboration. In agreeing to limit their own activities to America and Great Britain, respectively, ATC and ITC set up a jointly owed subsidiary called the British-American Tobacco Company (BAT) whose purpose was to develop the market for cigarettes across the rest of the world. By doing so, the two firms changed the shape of the international tobacco industry forever.

In 1907, concerned by the power wielded by ATC, antitrust authorities in the United States initiated proceedings against the company under the terms of the Sherman Act (1890). After four years of legal wrangling, the Supreme Court issued a decree on 29 May 1911 ordering the dissolution of ATC and obliging the company to sell off its institutional shareholding in BAT. The dissolution process was supervised by Duke himself and created an oligopolistic industry in America dominated by four firms: R. J. Reynolds, Liggett & Myers, Lorrillard, and a much-reduced ATC. The changes did nothing to reduce cigarette sales, which boomed following R. J. Reynolds's successful launch of their "Camel" brand in 1913. Duke, meanwhile, briefly took charge of BAT, whose rapidly growing activities in China, India, Australia, Canada, South Africa, and Germany had been further extended into Southeast Asia, Egypt, Mexico, Central and South America, and other parts of Africa by the 1920s.

Duke's legacy has been a curious one. Largely reviled in the United States, his activities and image helped to generate a climate of hostility and suspicion toward the tobacco industry that was greatly reinforced by the medical evidence concerning the adverse health effects of cigarette smoking. Since the mid-1960s, strict controls over advertising, coupled with a growing trail of litigation directed toward the industry in America, had by the 1990s thrown into question the very existence of the leading tobacco firms. Throughout much of the rest of the world, however, extensive advertising of American cigarettes after 1945 captured the imagination of vast groups of men and—increasingly—women, to the point where the machine-made cigarette is now the form of tobacco consumption chosen by the world's smokers, accounting for upward of 80 percent of all tobacco leaf grown and generating global sales of around 5.4 trillion sticks per annum.

Thus despite the growing difficulties faced by the tobacco industry in the United States since World War II, its leading tobacco firms—notably Philip Morris and R. J. Reynolds—were able to wrest from BAT its position as leading player in the global cigarette industry. Philip Morris in particular, through the extremely successful international marketing of its "Marlboro" brand, helped to maintain the popularity of American cigarettes throughout the late twentieth century. Nevertheless, sensing the limitations to continued growth of cigarette sales in the wake of the adverse health publicity, all of the largest, privately owned tobacco firms used their profits to diversify into other areas of business. By the early 1980s, the international tobacco industry had been subsumed into a group of multinational conglomerates.

A much more combative stance adopted against the industry by government bodies and international organizations—notably the World Health Organization—since the mid-1970s certainly acted to moderate the product's continued market growth within the developed industrial economies where controls against tobacco promotion have been greatest. By the late 1980s, it appeared that firms within the industry were entering a period of decline, with both ITC and R. J. Reynolds falling victim to corporate raiders while a similar bid for BAT narrowly failed. Since then, however, the collapse of communism, the moves toward deregulation of state-controlled markets, and the liberalization of international trade generally in the 1990s, have served to open up a range of new opportunities for the tobacco multinationals who, now largely shorn of their diversified business interests, experienced a period of relative prosperity.

[*See also* Tobacco.]

BIBLIOGRAPHY

THE AMERICAN TOBACCO INDUSTRY

Glantz, Stanton A., John Slade, Lisa A. Bero, Peter Hanauer, and Deborah E. Barnes. *The Cigarette Papers.* Berkeley, 1996. Based on a set of documents (approximately 10,000 pages) of the Brown & Williamson Tobacco Corporation (U.S. subsidiary of BAT) that were secretly removed from the offices of a law firm. The papers deal with various aspects of scientific research undertaken by the company from 1960s onward with regard to the effects of tobacco, including the possibility of creating a "safe" cigarette. Used by the authors to illustrate the constraints on the company's R&D activities caused by the possible legal implications that might ensue should such findings be used as evidence in a court of law.

Kluger, Richard. *Ashes to Ashes: America's Hundred-Year Cigarette War, the Public Health, and the Unabashed Triumph of Philip Morris.* New York, 1996. Popular, comprehensive account of developments in the American tobacco industry since the advent of machine-made cigarettes. Includes best available account of the corporate history of Philip Morris. Primary research is based on more than two hundred oral testimonies of leading figures involved with the industry. Superb index.

Tennant, Richard B. *The American Cigarette Industry: A Study in Economic Analysis and Public Policy.* New Haven, Conn., 1950. Essentially an account of the cigarette industry as a case study in industrial organization and market structure. Main purpose is an assessment of the issue of "tacit" collusion under the conditions of oligopoly created by the dissolution of ATC in 1911. Draws heavily on legal case histories involving tobacco litigation between 1890s and 1940s. Historical survey remains very useful, although analysis is somewhat dated.

Tilley, Nannie M. *The Bright Tobacco Industry, 1860–1929.* Chapel Hill, N.C., 1948. Invaluable study showing how the development of bright tobacco played a critical role in the transformation of tobacco manufacturing in the United States to a large-scale industry after 1885. Contains sections on cultivation, marketing, and manufacturing.

THE INTERNATIONAL TOBACCO INDUSTRY

Cochran, Sherman. *Big Business in China: Sino-Foreign Rivalry in the Cigarette Industry, 1890–1930.* Cambridge, Mass., 1980. Pioneering and well-received account of the British-American Tobacco Company's rivalry in China with the indigenous Nanyang Brothers Tobacco Company whose archive papers represent the main (but by no means only) primary source material. Adopts a critical approach based on notions of imperialism. A more recent approach by the same author to the issue is contained in chapter 3 of his book *Encountering Chinese Networks* (Berkeley, 2000).

Goodman, Jordan. *Tobacco in History: The Cultures of Dependence.* London, 1993. A collection of essays concerned with different aspects of tobacco (social, economic, political, cultural, and pharmacological) in varying historical eras and geographical regions. Particularly strong on premodern era. Contains an excellent bibliography of secondary sources on the industry.

Rogoziński, Jan. *Smokeless Tobacco in the Western World, 1550–1950.* New York, 1990. A rather misleading title since the book covers smoking tobacco as well as smokeless tobacco. Useful in its discussion of government involvement in the manufacturing of tobacco and for the broad range of countries covered.

BUSINESS/CORPORATE HISTORIES

Alford, Bernard W. E. *W. D. & H. O. Wills and the Development of the U.K. Tobacco Industry, 1786–1965.* London, 1973. Monumental but rather narrowly cast corporate history of Wills and, after 1901, the Imperial Tobacco Company (although the emphasis remains on the Wills branch of that company). Based mainly on the private business records of the firm. Good on early marketing of machine-made cigarettes.

Cox, Howard. *The Global Cigarette: Origins and Evolution of British American Tobacco, 1880–1945.* Oxford, 2000. Considers the role of BAT and its predecessors in the international expansion of the cigarette industry. Based on a variety of primary sources including papers from the company's private archive. Contains particularly detailed chapters of the development of the cigarette business in China and India. More concerned with production and distribution than consumption.

Durden, Robert F. *The Dukes of Durham, 1865–1929.* Durham, N.C., 1987. Traces the history of Duke's firm up until the early years of the American Tobacco Company. Leans heavily toward the biographical since it is based largely on the family papers deposited at Duke University library, and hence also covers the non-tobacco interests that the family developed in the twentieth century.

Tilley, Nannie M. *The R. J. Reynolds Tobacco Company.* Chapel Hill, N.C., 1985. Extensive commissioned study of the history of America's most successful Southern-based tobacco firm covering the period 1875 to 1963. Contains a detailed account of the "Camel" revolution. Particularly strong on labor issues.

ONLINE RESOURCES

Arents Collection of tobacco materials at the New York Public Library dealing with all aspects of its history <http://www.nypl.org/research/chss/spe/rbk/arents.html>.

Documents that were deposited with the principal author of *The Cigarette Papers* can be found at <http://www.library.ucsf.edu/tobacco>.

Papers relating to the Duke family business can be found at Special Collections Department, Perkins Library, Duke University <http://www.duke.edu/web/Archives>.

World Health Organization has a tobacco Web site with up-to-date statistics on the industry <http://tobacco.who.int>.

HOWARD COX

TOKYO. Development of the Tokyo area began in the early seventeenth century, when Ieyasu Tokugawa (1543–1616) settled the government (*Bakufu*) in Edo, which is the former name of Tokyo. Edo grew as the center of politics and administration, while another large city, Osaka, was the center of commerce. In the early nineteenth century, Edo became the largest city in the world with a population of more than one million.

After the Meiji Restoration, the new government changed the city's name from Edo to Tokyo in 1868, and the following year the emperor moved from Kyoto to Tokyo. While Tokyo temporally declined during the period of the Restoration, it soon began to develop into the capital

TOKYO. Towering neon signs and video screens in the city's Shinjuku District, 1988. (© Mike Yamashita/Woodfin Camp and Associates, New York)

of the modern state. Tokyo inherited from Edo the traditional consumer goods industry, which made such products as ornaments and clogs. Several other modern industries, including textiles, machinery, and printing, also began to develop during the early Meiji era.

Around the time of World War I, Tokyo changed in several ways. First, industrial development accelerated. The coast between Tokyo and Yokohama, where large factories of the heavy and chemical industries were constructed, was reclaimed. In turn, it brought about the development of a number of small and medium-sized factories as subcontractors of those large factories. Consequently, the huge industrial agglomeration known as the Keihin Industrial Belt emerged in the 1920s. The high ratio of the medium- and small-sized factories has been characteristic of Tokyo's industrial structure. Next, the 1923 Kanto earthquake destroyed Tokyo's physical appearance. Many middle-class people moved from the downtown area to the suburbs in the west and formed a new culture of "uptowners." Finally, an innovation took place in transportation. Uptown was connected to the downtown area by suburban electric railways. The city bus was introduced just after the earthquake, and the motorization of the city began.

World War II seriously damaged Tokyo. A large part of downtown was destroyed by U.S. strategic bombing, and the population was reduced. However, Tokyo quickly recovered from war damage. During the period of high economic growth, the Keihin Industrial Belt continued to expand, incorporating such new industries as automobile and consumer electric machinery. The Tokyo Olympics in 1964 symbolized Tokyo's recovery as well as Japan's comeback to international society. In preparation for the Olympics, construction of the city's infrastructure (the highways and drainage system) progressed substantially.

After the 1970s, the trend of the population and industrial production to concentrate in Tokyo ceased. However, major companies continued to concentrate their headquarters in Tokyo. Also, in the 1980s, Tokyo was expected to be the center of the international financial market under conditions of financial liberalization. A bubble in the real estate market, however, resulted in vast numbers of bad bank loans and contributed to a prolonged stagnation of the Japanese economy in the 1990s.

BIBLIOGRAPHY

Ishizuka, Hiromichi, and Ryuichi Narita. *Tokyo no hyakunen* (One Hundred Years of Tokyo). Tokyo, 1986.

Koshizawa, Akira. *Tokyo no Toshi Keikaku* (City Planning of Tokyo). Tokyo, 1991.

Mikuriya, Takashi. *Tokyo: Shuto wa kokka wo koeruka* (Tokyo: Will the Capital Go beyond the State?). Tokyo, 1995.

Nobuki, Mochida. "Toshi no Seibi to Kaihatsu" (Construction and Development of Cities). In *Sangyoka no Jidai* (Era of Industrialization), edited by Shunsaku Nishikawa and Yuzo Yamamoto, vol. 2. Tokyo, 1990.

Tokyo City. *Tokyo-shi Shi Ko* (Draft of the History of Tokyo City). Kyoto, 1973.

TETSUJI OKAZAKI

TORONTO, a port city on Lake Ontario. A combination of good location and decisions by early British colonial administrators explain why, by the mid-nineteenth century, Toronto was one of Canada's major cities. Toronto is situated at the southern end of a water and land shortcut between Lake Ontario and Lake Huron. In 1720, the French established a fort at the site to try to ensure that furs moved east toward the transshipment port of Montreal, not south to New York. In 1793, the governor of Upper Canada (John Graves Simcoe) decided to make what he named York a military stronghold and temporary political capital, since he considered it relatively free from the danger of invasion from the new United States of America. The governor also ordered the construction of a road north from the village (Yonge Street) to allow access to navigable rivers. Agricultural settlement proceeded fairly swiftly, but the population of York was only about 700 in 1812. With only brief gaps, York remained a colonial capital; as Toronto, it was made capital of the province of Ontario with Confederation (1867). Rapid settlement and the clearing of agricultural land after 1815 encouraged commercial development, and the town's population grew to almost 4,000 by 1831. York was renamed Toronto, and, by 1851, it had a population of more than 30,000. Railways were established in the 1850s that linked Toronto to Georgian Bay, Montreal, New York, Detroit, and Chicago. The city then had good land and water routes, both east to west and to the south.

By the late 1800s, Toronto's manufacturing sector included a range of light and heavy industries (especially food processing, clothing, and iron and steel products). Substantial tariffs on manufactured goods helped to ensure the profitability of Toronto's firms. By the early 1900s, Toronto firms could use hydroelectric power that was generated at Niagara Falls. Nonetheless, Toronto remained Canada's "second" city in the later nineteenth century, well behind Montreal as a financial and commercial sector, as well as in total population. These two cities dominated the rest of the country as locations for corporate head offices. By some measures, the concentration of nationwide businesses in Toronto roughly caught up to Montreal by World War I. The perception of Toronto's importance in national affairs was reinforced in English-speaking Canada from the 1930s, when it became the headquarters of the public Canadian Broadcasting Corporation (CBC). As the capital of Canada's most populous, and one of the richest provinces, Toronto and its economy also benefited from the growth of government during the twentieth century. With its concentration of white-collar and light-manufacturing employment, Toronto was spared the worst of the Great Depression of the 1930s, although many of the suburbs around the city went bankrupt under the strain of the relief (welfare) burden of the early 1930s. The population size of metropolitan Toronto overtook that of metropolitan Montreal around the end of World War II.

In the late nineteenth century, Toronto had become increasingly British and Protestant with population coming mainly from rural and small-town Ontario and from the United Kingdom. After 1900, small but highly visible communities of continental European immigrants developed; in the 1950s and 1960s, substantial inflows of non-English-speaking immigrants settled in Toronto. The city's several nicknames "Hogtown," "Toronto the Good," and "the Queen City" reflect the varied attitudes of residents and other Canadians to Toronto's role in Canada's society and economy.

BIBLIOGRAPHY

Careless, J. M. S. *Toronto to 1918: An Illustrated History*. Toronto, 1984.

Gentilcore, R. Louis, ed. *Historical Atlas of Canada*, vol. 2, *The Land Transformed 1800–1891*. Toronto, 1993.

Kerr, Donald, and Deryck W. Holdsworth, eds. *Historical Atlas of Canada*, vol. 3: *Addressing the Twentieth Century, 1891–1961*. Toronto, 1990. Several illustrations focus on aspects of Toronto's economic development.

Stelter, Gilbert A., and Alan F. J. Artibise, eds. *The Canadian City: Essays in Urban and Social History*. Ottawa, 1984.

MARY MACKINNON

TOTAL FACTOR PRODUCTIVITY. The concept of total factor productivity (TFP) has been very widely used in economic history. Most applications work with growth of TFP over time although a few studies compare levels of TFP between countries.

Definitions. In defining TFP growth, it is instructive to begin with a definition of labor productivity growth. Letting an asterisk above a variable denote a proportional rate of change, labor productivity growth (Y/L) is equal to the growth of output $(\overset{*}{Y})$ minus the growth of labor input $(\overset{*}{L})$:

$$\overset{*}{Y/L} = \overset{*}{Y} - \overset{*}{L} \tag{1}$$

For example, if output is growing at an annual rate of 3 percent while employment is growing at a rate of 1 percent per annum, then labor productivity is growing at a rate of 2 percent per annum. Similarly, capital productivity growth (Y/K) is equal to the growth of output minus the growth of capital input $(\overset{*}{K})$:

$$\overset{*}{Y/K} = \overset{*}{Y} - \overset{*}{K} \tag{2}$$

Total factor input (TFI) growth can now be defined as a weighted average of capital and labor input growth:

$$\overset{*}{TFI} = \alpha\overset{*}{K} + (1 - \alpha)\overset{*}{L} \tag{3}$$

where α is capital's share of income. In the case of these two inputs, TFP growth is equal to the growth of output minus the growth of TFI:

$$\overset{*}{TFP} = \overset{*}{Y} - \overset{*}{TFI} = \overset{*}{Y} - \alpha\overset{*}{K} - (1 - \alpha)\overset{*}{L} \tag{4}$$

This has an intuitive appeal since it means that TFP growth is a weighted average of labor productivity growth and capital productivity growth, with the weights reflecting how important the two factors are in production. In general, the weights should change over time to reflect changes in factor shares. In many historical applications, however, the weights are fixed owing to limited availability of information. Often, about two-thirds of income is paid out as wages and about one-third as a return to capital, so that α is commonly set at about one-third.

Another way of thinking about TFP is to recognize that labor productivity may be high because of a high level of capital per employee. An economy with expensive labor may choose to substitute capital for labor, for example. Although such an economy will have higher labor productivity than an economy with cheap labor that uses labor-intensive production methods, it will not necessarily have higher total factor productivity.

This definition of TFP, known as the primal measure, requires quantity information on output and inputs. The concept first surfaced during the 1950s in the work of Solomon Fabricant, Moses Abramovitz, John W. Kendrick, and Robert M. Solow. In many historical instances, however, reliable quantity information is not available, and it is necessary to use the dual measure of TFP, derived from information on prices and costs:

$$T\overset{*}{F}P = \alpha\overset{*}{r} + (1-\alpha)\overset{*}{w} + \overset{*}{p} \tag{5}$$

where $\overset{*}{r}$ is the growth of the cost of capital, $\overset{*}{w}$ is the growth of the cost of labor, and $\overset{*}{p}$ is the growth of the output price. In the primal measure, TFP growth is measured by the extent to which output grows faster than a weighted average of the inputs; whereas in the dual measure, TFP growth is measured by the extent to which the output price grows more slowly than a weighted average of the input prices. The two measures are in fact just two sides of the same coin; where output rises more than inputs, prices rise less than costs, that is, productivity growth is equivalent to real cost reduction. Although it is rarely noted by economists, the dual measure of real cost reduction was first published (posthumously) by G. T. Jones, a generation before economists formulated the primal measure of TFP growth.

Interpretation of the Residual as Productivity Growth. Calculated in the above way, it is clear that TFP growth is obtained as a residual; it is the growth of output that cannot be explained (in a proximate sense) by the growth of factor inputs. Some writers have tried to associate TFP growth with technical progress, but this relationship is unwarranted since in principle it captures anything that affects growth other than the growth of factor inputs. Indeed, Abramovitz famously described the residual as a "measure of our ignorance." Following this cautious lead, some writers preferred to abandon the term

TFP growth, preferring instead the more literal multi-factor productivity (MFP) or joint factor productivity (JFP) growth. This is an issue of semantics; but a number of debates have reflected substantive matters, as discussed below.

Debates. TFP growth has been treated in several ways.

Neoclassical assumptions and the radical critique. As noted earlier, it is usual for the weights on capital and labor to be derived from the respective shares of these inputs in income. Further, the weights often are held constant over time. Many writers have found this to be a natural procedure for deciding on the relative importance of factors, without setting down a precise theory of production. It turns out, however, that if an explicit theory of production is set out, this weighting procedure makes sense only if a set of strong assumptions is satisfied. In particular, the use of factor shares as weights requires constant returns to scale and perfect competition in product and labor markets so that firms are price takers, and factors are paid their marginal products. Technical progress also must be exogenous and Hicks-neutral, augmenting capital and labor at the same rate. The constancy of factor share weights requires the Cobb-Douglas form for the production function, with highly restricted substitution possibilities between inputs.

It is possible to derive alternative measures of TFP that take into account increasing returns, imperfect competition in product and factor markets, and endogenous or biased technical progress. It is also possible to derive optimally changing weights by using a flexible translogarithmic form of the production function. Nevertheless, for some radical writers, the whole concept is tainted by its association with neoclassical economics, particularly those for whom, following Joan Robinson, the whole concept of capital is problematic. This leads naturally to a consideration of the controversy between purist neoclassical writers and those of a more eclectic persuasion.

Purist and eclectic approaches. For purist neoclassical economists, the finding of a substantial residual provided a challenge since it appeared to indicate the possibility of growth without sacrifice in the form of factor inputs. This opened up a line of research associated particularly with Dale Jorgenson and his colleagues, where the residual was reduced by a detailed treatment of output and inputs at a sectoral level, allowing for changing relative prices, structural change, and quality effects, while retaining a consistent neoclassical production framework. Other researchers, such as Edward F. Denison and Angus Maddison, took an eclectic approach, reducing the residual by making adjustments for particular factors, without explicit reference to a unified theoretical framework. The eclectic approach is clearly less satisfactory than the purist approach from a theoretical point of view, but for economic historians it has the merit of making somewhat less stringent data requirements.

Whatever the problems with its theoretical underpinnings, many economic historians have continued to use TFP growth in an eclectic fashion. As a weighted average of labor productivity and capital productivity it has an intuitive appeal, and the possibility of calculating it via the cost dual measure allows economic historians to shed light on the growth process where little information on quantities is available.

Yeast and mushrooms. If TFP growth is treated as a genuine measure of productivity growth or real cost reduction and not just an arbitrary residual, an interesting issue arises, concerning whether this real cost reduction is spread evenly across the economy or concentrated in a few sectors at particular times. Arnold Harberger has drawn an instructive analogy with yeast and mushrooms. He suggests that if real cost reductions are spread evenly across the economy, the growth process can be likened to the effect of yeast on bread, with the yeast causing the bread to expand evenly, like a balloon being filled with air. If, on the other hand, real cost reductions suddenly spring up in one or two sectors during one period and then die out, with the growth process being taken forward by real cost reductions in several different sectors in the succeeding period, the growth process resembles the appearance of mushrooms in a field, popping up almost overnight in a fashion that is not easy to predict. Harberger presents evidence in favor of growth as a mushroom process in U.S. manufacturing between 1970 and 1990. However, it is clearly possible that growth looks like a yeast process at other times and in other countries or sectors.

Applications. TFP growth may be considered in a number of historical contexts.

Britain, 1700–1860. Estimates of British national income, factor inputs, and factor shares are available for the Industrial Revolution period. Table 1 presents a growth-accounting exercise for Britain during the period 1700–1860, divided into four subperiods, using the most recent data of Nicholas F. R. Crafts and C. Knick Harley, and illustrates effectively how TFP growth is obtained as a residual. During the period 1700–1760, for example, output grew at an annual rate of 0.69 percent. Since agriculture was the most important economic activity at the time, it is necessary to include land as a factor input in addition to capital and labor. Wage payments represented approximately 50 percent of national income and land rents an additional 15 percent, leaving 35 percent as payments to capital. With capital growing at an annual rate of 0.7 percent and labor at 0.3 percent per annum, and land being brought into cultivation barely growing at all, the total factor input growth was approximately 0.4 percent per annum. TFP growth for this period is obtained as the difference between output

TABLE 1. *Aggregate British Economic Growth, 1700–1860*

	GROWTH RATE				CONTRIBUTION TO GROWTH			
	Y	K	L	R	K	L	R	TFP
1700–1760	0.7	0.7	0.3	0.05	0.24	0.15	0.01	0.3
1760–1800	1.0	1.0	0.8	0.2	0.35	0.40	0.03	0.2
1801–1831	1.9	1.7	1.4	0.4	0.60	0.70	0.06	0.5
1831–1860	2.5	2.0	1.4	0.6	0.70	0.70	0.09	1.0

Notes: Y = output; K = capital; L = labor; R = land; *TFP* = total factor productivity. Factor shares for the calculations are: capital 0.35; labor 0.5; land 0.15.
SOURCE: Harley, 1993, p. 198.

TABLE 2. *Sectoral Contributions to British TFP Growth, 1780–1860*

	SHARE OF GROSS OUTPUT	TFP GROWTH	CONTRIBUTION
Cotton	0.070	1.9	0.13
Worsteds	0.035	1.3	0.05
Woollens	0.035	0.6	0.02
Iron	0.020	0.9	0.02
Canals and railways	0.070	1.3	0.09
Shipping	0.060	0.5	0.03
Sum of modernized	0.290	1.2	0.34
Agriculture	0.270	0.7	0.19
All others	0.850	0.02	0.02
Total	1.410		0.55

SOURCE: Harley, 1993, p. 200.

growth and TFI growth, or approximately 0.3 percent per annum.

Note that between 1700–1760 and 1831–1860, output growth increased by approximately 1.8 percent per annum (from 0.7 percent to 2.5 percent). Over the same period, TFP growth increased by 0.7 percent per annum (from 0.3 percent to 1.0 percent). Hence the increase in output growth of 1.8 percent per annum can be split into an increase of 0.7 percent in TFP growth and an increase of 1.1 percent in TFI growth. Note that a sizable part of the increase in TFI growth was due to labor, as a result of rapid population growth. Capital accumulation also played a role, but there was little possibility of bringing a lot more land into cultivation. This all suggests that a large share of the increase in the growth rate came simply from using more inputs rather than improved utilization of those inputs. Hence one should not be surprised if it took a long time for living standards to increase significantly.

Another interesting issue that can be pursued with data on TFP growth at this time is the extent to which productivity improvements were concentrated in a few modern sectors or spread evenly across the economy. Table 2 evaluates the sectoral breakdown of TFP growth during the period 1780–1860. Note that the weights are based on sectoral shares of gross output rather than value added, and hence add up to more than one. This is so because the only available measures of output in some sectors include intermediate products, which thus are counted more than once. These estimates suggest that the modernized sectors contributed 0.34 percent per annum to TFP growth, out of a total of 0.55 percent per annum. Agriculture contributed 0.19 percent per annum; so these data imply virtually no TFP growth in the other sectors. Growth during the Industrial Revolution thus appears to be more of a mushroom process than a yeast process, as suggested by Harberger.

The United States, 1800–1967. The work that first made use of the concept of TFP growth was concerned with the growth of the U.S. economy between the late nineteenth century and the mid-twentieth century. Moses Abramovitz and Paul A. David extended this work both forward and backward in time, and their estimates for the period 1800–1967 are provided in Table 3. Although output growth was more rapid during the nineteenth century than during the twentieth century, the growth of output per unit of labor input continued to increase through 1967. What is striking here, however, is that crude TFP growth remained sluggish throughout the nineteenth century, suggesting that U.S. labor productivity growth during this period was largely a result of capital accumulation. David later labeled this the "grand traverse," as the economy moved toward a new steady-state growth path with a higher capital intensity.

France. Philip T. Hoffman provides an ambitious application of the dual approach to TFP calculation in his study of French agriculture during the three centuries preceding the French Revolution. Although data are lacking on the volume of output and inputs during this period, there is ample evidence on prices and costs, which Hoffman aggregates into a TFP index for a number of regions. Table 4 shows that although TFP growth reached 0.31 percent per annum in the Paris basin during the late eighteenth century, it was far more sluggish than that over the whole period 1520–1789, at 0.13 percent per annum. Furthermore, the spark of hope in the late eighteenth century was snuffed out by the subsequent upheavals of revolution and war. Elsewhere, TFP growth was generally more sluggish, with TFP growth in the west even being negative over the period as a whole. Overall, then, Hoffman concludes that French agricultural performance was disappointing, certainly in

TABLE 3. *Aggregate American Economic Growth, 1800–1967 (% per annum)*

	1800–1855	1855–1905	1905–1927	1927–1967
Output	4.2	3.9	3.3	3.2
Output per unit of labor input	0.5	1.1	2.0	2.7
Crude TFP	0.3	0.5	0.5	1.9
Refined TFP				1.3

SOURCE: Abramovitz, and David, 1973, p. 430.

TABLE 4. *TFP Growth in French Agriculture, 1520–1790*

		TFP GROWTH RATE (% P.A.)	
	YEARS COVERED	OVERALL	LATE EIGHTEENTH CENTURY
Paris basin	1520–1789	0.13	0.31
Northeast (Lorraine)	1550–1789	0.13	0.13
Normandy (near Caen)	1520–1785	0.01	0.01
West	1611–1790	−0.16	−0.16
Southeast	1580–1790	0.21	0.21

SOURCE: Hoffman, 1996, p. 130.

TABLE 5. *International Comparisons of TFP Growth, 1913–1984*

	FRANCE	GERMANY	JAPAN	NETH.	U.K.	U.S.
1913–1950						
Output	1.06	1.30	2.24	2.43	1.29	2.78
Crude TFP	1.45	0.89	1.11	1.39	1.27	2.12
Adjusted TFP	0.64	0.22	0.05	0.67	0.50	1.32
1950–1973						
Output	5.13	5.92	9.37	4.70	3.02	3.72
Crude TFP	4.22	4.67	6.22	3.53	2.35	2.08
Adjusted TFP	3.31	3.96	5.12	2.56	1.74	1.28
1973–1984						
Output	2.18	1.68	3.78	1.58	1.06	2.32
Crude TFP	2.00	1.78	1.66	0.99	1.38	0.70
Adjusted TFP	1.09	1.36	0.87	0.32	0.80	−0.09

SOURCE: Maddison, 1987, pp. 649–698.

comparison with what was being achieved at the same time in Britain.

International. International comparisons of TFP growth in history are necessarily restricted in temporal span and country coverage because of limited information on capital stocks. Maddison provides the best-known study, covering six countries between 1913 and 1984. Estimates of output, crude TFP, and adjusted TFP derived from this study are presented in Table 5. Crude TFP uses the quantity of labor and capital inputs, whereas adjusted TFP includes allowances for the quality of inputs. Adjusted TFP still leaves a significant residual for most countries in all three periods. Furthermore, the acceleration of output growth between 1950 and 1973 is largely explained by an acceleration in TFP growth in all countries apart from the United States. This adds weight to the interpretation of this "golden age" of growth as a period when Europe and Japan were catching up with the United States; faster output growth was not simply a result of faster input growth.

BIBLIOGRAPHY

Abramovitz, Moses. "Resources and Output Trends in the U.S. since 1870." *American Economic Review, Papers and Proceedings* 46.2 (1956), 5–23.

Abramovitz, Moses, and Paul A. David. "Reinterpreting Economic Growth: Parables and Realities." *American Economic Review* 63.2 (1973), 428–439.

Barro, Robert J. "Notes on Growth Accounting." *Journal of Economic Growth* 4.2 (1999), 119–137.

Crafts, Nicholas F. R., and C. Knick Harley. "Output Growth and the Industrial Revolution: A Restatement of the Crafts-Harley View." *Economic History Review* 45.4 (1992), 703–730.

David, Paul A. "Invention and Accumulation in America's Economic Growth: A Nineteenth Century Parable." *International Organization, National Policies and Economic Development*. Carnegie-Rochester Conference Series on Public Policy, edited by Karl Brunner and Alan Meltzer, vol. 6. pp. 179–240. Amsterdam, 1977.

Denison, Edward F. *Why Growth Rates Differ: Postwar Experience in Nine Western Countries*. Washington, D.C., 1967.

Fabricant, Solomon. *Economic Progress and Economic Change*. New York, 1954.

Harberger, Arnold C. "A Vision of the Growth Process." *American Economic Review* 88.1 (1998), 1–32.

Harley, C. K. "Reassessing the Industrial Revolution: A Macro View." In *The British Industrial Revolution: An Economic Perspective*, edited by Joel Mokyr, pp. 171–226. Boulder, Colo., 1993.

Hoffman, Philip T. *Growth in a Traditional Society: The French Countryside, 1450–1815*. Princeton, 1996.

Jones, G. T. *Increasing Return: A Study of the Relationship between the Size and Efficiency of Industries with Special Reference to the History of Selected British and American Industries, 1850–1910*. Cambridge, 1933.

Jorgenson, Dale W., Frank M. Gollop, and Barbara M. Fraumeni. *Productivity and U.S. Economic Growth*. Cambridge, Mass., 1987.

Kendrick, John W. *Productivity Trends: Capital and Labor*. New York, 1956.

Maddison, Angus. "Growth and Slowdown in Advanced Capitalist Economies: Techniques of Quantitative Assessment." *Journal of Economic Literature* 25.2 (1987), 649–698.

Matthews, Robin C. O., Charles F. Feinstein, and John C. Odling-Smee. *British Economic Growth, 1856–1973*. Oxford, 1982.

Nicholas, Stephen. "Total Factor Productivity Growth and the Revision of Post-1870 British Economic History." *Economic History Review* 35.1 (1982), 83–98.

Robinson, Joan. "The Production Function and the Theory of Capital." *Review of Economic Studies* 21.2 (1953–1954), 81–106.

Solow, Robert M. "Technical Change and the Aggregate Production Function." *Review of Economics and Statistics* 39.3 (1957), 312–320.

Thomas, Mark. "Accounting for Growth, 1870–1940: Stephen Nicholas and Total Factor Productivity Measurements." *Economic History Review* 38.4 (1985), 569–575.

STEPHEN N. BROADBERRY

TROTSKY, LEON (1879–1940), socialist thinker and activist, member of the Bolshevik government (1917–1927), exiled from the USSR in 1929, assassinated, on Stalin's orders, in Mexico in 1940.

Not a professional economist, Trotsky was interested in the link between economics and politics from a Marxist perspective. Around the turmoil of the Revolution of 1905, he argued that state-led economic development under the last tsars had created a class structure, principally a small but concentrated and strategically important working class and a weak bourgeoisie, that made a socialist revolution in Russia possible. However, Russia's backwardness, evident above all in a large and impoverished peasantry, would mean that socialism could not be built in Russia without technical aid from the more advanced West. It was Trotsky's hope that this aid would be provided by sympathetic socialist regimes.

Viewing the outbreak of the World War I as a revolt of the productive forces against the narrow confines of state frontiers, Trotsky became interested in the establishment of socialist transnational state structures, mainly a "United States of Europe" and a "Federative Balkan Republic," that could better manage economic progress. By guaranteeing ethnic and cultural rights, Trotsky also thought that these transnational states would end national conflicts and their negative impact upon economic growth.

After joining the Russian Social Democratic Workers' Party in 1917, Trotsky grappled with the problems of building a socialist economy in what, for him, were the worst possible circumstances: an isolated country with a low economic base following war, revolution, and civil war. In the Russian Civil War (1917–1920), Trotsky argued that the best solution lay in the militarization of labor and strict state control of the economy. Above all, the state should limit any signs of capitalist activity as a threat to a socialist economy. In the period of mixed state and market economics of the New Economic Policy (1921–1929), Trotsky pursued a contradictory policy of using market activity to foster economic reconstruction but simultaneously seeking to overcome capitalist practice with the superiority of planning. As head of the State Concessions Committee (1925–1927), Trotsky sought, without much success, to develop links with the capitalist world market while

LEON TROTSKY. (University for Social Research, Amsterdam/Snark/Art Resource, NY)

arguing for the overthrow of capitalist regimes and for limits on the operation of the law of value in the USSR.

Ultimately, Trotsky demanded the industrialization of the Soviet economy via state planning. He was critical of the form that this took under Stalin's crash-course methods of the Five-Year Plans from 1928 onward. In particular, collectivization of agriculture was undertaken when the economic prerequisites were clearly lacking. However, Trotsky was convinced that the economic gains made under even Stalin's misguided leadership, particularly in branches of heavy and military-related industries, were sufficient to establish a base for socialist construction in the USSR and to illustrate the advantages of planning compared with those of the free market. Whether the USSR would progress along socialist lines or regress into capitalism was left as an open question by Trotsky, dependent upon the fate of the world revolution. It is as a revolutionary socialist in a political sense, rather than as an economist, that Trotsky will chiefly be remembered.

BIBLIOGRAPHY

Deutscher, Isaac. *The Prophet Armed, the Prophet Unarmed, the Prophet Outcast.* Oxford, 1954–1963.

Day, Richard B. *Leon Trotsky and the Politics of Economic Isolation.* Cambridge, 1973.

Thatcher, Ian D. "Trotsky, the Soviet Union and the World Economy," *Coexistence* 30 (1993), 111–124.

Trotsky, Leon. *Towards Socialism or Capitalism?* London, 1976.

Trotsky, Leon. *The Revolution Betrayed.* Detroit, 1991.

IAN D. THATCHER

TRUSTS. *See* Cartels and Collusion, *subentry on* Historical Overview.

TUNISIA. *See* North Africa.

TURKEY *[This entry contains two subentries, on premodern and modern Turkey.]*

Premodern Turkey

Anatolia and the ancient Near East were sites of some of the earliest examples of settled agriculture, long-distance trade, trading communities, and use of money in the form of coins. During the Neolithic revolution that dates back to the tenth millenium BCE, hunters and gatherers began to plant and cultivate cereals and other crops, first in Anatolia and then in a few other locations around the world. In time, they switched from a nomadic to a sedentary lifestyle and acquired greater control over the food supply. Later, ancient civilizations located in Anatolia developed commercial agriculture, long-distance overland trade, maritime trade across the Aegean and the eastern Mediterranean, mining, and metallurgy. Overland trading colonies and trade routes played an important role in the rise of Hittites and Assyrians during the second millenium BCE. Money, in the form of silver or mixed silver-gold coinage first appeared in seventh century BCE Lydia, located on the western Anatolian coast, well within the trade networks of antiquity. The conquests of Alexander the Great were instrumental in the spread of the coinage of the Greek city-states to Egypt, the Persian Empire, and northern India.

Over the centuries, the large geographical area from Persia to western Europe, with the Mediterranean basin often providing the critical medium of interaction, has witnessed some of the liveliest exchanges in the evolution of commercial and monetary forms. As ancient Greek, Roman, Sassanian, Byzantine, Islamic, and western European civilizations traded with and borrowed institutions from each other, Anatolia contributed to and remained at the center of their exchanges.

Byzantine and Ottoman Empires. After the Germanic invasions, economy and commerce in the Mediterranean basin were divided into two branches. In the western provinces of the Roman Empire, population, trade, and the urban economy declined sharply. In contrast, the urban economy and general economic activity remained strong in Byzantine Anatolia and elsewhere in the eastern Mediterranean.

From the eleventh century on, Anatolia began to participate in the rise of intercontinental trade. A few principal routes through the eastern Mediterranean and the Near East linked Europe with locations in Asia: a northern route went through Constantinople to the Black Sea coast and then across Central Asia; the central route connected the Mediterranean with the Persian Gulf and the Indian Ocean via Anatolia and Iran or Syria and Baghdad; and a southern route linked the Mediterranean to the Red Sea and the Indian Ocean.

Taking advantage of Byzantine weaknesses, Mongols established control over the Black Sea region and much of Anatolia as well as the routes across Asia during the thirteenth century. Under Pax Mongolica, the northern and central routes became the principal conduits for east-west trade. As Turkmen tribes began to come into Anatolia from the east, the major east-west trade route in the peninsula ran from Tabriz in Iran to Konya and then to southern Anatolian ports such as Alanya. Later, a new route became important, running through Erzincan, Sivas, and Ankara, and thence west. The most important commodities carried on these routes were silks and spices from the east and silver from the west. After the Ottomans took control of these routes, they offered privileges to foreign merchants and promoted long-distance trade.

There were significant similarities in the attitudes of the Byzantine and Ottoman empires toward the countryside. Both states attempted to establish small peasant production as the basic fiscal and economic unit, protecting it, whenever possible, from locally powerful elements. During periods of weaker central authority vis-à-vis the provinces, however, local magnates obtained the upper hand, and larger holdings prevailed. For most of the Ottoman era, the peasant family farm remained the basic unit in the countryside with the help of relatively high land to labor ratios. The state established ownership over most of the land early on and did not relinquish it until the second half of the nineteenth century. Hereditary usufruct of the land was given to peasant households, which typically cultivated with a pair of oxen and family labor.

The share of urban population in the total remained close to or below 10 percent until the nineteenth century, and Istanbul accounted for about half of the total urban population. In the urban economy, manufacturing and trade were controlled by guilds, which sought and obtained the support of the government whenever merchants tried to organize alternative forms of production. There was also a considerable amount of tension between the government and the guild membership, both Muslim and non-Muslim. When the guilds tried to preserve their independence, the state viewed them with suspicion for the heterodox religious beliefs of their membership.

Long-Term Trends. From the Roman era to the second quarter of the nineteenth century, the population within the borders of present-day Turkey appears to have fluctuated between a lower bound of three to four million and an upper bound of seven to eight million. Plagues, most notably in the sixth and the fourteenth centuries but also in later periods, were the most important check on population growth. Peace and economic prosperity supported population increases, for example, during the sixteenth century, from approximately five to eight million. The end of the plague, improvements in standards of living, and immigration of more than five million Muslims from Crimea, the Caucasus, and the Balkans—areas seceding from the Ottoman Empire—all contributed to a doubling of the population, from about eight million in the 1830s to seventeen million on the eve of World War I.

The sixteenth century, at least until the 1580s, was a period of demographic and economic expansion. Population growth increased the density of exchange in the urban areas and incorporated large segments of the rural population into the local markets. The Anatolian economy and state finances began to face serious difficulties, however, toward the end of the century. As population growth began to exert pressure on land and the rural economy, the changing technology of warfare and the need to maintain large permanent armies created fiscal problems for the central government. Another adverse effect was the impact of the discovery of the sea route to Asia on the intercontinental trade routes. When the ocean route finally triumphed over the mainland route around 1600, Anatolian towns along caravan routes felt a serious decline in commercial activity.

The economic and fiscal problems lasted well into the seventeenth century, when demographic and economic troubles culminated in the social and political upheavals known as the Celali rebellions. As the peasants took flight or returned to nomadism, agriculture, especially commercial agriculture, and tax revenues were adversely affected. Population and economic activity stagnated, probably declining later in the seventeenth century.

Most of the eighteenth century was a period of relative peace, stability, and economic expansion. Although available evidence on production is limited, it indicates a trend for increasing agriculture and artisanal activity as well as investment in manufacturing in Istanbul and many parts of Anatolia. There also was considerable expansion in trade with central and western Europe. Until the nineteenth century, however, technological changes in agriculture, manufacturing, mining, shipbuilding, and other areas remained limited.

The nineteenth century was quite different from the earlier era. In the face of the growing European challenges and the territorial losses of the Ottoman Empire, it was characterized, on the one hand, by major efforts of the central government aimed at Western-style reform in administration, education, law, and justice, as well as economic, fiscal, and monetary affairs. It was also a period of integration into world markets and rapid expansion in trade with industrial Europe, which transformed the Ottoman economy into an exporter of primary products and an importer of manufactures. This process was facilitated by the construction of ports and railroads and the establishment of modern banking institutions, mostly with the help of European capital. Between 1830 and 1914, Anatolia's trade with Europe expanded about fifteenfold. On the eve of World War I, about one-quarter of its agricultural output in value terms was being exported, mostly to western Europe. Exports remained quite diversified, with tobacco, raisins, hazelnuts, cotton, and raw silk as the leading crops. Commercialization of agriculture proceeded most rapidly in western and central Anatolia and along the eastern Black Sea coast. The rural population was drawn to markets not only as producers of cash crops but also as purchasers of imported goods, especially cotton textiles (See Issawi, 1980; Pamuk, 1987).

Institutional changes and integration into world markets combined to create a slow but significant economic growth trend in the decades leading up to World War I, and possibly earlier. Per capita incomes probably rose at an average of about 1 percent per annum after 1880. Commercialized coastal regions, especially western Anatolia and the port cities, participated the most in this process. Estimates place per capita incomes for 1913 in the range of twelve to fourteen current British pounds sterling, or above one thousand dollars in purchasing power-parity-adjusted 1990 U.S. dollars. This would put average pre–World War I incomes within the present-day borders of Turkey below those of most countries in southeastern Europe, but above those of Egypt and Iran.

[*See also* Byzantine Empire *and* Ottoman Empire.]

BIBLIOGRAPHY

Faroqhi, Suraiya. *Towns and Townsmen of Ottoman Anatolia: Trade, Crafts and Food Production in an Urban Setting, 1520–1650.* Cambridge, 1984.

İnalcik, Halil, and Donald Quataert, eds. *An Economic and Social History of the Ottoman Empire, 1300–1914.* Cambridge, 1994.

İssawi, Charles. *The Economic History of Turkey, 1800–1914.* Chicago, 1980.

Pamuk, Şevket. *The Ottoman Empire and European Capitalism, 1820–1913: Trade, Investment and Production.* Cambridge, 1987.

ŞEVKET PAMUK

Modern Turkey

The modern state of Turkey was established in 1923 after the breakup of the Ottoman Empire. As the population of areas within the borders of present-day Turkey declined—from 16 million in 1914 to 13 million in 1925—then increased to 21 million in 1950 and 68 million in the year 2000—the economy experienced important structural changes, most notably urbanization and industrialization. Per-capita gross domestic product (GDP) increased fourfold to fivefold from 1914 to 2000, but the gap in purchasing power between Turkey and the advanced countries narrowed only slightly during this period.

Long-Term Trends. Domestic and international developments combined to create three distinct periods for Turkey's economy during the twentieth century. The first period, until 1950, was characterized by the reconstruction efforts of a new nation-state in the face of the Great Depression and two extended periods of wars and costly mobilizations. From the open-economy conditions of the Ottoman era, a shift was made to inward-oriented industrialization. If 1914 is taken as the benchmark, annual rates of growth of GDP per capita were modest, around 0.6 percent per year.

From 1950 to 1979, the postwar expansion of the world economy and the import substituting industrialization (ISI) strategy (relying on domestic products) combined to lead to the highest long-term rates of growth of GDP per capita of the century: 3.6 percent per year. Since 1980, Turkey's economy has been going through a slow and painful process of structural adjustment, shifting once again to an outward-oriented model, which includes a customs union arrangement with the European Union. Average rates of growth of per-capita GDP slowed down to less than 2 percent per annum in the following two decades. Growth of the urban economy in the postwar era was supported by rural to urban migration, which accelerated after 1950. Share of rural to total population declined from 75 percent in 1950 to less than 40 percent in 2000 (Table 1).

The Ottoman economy was mostly agrarian and increasingly oriented toward the export markets during the nineteenth century (see Ottoman Empire and Turkey: Premodern Turkey). For more than a decade, beginning in 1912, however, Anatolia was ravaged by a series of wars. The hostilities, destruction, and death that accompanied the Balkan Wars of 1912–1913, World War I, and the War of Independence (1920–1922) had severe and long-lasting demographic, social, and economic consequences.

Total casualties, military and civilian, of Muslims during this decade are estimated at close to 2 million. In addition, most of the Armenian population of 1.5 to 2 million in Anatolia was either forcibly deported, killed, or died of other causes after 1915. Finally, in the largest peacetime agreement of population exchange between two governments, approximately 1.2 million Greeks left Anatolia. In return, approximately half a million Muslims arrived from Greece after 1923. Ethnically speaking, the population of Turkey emerged as much more homogeneous than the Ottoman population in the same areas, with Muslim Turks and Kurds making up close to 98 percent of the total.

The former military officers, bureaucrats, and intellectuals who assumed positions of leadership in the new republic viewed the building of a new nation-state and modernization through Westernization as two closely related goals. Industrialization and the creation of a Muslim-Turkish bourgeoisie were considered the key ingredients of national economic development.

Industrialization. After the recovery of the 1920s, the Great Depression was strongly felt, especially in the foreign trade–oriented regions of the country. The government responded with interventionism, which failed to increase aggregate demand through devaluations and expansionary fiscal and monetary policies but did create a more autarkic economy and greater central control. Protectionist measures were followed, in 1932, by the adoption of etatism or import substituting industrialization (ISI) led by the state. Severe import repression was supported by the strong performance of agriculture despite sharply lower crop prices. These led to a reasonably strong economic recovery until World War II. The legacy of the 1930s profoundly influenced attitudes toward international trade. The degree of openness of the 1920s as measured by the exports/GDP ratio was not exceeded until the 1980s. For better or worse, etatism also proved to be inspirational for other state-led industrialization attempts in the Middle East after World War II.

After the end of World War II, domestic and international forces combined to bring about major political and economic changes in Turkey. Various social groups began to demand, *inter alia*, greater emphasis on private enterprise, agriculture, and a more open economy. The emergence of the United States as the dominant world power also played an important role in the shaping of new policies. A strategy of agriculture-led growth could not be sustained, however, after the world commodity boom associated with the Korean War subsided. The severe balance-of-payments crisis in the second half of the 1950s moved Turkey back toward ISI, this time led by the private sector. While foreign investment remained modest, large, family-owned conglomerates with numerous manufacturing and distribution companies, as well as banks and other service firms, emerged as the new leaders. The state sector continued to play an important, supporting role in industrialization until the 1970s.

Taking advantage of the opportunities provided by a large and protected domestic market, the ISI process brought about growth and structural change. Rates of growth of the manufacturing industry averaged more than 10 percent per annum between 1963 and 1977. Industrialization was not carried to the technologically more difficult stage of capital goods industries, however. More importantly, export orientation of manufacturing remained weak, which proved to be the Achilles' heel for ISI.

The ISI regime had become too difficult to dislodge because of the power of vested interest groups who benefited from the existing system of protection and subsidies. To shift toward export promotion in a country with a large domestic market required a strong government with a long-term horizon and considerable autonomy. These were exactly the features lacking in the Turkish political scene during the 1970s. Escalation of international oil prices and short-term external borrowing under unfavorable terms by fragile coalition governments led to another severe balance-of-payments crisis at the end of the 1970s.

A comprehensive package of stabilization, liberalization, and structural adjustment was adopted in 1980, putting the economy on an outwardly oriented course. Supported by the suppression of wages under the military regime, the new policies succeeded in raising exports from less than 3 percent to 10 percent of GDP within a decade. Manufactures, most notably textiles, clothing, and iron and steel products, accounted for approximately 80 percent of this increase. Since then, however, efforts to reduce the size of the public sector have made slow progress against political and legal opposition. By the end of the 1980s, large public sector deficits had ushered in rates of inflation above 80 percent per annum. Macroeconomic instability continued in the 1990s. On the more positive side, Turkey successfully entered a customs union agreement with the European Union and began to seek greater integration around the Black Sea region and with the Central Asian republics.

Agriculture. During the half century until the end of the 1970s, agricultural output per person in the country increased at an annual rate of 1.6 percent. This performance

ISTANBUL. View of the city with the Galata Tower in the background and the Galata Bridge over the Golden Horn, 1986. (© Robert Frerck/Woodfin Camp and Associates, New York)

has enabled Turkey not only to increase per-capita consumption substantially but also to remain self-sufficient in foodstuffs, a rare achievement in the Middle East. The availability of additional land until the 1960s was an important factor in this outcome. At least equally important was the success of small peasant ownership and production supported by government policies.

Since the 1970s, increases in output have depended on increases in yields through the intensification of cultivation, the use of high-yielding plant varieties, and the expansion of irrigated lands through expensive schemes such as the Southeastern Anatolian project. When combined with the decline of agricultural price-support programs in the structural adjustment era, this constraint slowed the rate of growth of agricultural output. By the end of the century, share of agriculture in the overall economy had fallen to 14 percent. Nonetheless, it continued to provide employment for more than 40 percent of the labor force.

Growth, Human Development, and Distribution. Turkey's long-term record of growth in the twentieth century parallels general trends in the world economy. Limited increases in per-capita income during the first half of the century were followed by unprecedented rates of growth during the postwar expansion. Growth rates slowed down after the 1970s. On the whole, Turkey's economy performed slightly above the averages for the developing countries as a whole.

Another important indicator of productivity and distribution is urban wages. Real wages in manufacturing did not exceed their 1914 levels until the 1950s. During the high age of ISI, they tripled until the end of the 1970s, keeping pace with increases in average incomes. In the era of structural adjustment and globalization since 1980, manufacturing wages first declined and then recovered to

TABLE 1. *Turkey's Economy in the Twentieth Century: Basic Indicators*

	Years			
	1914	1950	1980	2000
Population (millions)	16	21	44	68
Share of urban to total population (%)	26	25	44	65
Share of manufacturing to GDP (%)	11	13	21	22
Index of real wages in manufacturing	100	85	242	290
GDP per capita in PPP, adjusted 1990 U.S. dollars	1,100	1,400	4,050	5,600
Life expectancy at birth (years)	n.a.	43	62	68
Female illiteracy (%)	92	81	45	12

Average annual rate of change of GDP per-capita (%)	1914–1950	1950–1979	1980–2000
	0.7	3.6	1.9

return to their 1978–1979 levels despite the more than 40 percent increase in average incomes in these two decades.

Basic indicators of human development have also shown increases, especially during the second half of the twentieth century. Life expectancy at birth has risen from about 35 in 1935 to 43 in 1950 and 68 in 2000. Part of this increase was due to the decline in rates of infant mortality from the exceptionally high levels of 160 per 1,000 until the late 1960s. Basic indicators for education have registered considerable but not exceptional increases. Illiteracy rates for males and females have declined from 71 and 90 percent in 1935 to 68 and 81 percent in 1950, 33 and 45 percent in 1980, and 11 and 16 percent in 1990 (Table 1). The relatively slow progress in education remains probably the most important impediment to higher rates of increase in productivity and incomes.

The quality of information on how these gains have and have not been distributed is not very good. Nonetheless, the existence of large urban-rural and regional (west-east) inequalities in income, education, health care, and other government services is not disputed. Although some studies have argued that overall inequalities have not changed since the 1970s, urban-rural differences, inequalities within the urban sector, and the gap between the Kurdish southeast and the rest of the country appear to have widened during the last quarter of the twentieth century.

BIBLIOGRAPHY

Barkey, Henry J. *The State and the Industrialization Crisis in Turkey*. Boulder, 1990.

Boratav, Korkut. "Kemalist Economic Policies and Etatism," in *Ataturk, Founder of a Modern State*, edited by A. Kazancigil and E. Özbudun. London, 1981.

Hansen, Bent. *Egypt and Turkey: The Political Economy of Poverty, Equity and Growth*. New York, 1991.

Keyder, Çağlar. *State and Class in Turkey: A Study in Capitalist Development*. London and New York, 1987.

Öniş, Ziya, and James Riedel. *Economic Crises and Long Term Growth in Turkey*, Washington, D.C., 1993.

Owen, Roger, and Şevket Pamuk. *A History of the Middle East Economies in the Twentieth Century*, chapters 1 and 5. London and Cambridge, 1998.

Richards, Alan, and John Waterbury. *A Political Economy of the Middle East*. 2d ed. Boulder, 1996.

State Institute of Statistics, *Statistical Indicators, 1923–1992*. Ankara, 1994.

ŞEVKET PAMUK

TUSCANY. Tuscany comprises some 9,304 square miles (24,097 square kilometers) in central Italy and is bounded by the Tyrrhenian Sea to the east, the Apennine Mountains to the north and west, and the upper Tiber Valley to the south. The landscape consists of hills, fields, and pasture lands traversed by streams and waterways, the most important of which is the Arno River.

Throughout the ancient and early medieval period Tuscany was a relatively minor agrarian center, given primarily to animal raising and farming. The economy of the region became commercialized as a result of the great Europe wide demographic expansion from the eleventh century to the middle of the fourteenth century. Dramatic population increases brought an expansion of trade, the growth of a merchant class, and the rise of cities. Lucca, Pisa, Florence, Siena, and Arezzo all developed into important urban centers, as did even minor towns such as Pistoia and Prato. Tuscans engaged in long-distance trade and became early leaders in banking and the manufacture of silk and woolen cloth. The accumulation of wealth paved the way for leadership in the cultural and artistic revival known as the Renaissance.

The cities of Pisa, Lucca, and Siena were the initial leaders. Located on the Tyrrhenian Sea, Pisa engaged in long-distance trade. Its merchants benefited greatly from the Crusades (1095–1291), serving as middlemen for the transport of soldiers and supplies. Christian victories in the First Crusade (1095–1099) allowed Pisa to establish trading posts in the Middle East. Pisa's inland neighbor Lucca took advantage of its position along the Via Francigena, a principal highway running from southern France to Rome, to develop trade links beyond the Alps. Lucchese merchants also entered the fields of banking and silk cloth manufacture. Lucca grew rich from the latter and maintained its position as Europe's main producer until political unrest in the fourteenth century drove many highly skilled weavers outside the city. Siena, also located on the Via Francigena, derived its wealth from trade beyond the Alps and from indigenous metal-bearing hills just outside the city. In the twelfth and thirteenth centuries Sienese merchants established themselves as the principal bankers of the pope.

The city of Florence emerged as the economic leader of Tuscany in the middle thirteenth century and the fourteenth century. Florence took over the pope's accounts from the Sienese and coupled this with the establishment of a strong industrial base. Florence developed a vibrant woolen cloth business and later a silk cloth industry. A strong international banking sector facilitated the marketing of these products. In the fourteenth and fifteenth centuries, Florence was the leading European center for banking.

The outbreak of the Black Death in 1348, accompanied by famine and internecine wars, altered the economy of the region. Tuscan cities attempted to sustain themselves by shifting more decisively into the luxury market, which remained vibrant. The Florentines succeeded best and became more decisively the dominant economy of the region. Florence coupled economic leadership with political hegemony and by degrees seized all of Tuscany.

By the late fifteenth century and the sixteenth century Tuscany began to lose its position in the broader

European economy. A series of foreign invasions hurt trade, as did growing competition from Dutch and English merchants who outmaneuvered the Tuscans in the international market. By the seventeenth century the region reverted to an economy of small-scale producers. In the eighteenth century Tuscany fell under the control of the Austrians, and a century later it was incorporated into the French Empire by Napoleon. It became part of the Kingdom of Piedmont in 1860 and part of the Kingdom of Italy in 1861.

BIBLIOGRAPHY

Caferro, William. *Mercenary Companies and the Decline of Siena*. Baltimore, 1998.

Epstein, Stephan R. "Stato teritoriale e economia regionale nella Toscana del Quattrocento." In *La Toscana al tempo di Lorenzo il Magnifico: PoliticaEconomia Cultura Arte*, edited by Riccardo Fubini, pp. 869–900. Pisa, Italy, 1996.

Luzzatto, Gino. *An Economic History of Italy*. London, 1961.

Martines, Lauro. *Power and Imagination: City-States in Renaissance Italy*. New York, 1979.

WILLIAM CAFERRO

U

UGANDA. *See* East Africa.

UKRAINE. Ukraine came into existence as an independent state in 1991. With its 603,700 square kilometers and 48,150,000 inhabitants (2002), it is the second largest country in Europe. Virtually the entire land mass of Ukraine is covered by vast plains comprised of fertile soil (the so-called black earth *chornozem*).

Ukrainian historical development may be divided into six eras, named for the state entities that ruled the area: Kievan Rus'; Lithuania-Poland; Cossack state and Muscovy; Russian and Austrian empires; Soviet Union; and independent Ukraine. In all but the last era, Ukraine's economy was determined by the needs and policies of the state to which its territory belonged.

Until the nineteenth century Ukraine functioned primarily as a source of raw materials that were shipped to more economically advanced countries, from which artisan and manufactured goods were received in return. Even before the first historic era, Kievan Rus', Ukraine supplied grain to Greek trading cities along the northern shores of the Black Sea and the Crimean peninsula beginning about 500 BCE. Ukraine's trade relations with the Aegean and eastern Mediterranean world continued during the Kievan Rus' era, which lasted from the late ninth to the mid-fourteenth century. The Rus' state, based in Kiev (Ukraine's present-day capital), traced its origin to a trade route that stretched from the Baltic coast of Sweden through Ukraine to the capital of the Byzantine Empire, Constantinople, along the straits between the Black and Aegean seas. Ukrainian lands supplied hemp, hides, grain, and in particular furs and slaves to the Byzantine Greeks, in return for luxury items such as wine, silk fabrics, and Christian art works.

A major change in the Ukrainian economy came during the second historic era. With the gradual decline of Kievan Rus', its principalities located in Ukraine were annexed to the Grand Duchy of Lithuania in the fourteenth century and then to the Kingdom of Poland in 1569. Those two states functioned as the Polish-Lithuanian Commonwealth, whose vast, sparsely settled Ukrainian lands were gradually developed to produce grain that was shipped northwestward through Poland to its Baltic port of Gdańsk(Danzig) and from there to western Europe. Polish-Lithuanian prosperity in the sixteenth and first half of the seventeenth centuries depended largely on income from its trade in grain, which derived largely from Ukraine.

In 1648, Ukraine was the scene of a major revolt against Polish rule, led by Zaporozhian Cossacks living in the south-central part of the country. Within a few decades Ukraine was divided between Poland-Lithuania west of the Dnieper River and a Cossack state closely allied with Muscovy east of the river. During this era the grain trade toward Poland virtually ended, and the Cossack state survived by trading to the northeast with Muscovy, but especially by exporting raw materials to the Ottoman Empire, which had replaced Byzantium in the Black Sea–eastern Mediterranean region. The Cossacks also supported a small domestic industry in iron mining and processing.

When Muscovy was transformed into the Russian Empire in the early eighteenth century, the Cossack state lost its autonomy. At the same time most Ukrainian lands west of the Dnieper River were annexed to Russia. Between 1772 and 1795 Poland-Lithuania was partitioned, and Ukraine's far-western regions (Galicia, Bukovina, Transcarpathia) were annexed to the Austrian, later Austro-Hungarian, Empire. During the Russian-Austrian era, which lasted until 1917–1918, Ukraine's economy served as an appendage to the empires that ruled the country. The Russian Empire used grain exports to finance its own existence; and during the nineteenth century between 73 and 84 percent of its corn, wheat, rye, barley, and industrial sugar came from Ukraine. By the 1880s, coal mining and metallurgical and machine-building industries were rapidly developed in the Dnieper-Donbas area of eastern Ukraine. By contrast, far-western Ukrainian lands under Austro-Hungarian rule remained underdeveloped, subsistence-level, agriculturally based lands.

The Soviet era began at the close of the Russian Civil War in 1920 and lasted until 1991. Far-western Ukraine for a time was ruled by Poland, Romania, and Czechoslovakia, but at the close of World War II these territories were also made part of the Soviet Union. The Soviet era was initially characterized by economic experimentation (war communism, New Economic Policy), but in 1928 the government instituted a so-called command economy. This meant that the entire Soviet economy (including Ukraine) was integrated and directed by government bureaucrats who formulated what came to be known as five-year plans. The goals of these periodic plans were large-scale industrialization and collectivization of agriculture. By 1940, Ukraine was producing between 90 and 95 percent of the Soviet Union's coke, soda ash, iron ore, pig iron, and coal. In contrast, agricultural production had been severely undermined by bureaucratic inefficiency, drought, and forced collectivization, which led to the loss of millions of lives in the Great Famine of 1933. Until the end of the Soviet era, Ukraine's economy was inextricably linked to and dependent on the successes and failures of the state's economic planning boards.

Since its independence in 1991, Ukraine has tried to transform its economy. The government has not attempted large-scale or radical reform, nor has it adopted adequate laws and a tax policy that would encourage extensive private enterprise. Many Soviet-style industrial enterprises have collapsed; others have been taken over by a small number of former Soviet officials, known as oligarchs, who have amassed extensive personal wealth. High unemployment and a low gross national product are the primary characteristics of Ukraine's economy at the outset of the twenty-first century.

[*See also* Russia.]

BIBLIOGRAPHY

Friedgut, Theodore H. *Iuzovka and Revolution: Politics and Revolution in Russia's Donbass, 1869–1924.* 2 vols. Princeton, 1989–1994.
Kononenko, Konstantyn. *Ukraine and Russia: A History of Economic Relations between Ukraine and Russia, 1654–1917.* Milwaukee, 1958.
Koropeckyj, I. S. *Development in the Shadow: Studies in Ukrainian Economics.* Edmonton, 1990.
Koropeckyj, I. S., ed. *Ukrainian Economic History: Interpretive Essays.* Cambridge, Mass., 1991.
Magocsi, Paul Robert. *A History of Ukraine.* Toronto, 1996.
Shen, Raphael. *Ukraine's Economic Reform: Obstacles, Errors, Lessons.* Westport, Conn., 1996.

PAUL ROBERT MAGOCSI

ULSTER. Ulster is best known for its endemic ethnic conflict, rather like the Balkans, the Middle East, or Sri Lanka. Yet it was one of the early industrializing regions of Europe, giving rise to proud traditions of economic, scientific, and technical endeavor. All three were embodied in the SS *Titanic*—launched by Harland and Wolff in Belfast in 1912 at the height of Ulster's industrial might. Its subsequent tragic fate some might see as emblematic of the decline of the industrial economy of the region in the twentieth century.

Ulster is the most northerly of the Irish provinces, comprised of nine of the thirty-two counties of Ireland, and is situated strategically in relation to the nurseries of the Industrial Revolution in the west of Scotland and the north west of England. The sources of modern economic growth go back to the seventeenth century, when this turbulent, Gaelic province was finally incorporated into England's expanding colonial system. In 1600, on the eve of conquest, the province was thinly populated, poorly endowed with land resources, and economically backward compared to other parts of the island. A century later, much of Ulster had been settled by English and Scottish landowners, farmers and craftspeople, with the forcible and partial displacement of some of the indigenous peoples. Property rights were rewritten with the sword. Modern landlord-tenant relations replaced lineage-based systems of authority and landholding. Urban and market development, as in the plantation towns of Belfast, Coleraine, and Londonderry, mirrored capitalist development in early modern England. A new ethnic mosaic, enriched by the manufacturing and marketing skills of some of the newcomers, shaped the subsequent evolution of the province, economically as well as politically.

Though small-holding agriculture was the principal livelihood of most people during the eighteenth century, the dynamic sector was linen textiles. The spinning and weaving of linen, based on locally grown flax, began as an activity ancillary to farming, but linen manufacture soon established itself as a major source of earnings. By the close of the century, more than 40 million yards of linen cloth were being exported annually, and linens constituted the principal export of the region. This remarkable case of export-led growth, allied to improvements in agriculture, resulted in the transformation of the Ulster economy from the most primitive to the most advanced of the Irish regions. Underpinning this success was the political and institutional framework fashioned during the early plantation period and consolidated by the Glorious Revolution (1688). The settlement opened the way to the duty-free access of Irish yarn and linen cloth to England from 1696. Thus, on the demand side, the expanding English and later North American markets held the key to the industry's progress. On the supply side, the symbiosis of part-time agriculture and household production of yarn and cloth helped keep competitive the prices of Ulster linens. Specialization in the finer, higher-priced cloths was an advantage in the face of competition from continental European rivals and the coarser linen trade of Scotland.

The development of the linen industry conforms to some key features of the proto-industrial model, as sketched by F. F. Mendels and Hans Medick. The geographical setting was primarily rural rather than urban, with tens of thousands of household production units scattered across the

Ulster countryside. The technology was a handicraft one, using such simple capital items as spinning wheels and handlooms. Crucially, though, most of the output was destined for export markets rather than meeting local demand. Manufacturing was fitted, at least initially, into the slack periods of the farming year. Rapid population growth accompanied the rise of rural industry. So, in time, commercial farming zones came to supply part of the food needs of these peasant manufacturers. With the benefit of hindsight, we can say that proto-industrialization proved to be the formative phase in the industrialization of Ulster, but earlier and later stages were linked through an evolving configuration of probabilities rather than a set of deterministic relationships.

The link, in part at least, was via another form of textile production. The fledgling cotton industry introduced Belfast and its environs to factory industry at the end of the eighteenth century, but this proved an evanescent growth. Its more enduring significance, however, was that it smoothed the pathway to the mechanization of the linen industry. By the 1830s, cotton factories were being adapted for the purposes of the machine spinning of linen yarn; and with the advent of power-loom weaving in the 1850s, the transition to a factory-based linen industry was complete. The inevitable counterpart was the disintegration of handicraft industry in the countryside, which in part explains the severity of the Great Famine (1845–1849) in outer Ulster. The clustering of linen firms in east Ulster and around the port of Belfast was such that by 1914 the province was the largest linen-producing region in the world, with linkages to textile engineering and other spin-off industries.

With linen as the leading sector, Ulster in the early nineteenth century developed sophisticated banking and financial services, an improved infrastructure (including the deepening of Belfast harbor, which later proved so important to the development of shipbuilding), and an active business community centering on the Belfast Chamber of Commerce. Processes of cumulative causation accelerated the industrial development of the region. Contingency played its part. Edward Harland was deflected from Liverpool to Belfast in 1854 and four years later set up the world-famous shipbuilding partnership of Harland & Wolff. The major inputs—skilled labor, coal, and iron—all had to be imported. Yet the partnership flourished, because its design skills, technical innovation, effective networking, and marketing. By the end of the century, Harland & Wolff had one of the largest shipyards in the world, a success that bred emulation in the form of two other Belfast shipyards. In a series of related and sometimes complementary developments, a number of major engineering firms had also established themselves in this local crucible of the Industrial Revolution.

The tenfold increase in the population of Belfast between 1821 and 1914 (fourfold in the case of the second-largest city, Londonderry) is indicative of the striking economic success of the region. By the eve of World War I, the east of the province, with Belfast as its metropolis, was home to world-class industries in linen, shipbuilding, and engineering. The huge expansion in international trade after 1850 amplified the opportunities for growth, while scale economies and linkage effects strengthened Ulster's competitiveness in the international marketplace. There were benefits for employers also in the large reserves of low-wage, unskilled labor to be found in the rural hinterland, but this advantage was common to many other regions. Much more unusual was the fact that Ulster developed industry, including heavy industry in the second half of the nineteenth century, in the absence of local supplies of coal and iron. In this, and indeed in other respects, economic geography was fundamental. Belfast was well situated within the industrializing world of northwest Great Britain. It was linked by watery highways to the neighboring ports and hinterlands of Liverpool and Glasgow, while cultural affinities eased the flow, not only of raw materials and skilled labor but of entrepreneurship, technical knowledge, and capital between Great Britain and the North of Ireland. It is noticeable how many of the successful entrepreneurs outside the linen sector—in shipbuilding, engineering, rope and shirt making—hailed from Scotland or England. Success attracts success, it would seem, more especially where the physical and cultural distances are small. The cultural continuum facilitated social and business networks crisscrossing the Irish channel.

A specialized industrial structure, heavily dependent on world trade, fitted the needs of the regional economy less well after 1920. Despite the coincidence of timing, the emerging problems had nothing to do with the partition of the island between two states in 1921. Southern Ireland seceded from the United Kingdom to form the newly created Irish Free State (later the Irish Republic). Northern Ireland, consisting of six of the original nine counties of Ulster, remained within the United Kingdom but was accorded its own regionally devolved parliament. Constitutional changes notwithstanding, the problems of the economy were primarily international in origin. Increasingly competitive conditions but, more fundamentally, shifts in demand affected the staple Northern Irish industries. Linen textiles faced a secular decline in demand, as fashions changed and cheaper substitutes increasingly displaced linen goods. British shipbuilding and engineering, including Belfast's, entered a much more turbulent age: new competitors emerged in Scandinavia and Japan; growth in world demand was sluggish and spiralled downward when the global economy descended into a slump at the end of the 1920s. World War II provided a short respite, but the painful process of restructuring took on a fresh momentum in the succeeding decades. Massive redundancies in linen, shipbuilding, and engineering characterized the third quarter of the century. The Northern Ireland government enjoyed some success in attracting multinational companies to substitute for ailing traditional industry, though the postwar Golden Age of economic growth touched Northern Ireland only lightly.

Civil disorder along religious and ethnic lines dominated and disfigured the final three decades of the century. One effect was to paralyze the development strategy based on inward investment, an approach pursued with consummate success by the neighboring state of the Irish Republic. Deindustrialization set in with a vengeance after the first oil crisis from 1973 to 1974, though living standards in Northern Ireland were shored up by large subventions from the British exchequer. Varying estimates of the economic impact of terrorism exist. While the corrosive effects on industrial production, employment, and investment cannot be disputed, a comparative view provides some perspective. Deindustrialization was by no means unique to Northern Ireland. Other older industrialized regions, from Tyneside or Clydeside in Great Britain to the "rust belt" cities of the United States, experienced heavy losses of traditional industry in the later twentieth century. It is clear that forces other than those of atavistic nationalism were at play. Even in the case of Northern Ireland, there was life after deindustrialization: a services-dominated economy took shape, centered on a disproportionately large public sector, but with the potential for further transformation in the new century.

[*See also* Great Britain; Ireland; *and* Linen Industry.]

BIBLIOGRAPHY
Bardon, Jonathan. *A History of Ulster.* Belfast, 1992.
Green, E. R. R. *The Lagan Valley, 1800–1850.* London, 1949.
Kennedy, Liam, and Philip Ollerenshaw, eds. *An Economic History of Ulster, 1820–1939.* Manchester, 1985.
Ó Gráda, Cormac. *Ireland: A New Economic History, 1780–1939.* Oxford, 1994.

LIAM KENNEDY

UNEMPLOYMENT. The word *unemployment* did not come into general use until the 1890s although *unemployed* was used throughout the nineteenth century. However, for much of the century there was no agreed-upon definition of unemployed. Many commentators defined as unemployed all individuals who were not working, whether they were looking for work or not. Thus the unemployed included the elderly, the sick and disabled, and, in some cases, children above a certain age. A more "modern" definition was used by Carroll Wright, chief of the Massachusetts Bureau of Statistics of Labor, in 1878. In an attempt to estimate the extent of male unemployment in the state, Wright instructed assessors to count only "able-bodied males, over 18 years of age, . . . who really want employment." The U.S. Bureau of Labor Statistics currently defines as unemployed individuals who do not have a job, have actively searched for work in the previous month, and are available for work. An individual without a job but not searching for work is defined as "out of the labor force" rather than unemployed. This definition is essentially the same as that adopted by the International Labour Office although the definition of what constitutes seeking work differs across countries.

For most of the nineteenth century, middle-class observers believed that, except during severe downturns, the majority of those out of work were voluntarily unemployed. The unemployed were described as shiftless, unfit, or incompetent. Charles Booth (1892) argued that many of those who lived in poverty because of irregular employment "cannot keep work when they get it; lack of work is not really the disease with them." A shift in how the public viewed the unemployed occurred after 1890. The extent of this shift can be seen in the title of William Beveridge's influential book *Unemployment: A Problem of Industry* (1909). Beveridge rejected the view that any able-bodied adult who wanted to work could readily find a job. Unemployment was caused by cyclical and seasonal fluctuations in the economy and maladjustments of supply and demand for labor, not by the deficiencies of individual workers. This new explanation for unemployment played an important role in the adoption of national unemployment insurance.

Early commentators such as Sidney and Beatrice Webb (1929) maintained that widespread unemployment was a recent occurrence, a "disease of the modern industrial system." Such claims, however, focused attention on cyclical unemployment and ignored the problem of chronic underemployment in preindustrial societies. Historian Charles Wilson (1965) estimated that in the late seventeenth century a quarter of England's population was "permanently in a state of poverty and underemployment, if not of total unemployment," and similar results have been obtained from studies of agrarian societies in the twentieth century.

Types of Unemployment. One of the earliest attempts to classify the unemployed was made in 1893 by H. Llewellyn Smith, Britain's first commissioner of labour. He listed eight causes of fluctuations in labor demand, which describe seasonal and cyclical unemployment, unemployment due to changes in fashion or in the location of industry, and unemployment due to changes in production processes. Llewellyn Smith's types of unemployment are similar to the currently accepted classification scheme of frictional, seasonal, structural, and demand-deficient unemployment.

Frictional unemployment arises because unemployed workers and employers with job vacancies do not instantly locate each other. The frictionally unemployed consist of workers between jobs and new entrants or reentrants to the labor force looking for work. The extent of frictional unemployment thus is determined by the flow of workers into the labor market and by the speed at which the unemployed are able to find jobs. Nineteenth-century observers noted that the length of time workers were between jobs was excessively long owing to the disorganized nature of labor markets. Improvements in information flows and the reduction of transportation costs in the second half of the nineteenth century reduced the interval between jobs, and around the turn of the twentieth century European governments attempted further to rationalize the job-search process by adopting systems of labor exchanges where unemployed workers could register and employers needing workers could post vacancies.

Seasonal unemployment arises because of systematic fluctuations in the demand for labor during the year. Seasonality is an inherent characteristic of arable agriculture, and seasonal unemployment was ubiquitous in preindustrial agrarian economies. In industry, seasonal unemployment was especially pronounced in the building trades, but also existed in clothing, printing, chemicals, lumbering, and other trades. Engerman and Goldin (1994) estimate that in 1850 two-thirds of the American workforce was seasonally unemployed for up to four months each year. Seasonality remained a serious problem throughout the nineteenth century.

Structural unemployment exists when there is a mismatch between the skills or the location of unemployed workers and the skills demanded by or the location of employers. At any time the demand for some types of labor is increasing as the demand for other types is falling. Workers who lose jobs in declining sectors often do not have the skills needed to fill the vacancies in sectors where labor demand is increasing. In the nineteenth century, rapid technological change was a major cause of "mismatch" unemployment in manufacturing. A classic example of technological unemployment is the sharp decline in the demand for handloom weavers in northwestern England in the second quarter of the nineteenth century due to adoption of the power loom. Structural unemployment also is caused by the movement of jobs from one region to another. For example, the recent shift in location of jobs in the United States from the rust belt to the sun belt created unemployment in Northeastern cities and vacancies in the Southwest. Since World War II most Western economies have attempted to reduce structural unemployment by adopting publicly funded training programs for unemployed workers, relocation subsidies for workers who migrate from high-unemployment to low-unemployment regions, and tax incentives to firms that locate in depressed areas.

Demand-deficient or cyclical unemployment is a result of declines in the demand for labor caused by business-cycle downturns. It occurs when the aggregate demand for goods and services is too low, at existing wage rates, to provide jobs for all those seeking work. Business cycles are a characteristic of industrial economies; so cyclical unemployment is a relatively modern phenomenon. Before the 1920s, many economists, while admitting the existence of cyclical unemployment, argued that it largely was due to the downward inflexibility of wages. Workers lost their jobs during downturns because they refused to accept wage reductions; cyclical unemployment thus was to a large degree voluntary.

Widespread demand for policies to reduce cyclical unemployment began early in the twentieth century. In Britain, the Webbs and others argued that public authorities should "regularise" the national demand for labor by undertaking necessary development projects when private sector demand for labor was slack. Thirty years later John Maynard Keynes, in *The General Theory of Employment, Interest, and Money* (London, 1936), developed a theory linking the level of employment to aggregate demand, and argued that during downturns increases in government spending could be used to reduce unemployment. Although most Western governments made some attempt to reduce demand-deficient unemployment during the Great Depression, large-scale Keynesian demand-management policies became widespread only after World War II.

Pre-1914 studies often considered casual unemployment as a separate category. Casual unemployment existed in low-skilled occupations that were subject to rapid and irregular fluctuations in labor demand; for example, employers at the London docks adjusted their workforce to the exact state of demand, hiring laborers by the day or half-day. To assure a plentiful supply of labor, work typically was given out in rotation to laborers queued up at calling-on stands. This led to a chronic oversupply of casual labor, and a large share of dock workers were underemployed even in relatively prosperous times. Governments attempted to reduce casual unemployment by convincing employers to hire workers only through local labor exchanges and to eliminate the practice of rotating work.

Full Employment and the Natural Rate of Unemployment. There is no agreed-upon definition of full employment although it is agreed that full employment does not mean zero unemployment. Many early commentators claimed that under a capitalist system there would always be an excess supply of labor, so that even during prosperous times there was an "irreducible minimum" below which unemployment would not fall. The idea that capitalism required "an unemployed reserve army of workers" can be traced back to Friedrich Engels, in his *The Condition of the Working Class in England* (Leipzig, 1845). Engels, and later Karl Marx, maintained that the reserve army would be depleted only during periods of "highest prosperity." However, late-nineteenth-century unemployment statistics revealed that a core of unemployed workers remained even during booms. Beveridge (1909) concluded from his study of trade-union data that unemployment in skilled trades seldom if ever fell below 2 percent, and that minimum unemployment rates among the unskilled were even higher. A study of unemployment in American cities in 1902–1917 found that as a result of seasonality, workers changing jobs, and other factors, unemployment never fell below 4 percent. Such studies led the Massachusetts Bureau of Labor Statistics to conclude in 1911 that "there is always a 'reserve army' of the unemployed."

Beveridge, in *Full Employment in a Free Society* (1945), defined full employment as existing when there are "more vacant jobs than unemployed" workers, and the number unemployed is "not excessive." Numerically, he estimated that because of seasonal and frictional unemployment the minimum achievable unemployment rate would be about 3 percent. Most economists today would argue that Beveridge's definition of full employment is far too ambitious. In fact, within economics the term *full employment* largely has been replaced by *natural rate of unemployment*, or, more recently, *NAIRU* (nonaccelerating inflation rate of unemployment). Milton Friedman (1968) defined the natural rate as the level of unemployment that is "consistent with equilibrium in the structure of *real* wage rates." His definition takes into account structural characteristics of the labor market, and the natural rate typically is measured as the level of frictional, structural, and seasonal unemployment. A country's natural rate of unemployment is determined by its economic and institutional characteristics; the natural rate can shift over time because of changes in government policies or because of supply shocks.

Improvements in information flows, declining transportation costs, and the adoption of public employment exchanges and publicly funded training programs should have caused the natural rate of unemployment to decline during the late nineteenth and early twentieth centuries. On the other hand, the adoption of national unemployment insurance (UI) policies in the twentieth century probably caused the natural rate to increase. The payment of UI benefits to unemployed workers reduces the cost of searching for work, and causes some unemployed workers to increase their minimum acceptable wage offer (reservation wage), which increases the average duration of unemployment.

The natural rate of unemployment reached a minimum in the late 1960s, when it was estimated to be 2 to 3 percent in western Europe and 3 to 4 percent in the United States.

It then increased in the 1970s for several reasons, including structural changes, a slowdown in productivity, external shocks, and changing labor-market institutions. Paul Samuelson and William Nordhaus (*Economics*, 12th ed., New York, 1985) put the U.S. natural rate at 6 percent in the early 1980s; it was at least that high in most European countries. The natural rate remained stuck at a high level in much of western Europe during the 1980s and 1990s, but declined in the United States, where by the late 1990s it again was estimated to be around 4 to 5 percent. One explanation offered by economists for the decline in the natural rate in the United States but not in Europe is that U.S. labor markets are more flexible and workers more mobile than those of western Europe, where institutional changes have created labor-market rigidities that have kept the equilibrium rate of unemployment from falling.

Long-Run Trends in Unemployment. For most countries, reliable data on unemployment rates before the 1920s do not exist. National unemployment estimates for the period before World War I, except for the United States, are derived from data reported by trade unions that offered benefits to unemployed members. Trade-union unemployment series exist back to 1855, for Britain 1887 for Germany, 1895 for France, 1903 for Denmark, and 1904 for Norway. Each of these series is based on a relatively small, nonrandom sample of industrial workers; so they are of limited usefulness as a measure of the level of unemployment at any given time, but probably are good measures of trends in unemployment. Unemployment rates for the United States for 1890–1930 have been calculated from estimates of the labor force and total employment. Several American states conducted periodic censuses of the unemployed, beginning with the Massachusetts survey of 1878. The only other unemployment estimates for the nineteenth century are for individual cities for short periods of time.

For the century from 1815 to 1914, a number of major business cycle downturns occurred in Britain (in 1819, 1826, 1841–1842, 1857–1858, 1878–1879, 1885–1887, 1893–1894, and 1908–1909) and in the United States (in 1818–1819, 1839–1843, 1857–1858, 1873–1879, 1893–1897, 1907–1908, and 1914–1915). The timing of downturns in Germany and France was roughly similar to that in Britain and America. The bits of data that are available indicate that urban unemployment often was quite high during the periodic downturns in the economy. For example, data for industrial cities in northwestern England collected by factory inspectors indicate that during the downturn of 1841–1842 unemployment among textile mill workers was 15 to 20 percent or higher. Estimates constructed from trade-union returns and other sources by Boyer and Hatton (2001) for 1870–1913 suggest that industrial unemployment in Britain exceeded 8 percent in 1878–1879,

UNEMPLOYMENT. British Labor Party poster, 1919. (Snark/Art Resource, NY)

1885–1887, 1893–1895, 1904–1905, and 1908–1909, and peaked at 11 percent in 1879.

There are few reliable estimates of unemployment in the United States before 1890. The Massachusetts Labor Bureau estimated that during the 1885 downturn the state's unemployment rate was 10.4 percent for males and 9.6 percent for females. Contemporary estimates of the number unemployed in the depression year 1893 ranged from one million to 4.5 million. A more recent estimate by David Weir (1992) put the number unemployed in 1893 at 1.67 million. Weir estimated that during the depression of 1893–1898 the civilian unemployment rate in the United States averaged 8.4 percent; for the same period, the private nonfarm unemployment rate averaged 15.2 percent.

Table 1 presents estimates of unemployment rates for ten countries for various periods from 1900 to 1998. The estimates for the period from 1964 to 1998 have been standardized by the Organization for Economic Cooperation and Development (OECD) using the International Labor Organization (ILO) definition of unemployment as a percentage of the total labor force, and can be used to compare unemployment rates across countries and over time.

The estimates for 1950 to 1963 were constructed largely from OECD sources and, for the most part, should be compatible with those for 1964 to 1998. The estimates for 1900 to 1938 are from sources of varying quality, and comparisons both across countries and with later time periods must be made with caution. For the United States between 1900 and 1913, the estimate in row (a) refers to nonfarm unemployment and that in (b) to civilian unemployment. For Britain from 1900 to 1913, Feinstein's estimate in row (a) relies solely on trade-union unemployment rates, whereas that of Boyer and Hatton in row (b) includes sectors for which union data are not available. Where two estimates are reported for 1921–1938, the higher estimate is for nonfarm/industrial unemployment, and the lower estimate is for economy-wide unemployment. Eichengreen and Hatton (1988) contend that the reported economy-wide unemployment rates for Germany, Belgium, and Sweden from 1930 to 1938 do not adequately measure unemployment for certain sectors or demographic groups, and therefore underestimate the true unemployment rate.

Economy-wide unemployment was relatively low for 1900–1913 except, perhaps, in Britain. In the 1920s, economy-wide unemployment remained below 5 percent in every country except Britain and Australia, but industrial unemployment exceeded 7 percent in five of eight countries. During the Great Depression industrial unemployment was exceptionally high in every country except France. The United States was hardest hit; from 1932 to 1935, industrial unemployment averaged 34.2 percent, and economy-wide unemployment averaged 22.9 percent. However, if the U.S. data are adjusted to count workers on public-work relief projects as employed rather than unemployed, following Michael Darby (1976), the economy-wide unemployment rate from 1930 to 1938 falls to 14.5 percent, only marginally higher than the unemployment rates in Canada and Australia.

From 1950 to 1973, western Europe and North America enjoyed a golden age of rapid economic growth and low unemployment. Average unemployment rates were below 4 percent in all but three countries: the United States, Canada, and Italy. There were no major episodes of high unemployment comparable to those before World War II or after 1973. In the United States, unemployment peaked at 6.6 percent in 1958; in Italy it peaked at 8.7 percent in 1956. In Britain, France, Germany, Sweden, Spain, and Japan, unemployment was below 4 percent in every year from 1956 to 1971.

The mid-1970s were a watershed for postwar unemployment. Largely because of the oil shocks of 1973 and 1979–1980, unemployment rates increased sharply in every country except Sweden and Japan. In the recession of the early 1980s unemployment peaked at 9.7 percent in the United States, and reached double digits in Britain, France, Belgium, Spain, Canada, and Australia. Although

TABLE 1. *Unemployment Rates 1900–1998, Selected Countries*

YEAR	U.S.	BRITAIN	GERMANY	FRANCE	ITALY	CANADA	JAPAN	AUSTRALIA	BELGIUM	SWEDEN	SPAIN
1900–13 (a)	10.0	4.4	3.6	2.8							
1900–13 (b)	4.7	7.2									
1921–29 (a)	7.7	12.0	9.2	3.8		5.5		8.1	2.4	14.2	
1921–29 (b)	4.6	9.1	4.1			3.5		5.8	1.5	3.4	
1930–38 (a)	27.9	16.5	21.8	10.2		18.5		17.8	14.0	16.8	
1930–38 (b)	18.6	12.8	8.8			13.3		13.5	8.7	5.6	
1950–63	4.8	2.6	3.8	1.9	6.1	4.7	1.9	2.1	3.6	1.7	2.1
1964–73	4.5	3.0	0.8	2.2	5.5	4.8	1.2	1.8	2.3	2.0	2.6
1974–79	6.7	5.0	3.2	4.5	6.6	7.2	1.9	5.0	6.3	1.9	5.2
1980–89	7.3	9.8	5.8	8.8	8.0	9.4	2.5	7.6	9.8	2.6	17.5
1990–98	5.9	8.5	7.4	11.2	10.5	9.8	2.9	9.0	8.7	7.3	20.3

SOURCES: 1900–13 (a): For U.S., Lebergott, 1964, p. 512, unemployment rate for nonfarm employees. For U.K., Feinstein, 1972, Table 57, pp. T125–126. For Germany, Galenson, and Zellner, 1957, p. 455. Data for Germany for 1903–13. For France, calculated by author from data reported in Galenson and Zellner, pp. 509, 516.
1900–13 (b): For U.S., Lebergott, p. 512, unemployment rate for civilian employees. For U.K., Boyer and Hatton, 2001, Table 4.
1921–38 (a): For U.S., Lebergott, p. 512, unemployment rate for nonfarm employees. For U.K., Feinstein, Table 57, pp. T125–126. For other countries, Galenson and Zellner, pp. 455, 523, unemployment rate for industry.
1921–38 (b): For U.S., Lebergott, p. 512, unemployment rate for civilian employees. For U.K., Feinstein, Table 57, pp. T125–126. For other countries, Maddison, 1991, pp. 260–261.
1950–63: Maddison, pp. 262–263.
1964–98: OECD, *Historical Statistics*, various years.

U.S. unemployment declined to 5.5 percent in 1988–1990, in several European countries unemployment fell little in the late 1980s before increasing again in the recession of the early 1990s. French unemployment peaked at 10.2 percent in 1985–1987, and then fell slightly to 9.0 percent in 1990 before increasing to 12.2 percent in 1994–1997. Spanish unemployment increased from 5 percent in 1976–1977 to 21.5 percent in 1985–1986, and then fell to 16.3 percent in 1990–1991 before peaking at 24.1 percent in 1994.

Unemployment trends in the 1990s differed significantly across countries. In the United States, unemployment declined to below 5 percent in 1997–1998; the average unemployment rate for the 1990s was below that for 1974–1979. On the other hand, in every European country unemployment in the 1990s was significantly higher than it had been in 1974–1979, and in five of seven countries higher than it had been in the 1980s. Several explanations have been offered for the persistence of high unemployment in Europe, including a slowdown in productivity growth, increasing structural problems caused by a decline in traditional manufacturing industries, excessively generous unemployment benefits, and labor-market rigidities caused by government regulations such as mandatory severance pay.

The Incidence and Duration of Unemployment. The nature of unemployment cannot be understood simply by examining annual unemployment rates, which tell nothing about the rates of flow into and out of unemployment or the duration of unemployment. An unemployment rate of 5 percent could result from 5 percent of the workforce being unemployed for the entire year, from 20 percent of the workforce being unemployed for three months, or from half of the workforce being unemployed for five weeks; that is, any given unemployment rate can reflect high turnover and short duration or low turnover and long duration. A labor market in which many workers are unemployed for a short duration functions much differently, and has different implications for the welfare costs of the unemployed, compared to one in which a smaller number of workers is unemployed for a long period of time.

Available data from state labor bureaus and the federal census suggest that, in the United States, the probability of becoming unemployed was higher, and the average duration of unemployment lower, in the decades before World War I than in the late twentieth century. In California in 1892, 32.2 percent of male manufacturing workers experienced some unemployment, as did 51.6 percent of manufacturing workers in Maine in 1890. The annual unemployment rates in the two states were 6.5 percent and 12.3 percent. For the United States as a whole in 1910, some 31.9 percent of male manufacturing workers experienced some unemployment, and the unemployment rate was 7.7 percent. The high incidence of unemployment was countered by a relatively low average duration of unemployment, as the mean duration of U.S. unemployment in 1910 was 3.5 months. It was 2.6 months in California in 1892, and 2.8 months in Maine in 1890. By contrast, in 1977–1979, some 14.9 percent of U.S. workers experienced some unemployment, with an unemployment rate of 4.7 percent; the mean duration of unemployment was 5.2 months (Goldin and Margo, 1991). The high incidence and low duration of unemployment in the late nineteenth century were caused in part by the pervasiveness of seasonality. Large numbers of manufacturing and construction workers were laid off for one or two months each year during slack seasons. As the extent of seasonality declined over time, the number of seasonal layoffs declined. Another reason for the long-term decline in incidence was a shift in the occupational composition of the labor force, in particular, an increase in low-incidence white-collar jobs.

Data on labor turnover in manufacturing for the United States in the interwar period show that during the 1920s most job separations were in the form of quits (which included miscellaneous separations caused by retirement, death, and military duty). Hiring rates, and therefore labor turnover rates, were quite high. In the early 1930s the separation rate increased sharply, owing to an increase in layoffs. Surprisingly, the hiring rate remained quite high even during the early years of the Great Depression. Data for Britain on vacancies filled by labor exchanges also suggest that hiring rates were relatively high throughout the 1930s. The rise in unemployment in Britain and the United States during the Depression was due to an increase in separations, not a decline in the rate of job creation.

For Britain it is possible to examine movements in unemployment duration over the course of the Great Depression. The average interrupted spell of unemployment increased from 12.3 weeks in 1929 to 41.3 weeks in 1936, before declining to 31.2 weeks in 1938. The increase in duration largely was caused by a sharp increase in the number of long-term unemployed: in 1929, some 4.7 percent of applicants for unemployment benefits had been out of work for more than a year, whereas 23.3 percent of applicants had been unemployed for more than a year by 1936. Long-term unemployment was a serious problem in other countries as well. In 1939 in Australia, 25.3 percent of those unemployed had been without work for more than a year; in 1940 in the United States, 33.6 percent were unemployed for at least a year; whereas in 1937 in Belgium, 50.4 percent of the unemployed had been without work for more than a year.

Various factors caused the sharp increase in long-term unemployment. Data for Britain show that the probability of leaving unemployment declined with the length of time

unemployed; those workers unemployed for less than three months were much more likely to find a job within a specified time than those unemployed for a year or more. Although this might reflect differences in worker quality—high-quality workers who lost their jobs were quickly re-employed, whereas low-quality workers were not—Crafts (1987) concludes that *individuals'* reemployment probabilities declined over time. This "duration dependence" was caused by a combination of three factors: a decline in skills; "depression and apathy," which led the unemployed to give up hope of finding work and therefore to stop searching; and an unwillingness of employers to hire the long-term unemployed. There also were regional and demographic aspects to the problem; long-term unemployment was more likely for males aged fifty-five years and over living in "outer Britain" than for younger males living in the south and the midlands.

In the 1980s long-term unemployment again became a serious problem in parts of Europe. In Britain, from 1975 to 1987 the unemployment rate tripled despite the fact that the rate of inflow into unemployment remained roughly constant. Thus, the increase in unemployment was entirely due to an increase in unemployment duration; the average interrupted spell of unemployment went from 7.2 months in 1975 to 24.5 months in 1986–1987. In 1989, some 41 percent of the unemployed in Britain had been without work for more than a year, as had 49 percent of German unemployed and 44 percent of the unemployed in France. In contrast, only 6 percent of the U.S. unemployed had been without work for more than a year. Some economists maintain that these high rates of unemployment duration are a result of generous social security programs in western European countries, which led to the development of a "culture of unemployment" after the 1979–1980 oil shock. In Germany and Britain unemployed workers can collect government benefits indefinitely, and in France benefits continue for at least thirty months. As a result, the unemployed may feel under little compulsion to search for work. Such a culture does not exist in the United States, where unemployment benefits typically continue only for six months.

The Makeup of the Unemployed. At any time within a country, unemployment rates differ across industries and regions, across age groups and skill levels, and between sexes. In some industries, employment is very sensitive to the state of the trade cycle, with unemployment increasing sharply during recessions. In late-nineteenth-century Britain, unemployment was especially volatile in shipbuilding, engineering, and metals. On the other hand, employment was relatively stable in clothing, textiles, railways, and the service trades. Differences in unemployment rates across industries were especially pronounced during downturns. In Massachusetts in 1885, when the male unemployment rate was 10.4 percent, it exceeded 20 percent for boot- and shoemakers, masons, and plasterers; was 16.2 percent for iron- and steelworkers; and was less than 5 percent for railway workers, paper mill operatives, compositors and printers, and clerks. In Britain throughout the interwar period, unemployment in the staple industries of coal, iron and steel, shipbuilding, and textiles was approximately double the national average. At the height of the Great Depression in 1932, when the overall unemployment rate was 22.1 percent, it was 62.0 percent in shipbuilding, 47.9 percent in iron and steel, and 34.5 percent in coal mining.

Unemployment rates also differ across regions within countries, in part because of differences in unemployment across industries. In interwar Britain, the depressed staple industries were concentrated in the north, Wales, and Scotland, whereas the new growth industries were located in the south. As a result, in 1929 unemployment was below 5 percent in London and the southeast but nearly 13 percent in northern England and 18 percent in Wales. This regional disparity in unemployment was even more pronounced in the Depression year 1932, and it continued into the late twentieth century, with unemployment rates in the south remaining far below those in "outer Britain." In the postwar period, regional differences in unemployment also have been highly persistent in Germany, Italy, and Japan. On the other hand, there has been little if any persistence in the United States in recent decades, largely because of a high rate of interregional migration.

Many nineteenth-century observers claimed that unemployment was more prevalent among unskilled laborers than skilled workers, and twentieth-century data support this contention. Unemployment rates are consistently lower for white-collar workers than blue-collar workers, and lower for skilled manual workers than unskilled workers. In 1931 in Britain, 21.5 percent of unskilled manual workers were unemployed, compared to 12 percent of skilled and semiskilled manual workers and less than 6 percent of managerial and professional workers. In 1985, the ratio of manual to nonmanual unemployment rates was 2.5 in Britain, 2.4 in the United States, 2.1 in Australia, 1.9 in Canada, and 1.5 in Germany. A comparison of unemployment rates by educational attainment yields similar results. In the United States between 1995 and 1998, some 10.0 percent of persons aged twenty-five to sixty-four with less than a high school diploma were unemployed, compared to 5.2 percent of high-school graduates (no college) and 2.1 percent of college graduates.

The relationship between age and unemployment has not been so consistent over time. Prior to World War II, the age profile of unemployment in many countries was U-shaped, with unemployment rates higher for the young and the old than for prime-age workers. In Massachusetts

in 1885, unemployment rates varied from 8.8 percent for males aged thirty to thirty-nine to 11.5 percent for those aged sixty to seventy-nine and 14 percent for those aged fourteen to nineteen. During the Great Depression, Australia, Canada, and the United States retained U-shaped distributions. For Britain in 1931, the age profile was U-shaped for workers aged twenty and over, but unemployment was exceptionally low for juveniles. For Belgium in 1937, unemployment was lowest for males aged fifteen to nineteen, and then increased to a plateau for those aged twenty to thirty-nine, before increasing with age. The exceptionally high rates of unemployment for males aged fifty-five and over in both Britain and Belgium mainly were due to their low reemployment probabilities. In Britain in 1938, the average interrupted spell of unemployment for out-of-work males aged sixty to sixty-four was seventy-three weeks; for those aged twenty-five to thirty-four it was twenty-six weeks. In Belgium in 1937 the average duration of unemployment for out-of-work males aged sixty and over was nearly three years.

By the mid-1970s the age profile of unemployment was significantly different from that before 1940, as a result of both a sharp increase in the unemployment rate of teenagers and a decline in the unemployment rate of those aged fifty-five or older relative to prime-age adults. In the United States in the recession from 1982 to 1983, the unemployment rate for sixteen- to nineteen-year-olds was 23.8 percent, compared to 7 percent for those aged thirty-five to forty-four and 5.8 percent for those aged fifty-five to sixty-four. The increase in teenage unemployment occurred throughout the OECD countries. In 1993, the unemployment rate for teenagers was 19 percent in the United States and Britain, 23 percent in Australia, 27 percent in France, and 50 percent in Spain.

Little information exists on female unemployment before the 1920s. Data for Massachusetts suggest that the female unemployment rate was slightly below the male rate in 1885 and 1890, and equal to the male rate in 1900. During the Great Depression, female unemployment rates were below male rates in all countries for which data are available. In Britain in 1931, some 14.7 percent of male workers were unemployed, compared to 9.4 percent of female workers. Even larger differences in male-female unemployment rates existed in Australia, Belgium, and Canada, where in 1931 some 20.8 percent of males and 8.2 percent of females were unemployed. The male–female differential was much smaller in the United States. The relatively low unemployment rates of females partly was a result of their tendency to be concentrated in low-unemployment occupations such as clerical and service jobs. In addition, females were more likely to drop out of the labor force after a spell of unemployment, and therefore not to be counted as unemployed.

In the postwar era, the relationship between male and female unemployment rates has differed across countries. In the United States, the female unemployment rate was higher than the male rate throughout the 1960s and 1970s, but since 1980 the two rates have been almost identical except that male unemployment has exceeded female unemployment in recession years. In Britain, female unemployment has been significantly below male unemployment throughout the postwar era. For the decade 1980–1989, female and male unemployment were within one percentage point of each other in the United States and Canada; female unemployment exceeded male unemployment in France, Germany, Belgium, and Australia; and male unemployment exceeded female unemployment in Britain.

The Relief of the Unemployed. Prior to the adoption of unemployment insurance by the industrialized economies in the first half of the twentieth century, there were no permanent institutions for dealing with unemployment relief. Local authorities and private charities provided cash and in-kind payments to the unemployed, but benefits seldom were generous enough to provide subsistence for a worker and his or her family, and had to be supplemented by the earnings of other family members, savings, and credit from landlords and shopkeepers.

In England in the first half of the nineteenth century, the poor law was an important source of income assistance to seasonally unemployed agricultural laborers and cyclically unemployed factory workers in industrial towns. Despite Parliament's attempt to restrict relief for able-bodied workers, local relief authorities continued to assist the unemployed for two or three decades after 1834. However, during major downturns, as in 1841 to 1842, the poor law was unable to support all who needed assistance, and in many cities private charitable organizations mobilized to raise money for the unemployed. Similar systems of poor relief did not exist on the Continent, but several European cities provided assistance to unskilled and casual laborers who were unemployed during downturns and harsh winters. Benefits also were provided by private, often church-related, charities. In early-nineteenth-century Amsterdam, unemployed workers were assisted by the municipal government and by Reformed (Calvinist), Catholic, Lutheran, and Jewish charities (van Leeuwen, 2000).

The role played by poor relief in aiding the unemployed declined after 1860, and in both Britain and the United States during major downturns local governments and voluntary agencies adopted ad hoc measures for relieving the unemployed. In the depression of 1893–1897, cities throughout Britain and the United States set up temporary work-relief projects; the forms of work relief included road repairing, road sweeping, snow removal, leveling land, and planting trees. In some cities charities worked together with local authorities in funding relief projects.

The amount of assistance offered to individual workers typically was quite small, and only a minority of the unemployed—mostly unskilled laborers—applied for and received relief.

Trade unions became a major source of unemployment benefits for skilled workers in late-nineteenth-century Britain. In return for an additional contribution to their membership dues, workers when unemployed received a weekly payment from their union branch, typically equal to between a quarter and a third of their earnings. The weekly benefit was too small to support a worker and his family, but it generally was enough to enable unemployed members to avoid having to turn to charity or the poor law for assistance. In 1908, some 1.47 million workers (62 percent of all union members, 12 percent of the adult male workforce) were eligible for unemployment benefits. Trade-union unemployment schemes also existed on the Continent, especially in France, Denmark, the Netherlands, and Germany, where in 1908 approximately 1.6 million workers were eligible for benefits from their trade unions. On the other hand, union schemes were rare in the United States; in 1908 only sixty-nine thousand of 2.1 million union members were insured against unemployment.

In 1901 the city of Ghent, Belgium adopted a voluntary unemployment insurance scheme, in which the municipality subsidized the provision of unemployment insurance by trade unions. Ghent-type systems quickly spread to cities throughout western Europe, and by 1908 national schemes for subsidizing voluntary (mainly trade-union) unemployment-insurance funds were adopted by France, Denmark, and Norway. The size of the state subsidy varied across national schemes, from one-third to 100 percent of benefits paid/contributions made by unions. It was hoped that government subsidies would lead additional unions—including unions of low-skilled workers—to offer unemployment benefits to their members, but in this regard the plans were not especially successful.

The first national compulsory unemployment-insurance scheme was adopted by Great Britain in 1911. It initially covered a limited number of industries, including about 20 percent of employed males. In 1920, the system was extended to cover virtually all workers except the self-employed and those in agriculture or domestic service. The system was financed by contributions from workers, employers, and the state. Benefits were relatively modest and could be collected for a maximum of fifteen weeks per year. Italy adopted compulsory unemployment insurance in 1919, followed by Austria in 1920 and Germany in 1927. In the United States, Wisconsin adopted a compulsory system in 1932; a national system of unemployment insurance, to be administered by the states, was enacted in 1935. By 1940, all major industrialized countries had adopted either voluntary or compulsory unemployment-insurance schemes. In the postwar era the generosity and the duration of unemployment benefits have increased in most countries.

Unemployment insurance, along with other forms of social insurance, helped to reduce the insecurity faced by wage laborers. Despite rising wage rates during the nineteenth century, most manual workers had little if any savings, and spells of unemployment lasting more than one or two months created severe hardship for their families. By reducing the cost to workers of a spell of unemployment, national insurance significantly improved the welfare of the unemployed.

[*See also* Business Cycles; Insurance, *subentry on* Unemployment Insurance; *and* Phillips Curve.]

BIBLIOGRAPHY

Aerts, Erik, and Barry Eichengreen, eds. *Unemployment and Underemployment in Historical Perspective*. Leuven, 1990. A collection of papers from the Tenth International Economic History Congress. Contains useful chapters on pre-1914 unemployment in the United States and Great Britain.

Beveridge, William H. *Unemployment: A Problem of Industry*. London, 1909. An extremely valuable and influential early study of unemployment, in which the author argues that unemployment was caused by short-run maladjustments between the supply of and demand for labor, not by the deficiencies of individual workers. When the book was published, the author was a civil servant in Britain's Board of Trade.

Beveridge, William H. *Full Employment in a Free Society*. London, 1945. Although this volume is remembered mainly for its super-Keynesian policy prescriptions, Parts II and III and Appendix B present a detailed discussion of unemployment in Britain before and during World War II.

Booth, Charles. *Life and Labour of the People of London*. London, 1892.

Boyer, George R., and Timothy J. Hatton. "New Estimates of British Unemployment, 1870–1914." Unpublished manuscript, Cornell University 2001.

Crafts, Nicholas. "Long-Term Unemployment in Britain in the 1930s." *Economic History Review* 40 (August 1987), pp. 418–432.

Darby, Michael. "Three-and-a-Half Million U.S. Employees Have Been Mislaid: Or, an Explanation of Unemployment, 1934–1941. *Journal of Political Economy* 84 (1976), pp. 1–16.

Eichengreen, Barry, and Timothy J. Hatton, eds. *Interwar Unemployment in International Perspective*. Dordrecht, 1988. The best available introduction to unemployment between the world wars. Especially noteworthy are the introductory chapter by Eichengreen and Hatton, Mark Thomas's chapter on Britain, Robert Margo's chapter on the United States, Alan Green and Mary MacKinnon's chapter on Canada, and Goossens et al.'s chapter on Belgium.

Engerman, Stanley, and Claudia Goldin. "Seasonality in Nineteenth-Century Labor Markets." In *American Economic Development in Historical Perspective*, edited by Thomas Weiss and Donald Schaefer, pp. 99–126. Stanford, 1994.

Feder, Leah H. *Unemployment Relief in Periods of Depression: A Study of Measures Adopted in Certain American Cities, 1857 through 1922*. New York, 1936. Examines public and private measures to relieve and to create work for the unemployed before the Great Depression. The author's detailed discussion of relief measures during the 1893–1897 downturn is especially valuable.

Feinstein, Charles. *National Income, Expenditure, and Output of the United Kingdom, 1855–1965*. Cambridge, 1972. Constructs the "standard" estimates of British unemployment rates for the period 1855–1913, based on the Board of Trade's time series of trade-union unemployment. A new unemployment series, which reworks the trade-union data and includes sectors of the economy for which trade-union data are not available, is given in Boyer and Hatton (2001).

Friedman, Milton. "The Role of Monetary Policy." *American Economic Review* 58 (1968), pp. 1–17.

Galenson, Walter, and Arnold Zellner. "International Comparison of Unemployment Rates." In *The Measurement and Behavior of Unemployment*, pp. 439–581. Princeton, 1957. Presents estimates of industrial unemployment rates in 1900–1950 for nine countries. The appendixes provide a detailed discussion of the unemployment data for each country.

Garraty, John. *Unemployment in History: Economic Thought and Public Policy*. New York, 1978. Surveys the changing views of the causes of unemployment and the methods of unemployment relief from medieval times to the present.

Goldin, Claudia, and Robert Margo. "Downtime: Voluntary and Involuntary Unemployment of the Past and Present." Paper presented at NBER-University of Kansas–University of California Conference on Late Nineteenth Century State Bureau of Labor Statistics Data. Lawrence, 1991.

Harris, José. *Unemployment and Politics: A Study in English Social Policy, 1886–1914*. Oxford, 1972. The best available analysis of the development of government policy to combat unemployment, leading up to Britain's adoption of national unemployment insurance in 1911.

James, John. "Reconstructing the Pattern of American Unemployment before the First World War." *Economica* 62 (August 1995), pp. 291–311.

Keyssar, Alexander. *Out of Work: The First Century of Unemployment in Massachusetts*. Cambridge, U.K. 1986. A detailed discussion of unemployment in Massachusetts focusing on the period from 1870 up to World War I. The author presents data on unemployment rates by occupation, location, sex, and place of birth for certain years using surveys of the unemployed done by the Massachusetts Bureau of the Statistics of Labor.

Layard, Richard, Stephen Nickell, and Richard Jackman. *Unemployment: Macroeconomic Performance and the Labour Market*. Oxford, 1991.

Lebergott, Stanley. *Manpower in Economic Growth: The American Record since 1800*. New York, 1964. Contains estimates of the unemployment rate for the civilian labor force and for nonfarm employees for 1900–1930. Although the author's estimates were considered the "standard" measure of unemployment for several decades, they have recently come under criticism; see Weir (1992).

Maddison, Angus. *Dynamic Forces in Capitalist Development: A Long-Run Comparative View*. Oxford, 1991. Appendix C contains unemployment estimates for fifteen countries for 1920–1938 and sixteen countries for 1950–1989. Eichengreen and Hatton (1988) contend that the author's numbers for several European countries for the 1930s underestimate the true unemployment rate.

van Leeuwen, Marco. *The Logic of Charity*. London, 2000.

Webb, Sidney, and Beatrice Webb. *English Poor Law History. Part II: The Last Hundred Years*. London, 1929.

Weir, David R. "A Century of U.S. Unemployment, 1890–1990: Revised Estimates and Evidence for Stabilization." *Research in Economic History* 14 (1992), pp. 301–346. This study presents a consistent unemployment series for 1890–1990. The author revises Lebergott's (1964) estimates for 1900–1930, and constructs a new unemployment series for 1890–1899.

Wilson, Charles. *England's Apprenticeship, 1607–1763*. London, 1965.

GEORGE R. BOYER

UNIONS. The earliest trade unions emerged in Britain before the Industrial Revolution. The term *trade unions* dates from the eighteenth century, but there are records of complaints against organized groups of journeymen (skilled craftsmen) going back well into the Middle Ages. Although the early references almost certainly do not relate to lasting organizations, there do appear to have been partially organized groups appearing for short periods among urban craftsmen.

Before 1900. In contrast to Sidney and Beatrice Webb who were emphatic in their classic *History of British Trade Unionism* (1894, revised ed., 1920) that "in no case did any trade union in the United Kingdom arise, either directly or indirectly, by descent from a craft guild," recent historians have been open to considering possible indirect descent from the guilds. Where guilds survived into the mid-seventeenth century in Britain, there are instances of at least groups of members acting together to defend their position as wage earners. The guilds often had similar concerns to the later skilled unions: control of entry to membership (which increasingly emphasized the exclusion of women), control of prices, mutual aid, maintenance of the craft's customs and practices, and providing a sense of dignity to labor. In Britain, guilds mostly had faded in significance by the end of the seventeenth century. In France, they survived until the French Revolution, and in Central Europe they were abolished in 1859 (Austria) and the 1860s (Germany).

In Britain, there were also brief combinations of journeymen from the Middle Ages. The most famous reference is to a 1381 Act, which prohibited all "alliances and covignes des Maceons & Carpenters." There are records of bodies threatening and organizing strikes, with such threats from skilled building workers in northern England playing a part in wage negotiations. The eighteenth century saw continued urbanization and continuing rising real wages for most urban workers.

A further element in the background to the early English trade unions was the fact that the state had intervened in labor matters from the Tudor period until the eighteenth century. As a result of the Statute of Artificers (1563) and other Elizabethan social legislation, English craftsmen in the eighteenth century often struggled to hold on to what they held to be their traditional legal rights, and they could petition for a return of such rights, even a return to a golden age before unrestricted market forces became the ideology of many British entrepreneurs. A major aspect of the 1811–1812 Luddite unrest was an attempt to enforce craft practices in hand loom weaving in the face of falling wages and the use of unskilled labor. The craftsmen's beliefs in ancient legal rights were abruptly shaken by the repeal of the apprenticeship clauses of the 1563 Statute of Artificers in 1813.

The widespread acceptance of a free market ideology and fear of French revolutionary subversion in Britain were major contributors to the passing of the Combination Acts (1799 and 1800), which consolidated earlier legislation banning employees' collective action in particular trades into a general ban. Although not rigorously enforced, these acts did disadvantage employees in their efforts to gain improved wages or conditions. The Combination Acts were repealed in 1824 and 1825.

The early trade unions were urban phenomena. They arose among craftsmen coming together for mutual benefit, which included trying to control entry to the local labor market and providing some welfare. Craft control often involved apprenticeships, but it was often effective without; either way, the unions were protecting property in the form of a skill. During the eighteenth century, male trade unionists seem to have squeezed out women from apprenticeships. The early unions were often centered on alehouses, which were frequently centers for "box clubs" (which involved joint payments of pence into a club, with sickness, funeral, and widow benefits paid out and the funds kept in a secure chest).

Box clubs often did not become trade unions, but many unions seem to have built on them. Such alehouses could be "houses of call" for traveling artisans. There were networks well established in the eighteenth century for wool combers, shoemakers, tailors, hatters, and many other skilled workers to move away from an overcrowded labor market to seek employment in an area of skilled labor shortage. This practice became widespread in Britain in the first six decades of the nineteenth century. It was even more notable in France, with the artisans' tour de France. The early trade unions would try to negotiate the ending of grievances. However, where the community was affronted by a particular employer's intransigence, there could be, to use Eric Hobsbawm's phrase, "industrial relations by riot." This was often linked to attempts at collective bargaining and was by no means always a primitive alternative.

Whereas the Webbs and others argued that collective bargaining only became common in Britain in the late nineteenth century, James Jaffe has recently shown in detail that local bargaining was widespread well before 1870. Although there was much legislation hostile to trade unionism in Britain after 1825, notably the Masters and Servants Acts and many ancient statutes, trade unionism could exist openly. The Trade Union Act (1871), the Conspiracy and Protection of Property Act (1875), and the Employers and Workmen Act (1875) gave the British trade unions legal protection, freed them from the danger of being prosecuted for restraint of trade or for strikes, and ended employees' criminal liability for breaking employment contracts. By 1875, the trade unions were recognized by the state and were free to engage in collective bargaining with the ability to withdraw labor.

This was a very different situation from continental Europe. In France, trade unionism was banned under the Le Chapelier law (June 1791) and under the Penal Code of 1810 (reinforced in 1834). Legal penalties against strikes were lifted in 1864. The 1791 legislation was repealed by the Waldeck-Rousseau law in 1884; the existence of the trade unions was recognized, but there were substantial restrictions on trade unions until 1901. After the French Revolution, the nineteenth-century Republican state and its laws focused on the freedom to work, thereby giving ample opportunity for litigation against unions to succeed.

In Germany, although there was legislation, such as the Prussian Association Law (1850), which underpinned freedom of association and assembly, there were also bans on workers' associations with political aims in the 1850s and the Anti-Socialist Law (1878–1890). Moreover, there were ample legal opportunities for the police to harass trade unionists. In Russia, trade unions were illegal until after the 1905 revolution. In the United States, English common law was drawn on to break trade unions for conspiracy or for coercion and intimidation. In New York and elsewhere, there was also legislation that banned acts injurious to trade or commerce. Beginning in the 1880s, federal courts granted injunctions against trade unions ostensibly to prevent violation of the Interstate Commerce Act, and later the Sherman Antitrust Act (1890). These were intended to prevent strikes, pickets, and boycotts.

In Britain, skilled male workers in industrial sectors added to the numbers of male trade unionists in crafts. In France, there were similar groups that unionized early on: hat workers, tailors, shoemakers, cabinetmakers, building crafts, and printing. In Germany, two of the early unions were in printing and cigar making. With the spread of industrialization there were increasing numbers of trade unionists in engineering and textiles. Trade unionism remained weak among women and white-collar workers and in the countryside.

Figures for nineteenth-century trade unionism are mostly estimates. In Britain, it is estimated that 10 percent of male workers belonged to trade unions, with more, perhaps up to 14 percent, unionized among skilled building workers, engineers, and other metal trades. In 1859, there may have been some 600,000 trade unionists, rising to 750,000 in 1888. The official union membership figures begin in 1892, with 1.47 million in 1892 and 1.9 million in 1900, of which less than 7 percent were women. In terms of trade union density (the percentage of those in trade unions out of those who are legally free to join), the British figures were 10.6 percent for 1892 and 12.7 percent for 1900. In France, there were some 120,000 to 140,000 trade

unionists in 1870, half in Paris. After falling, membership grew markedly from the late 1880s: from about 100,000 in 1886 to 200,000 in 1890, 400,000 in 1892, and 500,000 in 1900.

In Germany, there were some 47,000 free trade unionists in 1869, with a further 30,000 members of the Hirsch-Duncker Trade Associations, the number dropping after the Franco-Prussian War. By 1885, there were 85,687 free trade unionists and 51,000 members of the trade associations. These numbers grew rapidly after 1888. In 1891, the total German trade union membership was 343,300, rising to 848,800 in 1900. In the United States, trade union membership remained weak until the twentieth century. In 1900, union density among nonagricultural workers was only about 6 percent, with union membership around 800,000.

Trade unions in the nineteenth century sought to bargain for better wages and conditions of work. Even though aggregate national figures for trade union membership remained relatively small, the unions often could exercise much influence on behalf of their members because of the concentration of membership in certain skilled trades. For example, in Britain in 1900, union density was as high as 59.5 percent in coal mining, 31.9 percent in engineering and metals, 27.7 percent in printing, 25.4 percent in footwear, and 23.9 percent in gas. Although most disputes over wage demands were settled other than by strikes, there were major strikes in the nineteenth century in Britain. A major builders' strike in London in 1859–1860 was resolved without victory for either side, but it led to the formation of the London Trades Council. In 1871, there was a five-month engineering strike in northeastern England for the nine-hour workday, which was notable for much public support and for the victory of the trade unions. The 1889 London dock strike was a major success for unskilled workers and was a high point in their unionization.

The British unions were unsuccessful in major disputes in coal (1893) and engineering (1896) but secured a compromise settlement in cotton textiles (1893). In France, the unions were frequently unsuccessful in major strikes, the state and the employers being too strong. In Germany, the state was willing to use troops against strikers, as in 1889 against miners in the Ruhr, with five workers killed and nine wounded. However, this strike demonstrated that the Anti-Socialist Law could not eradicate strikes, and after a month the strike resulted in a compromise settlement, assisted by the kaiser.

In the United States, the unions were relatively weak, but occasionally union-led strikes were supported by large numbers of nonunion workers. For example, in an anthracite miners strike in 1900, the United Mine Workers had about 8,000 members in the area, but 100,000 miners came out on strike, with the stoppage leading to victory for the miners. In the United States, however, employers were frequently too strong for the unions. In 1892, the Amalgamated Association of Iron Workers lost in the Homestead strike at the Carnegie Steel Plant in Homestead, Pennsylvania. Violence resulted in the deaths of ten people when Pinkerton detectives, hired by the company, sought to break the union. Another notable union defeat was the Pullman strike of 1894, a rail strike arising from an attempt to force the restoral of earlier wage rates on the Pullman Palace Car Company.

The Twentieth Century. Trade unionism grew, albeit at an uneven pace, during the first two-thirds of the twentieth century. This growth was not only in western Europe and North America, but also in many parts of the world. The unions pressed more successfully than in the nineteenth century for improved working conditions and also pushed for social welfare and to have a say in economic and social policymaking.

Trade unionism's strength often waxed and waned across national frontiers at similar times in the twentieth century. This reflected conditions in the international economy. There had been some indications of such patterns in the nineteenth century, such as in the economic upturn of 1888–1890, but this feature was more marked in the twentieth century.

Trade unionism continued to grow strongly in Europe and North America before 1914. This growth was marked in the period from 1910 to 1914, when there was an upturn in economic conditions. In Britain, trade unionism's legal status was undermined by the Taff Vale Judgment (1901), which, contrary to previous understanding of the 1871 and 1875 legislation, made the major railway union liable for huge damages arising from a strike. It was later secured by the Trades Disputes Act (1906). This legislation gave trade unions complete immunity for their funds from civil actions and legalized peaceful picketing. That the measure went so far was due to the political situation. The Trades Union Congress (set up in 1868 as an annual forum for trade unions, with a political committee to lobby government) responded in 1899 to adverse legal decisions by taking steps that led to the setting up of a body (the Labour Representation Committee, 1900, which became the Labour Party from 1906) to achieve better labor representation in Parliament. In the 1906 general election, twenty-nine independent Labour Party MPs were elected, while the Liberal Party enjoyed a landslide victory, thus providing the political conditions for legislation along the lines sought by the Trades Union Congress.

Political change also assisted the growth of trade unionism in Russia. One of the major reforms arising from the 1905 revolution was the legalization of trade unions, although the czarist state wished to restrict their activities to health, safety, and welfare issues.

Trade unionism grew considerably between 1900 and 1913. In Germany, trade unionism increased three and a half times (excluding salaried employee associations), reaching 3,023,100 members (union density rising from 5.7 to 16.4 percent). In Britain, trade union membership more than doubled in these years, reaching 4,107,000 members in 1913 (union density rising from 13.1 to 24.8 percent). In Sweden, union membership more than doubled, reaching 149,300 in 1913 (union density rising from 4.8 to 9.4 percent). In Denmark, membership rose by over half, reaching 152,000 (a density of over 15 percent), and in Norway, membership probably trebled, from 20,100 to 63,800. In the United States, according to the National Bureau of Economic Research statistics (which are often on the low side), trade union membership tripled, reaching 2,588,000 members in 1913 (a density of 10.3 percent). In Australia, membership nearly multiplied by five between 1901 and 1913, reaching 497,900 members (a density of 31.2 percent).

In all countries, trade unionism was heavily male orientated before 1914, as it was until well into the second half of the twentieth century. For example, in Britain in 1913, there were only 430,000 female trade unionists (a union density of 8.5 percent); in Australia, 20,300 (a union density of 6.2 percent). Many women who worked were young, between school and marriage. Their employment opportunities were mostly restricted to work segregated as female work, and as such deemed less skilled and lower paid. Union meetings, even if not held in pubs, were male oriented and held at unfavorable times and rarely discussed matters of specific concern for women.

The period covering World War I and the postwar boom (1914–1920 for most countries) saw a massive growth in trade union membership, both male and female, in belligerent nations and neutrals. In belligerent countries, organized labor was in a potentially very powerful position in labor markets from which millions of men had been withdrawn from the armed forces. In Britain, trade unionism during the war spread to areas previously lightly unionized and overall grew from 4.1 million to 6.5 million members (union density rising from 24.7 to 38.1 percent). In Germany, where the old bans on trade union membership in the public sector ended, trade union membership nearly doubled by the end of the war, up from 1.8 million to 3.5 million. In France, membership in the Confédération Générale du Travail rose from 0.3 million to 1.5 million (1914–1919). In the United States, trade union membership rose by 22 percent between 1916 and 1918, from 2,605,000 to 3,186,000 members.

The expansion of trade unionism continued after the end of the war. In Germany, with the democratic Weimar Republic, there was a favorable political and legal climate in which trade unionism expanded to 9.4 million members (a density of about 46 percent). In Britain, the removal of the restraint of war encouraged trade unions to recover the wartime fall in real wages and to secure shorter working hours. Their membership reached 8,253,000 members, a density of 48.2 percent. In the United States, trade union membership grew by half to 4,775,000. However, in the United States, there was an anticommunist backlash, with far more strikes being lost than in the war years.

The international economic and political impact of World War I and the postwar boom provided favorable conditions for labor movements to expand elsewhere. For example, in Bolivia, there was a successful nationwide railway union, the Liga, in 1919–1920, and there was an attempt to form an effective mining union in 1923. In Japan, there was an upsurge of labor unrest toward the end of World War I, with strikes averaging over 62,000 per year from 1917 to 1919. There was a move to industrial unionism, an increase in unskilled trade unionism, and a proliferation of trade unions (from 108 to 432) from 1918 to 1923. In 1919, Japanese trade unions had up to 100,000 members.

In several European countries between the world wars, organized labor was a major part of governments. In Britain, Arthur Henderson, J. R. Clynes, and other trade unionists gained major office in minority Labour governments in 1924 and from 1929 to 1931. In Germany, the Social Democrats were frequently in office, mostly in coalition governments, and there were socialists in office in Austria, Belgium, Spain, and other countries. However, the rise of fascism saw the suppression of free trade unionism in Italy, Germany, Austria, and Spain, with many trade union activists murdered or imprisoned. In Britain, the second Labour government collapsed and the Labour Party was heavily defeated in the 1931 general election. Much influence in policymaking went to the trade union leaders, notably Ernest Bevin, the General Secretary of the Transport and General Workers' Union. He was a powerful political figure as minister of labor in Winston Churchill's wartime coalition government (1940–1945) and as foreign secretary in Clement Attlee's Labour government (1945–1951).

World War II revived trade unionism in most free countries. In Britain, as in World War I, trade union membership rose substantially in spite of roughly a third of the male labor force going into the armed services. Between 1939 and 1945, trade union membership rose by 24 percent to 7,684,000 (with density rising from 31.9 to 40.7 percent, 1939–1942, the wartime peak level). In the United States, trade union membership rose markedly from 1937, more than doubling by 1944 (from 5,563,000 to 12,153,000, and density rising from 13.6 to 28.6 percent). In Australia, trade unionism grew by a third between 1939 and 1944 (with the density rising from 39.2 to 46.1 percent).

Trade unionism continued to flourish in the "golden age" of the international economy (1950–1973). Bruce Western (1997) has argued that in these years rapid trade union growth was facilitated by working-class parties holding government office and favoring the trade unions; centralized industrial negotiations that enabled the trade unions to effectively coordinate their endeavors; and trade union management of welfare schemes, enabling them to hold the loyalty of those in a weak market position. In Britain, trade unionism grew to its greatest strength in 1979, reaching a membership of 12,639,000 (a density of 53.4 percent). Expansion took place under both Labour and Conservative governments but was most rapid from 1968 to 1979 under Labour governments and the economic expansionist Heath Conservative government. The period from 1945 to 1979 was marked by much centralized collective bargaining.

The Scandinavian trade unions, already strong before World War II, continued to grow afterward. Trade union membership rose from 1,356,700 between 1945 and 1977, with trade union density reaching a peak in 1986, at 86 percent. In Denmark, trade union membership rose markedly from 1,303,500 in 1975 to 2,066,400 in 1989, density rising from 63.5 to 79.4 percent (with the peak in 1985). In Norway, levels were lower, with membership rising from 645,000 to 917,900 between 1958 and 1976, but density generally staying in these years in the 58 to 63 percent range, with a peak in 1964 and 1965 and dropping to 57 percent in 1990. In these countries, social democratic governments were frequently in power: in Sweden, 1932–1976 and 1982–1991; in Denmark, 1929–1943, 1947–1950, 1953–1968, 1971–1973, and 1975–1982; and in Norway 1935–1965, 1971–1972, 1973–1981 and 1987–1989. In Sweden and Denmark, there was centralized collective bargaining, welfare benefits linked to union membership, and much industrial democracy, at least until the 1980s, when there were moves to decentralization of wage bargaining.

Other than Sweden and Denmark, trade unionism declined in the harsher international economic climate of the 1980s. The often severe decline of manufacturing and other basic industrial industries hit hard the old strongholds of male trade unionism in much of Europe, North America, and other industrial economies. In hostile economic and political climates, private-sector trade unionism weakened very markedly in the United States, Britain, and elsewhere, while public-sector trade unionism was less affected, notably in Britain, Italy, Sweden, and Portugal. The most severe declines in union membership were in such countries as France and Spain, which had low densities before the 1980s.

French trade unionism has faced much state hostility, only being legalized in 1884 and with closed shops illegal. The unions also faced effective employer opposition. They were notable for fragmentation between Marxist, anticommunist, Catholic, and others. Trade union density fell from

UNIONS. Union leader addressing strikers at a meeting, Yabucoa, Puerto Rico, 1941. (Jack Delano/ Prints and Photographs Division, Library of Congress)

20 percent in the mid-1970s to about 9 percent in the late 1980s. In Spain, trade unionism developed after the death of Francisco Franco in 1975, with the two largest unions having 2.6 million members in 1978, and an overall density of about 40 to 45 percent. This fell to about 20 percent in 1982 and below 15 percent by the early 1990s. To the general causes of decline of the heavily unionized industrial sectors and rising unemployment, trade union weakness in Spain owes something to low union income and poor organization.

U.S. trade union membership had peaked in terms of density in the early 1950s, reaching 31.6 percent in 1953. As in much of Europe, there was a rise in union numbers in the public sector in the 1970s but a decline in manufacturing. In the 1980s, the Reagan administration was notably hostile to the trade unions, and unfavorable economic circumstances, employer hostility, and the trade unions' failure to impress sufficient young, female, or black workers all contributed to union density falling below 20 percent by the mid-1980s. Trade unions in the United States avoided the ideological and religious fragmentation of many of their European counterparts, but they suffered through links to crime and in some cases a failure to give equal treatment to black workers. The best-known racketeering was linked to Jimmy Hoffa and the Teamsters Union, Hoffa being jailed in 1957, but it was also present in the docks, coal-mines, construction, clothing, and food and service industries. Although white trade union leaders such as George Meany, president of the AFL-CIO, acted against blatantly racist unions, racism nevertheless obstructed trade union membership.

By the late twentieth century, trade unionism everywhere was faced with a growing proportion of the workforce being female. Between 1955 and 1995, there were substantial rises in the percentage of women of working age (age fifteen to sixty-four) who were in the labor force: in Belgium, from 33.6 to 56.1 percent; Denmark, 48.9 to 73.6 percent; France, 45.8 to 59.4 percent; Italy, 27.4 to 43.3 percent; the Netherlands, 29.1 to 59.0 percent; Great Britain, 45.9 to 66.6 percent; and the United States, 38.3 to 70.7 percent. The trade unions had often been dilatory in recruiting women workers before the 1980s, but from that decade such recruitment became imperative in many countries for survival. In Britain, in 1999, union density among women workers was 28 percent, whereas that for men was 31 percent. As the loss of membership was halted, even reversed a little, most of the increase came from recruiting part-time female workers. In the United States, after 1960, union growth was strong in the public and health care sectors, where many employees were female. By 1990, nearly a third of union members were female, but of women working, only 16 percent were in unions.

From the eighteenth century, perhaps from their inception, trade unions have attracted strong criticism, not least from those who have seen them as obstacles to free market competition. Such criticisms reemerged in the politics of the last quarter of the twentieth century. In answer to the question, What do trade unions do?, some argued that they raised wages, hindered productivity, and made industries less competitive, thereby increasing unemployment. Although there has been agreement that trade unions have secured higher wages, (the union mark-up), there have been views that this could be bad in some instances (discouraging investment and innovation, affecting productivity adversely), but in other cases could be a pressure on management to change work processes for the better.

There has also been an argument that unions have exercised a "sword of justice" role, securing better wages for unskilled, female, black, and disabled workers and better health and safety conditions. However, by the start of the twenty-first century, it was becoming less credible to ascribe various problems of the U.S. and U.K. economies to trade union power when trade union densities and strike levels had dropped substantially.

[See also Bargaining, Collective; Employers' Associations; and Industrial Relations.]

BIBLIOGRAPHY

Baglioni, Guido, and Colin Crouch, eds. *European Industrial Relations: The Challenge of Flexibility*. London, 1990.

Bain, George S., and Robert Price. *Profiles of Union Growth*. Oxford, 1980.

Bamber, Greg J., and Russel D. Lansbury. *International and Comparative Industrial Relations*, 2d ed. London, 1993.

Chase, Malcolm. *Early Trade Unionism: Fraternity, Skill and the Politics of Labour*. Aldershot, U.K., 2000.

Clegg, Hugh A. *A History of British Trade Unionism since 1889*, vols. 2 and 3. Oxford, 1985, 1994.

Clegg, Hugh A., A. Fox, and A. F. Thompson. *A History of British Trade Unionism since 1889*, vol. 1. Oxford, 1964.

Crouch, Colin. *Industrial Relations and European State Traditions*. Oxford, 1993.

Ferner, Anthony, and Richard Hyman, eds. *Industrial Relations in the New Europe*. Oxford, 1992.

Garon, Sheldon. *The State and Labor in Modern Japan*. Berkeley, 1987.

Hobsbawn, Eric J. *Labouring Men*. London, 1964.

Jaffe, James A. *Striking a Bargain: Work and Industrial Relations in England, 1815–1865*. Manchester, 2000.

Kirk, Neville. *Labour and Society in Britain and the USA*. 2 vols. London, 1994.

Lora, Guillermo. *A History of the Bolivian Labour Movement*. Cambridge, 1977.

Lorwin, Val R. *The French Labor Movement*. Cambridge, Mass., 1954.

Renshaw, Patrick. *American Labour and Consensus Capitalism, 1935–1990*. London, 1991.

Robert, J.-L., F. Boll, and A. Prost, eds. *L'invention des syndicalismes*. Paris, 1997.

Schneider, Michael. *A Brief History of the German Trade Unions*. Bonn, Germany, 1991.

Western, Bruce. *Between Class and Market: Postwar Unionization in the Capitalist Democracies*. Princeton, 1997.

Wrigley, Chris. J., ed. *A History of British Industrial Relations*. 3 vols. Brighton, and Cheltenham, U.K., 1982–1996.

Wrigley, Chris J. *British Trade Unions since 1933*. Cambridge, 2002.

CHRIS WRIGLEY

UNITED STATES *[This entry contains four entries, on the economic history of the United States during the precolonial, colonial, antebellum, and modern periods.]*

Precolonial Period

Before 1600 the territory that later became the United States was populated by hundreds of indigenous nations as well as some Europeans who had migrated to North America after the exploratory ventures of Christopher Columbus at the end of the fifteenth century. Over the course of the sixteenth century, wherever natives met newcomers, they invented new economic relationships, often based on trade. By the time the English established what became their first permanent colony at Jamestown, Virginia, in 1607, the peoples of North America had created and sustained a variety of economies.

By 1492, indigenous peoples across the Americas had developed their own economies. Though there is no evidence of trade connecting Native Americans with peoples across either the Pacific Ocean or the Atlantic, archaeological evidence suggests that goods moved through North America along aboriginal trade routes. Unlike the commercial systems created by Europeans, this native commerce was likely a series of short-distance exchanges. Thus wampum, a bead made from a shell native to Narragansett Bay and Long Island Sound, spread across much of the interior to peoples who had no direct access to the Atlantic coast. In exchange, those who proffered wampum received goods to which they otherwise had no access, such as the hides of certain animals or stones used for decoration or as tools.

Scholars differ in their estimates of the pre-1492 population of North America, suggesting that the indigenous population was between 1.2 million and 2.6 million. Most of these people inhabited small communities. There were no large cities north of Mexico when Europeans arrived, although permanent communities did exist. In the southwest, for example, the Pueblo peoples created durable settlements by building adobe houses atop mesas and developing irrigation systems to maximize their water supply. However, Cahokia, the largest city in precontact North America (near modern-day East Saint Louis, Illinois), which once had a population estimated by archaeologists at perhaps thirty thousand, had already disappeared by the time Europeans arrived. Like the great cities of Mesoamerica (such as Tenochtitlán, Chichén Itza, or

Palenque), Cahokia had thrived because those in control of the city organized enormous expenditures of labor to produce the pyramids that dominated it. The so-called Monk's Mound, the largest surviving structure at Cahokia, took hundreds of thousands of hours of labor to construct, and the supplies for building it came from many miles away. However, Cahokia's residents had dispersed before 1500, and the descendants of the Mississippian peoples who had once inhabited that city organized economies similar to those of other eastern woodlands natives who eschewed the construction of large cities.

The indigenous peoples of eastern North America tended to live in semi-permanent communities. From spring to autumn, these Native Americans tended to cluster together in areas suitable for maize agriculture. After the harvest, settlements broke into smaller groups, usually defined by kin relationships, and dispersed for the winter. This strategy made sense to Indians who maximized their production of food and decreased their labor demands by adopting a transhumant lifestyle. In areas where maize agriculture was unreliable because of the shortness of the growing season (north of the Saco-Kennebec watershed in the east, for example), indigenous peoples tended to concentrate their efforts on hunting, fishing, and gathering wild plants. In the west, indigenous peoples also responded to environmental conditions in ways that made sense. Thus in the southwest most natives tended to inhabit the same towns year-round, whereas across the plains many peoples migrated to follow the bison herds, which provided much of their sustenance. Wherever they lived, Native Americans' economic activities modified the environment, though the changes that indigenous peoples wrought paled in comparison to the later colonial reshaping of the landscape.

When Europeans arrived in North America in the sixteenth century, they believed that they had found a continent overflowing with marketable commodities. Columbus had informed his supporters that the West Indies lay waiting to be exploited, and Spanish conquistadors who had conquered Moctezuma's Aztec empire based in Tenochtitlán had sent great hauls of gold and silver across the Atlantic. The Spaniards who arrived in the Western Hemisphere did more than bring Europeans' attention to a "New World"; they also established an economic precedent: whatever existed in the Western Hemisphere could either be traded for or taken, especially since the indigenous peoples of the Americas were, to the newcomers, uncivilized.

Wherever they went, Europeans hoped to extract mineral wealth. The conquistadors who expanded the boundaries of New Spain northward into modern-day New Mexico, Arizona, and California believed that they would find Cíbola, a mythic city of gold and jewels. Though they failed in that pursuit, many of the explorers continued to believe that great riches would come to the Europeans

who managed to find the minerals that Spaniards believed existed in North America.

By contrast, the Europeans who arrived along the Atlantic coast during the sixteenth century often had more mundane hopes. To be sure, the French and the English each wanted to find mineral wealth, but they failed. The English explorer Martin Frobisher, who sailed west of Greenland and into modern-day Frobisher Bay, thought he had found gold on his three expeditions in the 1570s; but when he returned home, the ore he had transported turned out to be worthless. Still, Frobisher and others had another economic goal in mind: they hoped to find a "Northwest Passage" that would provide a quick water route through North America to the Pacific and thus to the rich markets of east Asia, previously approachable only via a very long and expensive journey around Africa and India. However, no such route could be found, despite repeated European exploratory ventures into frigid northern waters.

Despite their failure to find rare minerals or a shortcut to the East, the French and the English who traveled to North America during the sixteenth century nonetheless managed to find sources of wealth. The most successful among them were probably cod fishermen, many of whom embarked from the English port of Bristol and sailed across the North Atlantic to the plentiful cod populations around the Grand Banks (off modern-day Newfoundland) and Georges Banks (off modern-day New England). Some of those fishermen landed on the shores of North America, and they began to trade with local peoples. Though there is no precise documentation for the origins of what became the fur trade, there is no doubt that Europeans were trading manufactured goods for the hides of beaver, otter, and other furbearers during the early sixteenth century. Over time, the fur trade became a dominant economic pursuit. Native Americans who wanted European goods—such as certain types of clothing, tools, and materials for personal adornment—killed thousands of animals and hauled them to coastal entrepôts. Long before the English established permanent settlements in North America, they benefited from a commercial system that brought them furs (which had become rare in Europe when the aboriginal populations of Russian fur-bearing animals had dwindled from overhunting). Unfortunately for the indigenous peoples, the spread of the fur trade also meant sustained exposure to Old World diseases such as smallpox, which devastated Native Americans who had no prior exposure to such pathogens. They succumbed in horrific numbers to the accidentally imported scourges.

Sixteenth-century European reports about North America often emphasized the potential fertility of the region. Travelers told tales, some perhaps too fantastic to be believed, about the great beasts that inhabited American forests and the vast schools of fish that swam in American rivers. More commonly, visitors recognized the abundant crops that Native Americans were able to produce. Perhaps the most significant visitors to North America during the sixteenth century were the English, who arrived at Roanoke, an island off the coast of modern-day North Carolina, in the 1580s. The migrants had hoped to create a permanent colony in North America, but they failed to do so; their disappearance in the late 1580s sent a message that colonization was not always an easy business. Still, among the travelers were Thomas Harriot, a young mathematician and ethnographer, and John White, a skilled painter. Working together, they created a memorable book, published in London in 1590 as *A Briefe and True Report of the Newfound Land of Virginia*. That book provided the English (and other Europeans) a keen sense of the economic bounty to be had in North America. In the hands of avid promoters of colonization, Harriot's text and White's pictures circulated along with other information about American resources. Taken together, the promotional material solidified certain ideas in the minds of potential colonists. First, the reports suggested, the soil in America could sustain agriculture. Second, there were large populations of useful animals and fish that could be harvested. Third, the native peoples could be converted to Christianity and thus "civilization," which meant that they also would adopt the logic of the market and become avid trading partners. Fourth, land could be acquired from the natives, presumably through treaties and purchases. For Europeans who inhabited a continent in which the rural population had long since grown too large to be sustained in the countryside, the vast resources of North America beckoned.

By the end of the sixteenth century, the French had established themselves in the Saint Lawrence Valley, though they were never able to attract many colonists to their North American holdings. The Spanish had created settlements in New Mexico and Florida, though neither proved to have a substantial economic effect on the Spanish empire. By contrast, the English had yet to succeed at all in territory that would become the United States. However, they had information about American resources, and in the early seventeenth century they used that knowledge to launch what became the most successful colonization efforts in North America.

[*See also* American Indian Economies.]

BIBLIOGRAPHY

Axtell, James. "At the Water's Edge: Trading in the Sixteenth Century." In *After Columbus: Essays in the Ethnohistory of Colonial North America*. New York, 1988.

Axtell, James. "The First Consumer Revolution." In *Beyond 1492: Encounters in Colonial North America*. New York, 1992.

Calloway, Colin G. *New Worlds For All: Indians, Europeans, and the Remaking of Early America*. Baltimore, 1997.

Cronon, William. *Changes in The Land: Indians, Colonists, and the Ecology of New England*. New York, 1983.

Elliott, John H. *The Old World and the New, 1492–1650*. Cambridge, 1970.

Kennedy, Roger G. *Hidden Cities: The Discovery and Loss of Ancient North American Civilization*. New York, 1994.

Mancall, Peter C., ed. *Envisioning America: English Plans for the Colonization of North America, 1580–1640*. New York, 1995.

Quinn, David B. *North America from Earliest Discovery to First Settlements: The Norse Voyages to 1612*. New York, 1975.

Quinn, David B. *Explorers and Colonies: America, 1500–1625*. London, 1990.

Redman, Charles L. *Human Impact on Ancient Environments*. Tucson, Ariz., 1999.

Silver, Timothy. *A New Face on the Countryside: Indians, Colonists, and Slaves in South Atlantic Forests, 1500–1800*. Cambridge, 1990.

Weber, David J. *The Spanish Frontier in North America*. New Haven, 1992.

PETER C. MANCALL

Colonial Period

In 1600, the territory that later became the United States was populated by Native Americans, a small number of Spanish colonists in New Mexico and Florida, and an even smaller number of French settlers who inhabited nascent villages in the Saint Lawrence Valley. By 1775, when the Revolutionary War began, there were approximately two million people inhabiting territory controlled by the English in eastern North America; the Spanish had expanded their holdings in the southwest and Florida; French settlers (whose numbers had grown to perhaps sixty thousand) remained in their old territory as well as the Mississippi Valley; and the number of indigenous peoples had decreased to perhaps one-tenth of what it had been in 1492, though most of the continent remained Indian country. A man or a woman traveling along the east coast in 1775 would have encountered the descendants of migrants from the Netherlands, Sweden, Finland, the German-speaking regions of central Europe, Africa, Ireland, and Scotland, all of them inhabiting territory in the British Empire. According to many scholars, the economy that this diverse population created was among the most productive in Western history.

After trying to establish colonies in Newfoundland, Guiana, and Roanoke in the sixteenth century, the English finally managed to create a permanent overseas community when they founded Jamestown, Virginia in 1607. Though many of the first colonists succumbed to local diseases—about 50 percent of them died of typhoid fever, dysentery, or possibly malnutrition within four years of their arrival—organizers of the settlement managed to convince enough young English men and women to migrate there for the village to survive. The economic base of the colony remained precarious until the mid-1610s, when settlers, desperate to find a profitable export, began to experiment with tobacco production. The crop succeeded, and planters in Virginia, and later Maryland, prospered as a result. The vast majority of immigrant men (approximately 85 percent) and women (almost 100 percent) arrived as indentured servants, and during the early decades of settlement many found economic opportunity after the end of their service. However, even with the boom in the tobacco trade, many of the migrants never survived their initial indenture, and by midcentury those who did complete their service discovered that much of the best land in the tidewater was no longer available.

In all, approximately 116,000 migrants traveled from England to the Chesapeake during the seventeenth century, the vast majority sailing across the Atlantic before 1660. After midcentury, however, opportunity declined, and, eventually, so did immigration, as potential colonists chose instead to remain in England (where the plague and the Great Fire of London in the mid-1660s provided new employment opportunities) or to migrate to other colonies where the possibilities for obtaining land and work seemed greater. For their part, tobacco planters who looked for labor for their holdings began to purchase African slaves. Although the Chesapeake magnates did not invent the slave trade, which by the mid-seventeenth century had existed in the Atlantic basin for many decades, their decision to import slaves to work on tobacco farms reoriented the economy and culture of the southern mainland English colonies. Once established, slavery remained a dominant component of the regional economy until the Civil War, in the mid-nineteenth century.

English migrants also established outposts in New England. After the initial Pilgrim colonization of Plymouth, which began in 1620, large numbers of Puritans traveled to New England during the so-called Great Migration, from 1630 to 1642. During that period, approximately twenty-one thousand English men, women, and children moved to Massachusetts. Although they never created a substantial export-oriented economy—their most important trade goods being furs purchased from local Native Americans—the colonists inhabited healthy environments. As a result, their populations swelled; family size in many New England communities was, on average, eight to ten individuals. Still, demographic success did not promise wealth. Instead, the great fecundity of the colonists led to overpopulation and land shortages, and by the third generation of settlement (approximately the final third of the seventeenth century), many grown children chose to migrate from their home communities to found new satellite villages. Such internal migration made sense from an economic perspective, but it did not always please the Puritan clerics, who had envisioned the creation of communities in which families would be able to remain close together.

By the late seventeenth century, the English had expanded their settlements along the Atlantic coast. Victory over the Dutch in the 1660s allowed the English to take control of the colony of New Netherlands, which they renamed New York. In 1681, King Charles II granted an enormous tract of land to William Penn, who created the colony of Pennsylvania. The English also created colonies in North and South Carolina, in East and West Jersey (later combined into New Jersey), and across New England (New Hampshire, Connecticut, and Rhode Island). The creation of the colony of Georgia in 1732 represented the final territorial expansion of the English during the colonial period.

Scholars who have examined the economy of the mainland colonies of British America often have focused on the staple crops produced in particular regions. Such an approach demonstrates the intense regional differences that existed. In low-lying areas in the southern colonies, notably South Carolina and Georgia, planters imported thousands of slaves to produce rice, a crop that they then exported to English ports, where merchants typically arranged to ship it again, to the Iberian Peninsula, where rice was always in great demand. Over time, southern colonists added indigo to their exports, as well as deerskins, which they obtained from the native Choctaws, Cherokees, Chickasaws, and Creeks (Muscolges) who survived the demographic catastrophe wrought by the arrival of Old World diseases. Tobacco dominated exports from Virginia and Maryland, though by the late-colonial period planters also had begun to export wheat. New York, Pennsylvania, and New Jersey became the center of cereal exports. Unlike the south, most of the agricultural exports produced in the middle colonies came from farms worked by free laborers, either the owners themselves, their children, or hired help (including, at times, the work of indentured servants, many of whom came from the Rhineland). Planters in the middle colonies shipped much of their produce to the English outposts in the West Indies, a trade that planters in the islands needed in order to concentrate their land and slave-labor supply on the production of sugar. In terms of exports, New England lagged behind the other regions, though the merchants of Boston, Newport, and Salem took a direct hand in organizing the shipments of goods across the Atlantic basin.

Throughout the colonial period, the economy remained rural. As late as 1790, the time of the first census of the United States, over 90 percent of the population inhabited farms or small rural communities. Yet even with the urban share of the population relatively slight, the cities that did exist became crucial for organizing economic activity. Merchants who clustered in Philadelphia and New York City, along with others in the coastal ports of New England and Charleston, South Carolina, played a dominant role in determining the imports that other colonists would find in their local stores. They also created the financial infrastructure to support commerce across English America.

Viewed from a distance of over two hundred years, the economy of the English colonies appears a great success.

COLONIAL UNITED STATES. View of long wharf and part of Boston Harbor, painting by Lieutenant Richard Byron, 1764. (Courtesy of The Bostonian Society, Boston)

The English never suffered the kind of defeat that the Spanish experienced in New Mexico during the Pueblo Revolt of 1680, an indigenous uprising that forced Spanish colonists back into Mexico, at least for a time. The English colonies also had a reputation for being an excellent place to find work, a "best poor man's country," as Pennsylvania was called in the eighteenth century; and the territory thus became a great magnet for migrants during the early-modern period. Hence Europeans flocked to the Anglo-American colonies and avoided New France; even poverty-struck French men and women refused to go to their nation's American settlements, leaving them mostly in the hands of soldiers and missionaries. Though English expansion had a catastrophic impact on the native peoples of eastern North America, Indians remained as trading partners and often neighbors of European colonists. By the mid-eighteenth century, if not earlier, Native Americans had experienced a

commercial revolution: they had become eager consumers of European goods such as manufactured clothing, guns and powder, metal tools, and alcohol, a commerce that began in earnest after 1650.

In recent times some scholars have questioned the nature of the economic success experienced by the English. There is no doubt that the prosperity colonists enjoyed often came from exploiting the labor of African and African-American men, women, and children kept in slavery, and from the purchase and appropriation of lands earlier tended by indigenous communities. However, close examination of the lives of urban denizens also suggests that many working people never enjoyed the prosperity they had hoped to find in North America. Further, the lack of large sets of statistics makes it difficult to provide measures for entities such as output per capita. Still, whatever the rate of economic growth, the Anglo-American colonies provided enormous opportunity to European colonizers and their descendants.

BIBLIOGRAPHY

Bailyn, Bernard. *The New England Merchants in the Seventeenth Century*. Cambridge, Mass., 1955.

Bailyn, Bernard. *The Peopling of British North America: An Introduction*. New York, 1986.

Bushman, Richard L. "Markets and Composite Farms in Early America." *William and Mary Quarterly* 3d Ser., 55 (1998), 351–374.

Canny, Nicholas. "English Migration into and across the Atlantic during the Seventeenth and Eighteenth Centuries." In *Europeans on the Move: Studies on European Migration, 1500–1800.* edited by Nicholas Canny, pp. 39–75. Oxford, 1994.

Clemens, Paul G. E. *The Atlantic Economy and Colonial Maryland's Eastern Shore: From Tobacco to Grain*. Ithaca, N.Y., 1980.

Coclanis, Peter A. "The Wealth of British America on the Eve of the Revolution." *Journal of Interdisciplinary History* 21 (1990), 245–260.

Davis, Lance, and Stanley Engerman, eds. "The Economy of British North America." *William and Mary Quarterly* 3d Ser., 56 (1999), 1–181.

Doerflinger, Thomas. *A Vigorous Spirit of Enterprise: Merchants and Economic Development in Revolutionary Philadelphia*. Chapel Hill, N.C., 1986.

Egnal, Marc. *Divergent Paths: How Culture and Institutions Have Shaped North American Growth*. New York, 1996.

Galenson, David. *White Servitude in Colonial America: An Economic Analysis*. Cambridge, 1981.

Greene, Jack P., and J. R. Pole, eds. *Colonial British America: Essays in the New History of the Early Modern Era*. Baltimore, 1984.

Heyrman, Christine Leigh. *Commerce and Culture: The Maritime Communities of Colonial Massachusetts, 1690–1750*. New York, 1984.

Innes, Stephen, ed. *Work and Labor in Early America*. Chapel Hill, N.C., 1988.

Jones, Alice Hanson. *Wealth of a Nation to Be: The American Colonies on the Eve of the Revolution*. New York, 1980.

Lemon, James. *The Best Poor Man's Country: A Geographical Study of Early Southeastern Pennsylvania*. Baltimore, 1972.

Mancall, Peter C. *Valley of Opportunity: Economic Culture along the Upper Susquehanna, 1700–1800*. Ithaca, N.Y., 1991.

Mancall, Peter C., and Thomas Weiss. "Was Economic Growth Likely in Colonial British North America?" *Journal of Economic History* 59 (1999), 17–40.

McCusker, John J., and Russell R. Menard. *The Economy of British America, 1607–1789*. Chapel Hill, N.C., 1985.

Perkins, Edwin J. *American Public Finance and Financial Services, 1700–1815*. Columbus, Ohio, 1994.

Perkins, Edwin J. *The Economy of Colonial America*. 2d ed. New York, 1988.

Shammas, Carole. *The Pre-industrial Consumer in Britain and America*. Oxford, 1990.

Smith, Billy G. *The "Lower Sort": Philadelphia's Laboring People, 1750–1800*. Ithaca, N.Y., 1990.

PETER C. MANCALL

Antebellum Period

The present preeminence of the U.S. economy might make such achievement appear to have been inevitable. One might think that once the shackles of the British empire were thrown off, industrious and well-motivated citizens would have taken full advantage of the country's abundant natural resources, and the economy would have moved ahead swiftly and inexorably. As plausible as this thesis may seem now, such an outcome was very much in doubt at the nation's start. As Henry Adams stated in *The United States in 1800* (Ithaca, N.Y., 1955, p. 12), "The man who in the year 1800 ventured to hope for a new era in the coming century, could lay his hand on no statistics that silenced doubt." The idea of inevitable success has long been discarded, and indeed was proved wrong early in the nineteenth century.

The Facts. The new nation did not maintain the sorts of economic records now kept; so knowledge of the economy's performance between the American Revolution and the Civil War has come from a variety of documentary evidence and from a fragmentary statistical record that is continually being developed by economic historians. Although these records are not so reliable and complete as current national income statistics, the figures nevertheless show the main trends in both the extensive and the intensive growth of the economy.

Extensive growth, measured by increases in the real value of all the goods and services produced in the nation's economy, was very robust. Real Gross Domestic Product (GDP) rose at an average rate of nearly 4.0 percent per year between 1774 and 1860 (see Table 1). Growth was slower than this before 1800; but even in the closing quarter of the eighteenth century, when the economy had to contend with the Revolutionary War and the disruptions immediately thereafter, the rate of growth exceeded 3.0 percent per year. Intensive growth—a more useful measure of a nation's progress than extensive growth because it separates out the growth of the population and indicates whether people on average are becoming better off—was positive but much more modest, although it did accelerate over the period. Whereas real GDP per person rose over the entire period from 1774 to 1860 at an average rate of 0.7 percent per year, near the end of the period the rate of increase was noticeably higher than this.

It is less certain when exactly the nation started on the path of sustained intensive economic growth, and whether it did so gradually or abruptly. In the years shortly after World War II, as the study of economic development increased, the U.S. transition to sustained growth was seen as a sharp upward movement, a takeoff triggered by some major undertaking, such as the railroad boom after 1843. More recent work, however, shows that the transition was much more gradual, as can be best seen in Table 1 by looking at the rates of growth in overlapping twenty-year periods, which help smooth out some shorter-term fluctuations. The rate of growth of GDP per capita appears to have accelerated rather steadily from 1800 to 1860, from an average of 0.4 percent in the first twenty years of the nineteenth century to 0.6 percent per year between 1810 and 1830, rising again to 1.2 percent between 1820 and 1840

TABLE 1. *Selected Economic Statistics for the United States, 1774–1860*

YEAR	GROSS DOMESTIC PRODUCT (MILLION $)	POPULATION (THOUSANDS)	GDP PER CAPITA ($s)	LABOR FORCE (THOUSANDS)	OUTPUT PER WORKER ($s)	LABOR FORCE PARTICIPATION RATE	AGRICULTURAL SHARE OF THE LABOR FORCE
			(dollar values expressed in prices of 1840)				
1774	145	2,419	60	844	172	0.35	0.76
1790	NA	3,929	NA	1,279	NA	0.33	NA
1800	348	5,297	66	1,712	203	0.32	0.74
1810	500	7,224	69	2,337	214	0.32	0.72
1820	689	9,618	72	3,150	219	0.33	0.71
1830	1,017	12,901	79	4,272	238	0.33	0.70
1840	1,553	17,120	91	5,778	269	0.34	0.67
1850	2,318	23,261	100	8,192	283	0.35	0.60
1860	3,905	31,513	124	11,290	346	0.36	0.56
			Average annualized rates of growth				
1774–1800	3.4	3.1	0.4	2.8	0.6	−0.3	−0.1
1800–1860	4.1	3.0	1.1	3.2	0.9	0.2	−0.5
1774–1860	4.0	3.1	0.9	3.1	0.8	0.0	−0.4
			Overlapping twenty-year periods				
1800–1820	3.5	3.0	0.4	3.1	0.4	0.1	−0.2
1810–1830	3.6	2.9	0.6	3.1	0.5	0.1	−0.2
1820–1840	4.2	2.9	1.2	3.1	1.0	0.2	−0.3
1830–1850	4.2	3.0	1.2	3.3	0.9	0.3	−0.8
1840–1860	4.7	3.1	1.6	3.4	1.3	0.3	−0.9

SOURCES: Weiss, Thomas. "U.S. Labor Force Estimates and Economic Growth, 1800 to 1860." In *American Economic Growth and Standards of Living before the Civil War*, edited by R. Gallman and J. Wallis, Chicago, 1992; Mancall, Peter C., and Thomas Weiss. "Was Economic Growth Likely in British Colonial North America." *Journal of Economic History* 59 (1999), 17–40; and worksheets underlying those papers. GDP excludes the value of home manufacturing and farm improvements.

and between 1830 and 1850, and finally increasing to 1.6 percent in the years 1840 to 1860.

This index of growth, however, does not adequately measure changes in all aspects of social welfare. This rise in material output per person may have come at the expense of health and well-being, as evidenced by changes in the stature of the population. The long-run trend in the average height of the U.S. population, like the trend in output, has been positive—that is, the population has on average become taller as well as richer over time; but this appears not to have been the case between 1830 and 1880. In that period, the evidence on stature and that on GDP present a contradiction: the population was getting shorter while output per person was rising. This "antebellum paradox" is one of the more intriguing puzzles confronting scholars, and a number of possible explanations have been proposed. Urbanization, factory employment, and immigration, for example, took their toll by exposing people to disease and a more intense work regime. Whatever the full explanation may be, Costa and Steckel (1997) estimate that the gain in income achieved during this period was not great enough to offset the imputed value of the decline in health.

Sources of Growth. The full explanation for intensive economic growth would be complex, and it is not yet known. In simpler terms, however, it is known that output per person is equal to average output per worker times the labor force participation rate, that is, the proportion of the population that is working; and growth occurs when either or both of these increase. As can be seen in Table 1, the participation rate declined in the last decades of the eighteenth century, but became a positive force for growth in the nineteenth century. Output per worker, on the other hand, was a positive force throughout the entire period of 1774 to 1860.

Other Economic Changes. The factors increasing the nation's output per worker before the Civil War were varied, and are not easily identified and measured. Productivity growth stemmed in part from a shift in the composition of the economy toward nonagricultural industries, where average output per worker was about two to two and one-half times as great as that in agriculture. Because of this large sectoral difference in productivity, the national average output per worker rose as an increasing share of the labor force worked in the more productive sector. This structural influence alone would have pushed up the national figure by about 25 percent. The rest of the increase in output per worker reflects improvements in productivity within the various agricultural and nonagricultural industries. Although some technological advances took place, mechanization was not a great source of productivity improvements, especially in agriculture. Advances such as the mechanical reaper and the seed drill emerged before the Civil War, but their impact was not felt until afterward, when they became more widely diffused. Productivity advances in this period stemmed more from advances in knowledge about farming practices, and the wider diffusion of that knowledge through burgeoning agricultural periodicals, than from advances in technology. The situation was somewhat similar in manufacturing. Although the introduction of sophisticated capital equipment and capital deepening occurred, the leading sources of productivity growth were changes in labor organization and increased intensity of work.

Although the trend in the economy was upward, and acceleration appears to have been persistent, the economy had its ups and downs. The period after the Revolutionary War was a trying time. Markets and trade patterns had been disrupted when Great Britain cut off trade with its former colonies, and relations with other trading partners had yet to be established and would have to be started in the face of a variety of duties and restrictions upon the trade and without the protection of the British navy. Moreover, the political structure and rules governing commerce laid down in the Articles of Confederation proved to be a detriment to the smooth functioning of the economy. The U.S. Constitution, adopted in 1789, was aimed in part at correcting the economic flaws in the Articles of Confederation; and although there seems little doubt that it did so in the long run, the enormous and long-lasting success that would ultimately occur was not obvious at the time.

The nation might have struggled longer had it not been for a series of wars in Europe, beginning with that between England and France in 1793. United States exporters and traders exploited the markets in each belligerent country, and exports and shipping activity boomed between 1793 and 1807. During this period of success, however, the U.S. Congress passed the Embargo Act of 1807, cutting off all foreign trade. Although Congress quickly revised this decision with the Non-Intercourse Act of 1809, which

ANTEBELLUM UNITED STATES. *Cotton Plantation on the Mississippi,* lithograph by Currier and Ives, nineteenth century. (Museum of the City New York/Scala/Art Resource, NY)

allowed trade with all countries except England and France, the damage had been done. The export boom had been brought to a screeching halt; and although it revived somewhat after 1809, that expansion too was aborted, by the War of 1812. At the end of this war, the nation in 1815 stood roughly where it had been in 1790. From then on, the economy moved ahead more consistently than it had, albeit not without some setbacks. Economic crises recurred, notably in 1837, 1839 and 1857, but were less precipitous than that of 1807 and to a large extent were financial panics that did not entail significant declines in real output.

The extensive growth of the economy went hand-in-hand with land expansion, rapid increases in the population, and westward movement. In 1790, the year of the nation's first census, 3.9 million people occupied some 865,000 square miles of land, located along the eastern seaboard. Population increased rapidly, its growth averaging about 3 percent per year for the entire period from 1774 to 1860; and at the close of the period, 31.5 million people were spread over nearly 3 million square miles.

The population was predominantly rural at the nation's beginning. In 1790, only around 5 percent of the population lived in twenty-four cities of twenty-five hundred or more inhabitants. By 1860, there were 392 cities, totaling over six million inhabitants and accounting for nearly 20 percent of the population. Although urbanization proceeded rapidly overall, there were noticeable differences among regions and cities. New York and Philadelphia were the two most prominent cities in both 1790 and 1860, but other cities grew dramatically. The village of Brooklyn had become the nation's third largest city by 1860. Cincinnati, Saint Louis, and Chicago sprang up as the nation moved westward. Charleston, on the other hand, which was the fifth largest city at the start of the nineteenth century, saw very slow population growth.

The shift in population from rural to urban areas paralleled a change occurring in the industrial composition of the economy. In 1790 and earlier, agriculture formed the bulk of the economy, employing around 75 percent of the labor force; but it had dwindled to only 56 percent by 1860. The shift was entirely relative; throughout the period the agricultural sector increased, but it simply fell in relative importance to the faster-growing manufacturing and service industries. This shift was part and parcel of the economic growth that was taking place. In part, it represented the shift in consumption away from food and toward manufactured goods and services that took place as people's incomes rose. At the same time, the shift helped to sustain economic growth, as noted earlier, by its effect on average labor productivity.

In 1790, manufacturing was of little consequence, owing to the restrictions that had been imposed on it under British rule. Although one could find sawmills and flour mills everywhere, other sorts of manufacturing were scarce, and much of the manufactured output was produced in households, not factories. The Embargo of 1807 and the War of 1812 provided a boost to the development of manufactures, but it was temporary. A sustained rise of manufacturing began when the textile industry took hold in New England with the establishment of large-size mills, such as the Boston Manufacturing Company in 1814, and the adoption of power looms, which allowed U.S. firms to compete with the British. The rise of manufacturing and its attendant service industries is reflected most clearly in the decline in the agricultural share of New England's labor force from 67 percent in 1800 to only 31 percent in 1860. Massachusetts and Rhode Island were far and away at the forefront of this structural shift, as their farm shares were only 17 and 19 percent in 1860.

The service industries also grew rapidly in this period, and changed in other ways as well. In transportation there was a revolution. At the end of the eighteenth century, overland transportation was extremely costly and slow, with the result that markets were small in scope and limited mostly to areas that could be served by ocean transportation as well as products that could be shipped downriver. The development of canal transportation, and in particular the completion of the Erie Canal in 1825, brought major changes. The Erie, as well as many less successful canals, reduced the costs of interregional trade and fostered the westward movement of the population. Railroads served to improve transportation even more, not so much by reducing shipping costs as by increasing the speed and the regularity of shipping, and by reducing cargo loss.

The growth and the development of banking and financial systems were noteworthy as well. Banking history in the antebellum period was marked by a constant tension between the desire for a sound currency that could facilitate interregional commerce and the demand for an expanding money supply that could stimulate investment and economic growth. These tensions were manifest in financial booms and busts, such as those in 1837 and 1857, and gave rise to various experiments in banking, such as the free banking systems that began in Michigan in 1837 and spread to about half the states in the 1850s. The tension was most pronounced in the political dispute over the Second Bank of the United States (see Temin, 1969 or Bodenhorn, 2000). Despite these problems, the banking system expanded noticeably, from three chartered commercial banks in 1790 to over fifteen hundred national and state banks by 1860. Other parts of the financial system, such as the markets for stocks, bonds, and commercial paper, flourished as well and helped to accelerate the nation's rate of capital formation.

In summary, modern economic growth in the United States had its origins in the antebellum period. Although it is not possible to date precisely when growth of output per person rose above 1 percent per year, there is little doubt that it occurred before the Civil War. While that acceleration was taking place, the nation struggled to find its place in the world and to contend with the fluctuations inherent in a burgeoning market economy. The period can be thought of as a prelude to post–Civil War expansion; the structural changes and institutional developments that occurred became the foundation on which longer-term economic success rested. However, the period was more than just prelude; there was notable economic success as well. Despite all the fits and starts, the material standard of living improved substantially, and economic growth had become the normal course of events.

BIBLIOGRAPHY

Bodenhorn, Howard. *A History of Banking in Antebellum America: Financial Markets and Economic Development in an Era of Nation-Building.* New York, 2000. Stresses the role of banks in fostering economic growth.

Costa, Dora, and Richard Steckel. "Long Term Trends in Health, Welfare and Economic Growth in the United States." In *Health and Welfare during Industrialization*, edited by Richard Steckel and Roderick Floud, pp. 47–90, Chicago and London, 1997.

David, Paul. "The Growth of Real Product in the United States before 1840: New Evidence, Controlled Conjectures." *Journal of Economic History* 27 (1967), 151–197. A pioneering work in the estimation of national income for the period before 1840.

Engerman, Stanley, and Robert Gallman. "U.S. Economic Growth, 1783–1860." *Research in Economic History* 8 (1983), 1–46. A bit dated but comprehensive review of the meaning, measurement, and sources of economic growth before 1860.

Gallman, Robert, and John Wallis, eds. *American Economic Growth and Standards of Living before the Civil War.* Chicago, 1992. A collection of articles that present much of the most up-to-date quantitative evidence about major aspects of the economy before 1860.

North, Douglass. *The Economic Growth of the United States, 1790–1860.* Englewood Cliffs, N.J., 1961. A pioneering work in quantitative economic history that stresses the role of exports in stimulating economic development.

Rostow, W. W. *Stages of Economic Growth.* Cambridge, 1960. Argues that a "takeoff" was brought about in the United States by the railroad boom after 1843.

Sellers, Charles. *The Market Revolution: Jacksonian America, 1815–1846.* New York, 1991. A historian's view of the booms and busts associated with the spread of the market economy.

Smith, Walter B., and Arthur H. Cole. *Fluctuations in American Business, 1790–1860.* Cambridge, 1935. The most comprehensive source of information on U.S. fluctuations before 1860, although limited mostly to prices and financial statistics.

Sokoloff, Kenneth. "Productivity Growth in Manufacturing during Early Industrialization: Evidence from the American Northeast, 1820–1860. In *Long-Term Factors in American Economic Growth*, edited by Stanley Engerman and Robert Gallman, pp. 679–729. Chicago and London, 1986.

Steckel, Richard. "Stature and the Standard of Living." *Journal of Economic Literature* 33.4 (December 1995), 1903–1940. Provides an excellent summary of the evidence on stature and its interpretation in relation to economic growth.

Sylla, Richard, Jack Wilson, and Charles Jones. "U.S. Financial Markets and Long-Term Economic Growth, 1790–1989." In *American Economic Development in Historical Perspective*, edited by Thomas Weiss and Donald Schaefer, pp. 28–52. Stanford, Calif., 1994. Presents long-term series on stock and bond yields and argue that financial developments after 1815 fostered growth of the realeconomy.

Temin, Peter. *The Jacksonian Economy.* New York, 1969. The best comprehensive treatment of the panic of 1837 and the economic downturn of 1839–1843.

Thorp, Willard L. *Business Annals.* New York, 1926. Collection of contemporary descriptions of economic conditions gleaned from newspapers and periodicals and arranged annually from 1790 to 1925.

U.S. Bureau of the Census. *A Century of Population Growth: From the First Census of the United States to the Twelfth, 1790–1900.* Washington, D.C., 1909. Remains a fundamental summary source of evidence and a guide to census data.

THOMAS WEISS

Modern Period

The performance and the structure of the U.S. economy always have been exceptional by world standards. In 1860, the U.S. economy stood apart from others because of its high level of output per capita, its rapid adoption of new capital-intensive technology, and an agricultural system dominated by owner-occupied farms in the North and slavery in the South. By 1900, this economy had become the world's largest, its growth fueled by high immigration and extensive private-sector investments in physical capital, natural resources, and new technologies. By 1950, the United States had become the world's technological leader. With an output per person far above that of any other region of the world, it took the lead in rebuilding the world economy after World War II and exporting its economic system to the rest of the world. At the beginning of the twenty-first century, the United States continues in its role as the world's largest and most productive economy, relying upon high education levels and technological superiority but distinguished by a relatively small governmental sector.

Because the central theme in the history of this economy is growth, this article first examines measures of economic growth and then turns to the causes of the growth, exceptions to it, and consequences of this set of economic changes. Distributional issues and the growth of government and the welfare state also are discussed.

American Economic Growth. The U.S. gross domestic product (GDP) per capita (in 1999 dollars) was roughly $2,737 in 1860. It climbed to about $4,952 in 1900, $11,575 in 1950, and $34,576 in 1999. These estimates are hampered by measurement problems, but most economic historians believe they give a fairly clear picture of economic growth. They demonstrate that real output per person in the United States has soared since 1860, when output per person was roughly equal to what it is in the Philippines today, or about half that of modern Mexico. At that time, however, the United States was among the richest countries in the world. Britain's GDP per capita was about 30 percent higher, but the U.S. level was three or four times higher than that in the non-European world, and about 20 percent above the western European average. By 1900, the U.S. level was about 10 percent below that of Britain and about 40 percent above the western European average. In 1950, the U.S. economy achieved an unprecedented relative position, about 75 percent above the average of western Europe. At the end of the twentieth century, the United States maintained its position as the most productive economy in the world, with a per capita output level about one-third higher than the levels in western Europe and Japan.

These estimates suggest that U.S. per capita output growth since 1860 has accelerated, averaging about 1.5 percent per year between 1860 and 1900, 1.7 percent per year between 1900 and 1950, and 2.3 percent per year since 1950. Moreover, these estimates may understate the acceleration of growth because they do not completely adjust for the arrival of new goods and quality improvement in old goods, which have accelerated over time.

Factors Contributing to Economic Growth. Growth accounting estimates using the production function approach show that between 1860 and the Great Depression, about half the growth in U.S. output per capita was due to increases in capital and about half to improvements in total factor productivity—which depends mainly on technological progress and rising education. Since 1940, most of this growth has been due to improvements in total factor productivity, with less than one-quarter due to increases in capital. In both periods, technological gains generally have been embodied in new capital and facilitated by rising education levels. Technological advances have occurred across a wide spectrum of economic sectors, including almost every industry, as well as agriculture and the service sectors.

In the late-nineteenth and early-twentieth centuries, the United States emerged as the world's preeminent manufacturing nation. Its share of world manufacturing output, which had been 7 percent in 1860, rose to 24 percent in 1900 and 39 percent in 1928. This success relied upon an uncountable number of mutually interdependent elements. The United States developed its comparative advantage, as demonstrated by the products that it exported, in goods whose production used high capital-to-labor ratios and relied extensively on nonrenewable natural resources. Simultaneously, the United States became the world's leading producer of nonrenewable natural resources. In 1913, it produced more than half of the world output of natural gas, petroleum, and copper and was also the top producer of phosphates, coal, zinc, iron ore and

lead. Its leading exports before the Great Depression—including iron and steel products, machinery, and automobiles—directly or indirectly used these resources. American industrial success was not derived simply from an abundance of resources, however. Hindsight reveals that the United States did not possess exceptional quantities of these resources. Instead, it was the first nation to exploit its hidden natural resources. Aided by government authorities, entrepreneurs systematically searched for the resources and were able to secure well-defined rights to the land containing them. Businesses then used the nation's well-developed and integrated financial markets to acquire capital (much of it before 1890 from western Europe), and used capital-intensive methods to extract the resources, transport them across the continent, and process them into finished goods.

A substantial proportion of the production workers in these industrial sectors were newcomers to the nation; in 1910, the foreign-born and children of foreign-born comprised more than 60 percent of U.S. machine operators and more than two-thirds of the laborers in mining and manufacturing. The United States experienced one of the largest transfers of population in human history during this period, as over twenty-six million immigrants arrived between the Civil War and World War I. This influx came primarily from northern and western Europe before 1890, then primarily from southern and eastern Europe until restrictions on immigration were enacted in the 1920s. (After World War II, immigration levels rose again, with immigrants arriving increasingly from Latin America and Asia.) By 1910, immigrants and their U.S.-born children made up 35 percent of the population.

Economywide figures show how unusually capital-intense the U.S. economy was during this period. In 1890, for example, the ratio of machinery-and-equipment capital to GDP in the United States was 0.46, well above ratios of 0.11 in Britain and 0.10 in Japan. Likewise, the ratio of capital in the form of nonresidential structures to GDP was 2.59, considerably higher than ratios of 0.72 in Britain and 0.61 in Japan. An important and visible component of this capital stock was the nation's transportation infrastructure. The number of miles of railroad rose from 31,000 in 1860 to 128,000 in 1885 and to 266,000 in 1910, as railroad ton-miles increased ninety-eight-fold. Railroad construction accounted for 20 percent of gross capital formation in the 1870s, 15 percent in the 1880s, and 7.5 percent in the decades from 1890 to 1920.

Throughout the nineteenth century and the first decades of the twentieth century, the United States was a technological follower, generally adopting new technologies developed in western Europe. However, it succeeded remarkably in adapting these technologies. Tapping a pool of workers skilled in making machinery and machine tools,

MODERN UNITED STATES. *Across the Continent: Westward the Course of Empire Takes Its Way,* lithograph by Currier and Ives, nineteenth century. (Museum of the City of New York/Scala/Art Resource, NY)

American firms achieved greater productivity than elsewhere by pioneering continuous-process, mass-production methods to tap into the immense economies of scale available in making standardized products for the large, relatively affluent American market—a market free of internal trade barriers. These economies of scale were obtained through the development of a new hierarchical system of management, which was pioneered by the railroads. By the 1860s, steam engines provided the majority of the power for these energy-intensive production systems; but after the turn of the century, electrification allowed for a restructuring of industrial processes and great improvements in productivity. In 1899, electrical motors made up about 5 percent of manufacturing horsepower. This climbed to 25 percent in 1909, 55 percent in 1919, and 82 percent in 1929. Simultaneously, the development of the internal combustion engine (and with it the automobile and the tractor) boosted productivity. Both of these technologies were pioneered in Europe but extensively commercialized in the United States. Improvements to moving assembly lines, which were adopted throughout the manufacturing sector, also boosted productivity in the early twentieth century.

Agriculture was, perhaps, the most important sector affected by capital deepening and technological improvements in this period. Between 1869 and 1919, the agricultural labor force grew at only 0.9 percent per year, but output was able to grow at 2.0 percent per year. Cultivated acres grew twice as fast as the agricultural workforce because capital climbed by 2.0 percent per year, and machinery and equipment, which embodied technological advances, grew by 3.9 percent per year. In 1870, half of the workforce was employed in agriculture. Yet, because of this substitution away from labor toward capital, by 1920 agriculture employed only one-quarter of the workforce. During the twentieth century, agricultural capital and technology accelerated with a shift from animal-powered to gasoline-powered equipment and technological developments, such as fertilizers, pesticides, and bioengineered crops, that allowed yields to soar. For example, bushels of wheat per acre quadrupled and bushels of corn per acre tripled between 1910 and 1990.

By the middle of the twentieth century, the U.S. comparative advantage in resource-abundant production began to wane because of the development of global resource markets. However, by this time the United States had emerged as the technological leader in a wide range of fields, including chemicals, pharmaceuticals, telecommunications, electronics, and computers. Behind this success was the invention, in the United States, of the industrial research laboratory. Such research facilities often developed close ties to universities, which produced a growing stream of engineers and scientists and to the government, which aided technological development through strong and clear intellectual property rights and the funding of research. The U.S. research and development effort was massive by world standards. In 1969, for example, the U.S. expenditures were more than twice those of West Germany, France, Britain, and Japan combined. Large firms in fairly concentrated industries carried on much of this research; but smaller, dynamic entrepreneurial firms funded by venture capitalists, which were especially important in commercializing high technology, complemented this effort.

The influx of immigrants helped hold the wages of unskilled workers down around the turn of the twentieth century, but boosted the wages of better-skilled and -educated workers. In 1860, 51 percent of children aged five to nineteen years were enrolled in school. The same figure held in 1900. In the face of this stagnant supply of educated workers, the rate of return to education became exceptionally high, with white-collar workers earning 70 to 100 percent more than manual workers in 1914. In response to this demand for education, local governments began a rapid expansion of the supply of high schools, with high-school enrollment rates soaring between 1910 and 1935, climbing from around 25 percent to about 75 percent in most regions. A well-educated workforce was crucial to the development of the United States as the world's technological leader by the mid-twentieth century, allowing technological advances to permeate the economy and spurring productivity growth in traditional service sectors such as finance, wholesale, retailing, medicine, and government. It is estimated that from 1929 to 1982 human capital formation in the United States exceeded physical capital formation by almost 50 percent. After World War II, the workforce became increasingly college-educated, with the percent of persons aged eighteen to twenty-four years enrolled in college rising from 13 percent in 1952 to 32 percent in 1970. By 1995, some 48 percent of the adult population had attended college, 8 percent had completed advanced degrees, and over 60 percent of graduating high school students went on to higher education. These levels, the highest in the world, spurred continual improvements and leadership in productivity and technology.

American growth relied on individual workers and firms pursuing economic gains in the marketplace. However, various levels of government often played a key role in augmenting the market. This took many forms, such as federal land-grant subsidies to transcontinental railroads in the 1860s and 1870s and the establishment of the Weather Bureau in 1870. Direct spending on education rose from 1.7 percent to almost 7 percent of GDP during the course of the twentieth century, most of it financed through state and local governments. After the turn of the twentieth century, the federal government also took a key role in encouraging competition through enforcement of antitrust laws. These actions forbade cartelization of industry (which was common in other nations), broke up some of the largest monopolies (such as Standard Oil and American Tobacco in 1911) and induced many large corporations to protect and expand their market shares via innovation rather than merger and collusion. In some industries, however, it appears that firms were able to capture their regulators. Deregulation of airlines, trucking, railroads, banking, telecommunications, and natural gas in the last quarter of the twentieth century brought considerable efficiency gains.

Exceptions to the Growth. The Southern United States was an important exception to the national growth pattern. In 1860, this region was dominated by a system of slave agriculture, with cotton the major staple crop. Output per capita was about 20 percent below the national average in 1860—well below the average in the Northeast, but about 15 percent above the North Central average. After the Civil War, the emancipation of slaves brought a loss of economies of scale in plantation agriculture and a withdrawal of labor from production. Combined with continued reliance on cotton, these changes left the South far behind the rest of the country. Output per capita in the South was only about half the national average from the end of the Civil War to 1900. A number of factors blocked Southern convergence to the national level, including political domination by landlords who desired low-wage labor, the unwillingness of Southerners to welcome well-educated people and businessmen from outside the region, education levels that lagged behind the national average, and a failure of poor Southerners to leave the region. All of these conditions were tinged by racist attitudes of Southern whites toward the large population of Southern blacks. Southern manufacturing developed rapidly, but it began at a low base and was concentrated in low–value added sectors such as textiles. Population growth pushed the number of acres in Southern farms per rural population down from fourteen in 1880 to nine in 1930, as it rose in the Midwest from sixteen to twenty-three. Finally, starting around World War II, the South began a sustained process of catching up with the rest of the country, driven by a mobility of labor out and capital in, along with rising education and declining racism. By the end of the twentieth century, Southern output per capita was about 92 percent of the national average.

Overall, U.S. economic growth has rarely been smooth. From 1854 to 1913, the economy endured fourteen recessions. The length of the recessions averaged twenty-three months and expansions twenty-five months, so the economy was shrinking almost as often as it was growing. An especially deep recession began in 1893; unemployment may have climbed above 15 percent and probably exceeded 10 percent for five years running.

Between 1913 and 1948, there were eight business cycles, with recessions averaging seventeen months in length and expansions thirty-six months. The worst of these episodes, by far, was the Great Depression, which began in 1929 and hit bottom in early 1933. Real GDP fell by 29 percent, consumer prices fell by 28 percent, and the unemployment rate peaked at 25 percent. Unemployment stayed above 8.5 percent for twelve years, until the country entered World War II. The Great Depression was an international event, but it hit the United States and Canada harder than any other countries. Its causes are difficult to disentangle, but most economic historians cite problems in the functioning of the international gold standard, weaknesses in the American banking sector, and mistakes made by the U.S. central bank—the Federal Reserve. The downswing was hastened by a crash in the value of stock market shares and was pushed by declines in aggregate demand, which may have been tied to unusually high levels of household indebtedness and the structure of automobile loans. Recovery from the downturn was hampered by great uncertainty and some of the early policies of President Franklin Roosevelt's New Deal, especially the National Recovery Administration's moves to cartelize industry. The Depression had a profound influence on American institutions. Agencies and policies created during the New Deal of the 1930s, such as the Federal Deposit Insurance Corporation, the Securities and Exchange Commission, the National Labor Relations Board, the Social Security Administration, the minimum wage, and agricultural price supports, continued in existence into the twenty-first century.

From 1948 to 2001 there were only nine recessions, lasting an average of eleven months with expansions averaging more than fifty-nine months. The worst of these recessions came in 1982 when the unemployment rate hit 9.7 percent after the Federal Reserve deliberately slowed the economy in an attempt to reduce the inflation rate, which had hit 13.5 percent per year. This recession was part of a longer period of slow growth and unprecedented inflation that began in late 1973 with soaring petroleum prices. Increased international competition during this period also caused slower growth and a restructuring of U.S. industry. However, these rough patches cannot obscure the picture of long-term economic growth and dampening business cycles.

Consequences of Growth: International Leadership, Rising Standards of Living, and Changes in the Use of Time. The productive strength of the United States translated into military strength during World War II; and after the war the U.S. government took an active interest in preventing the recurrence of war and blocking the expansion of the authoritarian Soviet Union, which relied upon a centrally planned, communist economy. Because of its economic strength, the United States was able to take the lead in rebuilding the economies of Japan and western Europe through the Marshall Plan and establishing international institutions, such as the International Monetary Fund, the General Agreement on Tariffs and Trade, and the World Bank, designed to strengthen free-market, democratic regimes around the world. The openness of U.S. markets and the stability it gave to the international economic system allowed countries in western Europe and Japan to approach the level of the U.S. economy and allowed economies of less-developed countries, such as South Korea, Taiwan, and Mexico, to make a dramatic improvement in their standards of living as well.

Another major long-run consequence of American economic growth has been a rising material standard of living. Rising output per capita translates directly into rising incomes, which have greatly altered spending patterns. In 1875, about 60 percent of consumers' income was spent on food, with 15 percent on clothing, 16 percent on shelter, and little left for other things. By 1990, food made up only about 14 percent of consumer spending, housing 15 percent, and clothing a mere 6 percent. This change occurred even though these people ate more food of higher quality and greater variety than that of their forebears (much of it in restaurants), their clothing had become more varied, durable, and attractive, and their housing was much more spacious and contained more amenities such as indoor plumbing and electricity. Consumption exploded in categories such as health care, transportation, recreation, and appliances. In 1900, household appliances such as refrigerators, radios, televisions, washing machines, microwave ovens, and air conditioners did not exist; but by the end of the twentieth century almost all households had refrigerators, radios, and televisions, and well over half had the other appliances. In 1900, some 20 percent of urban families owned a horse, but virtually no one owned a car. Family auto ownership rates climbed to 26 percent in 1920 (a rate similar to that of many western European countries four decades later), 60 percent in 1930, and 79 percent in 1970.

However, initially, higher incomes did not translate into better nutritional status and health. In the 1860s, the life expectancy of American-born white males at age ten was about fifty years. Almost exactly the same life expectancy prevailed in 1900. This number was about six years less than in 1800. Only after 1900 did life expectancy climb steadily, gaining nine years by 1950. Another measure, average final heights, is an excellent indication of net nutritional status—nutritional intake minus claims on nutrition due to body metabolism, work effort, and the effects of disease. Adult male heights declined by about three centimeters for cohorts born in the generation before 1860 and may have fallen a bit more, hitting bottom for those born around 1880. Only after 1900 did heights rise appreciably, climbing about seven centimeters during the first half of the twentieth century. Several factors seem to have thwarted the translation of rising incomes into better biological well-being in the last half the of 1800s. Chief among them may have been a deterioration of the disease environment due to increased interregional trade, migration, and immigration, which exposed previously isolated populations to disease and rapid urbanization (which rose from 20 percent of the population in 1860 to 40 percent in 1900) in an era before knowledge about germs led to the adoption of public-health measures such as sewage systems and clean water supplies. After 1900, urbanization continued (by the end of the century it exceeded 75 percent), but nutritional status and longevity improved with declining real food prices and advances in public health and medicine.

Differences in income elasticities of demand and rates of productivity growth across sectors have brought substantial changes in the occupational mix of U.S. workers. In 1860, agricultural workers made up 53 percent of the labor force; this share fell continuously, to 40 percent in 1900, 12 percent in 1950, and less than 3 percent in 2000. Manufacturing and mining's share rose from 15 percent in 1860 to 22 percent in 1900, but peaked at 30 percent in 1920, falling to 25 percent in 1950 and 17 percent at the end of the century. Among the most rapidly expanding occupational groups were professional (which increased from 4.3 percent of employment in 1900 to 8.6 percent in 1950 and 15.1 percent in 1998), managerial (which rose from 5.8 percent in 1900 to 8.7 percent in 1950 and 14.5 percent in 1998), and clerical (which rose from 3.0 percent in 1900 to 12.3 percent in 1950 and 14.0 percent in 1998). In all, white-collar occupations increased from 18 percent of employment in 1900 to 37 percent in 1950 and 60 percent in 1998.

These occupational changes belie an even larger change in use of the time enabled by rising incomes. In 1860, the average workweek in manufacturing was about 66 hours. This fell to 55 hours in 1900, 48 hours in 1920, and 41 hours in 1950. Simultaneously, workers began to retire at earlier ages. The labor-force-participation rate of males sixty-five and over fell from about 77 percent in 1860 to 58 percent in 1900, 46 percent in 1950, and 12 percent in 1995. Owing to the shortened workweek, earlier retirement, and lengthening life expectancy, a typical adult male's lifetime hours of paid work declined from about 182,000 in 1880 to 122,000 in 1995, with leisure time quadrupling from about 44,000 hours to 176,000 hours. Women's leisure may have increased even more.

Perhaps the most significant shift in time use by women has been a move out of child rearing and household production and into the labor market. The fertility rate fell from about 5.5 children per ever-married woman for women reaching age twenty-five in 1860, to 3.4 in 1900, hitting bottom at about 2.3 during the Great Depression, but rebounding during the post-World War II baby boom, before falling to a level just above 2 at the end of the century. In 1890, the adult female labor force participation rate was about 19 percent. This climbed to 29 percent in 1950 and 60 percent in 1998. The rise has been even stronger among married women, whose participation rate in 1890 was slightly below 5 percent, but was 61 percent in 1998. This move into the market by U.S. women has been due, among other reasons, to the lure of rising real wages, rising education, dramatic improvements in household technology, and changing cultural norms. Economic development has also brought institutional changes such as the development of part-time jobs, paid day care, and an end to practices that denied employment to married women. As the real wage of women has risen, so has the relative wage. The female-to-male wage ratio in manufacturing was about 0.55 in the late 1800s; but with the rise of white-collar jobs, the overall female-to-male wage ratio climbed to about 0.65 by the 1920s, dipped below this level as inexperienced women rapidly entered the labor market after World War II, and then climbed to about 0.76 by the end of the twentieth century.

Distributional Issues. The relationship between economic growth and equality is very complicated, depending on the shifting supply and demand for inputs to production, including labor, skills, capital, and land. In the United States, economic equality seems to have decreased substantially during the years after the Civil War. Skilled workers' wages rose relative to unskilled workers' wages, wealth became increasingly concentrated in the hands of successful businessmen, and inequality became an important political issue. During the first half of the twentieth century, equality seems to have risen (although there were periods when the trend reversed), mostly because income came increasingly from human capital, which was becoming much more equally distributed than physical capital and land. Wage equality rose dramatically during the 1940s, and stayed near its historic high until the 1970s. At the end of the twentieth century, equality fell significantly, going back to the level that existed in 1940, as returns to education soared.

Upon emancipation, at the end of the Civil War, few blacks had marketable skills, and almost none owned property. Living mostly in the nation's poorest region, and faced with rampant racism and segregation, blacks made slow progress toward economic equality with whites up until about 1940, when black male earnings were only about 43 percent of white male earnings. After World War II, however, increased education and declining racism allowed blacks to achieve greater equality with whites, with blacks' relative earnings climbing to 70 percent by 1980.

High levels of inequality spawned radical political movements in the late nineteenth and early twentieth centuries in Europe. The United States has been exceptional because of the relative weakness of such movements. With the country's democratic processes, entrenched two-party system, high rates of property ownership, extensive upward economic mobility, and ethnic fragmentation, socialism never made serious inroads in the United States. Labor unions also have had limited success. The nonagricultural sector's unionization rate barely passed 8 percent in 1886 before the Knights of Labor collapsed. Under the American Federation of Labor, membership rates climbed from 4.5 percent in 1900 to 16 percent in 1920, but fell considerably during the 1920s. Only with the passage of the Wagner Act in 1935 did organized labor gain a firm legal standing, with the right to bargain collectively for workers who had voted for representation. The Congress of Industrial Organizations promoted unionization among less-skilled workers in heavy industry, and unionization reached 35.5 percent in 1945. Organized labor enjoyed bargaining successes and political clout during the 1950s and 1960s, and public-sector unionism spread, but the unions' overall membership share began to erode because of stiff employer resistance and declining worker interest. Unionization fell below 14 percent in 1998 (being only 9.5 percent in the private sector), the lowest rate in the developed world. Employers have been able to limit unionism by shifting away from a system based on managerial control over workers to methods using employment security, fringe benefits, employee feedback, and carefully crafted anti-union policies to create workplaces where workers tolerate and often respect, managerial authority.

The Growth of Government and the Welfare State. In 1860, national (federal) government expenditures made up about 5 percent of GDP in the United States. This figure increased substantially during wartime, but the general trend was a slow upward drift, so that the share was about 7.5 percent during the 1920s. During the Great Depression, federal spending climbed to about 15 percent of GDP, and expenditures shifted from state and local levels to the national level. By 1985, federal expenditures reached 23 percent of GDP with expansion of military spending and transfer programs such as Social Security, Medicare, and Medicaid. However, by the end of the twentieth century this figure had fallen below 20 percent of GDP; and throughout the century, the United States was an outlier, with significantly lower transfers than found in similarly developed countries. Americans never became as comfortable as others with big government and the welfare state.

In addition, the United States has been unique in its acceptance of privately owned business. Unlike other industrialized countries, it has had only minimal government ownership in the telephone, electric power, railroad, and airline industries; and its health-care sector continues to rely extensively on private insurance. Except during wartime, it has lacked a coordinated set of industrial policies, designed to steer resources into particular industries, and has generally avoided bailing out or nationalizing failing firms or industries. It has instead relied mainly on competition to expand output and consumer choice.

A backward glance suggests that the U.S. economy (and most economies throughout the world) will continue to grow into the foreseeable future. However, it is difficult to say how much rising incomes and economic development have translated into increased happiness for Americans. International surveys of happiness from the last half of the twentieth century indicate that self-assessed happiness increases strongly as average incomes rise up to a level around $10,000 per person (1999 dollars), a level that the United States reached around the end of World War II. Above this point there is only a weak increase in happiness as income rises. In fact, happiness in the United States appears to have declined since about 1970, and this change seems to be largely due to a decrease in lasting marriages, which may well be a product of recent economic developments.

BIBLIOGRAPHY

Atack, Jeremy, and Peter Passell. *A New Economic View of American History: From Colonial Times to 1940.* 2d ed. New York, 1994. Comprehensive textbook, which incorporates the latest research, with careful explanations of the most advanced cliometric work.

Carter, Susan B., Scott S. Gartner, Michael R. Haines, Alan L. Olmstead, and Richard Sutch, eds. *Historical Statistics of the United States: Millennial Edition, Colonial Times to the Present.* 3 vols. New York, forthcoming. Invaluable source containing an abundance of statistical evidence about the U.S. economy, with overviews written by leading economic historians designed to assist the reader in appreciating the origins, meaning, and historical significance of the data in the tables.

Costa, Dora L., and Richard H. Steckel, "Long-Term Trends in Health, Welfare, and Economic Growth in the United States." In *Health and Welfare during Industrialization*, edited by Richard H. Steckel and Roderick Floud, pp. 47–88. Chicago, 1997. An evaluation that includes extensive analysis of measures of biological standards of living.

Engerman, Stanley L., and Robert E. Gallman, eds. *The Cambridge Economic History of the United States*, vol. 2, *The Long Nineteenth Century*, and vol. 3, *The Twentieth Century*. New York, 2000. Comprehensive treatment of the most important themes in U.S. economic history, by the leading scholars in the field.

Fearon, Peter. *War, Prosperity and Depression: The U.S. Economy, 1917–1945.* Lawrence, Kans., 1987. Accessible explanation of the origins and effects of the Great Depression.

Fogel, Robert William. *Railroads and American Economic Growth: Essays in Econometric History.* Baltimore, 1964. Path-breaking work that uses economic theory and data to show that railroads played only a small part in nineteenth-century economic growth.

Fogel, Robert William. *The Fourth Great Awakening and the Future of Egalitarianism*. Chicago, 2000. Insightful analysis of American economic history by the 1993 Nobel Prize winner. Focuses on the interaction of technology, economics, politics, culture, and religion.

Goldin, Claudia. *Understanding the Gender Gap: An Economic History of American Women*. New York, 1990. The most important work on the subject, full of informative statistics, institutional information, and careful explanations.

Higgs, Robert. *Crisis and Leviathan: Critical Episodes in the Growth of American Government*. New York, 1987. Examination of the growth of American government, arguing that crises, especially the world wars and the Great Depression, played a key role.

Hughes, Jonathan, and Louis P. Cain. *American Economic History*. Reading, Mass., 1998. The most widely used textbook in the field, which provides comprehensive coverage.

Jacoby, Sanford. *Modern Manors: Welfare Capitalism since the New Deal*. Princeton, 1997. Well-documented analysis of industrial relations.

Lebergott, Stanley. *Pursuing Happiness: American Consumers in the Twentieth Century*. Princeton, 1993. Extensive and inventive documentation of extraordinary changes in consumption and the rise in consumption standards.

Maddison, Angus. *Monitoring the World Economy, 1820–1992*. Washington, D.C., 1995. Extensive statistics and analysis, comparing U.S. development with the rest of the world.

Mowery, David C., and Nathan Rosenberg. *Paths of Innovation: Technological Change in 20th-Century America*. New York, 1998. Overview of the institutionalization of innovation and development of the internal combustion engine, chemicals, electric power, and electronics.

Whaples, Robert. "Where Is There Consensus among American Economic Historians? The Results of a Survey on Forty Propositions." *Journal of Economic History* 55.1 (1995), 139–154. Essay identifying major agreements and disagreements among American economic historians.

Wright, Gavin. *Old South, New South: Revolutions in the Southern Economy since the Civil War*. New York, 1986. Authoritative explanation of why the U.S. South lagged behind, then caught up with, the rest of the nation.

Wright, Gavin. "The Origins of American Industrial Success, 1879–1940." *American Economic Review* 80.4 (1990), 651–668.

ROBERT WHAPLES

URBANIZATION. Where people live in relation to one another is an important aspect of their lives—economic, social and otherwise. Urbanism, with its spatial propinquity, brings them into close touch, perhaps at the cost of distending or diluting their ties with the natural environment. Human interactions, planned or not, then become more frequent and diverse though less personal. In terms of economics, both production and consumption activities are profoundly affected by urban concentration. For these reasons, the shift from a basically agrarian (to say nothing of nomadic or hunter-gatherer peoples) to a growing urban society represents a long-term, structural change, comparable in its magnitude and consequences to other great socioeconomic transformations: settled agriculture, industrialization, sustained growth in per capita output, monetization, or the demographic transition. Urbanization

has probably drawn the attention of economic historians less often than these others; and yet they have not ignored urban activities, since many subjects of inquiry—finance, many kinds of production, and most types of commerce—are scarcely conceivable in any but an urban context. To a lesser extent, economic historians have examined the workings of cities, from land and housing markets to the regulation of business activity. Still, the underlying phenomenon of growth—absolute and relative—in urban populations, has received comparatively little attention.

In the context of economic history, urbanization, or urban economies, can be looked at in two ways: as the products of economic change or as agents of economic change. The first perspective considers the forces, those that are economic in nature or mediated through economic effects, that shape the growth of cities and their changing fortunes, as well as the massive shift of population from rural to urban life. This appears to be a straightforward approach, since it draws directly on such well-studied phenomena as growth in agricultural labor productivity, the shift from primary to secondary and tertiary employment, evolving technology, mass production, and the increasing scale, reach, and sophistication of markets. Actual cases are more complex, reflecting the diversity of urban experiences and economic contexts. The second view, seeking to explicate the role of cities as agents in determining economic change, raises more difficult problems and has largely eluded serious analysis by economic historians. Other social scientists, since the nineteenth century, from Max Weber on, have been far more interested in the issue. Although the rise and spread of sustained per capita ("intensive" or "modern") economic growth is the dominant preoccupation of economic history, cities are more likely to be emphasized by historical sociologists examining the "rise of capitalism."

An important clarification is necessary: the present subject is *urbanization*—the unit of study or observation of the economy of a particular city or town or a set of them. Yet these are distinct concepts. The city has been defined and re-defined, whereas quantitative thresholds and functional criteria mean more to economic historians than do juridical or political criteria, since they offer their own share of conceptual and measurement issues. If the concept of a city is familiar enough, urbanization is another and more complex matter. The term can refer to (1) the absolute growth of town populations in a country or region; but it more often means (2) the growth of urban population *relative* to the whole; however, it can also be used to signify (3) the shift of employment away from primary (agricultural, etc.) production toward industrial, commercial, and service occupations; or (4) a move by household units away from self-sufficiency and toward specialization in production and systematic involvement in markets (the

URBANIZATION. Archaeological site at Mohenjo Daro, Pakistan, an ancient city of the Indus Valley civilization (c. 2600–1700 BCE). (Borromeo/Art Resource, NY)

implication here is that households thereby gain access to a greater variety of goods and, possibly, to a greater quantity as well, owing to gains from trade). A final and more recent use, at least of the adjective *urban*, relates to (5) the social pathology of modern society, centering on class or ethnicity or on the presence of psychological alienation.

Definitions 3 and 4 make it clear that residence in a town is not a necessary condition for involvement in urbanization. Similarly, cities can develop and grow or multiply without there being urbanization in the quantitative sense of definition 2, as long as the rural population increases at least at the same rate as the urban. The distinction can be made (at the expense of oversimplification) with an epigram: Many past societies have had flourishing and sizeable cities without the urban share of the population increasing—Renaissance Europe and late imperial China are cases in point. Today, large numbers of people in developed countries, particularly in the West, lead apparently fully urban lives (in the sense of definitions 3 and 4) while residing in small clusters or in scattered dwellings. In fact, the death of cities in the traditional sense is often announced. Consider: from cities without urbanization, then, to urbanization without cities? Nevertheless, in this article, the term *urban* will be used as an adjective that situates something within the context of a town or city (this last a loosely quantitative distinction, used somewhat differently in British and American English, and absent in French and German).

Without providing a great many numbers, a sense of the quantitative progress of urbanization may be given. The urban populations of preindustrial societies rarely exceeded 10 percent of the total, although ancient city-states were an exception. Then, too, as early as the Middle Ages, in parts of Europe (notably in Italy and the Low Countries) urban populations reached about 20 percent. England was approaching that level by the mid-eighteenth century, largely because of London's exceptional size. By that time, however, the North of Europe as a whole, though more dynamic overall than the South, still had a lower urban share; the Mediterranean lands had not "ruralized" as their economic power waned after the Renaissance. With the Industrial Revolution, the urban share grew in most nations, as the cities needed laborers. The 50 percent mark was reached in England around 1850, and Belgium was the only other country to do so before 1900. By the turn of the twenty-first century, only countries with limited industrialization retain a rural majority, although both their urban share and the population of their larger cities grew enormously after 1950. The metropolises of India, China, Brazil, and Mexico are now more populous (approaching 20 million) than the "global cities" of New York (8 million), London (7 million), and Tokyo (8.5 million). By contrast, only a very few cities approached the 1 million mark in the preindustrial world—Rome, Bagdhad, Byzantium (Constantinople), and Peking—while most were very much smaller. In 1700, only Paris, London, and Naples exceeded 200,000 inhabitants.

Historical Issues. For all the attention that historians and social scientists have devoted to cities, their origins and the economic circumstances that gave rise to them remain uncertain. The logical progression of growth from scattered settlements to villages to towns to large city is not truly explanatory. Since about 3500 BCE, the principal places of early urban settlement were in Sumer, along the Tigris and Euphrates river valleys, and they were developed only gradually. Yet ports or trade gateways often began the process of settlement along the Nile River and in China, to remain leading urban centers for thousands of years. The origin of many early cities was probably noneconomic. Religious, political, and military functions—often mingled in the early theocratic civilizations—demanded a secure, compact, and awe-inspiring site together with organized provisioning. In time, commercial and other activities found favorable settings there, as well as a ready market. Ancient cities are usually dominated by a palace, fort, temple, or other architectural showcase of power. In fact, the very word *city* (from Latin *civis*, *civitas*, meaning "citizen") initially referred to that salient core of the "urban" fabric (from Latin *urbs*, meaning "city"). Dwellings and the facilities for commerce, crafts, and other needs originally huddled in the shadow of citadel walls, though they might eventually be enclosed within later and larger sets of zonal boundaries or their own fortifications.

A defining characteristic of urban dwellers, and thus of cities, is that they do not produce their own subsistence, whether food or fuel. Exceptions arise, to be sure: kitchen gardens, places for farm animals, and commuting to nearby fields or fishing grounds. Yet if primary production occupies most of the inhabitants, then even a large settlement is basically a village. Thus any true urban settlement requires steady, reliable provisioning. In the theocratic city, this was handled by exacting some of the agricultural surplus from producers in surrounding areas, whether as plunder, tribute, taxation, religious offerings, or under some other label. With time and the development of urban commercial, craft, and service functions, this exaction took on the characteristics of an exchange. Cities do produce, although most of their output consists of services—intangible or public (collective) goods. Beyond such direct production, cities can stimulate investment, innovation, and expansion—in other words, growth—in those same surroundings. For example, the sophisticated irrigation systems of the ancient Near East arose alongside the earliest Sumerian cities and agricultural modernization in preindustrial Europe flourished earliest in the most urbanized zones, roughly from central England to central Italy. Mutual causation, or a reciprocity of factors occurs, since urban settlement requires a preexisting agrarian surplus—but the urban stimulus to rural development is very real.

If the origins of the first cities are not yet fully known, their growth and the later development of others have become part of history. Still, questions arise because urban life in general, and in specific cities, has survived through centuries, sometimes millennia, despite recurring crises—natural, economic, and/or military. If urban life is at the mercy of a steady supply of provisions from outside, as well as the dangers from fire and epidemic disease, this longevity cannot be taken for granted. Cities have been abandoned; in Africa, Central Asia, Mesoamerica, and other venues, their ruins lie silently beneath the jungle, sea, or desert, awaiting archeological rediscovery. Many have already been found and excavated, enriching our knowledge of prehistoric and early historic urban life. Economic history tends to deal with shorter time periods than archeology does, so cities and their longevity, the way they often hold their roles, their rank, and their size, becomes noteworthy. Their persistence is based on resilience, their ability to recover their numbers and to regain their functions after crises—sieges and sacks, epidemics and famines, or other crises. A corollary is that rural populations are usually willing, even eager, to find a place in cities, whether drawn there by narrowly economic incentives or for other reasons. Over time, to be sure, small towns are quite likely to lose their urban character, as functions and people migrate to larger cities, but past a certain size threshold the probability of decline or extinction becomes much smaller.

Within a territory in which there are already cities, new ones may arise, and larger ones may emerge from a subset of the smaller ones. Town formation has been initiated by rulers, whether for a new capital or court or to anchor their power in newly acquired lands; it can be spurred by merchants and industrialists, perhaps to take advantage of mineral resources or a convenient transshipment point. Also, intensive rural settlement can give rise to new market and administrative centers. Cities also exhibit varied rates of population growth, from the mushrooming of boomtowns to the somnolence of backwaters; differentiation and/or hierarchic size distributions are common. In addition, urban expansion can give rise to new entities and extinguish old ones, as nearby cities fuse or growing ones absorb their lesser neighbors, a process seen since the nineteenth century, which continues unabated. Such descriptive terms as *metropolis*, *megalopolis*, *conurbation*, and *urban region* are used to characterize "greater metropolitan areas" and urban entities that transcend the traditional concept of a city or overwhelm their original historic identities.

Urban populations are studied by urban geographers, historical demographers, or population historians more than by economic historians. Demographics also concern historians of migration, for at least two reasons. First, cities have historically relied on in-migrants to sustain their numbers, and certainly for most of their growth, since they experienced higher mortality rates than their surroundings in earlier times and almost always lower fertility. New migrants were especially likely to suffer early death and less likely to marry than natives. Second, town dwellers have generally been relatively mobile, in keeping with the place of exchange at the center of urban economic life. In addition to rural-to-urban migration, cities have smaller return to the country movements; they also harbor commuters, temporary and career migrants, travelers, and interurban migrants. These streams feed many of the most characteristic occupations, districts, and activities of cities: the servants and factory hands imported from the country, the persistently ethnic neighborhoods, and the civil servants—whether beginning their careers in a distant provincial outpost or crowning it in the capital.

Urban Economies. The growth and economic character (the structure of activity, its scale and profitability) of cities form suitable subjects of investigation for economic history, yet it is important to recognize that here, as in issues of demographic or political change, the examination of single cities is unlikely to prove fully enlightening. The fundamental point—that urban economies specialize in exchange, which provides much of the rationale for the investments, ongoing costs, and risks that cities entail—also implies that studying a single city (or type of city) as a closed entity cannot make sense of it. Nonetheless, certain aspects of urban economies tend to show interesting regularities throughout a range of time and space.

Historically, cities are of two types with respect to economic functions. Some, probably the majority, are balanced, with a relatively wide range of market, service, and control activities for their population size. In a given territory, a clear functional hierarchy can be established among them, congruent with size. The base includes the many simple market centers, each serving and administering its local surroundings; then there are the fewer but larger and more diverse cities that add wholesaling, educational services, specialized retailing, manufacturing, and other activities, along with higher-order political, religious, and service functions; at the top is the great provincial or national capital city. Not all cities or all regions fit within this pattern. Some cities can and do function well with a great degree of economic specialization; they may concentrate on manufacturing, on educational services, on a particular trade, on shipping, finance, or military activities (garrison or arsenal), even on recreation or tourism. This functional specialization is often associated with paired cities—one member having economic and the other political functions (Milan and Rome, São Paolo and Rio de Janeiro) or one specialized and the other a diversified service provider (Liverpool and Manchester, Antwerp, and Brussels).

A subtle set of issues concerns the way a city's economic structure changes with time, the type of inquiry at the core of economic history. Do cities tend to remain balanced or specialized or do they change from one to the other? How persistent is a given specialization? Can cities trade places, with a major center losing to a once-lesser one? Among balanced cities, this sort of switching appears to be rare, but among specialized cities, especially in long-distance trade and finance, it has been common. Loss of preeminence in a particular activity may result in stagnation or decline, but it may also be offset by the rise of a new focus. Commerce may thus give way to finance or to manufacturing. Such questions need to be addressed in the context of the subject city's exchange partners and rivals, as discussed in a systems framework below.

Economic historians have examined many other aspects of urban economies, from mechanisms for provisioning to tax systems, housing regulation, policing (in both the narrow and the wider sense of ensuring order and stability), and political or administrative control of various activities. Specifically urban institutions—from pawnshops to craft guilds, fraternal societies, orphanages, retail establishments, and hospitals—have also been researched. Such institutions tend to offer long-lived, systematic written documentation in otherwise data-poor times and places. A general observation can be made about such institutions. Cities have clearly led in the development of modern forms and patterns of economic organization and behavior—rational calculation; formal recordkeeping and accounting; money and credit; highly elaborated goods; the systematic production, storage, and diffusion of knowledge and information. All these are highly urban, as are most organized markets and the legal and informational apparatus that supports them. Yet cities have also historically housed resistance to the free play of markets and the competition they imply. In part, this is because urban dwellers have enjoyed many privileges denied the bulk of the rural people in their society, whether because of feudal or similar constraints or simply for want of variety and quality of consumption goods. Correspondingly, city life is often marked by a vigorous defense of the monopoly power of urban guilds, the legal privileges of citizenship, and the rents denied from limiting access to markets.

Rent-seeking does not explain everything; urban environments also pose an inherent challenge to the smooth workings of markets, owing to high spatial density and forced interdependence. Externalities ("neighborhood effects") are not incidental but pervasive. Water supplies, arrangements for food and fuel, sanitation and fire protection, even noise and crime control are public goods in the urban framework—so are honest government, the maintenance of military security, and a proper balance between liveliness and order in festivities. By contrast with farm land, whose value depends primarily on its surface area and quality, though location also plays a part, a parcel of urban land gets most of its value from external factors, such as the prosperity of the city, nearness to the center, and the use made of adjacent parcels. A true laissez-faire economy is a near-impossibility, even without the economic rents that urban dwellers seek to capture or preserve. This longstanding ambivalence regarding the workings of the unseen hand goes some way toward explaining why the role of cities in economic development is difficult to depict.

A similar ambivalence characterizes urban economies and technology, since technological change has been a driving force in urbanization. Cities have provided and elaborated many innovations responsible for growth, not least bourses, banks, and mass literacy. Yet the technology of urban life in such areas as construction, transport, and hygiene seriously lagged behind that of manufacturing—and that was especially noticeable during the dynamic nineteenth century. The combination of slow progress in managing cities, rapid growth in urban populations, and the new hard-to-control production techniques is responsible for much of the congestion, degradation, and suffering that observers have noted in early industrial-era cities (which continues to taint capitalism in so many eyes). It took the dual development of the germ theory of disease and electricity to bring real improvement to urban life, although massive investments in infrastructure and administration, as well as political reform, were also necessary. By contrast, the technologies of the twentieth century, most notably the automobile, have gone far to eviscerate cities even as they spread the urban way of life to many outside them. Ironically, the automobile was once hailed as a solution to the traffic congestion and the pollution resulting from animal-powered urban transport (animal wastes befouled streets and made them slippery, causing accidents and traffic congestion).

Urban Systems. Cities live by exchange, and their dependence on outside provisioning must go beyond the kind of specialization and trade that would naturally occur within a family, an isolated village, or an estate like the medieval European manor. Urbanites, in other words, must do more than take in each others' laundry. In an economy that depends on consensual exchange, a city must overcome its inherently high costs of fixed investment, as well as provisioning and congestion. Its advantages to its inhabitants and to the administration (or value added) must therefore be positive and substantial. A city thus needs to mix "basic," or export-oriented activities, with internal ("nonbasic") services. For this reason and to make sense of the historical development of varied and complex arrays of cities in different countries or regions, the relationships that cities maintain with outside entities, as well as their internal organization, must be considered. As B. J. L. Berry put it, "Cities . . . [are] systems within systems of cities." (*Papers and Proceedings of the Regional Science Association* 13 (1964), pp. 147–163).

Four types of external urban relationships have been distinguished. The first is between the city and its surrounding countryside, source of at least some of its food, fuel, raw materials, population, and other necessities (water, straw, disposal sites, etc.). Cities do not always obtain their subsistence from, or provide services and goods only to, nearby areas, and this was true long before the age of railways and oil tankers. Thus rural areas with raw materials, goods, and services are likely to enter into exchanges with nearby towns.

The second type of external urban relationship involves the city with the larger territorial entity of which it typically is a part: a province, nation, empire, or other political unit. In the process of long-term economic development, urbanization has paralleled the development of the modern nation state, which claims political control over its cities while relying on and stimulating many of their functions. Throughout history, the relationships between territorial powers and any more or less autonomous cities have blended interdependence and bitter rivalry, and there was a range of "outcomes"—from highly centralized empires to true city-states to the recent absorption of Hong Kong (nominally a colony of Great Britain, effectively a city-state) by the large nation of China when the British colonial lease expired in 1997. Autonomous towns have fostered capitalism to the point that the relative independence of European cities, relative to those in Asia, is an important factor in the earlier onset of Europe's modern economic growth. Yet, in its early stages, the Industrial Revolution not only bypassed many of the established leading cities but took place at a time, and in places, where centralized nation-states (Britain, France, Prussia) managed to limit urban autonomy. By contrast, the former urban core of Europe, better able to preserve urban autonomy because it lay between contending territorial powers, lagged behind, except where large coal deposits attracted the new heavy industry.

The third set of relations that cities engage in, notably in the economic sphere, is with other cities. These relationships—involving flows of goods, payments, persons, and information—most clearly comprise the idea of an urban system. All the concepts that apply to interactions among units of the same type come into play: complementarity, rivalry, dominance, collusion, hierarchy, and so on. Going back to the ties between a town and its surrounding area, any nonroutine transaction will probably involve both the nearby market center and a larger "center of centers" that houses the specialized hospital, the wholesaler, or the investment bank. The administrative/judicial/political

World's Ten Largest Cities, 1500

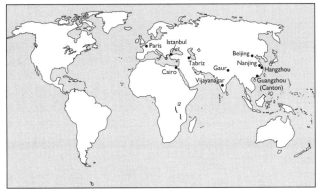

World's Ten Largest Cities, 1800

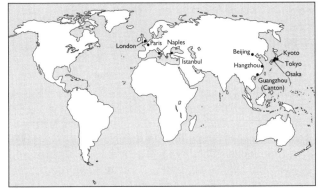

World's Ten Largest Cities, 1900

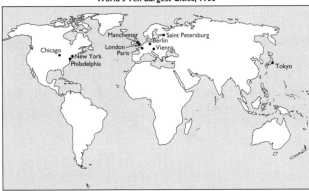

World's Ten Largest Cities, 2015 (estimates)

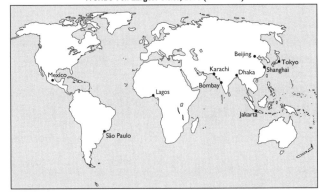

hierarchy also follows a branching tree of centers—out from the capital and back toward it. Larger cities also maintain close and complex relationships with far-flung correspondents, often other large cities. Networks of trade and finance have tied distant cities together at least since the Phoenicians sailed the ancient Mediterranean world; such networks have continued to flourish, or to adapt to difficulties, ever since. Colonial empires, caravan routes, urban leagues like the Hanse in late-medieval Europe, and the international financial empire of the Rothschilds, were built on such ties. Specialized interests have also forged links between and among cities, such as among royal courts or industrial centers, as well as between these and spas, resorts, universities, centers for the arts, theaters, libraries, and museums.

The fourth type of external urban relationship forges links between cities and distant nonurban places, such as mines, plantations, fisheries, and forests, which are not mediated by intervening cities. Typical would be the seventeenth- and eighteenth-century trade in tobacco or sugar between the French, English, or Dutch Atlantic and Channel ports and the plantations of the New World. Even so, for mines and plantations far from the coast, some colonial port would probably be used for transshipment, as was the case of the silver shipments to Spain from Peru or Mexico.

Given the importance of urban relations, and their consequences for urban economic fortunes and population size, how are cities linked into a system so that their properties and evolution may be studied? A size-distribution criterion has been used by some researchers to define an urban system—most notably a rank-size distribution, which supposedly characterizes a mature array of interacting elements that are subject to the many forces affecting their relative growth. The rank-size rule yields a stepwise distribution (one city of size p, and n cities of size p/n, where n goes from 2 to some lower urban threshold size, say 100 cities about 1 percent the size of the largest). With some "noise" in the distribution, a plot of rank (x) against the log of size (y) will approximate a straight line with a slope of -1. If the criterion holds, the range of the system can be determined empirically, by finding the geographic area whose cities fit the rule, be it a region, a nation, or a continent. Yet the logic behind the rank-size rule is far from compelling; it tends toward the conclusion that urban systems are comparatively recent, despite persuasive evidence of much earlier systematic links of the type outlined above.

The search for urban systems also uses spatial arrays that satisfy geometric patterns or that follow the topography of river basins. Those with geometric patterns are part of the *central-place system* (as elaborated in 1933 by

Walther Christaller, in *Central Places in Southern Germany*, translated by C. W. Baskin. Reprint, Englewood Cliffs, N.J., 1966). A site is central if it minimizes the average distance that economic agents must travel to reach it, whether to sell their crops or to obtain goods and services. A system arises insofar as central places (towns) trade among one another, with higher-order activities calling for "centers of centers." Economies of scale, of agglomeration (many producers or consumers of similar products), and of scope (related activities) underpin the model, in the sense that goods will be produced only where the demand justifies an adequate scale of production (considering the cost of spatial distribution). A complication of the model is that different functions (services, administration, transport), call for different spatial arrays of centers, while only one set of towns will develop in a given space, presumably a compromise among competing patterns. Since no ideal array can exist, path dependence, or historical specificity, remains a part of the picture in real-world central place systems. Although changes in efficient scale, economic structure, and institutions cause the system to evolve, the pull of the past, in the form of existing towns, remains strong. One seemingly robust trend, furthered by improvements in transport and not offset by increases in income and growing marketization (which intensify urban activities), has been steepening hierarchy in size distributions. This has often taken the form of *primacy*—with the largest city towering over the rest and many small places losing their centrality. In actuality, a central-place system will probably move toward a steeper size distribution than the rank-size rule predicts.

Many cities and groups of cities do not fit the central-place model, neither in the nature of their activities nor in their spatial groupings and size distributions. They can, however, usefully be seen as belonging to *networks*, with an emphasis on long-distance trade. Since water-borne commerce was able to overcome long distances much earlier than most land-based traffics (though caravans limited to carrying valuable commodities did so as well), most network cities, particularly the leading ones, have been ports, including some on rivers or lakes. Specializing in trade, finance, and trade-related processing industries, they maintain relations with specialized production sites and with other nodes and outposts of the networks. Inherently cosmopolitan, and needing at least a certain autonomy to compete successfully with rival poles, such cities could be more important than their size would suggest. For example, Amsterdam, when it dominated much of world trade in the seventeenth century, did not surpass 200,000 inhabitants. A city like London, however, capital of an empire and a leading port, has been at the summit of both sorts of urban system. Other cities have also been both nodal and central to varying degrees.

The above view of urban systems is not the only one, but it permits a system-based analysis of a wide variety of cases, certainly as far back as the Middle Ages or even ancient times, and over a range of countries and regions. Perhaps researchers should not ask whether, when, or where urban systems exist but, rather, what useful questions can be asked of historical evidence using a systems perspective.

Cities and Economic Development. What role have cities played in economic development? This question, posed at the beginning of the article, is considered here. Sustained growth in per capita incomes (*intensive* development as E. L. Jones calls it [in John Goodsblom, E. L. Jones, and Stephen Mennell's *Human History and Social Process*. Exeter, U.K., 1989]) ultimately results from advances in knowledge applied to economic activity, so cities have played a key role. The organizations that produce, transmit, record, or store knowledge have been primarily urban—printing and publishing, schools, libraries, museums, learned societies, and laboratories—as have been the major markets. Instruments, ships, and machine tools have mostly come from urban workshops. The innovators who propelled possible and profitable enterprise, who brought the love of adventure and risk into the toil of daily existence, who set higher store by calculation than by either pride or humility, by profit than by tradition, were also mostly urban and/or interacted in urban settings. What the pioneer sociologist Max Weber called the "spirit of capitalism" breathed city air.

Historically in the West, the initial working out of modern economic growth was done mainly outside established cities—although, in the process, that generated many agglomerated settlements that gradually took on more or less urban form. Knowledge had to be applied to natural resources: land, flowing and falling waters, deposits of minerals. Then investments and other fixed capital was needed for roads and, later, railways, dams, and ports. Crowded cities could not accommodate all forms of large-scale production, at least not without adding more disruption than urban elites and the authorities were prepared to countenance—whether from fire, fumes, and traffic or from unruly, demanding, potentially revolutionary workers. Most significantly, urban activity was traditionally regulated; that was to ensure quality but more often to restrict entry and otherwise limit competition. In surrounding villages and scattered cottages, there was cheap, undemanding labor, as well as the freedom from many labor regulations. Thus, well before the coming of mechanized factory industry, there was a move of manufactures outward from traditional urban craft centers to less regulated towns and to the countryside. This protoindustrial activity usually emphasized plain goods and relatively large quantities. It was organized by urban merchants, often entailed a complex division of labor with urban steps in the production process, and relied on cottage work. Farm families supplied labor in the off-season and year-round from partially redundant members (since age and sex mattered less than in farm work). Some have argued that what began as by-employment lightened controls on family formation and birth rates, which led to increased population densities that eventually made the handwork necessary for survival. The industrialization of rural areas (and the parallel development of urban workshops and nontraditional craft enterprises) generated a proletarianized workforce that became dependent on wages and therefore suitable for the discipline of factory work.

Despite the hardships of early industrial work, and the disamenity of living in towns that grew too fast, the flow of migrants to cities has not slackened since the nineteenth century; it is at least as strong today in third-world countries, where population growth has "benefited" from decreasing mortality brought by modern medicine and public health. Historically, protoindustrial activity loosened people's ties with the land, and its frequent displacement by factory-made goods finished the process of uprooting. At least that is the view of those who cannot believe that people would willingly move to congested, dangerous cities with chronically saturated labor markets. Since they keep arriving, greater motivation, powers of adaptation, and opportunities must exist (as well as a less idyllic view of rural life than researchers suggest). From the onset of mass rural-to-urban migration (including to overseas cities), many researchers have lamented the loss of rural vitality and its nefarious consequences, for morals and health, of the "rural exodus." In fact, in addition to many now-familiar urban ills, that population shift did empty some formerly well-populated countrysides—but for the most part in relatively poor agricultural areas. Still, the transitional difficulties, those aggravated by imbalances during business cycles, should not obscure technological and demand-structure changes that are associated with growth and that require a massive move from agriculture to manufacturing and services. The tendency for new migrants to concentrate in the largest metropolitan areas or only in some regions has prompted efforts at planned decentralization for regional balance in countries as varied as the Soviet Union and Great Britain—but market forces have tended to prevail.

Those in our own time who study economic development or who work to implement it have been suspicious of cities, especially of subsidies to urban production and consumption that drain human and financial capital at the expense of rural food producers. The past does not provide a simple answer to these fears—yet it offers no example of development without urbanization, as opposed to many cases of cities that foster change and enterprise.

[*See also* Internal Migration.]

BIBLIOGRAPHY

Bairoch, Paul. *Cities and Economic Development.* Chicago, 1988.
Braudel, Fernand. *Civilization and Capitalism.* 3 vols. Translated by Sîan Reynolds. New York, 1981–1984.
Chudacoff, Howard P., and J. E. Smith. *The Evolution of American Urban Society.* 5th ed. Upper Saddle River, N.J., 2000.
De Vries, Jan. *European Urbanization, 1500–1800.* Cambridge, Mass., 1984.
Fraser, Derek, and A. Sutcliffe, eds. *The Pursuit of Urban History.* London, 1983.
Gilbert, Alan. *The Latin American City.* London, 1994.
Hohenberg, Paul M., and Lynn Hollen Lees. *The Making of Urban Europe, 1000–1994.* Cambridge, Mass., 1995.
Holton, R. J. *Cities, Capitalism and Civilization.* London, 1986.
Mumford, Lewis. *The City in History.* New York, 1961.
Roberts, Hugh P. *An Urban Profile of the Middle East.* New York, 1979.
Skinner, G. William. *The City in Late Imperial China.* Stanford, Calif., 1977.
Vance, James A. *The Enduring City: Urban Morphology in Western Civilization.* Baltimore, 1990.
Van der Woude, Ad, et al., eds. *Urbanization in History: A Process of Dynamic Interactions.* Oxford, 1990.
Weber, Adna F. *The Growth of Cities in the Nineteenth Century.* [1899]. Reprint, Ithaca, N.Y., 1963.
Williamson, Jeffrey. *Coping with City Growth during the Industrial Revolution.* Cambridge, 1990.
Wrigley, A. E. *People, Cities and Wealth: The Transformation of Traditional Society.* Oxford, 1987.

PAUL M. HOHENBERG

URUGUAY. During the first decades after its independence, Uruguay suffered instability, precarious institutional building, and economic retardation. This was followed by a period of rapid economic growth from 1860 to 1910, led by the export of livestock products.

Productivity grew as a result of the steamship revolution, which reduced the price spread between Europe and America. Meanwhile, railways contributed to the unification of domestic markets and reduced domestic transport costs. The diffusion and adaptation to domestic conditions of universal innovations in cattle breeding and services increased productivity. There was a slow but constant process of institutional building and a strengthening of the coercive power of the state. In this period, Uruguayan population grew rapidly (a result of high natural rates and Latin immigration), and so did per capita output.

Wool, hides, and leather were exported mainly to Europe; salted beef (*tasajo*) was exported to Brazil and Cuba. Cattle breeding (mixed cattle and sheep) was intensive in natural resources and dominated by large estates. By the 1880s, the agrarian frontier was exhausted, and labor began to concentrate in urban areas, especially the port city of Montevideo, which played an important role as a regional (supranational) commercial center. By 1908, it contained 40 percent of the population and accounted for the bulk of all services, state employees, and the weak handicraft-featured manufacturing sector. Uruguay then had per capita income levels similar to the European leaders, real wages slightly lower, and a pattern of income distribution and educational attainment decidedly less equal than Europe's.

After the 1910s, the basis for Uruguayan competitiveness started changing. As the benefits of the old technological paradigm were eroding, the new one was not particularly beneficial for resource-intensive countries such as Uruguay. International demand shifted away from primary consumption, the population of Europe grew slowly, and European countries struggled for self-reliance in primary production in a context of soaring world productive capacity. In the 1920s, the cattle breeding sector showed a poor performance, owing to a lack of innovation away from natural pastures. In the 1930s, its performance deteriorated further, and export volumes stagnated until the 1970s, while purchasing power fluctuated with the volatile terms of trade.

The Uruguayan economy grew inward until the 1950s. The multiple exchange rate system was the main economic policy tool. Immigration ceased and natural population increases declined. Agrarian production was reoriented toward wool, crops, dairy products, and other industrial input. The manufacturing sector grew fast and diversified significantly, although it remained mainly light industry, without capital goods or technology-intensive sectors. Productivity growth depended upon technology transfers embodied in capital-goods imports and an intensive domestic adaptation process of mature technologies. Domestic demand grew also through an expanding public sector. The terms of trade regulated protectionism, productivity growth, and domestic demand. By the mid-1950s and relative to the European countries, Uruguayan per capita gross domestic product (GDP) had deteriorated somewhat, and the wage level, income distribution, and levels of educational attainment all had improved. Rent-seeking practices and a weak state, crowded by politically recruited voters, directed structural change toward inefficient management and extreme protectionism.

The obvious limits to inward-looking growth of a country with only 2 million inhabitants were exacerbated in the late 1950s as terms of trade deteriorated. Increasing social conflicts, complicated by strident ideological confrontation, could not be handled by the *clientelist* political system.

The dictatorship of 1973–1985 introduced a period of increasing openness and deregulation that continues in the present. A dynamic integration into the world market is still lacking. A first attempt to return to cattle breeding exports was hindered by the oil crisis. A raw-material- and cheap labor-based nontraditional industry was stimulated by the dictatorship, until the monetarist approach relied on fluent petrodollars in search of stability. Democratic regimes since 1985 have combined natural-resource-intensive exports to the region and other emergent markets with a modest intraindustrial trade mainly with Argentina and with financial capital inflow.

By the 1990s, Uruguay had a much worse position in relation to the leaders of the world economy in per capita GDP, real wage levels, equity in income distribution, and education than it had fifty years ago. The Mercosur project is still mainly oriented to price competitiveness and highly dependent on foreign capital inflow.

[*See also* Spain, *subentry on* Spanish Empire.]

BIBLIOGRAPHY

Barrán, José P., and Benjamín Nahúm. *Historia rural del Uruguay moderno*. 7 vols. Montevideo, 1967–1978.
Barrán, José P., and Benjamín Nahúm. *Batlle, los Estancieros y el Imperio Británico*. 7 vols. Montevideo, 1979–1985.
Bértola, Luis. *The Manufacturing Industry of Uruguay, 1913–1961: A Sectoral Approach to Growth, Fluctuations and Crisis*. Göteborg, Sweden, and Stockholm, 1990.
Bértola, Luis. *El PBI uruguayo 1870–1936 y otras estimaciones*. Montevideo, 1998.
Bértola, Luis. *Ensayos de historia económica: Uruguay en la región y el mundo*. Montevideo, 2000.
Finch, Henry. *A Political Economy of Uruguay since 1870*. London and Basingstoke, U.K., 1981.
Jacob, Raúl. *Depresión ganadera y desarrollo fabril*. Montevideo, 1981.
Jacob, Raúl. *Modelo Batllista: ¿Variación sobre un viejo tema?* Montevideo, 1988.

LUIS BÉRTOLA

USHER, A. P. (1883–1965), American economic historian.

The Harvard scholar Abbott Payson Usher will be remembered chiefly for three major monographs: *The History of the Grain Trade in France, 1400–1740* (Cambridge, Mass., 1913); *The Early History of Deposit Banking in Mediterranean Europe* (Cambridge, Mass., 1943); and *A History of Mechanical Inventions* (New York and Cambridge, Mass., 1929; 2d rev. ed., 1954; republished, 1988).

Usher began his scholarly career in 1905 with an article on the French Corn Laws that a few years later would lead to his book on the grain trade in France. Central in this still useful book are analyses of the organization of the market and the regulation of the grain trade. Although Usher would retain an interest in the subject, with subsequent publications on market speculation, food supply, and wheat prices, he soon became attracted to other topics. A research trip to Barcelona in 1929 allowed him to collect the material for an impressive book on the early history of deposit banking in Catalonia between 1240 and 1723. Although the subsequent volume, on the history of Italian banking, never appeared, Usher had completely reshaped the discipline with his knowledge of technology and modern financial theory.

But above all Usher was one of the pioneers of the history of technology. Together with such historians as Louis C. Hunter, Lewis Mumford, and Lynn White Jr., he further broadened a discipline that German engineeers had developed in the late nineteenth century. In what is perhaps his most important and certainly his most influential book (*A History of Mechanical Inventions*), Usher carefully examined the origins and development of inventions such as textile machinery, water wheels and windmills, clocks and watches, printing, and machine tools, always in the wider context of institutions, markets, banks, business firms, and public regulation. Here the history of technology is not merely the analysis of the accomplishments of individual inventors, but the explanation of the reasons for the progress of inventions.

Both in his own research and in his writings on theoretical and methodological issues, Usher showed a clear preference for empirical work. He did not like the general stage theories developed by Marxists, by the representatives of the Historical School (such as Karl Bücher, Gustav von Schmoller, and Werner Sombart) or by sociologists like Max Weber. At the same time, he also reacted sharply against the descriptive approach used by older economic historians (for example, John Clapham), which he called "unscientific." Although admiring the historical skill of these scholars, he accused them of not paying attention to quantification, economic theory, and causal reasoning. Usher himself, on occasion, has been accused of having always studied limited economic activities in the past (banking, specific inventions) and, even more, tangible objects with physical magnitudes that could be approached in exactly the same way as the engineer solves a mechanical problem. However true, the reproach certainly does not take into account the theoretical articles noted above, nor does it do justice to more general works, such as *An Introduction to the Industrial History of England* (1920) or *An Economic History of Europe since 1750* (1937, with W. Bowden and M. Karpovich).

Usher retired from Harvard in 1949, but continued to work and publish (for example, the important chapter on "Machines and Toolmaking" for *A History of Technology*, edited by Charles Singer) and teach (as a visiting professor at the universities of Wisconsin and Yale). He died on 18 June 1965. A few years earlier, the Society for the History of Technology established an annual Abbott Payson Usher Prize. In 1963, Usher received the Leonardo da Vinci Medal, the highest recognition from this society, to honor his outstanding contribution to the history of technology.

BIBLIOGRAPHY

J. C. B. Mohr, ed. *Architects and Craftsmen in History: Festschrift für Abbott Payson Usher*. Tübingen, 1956. Includes an important article on Usher by William N. Parker.

Smith, Thomas M. "Memorial: Abbott Payson Usher (1883–1965)." *Technology and Culture: The International Quarterly of the Society for the History of Technology* 6.4 (1965), 630–632.

De Roover, Raymond. "Review of *The Early History of Deposit Banking in Mediterranean Europe*." *Journal of Political Economy* 52 (1944), 367–368.

ERIK AERTS

USURY was defined historically as a charge for a loan. It denoted any rate of interest, not simply one that was excessive or illegal, and applied to loans of money and other fungibles, that is, things whose use consists of their consumption, such as grain and oil. Ordinary commercial profits and penalties for late repayment of loans were not considered usury.

Usury was permitted by Roman law but prohibited by Judaism, Christianity, and Islam. The Jewish prohibition derives from *Exodus* 22.25 and *Leviticus* 25.37, which forbade money loans at interest to fellow Jews, and *Deuteronomy* 23.19, which extended the ban to other goods. Usury ("excess") is also condemned in several passages of the Koran, most notably 3.130: "O you who believe, devour not excess, doubling and redoubling." Talmudic law extended the prohibition to possessory mortgages, partnerships in which only one party supplied the capital, and transactions in which usury was disguised as a price element, such as deferred-payment sales. Islamic jurisprudence added currency exchanges concealing interest and discounts for delayed delivery. The earliest Christian usury laws date from the Councils of Arles (314) and Nicea (325), which deposed clerics who lent at interest. The church fathers Ambrose (died 397), Jerome (died 420), and Pope Leo I (died 461) urged a universal ban; but the Christian emperors were reluctant to break with Roman legal and commercial practice. Constantine (died 337) confirmed the traditional maximum interest rate of 12 percent a year, reduced by Justinian (died 565) to 6 percent for commercial and 4 percent for consumption loans.

Usury remained legal in Byzantium, but in western Europe the prohibition was extended to the laity by Charlemagne at the Council of Aachen (789). It was, however, rarely invoked until the revival of trade in the twelfth century intensified the demand for credit. The church reacted to the new economic conditions at the Third Lateran Council (1179) and the Second Council of Lyons (1274), which deprived usurers of the sacraments, burial, and the capacity to make a valid will unless they first repaid interest to their debtors. The Council of Vienne (1311) excommunicated public authorities who licensed usurers and made it a heresy to maintain that usury was not a sin. The popes also ruled against several transactions designed to evade the prohibition, such as sales on credit, sales that concealed loans on security, and partnerships in which risk was unevenly shared. Similar measures were adopted by local synods and enforced in diocesan courts. The legal campaign was complemented by popular preachers, such as Jacques de Vitry (died 1240?), who denounced usurers and illustrated their damnation in lurid detail. Philosophers and theologians, such as Thomas Aquinas (died 1274) and Gerard of Siena (died 1336?), developed arguments to show that usury was a violation of natural law, a process aided by the recovery of Aristotle's *Politics*, where money is portrayed as a sterile medium of exchange rather than a source of profit in itself.

The rationale for the usury prohibition in all three religious traditions was the protection of the poor against exploitation, although in the Christian west it also reflected the hostility of feudal landowners and the clergy toward the new urban commercial classes. Its practical effects, however, are difficult to assess. The absence of formal credit institutions in the Islamic Middle East was probably due less to the prohibition than to the personal, informal character of commercial networks. By contrast, economic activity in western Europe was heavily dependent on access to credit. Pawnbrokers and moneylenders provided consumption loans at rates ranging from 12 to 43 percent a year. Because the Pentateuchal injunctions applied only within the Jewish community, such "public" usurers were often Jews; but in northern Europe Italians dominated the trade by the fourteenth century. Unpopular and barely tolerated, public usurers were often subject to violence, expropriation, and expulsion; and Christian moneylenders were also liable to prosecution in church courts and to legal penalties for usury. Merchant bankers, who lent capital to fellow merchants, and moneychangers, who provided exchange and deposit services, escaped more lightly than moneylenders because their activities were confined to restricted circles and cloaked under licit transactions, such as the bill of exchange. They were morally obliged to make restitution of illicit profits, but this could be enforced only through confession as a condition of absolution. Nevertheless, in the popular imagination the line dividing the merchant from the moneylender was vague: the usurers the poet Dante (1265–1321) consigned to Hell were all merchants (*Inferno* 17:43–78) and examples of restitution in surviving testaments show that even merchants as prominent as the Medici were sensitive to accusations of usury. It is also argued that the stigma attached to usury had the effect of focusing medieval banking on exchange, and that the prohibition retarded the development of capital markets by channeling wealth into religious bequests rather than productive investment.

In Europe, several factors contributed to the erosion of the usury prohibition. Purgatory, a state of purification after death defined in the thirteenth century, opened a route to salvation for repentant usurers. The policies of secular rulers were often at odds with church teaching. Public usurers usually operated under royal or municipal license, and the French kings regularly sanctioned interest rates of 16 to 20 percent in the fourteenth century. Florence, Venice, and Genoa openly paid investors 5 to 15 percent interest on public debt shares. Several theorists, notably the church lawyer Hostiensis (died 1271) and the theologians Peter John Olivi (1248–1298) and Bernardino of Siena (1380–1444), proposed grounds for compensatory interest that distinguished loans intended for commerce from consumption loans. The general reception of such views, however, was slow. With the exception of John Calvin (1509–1564), who endorsed interest on business loans, the Protestant reformers uniformly condemned the taking of usury. Nevertheless, by 1600 most Protestant jurisdictions allowed moderate interest on loans. The Catholic church tacitly abandoned the medieval prohibition in the early nineteenth century and formally redefined usury as an excessive rate of interest in the 1917 *Code of Canon Law*. The usury prohibition in its traditional form, however, remains in force in conservative Islamic jurisdictions.

BIBLIOGRAPHY

Galassi, Francesco L. "Buying a Passport to Heaven: Usury, Restitution, and the Merchants of Medieval Genoa." *Religion* 22 (1992), 313–326. Presents evidence that the usury prohibition constrained the development of capital markets in medieval Genoa.

Gilchrist, John T. *The Church and Economic Activity in the Middle Ages*. London, Melbourne, and Toronto, 1969. A basic introduction to the medieval church's economic teachings with a valuable appendix of documents in translation.

Helmholz, Richard H. "Usury and the Medieval English Church Courts." *Speculum* 61 (1986), 364–380. One of the few studies of the enforcement of the usury prohibition.

Kirshner, Julius. "Reading Bernardino's Sermon on the Public Debt." In *Atti del simposio internazionale cateriniano-bernardiniano: Siena, 17–20 Aprile 1980*, edited by Domenico Maffei and Paolo Nardi, pp. 547–622. Siena, 1982. Standard study of the controversy over usury and the public debts of Italian city-states.

Langholm, Odd. *Economics in the Medieval Schools: Wealth, Exchange, Value, Money and Usury According to the Paris Theological Tradition, 1200–1350*. Leiden, 1992. Most recent and comprehensive survey of scholastic economic theory, incorporating several sources unknown to Noonan.

Le Goff, Jacques. *Your Money or Your Life: Economy and Religion in the Middle Ages*, translated by Patricia Ranum. New York, 1988. Provocative study of changing social and religious attitudes toward usurers in the High Middle Ages.

McLaughlin, Terence P. "The Teaching of the Canonists on Usury (XII, XIII and XIV Centuries)." *Medieval Studies* 1 (1939), 81–147; 2 (1940), 1–22. Standard study of the canon law of usury.

Nelson, Benjamin. *The Idea of Usury: From Tribal Brotherhood to Universal Otherhood*. 2d ed. Chicago and London, 1969. Influential sociological account of the usury prohibition from ancient Judaism to modernity.

Noonan, John T., Jr. *The Scholastic Analysis of Usury*. Cambridge, Mass., 1957. Standard history of the Christian usury prohibition from the Middle Ages to modernity; should now be supplemented by Langholm and Spicciani.

Roover, Raymond de. *The Rise and Decline of the Medici Bank, 1397–1494*. Cambridge, Mass., 1963. Argues that the usury prohibition diverted medieval banking into exchange rather than pure credit transactions.

Shatzmiller, Joseph. *Shylock Reconsidered: Jews, Moneylending, and Medieval Society*. Berkeley, Los Angeles, and Oxford, 1990. Microhistorical study of a Jewish moneylender in fourteenth-century Marseilles.

Spicciani, Amleto. *Capitale e interesse tra mercatura e povertà nei teologi e canonisti dei secoli, XIII–XV*. Rome, 1990. Most recent study of the concepts of capital and interest in late medieval theology and law; an important supplement to Noonan.

Udovitch, Abraham L. "Bankers without Banks: Commerce, Banking, and Society in the Islamic World of the Middle Ages." In the Center for Medieval and Renaissance Studies UCLA, ed., *The Dawn of Modern Banking*, pp. 255–273. New Haven, Conn., and London, 1979. Provocative analysis of Islamic banking that downplays the importance of the Islamic usury prohibition.

LAWRIN ARMSTRONG

UZBEKISTAN. *see* Central Asia *and* Russia, *subentry on* Russian Empire

V

VANDERBILT FAMILY. The Vanderbilt family was one of the richest and best known families in the United States throughout the nineteenth and early twentieth centuries. The fortune of this colorful family, whose members collected art, engaged in yachting and horse breeding, and built grand mansions, came mainly from the steamship and railroad industries. Although they were competitive businessmen who always considered their own welfare first, the Vanderbilts became famous for their generosity and philanthropic activities.

Cornelius Vanderbilt. A highly competent self-made businessman and entrepreneur, Cornelius ("Commodore") Vanderbilt (1794–1877) was the first family member to become rich. Born in Staten Island, New York, he bought a small boat at age sixteen and began transporting passengers to and from New York City. During this time, he gained a reputation for honesty and reliability. In 1818, he began to work for a steamboat owner and in 1829, already a rich man, he decided to work on his own. Vanderbilt started a ship line from New York to Philadelphia before moving to the Hudson River and later to Long Island Sound. His strategy was to cut costs and prices below those of his competitors and to maintain a highly reliable service. More than once, his competitors bribed him to move his business elsewhere.

By 1848, Vanderbilt had already become a millionaire, but his competitive nature pushed him to the next adventure. The discovery of gold in California created a new demand for voyages from the East Coast to California, but existing routes were long and dangerous. Establishing the American Atlantic and Pacific Ship Canal Company in 1849, and the Accessory Transit Company (ATC) in 1851, Vanderbilt opened a new route passing through Nicaragua instead of Panama, which shortened the trip substantially and made it less hazardous. In the early 1860s, Vanderbilt quit the steamship industry and moved into railroads. By 1867, after gaining control of the Harlem Railroad, he had become the president of both the Hudson River Railroad and the New York Central, and then he merged the two. Vanderbilt failed to gain control of the Erie Railroads, but succeeded in connecting New York City to Chicago and in turning New York Central into the world's first four-track road. His contribution to the development of the transport

CORNELIUS VANDERBILT. Portrait by Nathaniel Jocelyn (1796–1881). (National Portrait Gallery, Smithsonian Institution, Washington, D.C./Art Resource, NY)

system of the northwest United States and southern Ontario was crucial, because many of his railways persisted long after he died. In 1873, he contributed $1 million to establish Vanderbilt University. Leaving behind an estate worth $100 million, the "Commodore" died as the richest man in the United States of his time.

William Henry Vanderbilt. William Henry Vanderbilt (1821–1885), the eldest of thirteen children, inherited most of his father's empire, but not before proving himself a competent businessman. In 1864, he was appointed vice-president of the New York and Harlem Railroad, and then, upon his father's death, became the president of the New York Central. He founded the College of Physicians and Surgeons, which is now part of the Health Sciences Division of Columbia University, and generously contributed to Vanderbilt University and Saint Bartholomew's Church as well as to other institutions. Expanding the family's railroad system, William Henry Vanderbilt doubled his father's fortune and left most of his estate to his sons Cornelius and William Kissam.

Cornelius Vanderbilt II, George Washington Vanderbilt, and Descendants. Cornelius Vanderbilt II (1843–1899), who started as an assistant treasurer of the New York and Harlem Railroad in 1865, became the chairman of the board of directors of the New York Central in 1883. Donating to various institutions, particularly to charities, Cornelius died at 56, leaving behind more than $50 million, most of it to one of his sons, Alfred Gwynne Vanderbilt. William Kissam Vanderbilt (1849–1920), who initiated the family's tradition of building luxurious houses, was a leading yachtsman and was active in the management of the family railroad business, especially after the death of his brother Cornelius II. George Washington Vanderbilt (1862–1914) was the youngest son of William Henry. A man of books and fond of art, he is famous for building the Biltmore estate in North Carolina in 1895, which was a grand country house and an important architectural creation.

Among fourth-generation family members, the better known are Cornelius II's children, Gertrude Vanderbilt Whitney (1875–1942), who organized art exhibitions and was a patron of American art, and Cornelius Vanderbilt III (1873–1942), who was a talented inventor. Consuelo Vanderbilt (1877–1964), William Kissam's daughter, became famous for being forced to marry a duke she did not love. Her brother, Harold Stirling "Mike" Vanderbilt (1884–1970), was a talented yachtsman who won the America's Cup three times and invented the game of contract bridge.

BIBLIOGRAPHY

Auchincloss, Louis. *The Vanderbilt Era: Profiles of a Gilded Age*. New York, 1989.

Croffut, William A. *The Vanderbilts and the Story of Their Fortune*. Chicago, 1886.

Lane, Wheaton J. *Commodore Vanderbilt: An Epic of the Steam Age*. New York, 1942.

Smith, Arthur D. Howden. *Commodore Vanderbilt*. London, 1928.

Wayne, Andrews. *The Vanderbilt Legend: The Story of the Vanderbilt Family, 1794–1940*. New York, 1941.

RAN ABRAMITZKY

VEBLEN, THORSTEIN (1857–1929), American economist.

During the thirty years that he held academic posts at the University of Chicago, Stanford University, the University of Missouri, and the New School for Social Research in New York, Veblen became the most influential and best-known dissenting economist in the United States. Veblen's heterodoxy was widely recognized by economists and sociologists after the publication of his *Theory of the Leisure Class* (1899), in which he developed his theory of status emulation. In this satirical study of the leisure class and the underlying social strata that emulate it, he argued that conspicuous consumption, conspicuous waste, and ostentatious avoidance of useful work were practices by which social status was enhanced.

As an economic historian and theorist of growth, Veblen is best known for his "institutionalism." In one sense, the term is misleading, because Veblen was critical of existing institutions, owing to their inhibitive impact on technological change. In his theory of cultural lag, he develops the idea that institutions are inhibitory and backward-looking, whereas science and technology are dynamic and oriented toward change. The question is whether institutions were or are sufficiently malleable to permit efficient exploitation of existing technological potential. As the "tool continuum" evolves, it may become absorptive of culturally cross-fertilized processes, which bring together more and different tools and make possible new technologies. Veblen explained the economic history of the West by linking cultural anthropology and social history with changes in the technoeconomic base; the main variables in his explanation are the degree of institutional rigidity and the force exerted on it by technology.

Veblen's theory of economic history was closely linked with his ideas regarding economic waste. He argued that the rate of economic growth cannot be maximized if all output is not serviceable and if efficiency is sacrificed to pecuniary interests. The rate of maximum growth is governed by technological advance, which controls the size of a nation's economic surplus, although this rate is also a matter of the disposition of the surplus between serviceable and disserviceable uses. In short, Veblen incorporated a theory of waste—that is, unproductive consumption, investment, and labor—within his theory of social change; this permitted him to show the conditions under which economic growth will stagnate and, also, the conditions under which growth will not contribute to the economic welfare of the community. The concept of economic efficiency was thus clarified and linked with the processes of social change and noninvidious economic growth.

Veblen's second book, *The Theory of Business Enterprise* (1904), contains his explanation of business cycles and an extended treatment of the cultural and social psychological significance of the machine process. Contrary to conventional analyses of business cycles, Veblen saw no natural equilibrating tendencies in the U.S. economy. Instead, he argued that instability was endemic in the U.S. business system, because of excessive capitalization and credit inflation. His analysis focused on the tendency of firms to borrow too much by exaggerating their future earning power.

nonpredatory traits; in short, the extent to which the sporting and pecuniary instincts have influenced the instincts of idle curiosity, parenthood, and workmanship.

Veblen's rejection of neoclassical value theory did not end in nihilism, for he outlined an alternative to both neoclassicism and classical Marxism. He wrote of the "generic ends" of life "impersonally considered" and of "fullness of life," which in his evolutionary—that is, "Darwinian"—mode of analysis, implied the existence of some transcultural set of values. What Veblen took from Charles Darwin's approach was not the conservative "social Darwinism," which glorified competition and economic predation, but a human sense of peacableness, critical intelligence, altruism, and proficiency of workmanship. Veblen's method studies humanity in its process of continuous adaptation to both its social and natural environment, and he sees the conditions of human existence as subject to ceaseless change. Yet he recognized that atavistic continuities, that is, "imbecile institutions," such as institutional religion and absentee ownership of property, might persist indefinitely. Thus, for Veblen, no socially consummatory or static condition of human existence lay on the horizon.

BIBLIOGRAPHY

Dente, Leonard. *Veblen's Theory of Social Change*. Introduction by James F. Becker. New York, 1977.
Diggins, John P. *Thorstein Veblen: Theorist of the Leisure Class*. Princeton, 1999.
Dorfman, Joseph. *Thorstein Veblen and His America*. New York, 1966.
Tilman, Rick. *Thorstein Veblen and His Critics, 1891–1963*. Princeton, 1992.
Tilman, Rick. *The Intellectual Legacy of Thorstein Veblen: Unresolved Issues*. Westport, Conn., 1996.

RICK TILMAN

THORSTEIN VEBLEN. Bronze sculpture (1982) by Bonnie Veblen Chancellor. (National Portrait Gallery, Smithsonian Institution, Washington, D.C./Art Resource, NY)

At some point, their creditors would recognize that loans made to these firms were unwarranted, because their earning power was less than anticipated. The loans would then be called in, with the inevitable consequences of liquidation and bankruptcy. A protracted period of economic depression would follow, characterized by large-scale unemployment and unused industrial capacity. Gradually, however, the earning power and credit rating of the firm would move toward convergence, so recovery would occur. A period of prosperity would then ensue until overcapitalization again occurred and the cycle was repeated.

Economic historians have responded sympathetically to such Veblenian concepts as "the penalty for taking the lead" in industrialization; the notion of "trained incapacity"; and the idea of "conscientious withdrawal of efficiency," which he used to explain retardation of economic growth. Veblen's erudition was evident in his further development of the phases through which he believed humanity had evolved—these included the savage, barbarian, handicraft, and industrial stages. What separates these stages from one another, in addition to the level of economic development they have reached, is the degree to which the predatory instincts have contaminated the peaceful or

VEGECULTURE. Vegeculture is largely the cultivation of corms and tubers of the *Araceae* (carohydrate-rich staple tropical crops like taro), *Dioscoreaceae* (yam), and *Zingiberaceae* (rhizomatous plants like ginger) families. Scholars have concluded that rhizomatous, cormous, and tuberous plant species were first cultivated in the humid tropics where their wild ancestors were distributed, rather than in the seasonally dry tropics, and adapted for longevity. They also recognize that a few dicotyledonous roots and tubers emerged in climatically seasonal environments.

Southeast Asia. Vegeculture originated in Southeast Asia in the humid tropics even though the distribution of nonseasonal rain forests and the changing pattern of sea-level and rain-forest distribution of our time may have left isolated populations of plants suited to both the humid tropics and the seasonal environments. The cultivation of cormous, tuberous, and rhizomatous crops was a progression from the wild populations that were found in isolated pockets of human activity central to Southeast Asian vegeculture. Oceanic agrarian systems were dominated to a large extent by root crops, and people established farms on small coral atolls and places where sandy soil permitted the growth of the coconut palm and other plants. The Polynesians dug pits, filled them with earth and humus, and turned them into gardens for the cultivation of breadfruit, taro, and other tubers. They cultivated yam species in the same way, thus creating ecological islands where re-created soil conditions permitted crop cultivation. These small plots produced enough for families. Because of a social system of obligations and reciprocity, such foodstuffs as sweet potatoes, manioc, second-grade taros and yams, papayas, bananas, and other crops were planted after the ceremonial tubers had been harvested.

Agriculture succeeded cultivation after domestication of these crops, and though native to tropical nonseasonal forests of the region, these roots and tubers have evolved to survive in seasonal tropics. Tuberous, rhizomatous, and cormous plants provided platforms for the growth of adventitious roots whose increased water intake and greater support permitted continuous growth in the tropical rain forest. Dormant apical buds replaced the parent plant laterally or vertically and enabled a continuous supply of buds that developed into shoots.

Vegecultural systems were frequently more diverse than grain-based systems. Many tropical vegecultural plants underwent morphological adaptations, which provided for mechanical protection, and thus established well-developed chemical defense systems as incidental domestication phased into specialized domestication. Southeast Asia boasted of a rich variety of root and tuber crops, fruits, and nuts. Staples that were vegetatively reproduced include taro (*Colocasia esculenta*), arrowroot (*Tacca leontopetaloides*), and yam (*Dioscorea alata, D. esculenta*). The major fruit and nut-producing species were the breadfruit (*Artocarpus communis*), jackfruit (*A. integrifolia*), coconut (*Cocos nucifera*), and sago palm (*Metroxylon*).

These root crops were adapted to survive long seasons and, therefore, were first domesticated in zones where dry seasons extended for more than three months. Other fruit and nut trees emerged in the margins of forests, along streams, and in clearings with adequate sunlight. Evidence has been adduced to show the emergence of indigenous agriculture before the introduction of rice into Southeast Asia. The discovery of buried meter-deep channels extending for a considerable distance in a New Guinea basin, while inconclusive, seems to suggest human construction and the probability of early root cultivation. Some archaeologists point to these as indications of efforts to modify the New Guinea landscape. Disturbance of pollen sequences some thirty thousand years old and the existence of large ground stone axes dating to about twenty-six thousand years are adduced as evidence of hunter-gatherers using stone tools to produce favored crops.

In Polynesia, the staple food plants were taro, banana, and breadfruit (*Artocarpus communis*). Whereas breadfruit dominated in the Marquesas, taros predominated in the southeastern Cook Islands. Breadfruit, the "staff of life" of Polynesia, was first seen by European travelers (Magellan, Queiros, Dampier) from the sixteenth century onward. These travelers found in Polynesia traditional food plants, including yams, bananas, coconuts, sweet potatoes, breadfruit, and arrowroot. Tree fruits, such as apples and breadfruits contributed to the agricultural system without being herbaceous plants. The latter occupied an important place in the diet of the South Pacific islanders. Captain Bligh, after a fruitless 1878 attempt, finally delivered breadfruit seedlings in Jamaica after West Indian planters petitioned King George II for breadfruit's introduction into the Caribbean as a cheap and nourishing food for slaves. Over time, the breadfruit, a Polynesian staple, became a Caribbean staple, too.

The coconut, a tall stately, monocotyledonous tree, is believed to have originated in the Indo-Malayan region and to the northwest of New Guinea—more than eighty insects associated with the coconut originated from there. It grew predominantly on shores, and ocean currents became a major agent of dispersal to tropical and subtropical lands, supplemented in a large part by human cultivation. The major coconut-producing areas of the world are the Malay Archipelago, Southeast Asian countries, India, Sri Lanka, Pacific Territories, East Africa, West Africa, Central and South America. Growing generally to 24 meters (nearly 80 feet) in height, the coconut's adventitious, fibrous roots, continually produced from a bulbous stem, are constantly replaced as they reach their maximum diameter quickly, and they die off. The tree thrives in warm, wet tropical climates with a minimum annual rainfall of 1250 millimeters (50 inches) evenly distributed, and high temperatures of 27 to 35 degrees Celsius.

South America. Farming societies had been long established in many parts of the Americas by the time the first Europeans arrived. In the vast tropical lowlands of South America, hunter-gatherers domesticated a variety of plants, including such root crops as manioc (*Manihot esculenta*) and sweet potato (*Ipomoea batatas*). There is little information about the archaeological record of this lowland rain forest agriculture, but the evidence shows that a distinctive highland agriculture unique to the Andes between 5,000 and 4,000 years ago, led to the emergence of the Inca and such plants as potatoes and quinoa. Though the Amazon forests have generally been proposed as the earliest center of agriculture in the Americas, the spine of the Andes has been largely regarded as the site of the emergence of distinctive agricultural economies based on high-altitude species of plants, such as potato and quinoa.

There is, however, little evidence as to whether they developed separately, were developed by different societies, or were part of the same developmental process. Of the four major tuber species domesticated in the Andes, the potato (*Solanum tuberosum*) has become a major food crop throughout the world. Studies of present-day wild and domestic potato point to a central Andes origin. Though the Lake Titicaca basin appears to be the place where potatoes were first cultivated, the *Solanum stenotomum* species grown in southern Peru and Bolivia are believed to be modern representatives of the earliest-known species. The potato was introduced into Europe in the sixteenth century and spread to many places before the Irish potato blight of the 1840s and other diseases almost killed it in Europe. About twenty desiccated and shrunken tubers believed to date between 4,000 and 3,200 years ago, found at the mouth of the Casma Valley in the Andes, proved to be potatoes on analysis. In the valleys and basins of the of the Andes, open-air settlements of societies that made the transition from herding to a farming way of life provide records of plant and animal domestication.

From Peru, Chile, and Mexico (where it was growing wild), the potato was introduced into Spain (in the sixteenth century), into England from Virginia by Sir Walter Raleigh (in 1586), and over the next century spread until the ravages of the Great Famine in Ireland in 1845.

West Africa. Scholars believe that the agricultural system of the forest margin complex first started in the savanna-forest zone and spread into the forest. Crops of the forest margin complex include kola, akee apples, and the African yam. The yam tubers, propagated vegetatively each year, are not truly annuals, but they annually mobilize food reserves at the beginning of the rainy season and store them for later use. This is an adaptation to savanna climates with pronounced dry seasons. Similarly, the African oil palm (*Elaeis guineensis*) a major source of oil (belonging to the palmae family with more than 225 genera and more than 2,600 species), has close ties to the savanna environment and thrives in regions with equitable rainfall distribution and a short dry season. It cannot do well in the dense rain forest, and as a wild plant it was more at home at the edge of the forest.

While some scholars maintain the American origin of the oil palm due to its spontaneous growth in coastal Brazil, many scholars accept the West African origin of the tropical palm—in a belt stretching from Senegal to Angola, and the Ruzizi plains between Lake Kivu and Lake Nyasa and on the Congo (now Zaire)-Uganda border. During the slave trade, it became widely established in Brazil; and in the 1960s, oil palm plantations developed in Latin America, having been introduced into Malaya from West Africa.

The oil palm grows in high rainfall tropical areas with 1500 millimeters (60 inches) of evenly distributed rain and temperatures of 27 to 35 degrees Celsius and high relative humidity. Though it is a lowland crop with a fibrous root system, it can also grow well up to an altitude of 900 meters (2,970 feet), certainly an adaptation to the forest-savanna farming complex.

Vegeculture, evolved as an adaptive strategy to ensure long life or long survival by tuberous plants, especially in humid tropical forests. Since yield was reduced by decrease in per capita productivity or in the number of successfully reproducing individuals, the number of seeds successfully dispersed occurred through conscious human activity. Such plants or vegetable crops developed large leaves and hyperdeveloped storage organs that made them important to humans as a source of food. In Southeast Asia, South America, and West Africa, the storage capabilities of vegetatively produced plants made them important to humans and facilitated conscious cultivation. The loss of evolutionary possibilities associated with sexual reproduction and the increase in vigor in hyperdevelopment of storage organs made nonsexual reproduction the major means of propagation.

BIBLIOGRAPHY

Barrau, Jacques. *Subsistence Agriculture in Polynesia and Micronesia.* Honolulu, Hi. 1961.
Cowan, C. Wesley, and Patty Jo Watson, eds. *The Origins of Agriculture: An International Perspective.* Washington and London, 1992.
Fisk, E. K., ed. *The Adaptation of Traditional Agriculture: Socioeconomic Problems of Urbanization.* Canberra, 1978.
Harris, David R., ed. *The Origins and Spread of Agriculture and Pastoralism in Eurasia.* Washington, D.C., 1996.
Rindos, David. *The Origins of Agriculture: An Evolutionary Perspective.* Orlando, Fla., 1984.
Smith, Bruce D. *The Emergence of Agriculture.* New York, 1995.
Wilder, G. P. *The Breadfruit of Tahiti.* Honolulu, Hawaii, 1928.

EDMUND ABAKA

VENEZUELA. During the last half century of the colonial period (1760–1810), Venezuela became a prosperous part of the Spanish Empire, exporting cacao and other commodities, such as tobacco, *añil*, and sugar. An increasingly centralized bureaucracy regulated the Venezuelan economy and its relationships with the world market either directly or through commodity monopolies in cacao and tobacco.

This relative prosperity connected Venezuela into the international export marketplace and nurtured local expectations for economic opportunities that might accompany independence from Spain, although the process of independence (1810–1830) first inflicted almost twenty years of economic dislocation. Between 1830 and 1858 Venezuela's producers reentered the international marketplace primarily as coffee and cacao exporters but with a deteriorated infrastructure (roads, port facilities, plantations), an impoverished internal capital market, and weak government and financial institutions.

Foreign investment through short-term commodity-based loans accentuated the dependence on export crops. The government, lacking the power to collect domestic taxes, relied on import-export duties. Together these situations made the economy and the various regimes highly vulnerable to fluctuations in commodity prices. Commodity export dependence and weak institutions produced constant economic and political instability, culminating in the Federal Wars of 1858–1863.

The subsequent period saw strong earnings from coffee exports that almost tripled between the mid-1860s and the mid-1870s and rose steadily until the collapse of coffee prices in the last years of the 1890s. This performance permitted the state to encourage foreign investment in economic infrastructure, such as roads, railroads, and ports, and Venezuela negotiated significant international loans secured by the state. However, the decline in coffee earnings near the end of the century once again plunged Venezuela into political crisis. Deteriorating economic conditions produced a major foreign intervention in 1902, when three of Venezuela's international creditor nations blockaded its ports and extracted a variety of concessions during the presidency of Cipriano Castro (1899–1908).

Venezuela's economic circumstances in 1910 appeared relatively unpromising until the international terms of trade shifted in the next decades as the rapid industrialization of the North Atlantic world and the two world wars created an increasing demand for petroleum. By 1925 the value of petroleum exports exceeded the combination of coffee and cacao, defining the end of the agricultural export era and the emergence of the petroleum economy. Venezuelan regimes subsequently focused their economic policies on capturing revenue from petroleum and distributing it to support economic development and the enrichment of favored classes and individuals.

The petroleum era began with the regimes of Juan Vicente Gómez (1908–1935) and saw a growing sophistication in the country's management of its oil wealth. Initially the exploitation of petroleum involved the distribution of concessions to international petroleum interests through the intermediary of regime supporters. This mechanism produced personal wealth for favored individuals, exceptional gains for the international firms receiving concessions, and increased government revenue well beyond previous levels.

A sequence of petroleum laws and regulations beginning with the 1943 Hydrocarbons Law increased the Venezuelan state's share in the value of petroleum extracted by international companies from 50 percent to 78 percent in 1976. After the nationalization of the industry in 1976, the state owned all the revenue from petroleum sales and shifted its focus to maintaining international prices and volumes at optimal levels using Organization of Petroleum Exporting Countries (OPEC) cartel arrangements. The state also sought favorable contracts with international companies for services essential to the continued competitiveness of the nationalized industry. Venezuela increased its participation in the vertical integration of this industry by investing in refining capacity and in the 1990s in the delivery of petroleum products to international consumers.

Venezuela's Hispanic tradition of centralized government responsibility for national economic activity rested on weak institutional structures inadequate to translate the national income resulting from petroleum into sustained economic growth. The variability of petroleum revenues and a concern over the finite character of oil reserves prompted a sense of urgency to spend and invest oil earnings as quickly as possible. Following the boom in revenues resulting from the dramatic increase in oil prices after 1973, the government rushed to transform the country into a stable, effective, and internationally competitive economic entity before petroleum reserves ran out.

Venezuela implemented large import substitution programs, public works, major industrial enterprises in steel, aluminum, and hydroelectric power, and wide-ranging social programs in health, education, and housing. With oil revenue subsidies, Venezuela raised its standard of living substantially throughout the last half of the century, especially after the 1970s boom, and created a number of competent if not internationally competitive industries. Successive governments subsidized economic difficulties rather than resolving them. Swings in oil revenue, produced by the 1973–1974 price boom and decline and again by the 1980 price spike, greatly exacerbated this process.

Economic programs scaled to match the ever-expanding revenue expectations of the mid-1970s proved extremely difficult to sustain when lower oil prices returned by the mid-1980s. The subsequent international borrowing to maintain these programs and purchase political stability brought Venezuela significant debt and financial difficulty by the late 1980s. As public expenditures rose far beyond revenues, the public debt rose from $470 million in 1973 to almost $5 billion by 1981 and reached well into the $30 billion range by the 1990s. Indeed debt service plus current expenditures exceed the earnings from petroleum revenues every year but one between 1977 and 1993.

The decline in Venezuela's economic circumstances and the necessary economic adjustments resulting from inflation, an overvalued currency, and the inability of petroleum revenue to sustain the high standard of living characteristic of earlier years produced riots at the end of the 1980s and two failed coups in 1992. These events signaled a collapse of the petroleum-financed political consensus that had prevailed since 1958, a repudiation of traditional party organizations, and a major regime change in 1998. The new regime, headed by Hugo Chávez, a military leader of the prior coup attempts and a master of revolutionary rhetoric, nonetheless pursued economic policies almost identical to those of its predecessors. An improvement in the international oil price in 2000 allowed the new regime to maintain its political base and subsidize preferred economic and social programs. However, the petroleum price rise of the early twenty-first century appears neither sufficiently large nor sustained to support a return to the halcyon days of the past.

The trajectory of Venezuela's economy illustrates these difficulties. The constant-dollar per capita GDP growth rate fell from 2.7 percent in the 1960s to a stagnant 0.1 percent in the 1970s, only to fall again to a negative (1.4) percent in the 1980s, recovering to a modest 0.2 percent in the 1990s. Although the first two years of the new century saw improved real GDP growth at 3.2 percent for 2000 and an estimated 3.3 percent for 2001, accompanied by a moderation of inflation and a slight improvement in other indicators, the continued dependence on oil subsidies from higher than normal prices and constant overexpenditures by the government offered little room for significant economy recovery.

Venezuela's twenty-first century economic prospects depend, as they have since World War II, on balancing the public expectation for prosperity derived from oil wealth with the realities of investing petroleum earnings into activities to create employment, export competitive industries, and establish a self-sustaining economy capable of resisting the inevitable variability of oil prices. The principal inhibitor of Venezuela's economic success remains its weak institutional infrastructure for resolving economic, political, and policy issues.

BIBLIOGRAPHY

Baptista, Asdrubal. *Bases cuantitativas de la economía venezolana, 1830–1989.* Caracas, Venezuela, 1991. Provides the most comprehensive estimates of Venezuelan economic data for the nineteenth century and the early twentieth century. While not everyone will find comfort in the methodologies used to compensate for the lack of consistency and completeness in the underlying data, the series often provides the only comprehensive data available for the period.

Ellner, Steve. "Recent Venezuelan Political Studies: A Return to Third World Realities." *Latin American Research Review* 32 (1997), 201–218. Includes both an exceptionally well informed analysis of the state of Venezuelan political and economic conditions and an effective evaluation of seven studies of Venezuela's modern history through the mid-1990s.

Izard, Miguel. *Series estadísticas para la historia de Venezuela.* Mérida, Mexico, 1970. Offers an early effort to collect historical statistics and is particularly useful for the nineteenth century, although both this and the Baptista item above necessarily rely on somewhat fragmentary and sometimes unreliable sources for many series.

Karl, Terry Lynn. *The Paradox of Plenty: Oil Booms and Petro-States.* Berkeley, 1997. Delivers an astute and perceptive analysis of the economic and political impact of petroleum in Venezuela. This work is especially valuable for its ability to put the Venezuelan economic experience within a context of both Latin American economies and the performance of non–Latin American petroleum states.

Martz, John D., and David J. Myers, eds. *Venezuela: The Democratic Experience.* Rev. ed. New York, 1986. Although now somewhat dated, gives an excellent overview of Venezuela's modern history.

Tugwell, Franklin. *The Politics of Oil in Venezuela.* Stanford, Calif., 1975. Delivers the best prenationalization account of the relationships between petroleum and Venezuelan political life.

Venezuela: Country Report: Economist Intelligence Unit. London, 1996–. Gives the best current and continuously updated data and analysis on the state of Venezuela's economy and is also available on-line by subscription at <http://db.eiu.com/>.

Wilkie, James W., et al., eds. *Statistical Abstract of Latin America,* vol. 37. Los Angeles, 2001. The best source for comprehensive comparative economic data on Latin America with time series back to the early twentieth century and for some data into the nineteenth century.

John V. Lombardi

VENICE. The Venetian economy must be understood not only in relation to the city of Venice itself (population c. 170,000 in c. 1550), but also to its extensive dominions on the Italian mainland (the "Terraferma," c. 1.6 million subjects) and in the Mediterranean (the "Stato da Mar," perhaps 600,000 people). The fortunes and significance of the entire state owed much to the environment of the city and to its geographical location. Although there is now some evidence to suggest an ancient Roman presence in the lagoon, the settlement that was, in Wordsworth's poem, to hold "the gorgeous east in fee" began as a community of refugees from the Lombard invasions of Italy in the later seventh century. The inhospitable environment may have offered shelter, but its salt waters made trade essential in order for the inhabitants to obtain corn.

The compensation of the location was the absence of a surrounding rural area, which enabled the state to develop without the interference of local magnates. In some ways, those environmental features were the foundations of Venice's renown: the prosperity of its commercial economy and the stability of its republican constitution. Venice's geographical location placed it at the exact center of the Mediterranean economy, which, until 1500, remained the economy of the world known to Europeans. Venice was a center of communications between Lisbon in the west and Damascus in the east. Its maritime trade routes linked Syrian cotton and Cornish tin, and its overland routes developed a thriving nexus with the markets of Germany.

The phases of Venice's economic history have a tidal quality, perhaps reflecting the city's amphibious position between sea and land. The initial flight to the lagoon was followed by the gradual establishment of trading links with the Italian mainland, and the settlers traded fish and salt for grain. From about the year 1000, when a measure of stability returned to European life after the invasions of Vikings, Saracens, and Magyars, a phase of trade and crusade opened that was directed to the sea and to the east.

The Venetians profited from crusading mathematics rather than crusading zeal, and in 1204 their provision of transport so exceeded the assembly of troops that the Fourth Crusade diverted to Constantinople and sacked it in order to pay the Venetians what they were owed. This period was one of intense rivalry with the Genoese for the markets of Byzantium and the Levant; the commerce and the conflict are exemplified in the career of Marco Polo (c. 1254–1324). The struggle with Genoa culminated in 1381 with a close Venetian victory in its own waters in the War of Chioggia. Soon afterward, it became clear that the advancing might of the Ottoman Turks could threaten Venice's commercial supremacy, so the Venetians turned westward.

In the course of the fifteenth century, the Venetians established a territorial state on the Italian mainland that stretched almost as far as Milan. At the same time, a major adjustment in the city's economic base saw the slow withdrawal from reliance on maritime commerce and the establishment of a high-quality manufacturing base in the city itself. With the Italian wars that began in 1494, the Venetians found themselves with nowhere to turn. The pressure of Turkish gains in the aftermath of the fall of Constantinople in 1453 was immeasurably compounded by catastrophic military defeat at the hands of a hostile European coalition at Agnadello in 1509. Venice's recovery of its mainland territories by 1516 was accomplished mainly by the divisions among the enemies of the Republic. All this took place just as the great horizons of the Atlantic were opening up to more westerly powers. The Venetians recognized the dangers posed by the Cape Route and engaged in negotiations with the Mamluks of Egypt to cut a canal at Suez. The Ottoman conquest of Egypt in 1514 put an end to such plans.

The Venetian economy withstood the complex of new economic and political pressures and adjusted to them, so that its history in the sixteenth century is one of remarkable survival rather than inevitable decline. The Mediterranean spice trade recovered in midcentury. The volume of spices that came from the Indian Ocean via the Red Sea to Alexandria may have equaled or even exceeded Portuguese imports. The disruptions of war on the mainland also enabled Venice to become a center of woolen cloth manufacture, and production peaked at around 28,000 cloths in about 1600.

Prosperity and its protection had long been symbolized by the gigantic shipyards of the Arsenal, a "factory of marvels," and perhaps the most advanced industrial complex in preindustrial Europe. Over half the Christian fleet of more than two hundred ships that defeated the Turks at Lepanto in 1571 had been built there. In the sixteenth century, Venice's advanced technologies were epitomized in the Mint (Zecca) and the Library. Standing at San Marco, the political and religious heart of the city, Jacopo Sansovino's buildings for Doge Andrea Gritti (in office 1523–1538) and a reminder of Venice's preeminence in the production of coins and books, the only items in the preindustrial economy that might be described as "mass produced." At the same time, the busy streets that linked San Marco to the Rialto—where the first giro bank (from the Italian for "circulation") was established early in the seventeenth century—became the heart of a booming retail sector of luxury goods.

The city enjoyed a symbiotic relationship with the peoples and wares of the mainland state and the maritime empire. Some figures suggest that the terra firma was as valuable to the Republic as the stato da mar by the early fifteenth century. Venice's Italian possessions were among the most urbanized areas in Europe and included cities like Padua (40,000) Verona (50,000), Vicenza (25,000), Bergamo (25,000), and Brescia (40,000). Immigrants from the Mediterranean regions and from Italy were vital in replenishing the population of Venice itself. Visitors' descriptions frequently remarked on the communities of Jews, Greeks, Slavs, Albanians, Turks, and others.

Venice suffered visitations of plague throughout the fifteenth century in the aftermath of the Black Death, and may have lost one-third of its inhabitants in the particularly devastating pestilence of 1575–1576. However, the plague of 1630 was worse; there was no complete demographic recovery. Although the numbers of people in the city rapidly returned more or less to the levels before the plague, they appear to have done so at the expense of the mainland. It is tempting to date the decline of Venice from this time, but the Republic did remain capable of sustaining a major war effort for almost a quarter of a century after 1645 in the struggle with the Turks for Crete.

In the economic history of the West, Venice retains enormous significance. It sheds light on what is often seen as the transition from feudalism to capitalism. In making economic adjustments in the fifteenth and sixteenth centuries, and in staving off decline in the seventeenth, the guilds of Venice proved remarkably adaptable to changes in the economic climate, and they helped construct a metropolitan economy based on both popular capitalism and an adherence to traditional standards of manufacture.

The nobility also adjusted to changes without betraying their entrepreneurial past. As the profits of maritime commerce began to shrink when the price of insurance against shipwreck and piracy soared in the later sixteenth century, patricians turned their attention to land. They did so because the returns were more assured, and the Palladian villas so often identified with a life of ease were strictly designed for efficient estate management.

VENICE. *The Reception of the Ambassador Count Bolagno,* painting by Giovanni Antonio Canaletto (1697–1768). (Collezione Aldo Crespi, Milan/Alinari/Art Resource, NY)

The Venetian achievement is also significant in the larger picture of what might constitute modernity. In the course of the Middle Ages, the Venetians established an empire that provides a prototype for the mercantilist powers of the seventeenth century, often depicted as innovative. Yet the Venetian empire in many ways set a pattern for the later empires of the English and of the Dutch. The Venetians did not seek to hold down vast areas of land, choosing instead to establish defensible coastal footholds. The state intervened to protect and further material gain with its war fleets in the open sea. The government shunned involvement in war in defense of abstract causes, withdrawing from the Holy League and ceding Cyprus to the Turks in 1573 because the recurrent defense costs were too high.

The commercial ventures of Venetian merchants were designed to spread cost and risk in ways that point toward the joint-stock company. It is perhaps significant that Sebastian Cabot was closely involved in the establishment of the first such enterprise in London, the Muscovy Company, in 1553. Indeed, his father, John (died 1498), native of Genoa, but a naturalized Venetian citizen, had planted the standard of Saint Mark as well as that of Henry Tudor on the coast of Newfoundland in 1497.

BIBLIOGRAPHY

Braudel, Fernand. *The Mediterranean and the Mediterranean World in the Age of Philip II*. 2 vols., trans. Sian Reynolds. London, 1972.

Chambers, David S. *The Imperial Age of Venice, 1380–1580*. London, 1970.

Lane, Frederic C. *Venice: A Maritime Republic*. Baltimore, 1973.

Lane, Frederic C. *Venice and History*. Baltimore, 1966.

Mackenney, Richard, *Tradesmen and Traders: The World of the Guilds in Venice and Europe, c. 1250–c. 1650*. London, 1987.

Pullan, Brian, ed. *Crisis and Change in the Venetian Economy in the Sixteenth and Seventeenth Centuries*. London, 1968.

Rapp, Richard T. *Industry and Economic Decline in Seventeenth-Century Venice*. Cambridge, Mass., 1974.

RICHARD MACKENNEY

VICKERS FAMILY. The Vickers' firm was founded in 1829 in Sheffield as Naylor, Hutchinson, Vickers and Company, an iron-and-steel mill. The founders of the company were William Vickers, the owner of an iron-rolling mill; George Naylor, the owner of an iron-and-steel firm; and John Hutchinson, who left the firm in 1841. In the 1830s, the demand for iron and steel in Great Britain escalated because of expansion in the railway system, especially in North America. As the company prospered, William withdrew from the firm; and his brother Edward Vickers, a flour mill owner, assumed leadership. In 1856, Edward's eldest son, Tom (1833–1915), took over technical control of the firm, and his younger son Albert (1838–1919) became the chief executive official. Tom was a brilliant scientist who developed many new processes for steel and iron work, while Albert was a gregarious commercial leader. The combination of their entrepreneurial skills led their firm into several industries, becoming one of Great Britain's largest businesses and foremost defense contractors. The Vickers brothers were clever entrepreneurs, adapting the firm's behavior to reflect changes in the market. In the financial panic of 1860, many British firms failed, but Vickers weathered the storm by becoming a limited liability firm called Vickers, Sons, & Co. George Naylor died in December 1861, and because he had no male descendants, his name was left out when Vickers, Sons & Co. was set up as a limited liability corporation in 1867.

In the 1860s, the demand for steel for railroads began to slow down because of an increase in U.S. tariffs, and Vickers moved into marine shafting, casting large shipyard components. When profits decreased during the 1880s recession, they moved into armaments.

Until the 1890s, Vickers remained predominantly a steel manufacturer with one foot in the defense sector, maintaining modest profits until the 1890s. When profits declined during the recession of the 1880s, Albert realized that the government needed extra artillery and armor for naval growth and boldly made the initial heavy investment for the move into armaments. His goal was to move more fully into armament manufacture, with the ambition of constructing an arsenal that could supply armor, cannon, and weaponry from light machine guns to heavy battleships. He saw that the supplier of a complete warship is more attractive to buyers than a supplier who offers only some components.

To achieve the goal of market control, Vickers began a multidimensional integration process in 1897, purchasing an artillery and ammunition works that produced light weapons, as well as a shipyard that would be a reliable buyer for heavy weaponry products. In 1900, they acquired large percentages of companies that produced gunpowder and armor plate. They also began building submarines in 1900 and began experimenting with aircraft before the war. By 1914, Vickers was one of the largest industrial concerns in Europe on sea and land. During World War I, Vickers sold several complete warships to the

British navy, and designed and built a better class of submarines. The Vickers machine gun was the army's most sought-after gun, comprising 30 percent of the total output of British machine guns during the war period.

Tom's son Douglas (1861–1937) became chairman in 1919, leading the company through difficult postwar times, as they expanded into civil aircraft, locomotives, merchant ships, and other industries. Many of their peacetime products were failures, but the firm survived with low profits. In 1934, Great Britain began the process of rearmament, and business improved. Vickers was in the lead of naval rearmament, constructing fifteen ships in 1937, several times as many as any other builder. They moved into smaller specialized ships in 1941. This program was their most important, producing 60 million pounds worth of naval orders in the early 1940s, while air and land orders totaled between 5 and 10 million pounds. Great Britain needed a new air force with up-to-date aircraft, and the Vickers Aviation company was among the strongest in design and production. It developed the Spitfire, the fastest and most efficient fighter plane in the world, as well as the Wellington, a twin-engine bomber. The thirty thousand planes the firm produced by 1945 helped Great Britain to win the war. It was the single largest supplier of weapons to the army in 1939, producing new designs of tanks and guns. However, the importance of the Vickers firm began to fade during this period, as World War II armaments turned toward an alliance of pure science and light industry, with the development of radar, rocketry, and other high-technology weapons. After Douglas's death in 1937, the firm passed out of the family's control, but Vickers has remained an important part of the shipbuilding, steel, engineering, and aircraft industries.

BIBLIOGRAPHY
Scott, J. D. *Vickers: A History*. London, 1962.
Trebilcock, Clive. *The Vickers Brothers: Armaments and Enterprise, 1854–1914*. London, 1977.

VIETNAM. *See* Indochina.

VINES AND VITICULTURE. Viticulture, the cultivation of the grape vine primarily to produce wine, has been an important commercial activity since the days of ancient Greece and Rome, contributing to the mercantile and agricultural expansion of early modern Europe, and to the rise of the modern mass-market economy. After the disastrous vine blight phylloxera and economic slumps of late-nineteenth-century Europe, viticulture in the late twentieth century expanded worldwide in regions with suitable climates and soils, usually between 30 and 50 degrees latitude north and south, such as California, Chile,

Argentina, South Africa, and Australia. The world's premier vine varieties are descended from or are hybrids of European *Vitis vinifera* vines, capable of producing quality wines. Viticulture requires technical skill; scientific understanding; determination against bad weather, vine pests and disease; and capacity to bear high costs for materials and labor, in exchange for sometimes uncertain returns and erratic markets. Thus we see the historical tendency for growers to seek quality wines fetching prices sufficient to bear costs of cultivation, processing, storage, and transportation.

Origins. Viticulture probably originated around 5000 BCE in Transcaucasia, perhaps when humans accidentally discovered that grapes stored in ceramic containers fermented spontaneously. It migrated to the ancient Near East and Egypt, then to Greece and Rome, where winegrowers developed cultivation practices remarkably familiar today: pruning, propagation by cuttings, intensive cultivation (Greece); grafting, treating for disease, vine trellising, and fertilizing (Rome). As perennials requiring high seasonal labor inputs, vines complemented agricultural routines of Mediterranean dry farming, particularly grains, olives, and sheep grazing. Imperial Rome transmitted viticulture into northern Europe and even to England. After economic disruptions and invasions of the Middle Ages, viticulture was revived by the princes, feudal landlords, and religious institutions of late Medieval Europe, with cultivation as far as Flanders, northern Germany, and Poland. Under the patronage of princes, the monks of medieval monasteries were instrumental in developing resilient vines adaptable to the cool, damp northern climate.

Vintage Viticulture. Following the collapse of medieval expansion, the seventeenth and eighteenth centuries saw the rise of finished vintage (cask-aged and bottled) wines, partly in response to rising costs and market barriers imposed by wars, economic competition, and trade embargoes by the Dutch and English. In Bordeaux, Burgundy, Rhineland, and Champagne, vintage viticulture was also a strategic response to a revolutionary innovation—distilling—and its ancillary, fortified (with brandy) sweet wines, such as port, sherry, and Madeira, hugely popular among the wealthy. By the late seventeenth century, modern regional vintages were emerging, each identified with specific vine varieties and cultivation routines (e.g., long or short pruning, bush or trellised support systems) to provide quality. A countertrend was competition from regions specializing in common, high-yield vines to supply growing urban mass markets with wine and distilled products. Efforts of royal governments to prohibit or even uproot common vines, seen as threatening to vintage growths, were generally unsuccessful. Important scientific contributions to viticulture were made by the industrialist Jean-Antoine Chaptal (1756–1832), viticulturalist Jules Guyot (1807–1872), and chemist Louis Pasteur (1822–1895).

Phylloxera. After decades of prosperity, reckless expansion of viticulture provoked vine disease and economic slumps in late-nineteenth-century Europe. Powdery mildew (oidium) yielded to spraying with copper sulfite. Far worse was another pest imported on resistant vines from America, phylloxera, a root-living vine aphid that eagerly killed *Vitis vinifera* vines. Phylloxera first appeared in southern France in the 1860s and traveled relentlessly across Europe, systematically destroying the entire continental rootstock between 1870 and 1910, an unimaginable catastrophe for viticulture. The only remedy was to replant with (resistant) American rootstock onto which European vines were grafted. The total costs and labor effort required for this undertaking were huge, forcing marginal producers in many areas to abandon viticulture, beginning a decline in European vineyard area that continues to this day. Tragically, pushed by high costs for replanting and for upkeep of fragile grafted vines, many growers stretched yields and output, harming quality and, in the face of stagnant demand, creating overproduction and a near permanent crisis in European and world viticulture in the 1900s to 1930s. The practical remedy was legislation that defined regional controlled appellations. These geographical delimitations of growths imposed strict controls on permitted vines and on yields, to protect quality, avert fraud, and cap production. Fully implemented in France during the 1930s, and since adopted by other countries in the European Union and beyond, controlled appellations have produced a marked revival in viticulture since the 1960s, though overproduction persists.

Turn to Quality. Following World War II, the turn to quality and decline of traditional viticulture in Europe inspired worldwide viticultural expansion in such regions as California, Australia, Chile, and South Africa, where viticulture had developed since colonial days. New World growers and their counterparts in Europe carefully selected post-phylloxera strains of classic vine varieties tested in the microclimates of their localities, creating new ecological identities for Old World vines—chardonnay, cabernet savingnon, merlot in California; shiraz and grenache in Australia; pinot grigio in Italy, and so on. New World viticulture also boldly combined technology and mechanization with scientific cultivation, especially in California where entrepreneurial growers worked closely with universities. Such innovation has produced comparatively high yields and greater global competition. Today, viticulture is a competitive, quality-oriented industry where corporate backing and strategic marketing characterize small and large producers alike. A recurrence of phylloxera in California in the 1990s and new vine diseases warn of future challenges.

[*See also* Horticulture and Track Farming *and* Wine and Wineries.]

BIBLIOGRAPHY

Billiard, R. *La vigne dans l'antiquité*. Lyon, 1913. Despite its age, an essential overview of ancient viticulture.

Dion, Roger. *Histoire de la vigne et du vin en France des origines au XIXᵉ siècle*. Paris, 1957. The classic account.

Huetz de Lemps, Alain. *Géographie historique des vignobles: Colloque de Bordeaux*, 27–29 Octobre 1977. Paris, 1978. 2 vols. Some essential if specialized articles, thirty-three in all; volume 1 is on France, volume 2 on Europe and other countries; good bibliography (mostly French).

Lachiver, Marcel. *Vins, vignes et vignerons: Histoire du vignoble français*. Paris, 1988. An invaluable modern treatment of French viticulture.

Ordish, George. *The Great Wine Blight*. 2d ed. London, 1987. Still the most useful account of phylloxera.

Unwin, Tim. *Wine and the Vine: An Historical Geography of Viticulture and the Wine Trade*. London, 1991. A thorough account; informative, extensive bibliography; multinational perspective.

HARVEY SMITH

VOLCANIC ACTIVITIES AND EARTHQUAKES.

Although seismologists and volcanologists have only recently understood the geologic forces behind earthquakes and volcanic eruptions, people have always known their destructive effects. Volcanic eruptions and earthquakes have caused death and suffering, destroyed structures of all kinds, and generally disrupted economies throughout human history. The legendary example is Italy's Mount Vesuvius, which erupted in 79 CE, wiping out Pompeii and killing twenty thousand of its inhabitants. Many times more lethal was the Calcutta, India, earthquake of 1737, which killed an estimated 300,000 people. Earthquakes and volcanic eruptions have the power to do more than devastate local populations, however; they have also brought economic and social distress to populations distant from the catastrophe. Large volcanic eruptions, for example, have induced short-term climatic change and brought on crop failure, famine, and social unrest.

Consider first the effects of earthquakes and volcanic eruptions on nearby populations. The deadliest earthquake on record occurred in Shensi, China, in 1556. Some 830,000 lives were lost. More is known, however, about the earthquake that struck Lisbon, Portugal, in 1755. That quake was, according to Voltaire, "a cruel piece of natural philosophy." Indeed, Europe already had known famine, war, and disease; but with its unprecedented destruction, the earthquake awakened Europeans more than ever to the potential for widespread human suffering. Almost all of Lisbon's magnificent city center was destroyed, and seventy thousand people in and around Lisbon lost their lives. The quake did damage as far away as Algiers. As with other earthquakes, extensive property damage came not from the tremors themselves but from fires that broke out and ravaged Lisbon for five days.

Volcanoes too have wreaked havoc on those living in their proximity. In 1883, Krakatau in the Indonesian islands (then the Dutch East Indies) erupted, destroying that island and several neighboring ones. Thirty-six thousand people perished, many by giant seismic ocean waves that inundated coastal villages. Also, in 1903, hot rock and ash flows from an eruption of Martinique's Mount Pelée buried the picturesque port city of Saint Pierre. All but two of the city's thirty thousand inhabitants died. Nonetheless, the Krakatau eruption stands apart. It left a permanent imprint on modern memory because for the first time the world had the means of communicating news of the disaster as it transpired (Simkin and Fiske, 1983).

An increasingly important question is the extent to which disasters—natural or otherwise—can have global economic consequences. Although nearby populations have always borne the brunt of earthquake and volcanic activity, distant communities and economies are, and always have been, susceptible. The Tambora eruption of 1815, history's largest, illustrates well the ways in which volcanic activity can affect remote economies by altering the earth's environment. First, the eruption on the Indonesian island of Sumbawa, killed twelve thousand people directly. At least another forty-four thousand people on neighboring islands later died of starvation.

Tambora's effects, however, spanned oceans and continents. Scientists estimate the volcano discharged at least 150 square kilometers of ash and gas and exploded with sufficient force to propel volcanic dust into the earth's stratosphere, thus veiling the earth from the sun. The consequence, most scientists agree, was short-term climatic change. Eastern North America and western and central Europe experienced abnormal cold and rain in the summer of 1816. The unusual weather was accompanied by widespread crop failures and a high incidence of mortality among livestock everywhere in the northern latitudes. The prices of farm goods naturally increased. Wheat, rye, and bread prices reached two to three times their 1815 levels. The poor harvests, according to Post (1974), resulted in not only diminished real incomes and economic hardship but also social unrest, as illustrated by bread riots in rural France.

Volcanic eruptions and earthquakes can affect remote economies through other means: capital markets can transmit the effects of natural disasters across regional and national boundaries. The San Francisco earthquake of 1906 and its aftermath provide the best example of this phenomenon. Compared to other earthquakes, the 1906 San Francisco earthquake was not especially deadly—only 498 people perished—but it did cause widespread destruction in property, again mostly by fire. Twenty-eight thousand buildings were destroyed, and over 350,000 people were left homeless. Property losses from the quake totaled

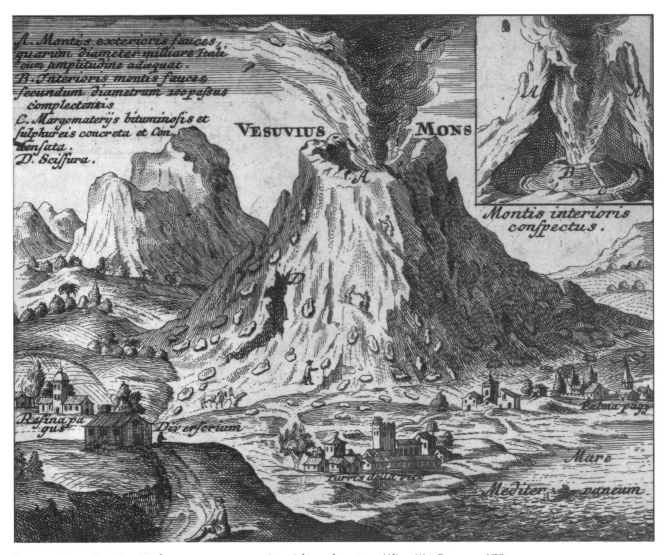

VOLCANO. Mount Vesuvius, Naples, anonymous engraving, eighteenth century. (Alinari/Art Resource, NY)

$350–500 million or 1.3–1.8 percent of the 1906 U.S. gross national product. According to Odell and Weidenmier (2001), the San Francisco quake reverberated through the international economy because risk to earthquake insurers was not sufficiently spread. British companies had been the principal fire insurers in San Francisco before the quake and thus were liable for approximately half of the fire insurance claims outstanding after the disaster. Payments by British insurers to American claimants resulted in large outflows of gold from Britain, which threatened the fixed sterling–dollar exchange rate and forced the Bank of England to raise its discount rates twice in the autumn of 1906. The bank's actions stanched the flow of gold from the United Kingdom but also choked off the flow of credit to the United States. This reversal in credit, the authors claim, contributed to the sharp economic downturn and bank panic of 1907.

Earthquakes and volcanoes continue to cause misfortune. In many parts of the world, little progress has been made in diminishing their destructive effects despite technological advances in prediction and earthquake-resistant construction. For instance, in 1976, an earthquake of magnitude 7.6 struck Tangshan, China, killing 250,000 people by official counts although in fact as many as 655,000 may have perished. In 1985, twenty-three thousand Colombians died when the volcano Nevado del Ruiz erupted. Even when there is not extensive loss of life, the economic costs of such events can be staggering. The 1995 Kobe, Japan, earthquake did $100 billion in direct damage to buildings, infrastructure, and personal property. Today, more and more of the world's population is inhabiting earthquake and volcano-active areas, making seismological monitoring and prediction a vital industry.

BIBLIOGRAPHY

Fisher, Richard V., et al. *Volcanoes: Crucibles of Change.* Princeton, 1997.

Odell, Kerry, and Marc D. Weidenmeier. "Real Shock, Monetary Aftershock: The San Francisco Earthquake and the Panic of 1907." Claremont Colleges Working Paper in Economics, 2001.

Post, John D. "A Study in Meteorological and Trade Cycle History: The Economic Crisis Following the Napoleonic Wars." *The Journal of Economic History* 34.2 (1974), 314–349.

Post, John D. *The Last Great Subsistence Crisis in the Western World.* Baltimore, 1977.

Sieh, Kerry, and Simon LeVay. *The Earth in Turmoil: Earthquakes, Volcanoes, and their Impact on Human Kind.* New York, 1998.

Simkin, Tom. "Distant Effects of Volcanism—How Big and How Often." *Science* 264.5161 (1994), 913–914.

Simkin, Tom, and Richard S. Fiske. *Krakatau 1883: The Volcanic Eruption and Its Effects.* Washington, D.C., 1983.

Strothers, Richard B. "The Great Tambora Eruption in 1815 and Its Aftermath." *Science* 224.4654 (1984), 1191–1198.

JAMES I. STEWART

W

WAGE LEGISLATION. Until the late nineteenth century, most wage regulation set maximum wages in an effort to curb rising labor costs. The earliest instance was the emperor Diocletian's (r. 284–305) edict of 301 CE, an effort to stabilize the weakening currency and rising prices. The edict fixed maximum prices of foodstuffs, raw materials, and manufactured goods and set maximum wages for workmen and salaries for professionals. Strict penalties for infringement, including death, did not deter raising prices, and enforcement was abandoned.

Medieval Period. The growth of cities and guilds created the development of a true labor market. Unlike many aspects of guild life and work, wages of journeymen and women were not regulated. An interesting exception is the Ordinance of the Carpenters, Masons, Plasterers, Daubers, and Tilers of London of Edward I (r. 1272–1307), which lists wages of all major types of construction workers. For prestigious crafts (e.g., carpenters) two wages per season were listed; if compensation included food, the specified wage was lower. Employers who overpaid were fined forty shillings. What effect this regulation had on actual wages remains unclear.

The Great Plague. The reduction in labor supply as a result of the plague put upward pressure on wages. The French responded with an ordinance in February 1351, the goal of which was price stability. Price ceilings were set on bread, wine, beer, and other foodstuffs; and wages were set at one-third above their preplague rates, with fines stipulated for violators. However, even this did not prevent further increases; mason workers' wages increased roughly threefold by 1352 (except for those hired by the king, for whom wages generally conformed to regulation).

In 1349, Edward III (r. 1327–1377) of England issued the Ordinance of Laborers that set wages and salaries for all workers at the preplague rates. The 1351 Statute of Laborers recognized that these rates were set too low and that wages had increased by two or three times the preplague levels. The statute set maximum wages for many rural and urban occupations. In an attempt to reduce labor movement and the bargaining power of workers, the statute set the minimum length of contracts to one year or season. Laborers were required by law to take an oath stating that they were aware of these rules. Those who broke their oath were punished by fines, ransom, or imprisonment. The fines were collected by commissions of laborers and counted toward the local community's tax obligations. Employers could sue their employees for the excessive wages. These measures increased the reporting of noncompliance and hence the ability to enforce the law. Indeed, wages remained almost constant at their postplague levels until 1402; however, nonwage benefits (such as food or the right of a hired hand to use his employer's plow on his own land) increased in quantity and quality during this period. Similar, though local, measures to control wages were taken in the Iberian Peninsula and in some Italian towns.

Tudor Period. The Statute of Artificers of 1563 added flexibility to wage legislation, as it required periodic adjustment of the regulated wage. Though the aim was to stabilize wages, it was understood that wages had to be in line with market forces. Assessments were made every Easter, on a local level, by justices of the peace in the counties and by mayors, bailiffs, and others in the towns, taking into account "the plenty or scarcity of the time." In 1597, an act was passed clarifying that the statute was not limited to farmworkers.

On the whole, the assessed wages were a binding maximum wage and were set below the market equilibrium. But in a few cases, they were set above the unregulated wages (as in 1604 in the textile industry), so as to counteract declining wages.

The assessments that exist from most of the counties and boroughs of England, and from all decades from 1600 to 1810, suggest that wage legislation was the norm until 1813, when the act was repealed. There are relatively few records of cases brought to court for violations. This may indicate either lax enforcement or high compliance. Some local studies refute the latter, suggesting instead that actual wages and legal wages diverged, especially during times of labor shortage.

The regulation of wages was accompanied by a requirement that all able bodies work. Anyone refusing to work at the assessed wage was punished. Evidence of enforcement of these laws is greatest for women and for part-time workers. The enclosures in the later decades of the seventeenth century limited nonlabor sources of income and increased labor supply. Consequently, the assessment system declined.

Modern Period. From the late nineteenth century, wage legislation was a part of the attempt by the post–Industrial Revolution labor movement to improve working conditions. There was growing concern that wages were too low for sustainable living and should be regulated to a "fair" or "living wage." In 1896, the Australian state of Victoria established industry wage boards, made up of employers and employees. Compulsory arbitration courts settled labor disputes and thus set de facto minimum wages within a given industry. With modifications, this system was followed by other Australian states and New Zealand.

England followed suit in 1909, establishing trade boards to set minimum wages in certain trades, including mining. France passed the first minimum wage act in 1915. It was limited in scope, covering only women engaged in the manufacturing of clothing in their home. In 1912, Massachusetts was the first U.S. state to regulate wages. This path-breaking, if timid, rule was limited to women and children—an attempt to avoid the unconstitutionality of intervening in contractual relationships by restricting the regulation to vulnerable groups needing the protection of the state. It relied, unsuccessfully, on voluntary compliance. With leadership from the National Consumers' League, many other states followed suit with more inclusive regulations. From the start, the state laws went under judicial review. This culminated with the U.S. Supreme Court decision in *Children's Hospital* v. *Adkins* (1923) that ruled the District of Columbia's law unconstitutional. The plaintiff in this case was a woman who was prepared to work for lower wages and whose output was too low to warrant the higher minimum wage. She objected to the state's disallowing a contract that was acceptable to both her and her prospective employer. This objection reflects the likelihood that binding minimum wages (i.e., wages above the market equilibrium) lead to unemployment as workers with low productivity may unsuccessfully seek employment at this wage.

The Great Depression aroused more sympathy toward workers, and the National Industrial Recovery Act (NIRA) of 1933 allowed minimum wages to be set by the president, instituted regulation against child labor, and set a maximum number of work hours per week. Though the NIRA was ruled unconstitutional in 1935, as the first federal regulation of wages it gave valuable experience. An important effect was the realization by unions that minimum wages need not hinder their expansion or influence.

In 1937, the Supreme Court overruled its objections to minimum wage laws. This opened the gate to the 1938 Fair Labor Standards Act, which covered about 43 percent of nonsupervisory workers and set the hourly minimum wage at twenty-five cents. The set wage did not vary by geography, industry, or occupation, nor by gender or age groups. But many occupations (e.g., executive, local retailing), industries (e.g., fishing and agriculture) and classes of workers (e.g., apprentices, handicapped) were exempt.

With time, the share of workers covered by this act expanded to approximately 88 percent of nonsupervisory workers. Because the wage is set within the statute of the law, any change to the minimum wage is a legislative process; and there have been long periods when the wage has not been increased to reflect inflation or productivity growth. Compliance with the law in the United States is low as punishment is limited to back pay of wages without, in most cases, punitive damages. Evidence of the law's effect on unemployment and poverty is mixed. Estimates suggest that a 10 percent increase in the minimum wage increases teenage unemployment by up to 3 percent. The effect on reducing poverty is limited by the fact that most minimum wage workers do not live in poor households. Laws similar to the U.S. law are now in place in most developed and many developing countries.

Recent wage legislation has attempted to close race and gender wage gaps. The U.S. Equal Pay Act of 1963 required employers to pay men and women equal pay for equal work. Critics have argued that few women hold the same jobs as men and thus the law is restrictive. A proposed solution is to require equal pay for "comparable" jobs. Comparability is measured by such criteria as skills, training requirements, responsibility, and mental and physical effort. An example is the 1988 Pay Equity Act of Ontario, Canada.

BIBLIOGRAPHY

Epstein, Steven A. *Wage Labor and Guilds in Medieval Europe.* Chapel Hill, N.C., 1991. A thorough review of the growth of guilds and the establishment of labor markets. Includes information on the French Ordinance of February 1351 and the English Statute of Laborers.

Minchinton, W. E., ed. *Wage Regulation in Pre-Industrial England.* Comprising works by R. H. Tawney and R. Keith Kelsall. New York, 1972. Two interesting essays on the Statute of Artificers. Note the good introduction. Unfortunately, not widely available.

Nordlund, Willis J. *The Quest for a Living Wage: The History of the Federal Minimum Wage Program.* Westport, Conn., 1997. A thorough and readable history of minimum wage regulation in the United States that covers economic, political, and legal aspects of the regulation.

Internet History Sourcebooks Project. "The Edict of Emperor Diocletian of AD 301." <http://www.fordham.edu/halsall/ancient/diocletian-control.html>

Internet History Sourcebooks Project. "Statute of Laborers, 1351." <http://www.fordham.edu/halsall/seth/statute-labourers.html.> Also found in *Source Problems in English History*, edited by Albert Beebe and Wallace Notestein. New York, 1915.

Grossman, Jonathan. U.S. Department of Labor. *Fair Labor Standards Act of 1938: Maximum Struggle for a Minimum Wage.* <http://www.dol.gov/dol/esa/public/minwage/history.htm.> Describes the political and legal background to the Fair Labor Act.

REBECCA M. STEIN

WAGES. Labor performed by a free person (in legal terms) for another person or an organization is generally compensated by a payment, the wage. This may take the form of goods, privileges, and money or a mixture of these. Broadly, there was an evolution toward the generalization of money wages according to the pace by which economies became more market oriented. Yet in present-day industrialized countries, goods are still a form of pay (for example, meal vouchers). From the 1900s onward and particularly since the 1950s, the wage includes complex forms of "postponed" and indirect pay such as pension, sick care, and paid holidays. The mix of direct and indirect wages varies greatly from one country to another, but everywhere the latter tends to grow in importance. For example, in France in the 1930s the indirect wage accounted for 10 percent of the total wage, against 30 percent in 1990. The direct wage may be divided into a gross and a net wage, the latter being the sum of money that employees actually obtain after deductions for taxes and national insurance contributions ("take-home pay"). In many countries, both deductions appeared for the first time in the 1920s.

Apart from different forms and meanings, *wage* has been used interchangeably with words such as *earnings*, *pay*, *wage rate*, or *salary*, although it may refer to quite distinct notions such as hourly pay, contract wage, or piece rate. Agricultural laborers have contracts of several months that include money and in-kind wages (board, lodging, and goods). Prepayments in money may be obtained. Some are paid by the day, with an outspoken difference between seasons. Wages of domestic servants are similar to agricultural wages. Industrial workers have a basic wage (the rate), which is a remuneration for input of labor in terms of time or piece. To compute the earnings per week, the wage rate is multiplied by the working time or the quantity of production. Additions for overwork and premiums or deductions for fines, broken material, and "inferior work" may intervene. Some workers, mostly overseers, have a fixed weekly pay. Usually, mill workers are paid each week or fortnight, and cottage workers are paid per piece. Salaries refer to white-collar workers who are commonly paid by the month and according to scales and seniority.

Historical Wage Research and Economic Theory. Price increases during the last decade of the nineteenth century led historians to study the evolution of workers' wages in connection to economic change. Researchers used documents that contained money wage rates, neglecting nonmonetary wages, working time, or premiums and assuming that wage earners worked full time and had no other income sources. Two types of wage series were collected: data for construction workers since the thirteenth century and data for a wide variety of occupations since the mid-nineteenth century. This work was largely empirical and spoke only indirectly to the available theories of

WAGES. City employees receiving their salary, Siena, Italy, fifteenth century. (Archivio di Stato, Siena, Italy/Scala/Art Resource, NY)

wage formation. Classical economics assumed that a subsistence (or natural) wage existed, which equaled the biological minimum and differed according to time and place. In the long run, wages evolve between the tension of the market price of labor and its natural price, and they depend on population fluctuations. In the short run, wages are limited by a wage fund, or the sum of available wages at a certain period. According to neoclassical theory, the market price of labor, or the interplay of demand and supply on the labor market, determines wage levels and differentials. For Karl Marx (1818–1883), the wage is the price of the value of labor. And via the difference between use value and exchange value of labor, the capitalist obtains surplus value; wages evolve according to the size of the reserve army of industrial workers.

Theoretical concepts were explicitly used in the 1920s and 1930s, a period of major changes in price level and high unemployment. The Cambridge economist John Maynard Keynes (1883–1946) launched hypotheses that directly inspired wage and price historians to learn about economic recurrences as well as influenced governmental policy. Keynes's interest in wages was part of his general theory of employment. He suggested a direct relationship between wages and output and between unemployment and wages, which led to debates that have not yet ended. The strong theoretical interests tended to push aside empirical study, and most historical statistics of wages and prices were cast into an economic model, whether inspired by neoclassical economics, Keynes, or Marx.

In the 1950s, a third generation appeared, putting the historical study of wages and real wages on top of the agenda for four decades. Three major developments occurred: a manifest ideological discord, a worldwide explosion of detailed investigation, and the introduction of new theories. The first led to a long-lasting debate in (mainly but not exclusively) British social and economic history writing: the question of the workers' standard of living in the Industrial Revolution (c. 1780–c. 1830). A pessimistic and an optimistic camp emerged (broadly, a Marxist and a neoclassical, although not all students would fit neatly in one of these). In the margin of this debate, more discussions came forth about pay inequality, the relationship between economic growth and purchasing power, and the cyclical pattern of wages.

The second development related to the growing discontent with existing west European wage statistics. In the Atlantic world, this led to the return to the sources and the presentation of multiple wage series for specific regions and cities, various occupations, women and men, or skilled and unskilled workers. The use of the wage rate was criticized. Instead, researchers wished to include working time, nonmoney wages, premiums, among other things, to learn about actual developments of earnings, not so much of the individual but of the family. Also, a sophisticated series of average earnings were proposed, especially for the nineteenth century, which incorporated changes in the composition of the labor force, overtime and premiums, as well as wages of occupations that had been omitted previously (e.g., dressmakers). In non-Western countries, the wage research expanded gradually. For instance, series for China, Japan, Latin American countries, the Balkans, Turkey, Egypt, (Soviet) Russia, and India were published, most of which covered the nineteenth and/or twentieth centuries. At the center of this were several concerns: unequal development within and between countries or continents, globalization, and international labor markets.

The application of new theories and insights was the third major development. The work on non-European countries and the criticism on the existing European series made clear that (real) wages have limitations as an indicator of the standard of living. Influenced by third-world theorists, historians turned to hard-to-grasp elements such as entitlements, capabilities, civil rights, and the definition, nature, and status of wage earning. For some historians, it became obvious that the study of wages is meaningful only in money economies. This restricts the field to only a few places in the preindustrial period and to industrialized countries since the late eighteenth century. Nonetheless, new theories with a long-run outlook have spread in the

1980s. Among these are neoclassical institutional models and the regulation-school, which stress the role of contracts, power relations on the shop floor, and especially the role of government and its institutions. More recently still, efficiency wage models appeared in economic theory, which tackle the question of downward wage rigidity and pay above the "market wage" in sectors where high wages guarantee high productivity (and not the other way round). Despite new theories, neoclassical and Marxist models and concepts continue to inspire many wage historians.

Aside from the three major developments, a differentiation between historians became apparent in the 1960s: Economic historians explicitly devoted attention to economic theory but seemed less preoccupied with the quality of the data. Social historians, in contrast, paid little attention to theory but considered detailed evidence and tended to neglect wage developments as an indicator of the living standard. Hence, they studied zealously the social and cultural history of the wage, which included wage systems, contracts and disputes, the meaning of the wage in terms of creditworthiness and status, and the perception of wage earning.

Methods, Index Numbers, and Difficulties. The above differentiation is certainly not absolute, yet it may entail different methods or, at least, accents. Both approaches require basic wage data from pay books, contracts, price lists, accounting registers, inquiries, or insurance documents. Obtaining homogeneous data for a well-defined type and quantity of labor is the most serious difficulty. Moreover, the shift from daily wage to piece rates, the incorporation of nonmonetary pay into the wage, a fortuitous change in the composition of the workforce, or new work or pay arrangements may influence the wage data without any relationship to economic factors. Primarily, wages from urban building industries were collected because of the availability of plentiful data over a long period, the social and economic importance of this industry, and the allegedly stable nature of the work. When earnings are looked at (weekly or even yearly), complex questions arise related to work time, pay for overwork, premiums, or fines. Such information is hard to find (generally, only pay books of modern factories contain all necessary data). And prior to the nineteenth century, series of earnings are scarce. Often, estimates of the working time are used to compute earnings. Wage rates can evolve at a different pace than earnings. For example, between the 1860s and 1910s the hourly wage of the printers in a leading Brussels printing mill increased by 85 percent, while weekly earnings rose by 40 percent.

When historians wish to study the wage development of more than one category of workers or a country's average, they compound several wage rates or earnings into one overall series. This may be done by calculating a simple average. However, to have significant series it is necessary to consider the composition of the workforce. This is done by applying more or less sophisticated formulae with weighing coefficients (which are the numbers of workers in each industry). Quite popular is the "aggregate" index number of Laspeyres ($\Sigma w1q0/\Sigma w0q0$), with w referring to wages, and q to weighing coefficients. This, however, tends to overstate a rise during longer periods; hence, the need to adapt the weighing coefficients, calculate a new series, and tie both together. Whatever formula is applied, index numbers are commonly used: One year or an average of several years equals 100 (1 or 10 have also been used), and all other years are expressed relative to the base period. The choice of this base is important and should ideally correspond to a normal or calm period. Average wage index figures may be refined by incorporating estimates for unemployment.

Index numbers reappear when a deflator is needed to construct real wages. A deflator may consist of the price of just one basic good (rye, wheat, rice). Real wages, then, express the value of the wage in quantities of a good, which has a theoretical as well as a practical significance ("135 liters of rye per year" is a clear notion that may have made sense to contemporaries). This method has frequently been used with regard to preindustrial societies, but as consumption became more complex in the eighteenth century, the use of the price of one good becomes inadequate. A price index number must be calculated, comprising prices of various goods and services, preferably weighted according to representative spending patterns. Ideally, a cost-of-living index number should be constructed that incorporates all expenditures to keep a family and is adequately weighted. This opens a wide field of investigation, involving the shopping basket and its changes, the nature of prices, the formulae (Laspeyres is mostly applied), and cost-of-living index numbers produced by official bodies from the late nineteenth century on.

The division of the wage index by the price index, commonly multiplied by 100 to obtain comprehensible figures, results in the real wage or the purchasing power of the wage rate or the earning. Here, the outcome differs from that of the division of the wage by the price of a single good, and the significance is purely theoretical ("127 points" or "89 points" make little sense in terms of purchased goods and services). Note that "points" are used and not "percent," which only applies when reference is made to the base year. Thus, real-wage indices have a precise and limited meaning: They measure the change of the wage in terms of the amount of purchasable goods and services related to a base period. The meaning reaches as far as the quality and the nature of the components, and not every series is of equal value. Real wages generally omit information about nonmoney wages and other income sources.

Economic historians ask questions about international competitiveness, worldwide labor migration, and living standards in various countries, fields in which real wage (rates) play a crucial role. Social historians tend to be more skeptical about international comparisons, fearing to neglect local characteristics of the wage, the work, the social relations, or the family. Some researchers convert local currencies (both wages and prices) into grams of silver (or U.S. dollars) to make meaningful comparisons. Others prefer to calculate the price of a basic shopping basket (sometimes limited to food) in each country and compare this to wages (the basic-need approach), while many favor a comparison in which real wages are expressed in relation to a reference year and country (the purchasing power parity, using a working-class budget in country A and prices in countries A and B, which provides a ratio for a meaningful comparison of wages).

Every step of the computation of real wages is subject to criticism. Thus, the British debate on the living standard during the Industrial Revolution often revolved around disputes about the base period, the lack of particular prices, the extrapolation of wage data, or the controversial weighing coefficients. Despite criticism, however, wages and real wages continue to be studied with perseverance and sophistication because they disclose crucial developments and express complex matters in simple terms.

Wage Evolution and Differentials. In 1955, H. Phelps Brown and S. Hopkins published the daily wage of craftsmen and laborers in the Southern English building trade from 1264 to 1954. Four features stand out: the infrequency of change (none in 500 of the 690 years), the rare declines (only three: 1887, 1920s, and 1930s), the stable differential (the laborer earned two-thirds of a craftsman's wage up to 1914), and the sensational increase in the long run (nominal wages multiplied by nearly 150). Recently, long-run series for other regions have been compiled. Year-to-year series for Flanders and Castile, for example, show the long-term increase and the periods of long stagnation as in England, but they follow a totally different path, with solid wage reductions and fluctuating differentials. Figure 1 depicts the daily wage of unskilled workers in three European regions for more than 500 years (graphs are drawn on a logarithmic scale to stress all movements). In general, these wage evolutions testify to many economic shifts, geographical as well as with regard to specialization (the shift from the Mediterranean to the Atlantic, the growth of complex commercial activities, and the industrialization process).

Many more long-run series of builders' wages have been constructed, which allows economists to situate wage evolution in a broad perspective. Based on such wages in twenty European cities, the existence of four "wage

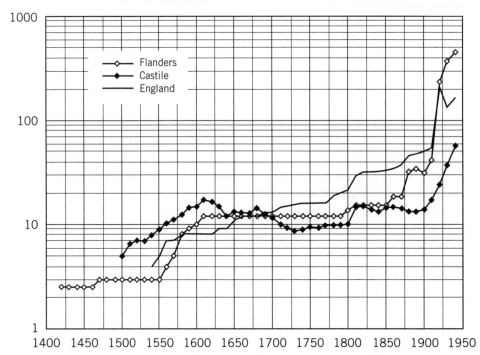

FIGURE 1. Daily wages of unskilled laborers. Flanders in stivers; Castile (and Madrid) index numbers (1790–1799 = 10); southern England in pence; logarithmic scale. SOURCE: Reher and Ballesteros, 1993, pp. 101–151; Vandenbroke, 1988, pp. 260–274; Phelps Brown and Hopkins, 1981.

regions" in Europe around 1500 was suggested: a central European, a North Sea region, Italy, and Spain. Converting the local currency into grams of silver to allow for meaningful comparisons, it appears that Spain's wages were on top in the sixteenth and a large part of the seventeenth century, while central European wages were among the lowest; in between were Italian and North Sea wages. In 1800, this hierarchy had totally changed, and the North Sea region took the lead, leaving only two broad wage regions. Wage differences were more marked in 1800 than in 1500. Nonetheless, important differentials within one region occurred. For example, in the Netherlands in 1819 the ratio between the lowest and the highest wage in forty agricultural districts reached 52 percent, with a variation coefficient (i.e., the standard deviation from the average) at 20 percent. These were large differences in a small country, particularly since high-wage regions bordered directly on low-wage regions. Similar huge regional wage differentials may be found in other parts of the world and in other times.

European wages diverged from the sixteenth to the nineteenth century, and they started to converge in the course of the twentieth century. Wage differences were investigated on a global level, too, particularly to find out whether an integrated global labor market operated. Non-European, often annual wage data—mostly starting around 1850—were compiled. For example, year-to-year wages were compared for Argentina, southeast and northeast Brazil, Colombia, Cuba, Mexico, and Uruguay from the 1850s to 1940 and for Manchester, Sydney, Chicago, San Francisco, Toronto, and Vancouver from 1879 to 1913. Within the third world, wages converged in the long run, while differentials among Europe, North America, and other regions lessened until 1913, grew to 1950, then tended to diminish again until recently.

Apart from geographical wage differences, huge gaps exist in one place when age, gender, trade, skill, or ethnicity are involved. Most of these categories are linked to each other. Thus, the gender wage gap is intertwined with the age wage gap and with the type of economic activity. When all occupations are taken together, young boys and girls receive nearly equal pay, but differentials grow sharply from the age of 18 onward. For example, for Finnish manufacturing workers around 1905 the following wage differences between men and women according to age were found: girls earned 88 percent of a boy's wage (below age 18), 68 percent (age 18–29), 56 percent (age 30–44), 55 percent (age 45–59) and 58 percent (above 60). Men's wages reached a top between age 30 and 44, after which a slow and then a more rapid (above 60) decline occurs. After the age of 18, women's wages hardly rose at all, while they started to drop moderately between age 30 and 44. There were important differences according to the industry, and taking all ages together, the male-female wage gap in Finnish industry ranged from 39 percent (glass works) to 66 percent (tobacco). In England during the Industrial Revolution (c. 1780–c. 1830), gender wage gaps were even more marked, reaching between 32 percent (silk factories) and 80 percent (lead mining); in agriculture, average ratios reached 45 percent, with a slowly growing gap after 1800. A rather stable gender wage gap of about 60 percent may be found in many past societies. For agricultural workers in Finland, for example, such a ratio remained the same for over two centuries. This ratio may also be found in advanced economies of the twentieth century, as in the United States in the 1960s, although it has improved since the late 1970s. Today, in many Western countries women earn on average between 70 and 80 percent of a man's pay. In Asian and Latin American countries, women earn between 40 and 70 percent of a male wage.

Wages differ according to ethnicity. Black/white wage ratios in the United States, for example, indicate a narrowing from 1939 to 1975 and a stagnation and slight widening after 1975 (a ratio of 45 percent in 1939, 74 percent in 1975, and 72 percent in 1992). If wages are adjusted for age, hours of work, and education, black/white ratios would exceed the above figures, indicating smaller pay differences. Nonetheless, even if other factors are included, such as number of children, marital status, and urban residence, there would still be a wage differential that reflects persistent discrimination.

Much of the above wage gaps are linked to jobs in different economic branches. There was a rather stable wage hierarchy between agriculture, industry, and services for a long time and in most regions. Industrialization changed this. In some countries, the growth of the industry and service sectors and the transformation of agriculture widened the wage gap in the nineteenth century and narrowed it in the twentieth century. Some historians, following the work of Simon Kuznets, claim the existence of an inverted U-shape of wage inequality accompanying any industrialization process. Often, wage inequality is measured through particular indicators that include all wage observations. Thus, the Gini coefficient (that ranges from 0.0 to 1.0, with 0.0 equal wage for all) for British male workers' wages reached 0.293 in 1827, it augmented to 0.358 in 1851, and then fell to 0.331 in 1901. Generally, wage differentials between industries and within one industry tend to follow the inverted U-shape of the general wage inequality. For instance, the variation coefficient for all Belgian male industrial workers rose from 19 percent in 1819 to 23 percent in 1846 and then fell to 13 percent in 1896; within each industry, the Gini coefficient dropped between 1846 and 1896. The strongest squeezing of wage gaps occurred in textiles.

Changes in wage gaps within one industry are partly caused by wage differences linked to skill. The Southern English building wage rates of craftsmen and laborers show a constant 66 percent ratio between 1400 and 1914, which then started to fall. Phelps Brown and Hopkins assumed that market forces alone were unable to keep this long stability, and they invoked "convention." Similar data for Holland between 1500 and 1800, however, do show flexible skill advantages: In 1500, unskilled laborers earned 80 percent of a craftsman's wage, but this gap widened to 60 percent in 1550. After 1610 and until 1800, the ratio fluctuated between 60 and 80 percent. Other observations indicate flexible rather than constant wage gaps between skilled and unskilled workers.

Explanations. A striking feature of Figure 1 is the strong wage increase in the sixteenth and the twentieth century. This was caused by inflation (i.e., the increasing quantity of money without an equivalent supply of goods). The huge supply of silver from Latin America in the sixteenth century caused a "price revolution," while the gigantic need for money to finance wars caused galloping inflation in the twentieth century. Apart from such vehement shocks, historians suggested the existence of a general consumption norm that may influence wage levels: changes in consumption in a particular period may lead to changes in the cost of living, which in turn may influence wages. For example, the spread of the potato as a basic food in many European regions in the nineteenth century, may help to explain moderately growing wages and rising rural-urban wage differentials. Yet in the long run, improved consumption norms may impose a stop to falling wages. During the inflation spurt from 1914 to 1920, wage indexation (wages that move according to fluctuations of a price index number) formally introduced the link of wage rates to a bargained consumption norm.

Most economic theories refer to the labor market as one of the strongest explanations of wage evolutions and wage gaps. Broadly, wages are high when demand for labor is high, and they are low when labor is abundant. This explains high wages in the United States and Australia in the nineteenth century and falling urban wages when rural migrants arrived in European towns during the economic crisis of the 1840s. However, not all wages evolve in one direction, nor with the same amplitude. Several kinds of wage gaps are related to different niches in the labor market (i.e., labor market segmentation). Being part of such a niche depends on dexterity, training, and effort but also on tradition, regulation, gender, and education. Thus, in explaining the narrowing wage gap between female and male wages in the West after 1970, improved access to education for women has been quoted as an important factor. Presently, the persisting pay differential between women and men and whites and nonwhites is viewed as a consequence not only of sheer discrimination but primarily of occupational segregation, different working time, and nonmoney pay.

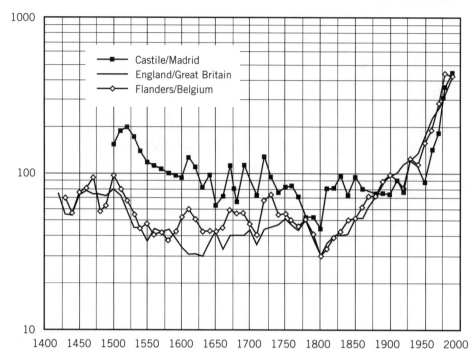

FIGURE 2. Indices of real wages for laborers. Flanders/Belgium, Castile/Madrid, southern England/United Kingdom (1913 = 100); logarithmic scale. SOURCE: Reher and Ballesteros, 1993, pp. 101–151; Vandenbroke, 1988, pp. 260–274; Phelps Brown and Hopkins, 1981.

In general, economic development exerts powerful pressure on the labor market. Thus, modern mills and workshops attracted labor at the onset of industrialization, which caused rising wages in specific industries and increasing wage inequality up to the 1850s. Mechanization reinforced both phenomena, while productivity rises also lead to increasing wages. The latter occurred directly if wages were linked to output, as for piece rates and premium systems, although wage rate cuts often accompanied new technology. When mechanization spread to most industries and to agriculture and services, wage differentials tended to narrow.

Wage rigidity in early modern times has been explained by "custom" as a move against labor market forces. Some historians claim that custom prevented wage cuts in the sixteenth century, although population rose and created a pool of labor. Yet, neither custom nor norms could stop wage cuts, as shown by the Castile example. Custom was subject to conflict and negotiation, which shows that neither employers nor employees remained passive in the process of wage formation. Wage bargaining on an individual basis happened constantly. This included not only wage rates but working time, pauses, measuring of production, and working conditions in general. On the whole, skilled male laborers had a rather strong bargaining position, while unskilled workers and especially women held a weak position. Men joined in associations that, among other things, strove to keep wages high by sending (young) associates on a tour trying to prevent a high labor supply. In the eighteenth century, wages had become the major topic in industrial relations that increasingly involved strikes. Maintaining wage rates was the reason for setting up modern unions in the nineteenth century. Around 1900, strong unions existed in particular trades, representing up to 90 percent of the workers. Unions bargained over collective work agreements that involved minimum wages, wage indexation, premiums, rates for overwork, and wage differentials.

In the process of wage bargaining, both sides often called on authorities. This took various forms, such as a plea to open guilds for "free" labor, an appeal to a high authority (such as a mayor or a member of government), or the introduction of a bill in Parliament. Local and national governments were present in wage formation, primarily to keep social order. From the middle of the nineteenth century, social policy dealt indirectly with wages (for example, limitations on unions, low import duties on basic food), while democratic pressure at the eve of the twentieth century led to direct interference. This included laws (for example, minimum wages), the installation of labor courts, the organization of national wage boards, or the establishment and refinement of an education system.

Researchers have tried to distinguish one particular factor to explain the unbridled movements of wages in the nineteenth and twentieth centuries. Economic factors were posited against institutional ones (particularly productivity gains versus trade union pressure). At first, historians tended to opt for the predominance of economic factors, but later the institutional seemed more persuasive. Yet, it appears to be impossible to select one set of explanations because of the complexity of wage formation and the reciprocity of diverse factors, which necessitates careful investigation at each occasion.

Real Wages. When compared with price trends or cost-of-living index numbers, wage rates or earnings rose to a much lesser extent than shown in Figure 1. Tying several series together, it is possible to present index numbers of real wages for three regions from 1420 to 1990. Figure 2 shows the graphs, using a logarithmic scale. Two broad movements appear: a decline from the fifteenth to the end of the eighteenth century and an increase thereafter. Real wages fell spectacularly in the sixteenth and the late eighteenth centuries and stagnated in between, with a moderate rise in England and Flanders. Extreme differences appeared in particular periods (for example, a fall by 36 points in Castile in 1650 or a rise by 27 points in Great Britain in 1960). In the long run, the rise of wages was eroded by fluctuations of the cost of living until the late twentieth century. Then, the wage spurt was powerful, while the price of consumer goods started to decline and the composition of the consumer's basket changed.

The time series in Figure 2 tell about changes in real wages in each region, but not about the relative levels among the regions. As noted above, meaningful comparisons in space and/or time are obtained by using specific techniques ("grain wages" prior to 1800, real wages adjusted by purchasing power parity after 1800). Such exercises lead to the following general picture (for wages of urban unskilled workers). Around 1500, the purchasing power of money wages was high in Vienna, somewhat lower in Holland, Flanders, England, Spain, and Paris, and much lower in Italy (daily wages converted in wheat). High real wages (in rye) were obtained in Poland. In all regions, real wages dropped around 1600 but stagnated. Some rose slightly around 1700. By 1800, all real wages lay below the 1500 level. The hierarchy had changed: Holland, England, and Paris took the lead, followed by Spain, Italy, Flanders, and Vienna. In Poland, "rye wages" had dropped by 60 percent. In the long run, real wage differentials tended to diminish moderately: Variation coefficients in nine European towns reached 29 percent in 1500, 27 percent around 1600, 36 percent around 1700, and 23 percent in 1800.

From the middle of the nineteenth century on, such comparisons may be done for non-European countries. Table 1 shows real wages in some countries between 1850 and 1913, expressed as a percent of the real wage in Great Britain in 1905, adjusted by purchasing power parity. Real

TABLE 1. *Real Wages Relative to Great Britain, 1850–1913*

	1850	**1870**	**1890**	**1905**	**1913**
Argentina	—	61	58	94	92
Brazil	40	39	68	94	87
Australia	124	127	131	124	128
Spain	63	51	49	48	51
Great Britain	69	69	97	100	110
Ireland	47	49	75	92	90
United States	106	115	145	167	169

(1905 = 100)

wages differed substantially in the middle of the nineteenth century, but they tended to converge from 1870 to 1913. A similar exercise has been done for the twentieth century, when wage data are more plentiful. For instance, within Latin America real wages converged between 1910 and 1990. But between Latin America and members of the Organization for Economic Cooperation and Development (OECD), real wages diverged.

Real wages will continue to be studied and debated widely. They have been used to account for manifold historical developments, ranging from consumption preferences, social and political unrest, demographic processes, economic growth, women's participation in wage labor, migration, and, in general, the standard and way of living, all of which are crucial issues in social and economic history.

[*See also* National Income Accounts, *subentry on* Wages and Labor Income; Wage Legislation; *and* Wage Systems.]

BIBLIOGRAPHY

Allen, Robert, C. "Real Incomes in the English-Speaking World, 1879–1913." In *Labour Market Evolution,* edited by George Grantham and Mary MacKinnon, pp. 107–138. London and New York, 1994.

Allen, Robert C. *The Great Divergence: Wages and Prices in Europe from the Middle Ages to the First World War.* Discussion paper 98-12, University of British Columbia. Vancouver, 1998.

Brenner, Yehojachin, Hartmut Kaelble, and Mark Thomas, eds. *Income Distribution in Historical Perspective.* Cambridge and Paris, 1991.

Burnette, Joyce. "An Investigation of the Female-Male Wage Gap during the Industrial Revolution in Britain." *Economic History Review* 50.2 (1997), 257–281.

Darity, William A., and Samuel L. Myers. *Persistent Disparity: Race and Economic Inequality in the United States since 1945.* Cheltenham, U.K., 1998.

Dean, Andrew. *Wages and Earnings,* vol. 13, *Reviews of United Kingdom Statistical Sources.* Oxford, 1980.

Filer, Randall, Daniel Hamermesh, and Albert Rees. *The Economics of Work and Pay.* New York, 1996.

Heikkinen, Sakari. *Labour and the Market: Workers, Wages, and Living Standards in Finland, 1850–1913.* Helsinki, Finland, 1997.

Phelps Brown, Henry, and Sheila Hopkins. *A Perspective of Wages and Prices.* London, 1981.

Reher, David, and Esmeralda Ballesteros. "Precios y salarios en Castilla La Nueva: La construcción de un índice de salarios reales, 1501–1991." *Revista de Historia Econòmica* 11 (1993), 101–151.

Reynaud, Bénédicte. *Les théories du salaire*. Paris, 1994.

Scholliers, Peter, ed. *Real Wages in Nineteenth and Twentieth Century Europe: Historical and Comparative Perspectives*. New York and Oxford, 1989.

Scholliers, Peter, and Vera Zamagni, eds. *Labour's Reward: Real Wages and Economic Change in Nineteenth- and Twentieth-Century Europe*. Aldershot, U.K., 1995.

Taft Morris, Cynthia, and Irma Adelman. *Comparative Patterns of Economic Development, 1850–1914*. Baltimore and London, 1988. Pages 353–366 contain references to series of historical wages and prices in twenty-three countries.

Vandenbroeke, Chris. "Werkinstrumenten bij een historische en sociaal-economische synthese, 14de–20ste eeuw." *Arbeid in veelvoud* (1988), 260–274.

Williamson, Jeffrey. "The Evolution of Global Labor Markets since 1830: Background Evidence and Hypotheses." *Explorations in Economic History* 32 (1995), 141–196.

Williamson, Jeffrey. "Real Wages, Inequality, and Globalization in Latin America before 1940." *Revista de Historia Económica* 17 (1999, special issue), 101–141.

Williamson, Jeffrey. "Real Wages and Relative Factor Prices around the Mediterranean, 1500–1940." In *The Mediterranean Response to Globalization before 1950*, edited by Sevket Pamuk and Jeffrey Williamson, pp. 45–75. London and New York, 2000.

Zanden, Jan L. van. "Wages and the Standard of Living in Europe, 1500–1800." *European Review of Economic History* 2 (1999), 175–197.

PETER SCHOLLIERS

WAGE SYSTEMS. Wage labor is compensated by a payment that can be done according to different systems. Broadly, two types of pay systems may be distinguished: payment by result and by time. A crystal-clear distinction cannot be made: the time needed to do a task is generally implicit in a piece wage, while the amount of output is considered in a time wage. This mixture appears clearly in the so-called contract wage, or the payment to an individual or a group for a specific task.

Around 1900, researchers started to study the history of wage systems. Some followed Karl Marx (1818–1883), who investigated changes of wage systems in relation to workers' exploitation under industrial capitalism, but a majority wished to situate new, complex wage methods (see below) in a historical perspective. These researchers assumed that time wages were the "natural," or at least traditional, remuneration system that was gradually replaced by piece wages under pressure of industrial capitalism. This view changed only recently when historians studied pay systems more methodically to improve their understanding of economic change, social protest, industrial relations, work effort, and economic organization.

The two main wage systems have existed next to one another since the emergence of wage labor. In agriculture, time wages seem to have prevailed from the Middle Ages until the late nineteenth century. Yet wage systems differed according to the status of the laborer, while it was not un-usual that one individual was paid via different systems. Live-in regular workers, often hired per year, obtained cash next to goods, board, and lodging. Nonresident regular workers were paid a daily or weekly wage alongside goods, the use of some land, and a house at low rent. Hourly wages were paid to both categories for exceptional tasks or well-defined overwork, while piece wages were given to nonresidents for doing specific tasks (reaping or digging). Casual or day laborers were paid by the day (mostly in cash), but during the nineteenth century they were increasingly paid on the basis of hourly wages and piece wages. In general, piece wages replaced gradually the more straightforward time wages, which may be explained by more efficient control possibilities of the work effort.

In industry since the Middle Ages, time wages were paid for labor where it was difficult or impossible to determine the amount of work of each laborer (for example, in construction or cloth finishing). Mostly day wages were paid, although contracts could include weekly, monthly, and even yearly wages. Also, aiming to attract and keep good workers, time wages were paid to highly skilled workers (such as overseers) or to workers in innovative industries (such as machine builders). In some remote regions or industries, a so-called truck system forced workers to spend their wages (or credit) in the company's store, a practice that persisted well into the twentieth century, and that tied workers to one company for a long period. However, piece rates seem to have prevailed in most industries. For the employer, piece wages did not necessitate much supervision, and they encouraged hard work; for the employee, piece rates allowed self-regulation of the work rhythm; for both, a precise wage rate could be paid for a well-defined output. With the success of the putting-out labor (employers providing raw material to workers who supply labor, tools, and a workplace) piece wages spread widely from the seventeenth century on.

Industrialization made wage systems more complex in the eighteenth century. Within one industry or one mill, various systems could coexist according to occupation and gender. In the textile industry of early-nineteenth century Europe, for example, a small majority of workers obtained piece wages, 30 to 35 percent got a daily wage, while the remaining 10 to 15 percent were paid fixed weekly wages. Some helpers got a weekly wage that was paid directly by the main worker, who was paid by result and could earn a higher wage by giving an arbitrary bonus to helpers. Toward the end of the nineteenth century, piece rates replaced time wages more and more, and hourly wages replaced daily wages, while the bonus became a formal part of remuneration. Such changes resulted from the employers' effort to increase productivity, and from the workers' goal of fair pay.

In the early twentieth century, wage systems with premiums spread. Much more than a simple incentive to work harder, premium systems arose out of complex combination of a basic piece rate, a conventional working time, a bonus and a fine, the meticulous measuring of output, and (collective) negotiation. Different premium systems existed, often named after their inventor (for example, F. A. Halsey, David Rowan, Charles Bedaux). In the European machine-building industry, for example, time wages were common up to the 1860s; then, a simple form of an individual premium wage was introduced (a fixed basic wage along with a moderate bonus linked to output); around 1900 a complex premium system was adopted for a "gang" of workers (a low basic wage, a very flexible premium that was linked to the output of a group of workers, and a penalty for not attaining requirements of output or speed); and in the 1920s, motion and time studies refined the whole premium system. Changes often appeared together with technological innovation. The success of sophisticated premium methods lessened in the 1960s because of deliberate moderation of effort (workers feared wage-rate cutting that often accompanied higher productivity). Fixed bonuses, according to a required standard norm of output, and profit sharing started to replace premium systems in the 1970s.

Most white-collar workers and workers in public sector receive a monthly salary, which is a "flat" wage that is more or less independent of output or hours of work. This involves close supervision, which produces a strict grade system of salaries ("classification"). Salaries differ according to skill, responsibility, and experience. After 1950 various incentive schemes appeared: in the United States, for example, bonuses for managerial employees became popular, while Japan introduced profit sharing (based on the firm's or a division's performance). These newer systems were meant to restrict high turnover of the labor force. Today a great variety of pay systems exist alongside each other, often with a mixture of a time wage (the basic pay) and a piece wage (a form of incentive) for each individual.

[*See also* Wages.]

BIBLIOGRAPHY

Bowey, Angela M., ed. *Handbook of Salary and Wage Systems*. Aldershot, U.K., 1982.

Brown, Charles. "Wage Levels and Method of Pay." *Rand Journal of Economics* 23 (1992), 366–375.

Dobb, Maurice. *Wages*. Cambridge, 1966 (especially 50–87).

Duplesis, Robert S., *Transitions to Capitalism in Early Modern Europe*. Cambridge, 1997.

Filer, Randall, Daniel Hamermesh, and Albert Rees. *The Economics of Work and Pay*. New York, 1996. Especially pp. 333–353.

Lupton, Tom, and Angela Bowey. *Wages and Salaries*. Harmondsworth, 1974.

Mottez, Bernard. *Systèmes de salaire et politiques patronales, essai sur l'évolution des pratiques et des idéologies patronales*. Paris, 1966.

Reith, Reinhold. *Lohn und Leistung: Lohnformen im Gewerbe 1450–1900*. Stuttgart, 1999.

Rule, John. *The Labouring Classes in Early Industrial England 1750–1850*. London, New York, 1986. Especially 107–129.

Scholliers, Peter, and Leonard D. Schwartz. *Experiencing Wages: Employers, Earners, Pay Systems, and Wage Forms in Europe since 1500*. Oxford, 2003.

PETER SCHOLLIERS

WALES. Wales comprises a central highland mass of predominantly acidic moorland surrounded on all sides by lowland fringes. To the west and south, steep-sided valleys flow toward the Irish Sea, while to the east, broad and generally fertile lowlands meet the English border. Apart from the island of Anglesey and the Llŷn Peninsula in the west, the predominant agricultural lowlands with relatively well-drained soils of low acidity are located to the northeast and southwest, although even here undulating relief imposes some restrictions on the practical business of farming. Whereas coniferous planting by the Forestry Commission after 1919 and, more recently, official encouragement of deciduous afforestation has tended to expand woodland cover, earlier deforestation was such that by the sixteenth century a mere 10 percent of the land remained under timber. The medieval Welsh texts and surviving legal material hint at an essentially livestock economy, which expanded with Cistercian monastic settlement in the thirteenth century. As sheep came increasingly to dominate the countryside, the woollen industry expanded, although subsequent to 1850, this most important of industries began to decline in the face of better-capitalized operations from northern England.

As the Acts of Union with England (1536–1542) rendered illegal the traditional system of partible inheritance in favor of primogeniture, opportunities were provided for the growth of landed estates and the establishment of the landlord-tenant system that prevailed until the rise of owner-occupation in the early twentieth century. Although arable agriculture was a major feature of the lowlands of the northeast, south, and southwest, livestock production, primarily for export to England, was the mainstay of the rural economy and continued to remain so into the twentieth century when dairy farming achieved vital importance.

By 1800, Wales remained overwhelmingly an agricultural country dominated by small, semisubsistence farming communities characterized by a high degree of mutual cooperation reinforced by religious nonconformity. The bulk of the population, which had risen from 422,000 in 1570 to 490,000 in 1750 and stood at 1.2 million a century later, was monoglot Welsh, with bilingualism very much the exception. English, however, viewed by many as the language of economic progress, was gradually encroaching; and with the demographic, urban, and industrial growth of the mid-nineteenth century, it rapidly began to spread with the inevitable cultural consequences. Migration from rural Wales, initially to the iron and copper smelteries of the southern valleys and subsequently to the burgeoning coal fields, meant that by 1911 some two-thirds of the people lived in the industrial south. The population of Glamorgan alone increased by 253 percent between 1861 and 1911. Combined, the effects of urbanization and industrialization, catalyzed by inward migration from England and Ireland, the development of the railways, and the promotion of tourism, led to a serious and apparently terminal decline in the Welsh language. However, subsequent to the nadir of the mid-twentieth century, the activities of language activists and politicians brought about significant changes in education policy and cultural outlook that have effected a renaissance in the use of Welsh as an everyday tongue to the extent that at the beginning of the twenty-first century, some 20 percent of the population of 2.9 million speak Welsh.

The later eighteenth and nineteenth centuries witnessed massive developments in industrial activity. As the population doubled between 1750 and 1850 and the total proportion engaged in agriculture fell to one-third, rural trades and occupations became relatively less significant contributors to the economy. Farming continued to play a vital role in the sustaining of rural communities, together with coastal trading activities; yet the economy as a whole became dominated by industrial concerns. The extension of the turnpike system, the proliferation of the railways, and the wholesale development of ports and docks at Cardiff, Newport, and elsewhere lay the foundation for quantum developments in iron, coal, and other extractive industries. Since Roman times, if not before, lead had been smelted in the west and north, and by the early-nineteenth century, the output from Welsh mines contributed to Great Britain's position as the world's leading producer of lead. However, dominance in the international market was gradually eroded, first by competition from Spanish silver-lead ore and subsequently by imports from the United States, so that the Welsh lead industry was largely in abeyance by 1900. The evolution of the tinplate industry since the seventeenth century followed a broadly similar pattern. The twenty-three tinplate works active in South Wales in 1843 had expanded to ninety by 1891, by which time annual output had peaked at 690,000 tons, some 448,000 tons being sold on the export market.

Concurrently, copper ore was being mined in Anglesey, while overseas copper ores found their way to the smelteries of Glamorgan, Monmouthshire, and south Carmarthenshire, which not only satisfied domestic British demand but supplied sources across much of the world. If the copper industry brought great wealth to Swansea, it yielded a legacy of environmental pollution of which vestiges still remain. The same can be said about the expansion of the iron, slate, and coal industries, which brought fortunes to their capitalist promoters but left behind spoil tips of unrelieved ugliness and townscapes of bleak monotony. The output of slate from north Wales peaked at 450,000 tons per year in 1882 but declined over the next century as tiles and concrete ousted traditional roofing materials. Iron and coal production, meanwhile, began to dwarf the other industries of the south. The annual output of coal, for example, had risen from 8 million tons in the 1850s to 57 million tons in 1923, after which, as overexpansion was followed by depression, there was a period of relative decline with devastating sociocultural effects on mining communities. A period of recovery during World War II preceded the closure of many high-cost coal mines and ironworks in the 1970s and 1980s and the final eclipse of the port of Cardiff.

By the end of the twentieth century, the extractive industries had given way to high-technology enterprises as key elements of the economy, while urban regeneration and "heritage" conservation became increasingly important. In the countryside, meanwhile, emphasis began to shift from the maximization of agricultural production to the development of sustainable farming systems, pluriactivity, the promotion of recreation and tourism, and the protection of the physical and cultural environment.

[*See also* Great Britain.]

BIBLIOGRAPHY

Bryan, Jane, and Calvin Jones eds. *Wales in the Twenty-First Century*. London, 2000.

Davies, John. *The Making of Wales*. Sutton, U.K., 1996.

Dodd, Arthur H. *The Industrial Revolution in North Wales*. 2d ed. Wrexham, Wales, 1990.

George, Kenneth D., and Lynn Mainwaring. *The Welsh Economy*. Cardiff, Wales, 1988.

Jenkins, Dafydd. *The Laws of Hywel Dda*. Llandyssul, Wales, 1986.

Jenkins, Geraint H., ed. *The Welsh Language and Its Social Domains, 1801–1911: A Social History of the Welsh Language*. Cardiff, Wales, 2000.

Jenkins, J. Geraint. *The Welsh Woollen Industry*. Cardiff, Wales, 1969.

Jenkins, Paul. *"Twenty by Fourteen": A History of the Welsh Tinplate Industry*. Llandyssul, Wales, 1995.

Lindsay, Jean. *A History of the North Wales Slate Industry*. Newton Abbot, U.K., 1974.

Linnard, William. *Welsh Woods and Forests: History and Utilisation*. Cardiff, Wales, 1982.

Midmore, P., and G. O. Hughes. *Rural Wales: An Economic and Social Perspective*. Aberystwyth, Wales, 1996.

Moore-Colyer, R. J. "Wales, 1850–1914." In *The Agrarian History of England and Wales*, vol. 7, edited by E. J. T. Collins. Cambridge, 2000.

Owen, D. Huw., ed. *Settlement and Society in Wales*. Cardiff, Wales, 1989.

Williams, John. *Digest of Welsh Historical Statistics*. Cardiff, Wales, 1985.

RICHARD MOORE-COLYER

WALLENBERG FAMILY. From the founding of Stockholm's Enskilda Bank (SEB) in 1856 until its merger with Skandinaviska Banken in 1972, the Wallenberg family maintained intact, and passed down through three generations a dominant block of shares in SEB. The bank's founder, André Oscar Wallenberg (1816–1886), was a naval officer and a devoted liberal who worked hard to modernize the Swedish banking system. It was the second-generation half-brothers Knut Agathon Wallenberg (1853–1938) and Marcus Wallenberg, Sr. (1864–1943), however, who shaped SEB's distinctive character as a banking house and industrial bank during their lengthy tenure as managing directors from the 1880s to 1920.

With the third generation, especially during the period from 1930 to 1960, the Wallenberg sphere of influence in Swedish industry grew substantially. Under the leadership of Jacob Wallenberg (1892–1980) and Marcus Wallenberg (1899–1982), both sons of Marcus Wallenberg, Sr., SEB became the center of the most influential business group in Sweden. In the late 1970s, more than 10 percent of all employees in the Swedish private sector worked for "Wallenberg" companies. Affiliated with SEB were a number of investment companies, the most important of which was Investor, established in 1916. The principal task of these investment companies, supported by Wallenberg foundations, was to provide an ownership platform for the business activities of the family.

Following the merger of Skandinaviska Banken and SEB (to produce S-E Banken) in 1972, restrictions on voting rights in the new bank caused the Wallenberg family to lose its dominant minority ownership position for more than two decades. After Marcus Wallenberg died, in 1982, and the fourth generation in the person of his son Peter Wallenberg (born 1926) took charge, the family business group was centered around the family's ownership base of investment companies and charitable foundations.

From its origin as a traditional investment company with a highly diversified portfolio, Investor evolved into a holding company with controlling positions that allowed it to exercise active ownership in a limited number of large firms. During the early 1990s, Investor acquired the other Wallenberg investment companies and took over the central role previously played by the old SEB. Following the financial crisis of 1992–1993, which had brought S-E Banken to the brink of bankruptcy, the Wallenberg family once more became a dominant and active minority owner of the bank. The voting restrictions were lifted in 1994. By 1999, the time was ripe for S-E Banken to be renamed SEB, the time-honored abbreviation used by the family bank prior to 1972.

The Wallenberg family's control of its "new but old" bank includes strong personal participation. Representing the fifth generation of the family, Jacob Wallenberg (born 1956), the son of Peter, is the chairman of the bank's board. Born in the same year as Jacob, his first cousin Marcus Wallenberg has served as CEO of Investor since 1998. As of 31 December 1999, the market value of Investor's core holdings totaled over 150 billion Swedish crowns. These holdings included fifteen of Sweden's best-known telecom and engineering firms, such as (Wallenberg percentage of group voting rights in parentheses) LM Ericsson (38), Scania (49), Atlas Copco (21), SKF (27), Electrolux (21), and the Finnish-Swedish forest company Stora Enso (24).

BIBLIOGRAPHY

Carlson, Rolf H. *Ownership and Value Creation: Strategic Corporate Governance in the New Economy.* London, 2001.

Lindgren, Håkan. *Aktivt ägande: Investor under växlande konjunkturer.* Stockholm, 1994.

Olsson, Ulf. *At the Centre of Development: Skandinaviska Enskilda Banken and Its Predecessors, 1856–1996.* Stockholm, 1997.

HÅKAN LINDGREN

WAQF. A property endowed to individuals or institutions for benevolent purposes is a charitable trust. In Arabic, the term *waqf* (pl. *awqaf*) is derived from the root *waqf*, which literally means to stop the ownership of property owned by the founder (*waqif*) from circulation and to discontinue the endowed property (*mawquf*) from becoming the property of a third person. The *waqf* is therefore inalienable and irrevocable property. The endowed property, *mawquf*, consequently becomes the property of God, according to the majority of Muslim jurists, although the Maliki school holds the opinion that the property in *waqf* remains the possession of the founder and his heirs. The incomes generated from *waqf* property often are endowed for religious institutions or charitable trusts. According to Islamic law, the *waqf* may be property endowed to individuals or institutions for religious benevolence or assigned for charitable purposes that are of a social or personal nature. Synonymous to *waqf* is *habs*, *hubus*, or *hubs* (pl. *ahbas*), which is often used for the most part by Maliki jurists, especially in North and West Africa. The French use of the term is also rendered as *habous*.

Waqf has been a subject of definition by various kinds of legal handbooks. Yet the question of what *waqf* is cannot be confined solely to the realm of legal theory as extracted from judicial handbooks. Throughout the various periods of Islamic civilization, *waqf*, originally a religious institution, has manifested itself beyond its legal traditional sense to include social and economic aspects. Therefore, it is part of a historical reality, and it touches upon the material and spiritual conditions of societies beyond the sphere of the legal system.

Origins. Although the *waqf* is an established religious institution in Muslim societies, and there is no reference to the term in the pre-Islamic era, some Muslim scholars hold the view that the idea of *waqf* predates Islam and, therefore, the first *waqf* was the building of the *Ka'bah*. This view conforms with the notion that when the Arab lands of the Byzantine spheres were conquered, the Muslims had before them many examples of charitable trusts among the Byzantines and Christians that could serve as models. In the beginning of the Islamic period, although there was no conclusive evidence of *waqf* in the Qur'ān, there is abundant evidence to suggest the *waqf* is divine in origin.

The earliest mention of *waqf* in the history of Islam goes back to the time of Muhammad. The mosque of Quba in Medina, built on the arrival of Muhammad in 622, has often been considered to be the first religious type of *waqf* in this period. Following Muhammad's death, the *waqf* attained institutional characteristics through a number of early Muslim practices. Among the numerous examples of the institutionalization of the *waqf* is that of the Caliph Umar I (634–644), who reportedly held that if conquered lands, waters, and peasants or serf-tenants were distributed among the conquerors as the property of individuals, future generations of Muslims would be deprived of this source of revenue. Similarly, Abu Bakr Muhammad Ibn Ali al-Madharai (d. 956) in Egypt turned his agricultural land into a *waqf* for the holy cities of Mecca and Medina and for other charitable reasons. These practices of the early Muslims gave rise to the creation of *miri* freehold land, or *mulk* state land *waqf*s.

Other kinds of *waqf* property may also relate widely to nonperishable property whose benefit can be extracted without consuming the property itself, such as copies of the Qur'ān, private libraries, agriculture, and machinery. Although Muslim jurists have grouped the various kinds of *waqf* into two main categories, in practice, this division has been impractical. Traditionally, the *waqf* may be for the benefit of the donor's family (*waqf ahli*) or for the benefit of a public institution (*waqf khayry*) with the intention of prohibiting any use or disposition of the property outside the specific purpose it is determined to have. Many of the *waqf al-khayry* were often employed as a revenue-generating source for several institutions in the Islamic world, including schools, mosques, hospitals, and the general public interest, such as libraries.

Socioeconomic Impact. Throughout the history of Islam, the institution of *waqf* has been of prime importance in the socioeconomic lives of many Muslims. *Waqf* has been considered to be social welfare, subsidizing the needs of the poor segments of society and establishing a certain socioeconomic infrastructure for the state. The economic importance of the *waqf* has been noticed by scholars and students of economic history of the Islamic world through a shift from a traditional sense of the institution in Muslim societies to more sophisticated socioeconomic machinery. This can be illustrated by a brief survey of the social and economic role of the *waqf* from the medieval to the modern period.

Studies of the institution of the *waqf* throughout these periods have shown that *waqf* played a crucial economic role in the centralization and consolidation of the Islamic states and the maintenance of their socioeconomic structures. In the Ottoman Empire, the *waqf* institution, particularly regarding state property defined as *miri* and *mulk* lands, played an important role in enterprise and economic development. *Waqf* and the landholding properties of the state or individuals were important contributors to the central treasury of the Ottoman State. During the reign of Mehmed II (1451–1481), out of a total revenue of 79.78 million akca, 13.64 million or 17 percent came from *waqf*, *miri*, and *mulk* lands in the province of Anatolia. This state property included a number of commercial facilities originally constructed or endowed as *waqf* property: bazaars, shops, and hospitals. The revenues from these sources were then redistributed to finance salaries of the religious class, religious seminaries, mosques, and schools.

The *waqf* institution was properly administered and carefully checked according to Ottoman bureaucracy. However, occasionally, the administrators of *waqf* were guilty of embezzlement and corruption. The mismanagement of the *waqf* often resulted in the extreme concentration of economic power in the hands of the *waqf* administrator (*nazir* or *mutawalli*) without effective supervision. This sometimes encouraged the populace, guided by practical economic considerations, to deviate from proper norms and legal procedure for administering their *waqf*s, or securing their property (especially *miri* and *mulk* lands) from expropriation by despotic rulers, and for gaining exemption from the payment of taxes.

In the modern period, many centralized Muslim states realized the economic, social, and political disadvantages of *waqf*; therefore, the institution of *waqf* went into decline. With the advent of colonial administrative systems in the Muslim world, the *waqf* was replaced in several Muslim societies by *Wizirat al-Awqaf* (the Ministry of Religious Endowment). However, the social and economic role of *waqf* became increasingly important for the popular religious orders, especially the Sufi and Muslim fundamentalist movements, due to the aid *waqf* could offer the needy in lieu of aid from the state.

[*See also* Emiri Lands *and* Mulk Lands.]

BIBLIOGRAPHY

Bilici, Faruk. *Waqf dans le monde musulman contemporain (XIXe–XXe siècles): Fonctions sociales, économiques, et politiques.* (Actes de la Table Ronde d'Istanbul, 13–14 No. 1992). Istanbul, 1994.

Çizakça, Murat. *A History of Philanthropic Foundations: The Islamic World from the Seventh Century to the Present.* Istanbul, 2000.

Deguilhem, Randi, and André Raymond. *Le waqf dans l'espace islamique: Outil de pouvoir socio-politique.* Damascus, Syria, 1995.

Inalcik, Halil, and Donald Quataert. *An Economic and Social History of the Ottoman Empire, 1300–1914*. Cambridge, 1994.

Van Leeuwen, Richard. *Waqfs and Urban Structures: The Case of Ottoman Damascus*. Leiden, 1999.

ISMAEL M. MONTANA

WAR AND ECONOMIC HISTORY. War has influenced economic history profoundly across time and space. Winners of wars have shaped economic institutions and trade patterns. Wars have influenced technological developments. Above all, recurring war has drained wealth, disrupted markets, and depressed economic growth.

Economic Effects of War. Wars are expensive (in money and other resources), destructive (of capital and human capital), and disruptive (of trade, resource availability, labor management). Large wars constitute severe shocks to the economies of participating countries. Notwithstanding some positive aspects of short-term stimulation and long-term destruction and rebuilding, war generally impedes economic development and undermines prosperity. Several specific economic effects of war recur across historical eras and locales.

Inflation. The most consistent short-term economic effect of war is to push up prices, and consequently to reduce living standards. This war-induced inflation was described in ancient China by the strategist Sun Tzu: "Where the army is, prices are high; when prices rise the wealth of the people is exhausted (Tzu Ssu, c. 400 BCE)." His advice was to keep wars short and have the money in hand before assembling an army.

Paying for wars is a central problem for states. This was especially true in early modern Europe (fifteenth to eighteenth centuries), when war relied heavily on mercenary forces. The king of Spain was advised that waging war required three things: money, money, and more money. Spain and Portugal imported silver and gold from America to pay for armies, but in such large quantities that the value of these metals eventually eroded.

One way governments pay for war is to raise taxes (which in turn reduces civilian spending and investment). U.S. revolutionary Thomas Paine warned in 1787 that "war . . . has but one thing certain, and that is to increase taxes." Another way to pay for war is to borrow money, which increases government debt, but war-related debts can drive states into bankruptcy as they did to Spain in 1557 and 1596. A third way to fund war is to print more currency, which fuels inflation. Inflation thus often acts as an indirect tax on a national economy to finance war.

Industrial warfare, and especially the two World Wars, created inflationary pressures across large economies. Increasingly, governments mobilized entire societies for war—conscripting labor, bidding up prices in markets for natural resources and industrial goods, and diverting capital and technology from civilian to military applications. World War I caused ruinous inflation as participants broke from the gold standard and issued currency freely. Inflation also accompanied the U.S. Civil War, World War II, and the Vietnam War, among others. War-induced inflation, although strongest in war zones, extends to distant belligerents, such as the United States in the World Wars, and, in major wars, even to neutral countries, owing to trade disruption and scarcities.

Present-day wars continue to fuel inflation and drive currencies toward worthlessness. In Angola's civil war (1975–2002), for example, the government currency became so useless that an alternative "hard" currency—bottles of beer—came to replace it in many daily transactions.

Capital depletion. In addition to draining money and resources from participants' economies, most wars create zones of intense destruction of such capital as farms, factories, and cities. These effects severely depress economic output. The famine and plague that accompanied the Thirty Years' War (1618–1648) killed as much as one-third of Germany's population, as mercenaries plundered civilians and civilians became mercenaries to try to survive. World War I reduced French production by nearly half, starved hundreds of thousands of Germans to death, and led to more than a decade of lower Soviet output. One estimate put World War I's total cost at $400 billion—five times the value of everything in France and Belgium at the time.

Battle casualties, war-induced epidemics, and other demographic disruptions have far-reaching effects. World War I contributed to the 1918 influenza epidemic that killed millions. Military forces in East Africa may have sparked the outbreak of what became a global AIDS epidemic. Quincy Wright estimates that "at least 10 percent of deaths in modern civilization can be attributed directly or indirectly to war (Wright, 1942). The U.S. "baby boom" after World War II continues decades later to shape economic policy debates ranging from school budgets to social security. Wars also temporarily shake up gender relations (among other demographic variables), as when men leave home and women take war jobs to replenish the labor force, as in the Soviet Union, Great Britain, and the United States during World War II.

Countries that can fight wars beyond their borders avoid the most costly destruction (though not the other costs of war). For example, the Dutch toward the end of the Thirty Years' War, the British during the Napoleonic Wars, the Japanese in World War I, and the Americans in both World Wars enjoyed this relative insulation from war's destruction, which meanwhile weakened their economic rivals.

Positive economic effects. War is not without economic benefits, however. These are not limited to having misfortune strike trade rivals. At certain historical times and places, war can stimulate a national economy in the short term. During slack economic times, such as the Great Depression of the 1930s, military spending and war mobilization can increase capacity utilization, reduce unemployment (through conscription), and generally induce patriotic citizens to work harder for less compensation.

War also sometimes clears away outdated infrastructure and allows economy-wide rebuilding, generating long-term benefits (albeit at short-term costs). For example, after being set back by the two World Wars, French production grew faster after 1950 than before 1914.

Technological development often follows military necessity in wartime. Governments can coordinate research and development to produce technologies for war that also sometimes find civilian uses, such as radar in World War II. The layouts of European railroad networks were strongly influenced by strategic military considerations, especially after Germany used railroads effectively to overwhelm French forces from 1870 to 1871. In the 1990s, the global positioning system (GPS) navigation system, created for U.S. military use, found wide commercial use. Although these war-related innovations had positive economic effects, it is unclear whether the same money spent in civilian sectors might have produced even greater innovation.

Overall, the high costs of war outweigh the positive spin-offs. Indeed, a central dilemma for states is that waging wars—or just preparing for them—undermines prosperity, yet losing wars in worse. Winning wars, however, can sometimes pay.

Conquest, Trade, and Accumulation. Nearly all wars are fought over control of territory, and sometimes over specific economic resources, such as minerals, farmland, or cities. The patterns of victory and defeat in wars through history have shaped the direction of the world economy and its institutions. For example, when Portugal in the sixteenth century used ship-borne cannons to open sea routes to Asia and wrested the pepper trade away from Venice, which depended on land routes through the Middle East, it set in motion a profound shift in Europe's economic center of gravity away from the Mediterranean and toward the Atlantic.

Wars of conquest can more than pay for themselves, if successful. The nomadic horse-raiders of the Iron Age Eurasian steppes found profit in plunder. Similarly, the seventeenth-to-eighteenth-century Dahomey Kingdom (present-day Benin) made war on its neighbors to capture slaves, whom it sold to Europeans at port for guns to continue its wars. War benefited the Dahomey Kingdom at the expense of its depopulated neighbors. Likewise, present-day armies in the Democratic Republic of the Congo and Sierra Leone are fighting to control diamond production areas, which in turn fund those armies. According to one controversial school of thought, states in undertaking

wars behave as rational actors maximizing their net benefits. However, wars are fought for many reasons beyond conquering valuable commodities.

Successful empires have used war to centralize control of an economic zone, often pushing that zone in directions most useful to continued military strength. Transportation and information infrastructures reflect the central authority's political control. When European states conquered overseas colonies militarily (in the sixteenth to nineteenth centuries), they developed those colonies economically to benefit the mother country. For example, most railroads in southwestern Africa were built—and still run—from mining and plantation areas to ports. Empires, however, inherently suffer the problems of centralized economies, such as inefficiency, low morale, and stagnation. Some scholars argue that empires also overstretch their resources by fighting expensive wars far from home, contributing to their own demise.

In recent centuries, the largest great-power wars have been won by ocean-going, trading nations whose economic style differs sharply from that of land-based empires. Rather than administer conquered territories, these "hegemons" allow nations to control their own economies and to trade fairly freely with each other. This free trade ultimately benefited hegemons as advanced producers who sought worldwide export markets. The Netherlands after the Thirty Years' War (1648), Great Britain after the Napoleonic Wars (1815), and the United States after the World Wars (1945) each enjoyed predominance in world trade. By virtue of superior naval military power, each of these great powers shaped (and to some extent enforced) the rules and norms for the international economy. For example, the international financial institutions of the Bretton Woods system grew out of U.S. predominance after World War II. As nations recover in the decades following a great war, however, their power tends to equalize, so a hegemon's raw power gradually matters less, and international economic institutions tend to become more independent—surviving because they offer mutual benefits and help resolve collective goods dilemmas. For example, the United States today, despite its military predominance, does not unilaterally control the World Trade Organization.

Naval power has been used historically to win specific trading and extraction rights, in addition to its broader uses in establishing global economic orders. When asked the reasons for declaring war on the Dutch, a seventeenth-century English general replied, "What matters this or that reason? What we want is more of the trade the Dutch now have." U.S. warships in the nineteenth century forced open Japan's closed economy. And in the mid-1990s, both Canada and Russia used warships to drive away foreign fishing boats from areas of the high seas that shared fish

WARTIME FRANCE. Women harnessed to plow, Oise, 1917. (Prints and Photographs Division, Library of Congress)

populations with Canadian and Russian exclusive economic zones as defined under the UN Convention on the Law of the Sea. In the last decades of the twentieth century, disputes over control of small islands, which now convey fishing and mining rights up to two hundred miles in all directions, have led to military hostilities in the South China Sea and the Falklands/Malvinas, among other places.

Military power has provided the basis for extracting tolls and tariffs on trade, in addition to its more direct role in conquest of resources and trade routes. Danish cannons overlooking the Baltic Sound for centuries gave the Danes a stream of income from tolls on the Baltic trade. Riverborne trade in Europe faced similar choke points where strategic military fortifications allowed tolls to be charged. The military defeat of the Ottoman Empire, by contrast, cost Turkey the ability to control or tax traffic from the Black Sea to the Mediterranean, which today includes a large and growing number of oil tankers.

War and the World Economy. Just as wars' costs and outcomes affect economic conditions and evolution, so too do economic conditions and evolution affect war. Casuality runs in both directions. For example, Dutch economic strengths in the early seventeenth century allowed rapid and cheap production of ships, including warships. The resulting naval military advantage in turn supported Dutch long-distance trade. The wealth derived from that trade, in turn, let the Netherlands pay and train a professional standing army, which successfully sheltered the Netherlands from the ruinous Thirty Years' War. This protection in turn let the Dutch expand their share of world trade at the expense of war-scarred rivals. Thus the evolution of warfare and of world economic history are intertwined.

War is the proximal cause of the recurring inflationary spikes that demarcate fifty-year "Kondratieff waves" in the world economy. Those waves themselves continue to be controversial. However, they may have some predictive value to the extent that they clarify the historical relationships between war and military spending on the one hand, and inflation and economic growth on the other. The 1990s mainly followed a predicted long-wave phase of sustained low inflation, renewed growth, and reduced greatpower military conflict. If this pattern were to continue, the coming decade would see continued strong growth but new upward pressures on military spending and conflict, eventually leading to a new bout of inflation in the greatpower economies. Since scholars do not agree on the mechanism or even the existence of long economic waves, however, such projections are of more academic than practical interest.

The relationship between military spending and economic growth has also generated controversy. Despite its pump-priming potential in specific circumstances, as during the 1930s, military spending generally acts to slow economic growth, since it diverts capital and labor from more productive investment, such as in roads, schools, or basic research. During the Cold War, high military spending contributed (among other causes) to the economic stagnation of the Soviet Union and the collapse of North Korea, whereas low military spending relative to GDP contributed to Japan's growth and innovation. During the 1990s, as real military spending worldwide fell by about one-third, the United States and others reaped a "peace dividend" in sustained expansion. However, effects of military spending are long term, and sharp reductions do not bring quick relief, as Russia's experience since 1991 demonstrates.

The global north-south divide—a stark feature of the world economy—is exacerbated by war. The dozens of wars currently in progress worldwide form an arc from the Andes through Africa to the Middle East and Caucasus, to South and Southeast Asia. In some of the world's poorest countries, such as Sudan and Afghanistan, endemic warfare impedes economic development and produces grinding poverty, which in turn intensifies conflicts and fuels warfare.

The role of war in the world economy is complex, yet pervasive. The shadow of war lies across economic history, influencing its pace and direction, and war continues to both shape economic developments and respond to them.

[See also War Finance.]

BIBLIOGRAPHY

Brandes, Stuart D. *Warhogs: A History of War Profits in America.* Lexington, Ky., 1997. A history of profiteering by Americans in wartime, through World War II.

Braudel, Fernand. *Civilization and Capitalism, 15th–18th Century*, vol. 3, *The Perspective of the World.* Translated from the French by Sian Reynolds. New York, 1984. Detailed macrohistory of the evolution of the Eurocentric and war-prone world system.

Cipolla, Carlo M. *Guns, Sails, and Empires.* New York, 1965. Describes the European conquest of the rest of the world.

Cranna, Michael, et al., eds. *The True Cost of Conflict.* New York, 1994. Descriptions of the economic, social, and environmental consequences of seven armed conflicts—the Gulf War, East Timor, Mozambique, Sudan, Peru, Kashmir, and former Yugoslavia—based on a study by six humanitarian organizations.

Gilpin, Robert. *War and Change in World Politics.* Cambridge, 1981. A political scientist's theoretical and historical account of how power and economics interplay in the rise and fall of great powers.

Goldstein, Joshua S. *Long Cycles: Prosperity and War in the Modern Age.* New Haven, Conn., 1988. A comprehensive review of the literatures on Kondratieff cycles and hegemony, with historical interpretations and empirical analysis of economic time-series.

Hamilton, Earl J. *War and Prices in Spain, 1651–1800.* Cambridge, Mass., 1947. An extended analysis of inflationary effects of war in one location and period.

Howard, Michael. *War in European History.* Oxford, 1976. A short, readable overview of war's evolution with attention to economic aspects.

Kennedy, Paul. *The Rise and Fall of the Great Powers: Economic Change and Military Conflict from 1500 to 2000.* New York, 1987. A historian uses several key cases to argue that great powers overstretch

themselves militarily and thereby economically undermine their own success.

Keynes, John Maynard. *The Economic Consequences of the Peace.* New York, 1920. Discusses the negative economic impacts of the Versailles Treaty and World War I on Germany.

Koistinen, Paul A. C. *Beating Plowshares into Swords: The Political Economy of American Warfare, 1606–1865.* Lawrence, Kans., 1996. First of a five-volume series detailing the economic underpinnings of U.S. military might. *Mobilizing for Modern War* covers 1865–1919; *Planning War, Pursuing Peace* covers 1920–1939.

Rabb, Theodore K., ed. *The Thirty Years' War.* New York, 1981. Collection of essays that enumerates the economic catastrophe of 1618–1648, notably in Rabb's own chapter on economic effects of the war.

Rasler, Karen A., and William R. Thompson. *The Great Powers and Global Struggle, 1490–1990.* Lexington, Ky., 1994. Develops theoretical and empirical arguments about the economic ascent and decline of great powers and hegemons, especially through global wars.

Seligman, Edwin R. A. "The Cost of the War and How It Was Met." *American Economic Review* 9 (1919), 739–770. An interesting review of the unprecedented expenses incurred by World War I, written in its aftermath.

Silberner, Edmund. *La guerre dans la pensée économique du XVIe au XVIIIe siècle.* Paris, 1939.

Silberner, Edmund. *The Problem of War in Nineteenth Century Economic Thought.* Princeton, 1946. Survey of economists' efforts to tackle the economic effects and causes of war.

Tilly, Charles, ed. *The Formation of National States in Western Europe.* Princeton, 1975. Sociologists discuss the connections of war making, taxation, and state formation in early modern Europe.

Tracy, James D., ed. *The Political Economy of Merchant Empires: State Power and World Trade, 1350–1750.* New York, 1991. Traces the importance of trade-based wealth in the emergence of the modern state system.

Wright, Quincy. *A Study of War.* Chicago, 1942.

JOSHUA S. GOLDSTEIN

WAR FINANCE. War finance, providing "the sinews of war," has usually determined a war's outcome. Fear of military defeat stimulates innovations in finance (among other reactions), which may have lasting consequence whether victory or defeat follows. Many, if not most, of the lasting innovations in the way governments have collected taxes, managed the money supply, controlled wages and prices, serviced their debts, and regulated trade have emerged under the duress of war.

Innovations in war finance fall under the three ways governments can finance their expenditures: taxes, debt, and seigniorage (money creation). Perhaps the earliest example is the creation of coinage, originating in Lydia in the seventh century BCE. The use of coins allowed more efficient collection of taxes and tribute by military leaders. It also allowed governments to hire mercenaries instead of maintaining standing armies. It is a matter of conjecture whether coins or mercenaries came first, but it is indisputable that they spread together throughout the Middle East and the Mediterranean. Coinage also facilitated the collection of taxes, including tribute from foreigners.

The first financial innovation to appear after coins was recoinage by the victor of his opponent's money supply, which could bring substantial payoffs. In the later Roman Empire and in medieval Europe, recoinage of one's own money was an occasional expedient of princes or cities under duress. During the military revolution of the sixteenth and seventeenth centuries, people relied upon it increasingly, culminating with the issue of fiat money (the value of which was determined by decree, rather than by the metallic content). This became standard by the end of the eighteenth century. Regular taxes paid in storable coin could lead to the accumulation of a "war chest" sufficient to pay for the troops and supplies for the next war.

Credit had to be extended on occasion, even in the wars of antiquity, from the mercantile community. But it took the pressure of the "military revolution" in Europe during the sixteenth and seventeenth centuries to make credit the most important share of war finance. Spain's Philip II at first used foreign bills of exchange, backed ultimately by tax receipts, to maintain the Army of Flanders. As the expenses of warfare grew, Philip II and his successors were forced into repeated bankruptcies. These amounted to forced refunding of the accumulated masses of short-term debt, *asientos*, which assigned to the lender specific extraordinary revenues granted for the war, into longer term debt, *juros*, which assigned him ordinary revenues that continued after the war. This stratagem eased the immediate liquidity problem of the Spanish ruler and recovered use of the extraordinary revenues for the war. But used repeatedly—1560, 1575, 1596, 1607, 1627, 1647, and 1653—it inhibited merchants from giving credit again. During the Thirty Years' War (1618–1648), capital levies were imposed on cities and towns by both sides. These *Kontributionen* were borne indefinitely by the cities from their local tax base. The discovery that taxes collected regularly by a permanently existing governmental unit, such as a city, could be leveraged up by assigning them to the service and repayment of a specific war debt laid the basis for far-reaching innovations in public finance throughout Europe in the second half of the seventeenth century.

The Glorious Revolution of 1688 allowed the English Parliament to extend to an entire kingdom financial techniques previously confined to cities. Even so, the final step was not taken until the traditional means of finance had failed in the War of the League of Augsburg. The recoinage crisis of 1696, caused by the flight of silver from Great Britain to finance the war effort on continental Europe, demonstrated that "funded debt," first held by the Bank of England established in 1694, had to be expanded. In the War of the Spanish Succession and thereafter, the national debt grew in each war to the extent that by the end of the eighteenth century, not only was the British national debt larger than its national income, but anywhere from one-

WAR FINANCE. Advertising poster for bonds issued by the German savings bank during World War I. (Scala/Art Resource, NY)

third to two-thirds of government revenue had to be applied to it. As a consequence, Britain won its "second Hundred Years' War" with France, and the restored Bourbon monarchy in 1815 quickly adopted the elements of British finance—a permanent national debt secured by specific taxes levied by a continuously sitting legislature.

Over the course of the nineteenth century, other emerging industrial nation-states followed suit—the United States with the Civil War, Germany after the Franco-Prussian war of 1870, and Japan after the Meiji Restoration in 1868 and victory in the Sino-Japanese War of 1895. Many other states attempted to follow—Tsarist Russia, Greece, and Spain—but military defeats thwarted them.

In the twentieth century, the success of the Allies in World War I in mobilizing external finance, especially from the United States, stood in contrast to the Axis powers, whose domestic tax base was diminished by the war effort and whose access to foreign loans was nil. The result at the end of the war was a huge stock of inter-Allied war debts among the victors and an overwhelming stock of domestic debt owed by the separate Axis powers. Their domestic tax bases were further diminished by the terms of the peace treaties and the reparations demands.

The lessons learned were applied in World War II. On the Allied side, the United States supplied war materials under the Lend-Lease Act to avoid inter-Allied debts at the end. On the Fascist side, heavy occupation taxes were levied upon each conquered country as well as levies of forced labor. At the conclusion of hostilities, the method chosen by the United States to minimize its outlay on occupation costs and reconstruction expenses led to the economic revival and miraculous export-led growth of Japan, West Germany, and Italy. Meanwhile, the attempt of the Soviet Union to imitate the economic and financial policies of wartime Nazi Germany in its occupation zones in Central and Eastern Europe led ultimately to economic collapse. For the Soviets, military victory led to economic ruin, while for the Japanese and West Germans, military defeat led to economic triumph.

BIBLIOGRAPHY

Dickson, P. G. M., and J. G. Sperling. "War Finance, 1689–1714." In *The New Cambridge History*, vol. 6, *The Rise of Great Britain and Russia (1688–1715/25)*, edited by J. S. Bromley. Cambridge, 1970.

Ferguson, Niall. *The Cash Nexus: Money and Power in the Modern World, 1700–2000*. New York, 2001.

Neal, Larry. *War Finance*. 3 vols. Aldershot, U.K., and Brookfield, Vt., 1994.

LARRY NEAL

WATER CONTROL. Prior to the Industrial Revolution only one investment promised rapid increases in output: water control (which here includes irrigation, drainage, and flood control). Like the factories of capitalism, water control required institutional innovation; in particular, mechanisms to channel savings into productive investment. Unlike the Industrial Revolution, the expansion of water control was usually publicly funded and did not diffuse from any one geographical center. Water control is never the main event of a narrative of economic growth; people digging ditches and raising levees conjure little of either the dialectic of class warfare or the epic of entrepreneurship. Nevertheless, improved water control was a critical means of raising agricultural output over several millennia, and the distribution of water resources remains an important policy issue.

Water control here leaves aside urban water supply, electricity production, transportation canals, and well- or aquifer-based irrigation. This division is somewhat arbitrary. During the past century, dams that have supplied water to agriculture have often produced electricity, and irrigation projects have frequently shared infrastructure with urban water projects. These conjoined projects often include cross subsidies to the benefit of agriculture, but they are too recent to feature in this essay.

Institutions are important to water control both because of characteristics of the industry and because of the complexity of property rights to land and water. In all cases there are economies of scale and externalities. Therefore, the geographical scope of water control authorities matters. Further, water control often has public-good aspects. Since these issues vary depending on type of water control, each type is considered separately. In the case of flood control, economies of scale arise because the least costly way of building a levee is along a level line, protecting all the higher ground, so that average cost falls as a project gets larger along a given level line. Levees tend to exacerbate the flooding problems along another part of the river, creating externalities. Finally, it is often difficult to protect some fields from flooding without protecting others. It is, therefore, difficult to realize all the gains from flood control through simple private provision. Institutions must provide incentives for individuals to contribute to projects. Hence the institutions that matter most to flood control are those that permit the flood control authority to assess the beneficiaries, and those that allow different areas along a river to coordinate their improvements.

Irrigation also features economies of scale in water delivery as the cost of the main canal that brings water to a set of fields does not increase proportionally with its size. Further, the least costly way of building that canal is along a level line, irrigating all the land below the line. Externalities arise because when one draws water from a river, one generally lowers its level, thereby increasing procurement costs for downstream canals; if a dam is put in place in a river, then it may increase flooding above the irrigation project. Yet it is always feasible to exclude fields from irrigation. Realizing all the gains from irrigation again requires a set of institutions to allocate available water among competing claimants, and to provide rights of way to builders of the main canal.

Drainage is somewhat different from other types of control. Water is removed from an area, either by digging a ditch from its lowest point through a rise so that the water can flow out, or by pumping (as in the case of Dutch polders). Drainage can be assimilated into a local public good; indeed it is much more costly to drain half a marsh than the whole of it. In all cases, because the water level tends to equalize between drained and undrained areas, any improvement in one field affects the adjoining ones. Again institutions will dictate the extent to which claimants will be willing to participate in a project. Compounding the problem for marshes, property rights to land in marshes are often unclear, and institutions must allocate the improved land among legal owners and those with use rights.

In many cases it is efficient to increase several types of water control at once. For instance, coastal lowlands require simultaneous drainage and flood control, whereas in drier zones irrigation and flood control come together. Finally, in the case of irrigated rice, all three services must be provided at once for low-lying fields. In these cases the problem of coordination throughout a river basin becomes especially daunting.

Historical Development. Problems of economies of scale, externalities, and local public goods would not arise if water basins were under the control of a single entity or very few owners. In California, for instance, irrigation proceeded smoothly up to the end of the nineteenth century precisely because there were few claimants to water, and land was very concentrated. A recent analysis of the development of water control institutions in California argues that as settlement increased, problems of property rights grew, and the development of irrigation depended upon new institutions.

In Europe, Asia, and elsewhere, however, the development of water control often occurred in populated areas. In such regions, promoters of water control projects were often stymied by conflicts among owners of claims on land and water. Conflict arose over changes in the flow of water, the use of land, and the distribution of the costs and the benefits of projects. For projects to go forward, three key institutions had to be put in place: (1) rules that incited landowners to participate (typically costs were shared on the basis of land improved, and the benefits were simply the change in land value); (2) rules that decided compensation for either lost property or rights (compensating for land was relatively simple because eminent domain procedures could be used, but use rights were a very thorny issue); (3) rules for granting rights over water to projects.

Historically, public authorities have provided these institutions with varying degrees of success. Inefficiencies generally have stemmed from conflicts among different authorities over who has jurisdiction and from delays that reflect the incapacity of some political systems to avoid litigation. Beyond these general principles, understanding the development of water control institutions requires one to abandon the general logic of economics to delve into the historically contingent process of political development.

Take, for instance, the problem of land. Carrying out a water control project requires access to land to build levees or ditches. In addition, once a project has been executed, there is a great urge to "privatize" the improved land (eliminating most of the access rights, for instance). The right of authorities to grant powers of eminent domain or the right to "privatize" improved land varies. In the cases of the Low Countries and Italy, provinces and cities retained the political and legal authority to promote water control. Until the nineteenth century local sovereignty was not called into question, and it proved sufficient to produce the highest levels of investment in water control in Europe. In the Netherlands, where the dominant problem was to ally flood control and drainage, reclamation projects were an important part of local public finance and played a role in the development of local capital markets. In Italy, the Po valley had to be protected from flooding, and many areas also developed irrigation. Across the rest of continental Europe, from Spain and Portugal to areas in central Europe, local authorities in the Middle Ages assured early development of water control. These local authorities (cities or feudal lords) would secure water rights from the sovereign and use their local feudal powers to secure rights of eminent domain. Yet after the Renaissance, local development came into conflict with the rise of centralized states.

Water control itself had little to do with how these conflicts were resolved, but its further development was arrested until states effectively assumed control in these matters. Consider England, where in the Middle Ages drainage was largely under the purview of lords. They improved land on their manors without fuss because such drainage rarely affected the flow of water. By the seventeenth century, projects encountered opposition from villagers who used marshes as common land and from millers for whom marshes were often water reservoirs. To limit such opposition, promoters sought charters from the national authorities, and water control became embroiled in the conflict between Crown and Parliament. Both the Crown and Parliament claimed jurisdiction. Hence promoters might secure a charter from the Crown only to see Parliament later annul their privilege, or a parliamentary charter might run into opposition in royal courts. The Glorious Revolution (1688) unified political control over all issues related to water improvements into the hands of Parliament. In the eighteenth century a wave of water control projects closely followed the more famous wave of enclosures.

France had a similar medieval history to that of England, but by the seventeenth century divergence set in. When conflicts arose in the seventeenth century, neither the Crown nor local authorities had sufficient authority to push projects forward. The judiciary was largely responsible for the stalemate. As part of a larger struggle against the centralizing tendencies of the Crown, judges interpreted both customary rights and medieval charters as requiring that projects secure the approval of all concerned. The Revolution changed all this by vesting all eminent-domain authority in the central government and tilting the balance of power away from the judiciary and toward the executive and legislative branches. In the first half of the nineteenth century, France experienced a wave of water control projects that depended upon a strong central state.

Politics and Water Control. Europe has been closely studied by economic historians, yet in considering water control institutions Asia proves to be both a leader (in terms of technology and investment) and in many cases the counter example to many easily adopted conclusions. This is true, in part, because too often the literature reduces Asia to China, thereby oversimplifying the connections between politics and water control.

In China, the emperor formally had unlimited authority over water control. It is clear, however, that local officials had considerable leeway over maintenance and local expansion of water control. The central government did coordinate water control campaigns (principally flood control) on a scale not seen in Europe, where political boundaries interfered. The central government also coordinated the northward spread of irrigated rice and the attendant expansion of the irrigation network. Yet despite all this centralization, projects often went ahead based on local initiative, leaving central officials with the delicate task of ensuring cooperation among localities. Finally, even though the imperial government was heavily involved in coordinating, and at times subsidizing, initial investment, there was an expectation that local resources and personnel would be responsible for long-term management and maintenance. Periods of political strife were, not surprisingly, associated with declines in water control efficacy.

In the rest of Asia (e.g., Japan or Thailand) water control was also of great importance. In the absence of an empire, however, the institutions that provided water control were far more local. Nevertheless, as in Europe and China, the connection between politics and investment in water control is pervasive. Times of political stability and strong central government were good for water control in these countries as well. Whether politics mattered because stability increased the return on investment or because stability was required for the political system to promote water control is an important question. Yet, a systematic answer remains elusive for East Asia as well as for the rest of the world.

In the preceding discussion the political regime was regarded as exogenous to the provision of water control. Yet there is an important literature in economic history that argues that endowments shape institutions. In particular, this literature seeks to show that certain forms of endowments favor either unequal societies or despotic ones. For water control the argument was brilliantly put forth by Wittfogel some five decades ago. Water control networks feature economies of scale and externalities such that efficient administration is very valuable. Civil peace, providing a guarantee that the gains to the network will be realized, is also very valuable. Hence, Wittfogel reasoned, the individual who controls the administration of the network has power that few can rival. Peasants can ill afford to exit the system since returning to dry-land farming is unattrac-

tive. Administrators are kept in check by a complex system of monitoring and competition. The emperor thus has free reign over his domain to be a cruel despot or a benevolent dictator. The historical context of the theory of hydraulic societies (Wittfogel's career spanned the years of Stalin's domination of Russia) is at least as important as its empirical validity. Although Wittfogel was careful to note that water control offered an opportunity (rather than a necessity) for despotism, he made little effort to explain why few places in the world ever experienced the despotism of hydraulic societies.

There are too many uncomfortable exceptions to the rule to allow historians casually to turn Wittfogel's opportunity into necessity. Consider Egypt: there despotism arose around access to the Nile's water without an irrigation network. Consider western Europe: there heavy investment in water control (Low Countries, Northern Italy) coincided with the most fragmented form of polities, and much of it occurred during periods of representative governance. Consider that the network's geographical limits rarely match political boundaries. China is persistently too large, spanning multiple hydrographic basins; every other region in the world's states is persistently too small. Water endowments offer possibilities for institutions, but they are not fate.

BIBLIOGRAPHY

Allen R. C "Agriculture and the Origins of the State in Ancient Egypt." *Explorations in Economic History* 34.2 (April 1997), 135–155.

Ciriacono. Salvatore, ed. *Land Drainage and Irrigation*. Aldershot, U.K. and Brookfield, Vt., 1998.

McDevitt, Edward Paul. "The Evolution of Irrigation Institutions in California: The Rise of the Irrigation District, 1910–1930." Ph.D. diss., University of California, Los Angeles, 1994.

Ostrom, Elinor. *Governing the Commons: The Evolution of Institutions for Collective Action*. New York, 1990.

Perdue, Peter C. "Official Goals and Local Interests: Water Control in the Dongting Lake Region during the Ming and Qing Periods." *Journal of Asian Studies* 41.4 (August 1982), 747–765.

Rosenthal, Jean-Laurent. *The Fruits of Revolution, Property Rights, Litigation, and French Agriculture (1700–1860)*. New York, 1992.

Vries, Jan de, and Ad Van der Woude. *The First Modern Economy: Success, Failure, and Perserverance of the Dutch Economy, 1500–1815*. Cambridge, 1997.

Will, Pierre Etienne. "State Intervention in the Administration of a Hydraulic Infrastructure: The Example of Hubei Province in Late Imperial Times." In *The Scope of State Power in China*, edited by Stuart Schram. New York, 1985.

Wittfogel, Karl August. *Oriental Despotism: A Comparative Study of Total Power*. New Haven, 1957.

JEAN-LAURENT ROSENTHAL

WATER ENGINEERING. Although the early stages of irrigation, flood control, and land drainage are lost from view and are thus the subject of speculation, a number of hypotheses seem reasonable. On the basis of anthropological studies of food-gathering societies, it seems likely that irrigation preceded agriculture. In the twentieth century it was observed that pre-agricultural communities often sought to increase the yield of natural grasslands by diverting onto them water from streams or runoff from rainstorms. In the remote past some pre-agricultural peoples probably also watered the grains they gathered or the grasses on which their animals fed. With the coming of agriculture, increasingly more elaborate projects must have followed. Where agriculture depended on rainfall, this could be supplemented by digging small ditches to channel water from hillsides, rivers, lakes, and springs. In regions where agriculture appeared on lands flooded annually by great rivers, the timing and amount of watering could be controlled in varying degrees by the construction of simple dams, embankments, and canals, which limited floods, drained flood land for the benefit of agriculturalists, and brought water onto cropland. Still other projects to extend cultivation into wetlands by digging primitive drainage canals and damming inflows cannot have been far behind.

The Ancient World until 150 CE. Agriculture was probably first invented about 8000 BCE in the Fertile Crescent of west Asia, and by 7000 BCE it was firmly established in a good number of places. Many were upland sites that could have depended entirely on rainfall to provide adequate yields in an average year, though it seems likely that even there artificial watering could have increased yields. Other sites required irrigation from the beginning. Thus at Jericho, where there appears to have been a settlement of over two thousand people around 8000 BCE and where remains of domesticated wheat and barley from this early time have been found, agriculture—if it was practiced—would have had to depend entirely on irrigation. By the sixth millennium BCE there is clear evidence of settlements depending on fields irrigated by canals in the middle valley of the Tigris and the Euphrates, and similar settlements appeared in the alluvial plains farther south during the fifth millennium BCE. Shortly after the invention of writing around 3100 BCE, there is literary evidence of the construction of canals by the rulers of Sumerian cities. By this time there is enough evidence to allow glimpses of a system of flood control and irrigation that used longitudinal dykes on river banks to prevent undesirable flooding, large canals to take water by gravity flow into reservoirs, and a complex network of large and small canals to spread water onto cultivated fields. A cylinder seal dated about 2300 BCE depicts a *shadūf*, a human-powered device consisting of a pail attached by rope to a pole that is pivoted in the middle and counterweighted at the other end; this was used to provide limited amounts of water to higher lands that could not be reached by gravity flow. In the first millennium BCE, probably during Achaemenid rule (c. 600–331 BCE), at least one large transverse canal was built in the northern alluvial

plains, linking the Euphrates with the Tigris. By the end of that millennium, there is evidence of considerable settlement, depending on irrigation, along the Tigris.

These accomplishments seem all the more remarkable when it is remembered that irrigated agriculture in the region faced great difficulties. The floods of the Tigris and the Euphrates varied greatly from year to year, sometimes bringing too little water and sometimes too much. Excessive floods were often violent, destroying dams, dykes, canals, and agricultural land and sometimes—because of heavy deposits of silt in relatively flat lands—causing rivers to change their course. Even in more normal years silting was considerable, necessitating the annual cleaning of canals and the periodic cleaning of basins and reservoirs. The flood moreover came in the early spring, when winter crops—virtually the only crops—were near harvest. To be useful to cultivators, floodwater had to be captured and stored behind dams or in reservoirs for use in the autumn and winter. Before the water could be distributed over fields by gravity flow, these had to be leveled and sometimes terraced. By the time it was needed, water was sometimes so low that it could not flow onto fields; it had to be painstakingly lifted into canals at a higher level. Finally, the waters of the rivers were somewhat saline, as was the silt, and after years of irrigation—particularly when this was heavy and raised water tables—land could become too salty for cultivation. Unless the salts could be flushed out or scraped off, the land might have to be abandoned. Perhaps for all these reasons the development of agriculture was limited. Farmland was almost everywhere interspersed with large areas of desert and marsh, and biennial fallowing was usual.

In Egypt the timing of the flood of the Nile accounts for the development of a quite different system of flood control and irrigation. As the Nile rises in the summer months and reaches its maximum height in September, lands along the shore and in basins behind the river's banks are sufficiently wet in the autumn, after the flood has receded, to allow growing winter crops without further irrigation. Thus settlements along the Nile, dating from the late sixth millennium BCE, produced various grass crops, including panic, without flood control or artificial irrigation. By the fourth millennium BCE, however, perhaps under the pressure of increasing population, efforts were made to control the river's flood and to channel water into basins along the river's shore. Appearing first on the west bank of the Nile in Upper Egypt, the irrigation system used canals to take water across the river's banks and into low-lying basins on the other side; typically a series of basins could be flooded from one canal and the flow between higher and lower basins controlled by artificial dykes with masonry openings.

Basin irrigation was slowly extended, as farming systems based on emmer and barley were introduced from the Fertile Crescent. It expanded northward along the west bank of the Nile and into the southern part of the delta during the third millennium BCE. Under the first ruler of the Middle Kingdom, Amenemhet I (2000–1970 BCE), and his successors, the "engineer kings," basin irrigation was also brought to the desert margins of the delta, to the Faiyūm oasis, and to the east bank of the Nile. Extension into the east bank was achieved through construction on the river banks of large longitudinal dykes, which controlled flooding, and digging canals, which pierced the banks and delivered floodwater to basins. Under Ptolemy I (323–285 BCE) the area of irrigated land in the Faiyūm was greatly enlarged by reducing inflow into the oasis and increasing drainage. By lowering the water level 22 meters, he increased the area of irrigated land in the oasis by about 130,000 hectares. Although the Faiyūm, after Ptolemy's initiative, was irrigated by a system of radial canals similar to those in Mesopotamia, the Nile Valley and the delta knew only basin irrigation—a simple system of irrigation that dominated Egyptian agriculture until the nineteenth century.

The introduction of water-lifting devices attenuated to some extent the limitations of basin irrigation. The *shadūf,* already in use in Mesopotamia, appeared in Egypt around the middle of the second millennium BCE; it was considerably more efficient than the manual lifting of water in buckets and pots. Where conditions permitted, a further increase in productivity was achieved by the screw attributed to Archimedes (third century BCE) but perhaps known somewhat before his time. This consisted of a wooden screw inside a cylinder; turned by a human-powered treadmill, the screw produced a continuous flow of water. By the second century BCE, if not earlier, other machines had appeared that used animal power (the *sāqiya*) and waterpower (the *noria*) and could lift water considerably higher than the earlier machines powered by human beings. Their use, however, may have been largely confined to ornamental gardens and small plots of specialty crops.

By the late fourth millennium BCE agriculture also had been diffused eastward across the Iranian Plateau and into the Indus Valley, where during the third millennium BCE the remarkable Harappan civilization arose. The demands of its large urban population, living in two major cities, Mohenjo-Daro and Harappa, and in numerous smaller towns, almost certainly led to attempts to manage the autumn flows of the many branches of the Indus in order to raise yields of a variety of winter crops diffused from the Fertile Crescent. And both irrigation and flood control were essential for growing summer crops, such as sesame, cotton, and finger millet. For reasons that are not well understood, the urban civilization of the Indus Valley disappeared during the first half of the second millennium BCE, though remnants of Harappan culture survived elsewhere.

Much has been written about the organization of irrigation and flood control in these ancient civilizations. The late Karl Wittfogel argued that the development of integrated irrigation systems in the great river valleys of the ancient world gave rise to strongly organized "despotic" states. These had large bureaucracies to direct the construction and maintenance of dams, embankments, and canals, for which involuntary, corvée labor was used. These states also provided protection, settled disputes among users, and taxed users heavily. The three river valley civilizations discussed above do not fit this model well. In Egypt and Mesopotamia projects to irrigate lands and control floods were small in scale and discontinuous. There was no large-scale integrated system for river valleys or even major parts of them. Projects appear to have been undertaken by local communities acting independently and using, to a considerable extent, voluntary labor. The ongoing maintenance of dams, canals, and embankments was also probably voluntary at first, though soon it must have become an obligation. Where the projects were undertaken on lands belonging to temples, great landowners, cities, or a nascent state, labor may have been recruited in other ways, about which there is little information, though it seems that in Mesopotamia some laborers were paid in kind. In any case the fact of corvée labor for the construction and maintenance of some irrigation works is hardly conclusive evidence of a despotic state. Medieval European peasants were often subject to heavy corvées at a time when kings were feeble and distant. In the Indus Valley, while no information bearing directly on the question exists, the apparent cultural homogeneity of the whole area might suggest a greater degree of centralization. Yet the disconnected nature of settlement and the apparent integration of individual towns with their surrounding villages and agricultural lands into what several scholars have described as "economic pockets" and "close circuits."

To be sure the spread of irrigated agriculture along river valleys facilitated the rise of chiefdoms and states. Increases in the amount of agricultural land and labor and in the productivity of these yielded larger agricultural surpluses that could be traded, given away, transferred as rent, or taxed, thus supporting the growth of various nonagricultural classes. Among these classes were rulers and their courts as well as literate bureaucrats engaged in collecting and distributing rents and taxes and in settling disputes over boundaries and water flows. Furthermore, as settlement became denser and more nearly continuous, communications improved, and it became easier to centralize irrigation, taxation, and defense. The problem is that in Mesopotamia, Egypt, and the Indus Valley the process of centralization does not seem to have gone far, and the irrigation works, in particular, seem to have remained disaggregated.

Although the spread of irrigation and flood control technologies along the great river valleys is the most spectacular manifestation of these technologies in the ancient world, they also appeared on a smaller scale in both neighboring and more distant regions during the millennia leading up to the current era. To give just a few of many possible examples, in the western parts of the Fertile Crescent, where the earliest agriculture could have relied entirely on rainfall, there are signs from the sixth millennium BCE onward that stream water and runoff from rainstorms were captured and spread onto terraces and fields. At roughly the same time irrigated agriculture seems to have spread eastward from Mesopotamia up the mountainsides of Khūzestān and onto the Iranian Plateau. During the late fourth millennium BCE urban centers appeared in southern and southwestern Iran that depended on the agricultural surplus of irrigated hinterlands. In Greece, near the city of Argolis, there are the remains of a dam, dated around 1300 BCE, constructed of massive "Cyclopean" stones.

By the first millennium BCE the ancient world could boast many peoples who undertook projects for irrigation, flood control, and drainage. Thus in Greece, where the science of mechanics was developing and, in the third century BCE, Archimedes (a Greek from Syracuse) was laying the groundwork for hydrostatics, irrigation projects appeared around the main cities. During the same period, on the mountain slopes of the Levant, the Phoenicians were developing extensive irrigated agriculture with cisterns, aqueducts, canals, and terraces; and it may be assumed that they took their knowledge of irrigation to their colonies in North Africa, Sicily, Sardinia, and Iberia. In the southeastern and southern Arabian Peninsula, from the seventh century BCE, the Himyaritic and other kingdoms constructed large dams in the upper reaches of the mountains above the coastal plains. Many of these dams supplied water not only to nearby agricultural lands but also to agricultural communities farther down the mountainsides, where smaller dams held water for short periods and released it into canals.

Irrigation, flood control, and drainage reached their apogee in the ancient world during the first two centuries CE, following the establishment of Roman imperial rule in 27 BCE. During this period population grew in size and became more urbanized. Projects, many ambitious in scale and requiring considerable knowledge of engineering, were undertaken in virtually every part of the empire, most sponsored by the imperial or provincial governments pursuing policies to promote cities and develop their agricultural hinterlands. Today in many of the lands of the former empire there can be seen the remains of Roman aqueducts (used to bring water to both city dwellers and farmers), dams of various sorts, cisterns, and canals, and archeologists have uncovered much more evidence of projects intended to develop countrysides capable of feeding larger or smaller cities. Particularly notable is the development of irrigated agriculture on the southern and eastern frontiers of the empire, in the semiarid and arid regions on the northern fringes of the Sahara, and in similar west Asian regions lying to the east of the margins of rain-fed agriculture. In general there is no convincing evidence that the climate of these regions in Roman times was not similar to that of today. The Romans it seems really did make the desert bloom.

To give only a few examples, in the province of Arabia, corresponding roughly to the present-day Negev, and in the most southerly parts of Jordan, the Romans built on earlier work by the Nabateans to create a large number of settlements, some of them frontier posts. All the wadis in the region, with the exception of the largest, which could not be controlled, were dammed. Many valleys had a series of dams, each averaging forty to fifty meters in length, going up the entire river valley. These captured not only water but also silt, which after some years of accumulation formed a flat bed in which crops could be grown after the flood waters receded. Smaller dams and canals diverted flash floods onto cultivated fields and olive groves. Similar works were built in the North African provinces of Libya, Cyrenaica, Africa, and Numidia.

Although for the most part the Romans used technologies developed earlier by the Greeks, Persians, and others, they apparently did invent two new and important types of dams: buttress dams, in which buttresses on the downstream wall of the dam help support the weight of water held in the reservoir, and arch dams, in which the wall of the dam gains strength by curving into the reservoir (a principle discovered by beavers at an unknown date but probably long before Roman times).

The Late Ancient World. The achievements of the Roman Empire—in water engineering as in other spheres—peaked by the middle of the second century CE, after which the empire entered a period of prolonged economic and political decline. This is most evident in the western part of the empire, where in the following centuries cities shrank and, in spite of migration from the cities to the countryside, there are almost everywhere signs of rural depopulation as well. Combined with a decline in slavery, this caused a manpower shortage and the widespread abandonment of agricultural land. The problem of *agri deserti* (deserted fields) was of great concern to a government that needed ever-greater resources to put down internal revolts and to defend itself against "barbarians" pressing more heavily on its borders on every side. In such circumstances the state could no longer take the initiative to launch new works of irrigation, drainage, and flood control. On the contrary, much that had been achieved was lost, as canals were left to silt up and dams were not repaired. When the last western emperor was murdered in 476 CE, almost the entire western empire was in the hands of Germanic tribes, who had little or no interest in the hydraulic achievements of the Romans and none of the skills or financial resources needed to maintain them.

The eastern part of the empire fared somewhat better than the western, though it too suffered from some of the factors leading to western decline. Parts of the eastern empire seem to have been affected by the same population loss experienced in the west during the third century CE. In Egypt, for instance, there is clear evidence of rural depopulation in the Faiyūm and along the Nile Valley in this period. As canals, weirs, and dykes fell into disrepair, there was a general retreat of settlement back to the areas that were easiest to irrigate, those along the river's shores, which could be flooded by simple basin irrigation. A shortage of labor in relation to land probably accounts for the gradual replacement from the fifth century onward of the human-powered devices for raising water, the *shadūf* and the Archimedes screw, by the water-driven *noria* and the animal-powered *sāqiya*.

In the sixth and early seventh centuries the whole of the eastern empire was devastated by the plague of Justinian, a pandemic that appeared in Constantinople in 541 CE and continued to ravage Byzantium, the Arab world, and western Europe for at least two centuries, though later visitations were probably less virulent. Population levels declined steeply. Some areas were hit particularly hard. Many Byzantine cities to the east of Aleppo were almost entirely abandoned by the early seventh century. During this same period huge amounts of silt descended the Levantine river valleys and accumulated in the plains and mouths of rivers—evidence it seems of widespread abandonment of terraced lands on the mountainsides, probably most especially those lands distant from villages. During the seventh century Egyptian agriculture was struck not only by the plague but also by two other natural disasters: low levels of the Nile floods during most of the century and the gradual subsidence and ultimate submergence of the northern and northeastern parts of the delta.

To the east of the Byzantine Empire, Mesopotamia and the Iranian Plateau seem to have prospered during much of the period of Sassanian rule (226 CE to 651 CE), only to decline precipitously in the seventh century. In the *Khudainama*, or Book of Kings, many rulers present themselves as builders of cities and irrigation works, though it is often not clear what irrigation projects they completed. There seem to have been two periods during which the greatest advances were made in irrigation and flood control systems: the third century CE, which was a time of consolidation, and the late fifth to early seventh centuries, which was a period of strong centralization. During these periods considerable repair and new construction were carried out

in Mesopotamia, while new dams and bridge dams were built on the Iranian Plateau or on its foothills, of which the most famous is that of Shādorvān on the Kārūn River. Sassanian prosperity seems to have ended by 627 CE if not earlier, as the empire fell prey to external attack and internal anarchy and as natural disasters struck. The plague of Justinian ravaged the empire in the sixth century and may have been particularly deadly in the early seventh century. Furthermore in the year 628 a huge flood on the Tigris and the Euphrates could not be contained, and many fields, embankments, canals, and dams—including the great Nimrud dam—were destroyed, leaving the lower reaches of the river system a marshy quagmire. No serious attempt was made to repair the damage.

Finally, in the southern and southeastern Arabian Peninsula the irrigation systems that supported once-prosperous kingdoms fell into disrepair during the fifth and sixth centuries. In the late sixth century the largest dam, Mārib, broke, and from that time onward there is no evidence of large irrigation systems in operation in the Himyaritic or any other kingdom of the region. In short, by the time of the Arab expansion into west Asia, North Africa, and Iberia from 632 to 714, the systems of irrigation and flood control in the regions the Arabs were to conquer were in an advanced state of decay where they were not in ruins.

The Islamic World until 1500. The Arab conquests of the seventh and early eighth centuries led to the creation of an Islamic nation, Dār al-Islām, which stretched from the Indus to the Pyrenees and thus united under one rule parts of the world that had never before been in direct contact. Because of the great movement through this world of scholars, pilgrims, soldiers, traders, settlers, and others, there was an unprecedented opportunity for the diffusion of existing technologies into regions where they had not previously been known or had been little used. The incentive to use to the full available irrigation and drainage technologies grew as from the eighth century onward rural populations began to increase and press more heavily on the land and as expanding cities, old and new, sought larger food supplies. The development of a substantial body of water law from the time of the Prophet onward and the machinery for enforcement also encouraged investment in waterworks. Thus many, though not all, regions the early Islamic period saw a revival of irrigation and drainage works and an intensification of agriculture. The extent of this revival has sometimes been underestimated by archaeologists relying on counts of surface shards, which, for the critical period of transition, cannot be dated, and by scholars using unreliable and confusing reports on taxation returns for Mesopotamia in pre-Islamic and Islamic times. The wealth of evidence, however, speaks for a strong revival of water-engineering projects after the conquests were over and the plague had receded.

In the valleys of the Tigris and the Euphrates, for instance, the repair and rebuilding of ancient works and the construction of new ones resumed as early as the late seventh century. As is well documented, the governor of the province of Iraq, Ḥajjāj ibn Yūsuf (d. 714) founded the city of Wāsiṭ, ordered the repair of the irrigation and drainage system between the two rivers, and had the al-Nīl canal built. Ziyād ibn Abīh, who was governor of two other new cities, Baṣra and Kūfa, each surrounded by newly irrigated hinterlands, ordered the construction of two large canals connecting Baṣra with the Shaṭṭ al-'Arab Recent archeological work in the middle Euphrates region has revealed the rebuilding of a long-abandoned ancient canal, Nahr Daurīn, in the late seventh century or early eighth century and the slightly later construction of an entirely new canal, Nahr Sa'īd. Many other examples could be adduced. Particularly interesting are many reclamation projects carried out by private developers in the Sawād in this early period.

In Egypt it is more difficult to track the development of irrigation works in the early Islamic period and to compare these achievements to those of earlier times because no comprehensive description of the state of Egyptian irrigation during either period exists. However, the writings of tenth-century geographers and historians, such as al-Kindī, al-Mas'ūdī, and Ibn Ḥawqal, tell of a strongly centralized government engaged in constructing and maintaining canals and dams in many regions. These writers also describe canal systems in every part of the country: those of Upper Egypt; the canal feeding into the Faiyūm, with its extensive irrigation system; another canal going from the Faiyūm canal back to the Nile; a canal leading from the capital, al-Fusṭāṭ, to the Red Sea, supplying water to the southeastern delta and also, along the first part of its course, to nearby lands; and the extensive system of the delta itself, fed by two principal canals that branched into mazes of smaller canals. It seems probable that the irrigation system described by these tenth-century authors surpassed any of the achievements of the ancients.

In Spain too there are many traces of hydraulic works built in Islamic times, most particularly for irrigation but also to control floods and drain swamps. Although an older school of Spanish historians stressed the continuity of Roman and Visigothic works into the Islamic period, it now seems clear that many pre-Islamic works had fallen into disrepair and that some were buried deep in silt. The evidence for extensive undertakings by Arabs and Berbers is of various types. Several studies have used the names of canals effectively. In a survey of these in Lorca, for instance, 68 percent of the names of irrigation canals were Roman, while the rest, mainly from peripheral regions, were Arabic. These findings suggest that after the Arab conquest the Roman system was brought back into use and extended outward. The Arabs and Berbers may have played a still more important role in developing irrigation in Valencia, where half of the major canals and branches have Arabic names, and in Murcia, where the proportion is 78 percent Arabic. The vocabulary for irrigation in both Castilian and Catalan is also in large measure of Arabic origin. Words for structures such as canals, dams, cisterns, and *noria*s derive from Arabic words, as does some of the vocabulary used in the distribution of water among users. Arab geographers from the late ninth to the thirteenth centuries describe extensive irrigation and drainage systems in the lower valley of the Guadalquivir and the lands south of the Sierra Nevada; in the *huertas* of Valencia and Gandía; and in the *vegas* of Granada, Murcia, and Játiva. Most of these seem to have been based on Syrian, Yemeni, and Egyptian models.

In addition to stimulating the construction of dams, weirs, embankments, canals, and cisterns, the Arab conquerors and those who followed them introduced a number of other technologies that had an important impact on the agriculture of the conquered regions. Most notable were the *sāqiya* and the *noria*, two devices for raising water from canals, wells, and cisterns. These were known in ancient times but were much more widely diffused in the Islamic world, in many parts of which they were essentially new. The Islamic world may also have seen the invention of, and certainly it witnessed the widespread transmission of, another hydraulic technology, the *qanāt*. This was an underground canal that tapped an aquifer and channeled water over shorter or longer distances—one *qanāt* in Iran is fifty kilometers long—toward communities that used the water for agricultural, industrial, and domestic purposes. Previously thought to have been invented at the beginning of the first millennium BCE, it now seems, after the research of Pierre Briant and others, that the *qanāt* may not have been known until Sassanian or even Islamic times. Whatever the date of its invention, clearly by the year 1000 the *qanāt* was widely used through much of Iran and Oman, where many communities depended on it for their agriculture, and from there the technology was carried through west Asia, across North Africa, and into Spain and Sicily.

The *sāqiya*, the *noria*, and the *qanāt* had special importance for the agriculture of west Asia and the Mediterranean basin. Not only did they bring water to lands that would otherwise have been dry, they also in most cases made water available through the entire year instead of during only one season. The importance of perennial irrigation was great, especially for the western part of the caliphate. It made possible the introduction of a considerable number of summer crops, including rice, sorghum, sugarcane, and cotton, grown at a time when in most areas both land and labor had lain idle. Perennial irrigation also enabled the planting of permanent crops that required heavy watering during the summer months, for example, bananas, plantains, sour oranges, and lemons.

The accomplishments of the early Islamic world in irrigation, flood control, and drainage, impressive as they may have been, were often undone in later centuries. It is possible that in some regions land was overcultivated or overirrigated, becoming in time too infertile or too saline to give good results. In other regions friable soils were vulnerable to erosion from floods, rains, and winds. Such lands came to be cultivated less intensively or were abandoned. Irrigation and flood control also depended for their success on the attitudes and circumstances of rulers. Periods in which strong rulers took an interest in maintaining and enlarging systems were followed, with almost monotonous regularity, by periods of neglect. Decline was particularly rapid following the invasions of various (mostly non-Arab) peoples: in the East the Saljūqs, the crusaders, the Ayyūbids, the Mongols, and the Ottomans and in the West the Banū Hilāl, the Almoravids, the Almohads, the Normans in Sicily, and the Christian conquistadores of Spain. The invasions themselves often damaged constructions and caused peasants to take flight, and the conquerors, familiar with agricultural systems that made less-intensive use of land, brought with them attitudes, laws, and institutions less favorable to irrigated agriculture. Once their conquests were consolidated, some of these invaders—for example, the Saljūqs and the later Īlkhānids (or Mongols) in Iran—attempted to repair and even extend systems of irrigation and flood control and thus ushered in times of relative prosperity, but they seldom restored all that had been lost. Finally, nearly the whole Islamic world fell prey to the Black Death, a catastrophic outbreak of the plague that began in the mid-fourteenth century and persisted through much of the fifteenth century, leaving cities and countrysides depopulated and making intensive agriculture unnecessary and uneconomic.

Medieval and Early Modern Europe. With the collapse of the western half of the Roman Empire in the fifth century and its replacement by weak and frequently changing successor states, many factors worked against the control of water for agriculture: the lack of security; the inability of the successor states to provide financing or a legal framework for irrigation and drainage works; the conquerors' lack of experience with hydraulic technology and irrigated agriculture; the gradual replacement of the slave labor forces of the latifundia by a tenant labor force composed of former slaves, or *servi casati*, and formerly free settlers, or *coloni*, both of which had tenancies and were thus less under the control of landowners; the decline of trade and the concomitant increase in self-sufficiency of rural estates; and the huge decline in population caused by the plague of Justinian in the late sixth and seventh centuries.

During the whole of the early Middle Ages, up to 1000, there is little sign of serious efforts in Europe to promote irrigated agriculture, flood control, or drainage. On the contrary, many existing works fell into disrepair. The main exceptions are Muslim Spain and briefly Muslim Sicily, where, as noted above, irrigated agriculture and drainage projects were actively promoted. When these areas were reconquered by Christians, some of the projects continued in operation, most notably the irrigation works in the *huerta* of Valencia. In many places, however, successful projects initiated under Muslim rule were neglected by the Christian conquerors, who had different agricultural traditions and needs.

In most of western Europe conditions began to change from the late tenth century onward, as external threats abated, the "feudal peace" descended, population began to increase, cities started growing, and trade revived. In these circumstances there was pressure to expand the area of agricultural land and to intensify land use. But the focus of work changed. Instead of being concerned mainly with irrigating semiarid lands in the Mediterranean basin, the medieval emphasis was on more temperate regions of Europe, where rainfall was heavier and the principal objectives were the control of floods and the drainage of swamps and coastal flats.

In the Lowlands (also known as Low Countries) the reclamation of fenlands seems already to have been underway by about 960, when an Icelandic account of a raid on the Frisian coast describes the land as flat and states that the fields and meadows were surrounded by drainage ditches full of water. In the three centuries that followed many small and large fens in both the Flemish and Dutch lowlands were drained by digging ditches and canals. In some areas dams also were constructed to prevent rivers from flooding lands downstream. Independent communities undertook some of the projects, while princes, counts, abbots, and bishops sponsored others. Perhaps the most impressive series of projects, known as the Big Reclamation, was undertaken in central Holland under the count of Holland and the bishop of Utrecht. Starting along riverbanks, the work pushed farther and farther into the fenland wilderness. By the fourteenth century most of the peat lands and clay-covered peat lands of the region had been reclaimed.

Poldering was another technique of land reclamation widely used in the medieval Netherlands. Lands along the coast or in low-lying, inland regions were surrounded by walls or dykes to create polders that could, if needed, be raised by the addition of soil from nearby. Canals might be dug outside the polders to facilitate drainage. The first recorded instance of poldering is in Flanders and dates from 1111 to 1115. By the end of the thirteenth century vast areas of inland marshes in Zeeland-Flanders had been turned into fields and meadows, while in the same period polder construction also led to impressive gains in many other parts of the Lowlands. By the thirteenth century it became necessary to construct polders in many areas where agriculture had long been practiced, as centuries of cultivation and drainage had caused land to subside.

Dykes were also used to protect low-lying fields from runoff from higher lands, to shore up riverbanks against floods and tidal waters, and to protect coastal areas against storms and tides. These were made from earth or clay, sometimes reinforced on the water side with seaweed or reeds. Coastal dyking became all the more important after storm surges in the twelfth century transformed the relatively small inland lake Almere into a large saltwater sea, the Zuiderzee, which brought tides much farther inland. Another great storm in 1287 caused heavy loss of life and land and made further protection necessary. Slowly there emerged a system of almost continuous dyking along the coast of Zeeland and South Holland. This extended cultivation considerably into some coastal areas, though in other parts much farmland was permanently lost in the ongoing battle with the sea.

During the twelfth and thirteenth centuries irrigation and drainage works were also undertaken in other parts of Europe, sometimes with the help of skilled workers from the Lowlands and generally under the direction of religious authorities. From 1113 onward the archbishop of Bremen and Hamburg signed a number of contracts with *Hollandenses* for the reclamation and settlement of fenlands in his archdiocese, while in England, under successive archbishops of Canterbury, work was begun on the reclamation of the Romney marshes along the southeastern coast. Records from Italy tell of projects to control floods and drain wetlands in twelfth-century Lombardy and thirteenth-century Emelia as well as a Cistercian initiative near Milan to use sewage water to irrigate cropland. In France the period of medieval expansion saw many projects—the precise nature of which is not always clear—in different regions: drainage in the Gulf of Saint Omer, dyking on the coast of Normandy, flood control along the Loire (where work was earlier initiated by Charlemagne), and reclamation of coastal lands of Poitou. Other references are to projects in Languedoc, Saintonge, and the Camargue. Particularly noted by travelers were the irrigated *hortas* or gardens of Rousillon, made on lands reclaimed from swamps in the eleventh and twelfth centuries.

In most of Europe the impetus to land reclamation weakened by the second decade of the fourteenth century, when population began to decline and falling agricultural prices made many projects uneconomic. And work virtually came to an end after the Black Death first struck in 1347. In the Lowlands, however, which seem to have been hit particularly hard by the increasingly stormy and wet weather of the late Middle Ages, the construction of polders and dykes continued through the fourteenth and fifteenth centuries, as lands subsided and severe storms—most particularly those that formed the great bays of Jade, Dollart, Biesbos, and Braakman—allowed the sea to encroach once more onto cultivated land. By the early fifteenth century drainage was made easier by the use of windmills to drive pumps; *wipmolen*, or hollow post mills, allowed the sails that caught the wind to turn to catch wind coming from any direction. Toward the end of the fifteenth century these were found in many parts of the Lowlands. By then another technological advance had been made in dyke construction. Where their walls were vulnerable to storms from the sea, dykes increasingly were reinforced by timber piles laid along the waterside. In Friesland, where the clay was not so strong and storms could be especially violent, the outer walls of dykes came to be protected by two rows of piles with faggots in between.

Similarly in the valley of the Po, where pre-Roman and Roman irrigation and drainage works had long ago fallen into disrepair, work continued through the fourteenth and fifteenth centuries. It became all the more necessary after a disastrous flood of the river in 1438. On the upper reaches of the Po and its tributaries, flooding was alleviated through embankments and canals. On the flood plains excess water was carried off in large canals, while smaller canals provided perennial irrigation to fields. By the end of the fifteenth century the main elements of the present-day system of flood control, irrigation, and drainage in the Po Valley were already in place.

In the Lowlands the dyking of coastal lands continued through the sixteenth and seventeenth centuries, accounting in the Netherlands for 80 percent of all land reclaimed during the two centuries. Slowly, however, attention turned to the draining of inland *meers* or lakes, some natural, some the result of peat digging, and some created by the subsidence of land previously drained. In the sixteenth century many of these projects were undertaken by "adventurers" or entrepreneurs out to make a quick profit. But their ultimate success depended on the creation of water boards with jurisdiction over ever-larger areas and mandates to establish communities, repair dykes and canals, and enforce their rulings on users. Progress in draining *meers* also depended on technological advances. Wind-driven scoop mills, for which 102 patents were issued in the Netherlands between 1560 and 1700, were often used in tandem, four or five lifting water to considerable heights. In the drainage of smaller *meers*, the Archimedean pump, a wind-powered version of the screw of antiquity, was also widely used. By the end of the seventeenth century the greater part of the work of reclamation in the Lowlands had been completed. The achievement was impressive. Today more than half of the land in the

Netherlands lies beneath sea level. The country's existence depends on the control of water established in this period.

England, France, and Italy had their own unique problems of flood control and drainage. In the sixteenth century these were studied, and some projects were attempted. But they were more effectively addressed in the seventeenth century. In England the most important project was the drainage of some 125,000 hectares comprising the Great Level of the fenlands in the coastal area around the Wash. Previous piecemeal work had been undertaken by various abbeys and, after the dissolution of the monasteries by 1540, by private speculators. But in 1589 Humphrey Bradley, from Brabant, submitted a comprehensive plan to drain the Great Level of the fens. After extensive surveying, Bradley showed that almost the entire region lay above sea level and could therefore be drained by canals leading to the sea without recourse to drainage mills. His proposals languished while financiers squabbled, but finally the work was completed between 1630 and 1653 under the direction of a Zeelander, Cornelius Vermuyden. (In time, however, subsidence of the drained land made the use of mills necessary after all.) In France the main problem was the large number of inland marshes created by the flooding of slow-moving rivers. At the intervention of a strongly centralized government, most particularly in the time of Henri IV (r. 1589–1610), and with help from three Lowland engineers, including Bradley, who was appointed Maître des Digues du Royaume, numerous swamps were drained in Saintonge, Poitou, Normandy, Picardy, Languedoc, Provence, and Puy-de-Dôme.

In Italy, where the main problems were the flooding of rivers rising in the central mountain ranges and floods and stagnant waters in the plains downstream, the leadership in attacking problems passed from the religious houses to the great landowners and polities, such as Venice, Milan, and the Papal State. These launched large-scale projects to control flooding in entire river systems using retaining walls, groynes and diversionary banks feeding into canals. Embankments were protected from erosion by piles, masonry walls, stone pitchings, and fasces. Some of the more ambitious projects of *bonifica* (reclamation) achieved in this period were in Brescia (1534), Aquileia (1561), Tuscany (1572), and Ferrara (1598). Attempts by the papacy to drain the seven hundred square kilometers of Pontine marshes southeast of Rome—after several near successes—in large measure failed.

During the sixteenth and seventeenth centuries the Lowlands and Italy produced a considerable literature on water engineering, which, in the form of printed books, not only aided in the diffusion of existing technologies and theory but also served as a platform for further progress. There were to be sure some earlier writings, most notably Book VIII of Vitruvius's *De architectura*, written in the first century CE, which outlined certain principles of hydraulics and described the construction of aqueducts and water-lifting machines, and the *Book of Machines* of al-Jazarī, written in 1206 and considered "the most important document on engineering from ancient times until the Renaissance" (Hill, 2001), in which the author described five water-lifting machines and a water-driven suction pump. Although the manuscript of Vitruvius's work was rediscovered in the fifteenth century, neither of these authors seems to have been known to the early modern writers, who based their writings largely on practical experience from which emerged a body of theoretical knowledge.

Among the more important Lowland writers were Andries Vierlingh of Brabant, whose *Tractaet van dyckagie* (written in 1578 but not published until 1920) codified sixteenth-century methods of constructing dikes and floodgates; Simon Stevin, whose *Nieuwe maniere van sterctebou, door spilsluysen* (published in 1617) is the oldest work on sluices and whose treatise on mills, *Van de molens* (1584) advanced original theories on statics and hydrostatics; Cornelius Janszoon Meijer, who wrote for Innocent XI a memoir (published in 1683) on how to drain the Pontine marshes as well as *L'arte di rendere i fiume navigable . . .* (1696), in which he prescribed methods for controlling floods in Bologna, Ferrara, and Ravenna; and Humphrey Bradley of Brabant, who wrote a treatise on the draining of the Great Level of the English fenlands. In Italy, Galileo (1564–1642) was responsible for pioneering work on hydraulics. Practical treatises, in which theories were also developed, were produced by the Florentine Antonio Lupicini, who wrote six books on flood control, including one published in 1587 on the Po Valley and another published in 1591 on the region of Florence; by Benedetto Castelli, whose book, *Della misura dell'acque corriente*, published in 1628, proposed ways of measuring water flows and controlling floods; by Domenico Guglielmini, who wrote *Della natura de fiume*, published in 1697; and by Giovanni Battista Barattieri, whose *Architettura d'acque* was published in 1699.

The Late Modern Period: 1750 to 2000. The last two and a half centuries have seen a proliferation of irrigation, flood control, and drainage projects driven by a worldwide demographic explosion, rising standards of living, many technological advances, the desire of European powers to reduce famine and flooding in their colonies, the promotion of key colonial export crops, and since 1950 aid projects to developing nations. Change was particularly rapid in the twentieth century. At the beginning of the century the area of irrigated land is estimated to have been 40 million hectares; this increased to 100 million hectares by 1950 and 270 million hectares by 1998. It may be assumed that there was also an increase in the average intensity of watering and a lengthening of the season of watering. At the end of the twentieth century about one-fifth of the world's agricultural land was irrigated. This yielded about 40 percent of agricultural production. In 2001 it was estimated that 1.5 trillion hectares of land were drained or protected from floods; most of this achievement was realized during the twentieth century.

Technological advances played an important role in this ongoing process. Although the technologies of ancient times continue in use, most particularly in developing countries, they have been and continue to be displaced by modern technologies with roots in the European Industrial Revolution. Perhaps the earliest relevant innovation was the reciprocating steam engine invented by James Watt in the 1770s and used later in the century for the drainage of Dutch polders. Results, however, were at first disappointing, and perhaps for this reason the use of steam power for drainage was adopted only slowly in England. But by the 1820s the steam engine was used widely in the Great Fens, and after the invention of the centrifugal pump in l852 steam engines came to be widely used in drainage projects. Further advances came in the 1880s and 1890s with the development of internal combustion engines powered by gasoline and diesel fuel; these were more mobile and more fuel efficient. And in the early twentieth century electricity was used to power pumps in some regions. Pumps could be used not only in drainage projects but also to raise water out of canals, cisterns, and wells—including deep wells. They could also force water through pipes and hoses, from which it would move into canals, onto furrowed fields, and into hoses providing drip irrigation. And the pressure of pumped water could drive a variety of types of sprinklers, most of which were portable and some of which were mobile while in operation. The spread of many of these innovations was rapid. By the end of the nineteenth century, for example, diesel-powered pumps were used in various parts of Mesopotamia.

There were also important innovations in dam construction. Portland cement, made of burnt limestone and clay ground together, provided a stronger building material upon its patent in 1824, and pressure cementation, developed through the nineteenth century, resulted in tighter constructions. Another advance was the invention of reinforced concrete, which was patented in l867; this involved the strengthening of concrete through the insertion of steel bars, rods, or mesh. The first dam with buttresses of reinforced concrete was built in l908. At the same time there were advances in the design of dams based on the developing science of mechanics and taking advantage of the stronger materials available. Most notable were the development through the nineteenth and early twentieth centuries of large dams supported by buttresses and multiple arches, which increasingly were constructed of concrete, and the development in France, under the leadership of François-Xavier Delocre and other engineers, of high arch dams needed for the control of floods. A remarkable multiple-arch dam was built in Hyderabad in 1804 under the direction of the French engineer Henry Rusle, and this was followed through the rest of the century by the construction of a good number of large dams—including arch dams, multiple-arch dams, and buttress dams—in France, Belgium, Germany, and England. Several collapses of large dams in France, England, and Spain, two at the cost of many lives, added to a growing body of theoretical and practical knowledge that allowed the proliferation of large dam construction in the first half of the twentieth century, most especially in western Europe and the American West.

In the second half of the twentieth century there was an explosion of large dam construction. Whereas in 1949 there were only 5,000 large dams (more than 15 meters in height) in the world, the majority in more-developed countries, by the end of the century there were about 45,000 large dams in 140 countries. The pace of construction was particularly rapid in the first half of the l970s, when on average one thousand large dams were constructed yearly. Although not all were used for irrigation (see below), they did supply water to about 30 to 40 percent of the world's irrigated farmland.

The incomplete world inventory of dams kept by the International Commission on Large Dams (ICOLD) listed 25,410 dams of over 15 meters in height in 1998; about 500 of these were over 100 meters high. Single-purpose dams account for 70 percent of the total inventory; nearly half of these are for irrigation and about 8 percent for flood control. The other uses are the generation of hydroelectricity (about 20 percent), domestic and industrial water supply, navigation, recreation, and fish farming. Of the multiple-purpose dams listed, nearly half store water for irrigation, and 39 percent play a role in flood control. These large dams are widely distributed over the world. Though the United States is the leader with of a quarter of the world's large dams, India has 15 percent, China 7 percent, and Spain and Japan over 4 percent each. The world's two highest dams are in Tajikistan, followed by dams in Switzerland, Georgia, Italy, and Mexico. The dams with the largest reservoirs are in Zambia-Zimbabwe, Russia, Egypt, Ghana, and Canada. In spite of technical advances in concrete and masonry construction, earth dams—most often faced with masonry or concrete—still account for 64 percent of all large dams. Most of these are under sixty meters in height, but the world's second highest dam (the Nurek dam in Tajikistan, standing three hundred meters high) is also an earth dam. Gravity dams, in which the upstream side is vertical and the downstream side slopes, account for 19 percent of the total, rock-fill dams are 8 percent, arch dams are 4 percent, and buttress dams are 1.4 percent.

In recent years the widespread construction of large dams has attracted much opposition. Critics admit that these dams play an important role in increasing the area of irrigated land and in prolonging the period of watering; they have thus helped to increase the world's food supplies. Critics also concede that the dams regulate the year-to-year flow of water, thus alleviating famine when rainfall in the catchment area is low and reducing floods in years of high rainfall. But they point out that most large-dam projects experience serious cost overruns, while the irrigation benefits are often less than estimated. Furthermore because of widespread removal of vegetation in the rain catchment areas, the reservoirs of large dams accumulate silt at a faster rate than expected, and the effective lifetime of many dams is thus shortened. The loss of silt downstream has adverse effects on farmers, who depended on it to renew soil fertility and have been obliged to turn to artificial fertilizers. Nearer the mouths of rivers the lack of silt causes the subsidence of deltas and the destruction of beaches, while the smaller flow of water into the sea, combined with sinking land levels, leads to invasions of saltwater behind seacoasts. Critics also point to many other adverse effects on the environment and note that the huge sums spent on dam construction and the development of irrigated agriculture have left rain-fed agriculture underfunded. Finally, they argue that the human cost has been great.

For all these reasons and also because most of the best sites have already been claimed, the pace of construction of large dams and hence the expansion of irrigated land slowed in the last two decades of the twentieth century. Some of the donor agencies, most notably the World Bank, once a proponent of large dams, are now more cautious in their support. They and the World Commission on Dams have proposed new criteria for designing, assessing, and selecting dam projects that should reduce the number of projects supported and attenuate their social and environmental costs.

A further constraint on the construction of large dams as well as on other initiatives to increase irrigation has been and will continue to be the growing shortage of water in the world. This has already been felt in countries such as Libya, Saudi Arabia, and Bangladesh as well as in the eastern Mediterranean countries, where nonrenewable aquifers are being depleted by deep wells and powerful pumps and groundwater levels are falling. In many parts of India and Pakistan water tables fall by one to two meters yearly, and in some areas groundwater is increasingly saline or polluted. The shortage is also evident in the great river valley systems, where increasing amounts of water claimed upstream deprive downstream users of needed water. Where aquifers and river valleys are shared by nations, the potential for conflict over vital water supplies looms. *The United Nations World Water Development Report* of 2003, prepared by twenty-three agencies of the United Nations, details the development of the world's water crisis over recent decades and predicts more widespread and serious shortages in decades to come. Exacerbated in many regions by the erratic weather patterns of the late twentieth century and probably also by global warming, the water crisis can only be attenuated by measures to use water less wastefully, in irrigation, for instance, by the reduction of seepage and evaporation in canals and by the less-wasteful distribution of water over fields through drip irrigation and other means. But with ever-rising populations in most parts of the world and increasing use of water for agricultural, industrial, and domestic purposes, the spread of water crises over much of the globe seems unavoidable—unless, that is, in the near future cost-efficient technologies can turn seawater into freshwater and move it to where it is needed.

BIBLIOGRAPHY

Adams, Robert M. *The Uruk Countryside: The Natural Setting of Urban Societies.* Chicago and London, 1972.

Adams, Robert M. *Heartland of Cities: Surveys of Ancient Settlement and Land Use on the Central Floodplains of the Euphrates.* Chicago and London, 1981.

Allchin, Bridget, and Raymond Allchin. *The Rise of Civilisation in India and Pakistan.* London and New York, 1982.

Allchin, F. R., and D. K. Chakrabarti, eds. *A Source Book of Indian Archeology*, vol. 2. New Delhi, 1997. A collection of a large number of short essays by practicing archeologists.

Bonneau, Danielle. *Le régime administratif de l'eau du Nil dans l'Égypte grecque, romaine, et byzantine.* Leiden and New York, 1993.

Briant, Pierre, ed. *Irrigation et drainage dans l'Antiquité: Qanāts et canalisations souterraines en Iran, en Égypte et en Grèce.* Paris, 2001. A collection of eight essays by various authors on ancient underground canals.

Butzer, Karl. *Early Hydraulic Civilization in Egypt: A Study in Cultural Ecology.* Chicago and London, 1976.

Christensen, Peter. *The Decline of Iranshahr: Irrigation and Environments in the History of the Middle East, 500 BC to AD 1500.* Copenhagen, 1993.

Ciriacono, Salvatore, ed. *Land Drainage and Irrigation.* Aldershot, U.K., 1998. Reprints of eighteen historical essays by various authors.

Dams and Development. World Commission on Dams. London and Sterling, Va., 2000.

Fahlbusch, H., ed. *Historical Dams.* New Delhi, 2001. A collection of nineteen essays by different authors on historical dams from around 2700 BCE until the early twentieth century.

Framji, K. K., and B. C. Garg. *Flood Control in the World: A Global Review.* 2 vols. New Delhi, 1976–1977. This work, like the one that follows, is an official publication of the International Commission on Irrigation and Drainage. Both publications begin with an introductory section that contains some historical material and a description of technologies, followed by a large number of studies of individual countries.

Framji, K. K., B. C. Garg, and S. D. L. Luthra. *Irrigation and Drainage in the World: A Global Review.* 3 vols. New Delhi, 1981–1983.

Glick, Thomas. *Irrigation and Society in Medieval Valencia.* Cambridge, Mass., 1970.

Hill, Donald R. "Mechanical Technology." In *Science and Technology in Islam*, edited by A. Y. al-Hassan, vol. 2, p. 177. Paris, 2001.

Lambton, A. K. S., et al. "Mā'." In *Encyclopaedia of Islam*, vol. 5, pp. 859–889. 2d ed. Leiden, 1960–. A collection of eleven articles in English by different authors. Most articles deal with aspects of irrigation.

Mehmet, Özay, and Hasan Ali Biçak. *Modern and Traditional Irrigation Technologies in the Eastern Mediterranean*. Ottawa, Canada, 2002. Nine essays by different authors.

Said, Rushdi. *The River Nile: Geology, Hydrology, and Utilization*. Oxford and New York, 1993.

Spooner, Brian. "Ābyārī." In *Encyclopaedia Iranica*, vol. 1, pp. 405–411. London, 1982–.

Subtelny, Maria. *Le monde est un jardin: Aspects de l'histoire culturelle de l'Iran médiéval*. Paris, 2002. The first lecture in this collection deals with the administration of waterworks in medieval Iran.

Von Wissmann, Hermann. *Zur Geschichte und Landeskunde von Alt-Südarabien*. Vienna, 1964.

Water for People. Water for Life. The United Nations World Water Development Report. UNESCO/World Water Assessment Programme. Paris, 2003.

Wittfogel, Karl. *Oriental Despotism: A Comparative Study of Total Power*. New Haven, 1959.

World Register of Dams, 1998. International Commission on Large Dams. Available as a CD from ICOLD. Also see <www.icold-cigb.org>.

ANDREW M. WATSON

WATER RESOURCES. Some of history's most impressive technological and institutional achievements have been in the provision of water and in the protection from water's extremes—drought and floods. Freshwater systems can most usefully be classified as surface water and groundwater systems. Surface water sources are essentially renewable when properly managed, while groundwater can be either renewable (when replenished by precipitation or from streams) or nonrenewable as found in some major aquifers deposited in prehistoric times.

The services provided by water systems can be classified as irrigation of crops; basic urban uses (residential, commercial, industrial); cultural and aesthetic uses (including water gardens, fountains, and recreation); and navigation on inland rivers and lakes. While irrigation is treated in a separate essay in this encyclopedia, it cannot be totally separated from the other water services because it has been so basic to human development in many parts of the world and because it consumes (historically and currently) by far the largest percentage of supplies.

The technologies through which these services have been delivered have varied from the simple capture of runoff in natural surface depressions to complex catchment, delivery, flood control, and artistic systems. These technologies have been developed and services provided within institutional settings ranging from community organizations and private initiatives to highly centralized legal/regulatory systems that prescribe processes for the allocation of water and water-related property rights.

Early Water Developments: Asia and Africa. Irrigation appears to have originated in the plains between the Tigris and Euphrates Rivers around 6000 BCE where settlers dug simple canals to bring water to their crops, thus extending the growing season. Multiple crops during the year became possible, producing the surpluses of food that allowed significant parts of the population to pursue other arts and crafts. Other inventions related to irrigation included various water-lifting devices (including the shaduf dating back to 3000 BCE) and sailing craft to ply the rivers (Postel, 1999, ch. 2).

Chinese efforts to manage the water resources of the north China plain are recorded by 4000 BCE. This plain of three hundred thousand square kilometers became the breadbasket of China for centuries. Its catchment area is the Loess Plateau, one of the most erodible regions on the earth, so the river carried huge sediment loads that raised the riverbed high above the plain. The river frequently broke through the dikes that contained it, causing devastating losses of life and crops. Yu the Great first controlled the river around 4000 BCE. Huge workforces were necessary to build the dikes and remove sediment, requiring highly centralized administrative powers, as had been the case in Mesopotamia. By the seventh century, grain production had shifted into the Yangzi Valley, where the water supply was greater and more reliable.

The Indus basin was settled around 3500 BCE, producing food surpluses and a powerful society by 2300 BCE. (Postel, 1999, p. 29). The central authority was able to mobilize vast numbers of workers in ways characteristic of Mesopotamia and the parts of China previously cited, but the society lasted only five hundred years, possibly disrupted by widespread deforestation that led to siltation, waterlogging, and salination of the soils.

While greatly increasing agricultural productivity, irrigation introduced new vulnerabilities: the vulnerability of the infrastructure to enemy attack, the need to assemble and control a large workforce to maintain the infrastructure, and the ultimate build-up of salinity in poorly drained soils. The latter was a major cause of the decline of the Fertile Crescent. Postel noted, "The overriding lesson from history is that most irrigation-based civilizations fail" (Postel, 1999, p. 12).

The social consequences of river developments like those cited above were the subject of Karl Wittfogel's analysis of "the hydraulic society," which presumably required the organization and discipline of a large labor force based on a highly stratified social structure, resulting in despotic political systems (Wittfogel, 1957). While discounted in recent times because of his failure to confront counterexamples or to extend his analysis to the modern scene, Wittfogel stimulated interest in the relationships between irrigation development and the evolution of social and political structures (Wescoat, 2000).

The Nile Valley and its great civilization presents a sharp counterexample to the Wittfogel hypothesis. It has sustained its agricultural foundation for five thousand years while withstanding conquest by the Persians, Greeks, Romans, Arabs, and Turks. Dating back to 3100 BCE, water management took the form of highly decentralized basin irrigation, which, along with the more predictable, silt-laden flows of the river, allowed irrigators to avoid the major problems of soil depletion and salinization. The political disruptions at the high levels appear not to have affected the irrigation basins directly. The water wheel was introduced around 325 BCE, while a system for measuring the height of the Nile flow allowed comparisons with past years. Thus, the localized system of basin irrigation was more stable hydrologically, agronomically, and socially than the systems noted above.

Early Developments in the Americas. Among cases of early water development in the Americas, two well-researched historic developments stand out: the Mesa Verde settlements of the Anasazi people in the Four Corners region of the United States (Colorado, Utah, New Mexico, and Arizona, now a national park) that started around 100 CE until the mysterious disappearance of the people around 1400; and Machu Picchu in the highlands of Peru (now an internationally protected historical site) that was occupied by the aristocracy of the Inca people during the period 1200 to 1400 (Bingham, 1930). Both sites have been extensively studied by paleohydrologist/anthropologist teams (K. Wright and Zegarra, 2000; R. Wright and Zegarra, 2001). Though occurring much later than the Asian systems noted above and employing less-sophisticated technologies, these societies exhibited advanced understanding of the climate-hydrology relationships in their areas: the Anasazis living in an extremely dry region and the Incas in the mountainous, well-watered terrain of Peru.

The peoples of Mesa Verde knew how to capture water in a region of occasional thunderstorms and how to distribute it through ditches to fields and to residential water-gathering sites. Research has shown that they maintained a system of reservoirs for at least the period from 750 to 1100. One canyon-floor reservoir diverted water from a river via a canal into a walled impoundment constructed to hold the water. Canal construction required an understanding of slope-flow rate relationships. Maintenance of the reservoir required knowledge of soil types and methods of compaction to reduce seepage into the soil. Sedimentation analysis has shown that the canal had to be regularly raised because the reservoir level continuously rose as sediments settled out.

Two other reservoirs at Mesa Verde have been identified on narrow mesa tops having no natural drainage basins.

They were located close to pueblo dwelling units of the Pueblo II era of 950 to 1180. The reservoirs had stone walls to catch the run-off from adjacent maize fields. This system was enhanced by foot compaction of the wetted soils. Run-off occurred only four to six times a year, so efficient capture was critical. Thus the Pueblo II people had extensive knowledge of basic hydrology and construction methods, passing the knowledge from generation to generation without the benefit of a written language.

Machu Picchu was started in the middle of the fifteenth century by the Inca ruler Pachacuti (1438–1471) as a sacred retreat for Inca royalty who traveled there from the Inca capital of Cuzco. It is located on a spectacular narrow ridge between two mountains at an altitude of 2450 meters. The terrain drops off sharply to the Urubamba River Valley far below. The site continued to be expanded and improved until the 1530s, when the Spanish destroyed the Inca Empire. Long known to local peoples, it was "discovered" by Hiram Bingham in 1911 (Bingham, 1930), who later cleared and photographed the site. The development of a water supply system to supply the town of several thousand persons was unusually challenging because of the steep terrain and the absence of a natural catchment area. The water was intended both for the usual human uses and for highly ceremonial and aesthetic uses involving an elaborate system of fountains and pools.

Inca engineers were able both to capture small supplies in difficult locations and to control large rivers, all without instruments or a written language. Their incredible stonework for walls, fortifications, temples, and residences is unmatched in the Western Hemisphere (K. Wright and Zegarra, 2000; R. Wright and Zegarra, 2001). In Cuzco, the Inca foundations on which the Spanish built their city have remained intact, while the Spanish structures have repeatedly been destroyed by earthquakes.

Urban Water Supply and Sanitation Developments. Roman aqueducts and water distribution systems have long been studied from technical and artistic viewpoints. The Roman administrator Marcus Agrippa (c. 63–12 BCE) installed three hundred statues in the fountains of Rome. In the various regions of the Empire, aqueducts were built and stood as symbols of Roman civilization and pride. Roman cities were initially supplied by wells and cisterns. The later construction of aqueducts was more a matter of luxury, with a constant flow of water into a central distribution tank or *castellum* (often ornate), thence to the baths (the largest use), public street fountains, and a few private businesses or homes.

Since there was little storage in the system, the constant flow helped flush sewage wastes out of the city. Sewers for the transport of human and kitchen wastes and drains for carrying off rainfall and all the wastes thrown onto the streets served parts of most Roman cities. Pompeii had one of the most elaborate systems, but it served only the forum area, while most towns simply had open sewers running in the middle of the street. Street drains might discharge into a central collector that carried the waste flow out of the town, where it was commonly discharged into a river or, in drier areas, onto fields that served to absorb the water and degrade the wastes.

A recent publication of the National Research Council cites a famous example of the early connections between water supply and public health:

> Experience with water supply management in England and particularly London is deserving of special attention because private water service began there in the late 16th century and continued for some 300 years . . . The 19th century saw the extensive growth of piped water services in cities, accompanied by the introduction of flush toilets which were responsible for the heavy pollution of the rivers in the cities. . . . Private water companies furnished piped water to various parts of the city, several taking their water from the heavily polluted Thames. Periodic cholera epidemics were responsible for high death rates among rich and poor alike, some quarter of a million people, mostly in London, died of cholera between 1848 and 1854. . . . The source of the cholera had not then been established; it had been attributed to inhalations from the foul air arising from the putrid Thames.
>
> Two private water companies had been serving households in the same area on the south side of the Thames when one elected to improve the taste and odor of its supply by moving its intake upstream of the city while the other continued to draw from its original intake. Dr. John Snow, physician to Queen Victoria and possibly the world's first epidemiologist, established that the cholera fatality rate of the latter in the summer of 1854 was 315 per 10,000 households, almost 9-fold greater than the rate among the customers of the company that had moved its intake. That study, along with his study of the cholera outbreak that occurred among people who carried water from a hand-pump on a well on Broad Street, were the first to establish that water was the source of cholera outbreaks. This was decades before the germ theory of disease had been recognized. (National Research Council, 2002)

Aesthetic and Cultural Uses of Water. The use of water for aesthetic purposes may have reached a peak in the early years of the Mughal Empire in India (1526–1858) with the development of highly refined pools, fountains, wells, and baths as the "skeletal and circulatory systems" of the elaborate Mughal gardens (Wescoat, 1989). The classic hydraulic pattern was a set of perpendicular channels dividing the garden into quadrants, shallow marble basins within an open pavilion at the center. Cascades of water rolled over carved surfaces of marble and sandstone. These dynamic features were combined with elaborate plantings and paintings to symbolize order and design in the world, to represent oases in a desert or places of peace

in a hostile environment. During the same era, irrigation system developments were taking place, yielding new techniques of water management at the macroscale.

In the southwestern United States, the old Spanish *acequia* system not only supported local agricultural needs, but also maintained social cohesion because maintenance of the canals and distribution of the water were community efforts (Crawford, 1988). In these old systems, the water rights typically belong to the community, so that communitywide decisions have to be made if water is to be sold and transferred outside the community.

The Evolution of Water Law and Water Markets. The evolution of water law provides a fascinating example of the responses of the law to changing social and economic conditions. The Code of Hammurabi (r. 1792–1750 BCE) had several laws related to irrigation covering the maintenance of works and payment of damages from careless flooding. The Assyrians' irrigation laws built on those of Hammurabi and covered the rights of landowners who shared a common water source, guaranteeing that those at the ends of canals received a fair share. Special courts were established to enforce these water laws.

Scott and Coustalin (1995) have provided the details of water law evolution from Roman times to the twentieth century. The law of prior occupancy (an early version of the priority doctrine), wherein the earliest water users had first call on available water, was adopted in England from Roman law. At the start of the Industrial Revolution, it became clear that these historical uses were preventing water access for the newer, more technical industries. To accommodate these needs, a "reasonable use" doctrine evolved, allowing new activities access as long as they did not "unreasonably" reduce availability for others or "unreasonably" degrade water quality. This was the "riparian doctrine" of English Common Law that was brought to the eastern United States by the English settlers.

The riparian doctrine was ill suited to the water allocation needs of western U.S. regions where water was much scarcer, much more variable in supply, and where uses were often removed from the streambank. The evolution of the "priority doctrine" in this setting has been well documented (e.g., Scott and Coustalin, 1995). Water rights (i.e., property rights in water) under the priority doctrine have the following characteristics:

1. They are considered personal property of the owner and can be sold or otherwise transferred to other owners and uses.
2. The priority of the rights is established by the date of first use and is transferred with the right.
3. The initial appropriation and subsequent transfers must prove that the water is being put to a "beneficial use."
4. Transfers of water rights are not allowed to damage other water users.

5. Rights usually are defined in terms of the diversion rate, dates of historical diversion, use of the water, whether the right is a direct flow right or a storage right and (sometimes) total volume of water allowed annually.

With these characteristics, the priority system has allowed water to move from older, lower-valued uses to emerging higher-valued uses and has allowed water users who highly value reliability of supply to obtain that reliability by buying senior (high priority) rights.

Spain has had "water auctions" for four centuries (Maass and Anderson, 1978). More recently, Australia has developed several unique forms of water markets, while Chile has moved strongly toward privatizing all water resources (Bauer, 1998).

[*See also* Water Engineering.]

BIBLIOGRAPHY

Bauer, Carl J. *Against the Current: Privatization, Water Markets, and the State in Chile.* Boston, 1998.

Bingham, Hiram. *Machu Picchu: A Citadel of the Incas.* New Haven, 1930.

Crawford, Stanley. *Mayordomo: Chronicle of an Acequia in Northern New Mexico.* Albuquerque, 1988.

Maass, Arthur, and Raymond L. Anderson. . . . *and the Desert Shall Rejoice: Conflict, Growth, and Justice in Arid Environments.* Cambridge, Mass., 1978.

National Research Council. *Privatization of Water Services in the United States: An Assessment of Issues and Experience.* Washington, D.C., 2002.

Postel, Sandra. *Pillar of Sand: Can the Irrigation Miracle Last?* New York, 1999.

Scott, Anthony, and Georgina Coustalin. "The Evolution of Water Rights." *The Natural Resources Journal* 35.4 (1995), 821–980.

Wescoat, James L., Jr. "Picturing and Early Mughal Garden." *Asian Art* (Fall 1989), 59–79.

Wescoat, James L. Jr. "Wittfogel East and West: Changing Perspectives on Water Development in South Asia and the United States, 1670–2000." In *Cultural Encounters with the Environment: Enduring and Evolving Geographic Themes,* edited by Alexander B. Murphy and Douglas L. Johnson, Chapter 5. Lanham, Md., 2000.

Wittfogel, Karl A. *Oriental Despotism: A Comparative Study of Total Power.* New Haven and London, 1957.

Wright, Kenneth R., and Alfredo Valencia Zegarra. *Machu Picchu: A Civil Engineering Marvel.* Reston, Va., 2000.

Wright, Ruth M., and Alfredo Valencia Zegarra. *The Machu Picchu Guidebook: A Self-Guided Tour.* Boulder, 2001.

CHARLES W. HOWE

WATER TRANSPORTATION. *[This entry contains five subentries, a historical overview and discussions of technological change, ocean shipping, canal transportation, and regulation.]*

Historical Overview

Although water acted as a barrier to the movement of early man, the use of crude boats, whether in the form of hollowed logs, skins stretched over a wooden frame, or bark or papyrus rafts, predates written history. Once rudimentary boats were developed, rivers and lakes offered an efficient means of transport. Notwithstanding technological developments in other modes of transport, water transport—via navigable rivers, improved (canalized) rivers, or artificial waterways (canals)—remains a means of inland cargo movement.

Over the centuries, the discovery of new lands and technological advances in ship construction and the art of navigation have steadily expanded the role of ocean-going transport. Despite advances in commercial aviation, technological progress within the shipping industry has enabled shipping to retain its role as the major carrier of international trade.

Technological and organizational innovations have played a major role in the continued growth of water transport. Prior to the nineteenth century, during the period when sail was the most important form of propulsion, gains came from improvements in ship construction, hull form, and sail capacity. Today's shipping industry is the product both of technological change—including the adoption in the nineteenth century of the marine steam engine and screw propulsion plus the use of iron and steel in ship construction—and of the enormous expansion of international trade following the Industrial Revolution.

Measured on a weight basis, 90 percent of international trade moves by sea transport. Basic raw materials (coal, minerals, fertilizers, and oil) and foodstuffs constitute a high proportion of seaborne cargo. A wide range of manufactured products also move by sea, although air transport competes for the carriage of high-value and/or time-sensitive cargoes.

To cope with rapid trade growth, as well as the immense variety of commodities and products shipped by sea, the shipping industry has had to develop new techniques and methods. The vessels themselves have become larger and more specialized: The tramp steamer has been replaced by the modern bulk carrier, the primitive oil tanker by the giant (200,000 deadweight tons) crude oil carrier, and the conventional cargo liner has been replaced by the container ship.

Early History, 3000 BCE–1500 CE. Three themes dominate the early history of water transportation: incremental changes in ship design; the extension of the known world through maritime exploration; and the slow growth of trade mainly, though not exclusively, in luxury commodities.

Technological developments. Archaeological evidence suggests that early civilizations in the Middle East, Mesopotamia, and Egypt used rivers as highways. The earliest use of sail is recorded in Predynastic (c. 3300 BCE) Egyptian rock carvings. While the fundamental character-

NAVIGATION. Three sailing ships maneuvered by young boys, Augustan Rome (c. 44 BCE–c. 14 CE). (Ny Carlsberg Glyptotek, Copenhagen, Denmark/Alinari/Art Resource, NY)

istics of Egyptian vessels altered little from those recorded in early rock carvings, their size increased, their seaworthiness improved, and there were technical improvements in the form of their mast, sails, and steering.

Ship design must fulfill certain essential requirements. The hull must slip through the water without creating disturbance behind the stern, which could cause following seas to break over the ship. Above the waterline, the vessel must be shaped so that waves are thrown aside rather than breaking on deck. Ships must be stable when loaded and in ballast. They must be able to carry sail safely. Finally, while the vessel must be tough and resilient, it must also be reasonably light.

The traditional shipwright begins by laying the keel and then sets up the stern and stem posts. The hull is constructed either by setting up frames or ribs and fastening planks to them, or by building up a shell with long planks attached to one end of the vessel, bent to the necessary curve, and then attached to the other end. The latter method, typical of Scandinavia, is known as clinker building, each plank of the shell being laid outside the plank beneath it and fastened to it with nails. The clinker-building technique spread throughout Europe in the ninth and tenth centuries CE.

By about 1200 CE, demands for greater cargo capacity meant that clinker building was no longer suitable. Northern European shipbuilders adopted carvel building, in which planks are laid edge to edge and fastened to ribs fixed to the keel. Heavier timber could be used, and shipbuilders could progressively increase the size of vessels. Larger vessels enabled European powers of the sixteenth and seventeenth centuries to cross the oceans and colonize distant continents.

International seaborne trade. Early man cautiously explored the oceans; archaeological evidence suggests that early seafarers voyaged across the Aegean Sea nine thousand years ago, although we have no means of knowing the types of vessels they used. Egyptian vessels are known to have traded with Crete circa 1500 BCE, while seafarers from Crete and the Aegean sailed westward to Spain, Ireland, and Wales.

Five hundred years later, the Phoenicians, Greeks, and Etruscans were the principal seafaring peoples. The Phoenicians colonized Cyprus by the end of the ninth century BCE. Settling in Spain by the seventh century, they may have sailed through the Straits of Gibraltar on trading voyages to Great Britain. By circa 600 BCE., they had founded a small trading colony at Essaouira, on the Atlantic coast of Morocco. Etruscan ships began by plying the Italian coast, while Greek merchants founded a commercial emporium at Al Mīnāon the north Syrian coast around 800 BCE.

Although Rome lacked a seafaring tradition when the republic began to expand rapidly through Italy in the third and fourth centuries BCE, the acquisition of new territories turned it into a major maritime power. Imperial Rome became the greatest maritime power the world would know until the Royal Navy imposed the Pax Britannica in the early nineteenth century.

The Vikings explored the coasts and rivers of northern Europe and Russia, in addition to colonizing Iceland and Greenland, eventually becoming the first Europeans to set foot in North America.

In the tenth and eleventh centuries, the Venetians traded with Constantinople and the Middle East, while the Genoese pioneered sea routes to the North Sea and the Baltic. In the thirteenth century, the Hanseatic League, centered in Lübeck, engaged in general trade along river routes to southern Germany, Poland, and central Europe.

Inland waterways. Although the primary purposes of river improvement and artificial channel construction in antiquity were irrigation or water supply, the improved waterways were used for transport purposes. The Assyrian king Sennacherib built an 80-kilometer (50-mile) stone-lined canal to bring fresh water to Nineveh in the seventh century BCE. The Phoenicians, Assyrians, Sumerians, and Egyptians also constructed elaborate canal systems, along which grain, timber, and stone were shipped. The Romans were responsible for extensive improvements to rivers and for the construction of canals in France, Italy, the Netherlands, and Great Britain for military purposes.

The technology of canal building also developed in China. Perennial flooding of China's great river systems, especially the Yangzi and the Yellow, renewed soil fertility but caused extensive downstream destruction. The Chinese learned to control the rivers by means of waterways. Between the third century BCE and the first century CE, an impressive canal network was built. For example, the Zheng Hou Canal, begun in 221 BCE, channeled the water of the Jingshui River across the Guanzhong Plain.

While canal building in Europe lapsed after the fall of the Roman Empire, it was revived by commercial expansion in the twelfth century and by the development of pound locks in the fourteenth century. However, China appears to have been ahead of Europe in canal building in the twelfth and thirteenth centuries.

The Early Modern Era, 1500–1800. In the early modern era, larger vessels were introduced as a result of technological innovation. Such vessels not only created new opportunities for trade, but they also led to an intensification of rivalry among seafarers in Portugal, Holland, France, and England.

Technological developments. By the end of the fifteenth century, three-masted sailing vessels had been adopted in northern Europe. The carrack was the largest merchant ship of the time. With its three or more masts, its bulging hull with tumble-home sides, and its fore and aft castles, the carrack's size increased from 360 metric tons to more than 900 metric tons during the course of the century. Originating in Spain, the galleon was narrower in the beam than the carrack. Although its towering stern made it appear top-heavy, the galleon proved capable of ocean voyaging.

The British East India Company influenced ship design throughout the sixteenth and seventeenth centuries. Built like warships but with additional width to improve cargo-carrying capacity, East Indiamen were particularly speedy. With the ending of the company's monopoly on trade with India, speed became important. The American clipper ship now offered real advantages.

In general, merchant ships remained relatively small, their dimensions limited by the size of the market, the depth of water available in ports, and by the need to minimize the number of crew members. Ships employed in Spanish-American trade were the exception. When trade began, a vessel of 135 or 180 metric tons was considered large; by the middle of the sixteenth century, vessels of 270 to 450 metric tons were employed.

Inland waterways. The development of the miter lock, the double-leaf gates of which pointed upstream when the lock was closed, heralded a period of extensive canal construction during the sixteenth and seventeenth centuries. By the eighteenth century, locks, inclined planes, and lifts had been developed to cope with changes in water level.

Extensive canal construction took place in Europe during the sixteenth and seventeenth centuries. In France, the Loire and Seine Rivers and, in Germany, the Elbe, Oder, and Wester were linked by canal, while the Canal du Midi linked Toulouse with the Mediterranean. In England, the canal-era proper dates from the construction of the Bridgewater Canal (1761) to carry coal from Worsley to Manchester.

Sail to Steam, 1800–1900. After centuries of relatively slow change in ship technology, the shift from sail to steam in the nineteenth century was one of the greatest revolutions in the history of shipping.

Technological developments. Experiments with steam propulsion began in the late eighteenth century. Patrick Miller and William Symington built and operated a small steamboat in 1788, while the Philadelphia-Trenton service operated in 1790 by a vessel built by John Fitch has claims to be the first regular steamboat service in the world. The first commercially successful use of steam on inland waterways was Robert Fulton's 1807 service on the Hudson River using the *Clermont*. Henry Bell's *Comet* operated as a service between Glasgow and Greenock for four years, commencing in 1812.

The first ocean-based intercontinental voyages by steam took place in the 1820s, the *Rising Star* sailing from England to Chile in 1821, although it is not known how long its engines were used during the voyage. In 1838, the *Great Western* and the *Sirius* raced across the Atlantic.

As long as shipbuilders were content to accept the limitations imposed by wooden hulls, paddle wheels and single-cylinder engines, steam was unable to compete economically with sail, particularly for the carriage of long-distance cargoes. However, between 1840 and 1870 the replacement of wooden ships by iron, the introduction of the screw propeller, and the use of the compound engine transformed the competitiveness of the steamship.

Experimental iron ships were built in the late eighteenth century. By 1830, iron steamboats were in relatively common use for short-haul voyages. Isambard K. Brunel's vision of a large, ocean-going iron ship came to fruition in 1844 with the *Great Britain*.

Efficient screw propulsion was developed in the 1830s. Although Robert Hooke (1681) and Daniel Bernoulli

(1738) proposed screw propulsion for ships and a patent relating to the driving of a screw by a steam engine was granted to Joseph Bramah in 1785, no evidence of successful innovation exists. Francis P. Smith and John Ericsson separately took out patents relating to screw propulsion in 1836. The Ship Propeller Company purchased Smith's patent in 1837, employing the technology in the *Archimedes*, later chartered by Brunel's Great Western Steamship Company. The ship's performance persuaded Brunel to adopt screw propulsion for the *Great Britain*.

The compound engine, introduced in the late 1850s and early 1860s, is said to have saved 30 to 40 percent of fuel compared with a single-expansion engine of the same power. P&O's first compound-engined vessel, the *Mooltan* (1861), was so successful that the company had ten such vessels in service by 1866. The triple-expansion engine, the standard engine for pre–World War I cargo vessels, dates from the 1880s, the shipbuilder Napier & Sons persuading G. Thomson & Company (Aberdeen Line) to fit a triple-expansion engine in the *Aberdeen* (1881).

Overseas water transport. Given the technological innovations noted above, steam came to be preferred to sail. At first suited only for short-sea passages, steam was widely adopted for deep-sea, intercontinental trades in the 1870s. The opening of the Suez and Panama Canals further enhanced steam's advantage, the opening of the Suez Canal (1869) shortening the sea route from Europe to India by more than 5,000 kilometers (3,100 miles). In lowering transport costs, the canal made Indian cotton competitive with American cotton in European markets.

Faced with intensifying competition from steam, shipbuilders designed larger and faster-sailing vessels. Three-masted ship-rigged American clippers came into service in time for the California gold rush of 1849, while clippers vied with steamships to deliver the first consignment of tea to the London market. Notwithstanding advances in sailing-ship construction, steamships—aided by the opening of the Suez Canal in 1869—drove clippers out of the China tea trade in the 1870s. Clippers now carried Australian wool, in competition with large, purpose-built iron-hulled sailing ships. When wool cargoes dwindled after 1890, sailing ships switched to the Chilean nitrate or Peruvian guano trades. The opening of the Panama Canal in 1914 led to the takeover of these trades by the ubiquitous tramp ship.

At the beginning of the twentieth century, the world steamship fleet totaled 22.5 million metric tons (25 million tons), while 5.8 million metric tons of sailing ships still engaged in trading. During the next fourteen years, steamship tonnage doubled.

Inland water transport. Industrialization in Europe and the United States encouraged canal building in the early nineteenth century. European industrial development led to the extension of Belgium's canal system and especially to the construction of canals to carry coal from Mons and Charleroi to Paris. Canal building in the United States, which had lagged behind Europe in the eighteenth century, now facilitated the opening up of America. The Erie Canal (1825) linked New York with the Midwest, carrying industrial goods westward and agricultural products eastward. Canals provided a southern route around the Allegheny Mountains and linked the Great Lakes with the Mississippi River.

With the development of rail transport in the mid-nineteenth century, canals declined as freight arteries, particularly in the United States and Great Britain. The impact of rail was less marked in continental Europe because the navigable rivers, linked by artificial waterways, formed an efficient and economical international transport network.

Growing Specialization, 1900–1970. The period from 1900 to 1970 was one in which ships not only became larger but also more specialized in function. The rapid growth in the volume of international trade in the years after 1945 created opportunities for shipbuilders and shipping lines to build special-purpose vessels such as crude oil carriers, specialized ore carriers, and refrigerated carriers.

Technological developments. The dramatic shift from sail to steam power was followed by almost a century of gradual change in cargo ship propulsion, instrumentation, and cargo-handling techniques. Despite experimentation in the late nineteenth and early twentieth centuries, the use of oil as marine fuel did not become common until after World War I. Conversion from coal burning was then rapid. Whereas in 1914, 97 percent of the world merchant fleet was coal fired, by 1939, 45 percent was coal fired and 30 percent was oil fired.

Marine turbine and marine diesel engines competed with the triple-expansion engine. Charles A. Parsons's experiments with marine turbines in the 1880s led to the building of the first turbine-powered vessel, the *Turbinia* (1894). The first turbine-powered liners, the Allen Line's sister ships, *Virginian* and *Victorian*, went into service in 1904. The marine diesel engine, pioneered by the Danish firm Burmeister & Wain, was first adopted in 1902. The first ocean-going diesel vessel was the *Selandia* (1912). By 1939, one in four ships was motor driven, with the diesel and the steam turbine competing for speed and economy.

Overseas water transport. During the first half of the twentieth century, the number and geographical spread of cargo-liner services increased substantially. A cargo liner operated a regularly scheduled service over a fixed route, carrying consignments of many different commodities. Cargo-liner services had begun in the late nineteenth century. The spread of industrialization, coupled with consumer demand for a wider range of products, created an

WATER TRANSPORTATION. Canoes between two locks along the Toeckfors River, Sweden, 1990. (© Urs Kluyver/Focus/Woodfin Camp and Associates, New York)

expanding market for cargo-liner services. By the 1950s, conventional general cargo-liners operated a dense network of routes serving both industrialized and developing countries. Until the 1960s, cargo-liners were multipurpose carriers, able to accept a huge range of commodities. They were replaced by container ships in the 1970s.

In the early twentieth century, the typical tramp ship was a relatively small and scruffy coal-burning vessel. On any given voyage, the tramp ship would carry a single cargo, perhaps coal or iron ore. Over its lifetime, such a vessel would carry many different bulk cargoes.

Following World War II, the demand for many bulk commodities (coal, iron ore, alumina, wheat) led to high-volume, continuous cargo flows. The specialized bulk carrier now replaced the tramp. From 1958 through the early 1970s, a dramatic increase took place in the world fleet of bulk carriers and in vessel size.

With changes in the types and quantities of goods carried, the need for specialized vessels grew. Over time, vessels were developed to carry refrigerated products, forest products, cement, automobiles, livestock, industrial waste, and heavy-lift cargoes. As a result, the cargo base available to tramps and conventional cargo liners eroded.

The Container Revolution. Containerization is the most far-reaching innovation in shipping since the introduction of steamships. Not only have cargo-handling costs been reduced drastically, but the size of vessels has also increased dramatically. Route structures have also changed radically and the industry has undergone considerable consolidation.

Technological change. The most recent maritime revolution, commencing in the 1960s, was associated with containerization, substantial increases in the size of vessels, and the further development of specialized cargo carriers. It was accompanied by the decline of tramping and conventional cargo-liner services and by the virtual elimination of line-haul sea voyages, as the airlines took over long-distance passenger transport.

Technological progress in ship construction and cargo handling has led to a dramatic increase in the size of ships. Whereas the early-twentieth-century tramp ship varied in size from 8,000 to 15,000 deadweight tons, vessel size increased rapidly from the late 1950s. Dry bulk carriers of over 200,000 deadweight tons now operate in the coal and iron ore trades. The size of oil tankers has also increased. The standard World War II oil tanker was the T2 of 16,400 deadweight tons. Following the war, there was a steady growth in tanker size, as the major oil companies took advantage of economies of ship size. Constraints imposed by the Suez Canal, which could accommodate only fully laden vessels of up to 70,000 deadweight tons, temporarily held back tanker size. The availability of an alternative route to Europe via the Cape of Good Hope eventually tipped the competitive balance in favor of very large crude carriers (170,000 deadweight tons).

Until recently, technological developments in shipbuilding have proceeded faster than cargo-handling technology. Prior to containerization, general cargo arrived at the wharf in boxes, packages, drums, or slings. As shipments had to be individually handled and stowed, cargo handling was labor intensive. Productivity was low and generally declining. During the 1960s, the cost of handling general cargo tripled.

The shipping industry responded by developing new cargo handling methods, especially containerization. This lowered the cost of cargo handling and increased vessel productivity, since a container ship replaced between four to six conventional cargo liners. The ability to tranship containers inexpensively between vessels and between sea and land transport has created more contestable transport markets. It has also led to a reevaluation of the transport chain: Whereas the vessel, train, or truck was formerly regarded as the focal point of the operation, the container is now the central component, with the ship, train, or truck merely providing motive power.

Overseas water transport. Over the past two decades, the container-shipping market has become globalized. Intense competition has forced owners to adopt innovative, productivity-enhancing, and cost-cutting strategies. Successively larger vessels have been employed on mainline east-west Northern Hemisphere trades. New service patterns have evolved, including "round-the-world," "pendulum," and "multistring" services. In their search for cost reduction and faster transit times, lines have reduced the number of port calls, leading to the growth of hubs or load centers and to the evolution of feeder networks. Very large ("mega") carriers are emerging, and lines are entering into strategic alliances.

The development of the container vessel removed economic, technical, and operational constraints that limited the growth in size of cargo liners. Whereas the capacity of early container vessels was under 1,000 twenty-foot equivalent units (TEU being the standard container recognized by the International Organization for Standardization), the average size of vessels now employed in the Europe-Asia trade is about 4,000 TEU. Maersk Sealand and P&O Nedlloyd currently operate containerships of up to 6,700 TEU. Containerships of 8,000 TEU are on the drawing board, and vessels of 15,000 TEU may appear early in the twenty-first century. Economies of vessel size and a competitive shipping market are driving change.

Container lines have sought to minimize costs by limiting the number of port calls. In so doing, companies rely on regional hub ports, notably Singapore and Hong Kong. Cargo to and from the region served by a hub port is handled by feeder shipping and/or by land transport. In archipelagic Southeast Asia, an extensive network of regional feeder services has evolved. These feeder networks are expanding geographically: Singapore's network serves Southeast Asia, the Indian subcontinent, the Persian Gulf, and Australasia.

Inland water transport. Since World War II, Europe has created an enlarged and integrated inland waterway network, including the Rhine-Main-Danube and Nord-Sud canals. Competition from road and rail has made it necessary to employ larger vessels on inland waterways in both Europe and the United States; the 270-metric ton barges typically employed on European waterways in the early 1900s are being replaced by vessels of 1,100 metric tons and above, while North American river operators have adopted large-scale tug and barge operations. European shipowners have introduced vessels capable of operating short-sea and inland waterway routes.

BIBLIOGRAPHY

Anderson, Romola, and R. C. Anderson. *The Sailing Ship*. London, 1947. Detailed discussion of the evolution of the sailing ship.

Bass, George F., ed. *A History of Seafaring Based on Underwater Archaeology*. London, 1972. Drawing primarily on archaeological evidence, this valuable and interesting volume traces the history of seafaring from earliest times to the advent of steam power.

Brooks, Mary. *Sea Change in Liner Shipping*. Oxford, 2000. Thoughtful and thorough study of today's container shipping market. Discussion focuses both on managerial decision making within the shipping company and the public policy implications of the industry's competitive dynamics.

Cipolla, Carlo M. *Guns and Sail in the Early Phase of European Expansionism, 1400–1700*. London, 1965.

Gardiner, Robert, ed. *The Shipping Revolution: The Modern Merchant Ship*, vol. 12, *Conway's History of the Ship*. London, 1992. The final volume in the twelve-volume encyclopedia. The series, with contributions from many leading maritime historians, is both informative and authoritative.

Gripaios, Hector. *Tramp Shipping*. London, 1959. The standard work on the development, organization, and working of the tramp trades.

Gwilliam, Ken W. *Current Issues in Maritime Economics*. Dordrecht, Netherlands, 1993. A valuable collection of papers focusing on three major areas: the rapid changes in the environment facing the shipping industry in the 1980s and 1990s, the relationship between market structure and competition, and the decision processes of firms faced with rapid change.

Rolt, L. T. C. *Navigable Waterways*. London, 1969. Descriptive account of the development of inland waterways.

Rowland, K. T. *Steam at Sea: A History of Steam Navigation*. Newton Abbott, U.K., 1970. Focuses on major technological innovations, such as the iron ship, screw propulsion, the compound engine, and the steam turbine.

Singer, Charles, et al., eds. *A History of Technology*. 5 vols. Cambridge, 1954–1958. Authoritative. Includes a number of chapters focusing on the history and development of water transport.

Skempton, A. W. "Canals and River Navigations before 1750." In *A History of Technology*, edited by Charles Singer et al., vol. 3, chap. 17. Cambridge, 1958. Useful discussion of canal development from earliest times to the middle of the eighteenth century.

Sletmo, Gunnar K., and Ernest K. Williams. *Liner Conferences in the Container Age*. New York, 1981.

KEITH TRACE

Technological Change

Single logs, then hollowed out logs, and then logs lashed together were probably the earliest vehicles of water transportation. First, paddles were added for propulsion; by 3500 BCE, sails were introduced and by 2500 BCE rowing replaced paddling on bigger Egyptian barges, about the same time that more complex hull construction made travel possible to Lebanon across the open sea. Moving beyond log rafts, Mesopotamian and Egyptian builders may have first experimented with vessels made with interwoven reeds.

There were serious problems of strength and integrity as vessels grew in size. To prevent hogging (i.e., drooping of the ends of the ship), builders stretched an adjustable truss from bow to stern. By 1190 BCE, such heavy ropes had disappeared from all vessels because Egyptians had learned to build strong hulls of planks, creating a watertight and buoyant container for goods. Building with planks raised the question of how to hold the planks together while keeping water out. By 2500 BCE, Egyptians sewed external planks together, a practice continued in waters around the Indian subcontinent and the Arabian Sea into the twentieth century. The lashings were hard to keep secure, especially with larger ships, and using them introduced holes in the planks. By 2000 BCE, Egyptian shipwrights built ships with planks flush and attached to each other by mortise and tenon joints. With the joints close together, the hull might be rigid, but it was also extremely strong and durable. This successful solution was followed in classical Greece and Rome.

Design Specialization. By 1600 BCE, shipwrights had developed variations in design, most obviously distinguishing between warships and cargo ships. Both carried a single square sail, but cargo ships had capacious hulls, whereas warships had narrow hulls and relied on oars as well as a sail for propulsion. The rowing arrangements on Greek warships have been a subject of extensive discussion. Each rower probably handled his own oar, with vessels built first of one, then two, then three banks of oars. The extra manpower increased potential speed and vessel size and was a great asset in fighting. In the fourth century BCE, an arms race led to the building of bigger warships, first with four oar banks, then five and six. Another big increase in the third century BCE led to the building of ships with as many as thirty banks of oars, but exactly how shipwrights chose to configure the rowers in such giants remains a mystery.

The big oared warships disappeared with the military and naval success of the Roman Empire. Roman domination of Mediterranean waters meant only small, low-profile warships, with one bank of oars and a single square sail on a single mast, were needed. There was also a small headsail, called an artemon, at the bow. Cargo vessels were of consistent design, with length-to-breadth ratios of about 3:1, and they could be very large, reaching on the order of 1,200 tons. Construction was the same throughout, with mortise and tenon joints set close together. The single square sail was equipped with brails, already known by 1190 BCE. Brails were lines running vertically through the sail, which made it possible to change its shape and so get maximum power from the wind. The design of classical ships appears to have been largely static for some centuries.

With the decline of the Roman economy from the third century CE, the size of Mediterranean ships declined. Instead of relying on the exterior planking for strength, shipwrights built up a skeleton for rigidity and then tacked the hull planks to the frame. The hull was not as sturdy or watertight, and it needed caulking between the planks and more frequent maintenance, but it was more flexible, easi-er to repair, and simpler and cheaper to build. Smaller ships could have a different kind of rig, with a triangular or lateen sail replacing the square one. Although the lateen sail originated probably in Indonesia, Greeks and Romans had long used lateens on smaller vessels. The lateen was harder to handle than a square sail but made it possible to sail closer to the wind, a great advantage if the vessel had to tack to overcome a contrary wind. By 1000 CE, Mediterranean shipwrights had produced a unique and unprecedented form of ship.

Viking Ships. In northern Europe, Scandinavian shipbuilders extended the capabilities of the German rowing barge. They retained clinker or lapstrake construction, overlapping hull planks with each strake riveted to the one below to provide strength. Around 700, Scandinavian shipwrights added a square sail and a heavy keel to the rowing barge, which combined to make the type an open sea sailor. The Viking long ship proved effective for raiding and fighting at sea, while the relatively shorter cargo version made regular voyages possible to islands in the North Atlantic. Builders retained oars, but on cargo ships there were very few, and they were used sparingly.

Alongside Viking ships, a number of Celtic types survived, including the cog, a flat-bottomed vessel with clinker-built sides suited for coastal shipping over tidal flats. In the thirteenth century, shipbuilders added a keel and made the cog a deep-sea trader. The bigger cargo ship with a box-like cross section proved well suited for carrying bulk goods. The straight sternpost proved the logical place to hang the rudder rather than having a steering oar or oars on the sides, as was the case with earlier ships. The modified cog of around 1400 was larger than before, commonly of 200 tons and more, but still carried a single square sail on a single mast as the only means of propulsion.

The cog was certainly well known in the Mediterranean by the early fourteenth century. Shipwrights there copied the cog but made a number of changes over time to the design, generating a very different vessel. The carrack had a Mediterranean-style skeleton-first hull but with the shape of a cog. It had not one but two masts, a mainmast in the middle with a large square sail, and near the stern a mizzenmast with a lateen sail that gave the carrack greater maneuverability. Carracks proved economical as bulk carriers in the Mediterranean as well as for voyages from the eastern Mediterranean to northwest Europe.

Rigging Improvements. The logical extension of adding a second mast was to add a third to balance the rig. The full-rigged ship with square sails on the foremast and mainmast and a lateen on the mizzen probably had its origins along the coast of Iberia at the end of the fourteenth century. The new rig combined with shell-first hull construction was the most significant innovation of the age of the sailing ship. It set the standard for seaborne transport up to the introduction of steam power in the nineteenth century. Full-rigged ships were more maneuverable and more reliable. Their lower labor requirement per unit of capacity made longer voyages possible and improved the potential profit from shorter ones.

In the fifteenth and sixteenth centuries, the mainsail became smaller relative to the size of the ship, while other sails got larger and new sails appeared above the mainsails. Captains got greater flexibility in deploying canvas. Because the maximum manpower needed to shift any one of the sails fell, manning requirements per unit of carrying capacity went down. Although the sternpost rudder was now standard throughout Europe, it could change the course little more than five or six degrees, so for anything other than fine-tuning, the navigator relied on trimming the increasingly divided sails.

About the same time that builders developed the full-rigged ship, they made major improvements in small boat rigs. They put two fore-and-aft sails, a staysail in front and a triangular or trapezoidal sail in back of a single mast, which made it possible for one man to handle a boat. All the rig improvements combined to make significant contributions to productivity of water transport in the fifteenth and sixteenth centuries.

The diffusion of the full-rigged ship brought modifications by local shipwrights. Unfamiliar with skeleton-first construction, builders in the north used various hybrid forms, combining features of the old with the new. The sixteenth century, but moreso the seventeenth and eighteenth centuries, was a period of elaboration of full-rigged design. The full-rigged ship proved highly effective as a platform for cannon, the new offensive weapon of naval warfare in the fifteenth and sixteenth centuries. Ships for use in trading along the all-sea route to the Far East typically carried guns; by the mid-seventeenth century, East Indiamen were similar to warships. The first vessels for shipping around the Cape of Good Hope were giant Portuguese carracks with full rig, the largest wooden ships ever built, reaching 2,000 tons or more. Their sheer size was their defense. In the seventeenth century, smaller, more handy, more reliable, but well-armed English and Dutch versions of the East Indiamen superseded the Portuguese giants. For voyages to the New World, Spanish shippers by the late sixteenth century preferred the galleon, a relatively long and fast cargo ship with guns ranged along the sides.

For cargo ships, the greatest modification in design came from the Netherlands sometime in the sixteenth century. There, builders produced the *fluit*, a vessel four or five times as long as it was broad with a boxlike cross section and simple rig. The bow was low, the stern high and tapered. *Fluiten* were typically unarmed or lightly armed and were well suited to regions of Europe where shipping was

relatively safe. They were slow because they carried less canvas than was feasible, to keep down crew size and make it possible to do some of the work setting sails from the deck. *Fluiten* were highly efficient in the carriage of bulk goods compared with earlier cargo types. They were also susceptible to adaptation for specific tasks, and shipbuilders in other parts of Europe imitated and adapted the design of those Dutch ships.

Asian Vessels. European ships with skeleton-first construction and full rig were superior for the carriage of cargo on long ocean voyages to vessels of the extensive Malaysian navigational tradition, which stretched from Madagascar to Polynesia. Similarly, European ships proved superior to the dhow, the lateen-rigged, relatively long and small cargo ship associated with Arab seafaring. The dhow was highly practical, but solely in the Arabian Sea, which was dominated by monsoon winds. The junk, a product of Chinese shipyards, proved better than its European competitors for a number of purposes. The balanced lug sail stiffened by battens and the vertical median rudder gave a relatively high degree of control. Three, four, five, and even more masts, each with its own sail, made it possible to build big junks. They reached 3,000 to 4,000 tons in the nineteenth century. Junks were capable of sea passages throughout the East and South China Seas and across the Indian Ocean and survived as the standard cargo ship of east Asia into the twentieth century.

By the middle of the eighteenth century in Europe, various experiments led to the evolution of something like a standard packet ship, a vessel of full rig of 300 to 500 tons, with vessels over 700 tons being rare. Shipbuilders made small improvements in handling and speed, for example, from the addition of staysails hanging down from the ropes holding the masts in place.

Shipbuilders made advances with a variety of other types of ships in the eighteenth century. The bark, long established as a vessel of full rig with typically a gaffsail on the mizzen, began to grow in size. The related barquentine appeared as well, with fore-and-aft sails on the main and mizzenmasts and traditional square rig on the foremast. The snow was the largest two-masted ship, reaching as much as 1,000 tons. Both of its masts carried square sails, and there was a fore-and-aft sail fitted on another mast set just behind and attached to the mainmast. The schooner, first built in North America in the early eighteenth century, originally carried both square and fore-and-aft sails on its two masts. Reduced to just fore-and-aft sails, schooners could add masts, getting to as many as seven in the last days of sail.

Other two-masted ships or even large single-masted ships with perpendicular sides, a single deck, and easily workable rig, such as the *smack*, the Dutch *tjalk*, and the *kof*, supplanted larger types of older design in intra-European trades in the north. Two-masters proved especially useful for coastal or regional trade, which enjoyed rapid growth in the eighteenth century, as with the English East Coast coal trade, where collier brigs grew to be able to carry 300 to 400 tons. The various two-masted ships sometimes proved useful for longer voyages and in various fisheries. They offered advantages of smaller crews per ton and less lumpy investment. By the eighteenth century, productivity gains were typically not to be found from the better design of the three-masted ship but rather from reductions in turnaround time and the exploitation of standardized and typically longer routes.

Advances in Navigation. There were also gains from the diffusion of better navigation techniques. The first mention of the pointing needle comes from around 1100. The compass was known by the twelfth century in both Europe and China, although development in the two regions seems to have been independent. By the thirteenth century in the West, books of sailing instructions indicated that sailors used the compass in steering. Combined with the hourglass to measure speed and the chart to plot a course, the compass made dead-reckoning navigation possible. The navigator used devices for calculation, used his own mathematical knowledge, and looked down at his charts as well as up at the sun and stars.

In the waters of northern Europe, navigators tended to rely more on lead and line, taking soundings to find out where they were. As some moved out from shoreline navigation after the development of the seagoing cog, they depended more on celestial navigation. That took on even greater importance in the fourteenth and fifteenth centuries, as Portuguese sailors made their way south along the coast of Africa, facing the problem of covering long north-south distances and of crossing the equator, which meant losing sight of the pole star. Navigators took the maximum altitude of the sun and then, comparing that with a table with the maximum altitude of the sun at Lisbon for any given day, they could establish latitude.

The astrolabe, a device known since antiquity, could generate the needed measurements, but for taking readings on a rolling ship's deck it was impractical. Around 1480, a much simpler mariner's version replaced the elaborate astronomer's astrolabe. More useful was the crossstaff, a simple device probably modeled on the very similar Arab *kamal*, which allowed measuring the elevation of any body above the horizon. The crossstaff did not get used in navigation until the sixteenth century, and at the end of that century it was supplanted by the backstaff, which performed the same function but eliminated a number of problems. By the eighteenth century, instrument makers produced the sextant, easier to use and much more accurate for measuring the height above the horizon of stars or the sun.

Sixteenth-century advances in mapmaking made setting courses easier and put less expensive charts in the hands of many more captains. Along with advances in mathematics, it was easier to apply spherical trigonometry to navigation. Knowledge of logarithms and of calculus, both products of the seventeenth century, proved absolutely necessary to the further development of navigation, but their effects would have to wait for the better sextant and better education. Captains sailing along shores still relied on soundings and landmarks to guide them. On long voyages, they had to take advantage of what winds there were, so only very occasionally did they make any effort to calculate their position, that is even if they had the proven ability to do so.

It might be possible to find a ship's latitude but it was not possible to determine longitude. Without the latter, the value of the former was severely restricted. Governments already in the sixteenth century offered prizes for a successful method of measuring longitude. John Harrison, an English instrument maker, found a solution when he produced a clock able to keep highly accurate time under varying weather conditions on a pitching ship over a period of months. Sea trials begun in 1761 proved that navigators, knowing noon at some location—for English navigators that was the site of the royal observatory at Greenwich—could compare that with local noon and so determine their longitude.

The quality of charts improved with standardization in the products of the British Admiralty in the nineteenth century. Royal Navy captains were directed to carry out hydrographic surveys as part of voyages of scientific investigation. Skilled practitioners like the English explorer James Cook provided the reliable information for charts that later became generally available at reasonable cost. The highly accurate methods of fixing position of the late nineteenth and twentieth centuries required comprehensive knowledge of geometry and trigonometry, so celestial navigation became an acquired skill gained only through extensive education. First the use of radio beacons at known points on shore in the 1940s and then in the 1960s the launching of navigational satellites, which yield a global positioning system based on the waves emitted by those satellites, generated astounding accuracy in measuring location and in easy-to-acquire form. Global positioning changed the basis for determining position and made obsolete long-standing navigational skills.

Steam Power. It did not take long after the development of a commercially viable steam engine for one to be placed on board a ship. Although the American inventor Robert Fulton generally receives credit for the first practical steam ship, operated on the Hudson River from 1807, early contemporaries like the American John Fitch and the Englishman William Symington experimented before

Fulton with different forms of propulsion. Early steam engines presented serious problems of reliability, of power per unit of weight, of required fuel that took up space otherwise destined for paying cargo, and of the best method of transferring the engine power. The first success with steam power came with tug boats. The ability to get vessels in and out of port on demand raised productivity significantly, since ships no longer had to wait for a favorable wind. The second success came with riverboats and canal boats, where sailing craft always had difficulties, especially with going upstream. Sometimes, the solution was to tow or row vessels, but steam made the hard labor of doing either unnecessary. Early seagoing steamships carried sails, the steam engine used only when the wind failed. As early as 1819 the steam-powered American ship *Savannah* crossed the Atlantic Ocean but used its sails for all but eight hours of the passage. It was more than a half-century before steamboats dominated major trading routes. As late as 1860, steamboats made up less than 10 percent of the tonnage of the United Kingdom merchant marine. In 1883, it was over 50 percent and by 1902, over 80 percent.

There were two principal reasons for the gradual adoption of steam at sea before the 1870s: the slow pace of technical advance in steam propulsion and marked improvements in competing sailing ships. The clipper, with its high ratio of length to breadth, lower wetted surface that decreased the resistance created by friction with the water, sharp stem, and relatively large sail area was developed from a Chesapeake Bay design. The first true clipper was built in 1845 in New York, and the design spread quickly after that to England, the Netherlands and other seafaring countries. Clippers were noted for speed, reaching an average of 22 knots on ocean crossings.

Sailing ships in general grew in size in the nineteenth century. Barks with four or even five masts fitted with fore-and-aft sails could be easily handled and so gained wider acceptance, growing in capacity to about 3,000 tons. The use of donkey engines on deck especially toward the end of the nineteenth century cut down on the need for sailors to go aloft and at the same time made it possible to fit bigger sails, thus making bigger ships possible. Despite productivity gains, sailing ships succumbed to the onslaught of steam after the 1870s.

The opening of the Suez Canal in 1869 promoted the development and use of the steam packet, a cargo ship made with an iron hull and a much more efficient steam engine. Pressures in steam engines rose, and by the 1860s they were five times what they had been early in the century. By the 1870s, pressures were twenty-five times greater. Tube boilers, which came into use after about 1835, lowered fuel requirements compared with earlier kettle boilers. The first operational compound marine steam engine that reused steam from the first cylinder in a second one dated from 1825. During the 1870s, reliable double, triple, and even quadruple expansion engines became firmly established, increasing cargo space and range because of more efficient fuel use. In the 1840s, experiments with British warships proved the superiority of the screw propeller. By 1865 the fundamental physical problems of screw propulsion had been solved. Single, twin, and even triple screws by 1862 had all but replaced sidewheels and sternwheels in seagoing ships.

Metal Construction. Long-term improvements in metallurgy made steam engines more dependable and also made it possible to replace wood with iron in ship construction. Already in the late eighteenth century, the introduction of iron frames, deckbeams, knees, and longitudinal girders created composite ships that had more internal room and less hull weight than all-wood ships. Composite building continued with clipper ships, but the trend was toward building entire hulls of iron. Wrought iron could be rolled into plates, and the first seagoing ships with hulls of riveted plates appeared around 1820. As the plates got bigger, larger ships became easier to build, as shown by the vessels of the English engineer I. K. Brunel. His *Great Britain* of 1843 was 100 meters long, and the *Great Eastern*, built in 1857, was 207 meters long with a length-to-breadth ratio of about 8:1 and a capacity of 18,900 tons. Though the *Great Eastern* was unique, in its time the direction of shipbuilding was undoubtedly toward greater size and length.

As steel replaced iron in the second half of the nineteenth century, the trend became even more pronounced. In poorer regions or where shipbuilding timber was easily accessible, shipwrights still turned out wooden ships into the twentieth century, just as sailing ships, like clippers and barks, survived in trades where winds were consistent and cargoes bulky, as in carrying nitrates from Chile to Europe, which went on into the 1930s. Wooden sailing ships also survived for inshore fishing, where crews were typically large and distances travelled short. The arrival of the marine diesel in the 1920s more or less meant the end of sail even along the coasts of Norway and later Canada.

The twentieth century was marked by the development of specialized ships, increases in the size of ships, mass-production techniques using new ways to fasten plates, changes in motive power, and the invention of alternatives to the simple single-hulled cargo vessel. Tramp steamers, which ran up to a maximum of about 8,000 tons, and even liners serving established routes especially after midcentury gave way to ships designed specifically to move containers of standard size. The ability to use containers for intermodal transport on land and sea made them the normal way of moving general cargo by the end of the century. Roll-on-roll-off ships with through decks and large doors carried automobiles across oceans as international trade in vehicles grew starting in the 1960. Ferries, similar in design and long known, increasingly came to be used to move automobiles rather than rail cars and took on longer routes. Shipbuilders developed methods of keeping large quantities of natural gas under pressure and refrigerated, making possible international shipment of the fuel. They also developed more fully the design of tankers to carry fluids, especially oil. Tankers appeared at the start of the century, when the rise in shipping volumes made it less feasible to carry oil in barrels. Growth in tanker tonnage was marked already in the interwar years, but the boom in tanker production came in the 1960s. The basic hull form remained that of the late nineteenth century, with some rise in the length-to-breadth ratios, reaching the range of 6:1 to 7:1.

Ship Size. From the 1960s, shipbuilders tested the boundaries of ship size. In the early twentieth century, steam ships of 5,000 to 10,000 tons were large compared with the biggest of sailing ships. World War II Liberty ships were 10,000 tons. Some 2,500 products of U.S. and Canadian shipyards were of a standard design, mass-produced to exploit the use of interchangeable parts and other practices of contemporary industry. Container ships by the late twentieth century approached 70,000 tons although a range of 40,000 to 60,000 tons proved optimal. Tankers in the 1960s already surpassed 200,000 tons, and in the mid-1970s, ultralarge crude-oil carriers even surpassed 300,000 tons. Shipbuilders found it possible to increase the scale of vessels without great sacrifices in integrity or durability. They could not, however, overcome the problems of navigating a vessel of such great size; the massive ships are difficult to get moving and, more important, extremely difficult to stop.

Steamships built for passenger travel were a product of the second half of the nineteenth century. Not dependent on vagaries of winds and tides, steamships opened new possibilities for regularly scheduled local, regional, and transoceanic passenger service. European countries, often with government subsidies, had national carriers on transatlantic, African, and Asian routes. Travel by sea could be luxurious, with elaborate dining and entertainment facilities for the better paying passengers, but this certainly was not always the case.

Jet aircraft capable of transoceanic flights made ocean liners obsolete for most passenger traffic. Owners converted many passenger ships into cruise ships. The growth in tourism in the late twentieth century led to demand for new cruise ships, even larger and more luxurious than their predecessors. Shipbuilders added stabilizers on cruise ships, and on larger ferries as well, to insure a more comfortable voyage. By the end of the century, cruise ships reached 100,000 tons.

Twentieth-Century Innovations. The English engineer Charles Parsons's strong advocacy of the steam turbine led to its adoption first on warships and then, after 1905, on many oceangoing cargo and passenger ships. The steam turbine offered fuel efficiencies, consistent power, higher speeds, and greater maneuverability, since multiple expansion turbines were often fitted on each of three propellers. The steam turbine was the typical source of power for larger vessels, but for medium-sized and smaller ships diesel motors increasingly came to be used to drive the propellers. At the end of World War I, only a minute percentage of larger ships were powered by diesel engines, but by 1939 nearly 25 percent of such ships used diesel power.

To gain greater control of the rotational speed of propellers, builders in the 1930s tried driving the shafts with electric motors, with the electricity generated by turbines. Turboelectric power also opened another possibility, especially for tankers and larger vessels. The rising use of diesel engines coincided with the shift from coal to oil as the source of power. Oil produced more energy per unit of weight and volume, was much easier to handle, and did not require large numbers of stokers, which reduced labor needs. Tradition, the existence of infrastructure for the use of coal, and some price advantages kept a place for coal in ocean shipping until about midcentury, but after that coal went the way of the sail.

In the 1930s, the electric welding of plates began to replace riveting in shipbuilding. The demand for rapid construction of Liberty ships during World War II led to the almost complete adoption of welding by midcentury. Welded hulls were 10 to 15 percent lighter than riveted hulls, and welding could be automated. Sections prefabricated under cover were welded together on a slipway in a short time. Prefabrication, the introduction of flow-line production, and the building of larger ships all involved significant capital expenditure for post–World War II shipyards, investment that not all shipbuilders made.

Polynesian sailors had for millennia used vessels with not one but two hulls, a logical extension of their use of outriggers. Twin hulls have the advantage of cutting down on wetted surface. In the second half of the twentieth century, a variety of builders began to experiment with twin hulls. By that time, catamarans had already gained some acceptance in small boats in Europe and North America. The design proved especially good for ferries, where speed was essential and cargo space could be sacrificed for that speed.

The first aluminum sailing boat was built in 1890, but aluminum has largely been limited to use in smaller vessels. Although aluminum hulls are 30 to 40 percent lighter than comparable steel ones, questions remain about the rigidity and durability of all-aluminum hulls and the considerably higher price of aluminum compared with steel.

For smaller vessels, especially for pleasure craft, reinforced plastics gained acceptance in the late twentieth century because of their lightness and malleability. For larger ships, however, that material proved impractical.

The hovercraft, made practical by the English engineer Christopher Cockrell in 1950, floats on a cushion of air forced downward by fans and kept under the vessel by a large skirt. Reaching a size large enough for commercial service as a ferry in 1968, the hovercraft proved to be noisy, unable to supply a smooth ride in rough seas, and expensive to operate. Its primary advantages are higher speed and the ability to go up on shore, eliminating the need for complex docking facilities. The hovercraft proved valuable for rescue work and began to be used for ferry services in the 1970s.

More successful as a passenger ferry has been the hydrofoil, a standard single-hulled ship equipped with wings attached below the hull. Once up to speed, the hydrofoil body rises above the water and rides only on the wings. Hydrofoils sharply decrease resistance and so are capable of significantly greater speeds, but wings cannot be fitted on vessels of any great size, so hydrofoils have found limited use.

The growth in size of ships and the standardization of the design of cargo vessels into specific categories has led to the concentration of shipbuilding and ship design in fewer places in the world. Despite experiments with different forms, the giant single-hulled vessel continues to dominate total tonnage built. The growth in the size of such ships, a process that started in the early nineteenth century and accelerated in the late twentieth, presumably will continue in the face of increasing demand for shipping services and in the presence of the technical ability shipbuilders have demonstrated to produce massive ships.

BIBLIOGRAPHY

Casson, Lionel. *The Ancient Mariners: Seafarers and Sea Fighters.* 2d rev. ed. Princeton, 1991.

Chapelle, Howard I. *The Search for Speed under Sail, 1700–1855.* New York, 1967.

Crumlin-Pedersen, Ole, ed. *Aspects of Maritime Scandinavia, AD 200–1200.* Roskilde, Denmark, 1991.

Gardiner, Robert, ed. *History of the Ship.* 12 vols. London, 1992–1995.

Guthrie, John. *A History of Marine Engineering.* London, 1971.

MacGregor, David R. *Fast Sailing Ships: Their Design and Construction, 1775–1875.* 2d ed. London, 1988.

Needham, Joseph. *Science and Civilization in China*, vol. 4, part 3, *Civil Engineering and Nautics.* Cambridge, 1971.

Parry, John H. *Discovery of the Sea.* London, 1975.

Rosenberg, Nathan. "Factors Affecting the Diffusion of Technology." *Explorations in Economic History* 10. 1(Fall 1972), 3–34.

Shepherd, James F., and Gary M. Walton. *Shipping, Maritime Trade, and the Economic Development of Colonial North America.* Cambridge, 1972.

Unger, Richard W. *Dutch Shipbuilding before 1800: Ships and Guilds.* Assen, 1978.

Unger, Richard W. *The Ship in the Medieval Economy, 600–1600.* London, 1980.

Williams, J. E. D. *From Sails to Satellites: The Origin and Development of Navigational Science.* Oxford, 1992.

RICHARD W. UNGER

Ocean Shipping

Ocean shipping, by allowing the exchange of goods between markets, permits specialization in production and so promotes economic growth. The first movement of goods over open seas in western Eurasia began around 3500 BCE. The addition of sails to boats made travel possible between Lebanon and Egypt. Traders presumably went north from the Nile Delta to get wood and wood products for shipbuilding and other uses. Continued improvements in the construction of ships contributed to the expansion of shipping to the Red Sea as well as farther north and west in the Mediterranean. Cargo ships carried many luxury goods but, from the earliest days of ocean shipping, also moved bulky goods, that is, goods of a low ratio of value to weight and volume. Wine and olive oil joined grain and wood by the middle of the first millennium BCE, though Greek and Phoenician shippers often carried goods of higher value, prominently people. The total volume of ocean shipping in the Mediterranean and the number of ports shippers visited rose through the first century BCE, as Greek sailors laid the foundation for later patterns of travel and commerce. Early in the Christian era, Roman shippers and the Roman state exploited the experience of their Greek predecessors, extending but more typically intensifying what had come before. The general growth in the population and the economy raised the demand for shipping services. In addition, the state, in order to supply grain to the capital, established regularly scheduled voyages between Egypt and Ostia, the port of Rome, using the largest ships built to that date creating what was in essence a liner service. The shipping network reached further afield as Romans traded through ports on the east coast of the Arabian Peninsula to India. Romans established partnerships, in which individuals bought shares, eighths, sixteenths, thirty-seconds, to distribute the high risk and also to raise the sizable capital needed to build and maintain ocean-going vessels. Divided ownership remained common; corporate ownership by joint-stock companies began in the early seventeenth century but was not common until the nineteenth century.

Ocean shipping declined in the late Roman Empire and the Middle Ages to about 1000 CE. By that time Chinese and Malaysian shippers made ocean voyages in the China Seas and the Indian Ocean and maintained more or less regular commercial contact. Chinese shipping reached the islands to the east and Southeast Asia, while Malaysian voyagers carried goods and people around the Indian Ocean and migrants to Polynesia. While before 1000 the

OCEAN SHIPPING. Loading steamers in Montreal harbor, late nineteenth century. (Detroit Publishing Co./Prints and Photographs Division, Library of Congress)

scope of ocean shipping in East Asia was far more impressive than that in and around Europe, early in the second millennium the difference narrowed. In the Mediterranean the movement of goods to the Levant from the West was aided by the traffic in pilgrims, including crusaders desiring to establish and maintain Christian rule in the Holy Land. Regular contact among different parts of the Mediterranean accompanied by improved exchange of information made more extensive shipping practical. The normal form was tramping with ships and shipowners, who were often merchants, intending to specialize in trade along one route or in one good but always flexible and open to any opportunity. Ships moved along coasts with the ultimate goal of reaching the home port, but they were easily diverted to carry a potentially profitable cargo. The growth in certain trades and government regulation in Italian commercial towns made shipping more predictable for both suppliers and users. In the late fourteenth century and the fifteenth century the government in Venice owned large oared sailing ships that traveled along defined routes at specific times of the year. Shippers leased space in the ships. While the voyages carrying pilgrims to the Holy Land are the best-documented, regular shipping services extended to the Black Sea, to England, and to the Low Countries, with ships carrying a variety of foods and industrial goods. In northern Europe, probably in the twelfth century, trade in bulk goods appeared alongside the existing carriage of luxuries. Shippers used cogs and other relatively short, round vessels to move goods like wood, salt, and grain across the open ocean. By the fifteenth century such vessels made trips to the Mediterranean, and Italian ships traveled to northwest Europe. The volume of ocean shipping declined dramatically after the massive demographic contraction in the mid-fourteenth century. The available tonnage for ocean shipping did not recover to the level of 1300 for a century and a half or more. The fall in the total volume of trade made tramping more difficult in all parts of Europe, but circumstances changed after 1500.

Expansion. The voyages of exploration begun in the fourteenth century bore increasing fruit. By 1500 Europeans, using new types of vessels such as two-masted lateen-rigged caravels and three-masted full rigged ships, which combined square and lateen rig, all equipped with sternpost rudders and navigational instruments, established shipping routes to the New World and Asia. After their arrival, Spanish sailors and ships quickly replaced the paddled vessels that existed in the Caribbean. In Asia, Europeans used force as well as technical superiority in shipping to supplement and then supplant indigenous shippers. The formation of East India and other trading companies in European states created institutions that owned ships, regulated and promoted trade, and regularly moved goods between Europe and Asia as well as within Asia. The growing volume of international commerce from Europe to the New World in the sixteenth century and to the East in the seventeenth century led to bigger and better ships and more regular movement of goods. The scale of investment involved and the high risk in the early days of colonial trades for Europe limited the numbers of individuals involved.

Gradual technological improvements in ships, the evolution of better commercial institutions (such as maritime insurance), and the expansion of trades both beyond and within Europe led to a more stable supply of shipping services. They also led to improvements in labor productivity onboard ships. The development of ports with facilities and personnel to handle cargoes and, in general, the better organization of trade on land lowered the number of people needed to carry on ocean shipping. Growth in the volume of trade made it possible to assemble cargoes more easily, decreasing turnaround times and enhancing exploitation of both capital and labor. Greater efficiency translated into falling freight rates and rapid growth in the total volume of shipping tonnage. Between 1500 and 1800 the size of the European merchant marine doubled per capita and then doubled again, increasing by more than 400 percent over those three hundred years. While shipping to distant points grew for Europeans, shipping in other parts of the world remained stable or declined. Within Europe the shipping patterns established in the Middle Ages intensified, with volumes rising significantly over time. In the North the movement of bulk goods, such as timber, naval stores, and grains from the Baltic, was joined by trade in coal, first coastal and then across seas and oceans. Northern European shippers by the end of the sixteenth century had established trades to the Mediterranean, so the two regions of northern and southern Europe were regularly connected. The greater frequency of such voyages and the falling costs of acquiring information decreased risk and increased utilization of existing resources. Investment in shipping became more common, especially in the ports of northwestern Europe, where sizable returns were possible. By the eighteenth century the new newspapers in those ports announced in advance the sailing of packet ships of somewhat standard design for specified destinations. Individuals came to specialize in providing ships and shipping services, forerunners of the shipping firms of the nineteenth century. The massive eighteenth-century increase in ocean shipping, fed by the rise in trade within Europe and in goods from the Americas, like sugar, tobacco, and rice; and from Asia, like spices and cotton cloth, was dwarfed by events in the nineteenth century.

Industrial Revolution. The Industrial Revolution spread to the oceans of the world slowly. The development of a new form of propulsion, steam, was not immediately effective. Rather, through the first half of the nineteenth century the emerging shipping firms had their greatest successes with sailing ships. The nearly regular and predictable services within much of Europe were supplemented by more standardized services to distant sites. The carriage of emigrants to the New World and to Australia was not as important as bringing in raw materials, such as cotton, and exotic goods, such as coffee, sugar, and especially tea onboard clipper ships from China. Sailing ships proved even more durable in shipping around Cape Horn, bringing guano and nitrates from the west coast of South America to Europe. The predictable winds and long reaches made it possible for them to survive in those trades well into the twentieth century. Nevertheless by around 1850 shipping firms increasingly moved over to the use of steam. The principal barrier to innovation was that carrying coal for fuel decreased the payload. Tugs or riverboats, which could refuel easily, did not experience this problem. But for long voyages over the ocean, steam engines needed improvements in efficiency to provide space onboard for cargo. An important element in that development was the perfection of the screw propeller in the late 1830s. Those gains, combined with the often greater speed of steamships, led to falling freight rates. The opening of the Suez Canal in 1869 was an important factor in steam's eventual dominance of shipping between the Far East and Europe, as steamships navigated canals more easily than sailing ships. But more importantly avoiding the long trip around the Cape of Good Hope reduced the distance, which dropped fuel requirements significantly. The canal and steamships cut dramatically the time for shipping to East Asia and Australia from Europe. On a smaller scale the opening of the Panama Canal in 1914 did the same for shipping between the east and west coasts of North America. From the 1850s on, iron and later steel replaced wood as the main shipbuilding material. While the largest ships that could be made of wood were 250 feet long, the *Great Eastern* launched in 1858, was almost 700 feet long. Larger ships again meant lower costs, as fuel costs and crew size increased more slowly than volume and thus cargo space. By 1891 over 80 percent of all ships were made of steel.

The effectiveness and the capital requirements of steamships led to the creation of larger and more easily identifiable steamship lines that competed vigorously with each other. The first and best-known lines operated regular liner routes across the North Atlantic. National postal services awarded mail contracts, and the critical profits from those contracts created a drive for greater speed among shippers. Firms like the American Collins Line and the British Cunard Line engaged in stiff competition for mail and for emigrants traveling across the North Atlantic. Firms from other western European and Scandinavian countries joined in the supply of regular liner services for goods and passengers not just on the North Atlantic but to all parts of the globe.

Twentieth Century. In the closing years of the nineteenth century shipping companies consolidated. While English firms dominated ocean shipping, they faced increasing competition from foreign companies, which were often supported by subsidies from their governments. These subsidies took a number of forms. The desire for foreign exchange earnings was linked to questions of national pride and promotion of domestic industry. The entrance of Japanese shipping companies into the search for cargoes between Asia and Europe complicated the market for services. To deal with what could be disastrous competition, many firms, in conjunction with governments, established shipping conferences, which were essentially cartels that restricted entry on specific routes or between specified parts of the world and set rates for the movement of goods. With their potential for disagreement about enforcement or equity, conferences were difficult to administer. They did succeed in keeping newcomers out of ocean shipping, and they also guaranteed profitable operations to those already in a conference. The protected environment tended to generate larger shipping firms though not necessarily larger ships or lower freight rates.

Shipping conferences came under increasing pressure from ambitious new firms and countries and from the disruption of two world wars, which led to ever-greater competition in ocean shipping. Bulk trades expanded rapidly after the middle of the twentieth century, especially in oil as demand for energy grew and tankers became larger and larger. Meanwhile the shipment of general cargo was revolutionized by the widespread adoption of standardized containers in the second half of the century, one of the most critical yet unnoticed innovations of globalization in the post-1945 era. The liner services carrying boxes that could be filled with anything heralded the decline and virtual disappearance of tramping. Goods were shipped to any destination by sea and on land in the same container. Smaller vessels searching ports for cargoes disappeared as intermodal transport made the irregular and occasional appearance of ships of no value. Goods went directly from origin to destination, spending part of the time on a ship. The greater capital requirements of giant tankers and container ships concentrated ownership of vessels in the hands of a smaller number of firms. The migration of shipping out of traditional regions into the periphery of the industrial world was the only force counteracting the tendency toward concentration. Shipping companies in Britain, the United States, the Netherlands, Germany, and Scandinavia tended to shrink and merge in order to compete with newcomers. Conferences no longer adequately served to protect them. The decision of the Soviet government to compete in international shipping after World War II led to a temporary challenge from countries of the Eastern bloc, but existing firms weathered the challenge.

More serious in both the short and the long term was the rise after 1945 of shipping first in southern Europe, particularly in Greece, generating a few large firms and massive fortunes for the owners, and then in Asia, primarily in Japan, Hong Kong, and Korea. Reacting to the lower costs of the new competitors, shipping firms resorted to flags of convenience. Firms, often with U.S. capital, operated with crews from poor countries and outside the increasingly stiff regulations of industrialized states by registering themselves and their ships in small states glad to offer a home to the industry. By the first years of the twenty-first-century ocean shipping was more extensive than ever before in terms of the potential volume that could be carried. At the same time the greater standardization of trade routes, with the volume between larger ports growing and that through smaller ports declining, and the introduction of more efficient transport on land, including pipelines and containers, led to a decline in the options open to shippers. The standardization of ships, packaging, routes and open competition simplified ocean shipping and undermined the great variety in the ways people and goods were moved on the seas of the world that had existed up to and through the Industrial Revolution.

BIBLIOGRAPHY

Casson, Lionel. *The Ancient Mariners Seafarers and Sea Fighters.* Princeton, 1991.

Davis, Ralph. *The Rise of the English Shipping Industry in the Seventeenth and Eighteenth Centuries.* London, 1962.

Gardiner, Robert, ed. *History of the Ship.* 12 vols. London, 1992–1995.

Harley, C. Knick. "Ocean Freight Rates and Productivity, 1740–1914: The Primacy of Mechanical Invention Reaffirmed." *Journal of Economic History* 48.4 (1988), 851–876.

Lucassen, Jan, and Richard W. Unger. "Labour Productivity in Ocean Shipping, 1500–1850." *International Journal of Maritime History* 12.2 (2000), 127–141.

Needham, Joseph. *Science and Civilization in China*, vol. 4, pt. 3, *Civil Engineering and Nautics.* Cambridge, 1971.

North, Douglass. "Sources of Productivity Change in Ocean Shipping, 1600–1850." *Journal of Political Economy* 76.5 (1968), 953–970.

Parry, John H. *Discovery of the Sea.* London, 1975.

Rosenberg, Nathan. "Factors Affecting the Diffusion of Technology." *Explorations in Economic History* 10.1 (Fall 1972), 3–34.

Shepherd, James F., and Gary M. Walton. *Shipping, Maritime Trade, and the Economic Development of Colonial North America.* Cambridge, 1972.

Unger, Richard W. *The Ship in the Medieval Economy, 600–1600.* London, 1980.

Wray, William D. *Mitsubishi and the N.Y.K., 1870–1914: Business Strategy in the Japanese Shipping Industry.* Cambridge, Mass., 1984.

RICHARD W. UNGER

Canal Transportation

In most countries, the main contribution of canals to economic growth occurred in the period when overland transport was still slow and expensive and before steam power had been applied to either land or water transport. Although the excavation of canals required heavy outlays of capital, the basis of their economic potential was clear and simple. In an age of horse or wind power, the average load of a single horse might be an eighth of a ton by pack, 2 tons by wagon (on the best surfaced roads), 8 tons by iron rail, 30 tons by riverboat, and up to 50 tons by canal barge.

Canals had specific advantages over navigable rivers, which were once the only alternative to bad roads. The water was confined to a purpose-built channel usually equipped with a towpath and largely free from the hazards of uncontrolled currents, flooding, weirs, water mills, and fishing nets. The most important new technical feature was the pound lock, normally a chamber enclosed at each end by double gates, which allowed transition between different water levels.

Many canals made other demands on civil engineering, such as cuttings, tunnels, and aqueducts. Unlike rivers, canals are not dependent on natural hydrology and could be designed to create the most useful possible artificial links. In principle, this meant cheap transport by water was taken to suitable manufacturing sites rather than vice versa. However, topography and the water table remained major constraints in many areas. Many canals were either of the contour type (relatively level, but circuitous) or of the undulating type (more direct, but with complex engineering and lockage).

The overall impact of canals was to reduce the cost of overland carriage by at least half, and often by far more. Their economic significance in industrialization was that they greatly facilitated the carriage of high-bulk/low-dispersion commodities, especially on short hauls. Canals were particularly well suited to the movement of the fuel that was indispensable to the first Industrial Revolution. The need to carry coal from pits distributed over a small area, in contrast to grain grown over a much larger region, translated into heavy loads passing along a small number of routes, rather than the opposite.

The best-known quotation in canal history is the duke of Bridgewater's remark that every canal "must have coals at the heel of it." Certainly coal was the principal cargo on a high proportion of the more successful British canals. National coal production expanded roughly sixfold from 1750 to 1830, while the real price remained stable or declined slightly. This increased output was mainly produced and consumed within limited areas of the country. Coal attracted all the manufacturing activities that needed heat or power; as a result, the industrial revolution in Britain could largely be defined geographically as the map of the coalfields. Cheap coal and good transport were the most fundamental characteristics shared by the industrializing areas. Canals made a particularly large and obvious contribution in South Lancashire, the West Midlands, and South Wales, but they were important elsewhere too, including the west of Scotland, Shropshire, and the Potteries.

Britain's Canal Age. The Canal Age in Britain was inaugurated by the Sankey Canal, which opened in 1757, and the Bridgewater, built by James Brindley for the third duke from 1759 to 1761. Both were short and were responses to the shortage of coal in Liverpool and Manchester, respectively. The first stage of the Bridgewater allowed coal from the duke's collieries at Worsley to be delivered to Manchester, less than 10 miles (16 kilometers) away, at four pence per ton instead of seven pence. The Sankey had a major impact in establishing access to the growing port city of Liverpool for the southern part of the Lancashire coalfield. The longer Leeds and Liverpool Canal (from 1774) enabled a rapid increase in supplies from the central part of that coalfield. The coal-based manufacturing of the area included copper, iron, salt and sugar works, breweries, distilleries, and potteries, plus the saltworks of Cheshire, and the glass, iron, and copper of Wigan and St. Helens. The Sankey's chief private backer was a Mersey saltmaster, John Ashton. By 1800, Liverpool was the third largest city in the country and was the hub of an integrated economic system that included almost the whole Lancashire coalfield.

It is now generally recognized that the British industrial revolution was essentially a regional phenomenon and that regional concentration was an important causal factor. The region has been compared to a system of walls in which new ideas reverberated and reinforced themselves instead of being spread ineffectively around the whole country. The role of canals in this perspective was as a provider of major intraregional benefits at a limited number of places. The nodes, terminals, and corridors along canal routes gained major advantages. Eventually, of course, the cost-reducing and market-widening effects benefited the national economy, but for some time they were felt primarily at regional level. The longer-term consequences included a changed balance of population and economic growth. Before the Canal Age, three of England's four largest cities were in the south, all on coastal or riverine sites; once canals were in widespread use, five of England's seven largest cities were located on inland coalfields. This transformation has been described as turning the economy "outside-in."

The regional character of the economic impact of Britain's canals lessens the force of the valid point that a national canal network developed only slowly and was

SUEZ CANAL. Ceremony for the inauguration of the opening of the canal at Port Said, Egypt, 17 November 1869. Painting by Edouard Riou (1833–1900). (Château de Compiegne, France/ Réunion des Musée Nationaux/Art Resource, NY)

incomplete until industrialization was well under way. As with the railways later, canals were built without any planning or coordination and to a considerable diversity of standards. A particular weakness was the large mileage in the Midlands that consisted of "narrow" canals, with an average lock width of only 7 feet. The system of ownership and tolls was fragmente d, and some longer journeys were complicated by the need for transhipment. All this mattered little to most users, since the average length of haul was short. Some other limitations of canal transport were, however, more serious. Canals were more vulnerable than roads to extremes of weather and could easily be closed by frost in winter or by drought in summer. This naturally detracted from their regularity of supply. Relatively low speeds meant that they did little to reduce inventory costs. Lack of security made them unattractive for-higher value goods. Nevertheless, the category of bulky, low-value goods was a wide one, comprising most foods and building materials, as well as industrial supplies.

The British canals were financed basically through joint stock companies, which succeeded in attracting funds on a national scale, with significant interregional capital flows. About £20 million was invested in around 3,000 miles of canal and improved river navigation projects from 1760 to 1830. Speculative elements were apparent at times, especially in the "canal mania" of the early 1790s, but for the most part investors responded rationally to the growth of trade. The returns to canal investment varied enormously. One estimate suggested that the ten most profitable canals

in 1825 were returning an average of over 27 percent to investors. Many others never justified their construction in terms of profit. The crucial variables were the burden of the original capital, the availability of suitable bulk mineral traffic, and the number of years of prerailway operation.

With few exceptions (mainly in Ireland and Scotland), the British government had little part in canal building, which may have confered an unintended advantage on the British economy. The only detailed and systematic comparison of transport in Britain and France (Szostak, 1991) produced the judgment that Britain experienced the first Industrial Revolution because it had the best transport system in the world by the late eighteenth century. Britain's primary advantage was not technological (France probably had more engineering expertise) or geographical (although here Britain had a slight advantage). The key factor was institutional: the decision-making process for transport investment was overcentralized in France, and therefore subject to inefficiency and mistaken priorities, whereas Britain relied to better effect on local initiatives, privately sponsored legislation, and arbitration of land prices.

Other European Canal Systems. State activity created an extensive canal system in several continental countries long before Britain's Canal Age and was often responsible for the continued vigor of canal transport long after its decline in Britain. The Netherlands, where geological conditions were perhaps more sympathetic than anywhere else, had created an extensive canal network before the end of the seventeenth century. Its medieval system of rivers and connecting canals was supplemented from 1632 to 1665 by a network of intercity canals intended mainly for passenger transportation. These routes were financed by the connected cities.

In France, the Canal de Briare of 1642 and the Canal du Midi of 1682 provided notably lengthy connections between the Loire and Seine and the Atlantic and Mediterranean, respectively. These certainly brought some benefits, the Midi Canal serving the local grain trade and the Briare helping the supply of coal to Paris. But these and other French watershed canals were of a type that usually reflected long-term government thinking rather than the more immediate pressure of existing demand. Such canals often suffered from poor water supply or inadequate gauges and struggled to justify the investments they represented.

The later Rhône-Rhine Canal of 1832 somewhat improved raw material supply to the textile industry of Alsace, but some difficulties were experienced until the arrival of the railways. On the other hand, the Saône-Loire Canal was a factor in the siting of the important Le Creusot iron works. France did, of course, eventually acquire many canals of a different variety, designed for specific traffic, especially coal or the supply of a large city. By the early nineteenth century, Paris was receiving about 25,000 boats a year, many through the canals of St.-Denis and St.-Martin.

French governments in the nineteenth century retained a dominant role in canal planning and construction, making good use of the highly trained engineers of the Corps des Ponts et Chaussées, who gained a reputation for their monumental style. The Becquey report of 1820 set out a program of canal building to ease transport bottlenecks, to be completed by both the state and concessionary companies. From 1821 to 1853, when canal mileage exceeded 4,000 kilometers, (2,480 miles), the state spent at least five times as much (over 500 million francs) as private companies on canals. Some of the advantages of a high level of state support became apparent after the onset of rail competition. The French government invested £56 million in waterways from 1830 to 1900. This was motivated by a belief that all modes of transport should continue to contribute to economic growth and that railways should face some pressure to keep their rates low.

The Freycinet Plan of 1879 set a target of an additional 2,000 kilometers (1,240 miles) of canals, of which only 400 kilometers (about 250 miles) were actually built, and promoted a long-term aim of standardization and improvement. The only major new work was the Canal de l'Est (Saône to Meuse), but total waterway tonnage increased by almost 60 percent from 1885 to 1894 and from to 1905 to 1913. Cargo consisted overwhelmingly of minerals and building materials and was carried mainly in the areas of highest regional density, the northern coalfields, and the basin of the Seine and its tributaries.

Canal development in Germany came later than in France and followed a pattern even more different from the British. In 1850, there were only about 750 kilometers (465 miles) of canals in the German states and double that length of navigable rivers, whereas by 1914 nearly 7,000 kilometers (4,340 miles) of waterways were in regular use. The Rhine, with its supporting tributaries and canals, was the most important element in the system, and Duisburg by far the biggest inland port. The Rhine was proportionately even more dominant in 1914, when it claimed 60 percent of national waterway traffic, than it had been in 1835, a trend that was closely related to the industrial development of the Ruhr.

Geography was, on the whole, more favorable in Germany than in France, with several large navigable rivers flowing broadly from southeast to northwest. Many of the canals were cut east-west to connect river routes, often with high capacity and relatively few locks. An important example was the Dortmund-Ems Canal of 1890, linking the Ruhr with the seaport of Emden in the northwest, carrying coal in one direction and grain and timber in the other. The 1,000-tonne (1,102 ton) Mittelland Canal, built in stages from 1905, connected the Rhine and the Weser, and eventually reached the Elbe. The Berlin area came to enjoy an advantageous transport situation, as the rivers Spree and Havel were reinforced by a number of linking canals. Some of these were of an early vintage, such as the Friedrich Wilhelm of 1669 (replaced by the Oder-Spree in the 1890s) and the Finow (modernized in the 1870s). Others, like the Ihle and Hohenzollern, were added after 1900. The German capital became the waterway center of a quadrilateral of cities: Hamburg, Magdeburg, Stettin, and Breslau. Berlin functioned as the principal market, Stettin and Hamburg as transshippers, and Breslau as a source of raw materials. The waterways plainly made a major contribution to German industrialization, with traffic growing continually from the 1830s to 1914, apart from a slight dip in the late 1840s. Although a crisis attributable to railway competition can be detected in the 1850s and 1860s, water transport enjoyed a renaissance from the 1870s, and in the decade 1895 to 1905 expanded more rapidly than either coal production or rail transport.

Canals in the United States. The United States had several of the same advantages as Germany. These included the favorable geography of the eastern third of the national territory, with its long, indented coast and the natural inland waterways of the Mississippi, Ohio, and Missouri Rivers and the Great Lakes. Canals were needed to enhance these assets. The United States also shared with France and Germany the support of the government for water transport projects of economic significance. Four thousand miles of canals were built from 1815 to 1890, mainly in the first half of that period. In 1808, the Gallatin report had unsuccessfully attempted to establish a federal program of integrated road and water transport. Public initiatives came, however, mainly at the state or city level, and were frequently motivated by competitive considerations, as established business communities in the eastern states sought to acquire for themselves the best possible links with the midwest.

The winner here clearly was New York, where the state government under DeWitt Clinton built the Erie Canal (1825) connecting the Hudson River to the Great Lakes. This was spectacularly effective in the development of New York's hinterland, carrying agricultural produce in one direction and manufactured goods in the other. Within ten years, the Erie Canal was used by more than 3,000 boats carrying 1.3 million tons of cargo annually. No other single canal was so successful; Pennsylvania's efforts to emulate New York in westward development achieved far less.

Nevertheless, a number of mainly short canals in the northeast had some important effects. Canal-borne anthracite coal influenced the output and location of several major industries in the 1830s and 1840s, a period that marked the beginning of rapid industrialization. Public support for canals was firmly based on recognition of their widely diffused benefits. Canals were responsible for a larger reduction in the cost of inland transportation than the railways, although economic growth would have been significantly slower from the mid-1800s onward without railways. A distinctive feature of American water transport was the early and large-scale employment of steamboats on inland rivers and lakes. Still, less effort than in continental Europe, though more than in Britain, was made to sustain the U.S. waterway system once it had been successfully challenged by the railways.

China's Grand Canal. Most historians in this field have focused on the contribution of canals to economic growth in Europe and North America, mostly in the period between the age of rivers and the age of railways. Britain has received particular attention because of the relationship between canals and the first Industrial Revolution. These boundaries, however, lead to the omission of much endeavor and innovation in times and places where the link with industrialization seems more remote.

In ancient civilizations, canals were used for both irrigation and transport, especially in the Egyptian and Roman empires. But by far the most spectacular example of preindustrial waterway engineering was the Grand Canal of China. This was a development of the earlier Pien Canal in Henan, which dated from probably the fourth century BCE. The Pien had been followed by the "Magic Canal" in Guangxi in 219 BCE, the first known contour transport canal. The Grand Canal was greatly extended by the Sui dynasty from between 581 to 617 CE and eventually reached a length of almost 1,750 kilometers (1,085 miles) between Hangzhou and Tianjin, which made it easily the longest canal in the world.

The Grand Canal of China was in fact a series of separate canals connecting sections of various rivers. From central China, it crossed the Yangtzi and Huang Rivers to reach Beijing and was used by both grain junks and passengers. The functioning of the grain transport system became important for tax collection, political control, and agricultural prosperity. The Grand Canal incorporated technical features, such as sluice gates, flash locks, capstans, winches, and pumps, that were impressive for their time. There is even evidence of the use of a version of the pound lock. But there is also evidence that the canal and its trade were in decline from the thirteenth century. Despite efforts to restore sections of the canal, it is now only of local importance.

BIBLIOGRAPHY

Crompton, G. W. "Canals and the Industrial Revolution." *Journal of Transport History* 14.2 (1993), 93–110.

Crompton, G. W., ed. *Canals and Inland Navigation*. Aldershot, U.K., 1996.

Goodrich, C. *Government Promotion of American Canals and Railroads, 1800–1890*. New York, 1960.

Hadfield, C. *World Canals: Inland Navigation Past and Present*. Newton Abbot, U.K., 1986.

Kunz, A. "The Economic Performance of Inland Navigation in Germany, 1835–1935: A Reassessment of Traffic Flows." In *Inland Navigation and Economic Development in Nineteenth Century Europe*, edited by A. Kunz and J. Armstrong, pp. 47–78. Mainz, 1995.

Meinig, D. W. *The Shaping of America*, vol. 2, *Continental America, 1800–1867*. New Haven, 1993.

Merger, M. "The Economic Performance of Inland Navigation in France: The Lower Seine and the Paris-Lens Route in Comparative Perspective, 1840–1914." In *Inland Navigation and Economic Development in Nineteenth Century Europe* edited by A. Kunz and J. Armstrong, pp. 181–212. Mainz, 1995.

Pollard, S. *Peaceful Conquest*. Oxford, 1981.

Szostak, R. *The Role of Transportation in the Industrial Revolution: A Comparison of England and France*. Montreal and Kingston, Ont., 1991.

Ville, S. *Transport and the Development of the European Economy, 1750–1918*. London, 1990.

Ward, J. R. *The Finance of Canal Building in Eighteenth Century England*. Oxford, 1974.

GERALD CROMPTON

Regulation

Waterborne transportation generally operates in economic environments that are conducive to the development of highly competitive markets. Early-day ships were individually owned, and they moved from trade to trade driven by opportunities to reap profits. Modern-day common carriers by water can operate over the same routes in competition with both contract and private carriers, and they typically make use of natural waterways or waterways improved by the government. In the absence of large fixed costs, such as those incurred by the railroads, capacity in water transportation can be adjusted quickly to changing demand. Under these competitive conditions, opportunity to charge monopoly prices and reap monopoly profits are limited. Hence, there is likely less political pressure placed on governments to enact price, entry, exit, and service-level regulations on waterborne transportation (Locklin, 1972, chapter 32; Johnson, 1919, p. 210).

In the United States until 1941, federal government regulation of inland waterways was confined to measures to promote safety. The United States, with more than twenty-five thousand miles of navigable waterways, has one of the largest networks of inland waterways in the world. Extension of economic regulation to carriers operating in the inland waterways came belatedly in 1940 with the passage of the Transportation Act of 1940, which extended the regulatory authority given to the Interstate Commerce Commission (ICC) over rail, highway, and pipeline transportation to include inland water transportation. Economic regulation of inland waterborne carriers was vigorously supported by the railroads and other overland carriers who were concerned about competition from barge lines (National Resources Planning Board, 1942). Nonetheless, numerous exemptions written into the Act, such as the exemption of the transportation of bulk commodities, meant that as late as the 1960s, nearly 95 percent of the freight ton miles carried on the inland waterways and Great Lakes were exempt from U.S. federal government regulation (Frankel, 1982, pp. 281–282).

With few major exceptions, international shipping has also been relatively free of government economic regulation. This is hardly surprising since the seas are open to ships from all nations. Ernest Frankel from the Massachusetts Institute of Technology observed that "Paradoxically, international shipping is one of the most and yet least regulated transportation industries. Its design, manning, cargo handling, stowage, and other technical and operational aspects are highly regulated. At the same time the industry is largely free of economic or management regulation" (Frankel, 1987, p. 87). Industry self-regulation has substituted for government regulation. Carriers in specific trade routes organized themselves into "conferences," offering regular sailing schedules; these liner conferences set rates and often allocated output among their members (Frankel, 1982, pp. 66–67). The first shipping conference was formed in 1875 in the United Kingdom–Calcutta trade (Ihedura, 1996, p. 123). While such agreements are transparently anticompetitive, the U.S. Shipping Act of 1916 exempted conference liners from American antitrust laws (Zeis, 1938, chapter XI). The 1964 United Nations Conference on Trade and Development concluded that "It was agreed that the liner conference system is necessary in order to secure stable rates and regular service" (Goss, 1968, p. 15).

Historically, many nations have maintained economic regulation over waterborne transportation to protect their nation's shipping industry from foreign competition. Protective legislation was enacted to achieve two goals: to promote economic development (that is, to provide shipping for the development of commerce) and to strengthen national defense. The earliest historical accounts of national protective legislation date back to seventeenth-century Europe when mercantilism was the prevailing economic doctrine. Mercantilism equated power with money (gold and silver), and the goal of a nation was to obtain as much money as possible. Constant warfare among the European states was an important factor in the rise of mercantilism. Europe was free from conflict for only eight years during the seventeenth century. Financing war required money; and if a country did not possess gold or silver from its own mines or from its overseas colonies, the only other way to obtain money was to maintain a favorable balance of trade with other nations. Active government intervention and regulation were believed necessary to maintain a favorable balance of trade. Regulation of maritime shipping served two complementary objectives: to retain earnings from shipping and to ensure the presence of a significant domestic merchant marine that could supply skilled sailors, shipbuilders, and ships to enhance the country's naval strength.

The most famous economic regulations imposed on maritime shipping during the seventeenth century were the British Navigation Acts, first passed by the British Parliament in 1651 as the Acts of Trade and Navigation (Harper, 1939, pp. 34–49). The 1651 legislation established a basic regulatory formula, which was to govern English navigation for nearly two centuries. The original law was modified and expanded several times (for example, in 1660, 1662, 1664, 1673, and later years). Trade with England's overseas colonies was a special concern of the Navigation Acts. The Acts stipulated that the trade of the colonies was to be carried in ships built, owned, and commanded by the English or their colonists, and manned by crews that were at least three-fourths English or colonial. The prohibition against the use of foreign shipping ensured that earnings from the inbound and outbound carrying trade were retained within the empire, even though goods could be shipped more cheaply on Dutch ships. England was not the only colonial power that imposed such regulations on overseas shipping. Similar restrictions were imposed by the Dutch, French, Spanish, and Portuguese (Heaton, 1948, p. 327). England's Navigation Acts were repealed in 1849.

Many nations continue to protect their national maritime shipping by maintaining cargo preference laws whereby some fixed percentage—usually 40 to 50 percent, but in some cases, 100 percent—of their international shipping is reserved for national carriers (Frankel, 1987, pp. 45–46; Bredima-Savopoulou and Tzoannos, 1990, 39–40). In some European Community (EC) countries such as France, Portugal, and Spain, all government cargoes, including imports by state enterprises, are reserved for national fleets. A 1970s survey conducted by the Ship Research Institute of Norway of fifty-five countries, including all the Organization for Economic Cooperation and Development (OECD) countries, as well as the most important developing countries (but excluding the eastern European states), found that twenty-four of them employed cargo preference policies to benefit their nation's carriers (Totland, 1980, p. 104). However, in most countries, actual practices are far less restrictive than stated in their policies, since they do not have sufficiently large national fleets to meet demand. Ernest Frankel has studied the impact of cargo sharing and reservation arrangements on U.S. liner trades and found that they significantly increased shipping costs and rates (Frankel, 1987, pp. 47–48).

Nations also have tried to protect their national shipping from foreign competition by reserving domestic, coastal, and intercoastal shipping for national carriers. Until their repeal, England's Navigation Acts closed the country's coastal traffic to all foreign vessels. The United States passed similar cabotage legislation to exclude foreign competition from its domestic trade in the Tonnage Act of July 20, 1789, and the Act of 1817 (Bauer, 1988, p. 104; Zeis, 1938; Johnson, 1919, p. 258). The Merchant Marine Act of 1920, widely known as the Jones Act, extended the domestic monopoly enjoyed by American shipping companies to include the insular possessions of the United States.

Most countries reserve domestic point-to-point shipping service for national shipping companies. A 1992 survey conducted by the U.S. Maritime Administration found that forty-four of the fifty-seven countries that responded to the survey maintained some form of cabotage law (U.S. General Accounting Office, 1998). Forty industrialized nations currently have cabotage laws, including Japan, Canada, France, and Germany (U.S. Maritime Administration, 12 June 1996). Cabotage restrictions are currently in force in nearly half of the EC countries. In comparing EC countries that have cabotage restrictions with those that do not, there appears to be no systematic relationship between the relative size of a country's maritime coastal trade and whether it reserves domestic shipping to national carriers (Bredima-Savopoulou and Tzoannos, 1990, p. 43). Britain, which has a large coastal trade relative to its international trade, does not have cabotage restrictions, but Greece and Spain do. By contrast, France and Ireland both have relatively small coastal trade in comparison with their overseas trade, but France maintains cabotage restrictions while Ireland does not. In

many countries (for example, the United States), national shipping engaged in international trade may not engage in their own domestic trade. The aim of the prohibition is to prevent government subsidized ships engaged in the international carrying trade from competing unfairly against unsubsidized vessels operating in the domestic carrying trade.

To date, no comprehensive analysis has been performed on the economic cost of shipping cabotage legislation around the world. The U.S. International Trade Commission (ITC) estimates that because of the higher cost of building and manning ships in the United States, the Jones Act cost the American economy approximately $1.32 billion in lost real national income in 1996 and $2.8 billion in 1993 (U.S. ITC, December 1995 and May 1999). The estimated losses clearly are not very large.

In sum, apart from certain governments' regulations intended to shield their nation's shipping industries from foreign competition, waterborne transportation has historically operated in environments subject to less stringent economic regulation than land transportation.

BIBLIOGRAPHY

Bauer, K. Jack. *A Maritime History of the United States.* Columbia, S.C., 1988.

Bredima-Savopoulou, Anna, and John Tzoannos. *The Common Shipping Policy of the EC.* Amsterdam, 1990.

Frankel, Ernest G. *Regulation and Policies of American Shipping.* Boston, 1982.

Frankel, Ernest G. *The World Shipping Industry.* London, 1987.

Goss, R. O. *Studies in Maritime Economics.* Cambridge, 1968.

Harper, Lawrence A. *The English Navigation Laws.* New York, 1939.

Heaton, Herbert. *Economic History of Europe.* Rev. ed. New York, 1948.

Iheduru, Okechukwu C. *The Political Economy of International Shipping in Developing Countries.* Newark, Del., 1996.

Johnson, Emory R. *Ocean and Inland Water Transportation.* New York, 1919.

Locklin, D. Philip. *Economics of Transportation.* 7th ed. Homewood, Ill., 1972.

Totland, Terje. "Protectionism in International Shipping and Some Economic Effects." *Maritime Policy Management* 7.2 (1980), 103–114.

U.S. General Accounting Office. "Maritime Issues: Assessment of the International Trade Commission's 1995 Analysis of the Economic Impact of the Jones Act." Report to the Chairman of the Senate Committee on Commerce, Science, and Transportation, 6 March 1998.

U.S. International Trade Commission. *The Economic Effects of Significant U.S. Import Restraint.* Washington, D.C., September, 1991. Also updates in November 1993, December 1995, and May 1999.

U.S. Maritime Administration. "The Jones Act." Statement of Maritime Administrator Albert J. Herberger. Before the Subcommittee on Coast Guard and Maritime Transportation Committee on Transportation and Infrastructure, U.S. House of Representatives, 12 June 1996.

U.S. National Resources Planning Board. *Transportation and National Policy.* Part II. Washington, D.C., May 1942.

Zeis, Paul Maxwell. *American Shipping Policy.* Princeton, 1938.

JAMES MAK

WATT, JAMES (1736–1819), Scottish inventor.

No life better illustrates the nature of the Industrial Revolution in Britain than Watt's. He came from a commercial family of solid middle ranking, and his father, a Scottish shipping merchant, had sufficient capital to send him to be an apprentice in London and to give him a good secondary-school education. While an apprentice, first with the job of cutting out numbers for the faces of clocks, young Watt acquired a mathematical tutor and became proficient in applied Newtonian mechanics. His life explodes the myth that the Industrial Revolution was in essence the work of semiliterate tinkerers. Watt was highly literate, highly numerate, and scientifically sophisticated.

More is known now about Watt's early life because in 1995 the Birmingham City Library obtained the vast Watt collection. Those papers add to the enormous collection generated by the firm of Boulton and Watt. From the 1780s on, it operated a factory in Soho on the outskirts of Birmingham and manufactured Watt's famous steam engine. Matthew Boulton had been a manufacturer of small metal objects, and their partnership became a template for the skills needed for industrial success: entrepreneurship and technological skill.

After his London apprenticeship, Watt turned himself into a civil engineer. His friend John Smeaton coined the term *civil engineer*, which represented a new breed of entrepreneurs: men with technical skills who could survey land, fix or build machines, or make scientific instruments, and most important, were possessed of sufficient business skill to make their way in the world or to team up with someone even more skilled at money. The profession of the independent civil engineer developed only gradually, barely emerging by the 1780s; but, by the 1750s and 1760s in Britain, men such as Watt were making their own living. Habits of discipline and thrift, born in a religious context, aided them in their struggle. Watt and his family were non-Anglican Protestants with Presbyterian origins.

An early invention changed Watt's life forever. Asked in the mid-1760s to repair an old Newcomen steam engine, Watt saw immediately that it wasted energy because the same cylinder or condenser of steam had to be heated and then cooled. Watt understood something about the chemistry of gases and atmospheric pressure, and could also work with his hands. He combined his technological and scientific skills, added a new and separate condenser to the engine, improved its horsepower easily by 35 percent, and got a patent for the device. The patent proved critically important, and Watt fought in court in the 1790s to protect it. By the 1790s, Watt and his business partner, Matthew Boulton, were rich men. They drew a lifetime income on a percentage of the costs saved by their engine to its users—in addition to what they charged to install it. There were cotton factories in Manchester that by 1800 had moved

JAMES WATT. (Prints and Photographs Division, Library of Congress)

from 16-horsepower to 45-horsepower engines in a matter of five years. By contrast, the first steam engine arrived at the cotton factories in Rouen, France, in 1810.

Watt saw himself as a man of science, and that meant being careful, disciplined, and inventing projects that could be replicated. When John Smeaton wanted to find out if Watt's engine did everything he claimed it could, he went home and built a tabletop replica for himself. Satisfied, he then recommended it to his entrepreneurial clients. The engine was particularly important for the draining of mines but also, when fitted with a rotating device that Watt invented, for the driving of spinning equipment in factories. That one device and its applications are at the heart of early industrialization in Britain: capital, coal, factories, new technology, and a vibrant scientific culture.

BIBLIOGRAPHY

Jacob, Margaret C. *Scientific Culture and the Making of the Industrial West.* New York, 1997.

MacLeod, Christine. "James Watt: Heroic Invention and the Idea of the Industrial Revolution." In *Technological Revolutions in Europe: Historical Perspectives*, edited by Maxine Berg and Kristine Bruland. Cheltenham, U.K., 1998.

Musson, Albert E., and Eric Robinson. *Science and Technology in the Industrial Revolution.* Foreward to the second printing by Margaret Jacob. New York, 1969.

MARGARET C. JACOB

WEBER, MAX (1864–1920), German sociologist.

Max Weber was the author of one of the most important theses for the emergence of modern capitalism in the West, *The Protestant Ethic and the Spirit of Capitalism.* Yet whether one would term him an economic historian is open to debate. Equally, there are those who would argue that Weber was not a sociologist—even though he is regarded as a founding father of sociology—but rather a human scientist whose writings belong to an older tradition of politics and *Nationalökonomie* (Hennis, 2000). Weber's writings traversed the fields of history, economics, sociology, politics, theology, and philosophy, and he kept up with the developments of his day in musicology, statistics, and literature. The key to understanding his work is through his methodology, which combined concepts of explanation, understanding, and causality taken from science and hermeneutics. Today we are only too aware of the ways in which disciplines can be sundered by methodological divides. With Weber, however, it is best to forget disciplinary divides and concentrate on methodological commonalities.

A brief outline of his intellectual biography makes some of this clearer. He was born in Erfurt, Germany, in 1864 into a leading political family closely linked to the Prussian school of history. Germany's history was told as the Prussian version of history—authoritarian, modernizing, centralizing, and Lutheran (as opposed to corporatist, particularistic, Catholic, and a culture of contentment rather than achievement). This narrative was crucial to the legitimacy of the new German nation established under Bismarck's leadership in 1871. In his commentary on contemporary politics, Weber was torn between his high regard for Prussia's modernizing role and his opposition to its unrepresentative authoritarianism (Beetham, 1974).

Weber's doctoral degree was in law and it showed how new legal forms in Ancient Rome were used to privatize communal land. His habilitation thesis (required for university teachers) investigated commercial law in medieval shipping enterprises and showed the spreading of risk and the rules of partnership. In 1894, he moved out of the fields of law and history (and Berlin) to accept a chair at Freiburg (in Baden) in economics, a subject in which he had little training. His reading lists for teaching, however, showed a familiarity with English political economy and Austrian marginalism, as well as the German historical approach to economics. As an economist, he conducted massive studies of the rural economy in Prussia and of the German stock exchanges.

In 1898, he entered a clinic, suffering from fatigue, and was gripped by a depressive illness from which he never really escaped. In 1902, he resigned from his chair in economics (*Nationalökonomie*) at Heidelberg, which he had taken up in 1896. It was only in the last year of his life (1919–1920) that he held a full-time university post at the University of Munich.

Effectively a private scholar, in 1904 he launched a journal, *Archiv für Sozialwissenschaft und Sozialpolitik,* with the banker Dr. Edgar Jaffé and the economic historian Werner Sombart. He published all his major essays, including the Protestant Ethic thesis, in its pages. Forced to defend why rationality as a special mentality became so privileged in the West, Weber expanded his studies to include a comparative study of world religions, which traced the linkage between religious ethics and economic behavior. Weber's unique contribution to science was to show how the causality of cultural meanings and their effect in the social world could be established. His scattered writings and unpublished manuscripts were collected together by his widow and other scholars only in the 1920s, an era when the international prestige of German science had been dimmed.

[*See also* Weber Thesis.]

BIBLIOGRAPHY

Beetham, David. *Max Weber and the Theory of Modern Politics.* London, 1974.

Hennis, Wilhelm. *Max Weber's Central Question.* 2d ed. Translated by Keith Tribe. Newbury, U.K., 2000.

Whimster, Sam. "Max Weber: Work and Interpretation." In *Handbook of Social Theory,* edited G. Ritzer and B. Smart, pp. 54–65. London, 2001.

SAM WHIMSTER

WEBER THESIS. In his comparative sociology of civilizations, Max Weber (1864–1920) seeks to understand the unique development of Western civilization, specifically in the economic sphere. Why did the Industrial Revolution occur where and when it did?

For Weber, it was a product of "modern Western capitalism": a very particular and revolutionary economic formation. Capitalism, in the sense of profit seeking through the market, is extremely ancient; a capitalist economy is not. Modern Western capitalism means profit seeking, indeed profit maximization; but it is not unbridled acquisitiveness. It does not, for example, use violence. Importantly, its motivating "spirit" is not straightforward self-interest: it is, for Weber, an ascetic and unnatural "ethos," with "ever-renewed profit" as an end in itself rather than a means to enjoyment: the capitalist eschews idleness and relaxation, limits consumption, and invests his surplus to accumulate more and more capital, and more and more profit. Such austerity contrasts markedly with the practice of other social classes—the extravagant display and lavish hospitality of feudal and post-feudal nobles, for example—and with earlier economic behavior. It requires an explanation.

Weber considered it no accident that the new style followed religious change: the Protestant Reformation.

According to Calvinism, every individual is divinely predestined, from the beginning of time, either to eternal bliss in heaven or to eternal torment. This doctrine—emphasizing our utter powerlessness in the face of God—Weber considered to be insupportable in its pure form. It was, however, possible to add what believers needed: a sign of assurance of salvation. According to Protestantism salvation is by faith alone, not works. Good works, however, remain necessary—not as a way of earning salvation, but as a sign of God-given, saving faith. Calvinists drew on, and modified, the Lutheran doctrine of the "earthly calling." One must perform faithfully a worldly task (or economic role) as part of God's plan for mankind, and thus glorify God. Add to this the characteristic puritanism of "ascetic" Protestantism—its hostility to idleness, extravagance, and display as sins of the flesh—and the result is the celebrated "work ethic" and avoidance of consumption that facilitate the capital accumulation and endless profit seeking of modern capitalism. This lifestyle, seen as a sign that one was saved, received an extraordinarily powerful psychological sanction—enough to overcome the resistance of human nature and custom alike.

But there is more to the "spirit of capitalism" and therefore the "Protestant ethic." It is one thing to glorify devotion to one's economic task, and another to glorify the "calling" of making money (the "providential interpretation of profit"). The work ethic, Weber noted, has precedents in pre-Reformation Christianity (notably the rule of St. Benedict, who required labor of his monks and famously proclaimed, *Laborare est orare*—to work is to pray); but a "profit ethic" seems to flout Christianity's traditional condemnation of avarice. Yet a Protestant profit ethic emerged, as Weber demonstrates by quoting Richard Baxter's seventeenth century *Christian Directory*. According to Baxter, failure to choose the more "gainful way" (when no other person is wronged thereby) is a failure to fulfil a duty of the calling: to act as "God's steward," putting resources to godly use. The businessman must pursue gain by all honest means, in order to maximize his ability to serve God. Profit, therefore, may be a sign not of avarice but of virtue.

The Weber Thesis has inspired intense controversy since it first appeared in 1904 and 1905. Undoubtedly, the most substantial contribution, given separate consideration below, is Tawney's *Religion and the Rise of Capitalism* (1926). Some recurrent objections are not particularly damaging. For example, Weber's thesis is said to be refuted by counterexamples, such as Scotland and Hungary (strongly Calvinist yet economically backward in the early modern period) and the Dutch Republic, where Calvinism and economic growth were both strong, but failed to coincide. What Weber's thesis asserts, however, is that Reformed Christianity promoted an economic revolution where it influenced an established bourgeois class: no such revolution occurred in the seventeenth-century Netherlands, where capitalism was essentially similar to that of pre-Reformation Europe. The existence of pre-Reformation capitalism is itself a frequent objection; Weber, however, considered it different in kind from modern Western capitalism. (Trevor-Roper, admittedly, endeavors to demonstrate their continuity.) Again critics point out that the "calling" and a work ethic appear in pre-Reformation Christianity, but the fact that Protestantism had its roots in earlier Christianity (as the Reformers emphasised) hardly shows that the Reformation made no difference. Another common objection cites frequent condemnations of avarice and acquisitiveness by Puritans and Reformed Christians (Hyma mentions a Dutch Synod's decision in 1574 to exclude bankers from the Lord's Supper). Often this objection is coupled with another: that after early hostility, Reformed Christianity later accommodated itself to developing capitalism (as did other confessions), producing such doctrines as Baxter's, which Weber misinterpreted. These last points are subsumed in the argument of Tawney's essay, and are best assessed in its light.

To the socialist Tawney, the rise of capitalism is synonymous with the triumph of "economic individualism": the uninhibited pursuit of gain, previously subject to religious and moral restraints. According to Christian morality, which was accepted as the ultimate authority before the sixteenth century, unlimited pursuit of gain was, precisely, the deadly sin of avarice: the epitome of selfish passion. By the mid-seventeenth century, it had become an inevitability to be accepted, even an element in God' providence. This, Tawney holds, was largely a result of the Reformers' influence, even if not their intention. Luther inveighed more vehemently than anyone against the traditional economic sins; but in practice, his doctrine of salvation by faith alone undermined those institutional sanctions by which the old church enforced its morality. Calvinism is a different, more complex case: whenever they could, Calvinists established a collectivist discipline of unprecedented ferocity over all aspects of life, including economics; but the Calvinist economic ethic was not exactly the traditional one. Finding the profit seeking life no longer suspect but acceptable in principle, Calvinism turned its fire against only the abuses and excesses of economic individualism. A life of laborious and virtuous wealth accumulation could be "a service acceptable to God," for wealth could be—must be—dedicated to God's service. Here Tawney echoes Weber; he differs from Weber in stressing that this individualistic side of Calvinism was originally only one-half of its economic ethic. Yet it was the half that prevailed, because it was acceptable to the socially powerful strata of an increasingly capitalist society in seventeenth-century England and elsewhere. The other half, the ferocious social and economic discipline, being unacceptable to them, faded away.

[*See also* Religion *and* Weber, Max.]

BIBLIOGRAPHY

Green, Robert W., ed. *Protestantism and Capitalism: The Weber Thesis and Its Critics.* Boston, 1959. An anthology with a useful bibliography.

Hill, Christopher. "Protestantism and the Rise of Capitalism." In *Essays in the Economic and Social History of Tudor and Stuart England*, edited by F. J. Fisher, pp. 15–39. Cambridge, 1961.

Hyma, Albert. "Calvinism and Capitalism in the Netherlands, 1555–1700." *Journal of Modern History* 10.3 (1938), 325–343.

Kitch, M. J., ed. *Capitalism and the Reformation.* London, 1967. A very useful anthology including both primary historical material and modern discussions, among them the articles by Hill, Hyma, and Trevor-Roper listed here.

Lessnoff, Michael H. *The Spirit of Capitalism and the Protestant Ethic.* Aldershot, U.K., 1994.

Robertson, H. M. *Aspects of the Rise of Economic Individualism.* Cambridge, 1933. Critical of the Weber thesis.

Tawney, R. H. *Religion and the Rise of Capitalism.* Harmondsworth, U.K., 1926.

Trevor-Roper, H. R. "Religion, the Reformation, and Social Change." In *Religion, the Reformation and Social Change and Other Essays.* London, 1972.

Weber, Max. *The Protestant Ethic and the Spirit of Capitalism.* London, 1930. Translated by Talcott Parsons from the 1920 edition. Reissued in 1920 as part of Weber's *Gesammelte Aufsatze zur Religionssoziologie*, with significant additions, including the author's introduction and replies to critics in footnotes.

Weber, Max. *The Sociology of Religion.* London, 1965–1966. Translated by Ephraim Fischoff from the 4th edition. Chapter VII is particularly relevant.

MICHAEL LESSNOFF

WEIGHTS AND MEASURES. Modern economic activity depends on common standards of weights and measures. Not only does industrial production depend on commensurate units of measurement, but fair exchange presupposes a means of verifying that the quantities exchanged match the parties' expectations. The key word here is *fair*. The balance has long symbolized justice. The Old Testament forbids shopkeepers from using two weights and two measures.

The ability today to refer without misunderstanding to 200 kilograms or ±0.01 millimeters of tolerance depends on the way these measures are instantiated in instruments (rulers, balances, surveying equipment), and the reassurance that these instruments are guaranteed by state-sponsored inspectors and (ultimately) by national and international guardians of metric standards (the United States Bureau of Standards, the International Metric Commission). The role played here by coordinating institutions suggests that the historical development of standard weights and measures has depended on the evolution of political authority as much as the spread of commerce or a drive for efficiency.

Differing Systems. The power to standardize measures is an ancient prerogative of authority. The civilizations of Mesopotamia, Egypt, China, and Rome all developed systems of measurement to administer their territories. The worldwide division of political authority meant that weights and measures differed in every corner of the globe until the twentieth century. Measures in feudal Europe differed not only from nation to nation, but from town to town and parish to parish. These differences were sometimes masked by the way a single unit—the "pound," for example—referred to diverse quantities. In eighteenth-century France, some 800 metrical names still referred to over 250,000 distinct quantities. The situation was similar in the rest of the continent. Measures differed not only by geographical area, but by trade and by good. In the final analysis, each unit of measurement referred not to an abstract length or capacity, but to a specific ruler in the town hall or a specific vessel in the seigneur's château. This vessel's dimensions affected its capacity since grain, for example, might be measured heaped, combed, or after being struck. Quantity, in these cases, depended on custom. Other measures were anthropomorphic in the narrow sense of being related to human anatomy: the "pace" as a human stride. And still other measures were anthropomorphic in the larger sense of being related to human invention and labor. Thus, the *aune* (a length of cloth in France) equalled the width of local looms. Or vinicultural land in France was measured in *journées*, the workdays needed to harvest the grapes, and farmland in *boisseaux*, the bushels of grain needed to sow the land.

This metrical diversity—often condemned as "irrational"—served the interests of local seigneurs, peasants, and traders. In return for guaranteeing the fairness of market weighings, seigneurs extracted a small tax on each transaction. Labor- and seed-based measures of land instructed peasants about the value and fertility of their holdings, while setting norms for farming practices. Moreover, in a just-price economy—where profit was suspect—a diversity of measures allowed producers and traders to buy at one measure and sell at a smaller one, keeping price constant and profits concealed. Finally, the idiosyncrasies of local measures obliged out-of-towners to pay conversion costs, favoring hometown sellers.

From a cosmopolitan point of view, however, metric diversity was reprehensible. It complicated travel and introduced myriad occasions for fraud. It frustrated metropolitan tax collection and the management of regions and colonies. It impeded landlords from assessing (and improving) the productivity of their land, and increased the cost of long-distance commerce. Hence, royal administrators urged their sovereigns to impose uniform measures. Important market towns induced their hinterland to adopt metropolitan units. And military and colonial administrators imposed standards on their subordinates. These metrical ambitions of royal bureaucrats also received an impetus from early-modern natural philosophers. Scientists reproducing the results of far-flung colleagues wanted common units. Several seventeenth-century savants proposed standards based on nature, which they touted for their universal appeal. In 1766, the French Academy replaced the old *toise* of the Châtelet—a well-worn ruler on the wall of the Paris courthouse—with an equivalent standard defined in terms of a pendulum beating one second at the equator. Yet oft-reiterated laws requiring nationwide use of the king's measures remained dead letter throughout the Old Regime.

Movement toward Uniformity. Implementation of metrical uniformity began to make headway when the French Revolution finally eliminated seigneurial privileges. Yet the metric system, created by French scientists between 1790 and 1795, added four additional features to the simple demand for uniformity. First, the unit of length—the neologism known as the "meter"—was defined by reference to nature, specifically one ten-millionth of the distance from the earth's pole to the equator. Second, all other weights and measures were systematically related to this foundational unit, such that a gram equaled a cubic centimeter of distilled water at maximum density. Third, all units were made divisible by ten to aid calculation (although some suggested base twelve as more suitable for commerce). And fourth, this decimal relationship was indicated by a systematic nomenclature of prefixes.

This hyper-rational system was the work of a coterie of illustrious French savants, including the mathematician Marie-Jean Antoine-Nicolas Caritat de Condorcet, the chemist Antoine-Laurent Lavoisier, the physicist Pierre-Simon Laplace, and especially two astronomers, Jean-Baptiste-Joseph Delambre and Pierre-François-André Méchain, who conducted the meridian survey (1793–1799), which defined the meter. This standard was then instantiated in a platinum meter bar housed in the National Assembly.

These men hoped a metric system derived from the dimensions of the globe would spur global agreement on measures. In the short run, this was not to be. Despite the backing of Thomas Jefferson, the United States refused to join the system, and the war with Great Britain ended any chance there. The further hope of these savants—who were influenced by the Physiocratic movement—was that the metric system would facilitate state administration and create a national free market. And their ultimate hope was that the metric system would transform the mentality of French citizens. By abolishing customary labor-based units and by undermining the just-price economy, the metric system would make productivity visible and establish price as the paramount variable in exchange. Along with the new system of centennial money, it would offer citizens daily instruction in right reasoning about economic matters. As

Condorcet noted, until citizens could calculate their own best interests, they would be neither equal nor free. In this sense, the reform of weights and measures also marks a deliberate step in the education of modern *homo economicus*.

No wonder then the reform met widespread resistance. Not only did it ask people to break old habits, but also to adopt abstract and (seemingly) arbitrary measures instead of units that served their local economy and society. The metric system nearly vanished like its sister reforms of decimal time and the revolutionary calendar. Frustrated with noncompliance, Napoleon returned France to the old Parisian units in 1812. The metric system was only reinstated in 1840 by Louis-Philippe, the procommerce constitutional monarch, and even then conversion was protracted. Like the hundred-year process by which peasants became Frenchmen, it depended on the spread of universal education, the expansion of trade via the railroad, and the breakdown of local economies.

The metric system is today one of the few economic institutions with (nearly) complete global reach. Yet the adoption of the metric system has tended to follow political rupture, rather than the spread of trade. That is because the initial conversion costs are high and must be superintended by coordinating institutions, themselves with a vested interest in the old measures.

Those countries formerly in the Napoleonic empire were first to rejoin the system. Holland and Belgium (1820–1830) led the way, followed by Spain (1849) and its former colonies (1848–1914), and unified Italy (1863). The turning point was the International Metric Commission of 1870 when Bismarck's German empire joined the system rather than impose Prussian standards on its newly united states. The international treaty of 1875 authorized the creation of a new platinum meter bar, made to match the old, to be housed in Paris in the new International Bureau of Weights and Measures.

One by one, the world's other nations have joined the metric system: Russia after the 1917 Revolution, China after the demise of the imperial system, Japan after its defeat in World War II, and the ex-colonies of Asia and Africa after their liberation movements of the 1950s and 1960s. The first large economy to join without political rupture was Great Britain. In the nineteenth century, inspectors there had imposed imperial measures in place of local ones. In 1963, with its accession to the European Union, Great Britain formally began to convert to the metric system. The United States remains the only nation outside the system, despite reform efforts (notably in the 1970s). Yet even American manufacturers are adopting metric standards as production becomes global.

In the meantime, the International Bureau of Weights and Measures has redefined the metric standards in terms of nature. In 1980, length was redefined as the distance traveled by light in a vacuum in 1/299,792,458ths of a second (with the second defined by an atomic clock), a value set to preserve the original (inaccurate) assessment of the meter as one ten-millionth the distance from pole to equator. But if there is no longer significant controversy regarding foundational units, disputes over measures still rage in many domains of consumption and production. The persistance of these disputes are signs that the right to set measurement standards remains a prerogative of authority—and that this authority remains contested.

[See also Markets.]

BIBLIOGRAPHY

Alder, Ken. *The Measure of All Things: The Seven-Year Odyssey and Hidden Error that Transformed the World*. New York, 2002.

Bigourdan, Guillaume. *Le système métrique des poids et mesures*. Paris, 1901.

Heilbron, John L. "The Measure of Enlightenment." In *The Quantifying Spirit in the Eighteenth Century*, edited by Tore Frängsmyr, John L. Heilbron, and Robin E. Rider, pp. 207–242. Berkeley, 1990.

Hocquet, Jean Claude, ed. *La métrologie historique*. Paris, 1995.

Kula, Witold. *Measures and Men*. Translated from the Polish by R. Szreter. Princeton, 1986.

Delambre, Jean-Baptiste-Joseph. *Base du système métrique décimal, ou mésure de l'arc du méridien*. 3 vols. Paris, 1806–1810.

Zupko, Roland. *Revolution in Measurement: Western European Weights and Measures since the Age of Science*. Philadelphia, 1990.

KEN ALDER

WELL-FIELD LAND SYSTEM. The well-field (*jingtian*) system is a Chinese model for the ideal distribution of land. The construct has been made to bear all that political economists in imperial China regarded as ideal: the closed rural community whose members promoted the welfare of the whole, the equitable distribution of land to cultivators according to household labor power, and the fair apportionment of modest levies on the community's productive members. The earliest references to the system, from the latter half of the first millennium BCE, indicate no connection to wells, though the idea of arranging private fields around a common plot may reflect the practice of sharing wells in the early agricultural communities of north China.

Instead, the word for well (*jing*) was used because the character, which resembles the pound sign (#), depicts the arrangement of nine fields laid out in a square of three by three. The classic account comes from the philosophical text of Mencius (also known as Meng-tzu) of the fourth century BCE: "A square *li* [0.16 square mile] constitutes one *jing*. The *jing* consists of 900 *mu* [1 *mu* = 190 square meters]. The middle of the nine fields is the public land. Eight families each hold 100 *mu*. They cultivate the public field together, and only after the public work is finished do they dare tend their own." The original well-field may have been a communal land-use arrangement facilitating tribute to an overlord, but Mencius's description adapts it the emergence of private landownership and the more bureaucratic forms of taxation that private land required.

For an economic institution that may never have existed, the well-field system has exerted an extraordinary hold on the imagination of Chinese policy makers. It expressed the hope that land should be in the hands of its cultivators, rather than landlords, who introduced inefficiency by siphoning off product that otherwise should have gone to cultivators or the state. It identified the family as the unit of production. It preferred that taxes be levied by communities rather than individuals, and that communities be trusted to assess their members' contributions equitably. Also it idealized the community as the fundamental building block of social and political order. Later policy analysts dreamed of reviving the system in order to restore the harmony of land, labor, and levy, but usually had to content themselves with limited intervention in land distribution. The equal-field (*juntian*) system, erratically imposed during the middle-imperial period, assumed that the state owned all land and empowered local officials to apportion that land to households on the basis of their labor, and to reapportion it regularly to adjust for changes in household composition, lest those with favorable land–labor ratios become landlords and drive able-bodied people into landlessness. Stymied by the presence of a market in private property, the system failed wherever it was tried. In the late-imperial period, political economists acknowledged that neither the well-field nor the equal-field system could offset the power of the market to skew property away from equitability. Their only recourse was to measure fields (*zhangtian*) in the more modest hope of ensuring that all landowners, whether they farmed or not, at least paid their fair share of taxes.

The power of this imaginative construct was manifested during the period of the People's Communes from the 1950s through the 1970s. The eradication of private property in land and the formation of large communes proceeded on the assumptions that the state had ultimate ownership of land, that land is most productive when it is held in common, and that communities rather than individuals should be taxed. What was represented as a program to bring communism to the countryside was also an attempt to bring the messy reality of the rural economy back into line with the well-field ideal. Even though most of the post-commune limitations on the ownership and sale of land introduced in the 1980s have disappeared, the vision of the solidary agrarian community as the best guarantee against risk, exploitation, and inefficiency continues to glimmer in the Chinese political imagination.

BIBLIOGRAPHY

Felber, Von Roland. "Die Utopie vom 'Brunnenfeld.'" *Wissenschaftliche Zeitschrift der Karl-Marx-Universitat Leipzig* (1965), 351–359.

Hori Toshikazu. *Kindensei no kenkyu* (Studies on Equal Field Systems). Tokyo, 1975.

Hsu, Chung-shu. "The Well-Field System in Shang and Chou." In *Chinese Social History: Translations of Selected Studies*, edited by E-tu Zen Sun and John de Francis, pp. 2–17. Washington, D.C., 1956.

TIMOTHY BROOK

WENDEL FAMILY, European nobility involved in the steel industry. The de Wendels came from Flanders and served as professional soldiers, first to the Holy Roman Emperor and then to the duc de Lorraine. Jean Martin, the founder of the business, began by hiring an ironworks. In 1704, he then purchased the ironworks in Hayange, which became the family enterprise. During the French Revolution of 1789, his factories were sold as a reprisal measure, because the iron-master Ignace de Wendel, who was also a *philosophe* and the former director of the Royal Arsenal, had chosen to emigrate with others who had served the deposed monarchy. His son François bought the Hayange ironworks back in 1803 and, by 1869, the firm was a leader in the French iron industry. After France's defeat in the Franco-Prussian War (1871), factories located in the province of Lorraine were in territory won and annexed by Germany. While the firm called The Grandsons of François de Wendel continued to run in Lorraine, the family set up a subsidiary under the name De Wendel & Co. in Joeuf, on the French side of the border. In 1913, the two companies produced 1.2 million tons of steel. During World War I, the factories were dismantled or confiscated and shared the same fate in World War II.

The de Wendels resisted the successive attempts to Germanize them, by being loyal to the Lorraine region. They relied on a work force that was strongly attached to the family, often for generations, and toward them they practiced a paternalism rooted in their Roman Catholicism and charitable works. The close-knit nature of the family was important, as shown by several strong-willed widows who acted as regents. They carried on their husbands' work, chose good sons-in-law, and provided sound training (the leading engineering schools and educational travel to Britain and the United States) for those who inherited the business. To that may be added a certain austerity, a constant check on the stability of the shareholders, and a policy of sharing out dividends that encouraged self-financing. In that way, internal conflicts were resolved and the gradual decline of a family business (known as the "Buddenbrooks effect") was avoided. Undoubtedly, they possessed a flair for technical innovation. The de Wendels were among the first in France to introduce techniques from the British steel industry, such as the use of coke for their smelting, puddling, and rolling mills. As early as 1879, they had acquired the Thomas patent for the dephos-phorizing of cast iron, which allowed the Lorraine region to exploit its enormous deposits of iron ore and embrace the steel revolution. In 1948, they were instrumental in the setting-up of Sollac, with the help of the U.S.-sponsored, postwar Marshall Plan, in order to apply modern techniques of continuous steel rolling.

The de Wendel family has strategic and symbolic importance to the steel industry, because of its long history, its economic success, and its geographical situation near the German border. The de Wendels also epitomize the archetypal "iron-master"—the aristocrat among French industrialists from the nineteenth century to the mid-twentieth. They were, as well, targeted by generations of French polemicists, from both the extreme right and extreme left, who spun legends around them that were taken for basic truths by readers and voters. In that way, they came to be falsely accused, in turn or simultaneously, of being "cannon merchants" (they had abandoned such manufacture by the 1820s), of putting pressure on the French military staff to prevent their factories from being bombed during World War I (to thus prolong the war), and of being "Germans," who delivered vast quantities of iron ore to Hitler's Germany until 1940, then sold their Moselle works to "Field-Marshall Goering in person." The Ironworks Committee, a union chaired from 1918 to 1940 by François II de Wendel (at that time a member of the French Parliament and a senator) was portrayed as a state within the state, manipulating ministers like puppets and dictating the policies France had to adopt. The "Saga of the Wendel Family" reached the United States in the film *Dealers in Death* (1934); there were then attacks in *Fortune* magazine, which were repeated in *Time* Magazine in 1949.

Since 1978, the fate of the family and that of the steel industry have parted company; the slump in the steel industry marked an end to its links with Lorraine. Their links with industry, however, have been maintained. Through Marine-Wendel holdings and Compagnie Générale d'industrie et de participations (CGIP), amalgamated in Wendel Investissement (June 2000), an international banking consortium firmly controlled by family shareholders has emerged around such traditional activities as metallic packaging (until 1998) or the production of abrasive shot. There is also increasing participation in "owner-shareholder" ventures in the promising sectors of exploration and exploitation of oil fields; computer and internet services; medical diagnostics; car equipment; certification and assessment; air transport; multimedia services, and electric equipment. Their importance to the French economy resulted in the chief executive, Ernest-Antoine Seillière (a Wendel on his mother's side), being elected chairman in 1997 of the Confederation of French Industry (the CNPF, now known as the MEDEF).

BIBLIOGRAPHY

Fritsch, Pierre. *Les Wendel, rois de l'acier français*. Paris, 1976.

Gangloff, Marcel. *Stiring-Wendel*, vol. 1, *Naissance d'une ville*. Stiring-Wendel, 1994.

Gordon, David M. "Le libéralisme dans l'empire du fer: François de Wendel et la Lorraine industrielle, 1900–1914." *Le Mouvement social* 175 (1996), 79–111.

Grosdidier de Matons, Marcel. *Histoire de la maison de Wendel*. 2 vols. 1940.

Jeanneney, Jean Noël. *François de Wendel en République: L'argent et le pouvoir, 1914–1940*. Paris, 1976.

Labouillerie, Geoffroy de. *La maison de Wendel: Évolution économique depuis 1918*. Thèse, Institut d' Études Politiques. Paris, 1953.

Léger, Alain. "Splendeur des de Wendel: Des forges de Hayange à la C.G.I.P. (1704–1992)." *Les Temps modernes* 558 (1993), 108–161.

Moine, Jean Marie. *Les barons du fer: Les maîtres de forges en Lorraine du milieu du 19e siècle aux années trente. Histoire sociale d'un patronat sidérurgique*. Nancy-Metz, 1989.

Moine, Jean Marie. "L' adoption du procédé Thomas par la sidérurgie lorraine. Sources nouvelles et conclusions définitives?" *Annales de l'Est*, 6th series, 49.1 (1998), 73–102.

Moine, Jean Marie. "Le Comité des forges pendant l'entre-deux-guerres: Contre-mesures au mythe d'un groupe de pression croquemitaine." Actes du colloque *Les groupes de pression dans la vie politique XIXe–XXe siècles*. Université Paris X Nanterre, 23–25 mars 2000.

Moine, Jean Marie. "La mythologie des 'marchands de canons' pendant l'entre-deux-guerres." Actes du colloque *Armement, stratégie, nation: De Gribeauval à la force de frappe*. Paris, 18–19 janvier 2001.

Sédillot, René. *Deux cent cinquante ans d'industrie en Lorraine: La maison de Wendel de 1704 à nos jours*. Paris, 1958.

Steines, Georges. *Le fer dans la peau*. Metz, 1977.

Versini, Laurent. *François Ignace de Wendel: Essais inédits*. Nancy, 1983.

JEAN-MARIE MOINE

WESTINGHOUSE, GEORGE (1846–1914), American inventor and industrialist.

George Westinghouse made significant contributions to transportation and energy. As the inventor of the compressed air brake, he made railroading safer; and he recognized and sought to harness the potential of alternating current electricity as an energy source.

Westinghouse was born in Central Bridge, New York. His father manufactured farm implements; so the young Westinghouse was immersed in mechanical processes. After serving in the Union army and navy, Westinghouse began inventing products for railroads, including a railroad frog (enabling trains to cross from one track to another) and a device for placing derailed rolling stock back on tracks. However, the compressed air brake was his first major invention. Prior to this invention, railroad crewmen often had to dash atop careening cars and manually apply the brakes. American railroads, like their steamboat cousins, compiled grisly safety records. Given the rugged terrain and long distances faced by American railroads, anything that economically enabled trains to increase speed and maintain or improve safety was a godsend. Thus, Westinghouse's invention, coinciding with completion of the transcontinental railroad, was timely. By 1874, many railroads had installed compressed air brakes upon thousands of railroad locomotives and cars. However, not all of the railroads were convinced of the air brake's value relative to its cost, and only action by Congress (Railroad Safety Appliance Act of 1893) fostered its universal dissemination.

Westinghouse formed the Westinghouse Air Brake Company to produce the new air brake. He also continued to improve the device, adding many patents to his portfolio. Other aspects of railroad safety intrigued Westinghouse, and he later formed the Union Switch and Signal Company to develop electrically controlled railroad-signaling systems. The company often improved existing equipment rather than inventing new equipment.

Because of the need for electricity to operate the signaling systems, Westinghouse recognized the need for a cheap, reliable way to produce and transmit electricity across long distances. He purchased patents covering electrical equipment from inventor William Stanley and formed Westinghouse Electric Company to produce the equipment. In addition, he bought an English patent covering alternating current and worked on developing transformers to distribute the electricity over long distances. He enlisted electrical inventor Nikola Tesla to develop a way to power motors, to resolve an early deficiency in the alternating current system.

Westinghouse's efforts were in some ways mirrored by the efforts of renowned American inventor Thomas Edison. Edison had developed a feasible electrical lighting system using direct current. Besides having already invested large sums of capital into generators producing direct current, Edison favored using it for safety reasons and because it was initially better adapted than alternating current for running motors. When alternating current was used in the first electrocution at New York's Sing-Sing Prison, Edison trumpeted the "dangers" inherent in using that system; he even advocated outlawing alternating current. The rivalry between the alternating and direct current systems culminated in Westinghouse's triumphant bid to provide lighting for the 1893 Columbian Exposition in Chicago. The lighting system was a great success, as were the Niagara Falls power stations that supplied power to Buffalo, New York in 1895. The alternating current system eventually became standard, especially once couplers such as the rotary converter allowed direct current systems to be synthesized with alternating current systems, and once General Electric and Westinghouse established a patent exchange agreement in 1896. Ironically, Westinghouse did not prosper greatly from these developments, as he faced extensive litigation, and the Panic of 1907 weakened Westinghouse Electric's finances.

Still, electricity eventually transformed American society and replaced steam as the primary source of energy.

After 1890, industry was the heavier producer and user of electricity until World War I. Thereafter, electric utilities began to produce the bulk of electric power. Nonindustrial commercial use of electricity outstripped residential use until the 1930s. Indeed, even with the economies of scale inherent in centralized alternating current power plants, rural electrification was not widespread until the late 1930s, and it often required government mandates and subsidies.

Given that other inventors were working with alternating current, its diffusion might have transpired without Westinghouse's efforts. Still, his efforts undoubtedly hastened its diffusion and the associated social savings. Also, Westinghouse Electric continued to invent important new technology, after its founder's death, including steam turbines for electrical utilities, television camera tubes, and an early tungsten lamp. Thus the company's inventions continued George Westinghouse's legacy.

BIBLIOGRAPHY

DuBoff, Richard B. *Electrical Power in American Manufacturing, 1889–1958*. Manchester, N.H., 1964. Provides an economic history of the electrical industry and manufacturing.

Hughes, Thomas P. *Networks of Power: Electrification in Western Society, 1880–1930*. Baltimore, 1983.

Levine, Israel E. *Inventive Wizard: George Westinghouse*. New York, 1962.

Prout, Henry G. *A Life of George Westinghouse*. New York, 1921.

DAVID G. SURDAM

WHALING. The whaling industry has a long history in Western civilization, dating from the eighth century in and around the Bay of Biscay. At the peak of the industry's importance, in the decade before the American Civil War, whales were primarily hunted as a source of oil for illumination and lubrication. According to Lance Davis, Robert Gallman, and Karin Gleiter (1997), whaling ranked fifth among U.S. industries in total output in 1850. Indeed, at that time whaling accounted for roughly 1 percent of the value of U.S. nonagricultural output—about the same as pig iron production. An industry of that size today would account for roughly $95 billion in real gross product. Following the successful exploitation of petroleum in the 1860s, the industry underwent a period of permanent decline in the United States, but it revived somewhat among other countries in the twentieth century. Although the industry's size relative to the rest of the U.S. economy was never so large again as it was during the antebellum period, its absolute size, at least as measured by whales slaughtered, substantially exceeded earlier figures. Whaling began to decline again toward the end of the twentieth century and now is undertaken only by a handful of countries.

The word *whale* is generally, and often confusingly, applied to a wide range of mammals of the biological order Cetacea. Cetaceans can be divided into two suborders: odontoceti, or toothed whales, and mysticeti, or baleen whales. From the rise of pelagic whaling until the technological changes of the late-nineteenth century (see below), the sperm whale (*Physeter macrocephalus*) was the most extensively hunted of the toothed whales; whereas the right whales (*Eubalaena glacialis* and *Eubalaena australis*) and the bowhead (*Balaena mysticetus*) were the most important baleen whales—though just about every type of whale was pursued at one time or another. The main products of the sperm whale—sperm oil, spermaceti, and ambergris—differed somewhat from those of the baleen whales, which provided whale oil and baleen ("whalebone").

Before petroleum products emerged as successful substitutes, sperm oil was used primarily as a high-grade illuminant and an industrial lubricant. It was obtained either directly from the head (or "case") of the whale or by processing the whale's blubber. Spermaceti, a waxlike substance suspended, along with the sperm oil, in the whale's head matter and blubber, was used primarily for candles. Both sperm oil and spermaceti were obtained only after a laborious though uncomplicated process of refining. The oil from the whale's head, which was the purest, was scooped out and directly barreled. The blubber had to be flensed (stripped) from the whale in a process not unlike peeling an orange. It was then refined on board ship by heating it in large vats, a process referred to as trying out; and after cooling, the resulting sperm oil was barreled. Whaling voyages in the nineteenth century were typically multiyear affairs, and to keep the oil from spoiling, it was often offloaded in port or at sea on board a less-than-fully laden inbound ship. Once onshore, the oil was bagged and subjected to a series of pressings, which extracted the oil. The material that remained was spermaceti.

Ambergris, the other product generated by the sperm whale, was a by-product of the whale's digestion, and was either extracted from the whale's digestive tract or found floating on the sea or washed up onshore. Overall, production of ambergris was a small part of the whaling industry, but it was highly valued as a musklike component in the production of perfumes. Its price was variously reported at from twenty-five to four hundred dollars an ounce; however, during the peak of American whaling the entire industry probably produced little more than fifty pounds of ambergris a year.

Baleen whales also generated oil from their blubber; and it, like sperm oil, was used as both an illuminant and an industrial lubricant. However, whale oil was inferior to sperm oil in three ways: whale oil congealed at higher temperatures than sperm oil, it did not burn as brightly; and it gave off a foul odor. Like sperm oil, whale oil was extracted from the whale's blubber through the process of trying out. It was then barreled and, once onshore, pressed. Despite its drawbacks, whale oil was the most important whale product until the twentieth century, measured by volume. At the peak of the industry in the United States, roughly nine million gallons of whale oil entered the country annually. Although sperm-oil production was typically less than half this amount, sperm oil usually sold for more than twice as much as whale oil. Measured by value, the annual U.S. output in the early 1850s was $5.1 million (in 1850 dollars) of whale oil and $4.4 million of sperm oil.

Baleen whales also were valued for their baleen or whalebone—the material through which they strained food, such as krill, for consumption. Prior to the metallurgical improvements of the late-nineteenth century, baleen was used primarily for light, ductile goods such as buggy whips and corset stays. It was quite valuable, selling in the 1850s for around $0.43 per pound in the Nantucket market. After sperm oil and whale oil, it was the most valuable of the industry's products, yielding around $1.3 million annually in the 1850s. Exact figures on world production are unavailable; it is estimated that, by the 1850s, the United States was responsible for approximately 85 to 90 percent of the world's marketed whale products.

Prior to the mid-eighteenth century, whaling, in both Europe and America, was conducted from the shore, or occasionally from small shore-based boats, and focused on baleen whales. The whales were killed and then hauled to the nearest shore to be processed. Increasingly, however, such land-based hunting was replaced by pelagic whaling, with larger vessels used to find the whales—which now included sperm whales—and smaller boats deployed to pursue and kill the whales, which were hauled back to the larger vessels to be tried out. As the size of the ships reached several hundred tons, and as good whaling grounds were discovered far from the markets for whale products, these vessels often remained at sea for several years. A typical voyage would begin with the ship's hold filled with provisions; and as the provisions were consumed, it was hoped that the hold would be filled with whale products.

Throughout its long history, the whaling industry has tended to be dominated, at any particular time, by the whalers of a single country. Before the eighteenth century, the Dutch dominated the industry, only to be replaced by the British in the early 1700s. During the early decades of the nineteenth century, the British were challenged and ultimately eclipsed by American whalers; and late in the nineteenth century, the Americans eventually gave way to the Norwegians. Each of these transitions was associated with a major political, technological, or organizational change in the industry. The British replaced the Dutch at least partly as a result of government subsidies to British whalers and protective tariffs on foreign whale oil. Although the reason for the eventual dominance of Ameri-

can whalers continues to be disputed, Davis, Gallman, and Gleiter (1997) argue that the Americans simply drove the British out of the market by better management. Some of this "management" was actually mismanagement on the part of the British government, which imposed additional costs on British whalers in the form of higher labor costs and more bureaucratic restrictions. In any case, by the 1840s, the Americans dominated the industry.

Prior to the technological changes that ultimately led to the industry's twentieth-century resurgence, by most indicators the whaling industry reached its apex in the United States around 1850. The average annual tonnage of the whaling fleet peaked at just over 200,000 tons (roughly 650 vessels) between 1846 and 1850, and average annual output reached $12.3 million between 1851 and 1855—or 312 tons per ship and $50,000 per voyage. At that time, New Bedford was on its way to becoming the center of the world whaling industry, with nearly 40 percent of all U.S. ships registered in its port. By comparison, at its peak in the 1820s, the British industry did not typically exceed $3.0 million in annual output.

The U.S. industry began a period of long-run decline after 1860. Although the market for baleen remained strong until the end of the century, improvements in metallurgy eventually doomed it as well. By the first decade of the twentieth century, there were fewer than fifty registered U.S. whaling vessels. However, during this period the Norwegians began their long-run climb to dominance of the world whaling industry. This rise was facilitated by factors on both the demand side and the supply side of the market.

In the late-nineteenth century the industry experienced several technological changes that altered its organization at a time when whales of the Balaenidae family reputedly were scarce in the North Atlantic. Cannon firing explosive harpoons from steam-powered vessels became the dominant tool for killing whales. To pursue them, large cables fastened to the mast through the ship's hold were attached to steam winches. Finally, to keep the enormous animals from sinking once they were killed, the Norwegians learned to pump compressed air into the whale carcass. The killing power of the cannon and the strength of the vessels allowed the Norwegians to pursue the larger fast rorquals: sei, fins, and blue whales (members of the Balaenopteridae family). Among the largest and fastest of all whales, the rorquals were not typically hunted using the older whaleboat technology, since their speed and diving ability put the whaleboats' crews at risk. Importantly, the rorquals were found in abundance in the seas off Norway, particularly in the northern area known as the Finnmark. With their crews long-accustomed to sealing and fishing in the harsh North Atlantic, the rise of the Norwegians would seem a classic case of comparative advantage at work.

WHALING. Lithograph by Currier and Ives, between 1856 and 1907. (Prints and Photographs Division, Library of Congress)

These changes in the hunting and killing of the whales reduced the number of hands required on board by 60 percent or so; and because the hunting was largely conducted off the Norwegian coast, the processing of the whales was once again moved onshore. Rather than a three- or four-year affair, the whaling voyage became a daily fishing expedition. Once killed and brought alongside the steamer, the rorquals were hauled ashore; the meat and the bones were pressed for oil; and the remains were then ground for fertilizer and animal feed. Although petroleum had replaced whale oil for lighting and lubrication, the discovery of the hydrogenation process led to the growth of the margarine and soap markets, which in turn demanded enormous quantities of fat. Between 1868 and 1904, the Norwegians killed about six hundred whales a year, or roughly 20 percent of the nineteenth-century annual average for the entire world.

As a result of local overhunting and domestic conservation efforts, after 1904 the Norwegians expanded beyond the Finnmark. They were eventually joined by British, German, Russian, and Japanese whalers, and the primary hunting ground became the Antarctic. Shore-based whaling became a problem in the Antarctic for two reasons: the distances and harsh weather created logistical problems, and the British, who largely controlled the area, discouraged foreign whalers on conservation grounds and to protect their own whalers from competition. By the late-1920s, these factors led to the reemergence of pelagic whaling and the emergence of "factory ships." These vessels were enormous by previous industry standards, ranging from ten thousand to twenty thousand tons. After the whale was killed, a great door on the stern opened, and the whale's carcass was hauled on board and processed. By the 1930s, these innovations had led to slaughter on a scale previously unimagined, with the winter of 1937–1938 yielding the largest catch in recorded history, 46,039 whales—a figure equal to more than 10 percent of all the whales killed in the entire nineteenth century.

For both biological and political reasons, slaughter on this scale could not continue indefinitely. Whereas the annual harvests of the nineteenth century probably never were large enough to endanger the animals' existence, those of the twentieth century could not be sustained indefinitely without jeopardizing the long-run survival of the most-hunted species. The basic dilemma faced by the industry was the so-called common resource problem. Since the whales were not owned by any party, and since many parties hunted them, every party had an incentive to overhunt; that is, the whales were harvested at a rate that exceeded the socially optimal rate. Their rapidly diminishing stocks, which reflected the biological inability of the whales to reproduce and mature at rates rapid enough to maintain themselves in the face of the technology used to hunt them, turned conservationists into political activists. The member countries of the International Whaling Commission (founded in 1946) eventually suspended commercial whaling in 1986, and only Japan and Iceland continued their whaling activities thereafter, though Norway eventually rejoined them, ostensibly for scientific research. In any case, the industry once again faced a period of long-run decline—one from which it had yet to recover as the twenty-first century began.

[*See also* Common Goods *and* Fisheries and Fish Processing.]

BIBLIOGRAPHY

Allen, Everett S. *Children of the Light: The Rise and Fall of New Bedford Whaling and Death of the Arctic Fleet*. Boston, 1973.

Burton, Robert. *The Life and Death of Whales*. 2d ed. Totawa, N.J., 1983.

Craig, Lee A., and Robert Fearn. "Wage Discrimination and Occupational Crowding in a Competitive Industry: Evidence from the American Whaling Industry." *Journal of Economic History* 53.1 (1993), 123–138.

Craig, Lee A., and Charles R. Knoeber. "Manager Shareholding, the Market for Managers, and the End-Period Problem." *Journal of Law, Economics, and Organization* 8.3 (1992), 607–627.

Davis, Lance E., Robert E. Gallman, and Karin Gleiter. *In Pursuit of Leviathan*. Chicago and London, 1997.

Davis, Lance E., Robert E. Gallman, and Teresa D. Hutchins. "The Decline of U.S. Whaling: Was the Stock of Whales Running Out?" *Business History Review* 62.4 (1988), 569–595.

Davis, Lance E., Robert E. Gallman, and Teresa D. Hutchins. "Call Me Ishmael—Not Domingo Floresta: The Rise and Fall of the American Whaling Industry." In *The Vital One: Essays in Honor of Jonathan R. T. Hughes*, edited by Joel Mokyr, pp. 191–233. *Research in Economic History*, Suppl. 6. Greenwich, Conn., 1991.

Hohman, Elmo. *The American Whaleman: A Study of Life and Labor in the Whaling Industry*. New York, 1928.

Jackson, Gordon. *The British Whaling Trade*. Hamden, Conn., 1978.

Melville, Herman. *Moby Dick; or the Whale*. 1851. Reprint. Berkeley and Los Angeles, 1983.

Starbuck, Alexander. *History of the American Whale Fishery from Its Earliest Inception to the Year 1876*. Waltham, Mass., 1878.

Tønnessen, J. N., and A. O. Johnsen. *The History of Modern Whaling*, translated by R. I. Christopherson. Berkeley and Los Angeles, 1982.

LEE A. CRAIG

WHITE, LYNN (1907–1987), American medievalist and historian of technology, wrote *Medieval Technology and Social Change* (Oxford, 1962).

White received his B.A. from Stanford University in 1928; a master's degree from Union Theological Seminary in New York, also in 1928; and his Ph.D. from Harvard University in 1934. His teaching career included Princeton University (1933–1937), Stanford (1937–1943), and the University of California Los Angeles (1958–1972). From 1943 to 1958 he served as president of Mills College in Oakland, California.

White is generally considered the founder of all serious study in medieval technology, a field that was largely ignored before his lifetime. White's approach was not shaped by the history of science or economic history. He did not consider technology to derive from economic forces, nor did he think technology had much in common with science before the nineteenth century. To White, the study of technology was closer to cultural history or even to cultural anthropology. Trained as a historian of medieval religious institutions, White claimed that reading A. L. Kroeber's *Anthropology* (New York, 1923) changed his focus and led him to the *Annales* school of French historians, and above all to Marc Bloch, to whom he dedicated *Medieval Technology and Social Change*.

White first published on technology in 1940 under the title "Technology and Invention in the Middle Ages," but his *chef-d'oeuvre* was *Medieval Technology and Social Change* (1962), based on lectures he gave in 1957 at the University of Virginia. The work aroused great interest, and by 1973 it had appeared in Italian, German, French, and Spanish. *Medieval Technology and Social Change* retains the form of three long lectures on related themes, with what amounts to a second book beneath the first in the form of intricate, layered footnotes.

Having established the importance of the Middle Ages to Western technology, White wrote extensively from the early 1960s until the mid-1970s on the cultural foundations underlying medieval technology (see bibliography). He found these in two unlikely places, Western Christianity and East Asia. Throughout his life, White was a believing Christian, an active Presbyterian layman; and he saw Western technology as an expression of an action-oriented style of Christianity distinctive to western Europe. Like Max Weber, he emphasised the ways that religious belief compelled the believer to actions that had economic consequences. Unlike Weber, he focussed on Catholic, pre-Reformation Europe. He also emphasized the connection between the West and the East as a fertile source of technological innovation, seeing Europe as the beneficiary of technologies originating from Asia. His clearest expression of this came in 1960 in "Tibet, India, and Malaya as Sources of Western Medieval Technology."

The most significant—certainly the most controversial—piece of work from this period is the 1967 essay titled "The Historical Roots of Our Ecologic Crisis." By suggesting that Christianity bears a considerable share of the moral burden for our environmental woes because of its hostile and domineering attitudes toward nature, White aroused a storm of protest and counterargument that still resonates. He is regarded as one of the founders of "deep ecology," the belief that nature should be regarded as having spiritual value in itself and not merely as a storehouse of "resources." In this respect, White might even be regarded as an "antieconomist," someone who denies the utilitarian foundations of economics as a discipline.

Lynn White regarded himself as both a defender of an old faith and as a pioneer. His old faith was a twofold belief in Christianity and humane letters; his role as a pioneer was to place technology into an intimate connection with both.

BIBLIOGRAPHY

WORKS BY LYNN WHITE

"Technology and Invention in the Middle Ages." *Speculum* 15 (1940), pp. 141–159.

"Natural Science and Naturalistic Art in the Middle Ages," *American Historical Review* 52 (1947), pp. 421–435.

"Tibet, India, and Malaya as Sources of Western Medieval Technology." *American Historical Review* 65 (1960), pp. 515–526.

Medieval Technology and Social Change. London, 1962.

"The Historical Roots of Our Ecologic Crisis." *Science* 155 (1967), pp. 1203–1207.

Machina ex Deo: Essays in the Dynamism of Western Culture. Cambridge, Mass., 1968. Subsequently reissued by MIT as *Dynamo and Virgin Reconsidered.* Reprints of earlier papers not readily available elsewhere.

"The Iconography of *Temperantia* and the Virtuousness of Technology." In *Action and Conviction in Early Modern Europe: Essays in Memory of E. H. Harbison*, edited by T. K. Rabb and J. E. Siegel, pp. 181–204. Princeton, 1969.

"The Expansion of Technology, 500–1500." In *The Fontana Economic History of Europe*, vol. 1, *The Middle Ages*, edited by C. Cipolla, pp. 143–174. London, 1969. "Cultural Climates and Technological Advance in the Middle Ages." *Viator* 2 (1971), pp. 171–201.

"Medical Astrologers and Late Medieval Technology." *Viator* 6 (1975), pp. 295–308.

"Medieval Engineering and the Sociology of Knowledge." *Pacific Historical Review* 44 (1975), pp. 1–21.

Medieval Religion and Technology. Berkeley and Los Angeles, 1978. Reprints most of White's major articles.

OTHER REFERENCE

Hall, Bert S. "Lynn Townsend White, Jr. (1907–1987)" Obituary and bibiliography. *Technology and Culture* 30 (1989), 194–213.

BERT S. HALL

WHITNEY, ELI (1765–1825), American inventor.

Eli Whitney was both the inventor of the cotton gin and one of the pioneers of the American system of manufacturing. The epitome of the Yankee inventor, Whitney received his early training with machines in his father's workshop, which contained a forge, tools, and a lathe. He did not initially aspire to be an inventor, but set his sights on a formal education. After graduating from Yale in 1792, Whitney took a job as a tutor in Georgia; the tutoring position did not live up to his expectations, however, and Whitney turned to his Yankee friend Phineas Miller, then living on the estate of Catherine Greene, widow of General Nathanael Greene of Revolutionary War fame. Catherine Greene invited Whitney to stay at her estate on the Savannah River in late 1792. Over the next year, while observing workers separating cotton lint from seeds, Whitney devised his cotton gin. Miller saw the brilliance of Whitney's gin, and the two formed a partnership, bankrolled by Catherine Greene.

A relatively simple machine, the cotton gin consisted of wire teeth that separated the cotton lint from the seeds. Without it, the United States could not be competitive as a world supplier of cotton because U.S. soils were predominantly suited to short-staple cotton, which entailed much greater amounts of labor to separate the lint from the seed compared to the long-staple cotton grown in other parts of the world. The cost savings of the cotton gin came from substituting machine for hand labor. Whitney estimated that his machine, powered by a horse, could gin as much cotton as fifty laborers ginning by hand. It is difficult to overestimate the impact of the cotton gin on the Southern economy. The device propelled the United States from being a marginal producer of cotton to its place as one the world's largest producers. In 1791, U.S. cotton represented 0.5 percent of world production; twenty years later it accounted for 68 percent. Cotton output soared from three thousand bales before introduction of the cotton gin in 1790 to seventy-three thousand bales ten years later, and it continued to escalate, reaching 3,841,000 bales by 1860. By making growing cotton more profitable, the cotton gin also made slavery more profitable. One might plausibly argue that slavery would have died much earlier in the absence of Eli Whitney's cotton gin.

Despite the widespread adoption of the cotton gin, it was not a commercial success. President George Washington signed Whitney's patent for the cotton gin in 1794, but the invention was easily copied, and his patent rights were difficult to enforce. Whitney set up a factory in New Haven to manufacture the cotton gin, but a 1797 fire left him on the brink of bankruptcy. With no profits in sight for producing cotton gins, a desperate Whitney went to the federal government with an offer to produce arms (muskets, bayonets, ramrods, and other equipment). He received a contract for ten thousand stands of arms, which not only kept Whitney afloat but contributed substantially to America's development as an industrial powerhouse.

Whitney's innovation in the production of arms was the use of interchangeable parts, which allowed him to employ unskilled labor in assembling weapons and, more important, enabled weapons to be repaired quickly. However, producing the arms with interchangeable parts was not a simple task; standardized machines were required to make the parts. Thus a machine-tool industry was needed, which in Whitney's time did not exist. So he created machines to produce the interchangeable parts in his shop in New Haven. Whitney shared his knowledge of machine building with other inventors, in part because of his former experience with patents and also because he was simply too busy to apply for a patent. Constantly behind schedule in his manufacture of arms, Whitney did not complete the contract for ten thousand muskets until 1809. However, Whitney's pioneering use of standardized machinery and his use of interchangeable parts ultimately contributed two key ingredients in what became known as the American system of manufacturing.

BIBLIOGRAPHY

Hughes, Jonathan. *The Vital Few: The Entrepreneur and American Economic Progress.* New York, 1986.

Mirskey, Jeannette, and Alan Nevins. *The World of Eli Whitney.* New York, 1952.

Mokyr, Joel. *The Lever of Riches: Technological Creativity and Economic Progress.* New York, 1990.

LEE J. ALSTON

WINE AND WINERIES. Wine is among the oldest commodities of human production and exchange. Humans probably began producing wine around 5000 BCE in Transcaucasia, and the practice spread to the Near East and Egypt, around 3000 BCE, thence via Minoan Crete to Greece. In earliest civilizations wine was often a luxury reserved for religious and governing elites, and the masses drank beer or mead.

Antiquity. Wine was essential to Greek civilization and was associated with male sociability and urban culture and religion, as in the cult of Dionysus, god of wine, later the Roman Bacchus. Wine also became the sacramental beverage of Jews and early Christians. Greeks developed pruning and introduced the beam press, amphorae (ceramic jars to store and transport wine by ship), and resins and spices for preservation and flavor. Their extensive galley trade propagated winegrowing to coastal colonies around the Mediterranean, such as Massilia (Marseille). The Romans took wine beyond the Mediterranean to the far reaches of the continental Europe. Under the Republic, a wealthy senatorial elite invested heavily in vineyards, spurred by eager merchants and domestic demand (Rome reached 1 million inhabitants), and organized capital-intensive wine estates worked by slave gangs. They introduced the screw press, large ceramic storage vats (dolia), and grafting. They improved pressing, racking, and aging and pushed exports. Like the Greeks they recorded vintage names (Caecuban, Falernian) on ceramic containers but, unlike the Greeks, produced much mediocre wine for the masses. By the second century BCE the republic exported 120,000 hectoliters annually, primarily to Gaul. Imperial Rome carried viticulture to far-flung military and trading outposts along the Rhine and Danube and into Germany, Spain, northern France, and even southern England. From some of these sites sprang the great medieval vineyards. By the second century CE Rome was a heavy net importer of wines from Gaul and Spain, thereby reversing the trade flow but expanding provincial production. Romans cut wines with water, spices, and honey to improve flavor.

Medieval Transformation. The fall of Rome (476 CE) brought strife, invasions, declining population, and shrinking cities. But winegrowing survived on peasant and manorial properties, sustained by the medieval church, by the rise of medieval empires, and by the expansion of merchant trade in northern Europe. Along with textiles, wine became a leading commodity in the economic recovery of the late Middle Ages (twelfth and thirteenth centuries), especially maritime trade. The continental shift in trade toward the urban markets and merchant towns of northern Europe, away from the Mediterranean South, propelled this revitalization. For the church wine was essential for sacramental uses as well as the social prestige of bishops and popes. Monasteries were medieval wine labs where monks patiently improved vine varieties, refined processing, and introduced blending and cask aging. In Burgundy, Benedictines founded Cluny in 910 CE, and the Cistercians founded Clos Vougeot two centuries later. Many Rhineland vintages had monastic origins (Schloss Johannisberg). Ambitious medieval princes, such as the dukes of Burgundy, promoted their wines in Paris, Flanders, papal Avignon, and across the Channel in London. One consequence of medieval expansion was that vineyards spread well north of present-day limits into Flanders, northern Germany, and even Poland thanks partly to the church and the difficulty of overland transport. As Roger Dion notes, harsh northern climates and soils spawned fine wines in Ile de France, Champagne, Burgundy, and Rhineland, making leading wine centers of Beaune, Cologne, Bruges, Rouen, and the fairs of Champagne. The medieval maritime trade reached its height in the biannual flotillas of ships bearing "new clarets" from Bordeaux to Bristol and London in the thirteenth century, when Gascony was under English domain and Bordeaux merchants enjoyed special trade monopolies with the English Crown. By the early fourteenth century Bordeaux shipped about 700,000 hectoliters of wine annually, until the disruptions of the Hundred Years' War (1337–1453) and the black plague. Critical technical problems for medieval wine dealers were transport costs and spoilage. In an era before bottling, wine in casks deteriorated from exposure to air and had to be consumed within the year, or they turned bad. In medieval Bordeaux prices declined as wine aged.

Early Modern Revolutions. Following the medieval era, economic crises, warfare, and mercantile rivalries between national monarchies changed the institutional setting for wine making. In the fourteenth century population crises eroded production and prices, while the sixteenth-century population growth pressured grain production, devaluing wine. In central Europe winegrowing never fully recovered from the devastation of the Thirty Years' War (1618–1648). By the late seventeenth century Louis XIV's mercantilist trade wars prompted the Grand Alliance of Holland, England, and Spain to impose prohibitive tariffs and outright embargoes on French wines, devastating Southwest France. However, Dutch merchants revolutionized wine making there by introducing distilling to produce brandy, an economical, compact,

WINE MAKING. *Month of October*: *The Wine Press*, anonymous fresco, Italy, fifteenth century. (Castello del Buonconsiglio, Trent, Italy/Scala/Art Resource, NY)

stable liquor capable of extended ocean travel. The Dutch conveyed the practice to English and Iberian merchants, who used distilling and blending to produce fortified wines, port, and sherry. In Portugal the monarchy regulated production of port by organizing the first regional delimitation zone in the upper Douro Valley, while in Andalusia in southern Spain sherry production soared, as did production of fortified wines on Madeira. All three were hugely popular with English and European wealthy consumers in the seventeenth and eighteenth centuries. Meantime the geographical retreat of marginal northern European vineyards concentrated wine production in regions familiar today, for example, Burgundy, Champagne, and Hungary (Tokay). Responding to fortified wines and

tariffs, Bordeaux growers desperately pushed quality, carefully blending, finishing, and aging wines in small oaken casks. Merchants bottled and aged these wines, naming grower and vintage on the label to distinguish their products. In early-eighteenth century Britain the new Bordeaux "clarets" were a sensation, fetching prices that more than covered high duties and bringing fame to aristocratic wine estates in Médoc (Margaux, Latour, and Lafite) and Graves (Haut-Brion). Their reputations were enshrined in the famous Bordeaux classification of 1855, largely unchanged today.

Mass Markets. By the eighteenth century vintage wines faced mounting competition from cheap common wines for the urban middling and lower classes. Industrialization brought increased demand and disposable incomes, lower transaction and production costs, and improved road, canal, and (later) rail transport. These factors, along with the rise of urban wine shops and dealers, spawned a peasant cottage industry, largely self-financed, in growing *vins ordinaires* to meet demand. Authorities saw the explosion in popular viticulture as threatening vintage wine and grain production, but efforts to limit its spread were unavailing. Monarchies strapped for revenue soon found more value in taxing common wines than in prohibiting them. A direct consequence was the relatively late emergence in Spain, Italy, and especially southern France of regions devoted principally to table wines: the French Languedoc became the largest volume wine-producing region in the world. A growing differentiation based on comparative advantage separated regions of vintage and ordinary wines. Following the disruptions of the Napoleonic wars, the rapid expansion of both vintage and popular wines culminated in the historic production and price levels of the 1860s and 1870s, the "golden era" of old European viticulture. After the mid-nineteenth century free trade and improved equipment for pruning, plowing spraying, and processing increased efficiency, while the beginnings of market advertising attracted the respectable middle classes. The latter aided the meteoric rise of merchant houses in Champagne, such as Moët et Chandon and Veuve Cliquot, whose sparkling sweet white wines skillfully exploited popular associations with royalty and high fashion.

But the limits of consumption were also evident. In England, Germany, and much of the New World consumption of other alcoholic beverages, gin, rum, whiskey, and beer, far outpaced wine. There were also mounting concerns over alcoholism and social decay, leading to influential temperance movements in Protestant western Europe. The sagacious French wine industry associated itself with temperance by claiming that wine was a natural, healthy beverage while distilled alcoholic drinks were toxic, a distinction the temperance movements often accepted. Only in the United States did a Protestant, not to say puritanical, temperance movement win prohibition of all commercial alcoholic beverages with the Eighteenth Amendment (1920–1933), temporarily halting the rise of the California wine industry. More damaging still was vine disease, especially the phylloxera, a tiny root-dwelling aphid from America that killed European *Vitis vinifera* vines. Phylloxera devastated vineyards in France and throughout Europe from the 1870s onward, very nearly bringing the European wine industry to its knees.

Crisis and Recovery. By the 1890s European growers were overcoming phylloxera by replanting vineyards with (resistant) American rootstock onto which they grafted native vines, but this imposed higher production and operating costs. Moreover delicate grafted vines had to be sprayed, cultivated, and fertilized intensively. In response growers increased yields and output, employing industrial wine making techniques to produce oceans of mediocre (and sometimes fradulent) wines, which industrial processing facilitated. By the 1920s more wine than ever was produced on smaller acreage, leading to a chronic glut of wines in the 1930s, worsened by the Great Depression. In the end only government intervention saved the wine industry, and the French example was widely imitated. In 1935 the French established a national system of controlled wine appellations (*appellations d'origine contrôlée*) that established strict regional controls on permitted vine varieties, yields, processing methods, and labeling, thereby certifying quality and authenticity. Though not adapted in all wine districts, controlled appellations bolstered quality and reduced (but did not eliminate) overproduction, stabilizing the chaotic industry and after World War II forging the basis for a remarkable revival of wine.

Quality and Globalization. By the 1990s fully 43 percent of French wine output was in controlled appellation wines. Establishment of the European Union prompted the introduction or updating of similar appellations in Spain, Italy, Portugal, and Germany. The proliferation of growers' cooperatives also raised standards and restored public confidence, as did improved wine processing and scientific research in universities. The consequence was that even medium-sized producers sought quality and replanted with improved rootstock, while costs of modernization forced marginal growers out, leading to an upward shift in quality. The collapse in demand for common wines devastated growers of bulk wines in Languedoc and Italy though not merchants who used jug wine to stretch their vintage offerings. Postwar demand for estate-bottled vintage growths and champagne boomed, despite occasional speculative bubbles (for example, the price collapse in Bordeaux in 1974–1975 after a decade of huge increases).

On the global scale the revival of quality was advanced by the rise of reputable wines in former settler colonies, notably California, Australia, South Africa, and Chile, where winegrowing burst forth after long development. In California, Franciscans established the first vineyards around 1770. Commercial winegrowing began with the influx of European settlers in the 1830s, boomed after the gold rush, then suffered decades of boom-and-bust cycles and Prohibition. Only in the 1970s did the region come into its own as a premier wine region, largely by imitating and sometimes surpassing the great Burgundies and Bordeaux. Fueling the renaissance of New World vineyards was a global prosperity that created new consumers eager for sophistication and refinement. Also important were new production techniques pioneered or adapted by New World wineries (carbonic maceration, refrigerated fermentation, innovative machinery, including row-straddling tractors and mechanized harvesters), innovations subsequently taken up by Old World growers to stay competitive. The striking consequence has been a global convergence in wines, as success of California wines in tasting competitions with French vintages attests. But the flaw of modernization has been that yields have risen even for quality wines, sometimes spectacularly, threatening chronic overproduction. And per capita consumption has declined recently in face of competition from soft drinks and health concerns. The future of wine is an open question, but the era of secular increases in mass-produced, mediocre wines since the eighteenth century is over, bested by the revival of quality. As they have since Roman antiquity, wine production and marketing continue to reflect wider trends in the global economy.

[*See also* Vines and Viticulture.]

BIBLIOGRAPHY

Bennet, Norman R. "Port Wine Merchants: Sandeman in Porto, 1813–1831." *Journal of European Economic History* 24 (1995), 239–269. Focused but clear demonstration of vital role of export merchants.

Brennan, Thomas. *Burgundy to Champagne: The Wine Trade in Early Modern France*. Baltimore, 1997. Posits that wine brokers who controlled market networks were agents of commercial capitalism dominating peasant winegrowers.

Carosso, Vincent P. *The California Wine Industry: Study of the Formative Years, 1830–1895*. Berkeley and Los Angeles, 1951. Definitive treatment of the early years.

Carter, F. W. "Cracow's Wine Trade: Fourteenth to Eighteen Centuries." *Slavonic and East European Review* 65 (1987), 537–578.

Davis, Ralph. "The English Wine Trade in the Eighteenth and Nineteenth Centuries." *Annales Cisaplines d'histoire sociale* 3 (1972), 87–106. A valuable account despite the obscure source, in English.

Dion, Roger. *Histoire de la vigne et du vin en France des origines an XIXe siècle*. Paris, 1959.

Enjalbert, Henri. "Comment naissent les grands crus: Bordeaux, Porto, Cognac." *Annales: ESC* 8 (1953), 315–328, 457–474. An essential interpretation.

Enjalbert, Henri, and Bernard Enjalbert. *History of Wine and the Vine*. Paris, 1987. Elegant, wide-ranging summary of the Bordeauist *terroir* perspective.

Foster, Robert. "The Noble Wine Producers of the Bordelais in the Eighteenth Century." *Economic History Review*, 2d ser., 14 (1961), 18–33.

Guy, Kolleen M. "'Oiling the Wheels of Social Life': Myths and Marketing in Champagne during the Belle Epoque." *French Historical Studies* 22 (1999), 211–239.

James, M. K. *Studies in the Medieval Wine Trade*. Oxford, 1971. Masterful study of the Bordeaux claret trade.

Loubère, Leo A. *The Red and the White: A History of Wine in France and Italy in the Nineteenth Century*. Albany, N.Y., 1978.

Loubère, Leo A. *The Wine Revolution in France: The Twentieth Century*. Princeton, 1990. Emphasizes recent but profound impact of modernization, especially marketing and technology.

Pech, Rémy. *Entreprise viticole et capitalisme en Languedoc-Roussillon du phylloxera aux crises de Mévente*. Toulouse, 1975. Vital analysis of the seesaw economic rivalries dividing small growers and wine estates in a region of mass wine production.

Pinney, Thomas. *A History of Wine in America: From the Beginnings to Prohibition*. Berkeley, 1989.

Robinson, Jancis, ed. *The Oxford Companion to Wine*. 2d ed. Oxford and New York, 1999. Thorough and informative, with many historical sections.

Tchernia, André. *Le vin de l'Italie Romaine: Essai d'histoire économique d'après les amphore*. Rome, 1986. A pathbreaking analysis.

HARVEY SMITH

WOMEN IN THE LABOR FORCE. Women's involvement in the labor force seems a straightforward concept, readily captured in participation rates, which can then be used in historical and cross-sectional comparisons. Unfortunately, the labor force is defined not in terms of all work but only work done for wages as a market transaction, and so is ahistorical and androcentric. Participation benchmarks are hard to establish when activities shift from subsistence to the market, and women's work has always been more likely to be unpaid, done in the home, and directed toward caring for family members. To avoid misleading measurement across countries with subsistence sectors of various sizes, the United Nations defines economic goods and services as those produced for pay or profit, including self-provisioning, and the International Labor Organization defines the economically active in terms of this broader view. However, problems remain about which subsistence activities to include in estimates of the labor force. For the historian, the recovery and the valuation of unpaid work are not feasible. Indeed, the record often is not adequate to measure the labor force as conventionally defined. In the British case, not until the mid-nineteenth century were there national counts of working women and populations, by age group, from which to construct aggregate participation rates. Even then the prejudices of enumerators, as well as the difficulty of registering part-time, seasonal, and home work in one-shot counts, ensured the systematic underrecording of women's work. Conventions used to deal with these problems varied over time and across countries, making comparisons tricky. Attempts to compare European countries often turn to existing surveys, which go no further back in time than the 1890s and focus on women's share of the labor force by sector, not participation rates.

The spark needed to turn this mound of problems into a bonfire of controversy was provided by the implications of the history of women's work for explanations of women's social and economic subordination. Feminists looked to historical analyses for insight into the origins and the evolution of women's inferior status. What, they asked, were the long-run trends in women's participation in the labor force, and how did they relate to the rise of the male-breadwinner family and women's economic dependence on men? Was women's dependence the product of blind market forces or the rent-seeking activities of groups of men? What role did biology, particularly childbearing, child rearing and physical strength, play? Would the post–World War II increase in female participation rates eventually secure equality between the sexes? These were loaded questions, heavy with implications for feminist strategy, and historians struggled to answer them with their problematic and patchy records. Only in recent years have the fires of controversy shed light as well as heat, and only now has agreement begun to meld around some patterns of female labor force participation.

Neoclassical Analysis of Female Labor Supply and Historical Applications. In neoclassical economics, individuals decide whether or not to participate in paid employment and how many hours to work by comparing the value of their time in the labor force (indexed by the wage rate) with the value of their leisure (the reservation wage). As far as men's decisions are concerned, the analysis generally proceeds in a straightforward manner, with the usual convex preferences associated with outcomes marked by mixtures of work and leisure. Empirical evidence is consistent with the theory. Most adult men participate in and vary their hours of work with characteristics that can be interpreted as proxies for the relative returns of work and leisure.

In studying the female labor supply, labor economists had a definitional problem. The failure of paid work to encompass all productive activity meant that married women had a third possible use for their time: work in the home. Modeling this extra dimension of choice involved investigating the family context. Analysis of women's labor supply became inextricably bound up with the new household economics developed by Gary Becker. The probability of participation for married women became a function of: their own real wage; other real income, including their husbands' earnings (which affects the reservation wage); and a vector of variables to allow for constraints on the participation decision and for heterogeneous tastes.

Examples of the former include local employment opportunities, and of the latter, the number and ages of children, conventionally assumed to imply a "taste" for home production. The standard economic model left no role for the influence of ideological and institutional factors. The gender division of labor, by which women specialize in domestic labor and men in paid work, was taken either as "natural," to be included in "tastes," or as determined simultaneously with labor force participation. Women's relatively low market earnings explained why they specialized in home production; but, simultaneously, their relatively low market earnings were explained by their specialization in home production. Women rationally invested less than men in market skills because the return was lower, as they spent less time than men in the labor force, interrupting paid work to bear and raise children. Even new household economists fell back on biological arguments, women's comparative advantage in child rearing following from their biological (absolute) advantage in childbearing. But, one may ask, how appropriate is such a model in the context of historical labor markets, and how easily can it be estimated using historical data?

Testing the neoclassical model requires specific technical procedures and individual data on women's participation, wages, skills and human capital, family composition, and other earnings. Even in a contemporary context, it often makes impossible demands on available data. Large-scale suitable historical data sets simply are not available; so historical applications typically involve cross-sectional analyses of small data sets painstakingly recovered from historical records. Better data are available in the twentieth century and especially from 1945 on. Earlier studies are rare, and, if they have been conducted, often involve compromises and improvisations that cloud the findings.

The conclusions are often surprisingly supportive of the neoclassical model, in that the female labor supply is positively related to women's own wages and negatively related to other family earnings; an economic motivation seems universal. However, there are intriguing differences in terms of the impact of family structure. Although numbers of children can be seen to reduce married women's labor supply in both contexts, this is so because children's presence is assumed to be correlated with a "taste" for home work in the modern family, whereas historically older children were substitutes for mothers in paid work. Another key difference is that in contemporary studies the presence of an infant, all other things being equal, is the single most important structural inhibitor of the female labor supply; but several historical studies have shown the opposite. The presence of a baby, controlling for other household characteristics, historically suggests that the wife/mother is young and newly married, and so able and willing to earn before other children arrive with their demands on her time and eventual ability to substitute for her in the labor force.

Although the neoclassical model was useful in emphasizing the universality of economic considerations and linking the female labor supply to the family life cycle, its demands on historical data limited its applicability. Nor was it entirely suited to understanding changes over time. It was necessary to be cautious in generalizing from statistical relationships, significant in cross-section, to causal relationships over time. The negative effects of husband's earnings on wife's labor supply in cross-sectional studies did not mean that the female labor supply declined with prosperity, as commentators on 1950s America discovered. Moreover, several studies suggested that social norms and community values affected women's decisions to work, yet offered few clues about how these factors emerged and were reproduced. Moreover, the neoclassical elevating of the individual over the social or the structural in the hierarchy of causation hindered exploration of the effects of economic development and structural change on women's economic activity.

Feminists' concerns also highlighted the need for explicitly historical and institutional analyses. They were particularly sceptical of neoclassical accounts of gender specialization, especially arguments that rationalized the household division of labor as "efficient," as the best that could be achieved. Instead, feminists were inclined to see the rent-seeking activities of men, production for profit, and institutional rigidities, especially cultural norms, as implicated in the emergence and the entrenchment of gender divisions.

Another problem was the fixation on supply. Demand for women's labor entered analyses only through market wages; but over the long run, demand shifts with structural, technological, and organizational changes, which influence productivity. Such shifts, while partially exogenous, are also responses to existing constraints on profits. Changes in demand and supply needed to be studied together and in their cultural context.

Structural Analyses. Neoclassical economics was not the only theoretical framework available; other social sciences offered more eclectic and less technical approaches. Some historians described the history of women's work in terms of persistent structures of dominance and subordination, summarized as patriarchy. Others interpreted the extent and the form of women's work in terms of the development of capitalism, and framed the history of women's work in terms of the dominant "mode of production." A third group sought to combine these two approaches in a "dual systems theory," interpreting the history of women's work in terms of the interaction between a developing capitalist economy and entrenched patriarchal relations of dominance and subordination.

WOMEN AT WORK. Shoe workers, Lynn, Massachusetts, 1895. (Frances Benjamin Johnston Collection/Prints and Photographs Division, Library of Congress)

The structuralist-functionalist theories of Talcott Parsons inspired a history of women's work framed in terms of economic stages in the development of the family. Alice Clark argued that in the preindustrial economy women had access to a wide range of jobs since production itself was based in the household. "Family industry," as she denoted it, obliterated distinctions between work in the home and in the labor market and enabled women to join with men and children to produce a family subsistence. Louise Tilly and Joan Scott depicted trends in women's involvement in the labor force in terms of evolving links between the family and the economy. Their "family economy," where households combined reproductive and productive functions and directly produced their own subsistence, repeated the picture of democratic effort painted by Clark. However, with industrialization the "family wage economy," in which individual family members had recourse to the wider labor market to earn but then pooled their wages to support the group, became increasingly prevalent. The distinction, central to modern economics, between work in the home and participation in the labor market emerges as a relatively recent characteristic of economic life, but nonetheless one with profound importance for women. The divorce of home and work was seen to make it more difficult for married women with family responsibilities to participate fully in production. The origins of women's specialization in home production seemed to lie in the development of the market economy.

The family wage economy was not the end of the story. Tilly and Scott went on to describe the patchy and uneven development of a family, based not on the earnings of all its members but on the earnings of the male head of household. In this "male-breadwinner family," women's specialization in domestic production deepened as children spent longer in school and accumulated more human capital. The family became primarily a unit for organizing human reproduction, the socialization of children, and collective and individual consumption—"the family consumer economy."

Emerging Accounts of Women's Work. Decades of debate produced a conventional wisdom, though not one lacking bones of contention and gaps in knowledge. Most accounts identified a premodern era characterized by high levels of female economic activity, but scholars differed about which features of the underdeveloped economy fostered women's involvement. Some authors pointed to the dominance of the agricultural sector, which employed many women, as both paid and unpaid workers. Others drew attention to the ubiquity of household production and the seamless web of domestic and productive activities in which women could rather easily contribute to the family subsistence. Still others suggested that low productivity was the ultimate explanation; underdeveloped economies were simply too poor to provide for many noncontributors. Women and girls had to work.

There was also disagreement about the interpretation of this era of mutual and joint labor, over whether women's work improved their status in family and community and fostered a rough equality between men and women as they struggled side by side to subsist. Historians who emphasised the deep roots of patriarchy were sceptical about the egalitarian aspects of this "golden age" and argued that distinctions of sex and age structured the domestic labor process and correlated with an unequal division of household resources. Historians also suggested that "essential" female characteristics, lack of upper body strength and preoccupation with pregnancy and lactation, could inhibit women's involvement in production even if it was located in the home and organized through the family. The physical demands of production in an unmechanized era and the dangers women faced outside the protected domestic environment reduced women's value as workers even at a time when production was based in the home.

Whatever the particular features of the various versions of the golden-age hypothesis, historians agreed on a second historical pattern: economic development operated to undermine women's ability to participate in production. Although some groups of women in some times and places benefited from economic development, finding well-paid jobs in feminized branches of the burgeoning textile industries, for example, the conventional wisdom was that, in general, the economic changes termed the Industrial Revolution reduced women's labor force participation. The development of markets, commercial relations, the movement of production out of the home and into centralized workplaces, the decline of agriculture, the rise of industry, urbanization, increasing wealth, and mechanization were all associated with the demise of the golden age and women's loss of access to complementary productive resources. The Industrial Revolution gave rise to an era of female dependence on men and male wages.

As development proceeded, the sectoral composition of the economy continued to change. The service sector expanded, offering new opportunities for women and girls.

Simultaneously, an expansion in girls' education, along with declining fertility, less work in the home, and more opportunities to substitute market production for domestic production, transformed the conditions of the female labor supply. Demand and supply factors combined to promote increasing female participation, and the new conditions drew married women and then mothers into the workforce. As more and more women, wives and mothers included, entered the labor force, any residual stigma about their employment eroded, tipping societies toward higher levels of female labor participation. Greater economic independence also contributed to rising divorce rates, which in turn discouraged female detachment from the labor force. The speed and the scale of these changes since World War II have been described as "the social revolution of our time."

These three epochs, the golden age, the era of dependency, and the social revolution of our time, have been linked in a grand narrative. Together they imply that women's labor force participation follows a U-shaped pattern as development proceeds. Much empirical work has this hypothesis either implicitly or explicitly as its inspiration.

Empirical Themes. The extent to which there was a golden age of sexually egalitarian production relations has provided one focus of empirical research. Another has been the identification of early industrialization as the crucible of modern gender divisions. The separation of the home and the workplace, the development of large-scale centralized units of production, and the formalization of the length of the working day were all seen to inhibit women's involvement in production, burdened as they were with domestic responsibilities, such as pregnancy, lactation, child care, and domestic work, and accustomed to work at home in familial and sexually nonpredatory settings. However, most accounts of women's work identified institutional constraints, particularly social norms, as important forces molding gender stereotypes and underpinning the emerging divisions of labor. These constraints appeared particularly important in the rise of the male-breadwinner family system, which many authors located in the second half of the nineteenth century. Some constraints, for example, trade union's exclusive strategies, were readily related to the rent-seeking activities of groups of men, whose economic interest lay in excluding women from the labor force and securing their services in the private sphere of the home. Other building blocks in the traditional division of labor, such as the campaign for the family wage, seemed to have been pursued by both men and women and were perceived to have been in the latter's interest by the historic actors involved. Some employers were also seen to have had an interest in crowding women into certain sectors of employment and thereby cheapening their labor. The state, concerned with both social control and the orderly reproduction of the working class, was also identified as interested and instrumental in molding the division of labor. Individual authors presented variations of these themes, with particular interests and actions that had both intended and unintended consequences in promoting the division of labor, separate spheres of work, and the male-breadwinner family. Comparative accounts were framed in similar terms, with national experiences distinguished according to the extent to which economic development destroyed or tolerated features of the premodern economy that had been conducive to women's work, such as the family farm and domestic industry.

Given the fragmentary nature of the empirical evidence available for the early modern and early industrial periods, it is not surprising that debate persists over key features of the first two phases in the U-shaped trajectory. It is hard to generalize on the basis of the detailed case studies of communities facing economic change that remain characteristic of women's history.

The third phase in the U-shaped path of female participation faces no such dearth of quantitative evidence. Individual country studies and international comparisons have served to document increased female involvement and to identify and rank specific causal factors. Ever more sophisticated econometrics and better data will throw this recent experience into sharper focus, in comparison with the shadows through which earlier developments must be deciphered. This contrast between a recent past where events and their causes are clearly perceived and a more distant and less well-understood era raises its own problems. Grand narratives of women in the labor force run the risk of providing falsely homogenizing accounts, which are obsessed with mono-causality, outcomes, and finished worlds.

BIBLIOGRAPHY

Clark, Alice. *Working Life of Women in the Seventeenth Century*. London, 1919, 1982. A classic contribution locating trends in women's work in the evolving links between the family and the economy.

De Groot, Gertjan, and Marlou Schrover, eds. *Women Workers and Technological Change in Europe in the Nineteenth and Twentieth Centuries*. London, 1995. An excellent collection of articles highlighting the complex relationship between culturally constructed sex-role stereotypes and technological change, and the effects of this relationship on the demand for female labor.

Glucksmann, Miriam. *Women Assemble: Women Workers and New Industries in Inter-War Britain*. London, 1995. Fills a major gap in the history of women and work and raises questions about a periodization that draws a sharp line at 1945. It is notable also for the use of a wide variety of sources, including interviews with people who worked in assembly-line industries in the interwar period.

Goldin, Claudia. *Understanding the Gender Gap: An Economic History of American Women*. New York, 1990. A classic country study.

Goldin, Claudia. "The U-shaped Female Labor Force Function in Economic Development and Economic History." In *Investment in Women's Human Capital*, edited by T. Paul Schultz, pp. 61–90. Chicago, 1995. An empirical investigation of the hypothesis that female labor force participation has a long-run U-shaped trajectory.

Humphries, Jane. "Women and Paid Work." In *Women's History: Britain, 1850–1945*, edited by June Purvis, pp. 85–106. London, 1995. A survey article, which details the problems involved in measuring women's participation in the labor force as conventionally defined and developing a periodization consistent with mainstream accounts of economic change.

Honeyman, Katrina, and Jordan Goodman. "Women's Work, Labor Markets, and Gender Conflict in Europe, 1500–1900." *Economic History Review* 44 (1991), 608–628. An important article for the doubts it raises about whether the history of women's work fits neatly into the conventional stages of economic development.

Janssens, Angelique. *Family and Social Change: The Household as a Process in an Industrializing Community*. Cambridge, 1993. A case study of the effects of economic change on an industrializing community, combining demographic and economic data in an interesting and illuminating way. It is notable for its excellent theoretical introduction.

Pinchbeck, Ivy. *Women Workers and the Industrial Revolution, 1750–1850*. London, 1930, 1981. A classic contribution in the English empirical tradition, remarkable for its range and detail. Pinchbeck's vision is of a heterogeneous female experience in which women's specialization in the home brought benefits as well as costs.

Richards, Eric. "Women in the British Economy since about 1700, an Interpretation." *History* 59 (1974), 337–357. A seminal article that introduces the idea of the long-run U-shaped trend in female labor force participation.

Rose, Sonya O. *Limited Livelihoods: Gender and Class in Nineteenth Century England*. London, 1992. A contribution from a historical sociologist, particularly useful for its focus on cultural factors.

Ross, Ellen. *Love and Toil, Motherhood in Outcast London, 1870–1918*. Oxford, 1993. A recent contribution looking at the history of women's work from the standpoint of the home and motherhood. It is notable also for its use of autobiography and oral history.

Rotella, Elise. "Women's Labor Force Participation and the Decline of the Family Economy in the United States." *Explorations in Economic History* 17 (1980), 95–117. A good neoclassical analysis.

Sharpe, Pamela, ed. *Women's Work: The English Experience, 1650–1914*. London, 1998. A collection of important recent articles on women's experience, with an excellent introduction and commentary.

Simonton, Deborah. *A History of European Women's Work, 1700 to the Present*. London, 1998. A comparative survey of European experience, especially interesting for its discussion of training and the gendering of skills.

Snell, Keith. *Annals of the Laboring Poor, Social Change, and Agrarian England, 1660–1900*. Cambridge, 1985. One of the few economic history classics to include women's experience. Snell's work has been enormously influential in suggesting that the commercialization of the agricultural sector reduced women's economic opportunities.

Tilly, Louise A., and Joan Scott. *Women, Work, and Family*. New York, 1978. An influential book that extends Alice Clark's framework relating women's work to stages in the development of the family and the economy.

JANE HUMPHRIES

WOOD AS FUEL. It may seem bold to assert wood's crucial place in human evolution. But consider: trees have provided the material to make fire, the key to humanity's domination over all other animals. It allowed *Homo erectus*, from which *Homo sapiens* evolved, to migrate from their warm niche in equatorial Africa to lands throughout the Old World, where heat from fire made these colder climates habitable. Increasing the range of habitat gave humanity better odds for survival. Light from wood fires permitted *Homo erectus* to work after nightfall. Hence, the discovery freed humanity from the strictures of the diurnal cycle. Wood fires also enhanced humanity's access to food. With torches, *Homo erectus* hunted at night. This gave them the element of surprise in killing diurnal animals and added nocturnal animals to their diet. Fire also widened the types of available food, freeing them from the constraints of the hunt. Vegetable matter, such as tubers, when cooked over fire, became edible. A diet based on local plants promoted population stability, as humans no longer had to follow migrating herds to eat. A wider choice of food enhanced survival and proliferation. Fire also provided humans with greater security. They could safely live indoors out of harm's way now, having the means of illumination. Lighting warded off nocturnal predators. It also lessened the chance of stepping on venomous snakes or tripping over rocks by improving vision at night, Wood fires changed not only the social evolution of humanity but also its physical development. Eating food softened by cooking led to smaller molars. Although many animals like chimpanzees and otters have used tools as aids, no other animal except the human genus beginning with *Homo erectus* has ever built fires.

The Importance of Wood Fuel for Civilization. Only by cooking grains over wood-fueled fires do grains become edible. The development of wood-fueled fires, and thus cooked foods, enabled the agricultural revolution of the last 10,000 years. In charcoal-fueled kilns, potters turned earth into durable ceramics in which goods could be stored and shipped. Providing an efficient means of storage stimulated trade on land and sea. Charcoal-fueled fires also gave humanity the capability to extract metal from ore, resulting in tools and weaponry so revolutionary that historians categorize society's evolution according to the dominant metal in use at the time. Wood fuel, in fact, is the unsung hero of the technological developments that brought humanity from a bone-and-stone culture to the Industrial Revolution.

Wood Fuel Appreciated. Lucretius, probably the most scientifically oriented thinker of antiquity, believed that the discovery of fire made civilization possible. He conjectured that the technique of metallurgy was born when great fires "devoured the high forests and thoroughly heated the earth," melting metal embedded in rock. When people saw the hardened metal, "the thought then came to them," according to Lucretius, "that these pieces could be made liquid by heat and cast into the form and shape of anything, and then by hammering, could be drawn into the form of blades as sharp and thin as one pleased, so they

might equip themselves with tools." Tools, in turn, Lucretius remarked, made forestry and carpentry possible, enabling humans "to cut forests, hew timber smooth, and even fashion it with auger, chisel and gouge." By this process, in Lucretius' opinion, civilization emerged.

Ibn Khaldun, writing in the fourteenth century CE, discussed the crucial role wood fuel played in the world of Islam. "God made all created things useful for man," he wrote in *The Muqaddimah*, his major work, "so as to supply his necessities and needs. Trees belong among these things. They give humanity its fuel to make fires, which it needs to survive."

The English of the sixteenth and seventeenth centuries also recognized the crucial role of wood fuel in their lives. Gabriel Plattes, writing in 1639, observed that all "tools and instruments are made of wood and iron. Upon weighing the relative importance of the two materials, he chose wood over iron because without wood for fuel, "no iron can be provided."

Examples of Civilization's Use of Wood Fuel. Mycenaean Greece attained an unprecedented level of material growth during the late Bronze Age. Yet it did not have much copper to make sufficient quantities of bronze, the essential metal of the time. To sustain the booming economy of the Mycenaean states, abundant and reliable sources of copper had to be found. Fortunately, there was one area close by, Cyprus, that had lots of copper ore and plenty of wood with which to smelt and refine it. In response to this need, the Cypriots smelted as much copper ore as they possibly could for the overseas market. But the growing demand put a great burden on the island's woods, as charcoal was the fuel for smelting and refining copper. One hundred and twenty pine trees were required to prepare 6 tons of charcoal needed to produce one ingot of copper, deforesting almost four acres. Underwater archaeologists found on board a Bronze Age shipwreck some two hundred ingots of copper that had been mined and smelted in Cyprus. The production of just this shipload cost the island almost twenty-four thousand pine trees. The lively commerce in ingots during the fourteenth and thirteenth centuries BCE surely consisted of many such shipments and the concomitant deforestation of a large expanse of woodlands. The industry's consumption of wood deforested about 4 to 5 square miles of woods a year. Another 4 or 5 square miles of forest were cut to supply fuel for heating and cooking and for other industries such as pottery works and lime kilns. The cumulative effect of deforestation on such a scale must have been felt quite soon on an island of only 3,600 square miles.

In ancient Greece, the silver smelted at Laurion paid for the Athenian fleet that defeated the Persians at Salamis. To extract the silver from ore at Laurion required the burning of more than twenty-four million pines. So much fuel had to be used that barges full of trees sailed from Thrace to Attica to smelt the silver ore.

The Roman treasury gained perhaps its largest supply of bullion from the silver mines of Iberia. Its accumulation of wealth was accomplished at great expense to the Iberian forests. An army of lumberjacks had to be employed to keep the smelting furnaces fed with charred logs of holm oak. To the north, the Anglo-Roman iron industry consumed around 500 square miles of forest. The Romans also burned whole tree trunks to keep the temperature of their baths' sweating rooms above 71°C and not allow the air temperature in the warm baths to drop below 54°C. To keep Rome's nine hundred baths operating, the Roman government founded a guild with sixty ships at their disposal, whose sole responsibility was supplying wood for heating the baths. Usually, the ships had to make wood runs as far as North Africa and France.

In the sixteenth century, the English iron industry, centered in Sussex, consumed about 117,000 cords of wood each year. By the 1700s, the iron industry had deforested such a large area of southeastern England that the iron masters had to ration the amount of iron ore they could smelt. To increase iron production required learning to smelt ore with coal without adding its impurities to the finished metal. By discovering how to make coal as close to charcoal as possible, the English freed themselves from the constraints of dwindling forests and began the Industrial Revolution, an age that has qualitatively separated people living since the middle of the nineteenth century from the rest of history.

The American experience in the nineteenth century demonstrates the overwhelming quantity of wood burned for fuel compared with the number chopped down for building. Between 1810 and 1867, almost five billion cords had been consumed for fuel in fireplaces, industrial furnaces, steamboats, and railroads, whereas only 10 percent of that amount went to build houses, ships, railroads, bridges, wagons, waterwheels, and other objects.

Today, still half of the wood cut throughout the world goes for fuel. Eighty percent of all wood consumed for fuel occurs in the developing world. In fact, the majority of people in the developing world depend on wood as the primary energy source. Charcoal and firewood in the Cameroons, for example, account for 80 percent of all energy consumption in that country. The demand for firewood and charcoal is also increasing as the population climbs. In Africa, the amount of wood consumed for energy purposes rose from 250 million cubic meters in 1970 to 502 million cubic meters in 1994. In Latin America, too, the vast majority of the rural population uses wood as the primary fuel. The true danger to the forests of the developing world is that growing numbers of people exploit local forests, threatening their viability and forcing the popu-

lace to search greater distances for wood fuel. In general, one-half hectare of forestland can sustain one person; today, as many as fifteen people in developing countries are relying on one hectare of forestland. Such overexploitation will surely cause local supplies to quickly diminish, forcing people to seek wood in more distant forests. Demand for wood and charcoal in expanding urban areas of the developing world has introduced a new and growing problem: the industrialization of acquiring firewood and charcoal. Instead of individuals fanning neighboring woods to cut down trees for fuel, well-capitalized charcoal dealers search throughout the countryside for supplies. Bangkok's five million citizens obtain a large amount of their charcoal in this fashion from forests throughout Thailand. There is no question that as the population in the developing world grows, so too will the demand for firewood and charcoal, and deforestation will continue to accelerate.

[*See also* Forests and Deforestation; Timber and Logging Industry; *and* Woodworking Industry.]

BIBLIOGRAPHY

Bryant, D., D. Nielsen, and L. Tangley. *The Last Frontier Forests: Ecosystems and Economies on the Edge.* Washington, D.C., 1997.
Myers, N. "The Present Status and Future Prospects of Tropical Moist Forests." *Environmental Conservation* 7.2 (1980), 101–114.
Perlin, J. *A Forest Journey: The Role of Wood in the Development of Civilization.* Cambridge, Mass., 1991.
Richards, J., and R. Tucker, eds. *World Deforestation in the Twentieth Century.* Durham, 1988.

JOHN PERLIN

WOODWORKING INDUSTRY. The manufacture of, and the trade in, finished wooden components—either for other producers or as finished goods for consumers—has been central to human society. From its earliest days, woodworking has developed specialized operations that remain important and distinct. Prehistoric wooden items included spears, bows, arrows, boxes, traps, and other hunting and storage objects. Neolithic woodworkers produced substantial items—from boats and ships to houses and furnishings. The toolmakers produced items on a modest scale, but their skills, from planing to wheelmaking, from carpentry to turning and barrelmaking, have remained important. Highly specialized aspects of woodworking were developed worldwide, with the rise of civilization, including joining, dovetailing, veneering, and decorative inlays. In time, there were blockmakers, coachbuilders, gunstockers, musical-instrument makers, plowmakers, shinglemakers, and coffin builders. In addition to these, there are specialized scientific, transport, art, and engineering instrument makers.

One of the most ancient and important of the woodworking industries was that of shipwright. From c. 2500 BCE, wooden ships were built for trade and warfare in the

Mediterranean Sea, the Red Sea, the Indian Ocean, and the China Seas; various boats, canoes, kayaks, and seagoing rafts were used in the Americas and the South Pacific. They all remained an essential component of sea trade into the early twentieth century. Even older are the woodworking crafts associated with the creation of structures and equipping them. For centuries, the carpenter was the key worker in the construction of the frameworks of buildings. Today, a vestige of this connection exists in the preparation of shuttering or the forms used to cast concrete for modern buildings. For the detailed components of building, carpenters still install the internal woodwork, including doors, windows, flooring, roofs, and all the major construction work on houses.

The craft of joinery was established during the fourteenth century in Europe; it evolved as a more precise and careful version of carpentry. As it developed, it took two forms: one associated with internal woodwork and the other with furniture making, later called cabinetmaking. In the case of cabinetmaking, the development of skills from simple board construction to the demanding veneering and marquetry processes demonstrated responses to changing social patterns. Initially, while furniture was mainly utilitarian, nailed and boarded construction methods, based on the carpenter's experience in building houses, were sufficient. When demand for a more sophisticated interior grew, the joiner, working with woodworking tools and jointing methods, was able to provide furniture and woodwork with a finer standard of finish, often augmented by carved or turned work. During the sixteenth century, the revival of marquetry and cabinetmaking skills met the demand for highly decorative furniture that used increasingly rare timbers and other materials, often from Europe's new colonies in Africa, Asia, and the New World. By the eighteenth century, demand for furniture and furnishings increased, and the trade was organized in a sophisticated way, using imported exotic timbers, skilled woodworkers, and a wide range of ancillary crafts in a network of suppliers. During the nineteenth century, furniture making began to be industrialized in both Europe and the United States, especially in particular aspects, such as chairmaking. The example of the Thonet brothers in Austria and eastern Europe is a good example; by establishing factories close to timber supplies and working with semiskilled labor, they used simple but very effective jig mechanisms to produce large batches of a wide variety of chairs. These were made to be disassembled and so could be easily packed and exported. The business soon became international and spawned many imitators.

The development of the spoked wooden wheel must rank as one of the great human achievements, an outstanding example of woodworking skills that met the

WOODWORKING. Palace construction in progress, with several carpenters working in the foreground, India, Mughal dynasty, circa 1600. (Victoria and Albert Museum, London/Art Resource, NY)

needs of a wide range of other businesses. Known from about 2000 BCE, the chariot wheel was light but strong and was an advance over solid or two-part wheels. The wheelwright worked in conjunction with the wainwright (cart builder) and, later, the coach builder. Wheelwrights were an important part of the transport business until the beginning of the twentieth century—by that time, many of the processes were mechanized for the early automobile industry. Coopering, the craft of wooden barrelmaking is another example of a specialized industry that developed its own range of tools and skills. It was well established by Roman times, and it remained an important trade for making the casks that stored and delivered wet or dry goods in bulk well into the twentieth century. The craft of turning, practiced continuously in northern Europe, dated from pre-Roman times. The high point of the turner's craft was in the late seventeenth century, but turners remained important as suppliers to carpenters, cabinetmakers, and upholsterers, as well as to producers of a wide range of tools, implements, and household objects (including brushes, poles, and tableware).

Woodworking was based on the individual skills of artisans who either specialized or generalized; that division often depended more on locational factors than on skills. In towns, the division of labor was seen in the growing range of specialist woodworkers, but in rural areas, the general woodworker was often the norm well into the nineteenth century. Developing markets and new technologies then supported changes in industrial organization. Machines gradually changed the specialization of the artisan to a machinist and allowed for developments in specialized production, batch production, and mechanized processing. The industrialization was most rapid in the United States, where great natural resources, fewer restrictions, fewer master craftsmen and skilled workers, and an ever-increasing population encouraged invention, economies of scale, and machine production from the early nineteenth century. The development of a transport infrastructure, especially the railroad, ensured success for woodworking factories that moved west toward new sources of supply, away from the old established centers of New England and the Atlantic seaboard.

The factors associated with the location of trades are especially relevant to the woodworking industries. In the United States from the 1850s to the 1920s, New York State was a leading producer of furniture. The development of new timber resources in the Midwest ensured that Michigan, Illinois, and Indiana came to prominence, with Grand Rapids, Michigan, then the most famous furniture center. By the end of the nineteenth century, North Carolina developed furniture manufacture (again based on natural resources and inexpensive labor); today it remains a world center for the industry. In Europe, mechanization generally came later for woodworking, and although there were a number of large-scale enterprises, the survival of small workshops remained a European specialty trade well into the second half of the twentieth century. Small-scale furniture-making businesses that emphasize craft skills still operate successfully in Europe and North America.

Much of the development in most aspects of woodworking has depended on associated improvements in tools and machines. Many machines have been developed to apply a power source to a hand-operated model or to increase its size and flexibility. Early attempts at mechanizing the woodworking processes were to replicate the "to-and-fro" motion of the human arm. Later, the application of the rotatory principle enabled a new generation of machines to be developed, thus speeding the processes. In all woodworking industries, the first operation is timber conversion, and this was the first to be mechanized. The original method of converting a log to boards was by pit-sawing or trestle sawing. In England, that remained the most common method until the early-to-mid nineteenth century, when steam-powered sawmills were fully developed. As early as the seventeenth century, the growth of the timber trade from Europe and North America meant that the value of sawmills, operated by running water and built near stands of timber, had been well established. Soon, it was the only practical way to supply the increasing demand for cut boards. By the late eighteenth century, a number of patents were granted for woodworking machinery that were designed to replicate the basic woodworking processes of cutting, planing, shaping, and so on. Initially, these were intended for naval or military use, especially for the large-scale production of regularly shaped items. The 1791 and 1793 woodworking patents of British engineer Samuel Bentham, and Marc Brunel's successful plans for the British navy's blockmaking machinery at Portsmouth, as well as American inventor Thomas Blanchard's U.S. patent for producing rifle butts all testify to that. Despite the initial military purpose, their success meant that the machines were soon developed and adopted by the building trades and, later, by most parts of the woodworking industry.

In many situations, timber has not only been a scarce resource, it has also been inadequate on its own for some industry end uses—so a variety of composite wood products were employed. Such need created materials like veneer for cabinetmaking, laminates and plywood for chairmaking and the building of early airplanes, and particleboard and fiberboard for inexpensive furnishings. These composites are more stable and regular than timber (each tree species has its own peculiarities as to grain, curing time, and checking [cracking]), and they can be manipulated in a variety of ways not available with wood in its natural state. Composites have become of great economic importance to the woodworking industries. At the beginning of the twenty-first century, although there is still a craft element in woodworking, most work is based in factories that use the full benefits of scientific development in processing wood, including synthetic glues, panel products, laser cutting, and the integration of wood products with other materials. Much wood is grown on tree farms, as a renewable resource, but some wood is still being cut from South American, Asian, and African rain forests (both legally and illegally), to supply specialty needs for exotic hardwoods. Large, old street and garden trees are also sometimes sold or stolen worldwide for such specialties, including black walnut, hickory, boxwood, tuliptrees, oak, ash, maples, and various fruitwoods.

[*See also* Timber and Logging Industry.]

BIBLIOGRAPHY

Ettema, M. J. "Technological Innovation and Design Economics in Furniture Manufacture." *Winterthur Portfolio* 16 (1981).

Hindle, Brooke. *Material Culture of the Wooden Age.* Tarrytown, N.Y., 1981.

Kebabian P. B., and W. C. Lipke. *Tools and Technologies of America's Wooden Age.* Burlington, Vt., 1979.

Louw, H. "The Mechanisation of Architectural Woodwork in Britain from the Late Eighteenth to the Early Twentieth Century and its Practical, Social and Aesthetic Implications." *Construction History* 8 (1992), 21–54; 9 (1993), 27–50.

Nicolle, G. *The Woodworking Trades, A Select Bibliography.* Plymouth, U.K., 1993.

Oliver, J. L. *The Development and Structure of the Furniture Industry.* Oxford, 1966.

Sims, W. *200 Years of History and Evolution of Woodworking Machinery.* London, 1985.

Woodworking Techniques before A.D. 1500: Papers Presented to a Symposium at Greenwich in September 1980. Oxford, 1982.

CLIVE EDWARDS

WOOL INDUSTRY
[*This entry contains three subentries, a historical overview and discussions of technological change and industrial organization, markets, and trade.*]

Historical Overview

The manufacturing of woolen fabrics was, no doubt, an important economic activity in ancient Egypt, and during Hellenistic, and Roman times, but no evidence exists for the emergence of a large-scale, export-oriented urban or rural wool industry. The few documents imply that woolens were produced mainly for local markets. Only a few references to a trade in woolens for a broader regional market have been found: for example, sales of imported mantles on the *agora* of Athens, the production of woolens at Padua for sale on the Roman market, and woolens produced for export in northern Gaul (Amiens and Arras) during late antiquity. A similar pattern exists for the early Middle Ages; on the whole, production in Europe remained local. Only scarce evidence points to production for a wider (regional) market, in particular in regions where abbeys or lords began concentrating production in workshops (*gynecea*) on their domains. Even in such workshops, weavers operated the upright loom, known as the warp-weighed loom, in the same way as their predecessors for many centuries. The fabrics produced also remained similar to those of antiquity, exhibiting the chief characteristics of worsteds: the lozenge-twill or diamond-twill weaves, rather flat and light. In documents of the ninth century CE, mention is made of a long-distance export-trade of "Frisian" woolens—but no details on their structure are available.

Middle Ages. During the eleventh and twelfth centuries in Europe, however, technological change, organizational progress, product innovation, and a commercial revolution advanced the production of woolens and converted the industry into a major export sector. The traditional, relatively cheap, worsted-type fabrics of northwestern Europe became the object of an important long-distance trade to northern and eastern Europe, and still more spectacularly, to the Mediterranean and the Middle East. The introduction of the horizontal loom was an important factor in the export expansion, but more important were the declining transaction and communication costs, because of improved security and better juridical protection throughout Europe. Also crucial was the concentration of production into towns, which allowed for a more efficient division of labor. Originally, production was concentrated in some ancient and in many new towns in Picardy, Artois, Hainaut, and Flanders. The trade was initiated by merchants of the producing areas, organized in urban and interurban guilds and *hansas* (trade associations). Foreign merchants then took over the bulk of the trade. Merchants from the port cities of the German Hanseatic League increasingly controlled distribution in northern and eastern Europe (to Novgorod in Russia) and many Italian merchants crossed the Alps to visit the Champagne Fairs in France. There, they purchased large quantities of northwest European woolens (says, serges, and other worsted-type fabrics), which they distributed with an astonishing dynamism throughout the whole Mediterranean and Black Sea area.

Product innovation was another motor behind the fundamental changes in the European woolen industry. The introduction of the horizontal loom seems to have favored the emergence, in northwestern Europe, of a new type of woolen fabric: the standardized, heavily fulled, felted (pressed) and shorn woolens. The new product—woven from a selection of short-stapled fibers and characterized by a labor-intensive finishing-process—had a great potential for improved quality, especially when woven from extra fine English wools on a horizontal "broad" loom. The new loom was developed slowly in northern Europe from the original horizontal loom, and it made possible the weaving of "broadcloth," having a width of about 3 meters (9 feet). The new cloth (later to be called cloth from the "Old" Draperies) was gradually traded to the northern and southern markets alongside the generally less expensive worsted-type fabrics (later to be called fabrics of the "Light" Draperies).

The economic rents gained from the successful export expansion of both types of wool-based fabrics generated a trend toward imitation in northwestern Europe, as well as outside the area. In northwestern Europe, export-oriented textile centers soon emerged in the cities of Brabant, the Rhineland, the Meuse Valley, Normandy, England, and somewhat later in Holland. Beyond this area, similar urban textile centers emerged in the regions closest to the Mediterranean markets, such as Catalonia, Aragon, Languedoc, Provence, Lombardy, Tuscany, and South Germany, many also imitating the established textiles of northwestern Europe. Another trend in each region was the spread of production from the original cities or large towns into smaller towns and villages—even the transfer of the whole production process from urban to rural areas.

From the 1290s and, in particular, during the early 1300s, warfare and piracy in Europe and the Mediterranean region came to overshadow the commercial revolution of the previous centuries. The Italian trading states of Venice, Genoa, and Florence tried to maintain their commerce by sending heavily armed convoys of galleys north to Bruges and London, but without lasting success. Transaction and communication costs then increased so substantially that the mass export of cheap worsted-type fabrics from northwestern Europe to the south, to Baltic parts, and to other Hanseatic-zones virtually vanished. Many northern textile towns reacted to that crisis by focusing on the increased production of the heavily fulled, felted shorn woolens of the Old Drapery sector, which had higher value-to-weight ratios; they also improved their quality by rigorously enforcing high standards in fulling, shearing, dyeing, and the use of the finer English wools. That strategy made the product ultraluxurious and more expensive; but the northern towns hoped that the relative inelasticity of demand for such products would safeguard their export positions. Such expectations were met to a certain extent and the luxury segment of the Old Drapery sector survived the crisis relatively well for many more decades. Other factors helped—in particular, Flemish and Brabant producers took advantage of their sovereign's debasement policies to reduce real labor costs. But the reductions in real incomes generated, in the longer run, social revolts there; if successful, the revolts led to higher wage rates, higher production costs, unemployment, and a decline in the Old Drapery on the continent. Disturbing in the long run were the increasing and ultimately burdensome English taxes on the export of wool, which the kings levied as the principal means of financing their many wars against France (Hundred Years' War, 1337–1453). At the same time, this taxation policy, by exempting domestic producers, stimulated the recovery and expansion of the Old Drapery within England, in both towns and villages. It would eventually grow into the fierce and fatal competitor of the traditional continental urban draperies.

Some small textile towns on the River Leie (Lys) in West Flanders reacted to the crisis by introducing, as early as the first half of the fourteenth century, a New Drapery (*nouvelle draperie*), based on technological and technical improvements in the production processes. The New Drapery towns produced, as did the Old Drapery towns, heavily fulled and felted woolens; however, by replacing the combed wefts with carded wefts that were spun on the wheel (not by hand [drop-spindle]), the felting potential of the fabric was increased substantially, together with a reduction in production costs. Moreover, less costly English or Scottish wools could be used; at a later stage, the then even cheaper Spanish merino wools could be used as well. The strategy proved to be successful. The Flemish towns on the River Leie saw their exports expand during the late fourteenth and early fifteenth century, a time when the Old Drapery sector was entering a phase of overall decline. Not surprisingly, in the course of the fifteenth century, many centers of Old Drapery production took over the innovations of the New Drapery, not only in the Low Countries (in Brabant, Holland, the Meuse Valley) but also in the Rhineland, Italy (Florence in Tuscany, soon to be imitated by Venice), Spain (Segovia in Castile), and France (Amiens). The English cloth industry, urban and then rural, would follow suit. (John Munro, however, contradicts the traditional myth that this English cloth industry was then primarily rural in "The Symbiosis of Towns and Textiles: Urban Institutions and the Changing Fortunes of Cloth Manufacturing in the Low Countries and England, 1270–1570," *Journal of Early Modern History: Contacts, Comparisons, Contrasts* 3.1 [February 1999], 1–74.) Once the English industry had fully assimilated the New Drapery techniques of spinning and weaving, English merchants, in particular the London Merchants Adventurers, began sending broadcloths and kerseys to Antwerp for dyeing and further processing; from there, they very successfully organized the export of the finished woolens to the rest of Europe and, via Venice and Ancona, to the Levant. The comparative advantage of English cloth was soon so overwhelming that even the urban centers of New Drapery production on the continent were unable to compete. During the late 1400s, most of the New Drapery centers joined the Old Drapery towns in their decay: only a few Dutch centers were able to resist for a time, chiefly because their merchants and shippers had built up a strong maritime and commercial position in the Hansa trade area.

The decline of the traditional Draperies (Old and New) on the continent was also affected by factors of demand. In regions with an advanced economy—the Italian states and the Low Countries—the heavy, felted woolens went out of fashion. That same trend emerged later in other European countries. The continuing expansion of traditional English cloth exports until about 1550, despite a shrinking world market for fine woolens, can be explained only because rising incomes during that era in such traditional economies as those of central and eastern Europe and the Iberian Peninsula still maintained aggregate demand. (That demand weakened at the end of the sixteenth century because of war: English export trade suffered but recovered to reach a final peak, from 1600 to 1609.)

The ultimate fall in demand for heavy woolens was contrasted by the rising demand for lighter woolens, and growing interest was also for linen underwear and for cheaper quality textiles. An increasing demand for home-decoration textiles (curtains for windows and beds, coverlets, coverings for armchairs, pillows, and benches) was another factor. During the 1400s, the new fashion had consisted of a "resurrection" (according to Munro, 1994), in Artois and Flanders, of the urban Light Draperies of the 1100s and 1200s. Several towns and villages there started producing—and once again for export—a gamut of cheap says, serges, tammies, and other worsted-type fabrics of good quality, in which long-stapled combed wools predominated, and fulling was either absent or reduced to a minimum. At the same time, says from the rural or small-town Light Drapery of Hondschoote (located in the same area) gained renown. A drastic fall in European transaction and communication costs (principally from peaceful world conditions and important technical and organizational innovations in transport) made possible a forceful revival—by the land and sea—of export trade of inexpensive textiles. That success stimulated import substitution, in particular, from Italy, France, and Spain.

Sixteenth and Seventeenth Century. In the course of the sixteenth century, an entirely "New" Light Drapery emerged in several Flemish urban centers that had specialized in making the lighter textiles. They then engaged in diversifying the former Light Draperies by producing new woolen fabrics that imitated various silks (satins, velvets, or damasks); furthermore, they mixed wools with angora, camel hair, or goat hair and with other classic textile yarns, such as cotton, linen, and silk. In Hainaut, such draperies came to specialize in knitted woolen stockings. Other forms of export-oriented diversification also emerged, such as tapestries, hats and gloves, and ready-made apparel crafts. The New Light Drapery became a tremendous success, with the rise of imitation manufactures in Europe, especially in France, northern Italy, Saxony, and Silesia. In the Italian and German states, the rise of the Light and the New Light Draperies found significant support in the old regional tradition of producing mixed fabrics—in particular, fustians, using linen warps and cotton wefts. In France, import substitution emerged in the region adjacent to the Low Countries, such as Picardy (Amiens, Abbeville, Beauvais) and Champagne (Reims), but Normandy (Rouen, Elbeuf, Louviers) also emerged as an important production area. Until the end of the sixteenth century and notwithstanding this ongoing process of continental imitation, the textile towns of Flanders, Artois and Hainaut, remained the leading European exporters of the very fashionable Light and New Light Draperies, producing fabrics not only for apparel but also and increasingly for house decoration on a very large scale.

The revolt of the Low Countries, for independence from Habsburg Spain (1568–1648), changed the situation dramatically. The advanced industrial regions in the north and the south, to a large extent favorable to Protestantism, wanted to be free of Roman Catholic conservatism. After 1575, devastating military campaigns and religious terror in the South by Catholics and Protestants, pushed thousands of merchants, textile workers, and other artisans from both urban and rural homes. In Brabant, Antwerp's population fell from nearly 100,000 to 42,000 between 1568 and 1588. The weavers of the Flemish Light Drapery and New Light Drapery resettled throughout Europe; a good number of them in Protestant Holland (in Leiden and in other Dutch cities), often helping to restructure the local textile sector. The immigrant say-weavers of Hondschoote were the prime movers of industrial revival in Leiden; the export of says soon expanded there spectacularly. The export of many other fabrics of the Light Drapery, also from Leiden, turned the town—with the help of the nearby growing Amsterdam market—into the most prominent producer of textiles in Europe during the 1600s. Light Drapery could not maintain its predominance in Leiden's industrial expansion; from the 1660s, the New Light Draperies were favored (in particular those subsectors that produced the camlets—expensive, high-quality mixed wools with angora, camel hair, and goat hair). Gradually, the production of heavily fulled, felted woolens also revived, as supply and demand factors improved.

As early as the turn of the sixteenth century, some textile centers in West Flanders had sought to thwart their inevitable decline by adopting innovations in their New Drapery sector. Not only did they replace combed wefts with carded wefts, spun on the wheel (as had been the case in the New Drapery), but they also replaced combed warps with wheel-spun carded warps. Thanks to that technical innovation, West Flanders towns and villages—Armentières, Belle (Bailleul), Menen, and Nieuwkerke—were able to produce a new type of woolens, the very expensive fulled and felted *oltrafini* (ultra-fines). Those fabrics, woven with the finest wools available (not just the better-quality English wools, but the increasingly fine merino wools from Spain), were not quite as heavy as the traditional broadcloth and were considered the best of the traditional industry—true luxury goods. The Revolt of the Low Countries was disastrous for the new Flemish sector, but weavers from Belle, among others, emigrated to Leiden in Holland, there reviving the traditional Drapery on the basis of the new techniques. In Leiden, the revival of

Wool. Workers spinning and weaving wool, painting (c. 1600) by Isaac Claesz van Swanenburgh (1537–1614). (Stedelijk Museum "De Lakenhal," Leiden, Netherlands/Erich Lessing/Art Resource, NY)

exports of traditional woolens from the (New) New Drapery, during the 1650s and onward, was remarkable.

Eighteenth Century. Supply factors were, no doubt, crucial for the revival of traditional woolens, but demand should not be underestimated. The supply of silk fabrics from the Middle East and Asia and from import substitution centers in Europe (in Italy, France, Spain, Germany, the Low Countries, and England) had been enlarged so much that silk prices fell dramatically, turning silk fabrics and silk garments into the great popular fashion of the late 1600s. They were accompanied during the 1700s by the rising fashion for printed cottons (calicoes from India, then from England). The heyday of the Light and New Light Draperies was over, while the carded and felted woolens—in their new finer appearance—succeeded in making a comeback, especially for use in coats and capes. The urban production of these standardized woolens became more vulnerable to competition than did Light and New Light Draperies. Leiden quickly relocated the spinning and weaving of its woolens to rural areas, to the Tilburg area (Brabant) and the region along the Vesdre (the rural triangle between Eupen, Verviers, and Aachen). After a time, some towns that were within that triangle or at its periphery also took over Leiden's finishing techniques, thereby promoting its position of leadership in the European export production of traditional woolens (of the [New] New Drapery) during the eighteenth century.

After Holland, England was the second area in which a large-scale restructuring of the wool sector took place during the seventeenth century. At the end of the sixteenth century, Flemish Protestant weavers had settled not only in Protestant Holland but also in Protestant England, in large numbers, mainly in East Anglia (particularly Norwich). There, they introduced the Flemish techniques of the Light and New Light Draperies (which misleadingly would receive in English historiography the name "New Draperies," a terminology not used here, to avoid misunderstanding). The English Light and New Light Draperies became a very great success; by 1700, the bays, says, Norwich stuffs, perpetuanas, serges, and other light or mixed fabrics provided almost 60 percent of English textile exports by value, a market share that would rise in the following decades. Yet the sector soon faced increasing competition from the cotton calicoes, which weakened substantially the dynamism of its previous expansion. A similar development occured in the hosiery sector. Partly on the basis of William Lee's invention of a mechanical knitting frame at the end of the sixteenth century, the production of fine English worsted stockings had expanded throughout the seventeenth century; but competition from silk stockings during the eighteenth century halted that expansion. The development of the traditional woolens industry proved to be most expansive during the eighteenth century, after a twofold restructuring process. First, in the English West Country, by assimilating the technical innovations of the Belle–Armentières region (the [New] New Drapery) during the seventeenth century, England managed to maintain a satisfying level of exports, with the help of the Levant Company, and thus chiefly to the Ottoman Empire. Mainly in northern England, in the West Riding of Yorkshire, did a real change occur—a combination of the Flemish techniques of the (New) New Drapery and some home-bred innovations in preparation and finishing—which enabled that sector to take full advantage of the eighteenth-century fashion for fine, felted woolens that reappeared in Europe. Their production, and that of worsteds, too—both for the home market and for overseas exports—expanded rapidly.

In France and Germany, the fine-woolens sector also grew during the eighteenth century. In Germany, growth was strongest in Thuringia and Saxony. In France, the establishment of royal manufactories to foster import substitution was a crucial factor of growth; in Languedoc, fifteen such manufactories were set up to produce fine, felted fabrics from Spanish merino wools. In the north of France, the royal manufacture of Sedan was another example; the rural region near Lille focused on cheap imitations.

Industrial Revolution to Nineteenth Century. The Industrial Revolution in England was in many aspects a turning point for the wool-textile industry. Although some early inventions were designed for that industry, their first large-scale applications, and those of later inventions, were not in mechanizing wool-spinning—but, from the 1760s in spinning cotton. Wool-spinning was mechanized on a general level only in the 1820s and 1830s. Even when mechanized, the wool-spinning machines had to work more slowly than those spinning cotton (to keep from breaking the yarn). Mechanical spinning of long-staple, combed wool was also easier than spinning short-staple carded wool. General mechanization of spinning worsted yarn, therefore, preceded the definitive mechanization of spinning woolen yarn, thus giving a comparative advantage to the worsted sector. In the new cotton industry, mechanization of weaving was also much ahead in comparison with the wool industry. In the West Riding of Yorkshire, England, the transition to power looms in the worsteds sector took place only in the 1840s; and in the woolens sector, in the 1850s. The long-term effects of those time lags were disastrous for the wool industry. After so many centuries as the predominant textile industry, it lost that position to the upstart cotton industry. A similar development occurred in British overseas exports. A second effect was the reemergence of worsteds as the dominant sector of the wool industry at the expense of heavyweight woolens.

On the continent, Belgium took the lead in mechanizing its wool industry; at the end of the eighteenth century, the English engineer John Cockerill, successfully built a first set of mechanized spinning machines for a Verviers woolens firm. During the early 1800s, Cockerill and others built similar machines for firms in the Verviers region and in France; however, the woolens sector was not best suited for mechanized spinning. From the 1820s onward, therefore, the spread of mechanized wool spinning, especially in France, accelerated mainly via the worsteds sector, thus making worsteds the leader in the wool industry. Mechanization of weaving followed a similar trend; but the transition from hand looms to power looms was extremely slow—in Reims, Roubaix-Tourcoing, Saint-Quentin, and Elbeuf it took place only from the 1850s onward; in the luxury sectors of Sedan, Louviers, and Paris, even later. Despite this late transition, France would maintain its export position, mainly by diversifying its production and specializing in the finest gamuts of merino worsteds.

In Germany, mechanized spinning began and spread from the 1840s in the woolens sector—in the Aachen region, Saxony, and Silesia; but growth was not impressive. In contrast, mechanized weaving in the second half of the nineteenth century, and with the help of extra imports of British yarn, became a flourishing export industry in both the woolens and worsteds sectors.

Twentieth Century Seen with time and a global perspective, the future of the wool industry was not as bright as its mechanization had suggested. Although technological progress continued in the wool sector, the spectacular adoption of the chemical industry's synthetic fibers during the twentieth century, plus the evolution of fashion toward a more comfortable, casual appearance, weakened the relative position of wool still further. Only during the world wars was wool in demand—for uniforms and blankets. At the end of the twentieth century, wool represented just 4 percent of total world consumption of textile fibers. With global warming, cotton, linen, and silk have become the natural fibers of choice—cool against the skin and easy to launder.

[*See also* Clothing Trades; Sheep and Goats; *and* Textiles.]

BIBLIOGRAPHY

Aerts, E., and J. H. Munro, eds. *Textiles of the Low Countries in European Economic History.* Proceedings of the Tenth International Economic History Congress, vol. 19. Leuven, 1990.

Ashley, W. *The Early History of the English Woollen Industry.* Baltimore, 1887.

Boone, M., and W. Prevenier, eds. *Drapery Production in the Late Medieval Low Countries: Markets and Strategies for Survival (14th–16th Centuries).* Louvain, 1993.

Chorley, P. "The Evolution of the Woolens Industries, 1300–1800." In *The New Draperies in the Low Countries and England, 1300–1800,* edited by N. Harte and D. Coleman, pp. 7–33. Oxford, 1997.

Coornaert, E. *La draperie-sayetterie d'Hondschoote, XIVe–XVIIIe siècles.* Paris, 1930.

Doren, A. *Studien aus der Florentiner Wirtschaftsgeschichte.* Stuttgart, 1901.

Freudenberger, H. *The Industrialization of a Central European City: Brno and the Fine Woollen Industry in the 18th Century.* London, 1980.

Harte, N., and D. Coleman, eds. *The New Draperies in the Low Countries and England, 1300–1800.* Oxford, 1997.

Heaton, H. *The Yorkshire Woollen and Worsted Industries from the Earliest Times to the Industrial Revolution.* Oxford, 1965.

Iradiel Murrugarén, P. *Evilucion de la industria textil castellana en los siglos XIII–XVI.* Salamanca, 1975.

Israel, J. *Dutch Primacy in World Trade, 1585–1740.* Oxford, 1989.

Jenkins, D., ed. *Cambridge History of Textiles.* Cambridge, 2001.

Kerridge, E. *Textile Manufactures in Early Modern England.* Manchester, 1985.

Landes, D. S. *The Unbound Prometheus. Technological Change and Industrial Development in Western Europe from 1750 to the Present.* Cambridge, 1969.

Lebrun, P. *L'industrie de la laine à Verviers pendant le XVIIIe et le début du XIXe siècle.* Paris, 1948.

Mann, J. de Lacey. *The Cloth Industry in the West of England, 1640–1880.* Oxford, 1971.

Markovitch, T. J. *L'industrie française au XVIIIe siècle: L'industrie lainière à la fin du règne de Louis XIV et sous la Régence.* Geneva, 1968.

Milward, A., and S. B. Saul. *The Economic Development of Continental Europe, 1780–1870.* London, 1973.

Milward, A., and S. B. Saul. *The Development of the Economies of Continental Europe, 1850–1914.* London, 1977.

Mokyr, J. *The British Industrial Revolution: An Economic Perspective.* Boulder, 1993.

Munro, J. H. *Textiles, Towns, and Trade: Essays in the Economic History of Late-Medieval England and the Low Countries.* Aldershot, U.K., 1994.

Ponting, K. G. *The Woollen Industry of South-West England: An Industrial, Economic and Technical Survey.* Bath, 1971.

Posthumus, N. W., *Geschiedenis van de Leidsche lakenindustrie.* 3 vols. The Hague, 1908–1939.

Rahn Phillips, C., and W. Phillips. *Spain's Golden Fleece: Wool Production and the Wool Trade from the Middle Ages to the Nineteenth Century.* Baltimore and London, 1997.

Sella, D. *Commerci e industria a Venezia nel secolo XVII.* Venice and Rome, 1961.

Spallanzani, M., ed. *La lana come materia prima: I fenomeni della sua produzione e circolazione nei secoli XIII–XVIII.* Florence, 1974.

Spallanzani, M., ed. *Produzione, commercio e consumo dei panni di lana (nei secoli XII–XVIII).* Florence, 1976.

Thompson, I. A. A., and B. Yun Casalilla, eds. *The Castilian Crisis of the Seventeenth Century: New Perspectives on the Economic and Social History of Seventeenth-Century Spain.* Cambridge, 1994.

Van der Wee, H., ed. *The Rise and Decline of Urban Industries in Italy and the Low Countries: Late Middle Ages–Early Modern Times.* Louvain, 1988.

Van Uytven, R. *Production and Consumption in the Low Countries, 13th–16th Centuries.* Ashgate, 2001.

Vries, Jan de, and A. Van der Woude. *The First Modern Economy. Success, Failure, and Perseverance of the Dutch Economy, 1500–1815.* Cambridge, 1997.

HERMAN VAN DER WEE

Technological Change

The history of technological development in the wool industry is primarily one of constant adaptation. Because of the delicacy of the wool fiber, even when major technical or scientific discoveries were made, considerable time and tinkering were necessary to modify those discoveries so that machinery could replace the feel and flexibility of the human hand. Before the eighteenth century there were very few major technical breakthroughs in wool production, beyond the much earlier, medieval innovations in wool preparation (carding), spinning (spinning wheel), weaving (the horizontal treadle loom), and fulling (water-powered fulling mills), principally achieved during the eleventh, twelfth, and thirteenth centuries. From the later Middle Ages to the eve of the modern Industrial Revolution, the history of technology in this industry is one of gradual progression, within the context of well-established basic principles, and was aimed primarily at diversifying product.

In the eighteenth century technological experimentation within the industry became much swifter, although with some exceptions subsequent innovation was not fast. Much of that experimentation, and ultimate innovation where successful, was generated by the new technology of cotton manufacture and attempted to adapt machinery, invented to process the stronger cotton fiber, to cope with the more delicate wool fiber. Some technology was developed specifically for the needs of the wool industry, which in many respects was facing pressures similar to those in the cotton and other textile industries in the quest to expand production, to reduce bottlenecks in the sequence of processes, and to reduce costs in a more competitive marketplace. Mechanization, however, when it did take over, rarely altered the long-established principles of processing wool into cloth. The modern technological revolution, which started in the early eighteenth century, lasted for a little over a hundred years. From the late nineteenth to the mid-twentieth century there was a lull in significant invention, but the 1950s heralded further experimentation and change.

The processes of wool manufacture can be seen as encompassing five stages. In the first stage—the preparation of the wool—the fleece of the sheep is converted into individual fibers in a condition ready for spinning. The wool was sorted to divide it into qualities, a process that had always been carried out by hand: willeying to break up the fleece, particularly where it was heavy with impurities; scouring to remove the natural grease or lanolin; drying; picking and burring to remove any foreign matter from the wool; and blending to combine wools according to the requirements of the end product. This stage of preparation was entirely carried out manually until the nineteenth century.

Of various new processing techniques developed in the nineteenth century, the most significant were willeying machines to break up the wool from the fleece and acid carbonizing techniques to remove extraneous vegetable matter. An automatic scouring machine, invented by John Petrie, was available from the 1850s.

The second stage in wool processing is the conversion of fiber to yarn. Here the methods vary somewhat according to the length of fiber, which mainly determined whether the wool was destined for woolen or worsted manufacture. Broadly, the distinctions between the two are that woolen cloth is made from shorter fibers, scribbled and carded to disentangle them, twisted while drafting, and fulled after weaving to provide greater strength. Worsted cloth is made from longer fibers that have to be disentangled by combing. The longer fibers do not need to be twisted during drafting and do not require fulling.

Carding of wool was a slow hand process until carding machines were invented in England during the 1740s, separately by Daniel Bourne and Lewis Paul. Bourne's was the more successful. Richard Arkwright improved the machinery in the 1770s. In the 1790s Yorkshiremen John and Arthur Schofield started constructing wool carding machines in the United States. The machinery soon became very efficient and in the late eighteenth and early nineteenth centuries was rapidly accepted in the major centers of manufacture. Longer wool had to be combed—an even more laborious hand process that proved extremely difficult to convert to machinery. Late-eighteenth-century attempts, notably by the Rev. Edmund Cartwright, established some mechanical principles but were not commercially successful. Experimentation continued through the first half of the next century. Platt and Collier attained partial success with their machine, patented in 1827, but it was not until 1846–1856 that real progress was made. In that short period four different machines were invented, the Heilmann (otherwise known as French), Lister, Noble, and Holden combs. Each had merit for a different type of wool and was installed accordingly. They are all, with subsequent adaptations, still in use.

The major technical advances made in the eighteenth century were in spinning. The three major inventions—the jenny, the mule, and the frame—have long been celebrated as among the major inventions of the Industrial Revolution. Spinning had evolved over many centuries from the use of the painstakingly slow distaff and spindle, to the use of whorls to give twist, to the innovation of various spinning wheels—notably the great wheel in the early medieval period and the Saxony wheel from the end of the fifteenth century—and to the suggestion in 1519, by Leonardo da Vinci, of a flyer to enable continuous spinning.

The pressures to increase textile manufacture in the eighteenth century drove more experimentation. John Wyatt and Lewis Paul developed further mechanical principles, but it was James Hargreaves's spinning jenny, patented in 1770, that was initially of most benefit to the woolen industry. The machine was invented for the spinning of cotton but it proved adaptable for wool. It copied the principles of the simple wheel, drafting the yarn with twist and using many spindles, and it proved capable of spinning a level yarn from short fibers. The initial small machines were hand driven; not a great deal is known about their early innovation. However, their use was widespread in the major wool manufacturing centres by the end of the century. The spinning jenny gradually increased in size and was converted to mechanical power. The longer fiber used in the worsted industry was better able to stand the strains of mechanical spinning.

Arkwright's water frame, patented in 1769, also intended for cotton, proved difficult to convert to the spinning of worsted yarn, but gradual experimentation produced a competent machine that was being quickly adopted in the main manufacturing districts of Britain from the 1800s. Samuel Crompton's mule, which combined the drafting principles of the water frame and the spinning principles of the jenny, was also gradually adapted to cope with wool fiber. The mule, or "jack," finally used for wool spinning, was very different from the cotton mule. It was not really commercially viable until the 1830s, when it incorporated Richard Roberts's self-acting mechanism. Then it quickly superseded the jenny for woolen spinning and was used in England and on the continent of Europe for spinning softer worsted yarn.

In the United States shortages of skilled labor encouraged the development of the simpler throstle frame. In 1828 Charles Danforth of New Jersey and John Thorp of Rhode Island both patented continuous spinning devices. Danforth's "throstle" rapidly gained favor in the United States, but not in Europe. In the late nineteenth century the ring spinning frame evolved from the throstle and in the United States quickly dominated spinning. The British woolen industry continued to prefer the mule until well into the twentieth century. For worsteds, the mule, the cap frame, and the ring frame were all employed in Europe. After World War II centrifugal pot spinning, developed earlier for continuous-filament rayon yarn, found some favor in the worsted industry.

The third stage of manufacture is weaving, with the auxiliary processes of preparing the yarn for the loom. The warp required the most attention. It had to be made into hanks, strengthened through sizing to prevent breakage in the loom, transferred to the loom beam, and then threaded through the harnesses. These steps were all done by hand. Setting up the loom took a long time and accounted for a large portion of weaving costs. Handlooms gradually evolved in two forms—a horizontal loom and a vertical, or upright, loom. Warp-weighted vertical looms predominated until about the eleventh century, when the horizontal loom, operated by foot-powered treadles, became more popular in Europe.

The first great modern breakthrough in weaving was John Kay's invention of the so-called flying shuttle, a device patented in 1733 for driving the shuttle across the loom. This remarkably simple gadget improved the productivity of weavers, particularly for making broadcloth. No longer did a weaver have to move from one side of the loom to the other to throw the shuttle through the warps, or two weavers throw the shuttle to each other. The new device, which consisted of cords operating pickers at both sides of the warp to project the shuttle, enabled one weaver to operate comfortably and quickly from the center. Weaving went much more quickly. Indications are that its use was widespread by the later decades of the eighteenth century.

Applying mechanical power to weaving wool proved a considerable challenge, again because of the fragility of the wool fiber and the yarn it produced. Stronger worsted yarn was easier to work without breakage. Many rose to the challenge; a number of significant steps forward can be identified, including those by the Rev. Edmund Cartwright in the 1780s, by William Horrocks, at the beginning of the nineteenth century, and then by Richard Roberts in the 1820s. In the late 1820s enough progress had been made to make it commercially viable for the British worsted industry. But many adjustments had to be made before the power loom proved its worth over hand weaving. In woolens it was well into the second half of the nineteenth century before use of the power loom was widespread. The Jacquard loom, invented around 1801 in France by Joseph-Marie Jacquard, was systematically improved, gradually enabling fancier, more complex cloths to be woven by machine. Further technical steps in the 1890s in automatic cop changing, warp thread breakage detection, a warp let-off mechanism, and improved weft change effectively made the loom automatic and finally established its commercial advantage.

Automation of weaving-related processes continued in the twentieth and twenty-first centuries, including automatic winding machinery, invented in the United States in the 1930s, and automatic bobbin-changing mechanisms. Subsequent technical developments have significantly improved the power loom, most notably through better shuttle transmission. The rapier needle system, shuttleless weaving through air-jet transmission, and the Sulzer loom, invented in Switzerland in the 1950s, which projects the weft by means of small pellets, were the major technical, as opposed to scientific, developments in wool textile manufacture in the last century. Specialized loom technology was developed for carpet making, with the Jacquard playing a major role. Tufting machines, introduced in the 1950s, provided a much more rapid production for plainer carpets.

The fourth process is finishing the cloth according to its purpose. Technical developments were many but small over the ages, but significant steps can be identified. The use of fulling stocks, driven by water power to replicate the action of cloth walkers or stampers, dates from at least the twelfth century. That basic process remained essentially unchanged until the invention of the milling machine by John Dyer in the west of England in the 1830s. Subsequent rotary milling developments have been many, according to types of cloth, but the principles have remained broadly the same. In cloth finishing, the use of teasels to raise the nap, incorporated into the water-powered gig mill from the fifteenth century, was gradually replaced by wire-raising machines, the use of the teasle surviving longest for highest quality clothes.

Perhaps the most significant innovations in modern times have been mechanical shearing and rotary cutting machines, which began to replace cumbersome hand shears early in the nineteenth century. Many other mechanical and chemical processes have added to the complexity and range of cloth finishing, including various proofings and conditionings.

The final category of processing is dyeing, the technical development of which has been traced in great detail. Natural mineral and vegetable materials were used to color wool and cloth as far back as the Stone Age. Dyers persistently experimented with natural materials. Beginning in the nineteenth century two major dyeing discoveries affected the wool textile industry. The first, in the 1830s, discussed below, radically improved the ability to dye animal and vegetable fibers together. The other, starting in the 1850s, was the development of synthetic dyestuffs. W. H. Perkins's creation of synthetic mauve, which could be applied directly to wool without a mordant, was the first step. Synthetic acid dyes, initiated by Nicholson from 1862, improved color range. Graebe and Liebermann's synthesized alizarin, which quickly replaced madder as the source of red, was soon followed by other synthetic dyestuffs, most notably synthetic indigo, available as of 1897. These dyes improved consistency of color, color matching, and color fastness. Chemical developments in dyeing, including better mordant agents and reactive dyes, which chemically react with the fiber and improve permanency, continued through the twentieth century.

Technological development in industry normally focuses on production methods. But the wool textile industry also faced challenges in its supply of raw materials. To some extent these challenges required technical solutions. The phenomenal reduction in the price of cotton cloth, resulting from an immense increase in supply of raw cotton from across the north Atlantic and from the huge productivity growth from new manufacturing technology, widened the price gap between cotton textiles and wool textiles. The latter were severally disadvantaged, in spite of the technical improvements in preparing, spinning, weaving, and finishing wool.

Although wool textiles could sustain a significant price differential because of the different qualities of the product and different markets, the larger that differential the more wool textile manufacturers faced losing market shares to cotton. They needed to reduce the costs of their raw material, but in the nineteenth century there were constraints to an increase in the supply of wool. Early in the century a rising demand for meat directed sheep farmers to pay more attention to breeding sheep accordingly. That trend which had begun in the sixteenth century, was to the detriment of both wool quantity and quality, causing a concomitant industrial shift from woolens to worsteds. Even with the growth of wool supplies from the Southern Hemisphere, they were insufficient to push down the price of raw wool. For most of the nineteenth century wool prices rose. Only in the last quarter did they begin to fall.

The wool textile industry had to find other means of reducing its raw material costs. The ongoing process throughout the industry was to use the cheapest wool available consistent with the quality required of the final product. There was continual experimentation with blending different wools. But during the course of the nineteenth century three significant developments, all with a technological base, revolutionized the raw material supply to the industry.

The first, and arguably the most significant, was the manufacture of wool textiles with a substantial cotton content. Mixing wool and cotton in the manufacturing process was by no means new. But manufacturers faced a problem. The animal and vegetable fibers had very different dyeing qualities and the color in mixed cloth was far from satisfactory. Dyeing the cotton and wool yarn separately to be woven in the same piece of cloth, created color-matching difficulties. Arguably the first scientific development in the wool textile industry solved the problem very successfully, allowing mixed woven cloth to be dyed satisfactorily. In the 1830s Yorkshire dyers discovered that using bichromate of potash, instead of copperas, as a mordant, or fixing agent, enabled both cotton and wool fibers to hold the same dye. The numbers of colors obtainable increased, the speed of dyeing significantly improved, and costs were reduced.

The British wool textile industry rapidly converted its processes to use cotton warps. It was a compromise, but one that suited the British industry and its markets. By mid-century the British worsted industry was using cotton warps in most of the cloth it produced. Although the nature of the handle of the cloth changed, the stronger cotton fiber improved wearing qualities, and, of course, significantly reduced costs. The British woolen industry used cotton less extensively, but, gradually, a significant proportion of cloth woven was "union" cloth, appropriate for many hard-wearing purposes, particularly for work wear, but also for furnishing and industrial fabrics. Cotton warps were less common in other countries, but still widespread. Use was determined primarily by the qualities required of the final product. The incorporation of cotton was not seen as an adulteration of wool textiles, since it was recognized that cotton served extremely useful purposes in woolen and worsted cloth.

The second major technological development that reduced raw material prices for the industry was the ability to process reclaimed wool. Wool had always been recovered during processing. But early in the nineteenth century machinery was developed to pull apart knitted and woven fabric to reclaim the wool fibers. A worldwide trade in rags was developed, channeling them back to Europe—particularly to Great Britain. The reclaimed wool from soft rags, mainly knitted materials, became known as "shoddy." That recovered from harder woven materials, which were more difficult to grind, was known as "mungo." Besides sorting the rags for color and pulling them apart for the fibers, the recovered wool industry (in France "renaissance" wool) also faced the problem of removing nonwool fibers. Chemical science provided the solution. Wool withstands sulfuric acid well, but it dissolves cotton. Thus treatment by acid, known as carbonizing, removed the vegetable fiber. The recovered wool was generally shorter and weaker than the original virgin wool, but considerably cheaper. By blending it with new wool, according to the qualities required of the finish cloth, the woolen industry could use it successfully. The fiber was generally too short for worsted spinning. Reclaimed wool was very heavily used in the dominant British woolen industry, particularly in Yorkshire, and was widely used elsewhere in Europe for lower qualities of cloth—probably far more widely than manufacturers admitted. Manufacturers were coy about admitting use, because shoddy, as its name came to imply, had connotations of poor quality. But, as with cotton, its use was appropriate for many types of woolen cloth, particularly those that were heavily fulled. By the late nineteenth century recovered wool was probably as important as virgin wool as a raw material for the British woolen industry. It was used extensively in France; Vienne in the Rhône valley was the center of its production. It was also produced in Germany and later in large quantities in Italy.

The third development in the supply of raw material in the nineteenth century was the ability to increase the use of wool from the skin of dead sheep. Slipe or skin wool from fell mongering had long been used throughout the wool textile industry. However, the rise in the meat trade, both in the Northern and Southern Hemispheres, brought about an immense increase in the number of skins from which wool could be recovered. From the mid-nineteenth century, Mazamet in southern France effectively cornered the market for these woolen skins, importing vast quantities. Mazamet processors developed new chemical techniques for removing the wool. Some slipe wool was particularly useful for blending with reclaimed wool.

[*See also* Sheep and Goats *and* Textiles.]

BIBLIOGRAPHY

Bowden, P. J. *The Wool Trade in Tudor and Stuart England.* Oxford, 1962.

Burnley, J. *The History of Wool and Wool Combing.* London, 1889.

Clapham, J. H. *The Woollen and Worsted Industries.* London, 1907.

Cole, Arthur Harrison. *The American Wool Manufacture.* 2 vols. Cambridge, Mass., 1926.

English, W. *The Textile Industry: An Account of the Early Inventions of Spinning, Weaving and Knitting Machinery.* London, 1969.

Graham Clark, W. A. *Manufacture of Woolen, Worsted and Shoddy in France and England and Jute in Scotland.* Washington, D.C., 1909.

James, John. *History of the Worsted Manufacture in England.* London, 1857.

Jenkins, D. T. "Mazamet and the Skin Wool Trade, 1850–1913." *Textile History* 15.2 (1984), 171–190.

Jenkins, D. T., ed. *The Industrial Revolution,* vol. 8, *The Textile Industries.* Oxford, 1994.

Jenkins, D. T., and J. C. Malin. "European Competition in Woollen Cloth, 1870–1914: The Role of Shoddy." *Business History* 32.4 (1990), 66–86.

Jenkins, D. T., and K. G. Ponting. *The British Wool Textile Industry, 1770–1914.* London, 1982.

Jenkins, J. Geraint, ed. *The Wool Textile Industry in Great Britain.* London and Boston, 1972.

Jeremy, David J. *Transatlantic Industrial Revolution: The Diffusion of Textile Technologies between Britain and America, 1790–1830s.* Oxford and Cambridge, Mass., 1981.

Kerridge, Eric. *Textile Manufactures in Early Modern England.* Manchester, 1985.

Mann, J. de L. *The Cloth Industry in the West of England from 1640 to 1880.* Oxford, 1971.

Munro, John. "Textile Technology." In *Dictionary of the Middle Ages,* vol. 11, edited by Joseph R. Strayer et al., pp. 693–711.

Murphy, W. S. *The Textile Industries.* London, 1910.

Onions, W. J. *Wool: An Introduction to Its Properties, Varieties, Uses, and Production.* London, 1962.

Rainnie, G. F. *The Woollen and Worsted Industry: An Economic Analysis.* Oxford, 1965.

Ramsay, J. D. *The English Woollen Industry, 1500–1750.* Oxford, 1982.

Singer, C., E. J. Holmyard, A. R. Hall, and T. I. Williams, eds. *A History of Technology,* vols. 4 and 5. Oxford, 1958.

Spibey, H., ed. *British Wool Manual,* 2d ed. Buxton, 1969.

Textile Institute. *Textile Terms and Definitions,* 6th ed. Manchester, 1970.

Von Bergen, W. *American Wool Handbook,* 3d ed. New York, 1970.

Williams, Trevor I., ed. *A History of Technology,* vol. 4, *The Twentieth Century,* Part I. Oxford, 1978.

D. T. JENKINS

Industrial Organization, Markets, and Trade

At about 1000 CE, the wool-textile industry in Europe emerged as an important, export-oriented urban economic sector, its success based on progress in industrial organization. With changes in technology, in the use of raw materials, capital, and labor, and in marketing and transportation, there were significant reductions in costs. Cost savings from innovations that increased the "physical" productivity of labor were limited. More important was the effect of technological change on "quality" improvements and "product" innovation.

Technology. From 1000 to the 1200s CE, the horizontal loom was developed into the broadloom, which made possible a new product: the heavily fulled, felted, and shorn cloth, which evolved into woolen broadcloth. Three other innovations would support the successful expansion of the new product. First, from the early 1300s, carding fine short-stapled wools during the preparation made possible the use of carded wefts, then, from the late 1400s, the use of carded warps as well, thereby increasing the felting potential of the fabric. Second, the introduction of the spinning wheel in the wool sector (for yarn) was closely linked with the rise of carded woolens. Combed wool, in contrast, continued to be spun generally with the distaff and drop-spindle (known as the "rock") until the Saxony wheel (an improved version of the original spinning wheel, with an additional "flyer" bobbin) came into general use during late 1400s. The introduction of the spinning wheel generated significant gains in labor productivity; its main advantage was in promoting the use of carded wool, initially for wefts only (because wheel-spun yarns were too weak to serve as warps). Third, the water-powered fulling-mill, which had been used for the first time in Italy during the late tenth century, was adopted in northern Europe in the late eleventh century and the twelfth. Its contribution to the wool-textile sector was somewhat complex, since it dramatically reduced the time and labor involved in fulling and felting a broadcloth (from three to four days, with three men, to just under one day, with one man). Yet the rapid pounding of the heavy oaken hammers (fulling "stocks") was widely considered to be injurious to the quality of the finer woolens.

In the Low Countries, with their industrial reorientation toward luxury cloth production during the fourteenth century, some towns dismantled existing fulling mills; and all required the traditional methods of foot-fulling until well into the sixteenth century, to guarantee the highest standards for their "sealed" broadcloths. In England, the situation was different; with the revival of the broadcloth industry in the mid-fourteenth century, both the surviving urban and especially the newer rural draperies tried to keep costs of production low by using inexpensive raw materials and by reducing labor costs—whose most dramatic aspect was the spread of the fulling mills. Many English textile towns used these mills, and English cloth production remained as much urban as rural until well into the fifteenth century. On the continent, the more general spread of fulling mills, from the end of the Middle Ages onward, paralleled the expansion of the Light and the New Light Draperies (whose mixed woolen-worsted fabrics, especially those containing greased, carded wefts, still needed some fulling).

In the fifteenth and sixteenth centuries, some drapers added gig mills to the fulling mills, with rapidly rotating burred metal cylinders that raised the nap of the cloth for shearing (i.e., to displace the use of thistle-like teasels); but gig mills, despite an estimated ninefold gain in labor productivity, were widely distrusted for impairing the quality of broadcloths. The finishing process would be further mechanized by calendering machines for pressing the cloths; here, the goal of the innovation was more the improvement of quality and the creation of new products than the increase of labor productivity. During the earliest phases of the Industrial Revolution, the innovations like mule spinning in textiles, while greatly improving the quality of spun yarns—that produced by European wheel-spinners—achieved even greater gains in labor productivity. Mechanized wool-spinning, however, because of problems in maintaining quality, followed mechanized cotton-spinning after a long time lag, becoming widespread only from the late 1820s. The mechanization of weaving—again, first in cottons, then in worsteds, and finally in woolens—was not successful until the 1840s for worsteds, until the 1850s for woolens. In both, England was well ahead of the continent, especially in mechanized weaving, because of the standardized character of the English product, while weaving in other European countries remained widely diversified.

Wool. Before mechanization, raw materials were crucial to both product innovation and the determination of costs and prices. Originally, wool produced locally or in the vicinity was the main source of supply. Then the export of cheap worsteds from northwestern to central Europe and to the Mediterranean created a growing demand, which was increasingly satisfied by imports from England, Scotland, and Ireland. The rise of fulled woolens, which gradually became the predominant wool-textile fashion in Europe, added impetus to demand. The fulling and felting processes required high-quality short-staple wools, carefully selected. Regional specialization solved the problem: some regions in England—the Welsh Marches (Shropshire and Herefordshire), the Cotswolds, and Lincolnshire in particular—became famous for producing the finest short-staple wools, which were exported in ever greater quantities, first to nearby European producers, then to Italian producers. The reasons for the success of these short-and-curly wools are a subject of great debate: some contend that the determining factors involved environmental conditions—a chilly, moist climate and sparse nutrition—while others argue that the genetics of sheep breeding and skills in flock management—especially by the Cistercian abbeys—were critical in producing sheep with such fleeces. Probably all these factors were involved.

From about the mid-fourteenth century, the Spanish produced a rival short-stapled wool from the new merino sheep (European sheep crossbred with North African [Marinid] sheep). Originally, the quality of merino wools was not as high as that of the better grade English wools—but it was still good enough, when mixed with English wools, to be used in the New Draperies. The Italian draperies began importing merino wool in increasing quantities during the late fourteenth century; the Flemish and Brabantine New Draperies did so in the early fifteenth century, certainly from the 1430s onward. In the sixteenth century, the quality of Spanish merino wool had greatly improved—at the same time that the quality of so many English wools had deteriorated. Some contend that the reason in England was the great improvement in nutrition that Tudor-Stuart enclosures, with ensuing rich grasslands, brought to sheep raising; others argue that the enclosures facilitated and promoted the breeding of larger, heavier sheep for urban meat markets, thus sheep with longer, coarser fleeces. Soon, Spanish merino wool predominated in the European wool industries, even in England. Meanwhile, the rise of the light and new light draperies favored an increased demand for long-staple combed wool, one that was met mainly by local supplies and by imports from Scotland, Ireland, Zealand, Frisia, Pomerania, Mecklenberg, and Saxony. By the end of the eighteenth century, Saxony had succeeded in breeding its own merino sheep. During the nineteenth century, mechanization of the wool industry generated the large-scale, regional specialization in sheep breeding and wool production—as in the northeastern United States, Argentina, South Africa, Australia, and New Zealand.

The export of English wools began by shipping by Flemish, Brabantine, and Italian merchants. In the 1330s, Edward III seized control of the wool-export trade; then in 1363, to maximize his income from wool-export taxes, he established the Company of Merchants of the Staple, a cartel based in recently conquered Calais, to monopolize almost all English wool exports (except those shipped to Italy from Southampton). His motive was to shift the tax incidence from English wool growers to continental drapers. In 1558, when France reconquered Calais, the staple town was moved to Middleburg; but by that time, English wool exports were insignificant, with England's almost complete commercial transformation to cloth exports, which dominated the continental markets. In that era, Spanish wool exports remained impressive, but they would soon decline because of wars and the weakening demand for traditional heavy-weight woolens. From the thirteenth century, the production of a large part of Spanish wool had been organized by the king of Castile within the framework of a *mesta real*, an institution that received royal protection and the privilege to regulate the movements and pasturage of the huge herds of *mesta* sheep; in Castile and Catalonia, some local independent *mestas* were established, but the royal *mesta* was dominant. The export of Spanish wool was controlled by independent Castilian and Biscayan merchants, who shipped the wool to Bruges (now in Belgium), their main nothern staple market. In 1455, the Bruges magistrate subdivided the merchants and shippers into two separate "nations," the nation of Spain (Castile) and the nation of Vizcaya. In 1540, Charles V confirmed Bruges as the Spanish wool staple and the headquarters for the various Spanish *consulados* in the Low Countries. In the mid-1600s, the Amsterdam (Holland) staple market would replace Bruges.

Dyestuffs, alum, and potash were critical ingredients in wool manufacturing. Cloth could be dyed in the wool, in the yarn, or in the piece. Often, woolens were woven from wools that had been first dyed blue with woad (genus *Isatis*, plants of the crucifer family), and then redyed in the piece with other vegetable-based dyes: madder, mull, weld, saffron, and/or again woad. Woad was first grown in the cloth-producing areas or in the vicinity, such as Picardy near Flanders. From the fifteenth century, it was increasingly imported from Languedoc in southern France. Insect-based dyes, such as the very expensive grain (genus *Kermes*), were used for the production of the luxury reds and scarlets. From the sixteenth century, powerful and brilliant tropical dyes came into use, especially brazilwood (from trees originally imported from the East Indies, later from Portuguese Brazil) and cochineal (from insects imported from Mexico); both replaced kermes. Indigo, a plant imported from the East Indies and, then from the Caribbean and the Carolinas, became a substitute for woad. In the late nineteenth century, the vegetable-based and insect-based dyes were gradually replaced by chemical dyes. Potash, derived from Baltic-based wood ash, was used as a chemical catalyst to make woad water soluble. For fixing colors, a mordant was essential, alum. It was first available from Phocaea in Asia Minor; in the 1460s, from Tolfa in the Papal States; then, after the Moors were conquered in 1492, from Spain.

Labor. The management of labor was important to the organizational progress of the wool industry. A first decisive step was taken about 1000 CE, when some urban-based merchants trading in wool, dyestuffs, and/or finished textiles initiated a large-scale production of textiles for export, both in northwestern Europe and in Italy. To maximize efficiency, they organized production on the basis of a far-flung division of labor; in some towns, the production process was subdivided into more than thirty tasks.

Although merchants were always important to the rise and expansion of the urban wool-textile industry, because of their crucial role in financing production and in marketing the fabrics, the true industrial entrepreneurs were the drapers: called *drapiers* in France and the Low Countries, *lanaiuoli* in Italy, and clothiers in England. Most organized production, both urban and rural, through a domestic "putting-out" system. The drapers were usually subordinate to the merchants; drapers purchased wool and other raw materials from merchants on credit, received additional credit to finance their operations, then sold the manufactured but unfinished cloth to the merchants. In northern Europe, and especially in the Low Countries, many of the drapers had been master weavers, but some came from the finishing sector of the dyers or shearers; in Italy, most of the *lanaiuoli* had mercantile rather than industrial origins. The draper delivered the wool mainly to female employees, who for piece-work wages, sorted, beat (to separate fibers), washed, and greased the fine, short-stapled wools (to protect them in the spinning and weaving processes). The draper then "put out" the wool within the town or in the countryside, again mainly to female workers and for piece-work wages, to have it combed, carded, and spun. The draper then subcontracted the weaving to a male master weaver, who wove the cloth with some journeymen, in the draper's own workshop or in the workshop of the master weaver. The final step was to take this woven cloth to the master fuller, for foot fulling, or in Italy and England, to the nearby fulling mill. Fullers were responsible, as well, for tentering (stretching the cloth to remove wrinkles), repairing, and preliminary raising (teaselling) of the cloth, and then received a wage that was in part for piece work and in part time based. In most cases, the merchants then took over the subsequent stages of cloth finishing, by subcontracting them to master dyers and master shearers, generally independent professionals who worked for set fees. In rural industries, the organization of the production—from wool to fabric—was very similar, but often a wool brogger or wool dealer, took on part of the production financing and operated between the merchant and the small drapers.

As far as production is concerned, two important characteristics have to be mentioned. First, the highest status crafts became male dominated, as was especially striking in weaving. During the early and high Middle Ages, weaving had been undertaken mainly by female workers, using the vertical warp-weighted loom, as a secondary occupation within the rural household economy. During the late medieval commercial revolution, the wool-textile industry became more urban, and male weavers became dominant, converting the weaving craft into a primary occupation and raising its status. The rise of the heavily fulled, felted, and shorn woolens reinforced that tendency, thus elevating the status of fullers, dyers, and shearers, to make the primary crafts in cloth finishing essentially male. The other tasks in the wool-textile sector were the low-status occupations that remained female dominated. Closely connected with the gender distinction was the rise of the craft guilds. Merchants had first organized themselves in guilds or in *hansas* (interurban guilds), to protect themselves during their traveling and to receive commercial privileges when marketing their products in foreign countries. As merchant guilds gained success, they exercised a growing influence within their home town, enough to allow many to acquire very considerable, and sometimes predominant, political power in their town governments. Within the Low Countries, they used such powers to regulate the local draperies and prevented the creation of independent craft guilds. More so than in Italy or England, the high-status crafts of the Low Countries reacted against such mercantile controls; then, in the early fourteenth century, the Flemish and Brabantine textile artisans in most of the traditional drapery towns successfully rebelled against and overcame these mercantile "patriciates." Weavers, dyers, fullers, and shearers were allowed to form craft guilds, with rights of active participation in the town governments. In collaboration with other craft guilds, and even with the mercantile and rentier members of the town government, these textile guilds achieved a prominent role in industrial organization—especially in imposing industrial regulations (*keuren*) designed not just to safeguard their own status but also to improve, police, and guarantee the quality of the town's woolens. In this way, the craft guilds contributed to organizational progress but undermined their value, when, in becoming too conservative during the next century, they resisted necessary structural adjustments. In the younger drapery town of Leiden, however, as in the older Italian textile towns, the mercantile-dominated town governments, not the craft guilds, imposed and maintained even more meticulously detailed and restrictive industrial legislation. One advantage of the English cloth industry, especially in its rural sector, was the virtual absence of such industrial legislation—until the Crown began imposing national legislation in textile manufactures, from the reign of Edward IV (1461–1483).

Trade. Savings in marketing, transportation, and transaction costs are the final factors to be considered in promoting the great expansion of the wool-textile industry. Certainly organizational process was very important in marketing woolens. About 1000 CE, Flemish merchants, organized in trade guilds, crossed the English Channel to buy wool and crossed the Alps to sell their cloth in Italy. In the thirteenth century, Italian merchants and bankers, organized in "nations," traveled to the Champagne Fairs in northern France, principally to purchase the northern woolen and worsted textiles. In the fourteenth century, the Baltic, Rhenish, and other North German merchants, who organized themselves formally into the Hanseatic League, visited the Bruges and London markets to make their cloth purchases. During the fifteenth and sixteenth centuries, the Brabant Fairs in Antwerp and Bergen-op-Zoom (Low Countries) became the primary staple market for both English and Dutch woolens on the continent, linking the German and central European market via the fairs of Frankfurt am Main, the leader of a network of fairs for Leipzig, Breslau, Poznan, and others. The integration of the French market was first organized via the fairs of Geneva and Châlons-sur-Saone, but from the end of the fifteenth century, the fairs of Lyon became predominant. The integration of the sixteenth-century Spanish and New World markets took place via the fairs of Castile. The export of English woolens to the continent was organized by the Merchant Adventurers, who centralized purchases during the Bartholomew Fair at Smithfield in the City (of London) and during the Stourbridge Fair held near Cambridge, but later almost exclusively in Blackwell Hall at London. From there, the cloth was sent to the Brabant fairs for sale. In the seventeenth century, Amsterdam became the leading staple market for the sale of woolens from the Low Countries, England, France, and Italy; it was succeeded by London during the eighteenth century.

Transportation costs did not decrease in linear fashion, not even in a long-term perspective. By the 1200s, such costs were decreasing because of the following: risk-reducing improvements in security; a better infrastructure provided by large-scale investments by local lords and sovereign princes; better organized crossings of the Alps; and significant progress in shipping and seagoing navigation. The decrease in transport and transaction costs was sharply reversed during the fourteenth and early fifteenth centuries, mainly because of European wars and plagues, increasing piracy on the seas, and a debilitating sense of insecurity. From the 1450s, transportation costs resumed their decline as those negative factors were overcome—with improved security for traveling overland and by sea; important organizational innovations in sending goods by sea, but especially transcontinental transport; and important technical improvements in shipbuilding and nautical expertise. This declining cost trend weakened during the seventeenth century but accelerated during the eighteenth and into the nineteenth, with the advent of railroads and steamships. The decline in costs benefited the other textile sectors too, and they took advantage of it to help overcome wool's dominant position in the textile industry during the nineteenth century and the twentieth.

BIBLIOGRAPHY

Bowden, P. *The Wool Trade in Tudor and Stuart England.* London, 1962.
De Poerck, G. *La draperie médiévale en Flandre et en Artois: Technique et terminologie.* Bruges, 1951.
De Sagher, H., et al., eds. *Recueil de documents relatifs à l'histoire drapière en Flandre.* Brussels, 1951–1966.

Espinas, G., and H. Pirenne, eds. *Recueil des documents relatifs à l'histoire de l'industrie drapière*. Brussels, 1904–1920.

Klein, J. *The Mesta: A Study in Spanish Economic History*. Cambridge, Mass., 1920.

Lloyd, T. H. *The English Wool Trade in the Middle Ages*. Cambridge, 1977.

Melis, F. *Aspetti della vita economica medievale*. Studi nell'archivo Datini di Prato, *L'industria laniera*, pp. 455–729. Florence, 1962.

Munro, J. H. "The Symbiosis of Towns and Textiles: Urban Institutions and the Changing Fortunes of Cloth Manufacturing in the Low Countries and England, 1270–1570." *Journal of Early Modern History: Contacts, Comparisons, Contrasts* 31 (February 1999), 1–74.

Munro, J. H. "Medieval Woollens: Textiles, Textile Technology, and Industrial Organization, c. 800–1500." In *The Cambridge History of Western Textiles* (in press), edited by D. T. Jenkins.

Posthumus, N. W., ed. *Bronnen tot de geschiedenis van de Leidsche textielnijverheid, 1333–1795*. 3 vols. The Hague, 1910–1922.

Power, E. *The Wool Trade in English Medieval History*. London, 1941.

Ramsay, G. D. *The English Woollen Industry, 1500–1780*. London, 1982.

Rahn Phillips, C., and W. D. Phillips. *Spain's Golden Fleece: Wool Production and the Wool Trade from the Middle Ages to the Nineteenth Century*. Baltimore and London, 1997.

Unwin, G. *The Guilds and Companies of London*. London, 1938.

HERMAN VAN DER WEE

WRIGHT BROTHERS. Wilbur Wright (1867–1912) and Orville Wright (1871–1948) invented the world's first successful pilot-controlled powered aircraft. In succeeding decades their invention evolved into an important military weapon, the world's principal means of long-distance passenger transport, and a major global industry.

Wilbur and Orville, plus two older brothers and a younger sister, were born to the Reverend Milton Wright and Susan Catherine (Koerner) Wright. The elder Wright's career as a teacher, minister, religious editor, and bishop of the United Brethren Church in Christ took the family to Dayton, Ohio, and several other Midwest communities before the family returned permanently to Dayton in 1884.

Wilbur and Orville were intelligent, inquisitive, and remarkably versatile individuals who shared ideas and worked closely together on projects from a young age until Wilbur's death in 1912. Accidental injuries, illness, family crises, and business demands combined to prevent their formal schooling from extending beyond high school.

Although their father's gift of a rubber-band-powered toy helicopter in 1878 piqued the young brothers' initial interest in flight, they began their lifelong business collaboration in 1889 far afield from aeronautics—as job printers. For a short time they also published two neighborhood newspapers. In 1892 they diversified by opening a shop to sell and repair bicycles and in 1896 they began to manufacture their own brand of bicycles. This modestly successful business provided the financial means for the brothers to conduct their early aviation experiments.

The decisive event that renewed the Wright brothers' interest in the challenges of flight was a glider crash in 1896 that killed German aeronautics pioneer Otto Lilienthal. Wilbur's interest also was stimulated by a desire for more significant personal accomplishments than success as a small businessman.

After carefully studying all the information they could obtain on aeronautical subjects, the Wright brothers were convinced that mechanical flight by humans was possible. They began experiments to increase their knowledge of aerodynamics and to find solutions to the daunting problems of propulsion and flight control. Experiments began with a small biplane kite and progressed to a series of man-carrying gliders, which the brothers designed, built, and tested exhaustively on the windy coastal dunes near Kitty Hawk, North Carolina. They tackled problems systematically and kept meticulous records of their activities in the workshop and in the field.

The Wright brothers demonstrated their intellectual and mechanical genius in several pathbreaking ways starting with practical solutions to aircraft maneuverability and control in all three axes of flight—pitch, roll, and yaw. Similarly, when experimental flight test results conflicted with published aerodynamic data, they built an ingenious wind tunnel to retest their designs and correct the published data.

In 1903 Wilbur and Orville combined the theoretical knowledge and practical skill gained in more than 1,000 manned glider flights with two other extraordinary achievements. They designed an efficient propeller to provide airborne thrust and designed and built (with assistance from a machinist in their bicycle shop) an innovative lightweight gasoline engine to power a twin-propeller system. The culmination of their efforts occurred on 17 December 1903 at Kitty Hawk, when they made four successful controlled flights in their new machine ranging from 12 to 59 seconds.

Following their historic achievement, the Wright brothers moved forward with improved aircraft designs and efforts to secure patent protection for their invention both in the United States and Europe. After the basic U.S. patent for a flying machine was granted in 1906, Wilbur and Orville became increasingly active in flying demonstrations in the United States and Europe and sought to interest government officials and private investors in the future development of their invention.

A protracted series of patent disputes and Wilbur's death from typhoid fever in 1912 prevented the Wright brothers from gaining large immediate financial rewards from their invention. However, their pioneering contributions to aerodynamic theory and aircraft design and construction and their piloting skills brought them widespread fame and public recognition throughout the United States and Europe.

BIBLIOGRAPHY

Crouch, Tom D. *The Bishop's Boys: A Life of Wilbur and Orville Wright.* New York, 1989. The best recent biography of the Wright brothers.

Howard, Fred. *Wilbur and Orville: A Biography of the Wright Brothers.* New York, 1987. Good biography, especially helpful on developments after 1903.

Moolman, Valerie, and the editors of Time-Life Books. *The Road to Kitty Hawk.* Alexandria, Va., 1980. Excellent historical overview and photographs of the Wright brothers and other aeronautic pioneers.

Renstrom, Arthur G. *Wilbur & Orville Wright: A Chronology.* Washington, D.C., 1975. Helpful chronology developed from the extensive collection of Wright brothers papers and related documents in the Library of Congress.

RICHARD W. BARSNESS

Y–Z

YEMEN. *See* Arabia.

YOUNG, ARTHUR (1741–1820), agricultural improver.

Young was an influential writer and important public figure who promoted modern farming methods and agrarian policies, such as enclosure, which he believed would lead to a more productive agriculture. Young was also one of the first to carry out surveys to obtain information to guide public policy. His views on agrarian issues have profoundly influenced historical writing, and his surveys are critical evidence in establishing the truth of those opinions.

The son of a Suffolk rector, Young was sent to school at the age of seven, and at seventeen he was apprenticed to a merchant in Lynn. At school he began writing a history of England and learned to dance; as an apprentice, he continued dancing, wasted his money on clothing and balls, and wrote to support himself—the start of a lifelong enterprise. He turned his hand to farming when he was twenty-two and followed the plow until fifty-three.

In 1765, Young married Martha Allen of Lynn. They had four children, but the marriage was not a happy one. He was more enthusiastic about improved agriculture than about his wife, as shown by his memorial to her in which she is described as "the great-grand daughter of John Allen, esq., of Lyng House in the county of Norfolk, the first person . . . who there used marl." He had great affection for his children, especially his youngest daughter, Bobbin, and her death in 1797 plunged him into a melancholy that lasted the rest of his life.

Young wrote about forty books and innumerable articles on politics, economics, and agriculture. From 1765 to 1771, he published three tours of English farming districts. The books were nearly five thousand pages long, most of which consisted of the results of village-by-village and farm-by-farm surveys. Young thought that such detailed knowledge was necessary for sensible agrarian policies and spent many pages analyzing his surveys to see whether crop yields increased with farm size and so forth. He also recorded the dimensions of the rooms of stately homes he visited in a similarly obsessive fashion. In 1774, he published his most famous economic tract, *Political Arithmetic*. Later, Young published tours of Ireland, and a very famous volume on France, which he visited in 1787, 1788, and in 1789, the first year of the Revolution. In 1784, he began publishing the *Annals of Agriculture*, which continued almost until his death and included contributions from leading landed gentlemen and even King George III, who wrote under the name of his shepherd, Ralph Robinson. In 1793, William Pitt established the Board of Agriculture and appointed Young its secretary. For two decades, he supervised the publication of its county reports and wrote many of them himself.

Young's success with the aristocracy was aided by his quick wit, his affable disposition, and his agrarian views. He contrasted the "goths and vandals of the open fields" with the "civilization of enclosures"; he denounced peasant proprietorship; he defended high rents as a spur to efficiency; he created the cult of the improving landlord; and he claimed that modern agriculture increased farm employment rather than leading to depopulation.

Young's standing among historians has fluctuated widely. Lord Ernle relied on Young's commentaries to argue that enclosures, large farms, and great estates were the basis of agricultural modernization. Young's reputation suffered at the hands of historian Eric Kerridge, who found the surveys superficial. More recently, however, they have provided a unique data source that has been reanalyzed by econometric historians. Young's wish may yet come true: "I want several penetrating political arithmetricians at my elbow to point out the combinations between different, and seemingly distinct circumstances, too many of which will, I fear, escape me."

BIBLIOGRAPHY

Allen, Robert C. *Enclosure and the Yeoman.* Oxford, 1992. Reanalyzes Young's data and comes to different conclusions.

Allen, Robert C., and Cormac O'Grada. "On the Road Again with Arthur Young: English, Irish, and French Agriculture during the Industrial Revolution." *Journal of Economic History* 48 (1998), 937–953. Positive assessment of Young's findings based on a comparison with alternative sources.

Kerridge, Eric. "Arthur Young and William Marshall." *History Studies* 1 (1968), 43–65. The harshest critic of Young.

Mingay, G. E., ed. *Arthur Young and His Times.* London, 1975. A very useful collection of Young's writings with a good introduction to his life and thought.

ROBERT C. ALLEN

ZAIBATSU. The Japanese word *zaibatsu* is a combination of two Chinese characters: *zai*, which means "financial," and *batsu*, meaning "clique" or "faction." In the Japanese literature, the term *zaibatsu* means a collection of diversified enterprises under the ownership of a single family or an extended family consisting of a main line and branch lines. Occasionally, in the Western literature, one discovers the concept of zaibatsu broadened to combines of all types, not just those controlled by families.

The literature concerning the zaibatsu falls into three distinct groups: political economy, business history, and economics. Political economists, including Marxist economists, are especially interested in the power exercised by the zaibatsu. They focus upon the relationships between politicians, bureaucrats, and the zaibatsu leadership. For instance, they note that the zaibatsu system took root during the early Meiji period because the members of Meiji oligarchy favored the interests of powerful merchants, selling off government-owned companies at cheap prices to them during the Matsukata Deflation in the early 1880s and subsidizing their ventures in postal delivery, shipping, and shipbuilding. With the transition from oligarchy rule to democracy and a party system, the *zaikai*—epitomized by the Industry Club of Japan formed by the major zaibatsu in 1917 and initially headed by Mitsui's Takuma Dan—consolidated its power by financing the two main political parties, the Seiyukai and the Minseito (Mistui favored the Seiyukai, and Mitsubishi the Minseito). They also stress that during the 1920s and 1930s, the zaibatsu simultaneously tightened their hold over both the financial sector—the big city banks and trust and insurance companies—and secured dominant positions in the emerging iron and steel, machine tool, chemicals, and shipbuilding subsectors of manufacturing. For instance, in 1941 the big four zaibatsu—Mitsui, Mitsubishi, Sumitomo, and Yasuda—accounted for 25 percent of the paid-in capital for the financial sector and 18 percent of the paid-within capital in heavy manufacturing (the top ten zaibatsu accounting for about 30 percent of the paid-in capital in heavy manufacturing). In short, political economists emphasize zaibatsu aggrandizement of economic and political power.

As political economists tend to take a dark view of the zaibatsu, blaming them for Japan's militarism during the period 1931–1945, they view the zaibatsu system as a form of monopoly capitalism that encouraged Japanese expansion onto the Asian mainland. This argument is questionable. To be sure, the zaibatsu benefited from the military-related investment program of the late 1930s and early 1940s, increasing their proportion of total paid-in capital; but the old-line zaibatsu were basically internationalist in outlook, having profited from the World War I investment boom when Japan (nominally allied to England but basically a nonbelligerent) enjoyed a huge export boom due to the collapse of European trade. Indeed, the military cabinets of the 1930s attempted to bypass the older zaibatsu by encouraging the emergence of industrial combines such as Nissan and Nichitsu, which were active in developing infrastructure and manufacturing in Korea and Manchuria. These new combines are known as *shinzaibatsu*, meaning "new zaibatsu."

The business-history literature is concerned with the evolution of the zaibatsu from closed enterprises (e.g., partnerships) to open forms (e.g., joint-stock companies), and with the transition from family capitalism to managerial capitalism. As for the shift from closed to open structure, the literature stresses two factors: (1) institutional changes and (2) economic changes involving structural shifts in the nature of production and expansion in the scale of domestic private-capital formation. For instance, implementation of the Commercial Code in 1893 encouraged the zaibatsu management to set up either limited (*goshi gaisha*) or unlimited (*gomei gaisha*) partnerships for the enterprises that they controlled. Then, because of changes in the tax code and diversification into new industries between 1900 and 1920, the zaibatsu moved toward a holding-company/multisubsidiary form of organization in which the headquarters/holding company was treated as a partnership into which the family placed most of its assets, and the individual enterprises were turned into joint-stock company subsidiaries. After 1931, under political pressure from the military and right wing ultranationalists and because of their voracious demand for capital during the massive investment boom of the 1930s, the zaibatsu opened up the holding companies to public ownership, turning their headquarters into joint-stock companies. Finally, between 1945 and 1949 under the American Occupation, the holding companies were dissolved, and their stock was sold to the public by the Holding Company Liquidation Commission.

The evolution of zaibatsu management and ownership can be related to Japan's transition from family capitalism to managerial capitalism. In the case of the two oldest zaibatsu, Mitsui and Sumitomo, which date back to the late sixteenth and early seventeenth centuries (Sumitomo's "well frame" logo was created in 1590, and use of Mitsui's "three wells" logo goes back to 1615), the transition to managerial-style organization predates the Meiji Restoration. During the Tokugawa or early modern period (1600–1868), the Mitsui house, which was active in the dry goods and money exchange business, adopted a system whereby its assets were held in a family partnership (not to be divided up upon the death of individual members of the family entity), with the actual management of the company the responsibility of chief clerks (*banto*). In the zaibatsu newly created during the Meiji period—Mitsubishi, created by the entrepreneur Yatoro Iwasaki, and Yasuda, created by

Zenjiro Yasuda—transition to a form in which salaried managers assumed primary responsibility for the operation of the enterprises of the zaibatsu took place after the death of the founder. In short, there was a life cycle, with salaried managers acquiring increasing power over decision making once the founding generation of the zaibatsu family had passed away. A technological imperative also was important in promoting this transition: as the zaibatsu diversified into technology-intensive heavy industries during the World War I boom, the importance of technical engineering expertise for the daily management of zaibatsu enterprises received a strong boost. Thus, the stature of salaried managers grew, especially during the period after 1915.

The typical economist, interested in efficiency and long-run growth, sees the zaibatsu as an innovation that solved problems posed by scarcities—in entrepreneurial talent, in knowledge of Western technology and foreign languages, and in physical capital. Within a typical zaibatsu was a financial cluster (banks, trust and insurance companies), a general trading company (*sogo shosha*), and industrial enterprises (this cluster became increasingly important after the investment boom between 1910 and 1919). Knowledge about technology and organizational innovations was shared within the zaibatsu as was access to financial capital. Enterprises in old line-industries that were already profitable subsidized unproven ventures in new enterprises. In a resource-poor economy isolated geographically and culturally from the West, the zaibatsu were beachheads, facilitating the acquisition of knowledge about foreign markets and foreign technologies; and, acting upon this knowledge, they behaved like venture capitalists. Thus, the economist views the emergence of the zaibatsu as a response to scarcities in Japan. The economic historian adds to this insight the observation that there is path dependence, with the institutions that worked in the past serving as models for the future. Thus, the Tokugawa merchant houses, with their internal system of training young apprentices who subsequently competed for advancement to *banto* status, served as models for the development of the managerial system in zaibatsu, especially after 1900.

The economist also is interested in the issue of industrial organization, the question of whether the existence of powerful zaibatsu stifled competition by preventing new firms from entering industries. The answer seems to be no. Consider entry and exit by zaibatsu themselves. During the early Meiji period, when the zaibatsu were concerned mainly with raw materials and financial and transport infrastructure—banking, mining, shipping, railroad building, and real estate development—there were five "political merchant" zaibatsu (Mitsui and Yasuda in banking, Okura in trade, Fujita in sake and engineering, and Mitsubishi in shipping) and two based on mining (Sumitomo

and Furukawa). With the massive investment boom in electricity and railroads between 1904 and 1910, legions of local zaibatsu, active in building intercity electrical railroads and the sale of electrical power, entered the fray. Then during the World War I boom, new national zaibatsu—Iwai (steel, textiles), Murai (tobacco, banking, textiles), Matsukata (shipbuilding, real estate), Suzuki (textiles, banking), and Nomura and Kuhara (mining, shipping, real estate)—emerged as competitors facing off against the older zaibatsu. In the aftermath of the investment boom, the Japanese economy entered the slow-growth period of the 1920s, when a number of the weaker zaibatsu were wiped out. For instance, Suzuki collapsed when the Bank of Taiwan, upon which it depended, collapsed in the financial crisis of 1927; and, as noted earlier, during the investment surge of the 1930s *shinzaibatsu*, which focused on investments in military-related hardware and the empire, proliferated.

In sum, prewar Japan was characterized by competition amongst the zaibatsu, that is, competition among the few. Consequently, political and economic power were often, but not always, synonymous; public ownership of Japan's expanding industrial base developed slowly; and Japanese business was able to cope successfully with substantial scarcities during its transition from an economy centered around light manufacturing to a dualistic economy whose engine of growth was heavy industry.

BIBLIOGRAPHY

Bisson, T. A. *Zaibatsu Dissolution in Japan.* Berkeley and Los Angeles, 1954. This work focuses on the dissolution of the zaibatsu under the American Occupation, providing detailed accounts about how the assets of the holding companies were sold on the market by the Holding Company Liquidation Commission, and how the subsidiaries were reorganized through elimination of zaibatsu-controlled directors and divestiture of intersubsidiary stock holdings. It addresses an audience interested in the political economy of the zaibatsu.

Hadley, Eleanor H. *Antitrust in Japan.* Princeton, 1970. This work deals with both prewar zaibatsu and postwar *keiretsu*. It provides details on cross-shareholding of stock within financial *keiretsu* during the 1960s and contributes to the literature on the political economy of the zaibatsu.

Hayashi, Takeshi. *The Japanese Experience in Technology: From Transfer to Self Reliance.* Tokyo, 1990. The main focus of this work is technological innovation and the import of foreign technology in Japan. Because the zaibatsu played a pivotal role in importing and adapting Western technology, the author provides a useful discussion of management within the zaibatsu, and the role of the salaried managers in the technological development of zaibatsu-affiliated enterprises.

Hirschmeier, Johannes, and Tsunehiko Yui. *The Development of Japanese Business, 1600–1973.* Cambridge, Mass., 1975. One of the premier business histories of Japan, this work provides useful details about Tokugawa merchant houses, including the Mitsui house, and about the key role played by the chief clerks (*banto*) during the Tokugawa period and afterward. It has a particularly fine treatment of Meiji entrepreneurship, and of the role played by the nonmerchant (e.g., former *samurai*) founders of zaibatsu.

Miyamoto, Matao. "The Position and Role of Family Business in the Development of the Japanese Company System." In *Family Business in the Era of Industrial Growth: Its Ownership and Management*, edited by Akio Okochi and Shigeaki Yasuoka, pp. 39–91. Tokyo, 1984. Written from the point of view of modern business history, this article discusses the evolution of the zaibatsu from closed family-run proprietorships to quasi-open structures mixing partnerships with joint-stock subsidiaries whose equity was at least partially open for purchase on the market. It provides useful details about the impact of the Commercial Codes of 1890 and 1899 on the establishment of limited partnerships (*goshi gaisha*), unlimited partnerships (*gomei gaisha*), and joint-stock companies (*kabushiki gaisha*), and discusses why the zaibatsu decided to establish holding companies during the early decades of the twentieth century.

Morikawa, Hidemasa. *Zaibatsu: The Rise and Fall of Family Enterprise Groups in Japan*. Tokyo, 1992. One of the few studies exclusively devoted to history of the zaibatsu, this work is written from a business-history viewpoint. It chronicles the evolution of the zaibatsu from family-run businesses with limited diversification during the early Meiji period into massive empires structured along multisubsidiary lines controlled by holding companies and managed by technically trained salaried managers. The main thesis of the work is that the zaibatsu evolved because of structural changes in the Japanese economy, institutional changes (e.g., the creation of the Commercial Code and its revisions and the way the tax code treated personal income and corporate income), and the political relationship between the zaibatsu, bureaucrats, and politicians.

Nakamura, Takafusa. *Economic Growth in Prewar Japan*. New Haven, Conn., 1971. This classic economic history of prewar Japan provides useful quantitative evidence concerning the economic concentration of production and assets in Japan during the period between the world wars. It discusses the role of zaibatsu in the development of a dualistic capital market with the large zaibatsu-affiliated main banks providing long-term loans to capital-intensive heavy industries, as miniscule regional banks specialized in credit creation for small business and farmers.

Roberts, John G. *Mitsui: Three Centuries of Japanese Business*. New York and Tokyo, 1989. This work is written for the student of Japanese history interested in the political economy of Japan. It has little economic content, but does provide a useful overview of the development of one of Japan's most famous zaibatsu. It discusses specific historical personalities and events in detail.

Yasuoka, Shigeaki "Capital Ownership in Family Companies: Japanese Firms Compared with Those in Other Countries." In *Family Business in the Era of Industrial Growth: Its Ownership and Management*, edited by Akio Okochi and Shigeaki Yasuoka, pp. 1–33. Tokyo, 1984. This article reflects the views of a business historian who argues that as the ownership of an enterprise becomes collectivistic, individual owners turn their attention exclusively toward securing regular payment of dividends, thereby eschewing direct intervention in corporate affairs. He employs this hypothesis to explain why the zaibatsu families tended to turn their affairs over to chief clerks (*banto*) and salaried managers after the founder of the house had perished.

Yoshino, Michael Y., and Thomas B. Lifson. *The Invisible Link: Japan's Sogo Shosha and the Organization of Trade*. Cambridge, Mass., 1986. This work examines the economic rationale for the great trading companies (*sogo shosha*) that were typically part of zaibatsu. It argues that the great Japanese trading houses are diversified intermediaries that fill the role of missing link, providing an infrastructure through which information, ideas, commodities, and services are channeled. The argument is consistent with the notion that the general trading companies provide scale economies that facilitate

importing and exporting, the ferreting out of new technologies, and the systematic analysis of market conditions in the major regions of the globe.

CARL MOSK

ZAIRE. *See* Central Africa.

ZAMBIA. *See* Southern Africa.

ZHITIAN (in Mandarin, "salary land") was a form of land ownership in imperial China. It was originated in 485 CE, during the Northern Wei dynasty (420–534 CE). It existed for more than a millenium, until the Ming dynasty (1368–1644 CE). In principle, salary land belonged to the state and provided the income for state officials. The actual acreage was determined by the recipient's rank in the bureaucracy, as shown in Table 1 (figures converted to hectares [ha], the modern measure).

Once allocated, the land was then rented out for tenants to till, usually under a sharecropping arrangement. Each year the tenant paid rent to the state. From the official's point of view, the rent was his salary for his services to the empire. This arrangement formed an incentive triangle: the tenant was motivated to produce more and better for his own share; the official was motivated to monitor the farming process for his livelihood; and the state was motivated to maintain such an institution for stability. In addition, the state made savings, since the day-to-day surveillance of the estate was done by the official.

Although the *zhitian* occupied a large proportion of the land owned by the state (37 percent of total state-owned land in the eleventh century CE, for example), it accounted for only a tiny proportion of China's total land under cultivation (0.5 percent of the total at that time), owing to two factors. First, private land ownership was the long-term dominant form of ownership throughout the empire. Second, the bureaucracy was small relative to China's population (on a long-term average, bureaucrats were ± 5 percent of the total population). Still, the effect of *zhitian* on the economy was profound. It perpetuated the bond between the officials and agriculture, since it maintained the officials' interest in farming. Many officials became "agro-cats" engaged in finding and promoting the best farming practices. Some wrote books on agriculture to spread the best practice. It was both logical and beneficial for officialdom to be pro-agricultural. In addition, since the salary was paid in kind, it obligated the official to participate in market exchange to satisfy the range of his and his family's needs. Given the inelasticity in demand for food, the higher his rank, the greater the proportion of his salary depending on marketing. It was therefore logical for officialdom to tolerate the market as long as it did not upset the Confucian social order. Demise of the salary land occurred

TABLE 1. *Acreage of Salary Land*

PERIOD	LAND FOR HIGHEST RANK		LAND FOR LOWEST RANK	
420–534 CE	1,500 Wei *mu*	(75.0 ha)	600 Wei *mu*	(30.0 ha)
581–618 CE	500 Sui *mu*	(25.0 ha)	100 Sui *mu*	(7.0 ha)
618–907 CE	1,200 Tang *mu*	(64.8 ha)	200 Tang *mu*	(11.6 ha)
960–1279 CE	2,000 Song *mu*	(116.0 ha)	200 Song *mu*	(11.6 ha)
1127–1234 CE	3,000 Jin *mu*	(174.0 ha)	200 Jin *mu*	(11.6 ha)
1279–1368 CE	1,600 Yuan *mu*	(112.0 ha)	100 Yuan *mu*	(7.0 ha)
1368–1644 CE	1,600 Ming *mu*	(112.0 ha)	100 Ming *mu*	(7.0 ha)

during the Manchu Qing era (1644–1911). This was largely caused by monetization of the economy, which was facilitated by large quantities of imported silver, and more efficient taxation after a long line of reforms ranging from "one whip method" under the Ming to "combining poll to land tax" during the Qing. As a result, officials were paid in kind and, increasingly, in cash.

BIBLIOGRAPHY

Deng, Gang. *Development versus Stagnation: Technological Continuity and Agricultural Progress in Premodern China.* New York, London, and West Port, 1993.

Deng, Gang. *The Premodern Chinese Economy: Structural Equilibrium and Capitalist Sterility.* London and New York, 1999.

KENT G. DENG

ZIMBABWE. *See* Southern Africa.

ZOOS AND OTHER ANIMAL PARKS. It has become customary, following Loisel (1912), to divide the history of zoological parks into five periods. The first of these is the "Prehistoric Period" and is based on the work of Galton, who argued that before animals were domesticated, men captured and kept young animals for pleasure rather than food. As tribes became larger, collections of wild animals were assembled as a sign of status. Captive pigeons were kept in Iraq as early as 4500 BCE. Egyptian tomb paintings at Saqqara dating from 2500 BCE depict several species of antelopes in collars. Loisel postulated that this might have been an early form of royal menagerie.

The second period is the "Period of the Paradeisos," which is based on the Persian word for a very large walled park. The earliest record of such a park belonging to the Empress Tanki was in China around 1150 BCE; considerable evidence survives of the existence of such parks in Persia and in Egypt. These royal parks contained numerous animals kept in conditions of relative liberty. Most of the animals were wild, but undoubtedly some were tame. Animals presented to the monarch would be kept in such a park, as would animals intended as presents. Few zoos existed for educational purposes, but it is likely that the Greeks of Aristotle's time (fourth century BCE) were concerned with study and experiment. This idea of a royal "paradise" (the Garden of Eden is an idealized version of such a park) remained in the West until the fall of Rome, in China well into the nineteenth century, and Loisel reported relics of such parks in India and Thailand.

During the Middle Ages in Europe, members of the nobility occasionally kept wild animals. Charlemagne maintained a collection in the eighth century CE, as did Henry I in the twelfth century. Philip VI had a menagerie in the Louvre in 1333, and members of the House of Bourbon maintained collections at Versailles. What emerged from this is the third period, which Loisel termed the "Period of the Menagerie" from the French for a "place to manage" animals. The animals were usually grouped by order and kept in separate enclosures (e.g., all the felines or primates were housed together). There was no thought of creating a paradise. These menageries were little more than a symbol of the extent of the empire and, therefore, the importance of the nobleman. The most important example of this period was the collection of the Aztecs at Tenochtitlán, which had a staff of 300 keepers. Cortés destroyed the collection as part of his campaign against Montezuma in 1521. The Aztecs maintained a second menagerie at Tezcuco, the scientific center of their empire, with an adjoining library and natural history museum. That, too, was destroyed.

Loisel maintains that Europe did not have an equivalent zoological park for three centuries after this slaughter. However, the creation of European zoological parks for scientific purposes began much sooner. Francis Bacon wrote of such an idealized place in *The New Atlantis* (1617), and, in 1662, Louis XIV of France established the menagerie of Versailles, intending it to become the grandest in the world. The scientific use of the collection was assigned to the Académie des Sciences, whose members did the first important work in comparative anatomy. It is widely reported that King Louis attended the dissection of an elephant in 1681. Unfortunately, this menagerie declined under the remaining French monarchs and was destroyed during the French Revolution.

Zoos. Hippopotamus begging for peanuts. National Zoological Park, Washington D.C. (Prints and Photographs Division, Library of Congress)

The Revolution ushered in the "Period of the Classical Zoo." The classical zoo was an institution for public education and recreation. The remnants of the Versailles menagerie were taken to the newly named Jardin des Plantes in Paris by its superintendent. The National Menagerie of the Museum of Natural History was created there. This zoo would serve as the model for all similar institutions throughout the nineteenth century. Modern zookeeping is considered to have begun with the creation of the Imperial Menagerie at the Schönbrunn Palace in Vienna in 1752, which was opened to the public thirteen years later. The menagerie concept remained as animals lived in barred cages or some other small enclosures. Similar institutions arose in London (1828), Amsterdam (1838), Berlin (1844), and Antwerp (1848). In the United States, zoos developed in Chicago's Lincoln Park (1869), Philadelphia (1874), Washington, D.C. (1889), and New York (1899). National or municipal governments financed some zoos; others, like those in London and New York, were financed by a private, nonprofit zoological society; and still others were private, for-profit institutions. This pattern continues to the present.

Loisel's schema concludes with the "Period of the Modern Zoological Park." He considers this to have begun in 1907 with the construction of Carl Hagenbeck's Tierpark in Stellingen, outside Hamburg. Hagenbeck, a second-gener-

ation animal dealer, collaborated with Urs Eggenschwyler, a Swiss sculptor and architect, to build a park in which the animals were displayed in large enclosures surrounded by largely hidden moats. The enclosures were designed to re-create a natural habitat for the animals, one that would promote more natural behaviors and would permit biologists to study animal behavior. One immediate result was an improvement in the biological condition of the animals.

Despite Hagenbeck's innovations, many zoos continued to follow the classical model. As in the days of royal menageries, there continued to be tacit competition as to how many different species could be displayed. In the late 1960s, things began to change. As part of the ecological awakening that culminated in the United States with the passage of the Endangered Species Act of 1973, zoos and aquariums throughout the world transformed their display space from cages and tanks to habitats designed to promote normal behavior. In many cities, this involved moving the zoo from small quarters in a park near downtown to a larger space on the outskirts of the city. The menagerie mentality disappeared; the best zoos were no longer those with the most different kinds of animals. By helping to create an environment in which breeding took place, this investment in new capital helped promote a rededication to the preferred mission of zoo people—species preservation. And this transformation was not limited to exhibit space. To facilitate research, laboratories and libraries were expanded. To provide education, classrooms were constructed, and teachers hired.

Similar developments took place in aquariums. The first aquariums developed in the mid-1800s when glass technology became sufficiently advanced. Several of the early aquariums were private, for-profit enterprises; many of them failed. Zoos began to build their own aquariums in the late nineteenth and early twentieth centuries. The display of, and often entertainment built around, marine mammals led to a resurgence of independent aquariums in the latter half of the twentieth century.

BIBLIOGRAPHY

Bostock, Stephen St. C. *Zoos and Animal Rights: The Ethics of Keeping Animals*, ch. 2. London, 1993.

Galton, Francis. "Domestication of Animals." In *Inquiries into Human Faculty*. London, 1865, rep. 1911.

Hoage, R. J., and William A. Deiss. *New Worlds, New Animals: From Menagerie to Zoological Park in the Nineteenth Century*. Baltimore, 1996.

Loisel, Gustave. *Histoire des ménageries de l'antiquité à nos jours*. 3 vols. Paris, 1912.

DENNIS MERITT

THE OXFORD ENCYCLOPEDIA OF
ECONOMIC HISTORY

Topical Outline of Articles

The entries and subentries in *The Oxford Encyclopedia of Economic History* are conceived according to the general conceptual categories listed in this topical outline. Entries in the Encyclopedia proper are organized alphabetically. The outline is divided into eleven parts:

1. Geography: Countries and Regions
2. Geography: Cities
3. Agriculture
4. Production Systems, Business History, and Technology
5. Demography
6. Institutions, Governments, and Markets
7. Macroeconomic History and International Economics
8. Money, Banking, and Finance
9. Labor
10. Natural Resources and the Environment
11. Biographies

1. GEOGRAPHY: COUNTRIES AND REGIONS

EUROPE

Alsace
Austria
  Austria before 1867
  Austro-Hungarian Empire
  Modern Austria
Balkans
Baltic States
Bavaria
Belgium
Black Country
Catalonia
Czechoslovakia and the Czech and Slovak Republics
Danube
England
  Early and Medieval Periods up to 1500
  Early Modern Period
France
  Early and Medieval Periods
  Early Modern Period
  Modern Period
  The French Empire between 1789 and 1950
  The French Empire to 1789

Germany
  Early and Medieval Periods
  Early Modern Period
  Modern Germany
Great Britain
  British Empire
  Modern Period
Greece
  Byzantine and Ottoman Periods
  Classical Period and Earlier
  Modern Period
Hungary
Ireland
  Ireland before 1800
  Ireland from 1800 to 1922
  Ireland after 1922
Italy
  Classical Period
  Early Modern and Modern Periods (to 1861)
  Medieval Period
  United Italy
Lancashire
Lombardy

Cotton
Crop and Plant Diseases
Draft and Pack Animals
Dye Crops
Fiber Crops
Fur Trapping and Trade
Horses
Kola
Legumes and Pulses
Oil Crops
Opium and Narcotics
Pigs
Potato
Poultry
Sericulture
Sheep and Goats
Sugar
Tea
Tobacco
Vines and Viticulture

AGRICULTURAL TECHNOLOGY AND PROCESSES

Crop Rotation
Fertilizing
Processing Crops
Seed and Seed Varieties
Water Control

AGRICULTURAL INPUTS, PRODUCTIVITY, AND WAGES

Agricultural Credit
Agricultural Labor
Agricultural Wages
Crop Failures
Crop Yields
Famines
Farm Capital
Farm Management
Hedges and Fences
Irish Famine

4. PRODUCTION SYSTEMS, BUSINESS HISTORY, AND TECHNOLOGY

BASIC CONCEPTS AND PHENOMENA

Accounting and Bookkeeping
Capitalism
Chaebol
Command Economies
Corporatism
Domestic Industry
Economies of Scale

Economies of Scope
Entrepreneurship
Factory System
Feudalism
   Historical Overview
   Manorial System
   Taxation
Firm
   The Firm before 1800
   The Firm after 1800
Flexible Specialization
Habakkuk Hypothesis
Industrial Revolution
Keiretsu
Management
Marxism and Marxist
Mass Production
Multinational Corporations
Nationalization and Privatization
Patents
Social Savings
Technology

INDUSTRIAL ORGANIZATION

Antitrust
Cartels and Collusion
   Historical Overview
   Concentration and Entry
   Price-Fixing and Vertical Constriants
   Price Discrimination
Company Towns
Industrial Districts
Integration
   Horizontal Integration
   Vertical Integration
International Cartels
Market Structure
   General Introduction
   Competition
   Monopoly and Natural Monopoly
   Oligopoly and Monopolistic Competition

INDUSTRIES SURVEYS

Advertising
Air Transportation
   Historical Overview
   Technological Change
   Industrial Organization and Regulation
Antiques Trade
Arms Industry
   Historical Overview
   Industrial Organization
Art Markets

9. LABOR

BASIC CONCEPTS

Apprenticeship
Human Capital
Journeymen
Labor
Labor Productivity
Literacy

FORMS OF LABOR CONTRACTS

Contract Labor and the Indenture System
Serfdom
Slavery

LABOR MARKETS

Child Labor
Labor Markets
  Historical Overview
  Segmentation and Discrimination
  Integration and Wage Convergence
Labor Mobility
Unemployment
Women in the Labor Force

LABOR ORGANIZATIONS, UNIONS, AND INDUSTRIAL RELATIONS

Bargaining, Collective
Craft Guilds
Employers' Associations
Industrial Relations
Luddism and Social Protest
Unions

PAYMENT SCHEMES AND WAGES

Wage Legislation
Wage Systems
Wages

LABOR CONDITIONS

Labor Conditions and Job Safety
Labor Time
Retirement

10. NATURAL RESOURCES AND THE ENVIRONMENT

NATURAL RESOURCES

Fisheries and Fish Processing
Forests and Deforestation
Fossil Fuels
Natural Resources
  Historical Overview
  Property Rights
  Regulation
Nuclear Power
Quarries
Soil and Soil Conservation
Solar Power
Water Resources
Whaling
Wood as Fuel

ENVIRONMENT

Climate and Climate History
Environment
  Historical Overview
  Environmental Policies and Regulation
Fire Control
Pest Control
Pollution
Volcanic Activities and Earthquakes

11. BIOGRAPHIES

INVENTORS AND WRITERS ON TECHNOLOGY

Agricola, Georgius
Arkwright, Richard
Babbage, Charles
Bell, Alexander Graham
Bessemer, Henry
Boulton, Matthew
Brunel Family
Cort, Henry
Daimler, Gottlieb
Diesel, Rudolf
Eastman, George
Edison, Thomas A.
Gutenberg, Johannes
Haber, Fritz
Jacquard, Joseph-Marie
Kettering, Charles
McCormick, Cyrus
Newcomen, Thomas
Nobel, Alfred
Otto, Nikolaus August
Roberts, Richard
Singer, Isaac Merritt
Smeaton, John
Stephenson Family
Taylor, Frederick Winslow
Watt, James
Westinghouse, George
Whitney, Eli
Wright Brothers

ENTREPRENEURS, BANKERS, AND LABOR LEADERS

Agnelli Family
Armour Family
Astor, John Jacob
Bakunin, Mikhail
Brown Family
Brunner Family
Cadbury Family
Campbell, Joseph
Carnegie, Andrew
Chavez, Cesar
Chrysler, Walter
Coats Family
Cockerill, John
Courtauld Family
Debs, Eugene Victor
Deere, John
DuPont Family
Duisberg, Carl
Duke, James Buchanan
Dunlop, James
Ericsson, L. M.
Ford, Henry
Franklin, Benjamin
Gompers, Samuel
Gould, Jay
Gramsci, Antonio
Guggenheim Family
Guinness Family
Harriman, Edward
Hill, James J.
Kautsky, Karl
Krupp Family
Lenin, Vladimir Ilich
Lever, William Hesketh
Lewis, John L.
Liebknechts, The
List, Georg Friedrich
Luxemburg, Rosa
Mellon Family
Morgan, J. P.
Morris, William (Lord Nuffield)
Owen, Robert
Philips Family
Pilkington Family
Rhodes, Cecil John
Rockefeller, John Davison
Rong Family
Sassoon Family
Schlumberger Family

Schneider, Joseph-Eugène
Siemens Family
Slater, Samuel
Sloan, Alfred
Stinnes, Hugo
Swope, Gerard
Thyssen, August
Trotsky, Leon
Vanderbilt Family
Vickers Family
Wallenberg Family
Wendel Family
Zaibatsu

ECONOMISTS AND ECONOMIC HISTORIANS

Ashton, T. S.
Bloch, Marc
Braudel, Fernand
Chandler, Alfred D.
Clapham, John
Cliometrics
Fogel, Robert
Friedman, Milton
Gerschenkron, Alexander
Heckscher, Eli
Hughes, Jonathan
Keynes, John Maynard
Kindleberger, Charles P.
Lane, Frederic Chapin
Le Roy Ladurie, Emmanuel
Lewis, W. Arthur
Malthus, Thomas
Marshall, Alfred
Marx, Karl
Mill, John Stuart
Mumford, Lewis
North, Douglass Cecil
Pirenne, Henri
Polanyi, Karl
Postan, Michael
Power, Eileen
Ricardo, David
Schumpeter, Joseph
Smith, Adam
Sombart, Werner
Tawney, R. H.
Usher, A. P.
Veblen, Thorstein
Weber, Max
White, Lynn
Young, Arthur

Internet Sites

The following list includes websites where information on entries in this Encyclopedia can be found. Websites listed here were current as of spring 2003. The list is arranged by topical order. Only those entries for which a website is available are listed; for other topics, type the topic into a search engine.

1. GEOGRAPHY: COUNTRIES AND REGIONS

For information on individual countries, consult two resources available at the Library of Congress:
http://lcweb2.loc.gov (click on "Global Gateway")
http:// lcweb2.loc.gov/frd/cs

EUROPE

Austria: Austria before 1867
http://lcweb2.loc.gov/frd/cs/attoc.html
http://www.fortunecity.com/victorian/wooton/34/austria/contents.htm

Austria: Austro-Hungarian Empire
http://www.fortunecity.com/victorian/wooton/34/austria/contents.htm

Austria: Modern Austria
http://lcweb2.loc.gov/frd/cs/attoc.html

Balkans
http://www.lib.msu.edu/sowards/balkan/lect09.htm
http://www.lib.msu.edu/sowards/balkan/lect23.htm

Baltic States
http://www.ibs.ee/Business/index.html.en
http://www.ibs.ee/ibs/history/brief/brief1.html

Czechoslovakia and the Czech and Slovak Republics
http://lcweb2.loc.gov/frd/cs/cstoc.html

England: Early and Medieval Periods up to 1500
http://www1.enloe.wake.k12.nc.us/enloe/CandC/showme/medieval.html
http://www.fordham.edu/halsall/sbook1j.html

England: Early Modern Period
http://www.portsdown.demon.co.uk/dem.htm

France: Early and Medieval Periods
http://orb.rhodes.edu/encyclop/high/France/HMFrance.html
http://orb.rhodes.edu/encyclop/late/France/LMFrance.html
http://www1.enloe.wake.k12.nc.us/enloe/CandC/showme/medieval.html
http://www.fordham.edu/halsall/sbook1j.html

Germany: Early and Medieval Periods
http://www1.enloe.wake.k12.nc.us/enloe/CandC/showme/medieval.html
http://www.fordham.edu/halsall/sbook1j.html

Germany: Modern Germany
http://lcweb2.loc.gov/frd/cs/gxtoc.html
http://lcweb2.loc.gov/frd/cs/detoc.html

Great Britain: British Empire
http://www.britishempire.co.uk/science/science.htm

Great Britain: Modern Period
http://www.victorianweb.org/technology/technolov.html
http://mars.wnec.edu/~grempel/courses/wc2/lectures/industrialrev.html
http://www.let.leidenuniv.nl/history/econgs/uk.html

Greece: Classical Period
http://www.middlebury.edu/~harris/Classics/Economicsin-Greece.html
http://devlab.dartmouth.edu/history/bronze_age/lessons/22.html#13

Hungary
http://lcweb2.loc.gov/frd/cs/hutoc.html

Ireland: Ireland from 1800 to 1922
http://vassun.vassar.edu/~sttaylor/FAMINE/
http://www.adw03.dial.pipex.com/peel/econ.htm

Ireland: Ireland after 1922
http://www.geocities.com/CapitolHill/2419/partion.html

Italy: Classical Period
http://www.camelotintl.com/romans/trade.html
http://snafu.mit.edu/~bhslatin/history/trade.shtml

Italy: Medieval Period
http://www.fordham.edu/halsall/sbook1j.html

Low Countries: The Low Countries before 1568
http://www.le.ac.uk/hi/bon/ESFDB/BLOCK/block.html
http://www.jyu.fi/~jojuto/df_1585.html

Low Countries: Northern Netherlands between 1568 and 1815
http://www.coins.nd.edu/ColCoin/ColCoinIntros/Netherlands.html

Mediterranean Sea and Islands
http://myron.sjsu.edu/romeweb/TRANSPRT/shiptrav.htm
http://myron.sjsu.edu/romeweb/GLOSSARY/timeln/t02.htm
http://lcweb2.loc.gov/frd/cs/cytoc.html

Nordic Countries: Modern Denmark
http://www.pip.dknet.dk/~pip261/denmark.html
http://www.sv.uio.no/arena/publications/wp00_6.htm
http://www.ilo.org/public/english/employment/strat/publ/
etp53.htm

Nordic Countries: Modern Finland
http://lcweb2.loc.gov/frd/cs/fitoc.html
http://www.sv.uio.no/arena/publications/wp00_6.htm

Nordic Countries: Modern Norway
http://www.un.org/esa/agenda21/natlinfo/countr/norway/
index.htm
http://www.sv.uio.no/arena/publications/wp00_6.htm
http://www.cyberclip.com/Katrine/NorwayInfo/Articles/
HistNorw.html
http://www.state.gov/www/issues/economic/trade_reports/
europe_canada97/norway97.html

Nordic Countries: Modern Sweden
http://www.sv.uio.no/arena/publications/wp00_6.htm

Poland: Modern Period
http://lcweb2.loc.gov/frd/cs/pltoc.html

Portugal: An Overview
http://lcweb2.loc.gov/frd/cs/pttoc.html

Portugal: Portuguese Empire
http://lcweb2.loc.gov/frd/cs/pttoc.html

Provence
http://www.france.diplomatie.fr/label_france/ENGLISH/
REGION/PROVENCE/provence.html

Roman Empire
http://www.tulane.edu/~august/H303/currency/Dioclctian.htm
http://myron.sjsu.edu/romeweb/transport/shiptrav.htm

Russia: Early and Medieval Periods
http://www.ece.iit.edu/~prh/coins/PiN/ecm.html

Russia: Modern Period
http://lcweb2.loc.gov/frd/cs/rutoc.html
http://www.let.leidenuniv.nl/history/econgs/Rusland.html

Russia: Communist Russia
http://lcweb2.loc.gov/frd/cs/rutoc.html
http://www.emayzine.com/lectures/STALIN.html
http://econ161.berkeley.edu/TCEH/Slouch_Purge15.html
http://www.let.leidenuniv.nl/history/econgs/Rusland.html

Russia: Post-Communist Russia
http://lcweb2.loc.gov/frd/cs/rutoc.html
http://www.let.leidenuniv.nl/history/econgs/Rusland.html

Russia: Russian Empire
http://lcweb2.loc.gov/frd/cs/rutoc.html

Scotland
http://www.ex.ac.uk/~ajgibson/scotdata/
scot_database_home.html

Spain: Early and Medieval Periods
http://lcweb2.loc.gov/frd/cs/estoc.html

Spain: Modern Spain
http://www.nova.es/%7Ejlb/mad%5Fin90.htm
http://lcweb2.loc.gov/frd/cs/estoc.html

Spain: Spanish Empire
http://lcweb2.loc.gov/frd/cs/estoc.html

Tuscany
http://www.fordham.edu/halsall/source/1225florence?gig.html

Ukraine
http://www.odessit.com/general/ukraine.htm
http://rru.worldbank.org/viewpoint/HTMLNotes/
170/170summary.html.

Ulster
http://www.motherbedford.com/Irish4.htm

Wales
http://www.womeninworldhistory.com/lesson7.html

THE AMERICAS

American Indian Economies: Aztec Economy
http://www.utexas.edu/courses/wilson/ant304/projects/
projects98/morrisp/morrisp.html

Argentina
http://www.surdelsur.com/economia/indexingles.html
http://www.eclac.org/English/research/dcitf/lcl1129/
argeng.htm

Brazil
http://lcweb2.loc.gov/frd/cs/brtoc.html

Caribbean Region: Post-Emancipation Period
http://www.postcolonialweb.org/caribbean/caribov.html

Central American Countries
http://davem2.cotf.edu/earthinfo/camerica/CAeco.html

Central South American States
http://www.ciesin.org/decentralization/English/CaseStudies/
paraguay.html
http://www.state.gov/www/issues/economic/trade_reports/
latin_america97/bolivia97.html

Chile
http://lcweb2.loc.gov/frd/cs/cltoc.html

Colombia
http://lcweb2.loc.gov/frd/cs/cotoc.html

Cuba
http://lanic.utexas.edu/la/cb/cuba/asce/cuba2/nick.html
http://lanic.utexas.edu/la/cb/cuba/asce/cuba2/alvarez.html

Guyana
http://lcweb2.loc.gov/frd/cs/gytoc.html

Haiti
http://lcweb2.loc.gov/frd/cs/httoc.html

Jamaica
http://www.iadb.org/exr/sep/ja981.htm
http://www.tradeport.org/ts/countries/jamaica/

Mexico
  http://historicaltextarchive.com/
    sections.php?op=listarticles&secid=21
  http://lcweb2.loc.gov/frd/cs/mxtoc.html
  http://www.msu.edu/course/hst/384/xObstacles.htm

Panama Canal
  http://www.pancanal.com/

United States: Colonial Period
  http://www.coins.nd.edu/ColCurrency/index.html
  http://etext.lib.virginia.edu/journals/EH/EH34/brock34.htm
  http://earlyamerica.com/review/summer97/banking.html

United States: Antebellum Period
  http://web.uccs.edu/~history/index/
    antebellum.html#transportation
  http://odur.let.rug.nl/~usa/ECO/1991/index.htm
  http://web.uccs.edu/~history/index/
    antebellum.html#marketrev
  http://web.uccs.edu/~history/index/antebellum.html#banking

United States: Modern Period
  http://odur.let.rug.nl/~usa/ECO/1991/index.htm
  http://socserv2.socsci.mcmaster.ca/~econ/ugcm/3ll3/veblen/
    leisure/chap04.txt
  http://econ161.berkeley.edu/TCEH/Slouch_Crash14.html
  http://internationalecon.com/tradeimbalance/US.html
  http://www.mises.org/money/4s5.asp
  http://www.let.leidenuniv.nl/history/econgs/usa.html

Uruguay
  http://lcweb2.loc.gov/frd/cs/uytoc.html

Venezuela
  http://lcweb2.loc.gov/frd/cs/vetoc.html

ASIA

Arabia
  http://www.tradeport.org/ts/countries/saudiarabia/trends.html
  http://www.saudinf.com/main/000.htm

Bangladesh
  http://lcweb2.loc.gov/frd/cs/bdtoc.html
  http://www.theodora.com/wfb/bangladesh_economy.html

Byzantine Empire
  http://www.fordham.edu/halsall/source/550byzsilk.html
  http://www.shsu.edu/~his_ncp/265notes.html
  http://www.shsu.edu/~his_ncp/MunByz.html

China: Ancient and Feudal China
  http://library.thinkquest.org/23062/frameset.html

China: Tang, Song, and Yuan Dynasties
  http://www.crystalinks.com/china.html
  http://www.ess.uci.edu/~oliver/silk.html
  http://lcweb2.loc.gov/frd/cs/cntoc.html

China: Ming and Qing Dynasties
  http://www.cnd.org/fairbank/qing.html
  http://lcweb2.loc.gov/frd/cs/cntoc.html

China: Republican Period
  http://lcweb2.loc.gov/frd/cs/cntoc.html

China: Communist China
  http://lcweb2.loc.gov/frd/cs/cntoc.html

Hong Kong
  http://www.state.gov/www/issues/economic/
    trade_reports/1999/hongkong.html

India: Muslim Period and Mughal Empire
  http://lcweb2.loc.gov/frd/cs/intoc.html
  http://reenic.utexas.edu/asnic/countries/india/
    JohnRichards'Indian.html

India: Colonial Period
  http://lcweb2.loc.gov/frd/cs/intoc.html
  http://www.virginia.edu/~soasia/symsem/kisan/papers/land.html

India: Independent India
  http://lcweb2.loc.gov/frd/cs/intoc.html
  http://astro.temple.edu/~sanjoy/calpap.html

Indochina
  http://lcweb2.loc.gov/frd/cs/latoc.html
  http://lcweb2.loc.gov/frd/cs/vntoc.html
  http://lcweb2.loc.gov/frd/cs/khtoc.html

Indonesia
  http://lcweb2.loc.gov/frd/cs/idtoc.htm
  http://csf.colorado.edu/jwsr/archive/vol5/vol5_number1/
    v5n1a3.htm
  http://www.okusi.net/garydean/works/IndEcDev.html
  http://www.ilo.org/public/english/protection/migrant/papers/
    emindo/ch2.htm

Iran: Ancient Period
  http://lcweb2.loc.gov/frd/cs/irtoc.html

Iran: Islamic Period, 640–1800
  http://lcweb2.loc.gov/frd/cs/irtoc.html

Iran: Modern Period, since 1800
  http://lcweb2.loc.gov/frd/cs/irtoc.html
  http://ivl.8m.com/characteristics_of_labor_force.htm

Iraq: Ancient Period
  http://lcweb2.loc.gov/frd/cs/iqtoc.html

Iraq: Islamic Period
  http://lcweb2.loc.gov/frd/cs/iqtoc.html

Iraq: Modern Iraq
  http://lcweb2.loc.gov/frd/cs/iqtoc.html

Israel
  http://lcweb2.loc.gov/frd/cs/iltoc.html
  http://www.biu.ac.il/SOC/besa/books/kanov/chap2.html

Japan: Ancient and Medieval Periods
  http://lcweb2.loc.gov/frd/cs/jptoc.html

Japan: Early Modern Period
  http://lcweb2.loc.gov/frd/cs/jptoc.html
  http://www.unu.edu/unupress/unupbooks/uu36je/uu36je09.htm

Japan: Modern Period
  http://lcweb2.loc.gov/frd/cs/jptoc.html
  http://www.unu.edu/unupress/unupbooks/uu36je/uu36je09.htm
  http://www.let.leidenuniv.nl/history/econgs/japan.html

Japan: Japanese Empire
  http://lcweb2.loc.gov/frd/cs/jptoc.html
  http://www.let.leidenuniv.nl/history/econgs/japan.html

Korea: North Korea
  http://lcweb2.loc.gov/frd/cs/kptoc.html

Korea: South Korea
  http://lcweb2.loc.gov/frd/cs/krtoc.html

Levant: Modern Lebanon
  http://lcweb2.loc.gov/frd/cs/lbtoc.html
  http://www.tradeport.org/ts/countries/lebanon/trends.html

Levant: Modern Syria
  http://lcweb2.loc.gov/frd/cs/sytoc.html

Malaysia
  http://www.unu.edu/unupress/unupbooks/uu11ee/uu11ee11.htm
  http://www.state.gov/www/issues/economic/trade_reports/
    eastasia98/malaysia98.html

Myanmar
  http://www.riceweb.org/countries/myanmar.htm

Nepal
  http://lcweb2.loc.gov/frd/cs/nptoc.html

Ottoman Empire
  http://coursesa.matrix.msu.edu/~fisher/hst373/readings/
    inalcik8.html

Pakistan
  http://lcweb2.loc.gov/frd/cs/pktoc.html

Philippines
  http://lcweb2.loc.gov/frd/cs/phtoc.html

Silk Road
  http://ess1.ps.uci.edu/~oliver/silk.html
  http://library.thinkquest.org/13406/sr/

Singapore
  http://lcweb2.loc.gov/frd/cs/sgtoc.html
  http://www.unu.edu/unupress/unupbooks/uu11ee/uu11ee1a.htm

Sri Lanka
  http://lcweb2.loc.gov/frd/cs/lktoc.html

Taiwan
  http://www.tier.org.tw/apecc/hotnews/Discussion_Papers/
    wp0008.html

Thailand
  http://www.state.gov/www/issues/economic/
    trade_reports/1999/thailand.html

Turkey: Premodern Turkey
  http://www.turkishodyssey.com/turkey/history/history1.htm

Turkey: Modern Turkey
  http://lcweb2.loc.gov/frd/cs/trtoc.html

AFRICA

Central Africa: Central Africa from 1850 to the Present
  http://www.state.gov/www/background_notes/
    rwanda_0398_bgn.html
  http://www.state.gov/www/background_notes/
    zambia_0997_bgn.html

  http://www.state.gov/www/background_notes/
    gabon_0197_bgn.html
  http://www.state.gov/www/background_notes/
    cameroon_9912_bgn.html
  http://lcweb2.loc.gov/frd/cs/aotoc.html

Côte d' Ivoire and Ghana
  http://www.stanford.edu/~ankle/edge/3.html
  http://www.unu.edu/unupress/unupbooks/uu28ae/
    uu28ae0g.htm
  http://lcweb2.loc.gov/frd/cs/ghtoc.html
  http://lcweb2.loc.gov/frd/cs/citoc.html

East Africa: Colonial and Modern Periods
  http://lcweb2.loc.gov/frd/cs/mgtoc.html
  http://lcweb2.loc.gov/frd/cs/ugtoc.html
  http://www.unu.edu/unupress/unupbooks/80604e/
    80604E0b.htm
  http://lcweb2.loc.gov/frd/cs/sctoc.html
  http://lcweb2.loc.gov/frd/cs/mutoc.html
  http://lcweb2.loc.gov/frd/cs/mgtoc.html
  http://lcweb2.loc.gov/frd/cs/ugtoc.html
  http://www.unu.edu/unupress/unupbooks/80604e/
    80604E0b.htm
  http://www.state.gov/www/background_notes/
    tanzania_0598_bgn.html
  http://lcweb2.loc.gov/frd/cs/mutoc.html
  http://lcweb2.loc.gov/frd/cs/sctoc.html

Egypt: Ancient and Classical Periods
  http://www.reshafim.org.il/ad/egypt/trade/index.html

Egypt: Islamic and Modern Periods
  http://lcweb2.loc.gov/frd/cs/egtoc.html
  http://www.innogize.com/papers/egypt.html

Ethiopia
  http://lcweb2.loc.gov/frd/cs/ettoc.html

Maghrib
  http://www.ilo.org/public/english/protection/migrant/papers/
    migmagh/ch3.htm
  http://www.ilo.org/public/english/protection/migrant/papers/
    migmagh/index.htm
  http://lcweb2.loc.gov/frd/cs/dztoc.html
  http://lcweb2.loc.gov/frd/cs/dztoc.html
  http://lcweb2.loc.gov/frd/cs/mutoc.html
  http://lcweb2.loc.gov/frd/cs/mrtoc.html
  http://lcweb2.loc.gov/frd/cs/dztoc.html
  http://lcweb2.loc.gov/frd/cs/lytoc.html
  http://dosfan.lib.uic.edu/ERC/bgnotes/nea/morocco9411.html
  http://dosfan.lib.uic.edu/ERC/bgnotes/nea/tunisia9407.html

Nigeria
  http://lcweb2.loc.gov/frd/cs/ngtoc.html
  http://www.stanford.edu/~ankle/edge/2.html

Nile
  http://www-personal.umich.edu/~wddrake/smith.html

North Africa: Colonial and Modern Periods
  http://www.ilo.org/public/english/protection/migrant/papers/
    migmagh/ch3.htm

http://www.ilo.org/public/english/protection/migrant/papers/
     migmagh/index.htm
http://lcweb2.loc.gov/frd/cs/dztoc.html
http://lcweb2.loc.gov/frd/cs/mutoc.html
http://lcweb2.loc.gov/frd/cs/mrtoc.html
http://lcweb2.loc.gov/frd/cs/lytoc.html

Sahara
http://www.hf.uib.no/institutter/smi/paj/Masonen.html

Sahel
http://www.state.gov/www/background_notes/
     mali_0006_bgn.html
http://www.state.gov/www/background_notes/
     senegal_0298_bgn.html
http://lcweb2.loc.gov/frd/cs/ngtoc.html

Southern Africa: Modern Period
http://www.state.gov/www/background_notes/
     botswana_bgn_9710.html
http://dosfan.lib.uic.edu/ERC/bgnotes/af/
     mozambique9607.html
http://lcweb2.loc.gov/frd/cs/zatoc.html

Sudan: Western Sudan
http://geography.ou.edu/research/sudan.html

Sudan: Central Sudan
http://lcweb2.loc.gov/frd/cs/sdtoc.html

Suez Canal
http://www.wwnorton.com/college/history/worldciv/-
     resource/39suez.htm

OCEANIA

Australia
http://www.people.virginia.edu/~hms2f/internal.html
http://www.state.gov/www/background_notes/
     australia_899_bgn.html

New Zealand
http://www.people.virginia.edu/~hms2f/internal.html
http://www.state.gov/www/background_notes/
     new_zealand_899_bgn.html

Pacific Islands
http://www.boh.com/econ/pacific/fjaer.asp
http://www.oneworld.org/ecdpm/pubs/wp17_gb.htm
http://www.abc.net.au/ra/carvingout/issues/default.htm
http://www.state.gov/www/background_notes/
     png_899_bgn.html

2. GEOGRAPHY: CITIES

EUROPE

Amsterdam
http://www.bmz.amsterdam.nl/adam/uk/intro/gesch2.html
http://bewley.virtualave.net/credit.html

Bruges
http://www.brugge.be/toerisme/en/historye.htm
http://www.owlnet.rice.edu/~arch343/lecture9.html

Florence
http://www.owlnet.rice.edu/~arch343/lecture9.html
http://www.d.umn.edu/~aroos/jensen2.htm

Genoa
http://bewley.virtualave.net/credit.html

Hamburg
http://www.kfki.hu/~arthp/tours/gothic/history/hansa.html
http://members.bellatlantic.net/~baronfum/hansa.html

London
http://www.britarch.ac.uk/ba/ba45/ba45regs.html
http://www.dur.ac.uk/History/staff/RCMLECT.HTM

Lübeck
http://www.kfki.hu/~arthp/tours/gothic/history/hansa.html
http://members.bellatlantic.net/~baronfum/hansa.html

Manchester
http://www.spartacus.schoolnet.co.uk/ITmanchester.htm
http://www.macalester.edu/courses/geog61/manchester/
     history.html

Rome and the Papal State
http://snafu.mit.edu/~bhslatin/history/trade.shtml

Seville
http://enterprise.is.tcu.edu/~rwoodward/thalassa.htm

Venice
http://www.sjsu.edu/faculty/watkins/venice.htm
http://www.d.umn.edu/~aroos/jensen2.htm
http://bewley.virtualave.net/credit.html

THE AMERICAS

Mexico City
http://www.macalester.edu/courses/geog61/jpalmer/
     migration.html

Philadelphia
http://mcmcweb.er.usgs.gov/phil/
     philhistory.html#EconomicHistory
http://www.phlx.com/exchange/history.html

ASIA

Baghdad
http://www.albalagh.net/kids/history/abbasids.shtml

Bombay
http://theory.tifr.res.in/bombay/history/
http://theory.tifr.res.in/bombay/history/cotton.html

Calcutta
http://astro.temple.edu/~sanjoy/calpap.html

Istanbul
http://www.shsu.edu/~his_ncp/MunByz.html

Shanghai
http://www.mcgill.ca/mchg/mchg/qia/qiach1.htm

Tokyo
http://www.kouwan.metro.tokyo.jp/kowane/rekisi/rekisie.html

AFRICA

Timbuktu
    http://www.anthro.mankato.msus.edu/archaeology/sites/africa/
        timbuktu.html
    http://users.erols.com/gmqm/timbuktu.html

3. AGRICULTURE

BASIC CONCEPTS AND PHENOMENA

Agricultural Marketing: Agricultural Marketing Boards
    http://www.rdg.ac.uk/AcaDepts/ae/rjl/aemscfams/marketin.htm

Agricultural Policy
    http://www.usda.gov/history2/text11.htm

Agricultural Revolution: Asia, Africa, and the Americas
    http://museum.agropolis.fr/english/pages/expos/fresque/
        module_12.htm
    http://www.oldengine.org/members/ihc14/impliments.htm
    http://www.ssbtractor.com/features/Ford_tractors.html
    http://www.indiaonestop.com/Greenrevolution.htm
    http://www.theatlantic.com/issues/97jan/borlaug/speech.htm
    http://www.orst.edu/instruction/bi301/greenrev.htm
    http://www.webspawner.com/users/INDIAAGRIC/

Agricultural Risk Management: Historical Overview
    http://www.futuresbroker.com/development.htm

Agriculture: Historical Overview
    http://www.liang.8m.com/edu/hisagri.htm

Agriculture: Technological Change
    http://www.history.rochester.edu/appleton/a/agmac%2Dm.html

Agriculture: Main Tools and Implements
    http://www.usda.gov/history2/text4.htm
    http://www.history.rochester.edu/appleton/a/agmac%2Dm.html

Green Revolution
    http://www.indiaonestop.com/Greenrevolution.htm
    http://www.theatlantic.com/issues/97jan/borlaug/speech.htm
    http://www.orst.edu/instruction/bi301/greenrev.htm
    http://www.webspawner.com/users/INDIAAGRIC/

Open-Field System
    http://www.users.globalnet.co.uk/~chrisjs/drystone/
        drystonewalls.htm

AGRICULTURAL PRODUCTION SYSTEMS

Apiculture
    http://www.3838.co.jp/english/beepark/surprise/
        surprise_coin_e.html
    http://outdoorplace.org/beekeeping/

Dairy Farming
    http://www.dairycorp.com.au/milk/
        redirectme.htm#milk_history

Farming Intensity
    http://www.cnie.org/pop/marquette/marque3.htm

Irrigated Farming
    http://www.soilandhealth.org/01aglibrary/
        010102/01010216.html

Pastoralism
    http://www.unu.edu/unupress/unupbooks/80458e/
        80458E09.htm
    http://www.mc.maricopa.edu/academic/cult_sci/anthro/
        lost_tribes/hg_ag/pastor.html

Rice Farming
    http://www.admissions.carleton.ca/~bgordon/Rice/papers/
        zhimin99.htm
    http://www.riceweb.org/History.htm
    http://thecity.sfsu.edu/~sustain/bray.html

Swidden Agriculture
    http://www.unu.edu/unupress/unupbooks/80192e/
        80192E02.htm
    http://www.unu.edu/unupress/unupbooks/80192e/
        80192E05.htm

AGRICULTURAL PROPERTY RIGHTS AND TENURE SYSTEMS

Agricultural Rents
    http://cupid.ecom.unimelb.edu.au/het/whewell/lecture6.html
    http://www.yale.edu/lawweb/avalon/econ/rent.htm
    http://www.humboldt.edu/~jrp2/Documents/econpapr.html

Clan Land
    http://eserver.org/marx/1853?scot.clearings.txt

Collective Agriculture and Collectivization
    http://www.era.anthropology.ac.uk/Era_Resources/Era/
        Peasants/russia.html
    http://www.marx2mao.org//Stalin/RFFYP33.html
    http://www.marx2mao.org//Stalin/YGC29.html#c3

Cooperative Agriculture and Farmer Cooperatives
    http://www.aae.wisc.edu/aae323/history.html

Crofters
    http://www.umist.ac.uk/sport/jarvie.html
    http://www.caledonia.org.uk/socialland/history.htm
    http://www.alastairmcintosh.com/articles/
        1994_interculture.htm
    http://pages.eidosnet.co.uk/~skye/crofting.html

Homesteading
    http://www.homestead.org/hofaq.htm
    http://www.beatricene.com/homestead/world.html
    http://www.beatricene.com/homestead/history.html

Land Reform and Confiscations
    http://www.fao.org/WAICENT/FAOINFO/SUSTDEV/LTdirect/
        LTan0037.htm

Latifundia
    http://ideas.uqam.ca/ideas/data/Papers/nbrnberhi0096.html
    http://www.intl.pdx.edu/latin/economy/hacienda_ec.html

Mulk Lands
    http://www.socsci.mcmaster.ca/~econ/ugcm/3ll3/laveleye/
        PrimProp25.htm

Plantation System
    http://www.citinv.it/associazioni/CNMS/archivio/lavoro/
        teaplantation.html

http://www.unu.edu/unupress/unupbooks/80918e/80918E10.htm

http://instruct.uwo.ca/anthro/211/plantation.htm

Private Plots

http://www.polyconomics.com/searchbase/fles3.html

Sharecropping

http://www.unu.edu/unupress/unupbooks/80636e/
80636E0q.htm

State Farms

http://nt2.ec.man.ac.uk/multimedia/russia.htm

http://www.panasia.org.sg/nepalnet/policy/prop.html

http://www.wpb.be/icm/97en/97en05.htm

http://www.wiu.edu/users/miag/facstaff/jpc/jpcpap1a.htm

Tenant Right

http://homepage.tinet.ie/~beprepared/Ireland.htm

Waqf

http://coursesa.matrix.msu.edu/~fisher/hst373/readings/
inalcik8.html

AGRICULTURAL RESOURCES AND PRODUCTS

Cassava

http://www.globalcassavastrategy.net/asian_report.htm

Coffee

http://sovrana.com/libstory.htm

http://jrscience.wcp.muohio.edu/FieldCourses00/
PapersCostaRicaArticles/Coffee.ABitterDelight.html

Cotton

http://www.thoemmes.com/economics/cotton_intro.htm

Draft and Pack Animals

http://www.imh.org/imh/draft/drtoc.html

Fiber Crops

http://www.druglibrary.org/schaffer/hemp/indust/
INDHMPFR.HTM

Fur Trapping and Trade

http://www.whiteoak.org/learning/timeline.htm

http://www.gov.edmonton.ab.ca/comm_services/
city_op_attractions/fort/1846/fur_trade_history.html

Horses

http://users.erols.com/mmaidens/

Opium and Narcotics

http://history.binghamton.edu/hist130/docs/teaopium.htm

http://www.pbs.org/wgbh/pages/frontline/shows/heroin/etc/
history.html

http://www.opioids.com/opium/

http://www.hygra.com/teaand.htm

Pigs

http://www.cyberspaceag.com/pighistory.html

Potato

http://www.american.edu/projects/mandala/TED/
POTATO.HTM

Sugar

http://www.sucrose.com/lhist.html

Tea

http://www.stashtea.com/facts.htm

Tobacco

http://www.bell.lib.umn.edu/Products/tob1.html

http://www.tobacco.org/History/colonialtobacco.html

AGRICULTURAL TECHNOLOGY AND PROCESSES

Water Control

http://www.fao.org/docrep/T0231E/t0231e03.htm#TopOfPage

http://www.wcc.nrcs.usda.gov/nrcsirrig/Irrigation_Photos/
irrigation_photos.html

4. PRODUCTION SYSTEMS, BUSINESS HISTORY, AND TECHNOLOGY

BASIC CONCEPTS AND PHENOMENA

Capitalism

http://www.wsu.edu:8080/%7Edee/GLOSSARY/CAPITAL.HTM

http://hsb.baylor.edu/html/gardner/CESCH03.HTM

Entrepreneurship

http://www.ucc.uconn.edu/~LANGLOIS/SCHUMPET.HTML

Factory System

http://www.kentlaw.edu/ilhs/lowell.html

Feudalism: Historical Overview

http://www.britainexpress.com/History/
Feudalism_and_Medieval_life.htm

http://www.wsu.edu:8080/~dee/MA/FRENCH.HTM

http://melbecon.unimelb.edu.au/het/vinogradoff/feudal

Feudalism: Manorial System

http://www1.enloe.wake.k12.nc.us/enloe/CandC/showme/
manor.html

Feudalism: Taxation

http://www.fordham.edu/halsall/source/1133Hank1tax.html

Flexible Specialization

http://www.sfu.ca/~hayter/Flespec.htm

Industrial Revolution

http://www.fordham.edu/halsall/mod/modsbook14.html

http://www.fordham.edu/halsall/mod/modsbook35.html

http://mars.wnec.edu/~grempel/courses/wc2/lectures/
industrialrev.html

http://www.geocities.com/Athens/Acropolis/6914/index.htm

http://www.history.rochester.edu/steam/

http://members.aol.com/TeacherNet/Industrial.html

http://www.spartacus.schoolnet.co.uk/Textiles.htm

http://www.anglia.co.uk/angmulti/indrev/contents.html v

Mass Production

http://www.willamette.edu/~fthompso/MgmtCon/
Mass_Production.html

Patents

http://www.ladas.com/Patents/USPatentHistory.html

Technology

http://www.history.rochester.edu/steam/

INDUSTRIAL ORGANIZATION

Antitrust
   http://www.ftc.gov/bc/compguide/antitrst.htm
   http://www.apeccp.org.tw/doc/USA/Policy/sherman.html

Cartels and Collusion: Historical Overview
   http://www.let.leidenuniv.nl/history/rtg/cartels/
   http://www.antitrust.org/

Cartels and Collusion: Concentration and Entry
   http://www.antitrust.org/

Cartels and Collusion: Price-Fixing and Vertical Restrictions
   http://www.antitrust.org/

Cartels and Collusion: Price Discrimination
   http://www.antitrust.org/

International Cartels
   http://www.let.leidenuniv.nl/history/rtg/cartels/

Market Structure: Monopoly and Natural Monopoly
   http://home.att.net/~Resurgence/L-ausmon.htm

INDUSTRIES SURVEYS

Advertising
   http://etext.lib.virginia.edu/journals/EH/EH37/Murphy.html

Automobile and Truck Industry: Historical Overview
   http://www.autoshop-online.com/auto101/histtext.html

Automobile and Truck Industry: Technological Change
   http://www.toyota.co.jp/Museum/Tam/chart.html

Beer and Breweries
   http://www.alabev.com/brew.htm
   http://www.cohums.ohio-state.edu/history/projects/
      prohibition/brewing/

Bessemer Process
   http://www.history.rochester.edu/ehp-book/shb/hb11.htm
   http://www.history.rochester.edu/ehp-book/shb/hb12.htm

Coal Basins
   http://www.rwth-aachen.de/lek/Ww/aapg/640_480_v/
      sld002.htm

Computer Industry
   http://ei.cs.vt.edu/~history/TMTCTW.html

Cotton Industry: Historical Overview
   http://www.thoemmes.com/economics/cotton_intro.htm

Cotton Industry: Technological Change
   http://sweetmamapam.tripod.com/gin.html
   http://web.bryant.edu/~history/h364proj/fall_98/hulton/
      carding.htm

Domestic Service
   http://www.eh.net/Clio/Conferences/ASSA/Jan_00/
      rosenbloom.shtml

Electrical Industry
   http://www.americanhistory.si.edu/csr/powering/hirsh1/
      frmain.htm
   http://www.mcc.commnet.edu/cbt/staff/Russell/science/
      circuits/history/electricall.html
   http://acre.murdoch.edu.au/refiles/hydro/text.html

   http://www.americanhistory.si.edu/csr/powering/hirsh1/
      frmain.htm

Electronics Industry
   http://website.lineone.net/~ian_poole/articles/
      radio_history/radio_history.html

Fashion Industry
   http://www.marquise.de/

Food Processing Industry: Technological Change
   http://www.food-irradiation.com/florida.htm
   http://www.history-magazine.com/refrig.html

Food Processing Industry: Industrial Organization, Markets, and Trade
   http://www.stanford.edu/~mbucheli/unitedfruit.html

Gambling and Gambling Industry
   http://www.library.ca.gov/CRB/97/03/Chapt2.html
   http://www.library.ca.gov/CRB/97/03/Chapt6.html
   http://www.library.ca.gov/CRB/97/03/Chapt9.html
   http://www.library.ca.gov/CRB/97/03/Chapt11.html

Gas Industry
   http://www.geocities.com/Athens/Acropolis/4007/gsframe.htm
   http://www.eia.doe.gov/oil_gas/natural_gas/data_publica-
      tions/natural_gas_annual/nga.html
   http://www.eia.doe.gov/emeu/international/gas.html

Glass Products Industry
   http://inst.augie.edu/~gjhonsbr/glass.htm
   http://www.umich.edu/~kelseydb/Exhibits/WondrousGlass/
      glass.html

Gold and Silver Industry: Historical Overview
   http://www.ex.ac.uk/~pfclaugh/mhinf/mexico.htm
   http://www.ex.ac.uk/~pfclaugh/mhinf/nm_gold.htm
   http://www.silverinstitute.org/prodhist.html

Hard Fibers Industry
   http://www.gametec.com/hemp/IndHmpFrmg.htm

Health Industry: Historical Overview
   http://www.cl.utoledo.edu/canaday/quackery/quack-index.html

Health Industry: Technological Change
   http://www.mjm.mcgill.ca/issues/v02n02/aspirin.html
   http://www.midwifeinfo.com/history.html

Insurance: Historical Overview
   http://www.insurance4texas.com/crop1.htm

Insurance: Maritime Insurance
   http://www.acs.ucalgary.ca/MGMT/inrm/industry/marine.htm

Insurance: Health and Accident Insurance
   http://www.wa-ic.org/in_hist.htm

Insurance: Unemployment Insurance
   http://www.hrdc-drhc.gc.ca/insur/histui/hrdc.html

Jewelry Industry
   http://www.ex.ac.uk/~pfclaugh/mhinf/mexico.htm
   http://www.ex.ac.uk/~pfclaugh/mhinf/nm_gold.htm
   http://www.silverinstitute.org/prodhist.html

Jute Industry
   http://les1.man.ac.uk/multimedia/jute.htm

Linen Industry: Historical Overview
http://www.ulsterlinen.com/2.htm

Luxury Trades
http://www.artistictile.net/pages/Info/Info_Porcelain.html

Machine Tools Industry: Historical Overview
http://www.neo-tech.com/businessmen/part6.html

Magazines
http://www.kanzaki.com/jpress/mag-history.html

Meatpacking Industry
http://www.msstate.edu/dept/ads/Faculty/history.html

Metallurgic Industry: Historical Overview
http://neon.mems.cmu.edu/cramb/Processing/history.html

Mining: Historical Overview
http://www.ex.ac.uk/~RBurt/MinHistNet/
http://www.history.ohio-state.edu/projects/coal/
   AnthraciteDescription/AnthraciteRhone.htm
http://www.cohums.ohio-state.edu/history/projects/Lessons_US/
   Gilded_Age/Coal_Mining/default.htm

Mining: Technological Change
http://collections.ic.gc.ca/coal/mining/mining.html

Music Industry
http://www.soc.duke.edu/~s142tm01/history.html
http://www.soc.duke.edu/~s142tm01/history.html
http://history.acusd.edu/gen/recording/notes.html
http://www.soc.duke.edu/~s142tm01/competition.html

Newspapers: Historical Overview
http://www.newspaper-industry.org/history.html
http://www.discovery.com/guides/history/historybuff/library/
   refnews1692.html
http://www.discovery.com/guides/history/historybuff/library/
   refnews1792.html

Newspapers: Industrial Organization and Regulation
http://www.discovery.com/guides/history/historybuff/library/
   refnews1892.html
http://www.discovery.com/guides/history/historybuff/library/
   refnews1992.html

Oil Industry: Historical Overview
http://www.let.leidenuniv.nl/history/rtg/oilcrisis/index.htm
http://www.micheloud.com/FXM/SO/rock.htm

Oil Industry: Industrial Organization
http://www.micheloud.com/FXM/SO/rock.htm

Papermaking
http://www.ibfsrp.com/paper%5Fhistory.html
http://www.baph.freeserve.co.uk/information/papermaking.html

Power Technology
http://www.fordham.edu/halsall/mod/modsbook14.html
http://www.geocities.com/Athens/Acropolis/6914/index.htm
http://www.history.rochester.edu/steam/
http://telosnet.com/wind/early.html

Printing Industry
http://www.printersmark.com/Pages/HistLnks.html
http://www.donblacklinecasting.on.ca/pictures/
   pix-linotype.htm

Radio and Television Industry: Historical Overview
http://www.people.memphis.edu/~mbensman/history1.html
http://scriptorium.lib.duke.edu/adaccess/radio-history.html
http://scriptorium.lib.duke.edu/adaccess/tv-history.html

Radio and Television Industry: Technological Change
http://www.cedmagazine.com/retro/index.html
http://www.orbitsat.com/AboutSat/history.htm

Radio and Television Industry: Industrial Organization and Regulation
http://www.people.memphis.edu/~mbensman/history1.html

Railroads: Historical Overview
http://www.history.rochester.edu/steam/brown/
http://www.spartacus.schoolnet.co.uk/railways.htm
http://www.nationalrrmuseum.org/EdPacket/html/Tguide1.htm
http://www.aar.org/comm/statfact.nsf/5406ac733125e6c785256
   4d000737b60/38724e97801d66418525688000606540?Open-
   Document
http://mikes.railhistory.railfan.net/pindex.html
http://odur.let.rug.nl/~usa/E/ironhorse/ironhorsexx.htm

Railroads: Industrial Organization and Regulation
http://www.aar.org/comm/statfact.nsf/5406ac733125e6c785256
   4d000737b60/38724e97801d66418525688000606540?Open-
   Document

Road Transportation: Historical Overview
http://www.tfhrc.gov/pubrds/summer96/p96su10.htm
http://www.arches.uga.edu/~mgagnon/students/Brignac.htm
http://www.tollroads.com/history.htm

Road Transportation: Technological Change
http://myron.sjsu.edu/romeweb/TRANSPRT/land.htm
http://www.rockbinders.com/asphalt.html

Salt and Salt Making
http://www.saltinfo.com/all.htm
http://www.saltinstitute.org/38.html
http://www-geology.ucdavis.edu/~gel115/salt.html

Silk Industry: Historical Overview
http://www.ess.uci.edu/~oliver/silk.html
http://www.fasid.or.jp/public/paper3/e-2.html
http://www.spartacus.schoolnet.co.uk/TEXsilk.htm

Silk Industry: Technological Change
http://www.smith.edu/hsc/silk/History/jacquard.html

Spices and Spice Trade
http://www.theepicentre.com/Spices/spicetrd.html
http://www.astaspice.org/history/history_01.htm

Steelmaking
http://www.mri.on.ca/steel.html
http://www.hz.cz/steel/history.html
http://www.history.rochester.edu/ehp%2Dbook/shb/start.htm
http://www.newsteel.com/features/NS9911f2.htm
http://www.history.ohio-state.edu/projects/steel/

Synthetic Fibers Industry
http://www.fabriclink.com/History.html
http://www.fibersource.com/f%2Dtutor/history.htm
http://www.fabriclink.com/History.html
http://www.fibersource.com/f%2Dtutor/history.htm

Telephone Industry
  http://www.privateline.com/TelephoneHistory/History1.htm
  http://phworld.tal-on.com/history/ PORN

Textiles
  http://www.fabriclink.com/History.html
  http://www.thoemmes.com/economics/cotton_intro.htm
  http://www.spartacus.schoolnet.co.uk/Textiles.htm

Timber and Logging Industry
  http://collections.ic.gc.ca/Mississagi/industry/forestry/
    indexlog.htm

Tobacco Industry
  http://www.ibiblio.org/maggot/dukehome/family.html
  http://www.tobacco.org/History/Tobacco%5FHistory.html
  http://druglibrary.org/schaffer/LIBRARY/studies/nc/nc2b.htm
  http://www.tobacco.org/History/colonialtobacco.html

Water Transportation: Historical Overview
  http://www.cronab.demon.co.uk/china.htm

Water Transportation: Technological Change
  http://www.history.rochester.edu/steam/thurston/1878/
  http://www.history.rochester.edu/steam/
  http://www.geocities.com/Area51/Vault/1820/WSP/ships.html
  http://www.isa.dknet.dk/~janj/navigation.html
  http://www.history.rochester.edu/steam/parsons/
  http://www.mariner.org/age/evohist.html
  http://www.ulster.net/~hrmm/steamboats/steam.html
  http://home.pacifier.com/~rboggs/ENGINES.HTML

Water Transportation: Canal Transportation
  http://www.home.eznet.net/~dminor/Canals.html

Wine and Wineries
  http://www.history-of-wine.com/html/timeline.html
  http://www.eresonant.com/pages/history/
    history-winemaking.html

Wool Industry: Historical Overview
  http://infoplease.lycos.com/ce6/society/A0861998.html
  http://www.dfmg.com.tw/mirron/wool/industry.html

Wool Industry: Technological Change
  http://www.dfmg.com.tw/mirron/wool/processing.html
  http://www.dfmg.com.tw/mirron/wool/woolprocessing.htm

5. DEMOGRAPHY

BASIC CONCEPTS

Age Composition
  http://www.urban.org/aging/abb/agingbaby.html
  http://www.census.gov/ipc/www/idbpyr.html

Demographic Transition
  http://www.hsph.harvard.edu/Organizations/healthnet/SAsia/
    suchana/1299/h028.html
  http://academics.smcvt.edu/geography/sweden.htm

Household
  http://www.curtin.edu.au/curtin/muresk/publications/Fay/
    intramodel.htm
  http://les1.man.ac.uk/multimedia/theory7.htm

Malthusian and Neo-Malthusian Theories
  http://www.igc.org/desip/malthus/principles.html
  http://socserv2.socsci.mcmaster.ca/~econ/ugcm/3ll3/malthus/
    popu.txt

BIRTH

Baby Boom
  http://www.urban.org/aging/abb/agingbaby.html

HEALTH, MORBIDITY, AND MORTALITY

Mortality
  http://www.users.globalnet.co.uk/~rossm/Issue2/rob/
    migration.htm

MIGRATION

Immigration Policy
  http://www.ailf.org/polrep/1996/pr9613.htm
  http://www.queensu.ca/samp/transform/Peberdy.htm
  http://www.cato.org/pubs/policy_report/pr-immig.html

Internal Migration
  http://www.let.leidenuniv.nl/history/migration/chapter3.html
  http://www.users.globalnet.co.uk/~rossm/Issue2/rob/
    migration.htm

International Migration
  http://www.gober.net/victorian/reports/irish2.html
  http://www.let.leidenuniv.nl/history/migration/chapter52.html
  http://www.let.leidenuniv.nl/history/migration/chapter54.html
  http://www.let.leidenuniv.nl/history/migration/contents.html
  http://www.let.leidenuniv.nl/history/migration/chapter22.html
  http://www.let.leidenuniv.nl/history/migration/index.html

6. INSTITUTIONS, GOVERNMENT, AND MARKETS

INSTITUTIONS

Barter and Barter Economies
  http://www.wvculture.org/history/journal_wvh/wvh51-4.html

Espionage, Economic and Industrial
  http://www.iwar.org.uk/ecoespionage/

Poor Laws
  http://users.ox.ac.uk/~peter/workhouse/poorlaws/poorlaws.html

Poor Relief
  http://users.ox.ac.uk/~peter/workhouse/poorlaws/poorlaws.html

EXTERNALITIES, PUBLIC GOODS, AND COMMON GOODS

Sanitation: Water Supply
  http://www.ci.nyc.ny.us/html/dep/html/history.html
  http://www.theplumber.com/eng.html

Sanitation: Sewerage and Urban Drainage
  http://www.theplumber.com/eng.html
  http://www.ocpa.com/manual/history.htm

Water Engineering
  http://www.fisheries.freeserve.co.uk/fens.htm
  http://animation.schou.dk/

Weights and Measures
   http://www.cftech.com/BrainBank/OTHERREFERENCE/WEI
      GHTSandMEASURES/MetricHistory.html
   http://infoplease.lycos.com/ce6/sci/A0851771.html

PUBLIC FINANCE

Bank for International Settlements
   http://www.trade-center.com/trading/history1.htm

Central Banking
   http://www.bankofengland.co.uk/history.htm
   http://www.finanzbahnhof.de/b-lo3.htm

Domesday Book
   http://www.domesdaybook.co.uk/

Income Maintenance: Social Insurance
   http://www.ssa.gov/history/history.html
   http://www.vn.fi/stm/english/organ/systhist.htm
   http://www.hrdc-drhc.gc.ca/insur/histui/hrdc.html

Lotteries
   http://www.library.ca.gov/CRB/97/03/Chapt3.html
   http://www.naspl.org/history.html

Public Utilities: Electricity Supply and Networks
   http://www.eei.org/issues/comp_reg/

Public Utilities: Postal Systems
   http://www.usps.com/history/his1.htm
   http://www.usps.com/history/his2.htm
   http://www.fortunecity.com/marina/armada/367/hillrowl.htm

Taxation: Taxation and Public Revenue
   http://www.taxworld.org/History/TaxHistory.htm
   http://www.aca.ch/hisustax.htm
   http://www.faculty.econ.nwu.edu/faculty/witte/pf/handouts/
      taxhist.html
   http://www.house.gov/jec/fiscal/tx-grwth/estattax/estattax.htm
   http://www.inlandrevenue.gov.uk/so/so6.htm

REGULATION

Regulation: Control of Prices
   http://mars.wnec.edu/~grempel/courses/wc1/lectures/
      24guilds.html
   http://www.fordham.edu/halsall/sbook1j.html#The Rise of
      Towns

Regulation: Control of Quality
   http://mars.wnec.edu/~grempel/courses/wc1/lectures/
      24guilds.html
   http://www.infoplease.com/ce6/bus/A0858519.html

INSTITUTIONAL FEATURES OF TRADE

Beggar-My-Neighbor Policies
   http://www.csusm.edu/politicalscience/golich/
      money-module/history.html

Commercial and Trade Diasporas
   http://www.rrz.uni-hamburg.de/rz3a035/jew_history.html

Commercial Policy: Tariffs
   http://internationalecon.com/v1.0/ch90/ch90.html

Commercial Policy: Nontariff Barriers
   http://internationalecon.com/v1.0/ch90/ch90.html

Commercial Policy: Custom Unions
   http://www.factmonster.com/ce6/history/A0853484.html
   http://www.let.leidenuniv.nl/history/rtg/emu/

Corn Laws
   http://www.thecore.nus.edu.sg/landow/victorian/history/
      cornlaws1.html
   http://www.yale.edu/lawweb/avalon/econ/cornlaws.htm

Fairs: European Fairs
   http://www.dragonbear.com/champagne.html

Hanseatic League
   http://members.bellatlantic.net/~baronfum/hansa.html
   http://orb.rhodes.edu/encyclop/late/central/hanindex.html
   http://www.unibw-hamburg.de/PWEB/hisfrn/hanse.html

Jewish Diaspora
   http://www.fordham.edu/halsall/jewish/jewishsbook.html#The
      Jewish Middle Ages

Joint-Stock Trading Companies
   http://www.history.rochester.edu/steam/lord/1-6.htm
   http://www.infoplease.com/ce6/history/A0816597.html
   http://www.infoplease.com/ce6/history/A0824442.html

Mercantilism
   http://mars.acnet.wnec.edu/%7Egrempel/courses/wc2/
      lectures/mercantilism.html

Merchant Guilds
   http://mars.wnec.edu/~grempel/courses/wc1/lectures/
      24guilds.html
   http://www.infoplease.com/ce6/bus/A0858519.html
   http://www.fordham.edu/halsall/sbook1j.html#The Rise of
      Towns

Navigation Acts
   http://campus.northpark.edu/history/WebChron/USA/
      Navigation.html

Slave Trade
   http://www.monde-diplomatique.fr/en/1998/04/02africa
   http://www.juneteenth.com/mp2.htm

7. MACROECONOMIC HISTORY AND INTERNATIONAL ECONOMICS

NATIONAL INCOME ACCOUNTS

Inequality of Wealth and Income Distribution
   http://www.worldbank.org/fandd/english/0397/
      articles/0140397.htm
   National Income Accounts: Historical Overview
   http://www.chass.utoronto.ca/~reak/eco100/100_13.htm
   http://www.mines.edu/Academic/courses/econbus/ebgn412/
      readings/GDP.html

Total Factor Productivity
   http://ideas.uqam.ca/ideas/data/Papers/wopcenses91-3.html

BUSINESS CYCLES AND STABILIZATION POLICIES

Bubble Act of 1720

http://www.ex.ac.uk/~RDavies/arian/amser/chrono8.html

http://clarity.net/~jake/bubble.htm

Business Cycles

http://www.nor.com.au/users/mcminn/pages/bcnum56.htm

http://www.ak.planet.gen.nz/~keithr/rf98_GrowthCycles.html

http://cepa.newschool.edu/het/essays/cycle/cycle.htm

http://www-rohan.sdsu.edu/~rbutler/chart.htm

http://www.albany.edu/cer/bc/bc_essays.html

http://www-rohan.sdsu.edu/~rbutler/chart.htm

Financial Panics and Crashes

http://www.tulipsandbears.com/tulip.htm

http://www.sunwayco.com/news10.html

http://www.historyhouse.com/stories/south_sea.htm

Great Depression

http://memory.loc.gov/ammem/fsowhome.html

http://www.fordham.edu/halsall/mod/modsbook41.html

http://www.j-bradford-delong.net/TCEH/Slouch_Crash14.html

http://www.j-bradford-delong.net/TCEH/Slouch_Climb16.html

New Deal

http://newdeal.feri.org/

Phillips Curve

http://webnt.calhoun.cc.al.us/distance/internet/Business/eco231/lecnotes/app3.htm

ECONOMIC GROWTH AND ECONOMIC DEVELOPMENT

Economic Convergence and Divergence

http://faculty-web.at.nwu.edu/economics/chung/growth/

Economic Development: Historical Overview

http://www.cedarville.edu/employee/wheelerb/macro/ldc_theory/ecn_dev.html

http://global.cscc.edu/ssci/104/growth_notes.htm

Economic Development: Development Policies

http://www.kimep.kz/SSE/popdev-k/Topics/Conferences/Urbanization/Graphics/Lewismodel.html

http://www.cedarville.edu/employee/wheelerb/macro/ldc_theory/ecn_dev.html

http://global.cscc.edu/ssci/104/growth_notes.htm

http://www.bized.ac.uk/virtual/dc/copper/theory.htm

Economic Growth

http://www.kimep.kz/SSE/popdev-k/Topics/Conferences/Urbanization/Graphics/Lewismodel.html

http://www.bized.ac.uk/virtual/dc/copper/theory.htm

Labor Surplus Models

http://www.oswego.edu/~graham/devlew.htm

http://www.kimep.kz/SSE/popdev-k/Topics/Conferences/Urbanization/Graphics/Lewismodel.html

Marshall Plan

http://www.state.gov/www/regions/eur/marshall.html

http://www.usaid.gov/multimedia/video/marshall/marshallspeech.html

http://www.j-bradford-delong.net/TCEH/Slouch_Present19.html

INTERNATIONAL ECONOMICS AND TRADE

Balance of Payments

http://www.bea.doc.gov/bea/di1.htm

Economic Imperialism

http://venus.spaceports.com/~theory/economy_1.htm

http://www.marxists.org/archive/lenin/works/1916/imp-hsc/ch10.htm

Geographical Expansion

http://www.fordham.edu/halsall/mod/wallerstein.html

http://www.surrey.ac.uk/LIS/MNP/may2000/Barradas.html

http://www.louisville.edu/~jabusc01/worldsys.htm

Long-Distance Trade: Long-Distance Trade before 1500

http://www.metmuseum.org/toah/hd/trade/hd_trade.htm

http://www.ciolek.com/owtrad.html

http://www.hf.uib.no/institutter/smi/paj/Masonen.html

Long-Distance Trade: Long-Distance Trade between 1500 and 1750

http://www.ciolek.com/owtrad.html

INTERNATIONAL FINANCE AND EXCHANGE RATES

Bretton Woods System

http://www.econ.iastate.edu/classes/econ355/choi/bre.htm

http://netec.wustl.edu/BibEc/data/Papers/nbrnberwo4141.html

http://orlingrabbe.com/bretton_woods.htm

Exchange Rates

http://www.infoplease.com/ce6/bus/A0858874.html

http://www.colorado.edu/Economics/courses/econ2020/section13/section13-main.html

http://www.cba.uh.edu/~rsusmel/7386/ln1.htm

Gold Standard

http://www.libertyhaven.com/regulationandpropertyrights/bankingmoneyorfinance/goldstandard/

http://www.auburn.edu/~garriro/g4gold.htm

http://www.j-bradford-delong.net/TCEH/Slouch_Gold8.html

http://www.j-bradford-delong.net/TCEH/Slouch_Restoring11.html

Monetary Standards

http://www.libertyhaven.com/regulationandpropertyrights/bankingmoneyorfinance/goldstandard/

http://www.auburn.edu/~garriro/g4gold.htm

http://www.j-bradford-delong.net/TCEH/Slouch_Gold8.html

http://www.j-bradford-delong.net/TCEH/Slouch_Restoring11.html

http://www.columbia.edu/~ram15/LBE.htm

8. MONEY, BANKING, AND FINANCE

MONEY AND PRICES

Eurodollar

http://www.globalfindata.com/articles/euro.htm

European Monetary System
http://www.ex.ac.uk/~RDavies/arian/euro.html

Florin
http://www.24carat.co.uk/florinstory.html

Money and Coinage: General Overview
http://www.ex.ac.uk/%7ERDavies/arian/northamerica.html
http://www.ex.ac.uk/~RDavies/arian/amser/chrono.html
http://www.ex.ac.uk/~RDavies/arian/northamerica.html

Money and Coinage: Money and Coinage before 1750
http://www.ex.ac.uk/~RDavies/arian/origins.html
http://www.ex.ac.uk/~RDavies/arian/amser/chrono.html
http://www.ex.ac.uk/~RDavies/arian/northamerica.html

Money and Coinage: Money and Coinage after 1750
http://www.ex.ac.uk/~RDavies/arian/origins.html
http://www.ex.ac.uk/~RDavies/arian/amser/chrono.html
http://www.ex.ac.uk/~RDavies/arian/northamerica.html

BANKING

Banking: Classical Antiquity
http://www.ex.ac.uk/~RDavies/arian/origins.html

Banking: Middle Ages and Early Modern Period
http://www.howcreditworks.com/body_banking_among_the_g
reeks_and_r.asp

Banking: Modern Period
http://www.howcreditworks.com/body_banking_among_the_g
reeks_and_r.asp

Credit Cooperatives
http://www.ncua.gov/about/history.html

Glass-Steagall Act
http://www.cftech.com/BrainBank/SPECIALREPORTS/
GlassSteagall.html

CREDIT, FINANCE, AND INTEREST RATES

Bills of Exchange
http://www.best.com/~szabo/lex.html

Bonds
http://www.publicdebt.treas.gov/of/ofaicqry.htm

Futures Markets
http://futures.tradingcharts.com/tafm/tafm1.html

Real Bills Doctrine
http://minneapolisfed.org/research/sr/sr64.html
http://ideas.uqam.ca/ideas/data/Papers/
wpawuwpma9711001.html
http://www.cato.org/pubs/journal/cj14n3-5.html

9. LABOR

BASIC CONCEPTS

Apprenticeship
http://www.nwlink.com/~donclark/hrd/history/
apprenticeship.html
http://historymedren.about.com/homework/historymedren/
library/weekly/aa033001d.htm

FORMS OF LABOR CONTRACTS

Contract Labor and the Indenture System
http://www.eh.net/Clio/Publications/indentured.shtml
http://www.nv.cc.va.us/home/nvsageh/Hist121/Part1/
Frethorne.htm

Serfdom
http://www.manitoulin-link.com/medieval/history.html
http://www.infoplease.com/ce6/history/A0844486.html

Slavery
http://www.eh.net/Clio/Conferences/ASSA/Jan_00/
rosenbloom.shtml
http://www.innercity.org/holt/slavechron.html
http://www.fordham.edu/halsall/africa/africasbook.html#The
Impact of Slavery

LABOR MARKETS

Child Labor
http://www.historyplace.com/unitedstates/childlabor/index.html
http://www.earlham.edu/~pols/globalprobs/children/Laila.html
http://www.spartacus.schoolnet.co.uk/IRchild.htm

Women in the Labor Force
http://www.wic.org/misc/history.htm
http://www.thehistorynet.com/WomensHistory/
articles/19967_text.htm
http://www.redstone.army.mil/history/women/welcome.html
http://www.spartacus.schoolnet.co.uk/Wwork.htm
http://www.womeninworldhistory.com/lesson7.html

LABOR ORGANIZATIONS, UNIONS, AND INDUSTRIAL RELATIONS

Craft Guilds
http://www.infoplease.com/ce6/bus/A0858519.html
http://www.fordham.edu/halsall/sbook1j.html#The Rise of
Towns
http://mars.wnec.edu/~grempel/courses/wc1/lectures/
24guilds.html

Luddism and Social Protest
http://www1.octa4.net.au/linden/luddites.htm

Unions
http://www.thehistorynet.com/WomensHistory/
articles/19967_text.htm
http://natcahelp.natca.net/online/sup/supguide.htm
http://www.angelfire.com/ky/LaborUnions/Home.html
http://www.socialstudieshelp.com/Eco_Unionization.htm
http://www.umwa.org/history/hist1.shtml
http://users.otenet.gr/~makine/enghistorytuc.htm

PAYMENT SCHEMES AND WAGES

Wage Legislation
http://www.bu.edu/econ/faculty/cooper/rcplays/minwage/
MINWAGEwebez.htm

10. NATURAL RESOURCES AND ENVIRONMENT

NATURAL RESOURCES

Fossil Fuels
http://www.wtrg.com/prices.htm

http://www.bydesign.com/fossilfuels/links/html/
natural_gas/gas_history.html
http://www.flogas.com/natgashistory/
history_of_natural_gas.htm
http://www.bydesign.com/fossilfuels/links/html/coal/
coal_history.html

Nuclear Power
http://nuclearhistory.tripod.com/tableofcontents.html
http://starfire.ne.uiuc.edu/~ne201/1995/jurgovan/intro.html

Quarries
http://www.state.me.us/doc/nrimc/pubedinf/photogal/
economic/econphot.htm

ENVIRONMENT

Pollution
http://www.worldbank.org/nipr/work_paper/wheeler92/

Volcanic Activities and Earthquakes
http://www.geo.umass.edu/courses/geo510/economics.htm
http://www.sfmuseum.org/1906/recovery.html

11. BIOGRAPHIES

INVENTORS AND WRITERS ON TECHNOLOGY

Agricola, Georgius
http://www.ucmp.berkeley.edu/history/agricola.html
http://www.adh.bton.ac.uk/schoolofdesign/MA.COURSE/
LInfDes32.html

Arkwright, Richard
http://www.spartacus.schoolnet.co.uk/IRarkwright.htm
http://www2.exnet.com/1995/10/10/science/science.html
http://www.cottontimes.co.uk/arkwrighto.htm

Babbage, Charles
http://ei.cs.vt.edu/~history/Babbage.html
http://www.cbi.umn.edu/exhibits/cb.html
http://www.ex.ac.uk/BABBAGE/

Bell, Alexander
http://www.iath.virginia.edu/albell/homepage.html

Bessemer, Henry
http://www.history.rochester.edu/ehp-book/shb/start.htm

Boulton, Matthew
http://www.geocities.com/mboulton1797/
http://www.spartacus.schoolnet.co.uk/SCboulton.htm

Brunel Family
http://www.spartacus.schoolnet.co.uk/RAbrunel.htm
http://web.ukonline.co.uk/b.gardner/brunel/marcbrun.html
http://www.brunel.ac.uk:8080/depts/mech/ikb.htm
http://www.bris.ac.uk/is/services/specialcollections/
brunelchronology.html

Cort, Henry
http://www.bookrags.com/books/inbio/PART8.htm

Daimler, Gottlieb
http://stroked.virtualave.net/einspur.html

Diesel, Rudolf
http://www.invent.org/book/book-text/31.html

Eastman, George
http://www.kodak.com/US/en/corp/aboutKodak/
kodakHistory/eastman.shtml

Edison, Thomas A.
http://edison.rutgers.edu/
http://www.hfmgv.org/exhibits/edison/

Gutenberg, Johannes
http://www.fecha.org/gutenbergbio.html
http://www.uh.edu/admin/engines/epi753.htm
http://www.gutenberg.de/english/index.htm

Haber, Fritz
http://www.nobel.se/chemistry/laureates/1918/haber-bio.html
http://www.chemheritage.org/EducationalServices/chemach/
tpg/fh.html
http://www.woodrow.org/teachers/ci/1992/Haber.html

Jacquard, Joseph-Marie
http://www.csc.liv.ac.uk/~ped/teachadmin/histsci/htmlform/
lect4.html
http://history.acusd.edu/gen/recording/jacquard1.html
http://kzoo.edu/~k00et01/jacquard.html

Kettering, Charles
http://www.invent.org/book/book-text/61.html
http://www.flint.lib.mi.us/timeline/autohistory_0798/
ketteringC.html
http://vintagecars.miningco.com/autos/vintagecars/library/
weekly/aa082998.htm?terms=invent&COB=home

McCormick, Cyrus
http://www.vaes.vt.edu/steeles/mccormick/bio.html
http://www.invent.org/book/book-text/73.html

Newcomen, Thomas
http://inventors.about.com/science/inventors/library/
inventors/blnewcomen.htm
http://www.technology.niagarac.on.ca/courses/tech238g/
newcomen.htm
http://www.geocities.com/Athens/Acropolis/6914/newcome.htm

Nobel, Alfred
http://www.nobel.no/eng_com_will1.html
http://www.nobelchannel.com/life.html
http://sunsite.bilkent.edu.tr/oldnobel/alfred/biography.html

Smeaton, John
http://www.structurae.de/en/index.html?http://www.struc-
turae.de/en/people/data/des0108.html

Stephenson Family
http://www.thenortheast.fsnet.co.uk/Pioneers.htm#THE
STEPHENSONS
http://www.geocities.com/Athens/Acropolis/6914/stephe.htm
http://www.spartacus.schoolnet.co.uk/RAstephensonR.htm

Taylor, Frederick Winslow
http://www.pillowrock.com/ronnie/fwtaylor.htm
http://www.fordham.edu/halsall/mod/1911taylor.html

Watt, James

http://www.geocities.com/Athens/Acropolis/6914/watte.htm

http://www.history.rochester.edu/steam/carnegie/

http://level2.phys.strath.ac.uk/ScienceOnStreets/jameswatt.html

Westinghouse, George

http://www.georgewestinghouse.com/george.html

http://www.memagazine.org/backissues/october96/features/
westingh/westingh.html

Whitney, Eli

http://www.eliwhitney.org/ew.htm

ENTREPRENEURS, BANKERS, AND LABOR LEADERS

Astor, John Jacob

http://www.thehistorynet.com/AmericanHistory/
articles/1997/12972_text.htm

http://www.raken.com/american_wealth/realtors/
John_Jacob_Astor1.asp

http://www.astors-beechwood.com/JohnJacobAstor.html

http://history.acusd.edu/gen/st/~kalenius/john.htm

Bakunin, Mikhail

http://csf.colorado.edu/mirrors/marxists.org/reference/archive/
bakunin/

http://flag.blackened.net/daver/anarchism/bakunin/
bakunin.html

Cadbury Family

http://www.spartacus.schoolnet.co.uk/REcadbury.htm

Carnegie, Andrew

http://www.j-bradford-delong.net/TCEH/andrewcarnegie.html

http://www.ltbn.com/tribcarnegie.html

http://www.clpgh.org/locations/pennsylvania/carnegie/

http://www.carnegieclub.co.uk/carnegie_story1.html

Chavez, Caesar

http://latino.sscnet.ucla.edu/research/chavez/bio/

Courtauld Family

http://www.spartacus.schoolnet.co.uk/TEXcourtauldS.htm

Debs, Eugene Victor

http://www.indianahistory.org/library/manuscripts/
collection_guides/debs.html

http://www.allsands.com/History/People/
eugenevdebsbi_avg_gn.htm

http://www.cc.ukans.edu/kansas/pullman/texts/debs.html

Du Pont Family

http://www.chemheritage.org/HistoricalServices/
eminentchemists/EIduPont/eidupont.htm

http://www.academiecaen-scabl.com/anglais/dupont.htm

Ford, Henry

http://www.time.com/time/time100/builder/profile/ford.html

Franklin, Benjamin

http://www.incwell.com/Biographies/Franklin.html

http://www.lexrex.com/bios/bfranklin.htm

http://www.cs.mdx.ac.uk/wrt/siteview/index.html

Gompers, Samuel

http://www.inform.umd.edu/ARHU/Depts/History/Gompers/
web1.html

Gould, Jay

http://elections.harpweek.com/2biographies/bio-1884-
Full.asp?UniqueID=6&Year=1884

Gramsci, Antonio

http://www.charm.net/~vacirca/

http://www.marxists.org/archive/gramsci/index.htm

http://www.soc.qc.edu/gramsci/

http://member.nifty.ne.jp/katote/Jessop_on_Gramsci.html

Guggenheim Family

http://www.gf.org/gugg_fam.html

Harriman, Edward

http://www.sierraclub.org/john_muir_exhibit/writings/
edward_henry_harriman.html

http://www.icrrhistorical.org/edward.harriman.html

Hill, James J.

http://www.railserve.com/JJHill.html

Kautsky, Karl

http://www.marxists.org/archive/kautsky/

Krupp Family

http://www.saburchill.com/history/chapters/IR/049ft.html

http://alpha.uni-sw.gwdg.de/~hessman/MONET/krupp.html

Lenin, Vladimir Ilich

http://www.acerj.com/CommOnline/Leninbio.htm

http://www.marxists.org/archive/lenin/

Lewis, John L.

http://www.umwa.org/history/jll1.shtml

http://www.spartacus.schoolnet.co.uk/USAlewisJL.htm

http://www.buyandhold.com/bh/en/education/history/2001/
johnlewis1.html

http://www.buyandhold.com/bh/en/education/history/2001/
johnlewis2.html

Liebknechts, The

http://www.marxists.org/archive/trotsky/works/1940/profiles/
rosa.htm

http://www.spartacus.schoolnet.co.uk/GERliebknecht.htm

http://www.callnetuk.com/home/socrev1text/pubs/sr232/
birchall.htm

List, Georg Friedrich

http://www.socsci.mcmaster.ca/~econ/ugcm/3ll3/list/

http://members.tripod.com/~american_almanac/contents.htm
#list

http://www.cooper.edu/humanities/classes/coreclasses/hss3/
f_list.html

Luxemburg, Rosa

http://www.marxists.org/archive/trotsky/works/1940/profiles/
rosa.htm

http://www.marxists.org/archive/luxembur/

http://www.kirjasto.sci.fi/luxembur.htm

Ricardo, David
  http://www.fordham.edu/halsall/mod/ricardo-wages.html
  http://www.fordham.edu/halsall/mod/ricardo-summary.html
  http://cepa.newschool.edu/het/profiles/ricardo.htm

Schumpeter, Joseph
  http://www.utdallas.edu/~harpham/joseph.htm
  http://socserv2.socsci.mcmaster.ca/~econ/ugcm/3ll3/
    schumpeter/socialval.html

Smith, Adam
  http://socserv2.socsci.mcmaster.ca/~econ/ugcm/3ll3/smith/
    index.html
  http://www.blupete.com/Literature/Biographies/Philosophy/
    Smith.htm#Wealth
  http://cepa.newschool.edu/het/profiles/smith.htm

Sombart, Werner
  http://cepa.newschool.edu/het/profiles/sombart.htm

Tawney, R. H.
  http://www.lse.ac.uk/lsehistory/tawney.htm
  http://www.business.utah.edu/~fincmb/tawn.html

Veblen, Thorstein
  http://www.mnc.net/norway/veblen.html
  http://www.fordham.edu/halsall/mod/1902veblen00.html
  http://www.fordham.edu/halsall/mod/1899veblen.html

Weber, Max
  http://www.faculty.rsu.edu/~felwell/Theorists/Weber/
    Whome.htm

White, Lynn
  http://www.theaha.org/info/AHA_History/lwhite.htm

Young, Arthur
  http://www.trumanlibrary.org/oralhist/young.htm

Directory of Contributors

Edmund Abaka
University of Miami, Coral Gables, Florida
Alkaloids; Kola; Vegeculture

Ran Abramitzky
Northwestern University
Du Pont Family; Kettering, Charles; Lenin, Vladimir Ilich;
Lewis, John L.; Malthusian and Neo-Malthusian Theories;
Vanderbilt Family

David Abulafia
Gonville and Caius College, Cambridge
Levant: General Overview; Lombardy; Mediterranean Sea and
Islands

Thomas Adam
University of Texas, Arlington
Saxony

Akanmu G. Adebayo
Kennesaw State University
Pastoralism

Erik Aerts
Rijksarchief te Antwerpen and *Katholieke Universiteit Leuven,
Belgium*
Antwerp; Fairs: European Fairs; Long-Distance Trade: Long-
Distance Trade before 1500; Usher, A. P.

Catherine Albrecht
University of Baltimore
Slavic Central Europe

Ken Alder
Northwestern University
Weights and Measures

Robert C. Allen
Nuffield College, Oxford
Agricultural Prices; Agricultural Revolution: Europe; Engel's
Law; Young, Arthur

Lee J. Alston
University of Illinois, Urbana-Champaign
Property Rights in Land: Historical Overview; Sharecropping;
Tenant Farming; Whitney, Eli

Franco Amatori
Università Bocconi, Milan
Agnelli Family

Kym Anderson
University of Adelaide, Australia
Agricultural Marketing: International Trade

Lawrin D. Armstrong
University of Toronto
Sombart, Werner; Usury

Ashish Arora
Carnegie Mellon University
Synthetic Fibers Industry

Jeremy Atack
Vanderbilt University
New York

Gareth Austin
London School of Economics and Political Science
Côte d'Ivoire and Ghana; Economic Imperialism

Dudley Baines
London School of Economics and Political Science
Internal Migration

Daniel Barbezat
Amherst College
Cartels and Collusion: Historical Overview, Concentration and
Entry, Price-Fixing and Vertical Constriants, *and* Price
Discrimination; Stinnes, Hugo

Jo Ellen Barnett
Mount Sinai School of Medicine, New York
Clock Making and Time Measurement

Richard W. Barsness
Lehigh University
Wright Brothers

Jean-Pascal Bassino
Paul Valéry Université, Nîmes, France
Indochina

Joerg Baten
Universität Tübingen, Germany
Bavaria

Claude Beaud
Université de Paris IV, Paris-Sorbonne
Schneider, Joseph-Eugène

J. Joseph Beaulieu
Federal Reserve System, Washington, D.C.
Seasonality

Gérard Béaur
Centre de Recherches Historiques, École des Hautes Études en Sciences Sociales, Paris
Agricultural Policy

Hilary Beckles
University of the West Indies, Mona, Jamaica
Barbados

Shiferaw Bekele
International Livestock Research Institute, Ethiopia
Ethiopia

R. P. Bellamy
University of Essex, England
Gramsci, Antonio

Miriam Ben-Peretz
University of Haifa, Israel
Teaching Profession

Maxine Berg
University of Warwick, Coventry, England
Luxury Trades; Power, Eileen

R. Albert Berry
University of Toronto
Land Reform and Confiscations; Latifundia; Minifundia

Luis E. Bertola
Universidad de la República, Montevideo, Uruguay
Uruguay

Dianne C. Betts
Southern Methodist University
Slater, Samuel

Huw Beynon
University of Cardiff, England
Mining: Work Safety Regulation

Michael Bibikov
Institute of Universal History, Russian Academy of Sciences, Moscow
Russia: Early and Medieval Periods

Ian Blanchard
University of Edinburgh, Scotland
Consumption: Leisure; Livestock Leases; Postan, Michael; Sheep and Goats

Ivo J. Blanken
Royal Philips Electronics, Eindhoven, The Netherlands
Philips Family

Bruno Blondé
University of Antwerp
Low Countries: Southern Netherlands between 1585 and 1830

Howard Bodenhorn
Lafayette College
Harriman, Edward

Maria Bogucka
Institute of History, Polish Academy of Sciences, Warsaw
Poland: Early Modern Period

Andrea Boltho
Magdalen College, Oxford
Stabilization Policies

Alan Booth
University of Exeter, England
Collective Action

Anne Booth
School of Oriental and African Studies, University of London
Indonesia

Michael D. Bordo
Rutgers, The State University of New Jersey
Monetary Standards

Maristella Botticini
Boston University
Commercial and Trade Diasporas; Jewish Diaspora; Marriage Payments

Sue Bowden
University of Sheffield, England
Consumption: Consumer Durables; Corporate Finance

Brian Bowers
Science Museum, London
Electrical Industry

George R. Boyer
Cornell University
Unemployment

Fabio Braggion
Northwestern University
Glass-Steagall Act; Malthusian and Neo-Malthusian Theories; Seed and Seed Varieties

Loren Brandt
University of Toronto
China: Republican Period

Paul Brassley
University of Plymouth, Seale-Hayne, Devon, England
Fertilizing

Christopher Breward
London College of Fashion
Fashion Industry

Elise S. Brezis
Bar Ilan University, Ramat-Gan, Israel
Mercantilism

Asa Briggs
Worcester College, Oxford, and *Open University, Milton Keynes,*
England
Book Industry: Modern Book Publishing; Radio and Television
Industry: Historical Overview

Garland L. Brinkley
University of California, Davis
Diseases: Deficiency and Parasitic Diseases

Richard H. Britnell
University of Durham, England
Agricultural Marketing: Regional Trade; Domesday Book; Eng-
land: Early and Medieval Periods up to 1500

Stephen N. Broadberry
University of Warwick, Coventry, England
Labor Productivity; Total Factor Productivity

Janet Farrell Brodie
Claremont Graduate University
Birth Control and Contraceptives

Timothy Brook
University of Toronto
Well-Field Land System

Romain Brossé
Université d'Angers, Bouchemaine, France, Emeritus
Quarries

John C. Brown
Clark University
Public Health; Sanitation: Historical Overview *and* Water
Supply

John K. Brown
University of Virginia
Machine Tools Industry: Technological Change

Jonathan Brown
Rural History Center, University of Reading, England
Animal and Livestock Diseases; Crop and Plant Diseases

Kenneth D. Brown
Queen's University, Belfast
Leisure Industries: Hobbies Industry

Kristine Bruland
University of Oslo, Norway
Education; Habakkuk Hypothesis; Nordic Countries: Modern
Norway

James A. Brundage
University of Kansas, Lawrence
Tithe

Liam Brunt
St. John's College, Oxford
Crop Rotation; Mixed Farming

Henry J. Bruton
Williams College
Economic Development: Historical Overview

Lynwood Bryant
Massachusetts Institute of Technology, Emeritus
Diesel, Rudolf

Victor Bulmer-Thomas
Institute of Latin American Studies, University of London
Central American Countries

Joyce Burnette
Wabash College
Labor Markets: Segmentation and Discrimination; Mill, John
Stuart

Erik Buyst
Katholieke Universiteit Leuven, Belgium
Belgium; Housing, Investment in; Mortgage Banks

William Caferro
Vanderbilt University
Florence; Italy: Medieval Period; Tuscany

Louis P. Cain
Loyola University, Chicago
Armour Family; Chicago

Charles W. Calomiris
Columbia Business School
Banking: Modern Period; Hughes, Jonathan

Ewen A. Cameron
University of Edinburgh
Crofters

Forrest Capie
City University Business School, London
Central Banking; Clapham, John; Commercial Policy: Tariffs

Mauro Carboni
Università degli Studi di Bologna, Italy
Rome and the Papal State

Dominique Cardon
Centre National de la Recherche Scientifique, La Salle, France
Dye Crops

Ann M. Carlos
University of Colorado, Boulder
Joint-Stock Trading Companies

Ann G. Carmichael
Indiana University, Bloomington
Diseases: Infectious Diseases

François Caron
Université de Paris IV, Paris-Sorbonne
France: Modern Period; Paris

Albert Carreras
Universitat Pompeu Fabra, Barcelona
Catalonia; Spain: Modern Spain

Fred Carstensen
University of Connecticut
McCormick, Cyrus; Singer, Isaac Merritt

Michael R. Carter
University of Wisconsin–Madison
Farm Scale

Mark Casson
University of Reading, England
Entrepreneurship

Christopher J. Castaneda
California State University, Sacramento
Oil Industry: Historical Overview, Technological Change, Property Rights, *and* Industrial Organization

Myung Soo Cha
Yeungnam University, Kyungsan, South Korea
Korea: Korea before 1945 *and* North Korea

J. A. Chartres
University of Leeds
England: Early Modern Period

Kirti N. Chaudhuri
European University Institute, Florence
Geographical Expansion

Jean-Michel Chevet
Institut National de la Recherche Agronomique, Ivry, France
National Income Accounts: Rental Income

Paul Christesen
Dartmouth College
Italy: Classical Period

Federico Ciliberto
North Carolina State University
Economies of Scope

Gregory Claeys
Royal Holloway, University of London
Owen, Robert

Julia Clancy-Smith
University of Arizona
Maghrib

William G. Clarence-Smith
School of Oriental and African Studies, London
Cocoa

Gregory Clark
University of California, Davis
Agricultural Labor; Agricultural Wages; Agriculture: Agricultural

Inputs, Productivity, and Wages; Farm Capital; Farm Management

L. A. Clarkson
Centre for Social Research, Queen's University, Belfast
Domestic Industry

Karen B. Clay
H. John Heinz III School of Public Policy and Management, Carnegie Mellon University
Duke, James Buchanan; San Francisco

Piet Clement
Bank For International Settlements, Basel, Switzerland
Bank for International Settlements

H. M. Clifford
Victoria and Albert Museum, London
Jewelry Industry

John H. Coatsworth
David Rockefeller Center for Latin American Studies, Harvard University
Mexico; Mexico City

Sherman Cochran
Cornell University
Rong Family

Jon S. Cohen
University of Toronto
Marx, Karl

Francisco Comín
Universidad Complutense de Madrid, Spain
Government Borrowing: Government Borrowing after 1800; National Income Accounts: Public Expenditures

S. J. Connolly
Queen's University, Belfast
Ireland: Ireland before 1800

Catherine Coquery-Vidrovitch
Université de Paris VII, Denis Diderot
France: The French Empire between 1789 and 1950

Dennis D. Cordell
Southern Methodist University
Sahara

Metin M. Co gel
University of Connecticut
Property Rights in Land: Communal Control

Robin Cowan
Universiteit Maastricht, The Netherlands
Automobile and Truck Industry: Technological Change; Gould, Jay; Pest Control

Howard Cox
Centre for International Business Studies, South Bank University, London
Tobacco Industry

N. F. R. Crafts
London School of Economics and Political Science
Economic Growth

Lee A. Craig
North Carolina State University, Raleigh
Consumption: Non-Durables; Whaling

Gerald Crompton
Canterbury Business School, University of Kent
Water Transportation: Canal Transportation

Frederick W. Crook
Economic Research Service, Retired
Private Plots

Pierre Crosson
Resources for the Future, Washington, D.C.
Soil and Soil Conservation

Timothy Cuff
Saint Vincent College
Pigs

Hugh Cunningham
Rutherford College, University of Kent, Canterbury
Charities

Terence N. D'Altroy
Columbia University
American Indian Economies: Inca Economy

Eduard L. Danielyan
Institute of History, National Academy of Sciences of the Republic of Armenia
Armenia

Jim Davis
University of New South Wales, Sydney
Popular Entertainment

Tracy C. Davis
Northwestern University
Theater Arts

Paul De Grauwe
Katholieke Universiteit Leuven, Belgium
European Monetary System

Kent G. Deng
London School of Economics and Political Science
China: Tang, Song, and Yuan Dynasties; Diandi; Zhitian

Georges Depeyrot
Centre National de la Recherche Scientifique and Centre de

Recherches Historiques, École des Hautes Études en Sciences Sociale, Paris
Money-Changing: Ancient World and Early Middle Ages

José Luis de Rojas
Universidad Complutense de Madrid
American Indian Economies: Aztec Economy

Robert A. Dodgshon
University of Wales, Aberystwyth
Clan Land

Peter B. Doeringer
Boston University
Bargaining, Collective

Mauricio Drelichman
Northwestern University
Organized Crime; Radio and Television Industry: Technological Change

Margarita Dritsas
University of Crete
Greece: Modern Period

Robert S. DuPlessis
Swarthmore College
France: The French Empire to 1789

Alastair J. Durie
University of Glasgow
Leisure Industries: Historical Overview *and* Travel and Tourist Industries; Scotland

Peter Duus
Stanford University
Japan: Japanese Empire

Alan D. Dye
Barnard College
Commercial Policy: Nontariff Barriers

Christopher Dyer
University of Leicester, England
Ecclesiastical Estates

Richard A. Easterlin
University of Southern California
Baby Boom; Living Standards

William Easterly
New York University
Economic Development: Development Policies

Clive D. Edwards
Loughborough University, England
Woodworking Industry

Peter Edwards
Surrey University, Roehampton, England
Horses

Marc Egnal
York University, Toronto
Franklin, Benjamin

Robert B. Ekelund, Jr.
Auburn University
Rent Seeking

Ivana Elbl
Trent University, Peterborough, Ontario
Portugal: Portuguese Empire

Jari Eloranta
European University Institute, Florence
National Defense

P. C. Emmer
University of Leiden, The Netherlands
Low Countries: Dutch Empire

Stanley L. Engerman
University of Rochester
Capitalism; Caribbean Region: Pre-Emancipation Period;
Fogel, Robert

Omar A. Eno
York University, Toronto
East Africa: Colonial and Modern Periods

S. R. Epstein
London School of Economics and Political Science
Apprenticeship; Craft Guilds; Journeymen; Naples

Steven A. Epstein
University of Colorado, Boulder
Genoa

Aurelio Espinosa
University of Arizona
Merced

Emily Erikson
Columbia University
Taboos

Chris Evans
University of Glamorgan, Pontypridd, Wales
Bessemer Process; Blast Furnaces

Michael Everett
Quinnipiac University
Integration: Horizontal Integration

Malcolm Falkus
University of New England, Armidale, Australia
Gas Industry

Douglas A. Farnie
Manchester Metropolitan University
Cotton Industry: Historical Overview; Suez Canal

David Faure
Institute for Chinese Studies, Oxford
Guangzhou (Canton)

Jeffrey Fear
Harvard Business School
Thyssen, August

Giovanni Federico
Università degli Studi di Pisa, Italy
Jacquard, Joseph-Marie; Landlordism; Sericulture; Silk
Industry: Historical Overview, Technological Change, *and*
Industrial Organization and the State; Swidden
Agriculture

Charles Feinstein
All Souls College, Oxford
National Income Accounts: Investment and Savings

Wilfried Feldenkirchen
Friedrich-Alexander-Universitat Erlangen–Nuremberg, Germany
Siemens Family

Ann Harper Fender
Gettysburg College
Lotteries; Poultry; Smuggling

Niall Ferguson
Leonard H. Stern School of Business, New York
Rothschild Family

Joseph P. Ferrie
Northwestern University
Labor Mobility

Alexander J. Field
Santa Clara University
Land Ordinances; Telegraph

Carole K. Fink
Ohio State University
Bloch, Marc

Price Vanmeter Fishback
University of Arizona, Tucson
Company Towns

Caroline Fohlin
Johns Hopkins University and *California Institute of
Technology*
Investment and Commercial Banks

James S. Foreman-Peck
HM Treasury, Oxford
Daimler, Gottlieb; Long-Distance Trade: Long-Distance Trade
since 1914

Mathew Forstater
University of Missouri, Kansas City
Labor Surplus Models

Jon Fraenkel
University of the South Pacific
Pacific Islands

Michael French
University of Glasgow
Dunlop, James; Food Processing Industry: Food Safety
Regulation; Rubber: Natural Rubber

William Freund
University of Natal, Durban, South Africa
Southern Africa: Colonial Period

Tony A. Freyer
University of Alabama Law School
Antitrust

Amy Friedlander
Council on Library and Information Resources, Washington, D.C.
Bell, Alexander Graham; Telephone Industry

Gerald Friedman
University of Massachusetts, Amherst
Industrial Relations; Labor

Bruno Fritzsche
University of Zürich
Switzerland: Switzerland after 1815

Lionel Frost
La Trobe University, Bundoora, Australia
Fire Control

Dario Gaggio
Northwestern University
Diamond Industry: Historical Overview, Technological
Change, and Industrial Organization; Flexible Specializa-
tion; Gold and Silver Industry: Historical Overview,
Technological Change, and Industrial Organization;
Industrial Districts

Zoltán Gál
*Centre for Regional Studies, Hungarian Academy of Sciences,
Budapest*
Danube

Dick Geary
Nottingham University, England
Luxemburg, Rosa

David P. Geggus
University of Florida, Gainesville
Haiti

Thomas M. Geraghty
University of North Carolina, Chapel Hill
Babbage, Charles; Courtauld Family; Factory System;
Pilkington Family

Mark Gersovitz
Johns Hopkins University
Lewis, W. Arthur

Nicholas P. W. Goddard
Anglia Polytechnic University, Cambridge, England
Agricola, Georgius; Agriculture: Main Tools and Implements

Avi Goldfarb
Rotman School of Management, University of Toronto
Lever, William Hesketh

Joshua S. Goldstein
American University
War and Economic History

Douglas Gomery
College of Journalism, University of Maryland
Film Industry

Yadira González de Lara
Universidad de Alicante, Spain
Commercial Partnerships

David F. Good
University of Minnesota–Twin Cities
Austria: Austro-Hungarian Empire

Paul Gootenberg
State University of New York, Stony Brook
Andean Region

John Steele Gordon
New Salem, New York
Morgan, J. P.

Robert B. Gordon
Yale University
Metallurgic Industry: Technological Change

H. Roger Grant
Clemson University
Railroads: Industrial Organization and Regulation

George Grantham
McGill University
Agriculture: Historical Overview; Grassland Farming

Karl Gratzer
*Centre for Banking and Finance, University College of South
Stockholm*
Ericsson, L. M.

Alan G. Green
Queen's University, Kingston, Ontario
Immigration Policy

Liah Greenfeld
Boston University
List, Georg Friedrich

Paul R. Gregory
University of Houston
Command Economies

Richard T. Griffiths
Leiden University, The Netherlands
Marshall Plan

David Grigg
University of Sheffield, England
Agriculture: Agricultural Production Systems; Cattle

Richard S. Grossman
Wesleyan University
Bank Failures

Farley Grubb
University of Delaware
Contract Labor and the Indenture System

Timothy W. Guinnane
Yale University
Credit Cooperatives; Informal Credit; Rotating Savings Societies

Lynne A. Guitar
Student and Researcher Services, Santo Domingo, Dominican Republic
Cassava

Gerald Gunderson
Trinity College, Hartford
Rockefeller, John Davison

John Denis Haeger
Northern Arizona University
Astor, John Jacob

William W. Hagen
University of California, Davis
Prussia

Michael R. Haines
Colgate University
Fertility; Mortality

Nadav Halevi
Hebrew University, Jerusalem
Israel

Bert Hall
University of Toronto
White, Lynn

Martin Hall
University of Cape Town, Rondebosch, South Africa
Southern Africa: Early Period

Gillian Hamilton
University of Toronto
Montreal

E. A. Hammel
University of California, Berkeley, Emeritus
Family Structures and Kinship

Rolf Hammel-Kiesow
Forschungsstelle für die Geschichte der Hanse und des Ostseeraums, Lübeck, Germany
Hamburg; Hanseatic League; Lübeck

Mark Hammonds
BP Solar, Ltd.
Solar Power

Ibrahim Hamza
York University, Toronto
Emiri Lands; Mulk Lands

Susan B. Hanley
Jackson School of International Studies, University of Washington
Japan: Early Modern Period

Leslie Hannah
Ashridge Business School, Berkhamsted, England
Chandler, Alfred D.

David Hardiman
University of Warwick, Coventry, England
Famine Relief

Anne Hardy
Wellcome Trust Centre for the History of Medicine, University College London
Health Industry: Technological Change

George Harmon
Medill School of Journalism, Northwestern University
Newspapers: Industrial Organization and Regulation

Ron Harris
School of Law, Tel Aviv University
Bubble Act of 1720

Marjolein 't Hart
University of Amsterdam
Low Countries: Northern Netherlands between 1568 and 1815

R. M. Hartwell
University of Virginia, University of Chicago, and *Nuffield College, Oxford, Emeritus*
Capitalism

Alan Harvey
University of Northumbria, Newcastle upon Tyne, England
Byzantine Empire

Barbara F. Harvey
Somerville College, Oxford
Monasteries

Sylvia Harvey
Sheffield Hallam University, Sheffield, England
Radio and Television Industry: Industrial Organization and Regulation

Timothy Hatton
University of Essex, England
International Migration

Michel Hau
Université Marc Bloch, Strasbourg, France
Alsace

Michael J. Haupert
University of Wisconsin–La Crosse
Guggenheim Family; Sports and Sport Industry

Gary R. Hawke
Victoria University of Wellington, New Zealand
New Zealand

Peter Hayes
Northwestern University
Duisberg, Carl; Krupp Family

Peter B. R. Hazell
International Food Policy Research Institute, Washington, D.C.
Green Revolution

Daniel R. Headrick
Roosevelt University
Information and Communication Technology

Anthony F. Heath
Nuffield College, Oxford
Social Mobility

James Heitzman
Georgia State University
India: Early Indian Civilization

Santhi Hejeebu
University of Iowa
Fairs: Emporia and Bazaars; Firm: The Firm before 1800

Richard Hellie
University of Chicago
Russia: Early Modern Period

Rolf G. H. Henriksson
Stockholm University
Heckscher, Eli

P. W. R. B. A. U. Herat
Central Bank of Sri Lanka
Sri Lanka

Patrick Heuveline
University of Chicago
Demographic Methods

Kim Hill
University of New Mexico
Gathering; Hunting

Patricia Hillebrandt
University of Reading, England
Construction Industry: Historical Overview and Technological Change

Richard L. Hills
University of Manchester Institute of Science and Technology, Manchester, England
Railroads: Technological Change; Roberts, Richard; Smeaton, John

R. Bruce Hitchner
University of Dayton
Roman Empire

Riitta Hjerppe
University of Helsinki
Nordic Countries: Modern Finland

Jean-Claude Hocquet
Centre National de la Recherche Scientifique, Lille 3 University, France
Salt and Salt Making

Philip T. Hoffman
California Institute of Technology
Agriculture: Property Rights and Tenure Systems; France: Early Modern Period; Le Roy Ladurie, Emmanuel

Paul M. Hohenberg
Rensselaer Polytechnic Institute, Emeritus
Urbanization

Daniel U. Holbrook
Marshall University
Electronics Industry

Katrina Honeyman
University of Leeds, England
Gender Relations

Rosemary L. Hopcroft
University of North Carolina, Charlotte
Open-Field System

Sally M. Horrocks
University of Leicester, England
Food Processing Industry: Historical Overview *and* Technological Change

Allen M. Howard
Rutgers, The State University of New Jersey
Liberia and Sierra Leone

Charles W. Howe
University of Colorado, Boulder
Water Resources

Martha C. Howell
Columbia University
Merchant Guilds; Sumptuary Legislation

Michael Huberman

Université de Montréal
Arkwright, Richard; Cotton Industry: Industrial Organization, Markets, and Trade

Will Hughes

University of Reading, England
Construction Industry: Historical Overview and Technological Change

Peter Hull

Newbury, Berkshire, England
Morris, William (Lord Nuffield)

Staffan Hultén

Stockholm School of Economics
Automobile and Truck Industry: Technological Change

Thomas M. Humphrey

Federal Reserve Bank of Richmond
Phillips Curve; Real Bills Doctrine

J. Humphries

All Souls College, Oxford
Women in the Labor Force

William Huneke

Surface Transporation Board and *University of Maryland*
Railroads: Historical Overview; Road Transportation: Regulation

Edwin S. Hunt

University of Cincinnati
Medici Bank

Robert C. Hunt

Brandeis University
Irrigated Farming

John Hunwick

Northwestern University
Timbuktu

A. Magdalena Hurtado

University of New Mexico
Gathering; Hunting

Diane Hutchinson

University of Sydney, Australia
Brunner Family

William K. Hutchinson

Miami University of Ohio
Homesteading

Halil Inalcik

Bilkent University, Ankara, Turkey
Istanbul

Paul Israel

Rutgers, The State University of New Jersey
Edison, Thomas A.

Margaret C. Jacob

University of California, Los Angeles
Watt, James

Harold James

Princeton University
Bretton Woods System; Eurodollar

John A. James

University of Virginia
Economies of Scale

D. T. Jenkins

University of York, England
Textiles; Wool Industry: Technological Change

Hans Christian Johansen

University of Odense, Denmark
Nordic Countries: Modern Denmark

Richard R. John

University of Illinois, Chicago
Public Utilities: Postal Systems

C. Derek Johnson

Castle Rock, Colorado
Air Transportation: Technological Change

Paul Johnson

London School of Economics and Political Science
Great Britain: Modern Period; Insurance: Life Insurance

Louis D. Johnston

College of Saint Benedict, Saint John's University, Minnesota
Balance of Payments; Hill, James J.; National Income Accounts: Exports and Imports

Eric Jones

Melbourne Business School, Australia, and *University of Reading, England*
Book Industry: Historical Overview; Environment: Historical Overview; Natural Resources: Historical Overview

Sylvia Jones

Melbourne Business School, Australia
Book Industry: Historical Overview

Brooks A. Kaiser

Gettysburg College
Carthage; Environment: Environmental Policies and Regulation; Market Structure: General Introduction, Competition, Monopoly and Natural Monopoly, *and* Oligopoly and Monopolistic Competition; Product Safety Regulation

A. K. M. Abul Kalam

School of Urban and Regional Planning, University of Waterloo, Ontario, and *Jahangirnagar University, Bangladesh*
Bangladesh

Kenneth H. Kang

International Monetary Fund, Washington, D.C.
Korea: South Korea

Robert Kastenbaum
Arizona State University
Burial and Funeral Services

Kyle D. Kauffman
Wellesley College
Draft and Pack Animals

Liam Kennedy
Queen's University, Belfast
Tenant Right; Ulster

Alan J. Kidd
Manchester Metropolitan University
Poor Laws; Poor Relief

L. Lynne Kiesling
Northwestern University
Contract Enforcement and Legal Systems; Energy Regulation;
Smith, Adam

Dong-Woon Kim
Dong-Eui University, Pusan, South Korea
Coats Family

Maurice W. Kirby
Management School, University of Lancaster, England
Mining: Industrial Organization, the Environment, and Pollution

Edgar Kiser
University of Washington, Seattle
Tax Farming

Martin A. Klein
University of Toronto
Slavery; Sudan: Western Sudan

Franklin W. Knight
Johns Hopkins University
Cuba

Meir Kohn
Dartmouth College
Bills of Exchange

Anu Mai Köll
Stockholm University
Baltic States

Jozef Konings
Katholieke Universiteit Leuven, Belgium
Russia: Post-Communist Russia

György Kövér
Budapest, Hungary
Hungary

Olle Krantz
Umeå University, Sweden
Consumption: Services; Nordic Countries: Modern Sweden

Colleen E. Kriger
University of North Carolina, Greensboro
Central Africa: Ancient Period *and* Central Africa from 1500 to
1850

Andreas Kunz
Institut für Europäische Geschichte, Universität Mainz, Germany
Rhine

Timur Kuran
University of Southern California
Levant: Islamic Rule

Sumner J. La Croix
East-West Center, University of Hawaii, Manoa
Land Tenure

Pamela Walker Laird
University of Colorado, Denver
Advertising

Naomi R. Lamoreaux
University of California, Los Angeles
Firm: The Firm after 1800; Management

John R. Lampe
University of Maryland, College Park
Balkans

Janet T. Landa
York University, Toronto
Middleman Minorities

Ralph Landau
Stanford University
Synthetic Fibers Industry

Zbigniew Landau
Warsaw School of Economics
Poland: Modern Period

Erick D. Langer
Georgetown University
Central South American States

Richard N. Langlois
University of Connecticut
Computer Industry

George Michael LaRue
Clarion University
Egypt: Islamic and Modern Periods; Sudan: Eastern Sudan

A. J. H. Latham
University of Wales, Swansea
Rice Farming

Wolfram Latsch
Northwestern University
Central Africa: Central Africa from 1850 to the Present

Robin Law
University of Stirling, Scotland
Ouidah

Maxwell G. Lay
Melbourne, Australia
Road Transportation: Technological Change

Bill Leadbetter
Edith Cowan University, Mount Lawley, Australia
Levant: Roman and Byzantine Periods

Sergei Lebedev
Saint Petersburg Institute of History, Russian Academy of Sciences
Russia: Russian Empire

René Leboutte
University of Aberdeen, Scotland
Coal Basins; Cockerill, John; Steelmaking

Martin Legassick
University of Western Cape, Bellville, South Africa
Southern Africa: Modern Period

Beverly Lemire
University of New Brunswick
Clothing Trades

Clé Lesger
University of Amsterdam
Amsterdam; Staple Markets and Entrepôts

Michael Lessnoff
University of Glasgow
Religion; Weber Thesis

Timothy Leunig
London School of Economics and Political Science
Cotton Industry: Technological Change

Margaret C. Levenstein
University of Massachusetts, Amherst, and *Albion College, Michigan*
Integration: Vertical Integration

Wayne Lewchuk
McMaster University, Hamilton, Ontario
Automobile and Truck Industry: Industrial Organization and Regulation; Chrysler, Walter; Mass Production

Bradley G. Lewis
Union College, Schenectady, New York
Otto, Nikolaus August; Sloan, Alfred; Social Savings

Jane Lewis
Saint Cross College, Oxford
Family Policies

W. David Lewis
Auburn University
Air Transportation: Industrial Organization and Regulation

Gary D. Libecap
University of Arizona
Food Processing Industry: Industrial Organization, Markets, and Trade; Grazing and Ranch Farming; Hedges and Fences; Natural Resources: Property Rights *and* Regulation; Property Rights

Walter Licht
University of Pennsylvania
Philadelphia

Håkan Lindgren
Institute for Research in Economic History, Stockholm School of Economics
Wallenberg Family

Massimo Livi-Bacci
Università degli Studi di Firenze, Italy
Population

Jonas Ljungberg
Lund University, Sweden
Nordic Countries: General Overview

Roger Lloyd-Jones
Sheffield Hallam University, England
Manchester

James Lockhart
University of California, Los Angeles, Emeritus
Encomienda and Repartimiento

Jennifer Lofkrantz
York University, Toronto
Nigeria

John V. Lombardi
University of Massachusetts, Amherst
Venezuela

Jason Long
Northwestern University
Labor Mobility

Nancy Longnecker
Center for Legumes in Mediterranean Agriculture, University of Western Australia
Legumes and Pulses

James R. Lothian
School of Business, Fordham University
Exchange Rates

Paul E. Lovejoy
York University, Toronto
Plantation System

Rodney Lowe
University of Bristol
Income Maintenance: Social Insurance

Christian Lübke
Ernst-Moritz-Arndt-Universität Greifswald, Germany
Poland: Early and Medieval Periods

Ragnhild Lundstrom
Uppsala University, Sweden
Nobel, Alfred

Martin Lynn
Queen's University, Belfast
Oil Crops

Peter Lyth
London School of Economics and Political Science
Air Transportation: Historical Overview

Charlotte M. Lythe
University of Dundee, Scotland
Jute Industry

Debin Ma
GRIPS/FASID Joint Graduate Program, Tokyo
Shanghai

Joseph J. McAleer
Stamford, Connecticut
Book Industry: Libraries and Bookstores; Magazines

James C. McCann
African Studies Center, Boston University
Ethiopia

W. Patrick McCray
University of Maryland, College Park
Glass Products Industry

Stuart Macdonald
School of Management, University of Sheffield
Espionage, Economic and Industrial

Alan MacFarlane
King's College, Cambridge
Tea

Martin C. McGuire
University of California, Irvine
Public Goods

R. Marvin McInnis
Queen's University, Kingston, Ontario
Canada

Arthur J. McIvor
University of Strathclyde, Glasgow, Scotland
Employers' Associations

John P. McKay
University of Illinois, Urbana-Champaign
Brunel Family

Richard S. Mackenney
University of Edinburgh, Scotland
Venice

Mary MacKinnon
McGill University
Toronto

Ian W. McLean
University of Adelaide, Australia
Australia

John Macnicol
Royal Holloway, University of London
Retirement

Geoffrey McNicoll
Population Council, New York
Demographic Transition

Kim McQuaid
Lake Erie College, Cleveland, Ohio
Swope, Gerard

Gary B. Magee
University of Melbourne, Australia
Papermaking

Lars Magnusson
University of Uppsala, Sweden
Tawney, R. H.

Paul Robert Magocsi
University of Toronto
Ukraine

John Major
University of Hull, England
Panama Canal

James Mak
University of Hawaii, Manoa
Water Transportation: Regulation

Paolo Malanima
Università degli Studi di Catanzaro, Italy
Italy: Early Modern and Modern Periods (to 1861)

Peter C. Mancall
University of Southern California
United States: Precolonial Period *and* Colonial Period

Kristin Mann
Emory University
Lagos

J. G. Manning
Stanford University
Egypt: Ancient and Classical Periods; North Africa: Ancient Period

Morag Martin
State University of New York, Brockport
Cosmetics Industry; Personal Services

Herbert W. Matis
Institut fur Wirtschafts- und Sozialgeschichte, Wirtschaftsuniversität Wien, Vienna
Austria: Modern Austria

N. J. Mayhew
Ashmolean Museum, Oxford
Price Revolution

Maureen Fennell Mazzaoui
University of Wisconsin-Madison
Linen Industry: Overview

Christopher M. Meissner
King's College, Cambridge
Gold Standard

Tim Meldrum
Imperial College, London
Domestic Service

Joseph Melling
University of Exeter, England
Labor Conditions and Job Safety

John W. Mellor
Abt Associates, Inc., Washington, D.C.
Agricultural Credit

Rebecca Menes
George Mason University
Construction Industry: Industrial Organization and Markets *and* Regulation

Dennis A. Meritt, Jr.
DePaul University
Zoos and Other Animal Parks

Jacob Metzer
Hebrew University, Jerusalem
Levant: Palestine during the British Mandate

Peter Benjamin Meyer
United States Bureau of Labor Statistics, Office of Productivity and Technology, Arlington, Virginia
Cort, Henry; Machine Tools Industry: Historical Overview; Siemens-Martin Process

F. G. Michaud
University of Calgary
France: Early and Medieval Periods; Provence

Robert Millward
University of Manchester, England
Nationalization and Privatization

Paul J. Miranti Jr.
Rutgers, The State University of New Jersey
Stock Markets

Boris N. Mironov
Saint Petersburg Institute of History, Russian Academy of Sciences
Russia: Modern Period

Thomas J. Misa
Illinois Institute of Technology
Bessemer, Henry

David Mitch
University of Maryland, Baltimore County
Human Capital; Literacy

D. E. Moggridge
University of Toronto
Keynes, John Maynard; Marshall, Alfred

Fatemeh Etemad Moghadam
Hofstra University
Iran: Islamic Period, 640–1800; Iran: Modern Period, since 1800

Jean Marie Moine
Université François Rabelais, Fondettes, France
Wendel Family

Joel Mokyr
Northwestern University
Industrial Revolution

Ismael M. Montana
York University, Toronto
North Africa: Colonial and Modern Periods; Waqf

Michael Montéon
University of California, San Diego
Chile

Lyndon Moore
Northwestern University
Baghdad; Greece: Byzantine and Ottoman Periods; Iraq: Islamic Period; Levant: Modern Lebanon; North Africa: Independent Islamic Period; State Farms; Thailand

R. J. Moore-Colyer
Institute of Rural Studies, University of Wales, Aberystwyth
Wales

Michio Morishima
London School of Economics and Political Science, Emeritus
Ricardo, David

Peter J. T. Morris
Science Museum, London
Chemical Industries: An Introduction *and* Chemical Industries before 1850; Rubber: Synthetic Rubber

Carl Mosk
University of Victoria, British Columbia
Chaebol; Keiretsu; Zaibatsu

Bernardo Mueller
University of Brasília, Brazil
Property Rights in Land: Historical Overview

Reinhold C. Mueller
Università degli Studi di Venezia, Italy
Lane, Frederic Chapin

John H. Munro
University of Toronto
Gresham's Law

Roger Munting
University of East Anglia, Norwich, England
Gambling and Gambling Industry; Sugar

Johann Peter Murmann
Kellogg Graduate School of Management, Northwestern University
Chemical Industries: Chemical Industries after 1850

James M. Murray
University of Cincinnati
Bruges

John E. Murray
University of Toledo
Health

Rahmadi Murwanto
State Accountancy School, Jakarta, Indonesia
Accounting and Bookkeeping

Eric C. Mussen
University of California, Davis
Apiculture

Maria Giuseppina Muzzarelli
Università degli Studi di Bologna, Italy
Monte di Pietà

Barry Naughton
Graduate School of International Relations and Pacific Studies, University of California, San Diego
China: Communist China

Larry Neal
University of Illinois, Urbana-Champaign
Bonds; Capital Markets: Capital Markets before 1750; Government Borrowing: Government Borrowing: 1500–1800; War Finance

Daniel Nelson
University of Akron
Rubber: Manufacturing and Industrial Organization; Taylor, Frederick Winslow

John L. Neufeld
University of North Carolina, Greensboro
Public Utilities: Electricity Supply and Networks

Dianne Newell
University of British Columbia
Fisheries and Fish Processing

Carlos Newland
Universidad Argentina de la Empresa, Buenos Aires
Argentina

David Nicholas
Clemson University
Ghent; Pirenne, Henri

Omar Noman
United Nations Development Program, New York
Pakistan

Douglass North
Washington University, Saint Louis
Markets

Michaël North
Ernst-Moritz-Arndt-Universität Greifswald, Germany
Art Markets; Banking: Middle Ages and Early Modern Period; Fugger Bank; Germany: Early and Medieval Periods

Jeffrey B. Nugent
University of Southern California
Common Goods

John V. C. Nye
Washington University, Saint Louis
Corn Laws; Free Trade; North, Douglass Cecil

Allen Oakley
University of Newcastle, Callaghan, Australia
Schumpeter, Joseph

Kerry A. Odell
Scripps College, Claremont, California
Chavez, Cesar; Mellon Family

James M. O'Donnell
Huntington College
Financial Panics and Crashes

Gur Ofer
Hebrew University, Jerusalem
Russia: Communist Russia

Avner Offer
All Souls College, Oxford
Gifts and Gift Giving

Cormac Ó Gráda
University College Dublin
Famines; Ireland: Ireland from 1800 to 1922 *and* Ireland after 1922; Irish Famine

Maureen O'Hara
Cornell University
Postal Savings

Olatunji Ojo
York University, Toronto
East Africa: Colonial and Modern Periods; Nigeria

Tetsuji Okazaki
University of Tokyo
Tokyo

Andrezj Olechnowicz
University of Durham, England
Public Housing and Housing Policies

Nancy D. Olewiler
Simon Fraser University
Pollution

Martha L. Olney
University of California, Berkeley
Consumer Credit

John Orbell
ING Bank, London
Barings

David Ormrod
Rutherford College, University of Kent, Canterbury, England
Antiques Trade; Museums

W. M. Ormrod
University of York, England
Feudalism: Historical Overview, Manorial System, *and* Taxation

Kevin O'Rourke
Trinity College, Dublin
Long-Distance Trade: Long-Distance Trade between 1750 and 1914

Laura J. Owen
DePaul University
Debs, Eugene Victor

Fabio Padovano
Centro Studi di Economia delle Istituzioni, Dipartimento di Istituzioni Politiche e Scienze Sociali, Università Roma Tre
Corporatism

Bryan D. Palmer
Trent University
Marxism and Marxist Historiography

Colin A. Palmer
Princeton University
Asiento

Ransford W. Palmer
Howard University
Jamaica

Şevket Pamuk
Atatürk Institute, Bo azici University, Istanbul
Ottoman Empire; Prices; Turkey: Premodern Turkey *and* Modern Turkey

Robert Patch
University of California, Riverside
American Indian Economies: Maya Economy

Donald G. Paterson
University of British Columbia
Fur Trapping and Trade; Guinness Family

Robin Pearson
University of Hull, England
Insurance: Historical Overview; Insurance: Fire Insurance

Mark Pendergrast
Colchester, Vermont
Coffee

Peter C. Perdue
Massachusetts Institute of Technology
China: Ming and Qing Dynasties; Silk Road

Edwin J. Perkins
University of Southern California
Brown Family

John Perlin
Santa Barbara, California
Forests and Deforestation; Timber and Logging Industry; Wood as Fuel

Anne Pérotin Dumon
Institute of Latin American Studies, University of London
Piracy

Richard Perren
University of Aberdeen, Scotland
Agricultural Marketing: Agricultural Marketing Boards; Processing Crops

Karl Gunnar Persson
University of Copenhagen
Agricultural Risk Management: Historical Overview

Luciano Pezzolo
Università di Venezia–Ca' Foscari, Italy
Government Borrowing: Government Borrowing before 1500

Christian Pfister
University of Bern, Switzerland
Climate and Climate History

Peter Philips
University of Utah
Gompers, Samuel

Renate Pieper
Karl-Franzens-Universität Graz, Austria
Bullion

Toni Pierenkemper
Universität zu Köln, Germany
Labor Markets: Integration and Wage Convergence

J. P. Platteau
University of Namur, Belgium
Land Inheritance Patterns

Richard Pomfret
University of Adelaide, Australia
Settler Economies

Gilles Postel-Vinay
École des Hautes Études en Sciences Sociales, Paris
Agribusiness

Leandro Prados de la Escosura
Universidad Carlos III de Madrid, Spain
National Income Accounts: Wages and Labor Income

Om Prakash
Delhi School of Economics, India
Bombay; Calcutta; India: Colonial Period; Spices and Spice Trade

Gary John Previts
Weatherhead School of Management, Case Western Reserve University
Accounting and Bookkeeping

Jacob M. Price
University of Michigan
Tobacco

Daniel Raff
Wharton School, University of Pennsylvania
Automobile and Truck Industry: Historical Overview; Ford, Henry

Matthew Ramsey
Vanderbilt University
Health Industry: Medical Practitioners

Adrian Randall
University of Birmingham, England
Luddism and Social Protest

Mark J. Ravina
Emory University
Japan: Ancient and Medieval Periods

Evelyn S. Rawski
University of Pittsburgh
Educational Land

Christopher Read
University of Warwick, Coventry, England
Bakunin, Mikhail

Angela Redish
University of British Columbia
Money and Coinage: General Overview *and* Money and Coinage before 1750

Clyde Reed
Simon Frazer University, Canada
Pollution

Mahesh C. Regmi
Kathmandu, Nepal
Nepal

Jonathan Reinarz
Centre for the History of Medicine, University of Birmingham, England
Health Industry: Hospitals

Johannes M. Renger
Freie Universität Berlin, Germany
Banking: Classical Antiquity; Iran: Ancient Period; Iraq: Ancient Period; Levant: Ancient Period

Terry S. Reynolds
Michigan Technological University
Power Technology

Paul W. Rhode
University of North Carolina, Chapel Hill
Horticulture and Truck Farming

Bonham C. Richardson
Virginia Polytechnic Institute and State University
Caribbean Region: Post-Emancipation Period

David Richardson
University of Hull, England
Slave Demography; Slave Trade

Giorgio Riello
The Open University, Milton Keynes, England
Leather Industry: Tanning

S. H. Rigby
University of Manchester
Serfdom

James C. Riley
Indiana University, Bloomington
Health Industry: Historical Overview

Albrecht Ritschl
University of Zürich
Germany: Modern Germany

Brian K. Roberts
University of Durham, England
Settlement

Richard Roberts
Stanford University
Sahel

Hugh Rockoff
Rutgers, The State University of New Jersey
Friedman, Milton

Catherine Rollet
Université de Versailles, Guyancourt, France
Child Care

Jean-Laurent Rosenthal
University of California, Los Angeles
Water Control

Joan R. Rosés
Universidad Carlos III de Madrid, Spain
National Income Accounts: Wages and Labor Income

Robert I. Rotberg
Harvard University
Rhodes, Cecil John

Elyce J. Rotella
Indiana University, Bloomington
Pawnbroking and Personal Loan Markets

Geoffrey Rothwell
Stanford University
Nuclear Power

James A. Roumasset
University of Hawaii, Manoa
Crop Failures

Marie B. Rowlands
Wolverhampton University, Birmingham, England, Emerita
Black Country

Teofilo F. Ruiz
University of California, Los Angeles
Granada; Seville; Spain: Early and Medieval Periods

S. Ryan Johansson
Cambridge Group for the History of Population and Social Structure
Epidemics

Göran Rydén
Mid Sweden University, Härnösand
Coke Smelting; Metallurgic Industry: Historical Overview *and* Industrial Organization and Markets; Puddling and Rolling

Frank R. Safford
Northwestern University
Colombia

Osamu Saito
Institute of Economic Research, Hitotsubashi University, Tokyo
Age Composition

Victoria Saker Woeste
American Bar Foundation, Chicago
Cooperative Agriculture and Farmer Cooperatives

Ian Savage
Northwestern University
Public Utilities: Mass Transit

Larry Sawers
American University
Navigation Acts

Gary R. Saxonhouse
University of Michigan
Japan: Modern Period

Lorna Scammell
University of Newcastle-upon-Tyne, England
Ceramics

F. M. Scherer
Harvard University
Deregulation; Music Industry

Ekkehart Schlicht
University of Munich
Custom

Peter Scholliers
Vrije Universiteit Brussel, Belgium
Labor Markets: Historical Overview; Wages; Wage Systems

Harm G. Schröter
Universitetet i Bergen, Norway
Health Industry: Pharmaceutical Industry; International Cartels

Max-Stephan Schulze
London School of Economics and Political Science
Austria: Austria before 1867

Leonard Schwarz
University of Birmingham, England
London

George J. Sheridan, Jr.
University of Oregon
Lyon

Abdul Sheriff
Zanzibar Museums, Tanzania
East Africa: Precolonial Period

Pierre L. Siklos
Wilfrid Laurier University, Waterloo, Ontario
Barter and Barter Economies; Inflation and Hyperinflation

Cory Sinclair
University of Utah
Gompers, Samuel

John Singleton
Victoria University of Wellington, New Zealand
Arms Industry: Historical Overview *and* Industrial Organization

Vaclav Smil
University of Manitoba
Agricultural Revolution: Asia, Africa, and the Americas; Fossil Fuels

Anthony Smith
Magdalen College, Oxford
Newspapers: Historical Overview

Harvey Smith
Northern Illinois University
Vines and Viticulture; Wine and Wineries

Margaret M. Smith
University of Reading, England
Printing Industry

Michael E. Smith
State University of New York, Albany
American Indian Economies: General Overview

Richard M. Smith
Cambridge Group for the History of Population and Social Structure, Cambridge, England
Malthus, Thomas

Peter M. Solar
Vesalius College, Brussels
Fiber Crops; Linen Industry: Technological Change; Potato

Solomos Solomou
Peterhouse, Cambridge
Business Cycles

Jay Spaulding
Kean University
Nile

Peter Spufford
Queen's College, Cambridge
Florin

Alan M. Stahl
Dibner Institute for the History of Science and Technology, Massachusetts Institute of Technology
Ducat; Money-Changing: Middle Ages to the Present

Richard H. Steckel
Ohio State University
Anthropometric History

Mark Steele
Institute of Historical Research, School of Advanced Study, University of London
Cadbury Family

Gary P. Steenson
California Polytechnic State University
Kautsky, Karl

Rebecca M. Stein
University of Pennsylvania
Wage Legislation

James I. Stewart
Reed College
Deere, John; Mining: Historical Overview *and* Technological Change; Volcanic Activities and Earthquakes

Sean Stilwell
University of Vermont
Sudan: Central Sudan

Dietrich Stoltzenberg
Hamburg, Germany
Haber, Fritz

Nicolas Stoskopf
Institut d'histoire Moderne et Contemporaine, Paris
Schlumberger Family

Susan Mosher Stuard
Haverford College
Dowry Fund

Robert C. Stuart
Rutgers, The State University of New Jersey
Collective Agriculture and Collectivization

David Sugarman
Law School, Lancaster University, England
Legal Profession

Richard J. Sullivan
Federal Reserve Bank of Kansas City
Patents

William R. Summerhill III
University of California, Los Angeles
Brazil

Yun-Wing Sung
Chinese University of Hong Kong
Hong Kong

David G. Surdam
University of Chicago and University of Oregon
Carnegie, Andrew; Cotton; Taxation: Taxation and Public Revenue; Westinghouse, George

Nathan Sussman
Hebrew University, Jerusalem
Inflation Tax

James A. Swaney
Wright State University
Polanyi, Karl

Richard Sylla
Stern School of Business, New York University
Interest Rates

Rick Szostak
University of Alberta
Road Transportation: Historical Overview; Stephenson Family

Elaine S. Tan
Nuffield College, Oxford, and *University of Michigan Business School*
Land Markets

David W. Tandy
University of Tennessee, Knoxville
Greece: Classical Period and Earlier

Nicholas Tarling
New Zealand Asia Institute, University of Auckland
Malaysia; Myanmar

Joel A. Tarr
Carnegie Mellon University
Sanitation: Sewerage and Urban Drainage

Alan M. Taylor
University of California, Davis
International Capital Flows

Richard S. Tedlow
Harvard Business School
Eastman, George

Alice Teichova
Girton College, Cambridge
Czechoslovakia and the Czech and Slovak Republics

Peter Temin
Massachusetts Institute of Technology
Great Depression; Kindleberger, Charles P.

Patricia M. Thane
University of Sussex, Brighton, England
Income Maintenance: Transfer Payments and Public Assistance; Insurance: Old Age Insurance

Ian D. Thatcher
University of Leicester, England
Trotsky, Leon

John Theibault
Voorhees, New Jersey
Germany: Early Modern Period

Mark Thomas
University of Virginia
Beggar-My-Neighbor Policies; Comparative Advantage and Economic Specialization

Ross Thomson
University of Vermont
Leather Industry: Shoe and Boot Industries

Mark Thornton
College of Business, Columbus State University, Georgia
Taxation: Local Taxation

Atle Thowsen
Bergen Maritime Museum, Norway
Insurance: Maritime Insurance

Richard Tilly
Institut für Wirtschaftsgeschichte, Munich, and *University of Münster, Germany*
Capital Markets: Capital Markets after 1750; Commercial Policy: Customs Unions

Rick Tilman
University of Nevada, Las Vegas, Emeritus
Veblen, Thorstein

Marcel P. Timmer
University of Groningen, The Netherlands
Economic Convergence and Divergence

B. R. Tomlinson
School of Oriental and African Studies, University of London
Great Britain: British Empire; India: Independent India

Keith Trace
Monash University, Victoria, Australia
Water Transportation: Historical Overview

Stanley W. Trimble
University of California, Los Angeles
Soil and Soil Conservation

Werner Troesken
University of Pittsburgh
Public Utilities: Historical Overview *and* Gas Supply and Networks

Michael Turner
University of Hull, England
Agricultural Rents; Cereals; Crop Yields; Enclosures

Carolyn Tuttle
Lake Forest College
Child Labor; Children

Thomas S. Ulen
College of Law, University of Illinois, Urbana-Champaign
Regulation: Historical Overview, Control of Prices, Control of Quantity, Control of Quality, *and* Control of Entry and Exit

Richard W. Unger
University of British Columbia
Beer and Breweries; Water Transportation: Technological Change *and* Ocean Shipping

Deborah Valenze
Barnard College
Dairy Farming

Nuno Valério
Instituto Superior de Economia e Gestão, Universidade Tecnica de Lisboa, Portugal
Portugal: An Overview

Bart van Ark

University of Groningen, The Netherlands
Economic Convergence and Divergence; National Income Accounts: Historical Overview

Ilja van Damme

University of Antwerp, Belgium
Low Countries: Southern Netherlands between 1585 and 1830

Etienne van de Walle

Population Studies Center, University of Pennsylvania
Marriage

Herman van der Wee

Katholieke Universiteit Leuven, Belgium
Wool Industry: Historical Overview *and* Industrial Organization, Markets, and Trade

Pitou van Dijck

Centre for Latin American Research and Documentation (CEDLA), Amsterdam
Guyana

Jan C. van Ours

Tilburg University, The Netherlands
Opium and Narcotics

Raymond van Uytven

Katholieke Universiteit Leuven and *Universiteit Antwerpen, Belgium*
Low Countries: The Low Countries before 1568

Jan Luiten van Zanden

University of Utrecht, The Netherlands
Inequality of Wealth and Income Distribution; Low Countries: Northern Netherlands after 1815

François R. Velde

Federal Reserve Bank of Chicago
Money and Coinage: Money and Coinage after 1750

Andreas Venzke

Freiburg, Germany
Gutenberg, Johannes

Nick Von Tunzelmann

Science Policy Research Unit, University of Sussex, England
Boulton, Matthew; Newcomen, Thomas; Technology

Hans-Joachim KLR Voth

Universitat Pompeu Fabra, Barcelona, and *Centre for History and Economics, King's College, Cambridge*
Labor Time

Jan de Vries

University of California, Berkeley
Long-Distance Trade: Long-Distance Trade between 1500 and 1750; Peasantry

Richard Wall

University of Essex, Colchester, England
Adoption; Household

Immanuel Wallerstein

Yale University and *Binghamton University*
Braudel, Fernand

John Joseph Wallis

University of Maryland, College Park
New Deal; Public Administration

Claire Walsh

University of Warwick, Coventry, England
Retail Trade

Margaret Walsh

School of Canadian and American Studies, University of Nottingham, England
Meatpacking Industry

John R. Walton

University of Wales, Aberstwyth
Animal Husbandry

John K. Walton

University of Central Lancashire, England
Hospitality Industry; Lancashire

Andrew Watson

University of Toronto
Water Engineering

E. Juerg Weber

University of Western Australia
Switzerland: Switzerland before 1815

Simone A. Wegge

City University of New York
Inheritance Systems

Marc D. Weidenmier

Claremont McKenna College
Mutual Funds

Ron Weir

University of York, England
Distilleries and Spirits

Thomas Weiss

University of Kansas
United States: Antebellum Period

Allen Wells

Bowdoin College
Hard Fibers Industry

Robert Whaples

Wake Forest University
Cliometrics; United States: Modern Period

Sam Whimster

London Metropolitan University
Weber, Max

Harrison C. White
Columbia University
Taboos

Luise White
University of Florida
Prostitution

Noel Whiteside
University of Warwick, Coventry, England
Insurance: Health and Accident Insurance *and* Unemployment Insurance

William G. Whitney
Wharton School, University of Pennsylvania
Gerschenkron, Alexander

Olav Wicken
Center for Technology, Innovation, and Culture, University of Oslo
Nordic Countries: Modern Norway

Mira Wilkins
Florida International University
Multinational Corporations

Jeffrey Williams
University of California, Davis
Agricultural Risk Management: Agricultural Price Stabilization; Futures Markets

Samuel H. Williamson
Miami University of Ohio
Cliometrics

Tom Williamson
University of East Anglia, Norwich, England
Meadows and Water Meadows

Onn Winckler
University of Haifa, Israel
Levant: Modern Syria

André Wink
University of Wisconsin, Madison
India: Muslim Period and Mughal Empire

David M. Wishart
Wittenberg University

American Indian Economies: Indigenous North American Economy

Susan Wolcott
University of Mississippi
Campbell, Joseph

John Wong
East Asian Institute, National University of Singapore
Singapore

J. R. Wordie
University of Reading, England
Agriculture: Technological Change

Brian Davern Wright
University of California, Berkeley
Agricultural Risk Management: Storage

Robert E. Wright
Thomas Edison State College, Abington, New Jersey
Local Banks

Chris Wrigley
Nottingham University, England
Unions

Tsong-Min Wu
National Taiwan University, Taipei
Taiwan

Robin D. S. Yates
McGill University
China: Ancient and Feudal China

Bartolomé Yun-Casalilla
Universidad Pablo de Olavide de Sevilla, Spain
Spain: Spanish Empire

Vera Zamagni
Università degli Studi di Bologna, Italy
Italy: United Italy

David Zilberman
University of California, Berkeley
Farming Intensity

Index

Page numbers in boldface refer to the main entry on the subject. Page numbers in *italics* refer to illustrations, maps, figures, and tables. General and historical overviews of a subject are filed immediately following that subject.

government, *cont.*
  Japanese, history of, **3:**190–196
  land ordinances, **3:270–271**
  land reform and confiscations,
    3:271–274
  legal profession and, **3:**287
  leisure industry, **3:**291
  and licenses for monopoly or
    limited-term patents, **3:**444
  literacy and, **3:**338
  living standards and, **3:**348
  long-distance trade and, **3:**369
  lotteries, **3:378–380**
  measure of good governments, **4:**294
  and monopoly, **3:**442, 445
  national accounts and cost of, **4:**33
  national defense and, **4:30–33**
  nationalization and privatization
    and, **4:**54–58
  Nigeria, **4:**92–93
  and oligopolies, **3:**448–449
  origin of revenues, **4:**291
  ownership of productive resources
    and revenue, **5:**61
  planned economic development in
    Prussia, **4:**287
  property rights and, **4:**61–64
  public expenditure priorities of,
    4:39–41
  public health and, **2:**225–226
  and public housing, **4:**303–304
  and pure competition, **3:**441
  regulation of economy after Great
    Depression, **2:**466
  rent seeking and, **4:**365–366
  and restoration of pure competition,
    3:441–442
  road transportation and, **4:**384–385
  size, **4:**288–290
    historically, **4:**290–293
  sources of revenue, **5:**61
  in South Korean development,
    3:224–226
  structure, **4:**288–290
    historically, **4:**290–293
  tourism and, **3:**294
  Venezuela, **5:**192
  and water control, **5:**220
government bonds. *See* bonds
government borrowing, **2:437–445**.
  See also public debt
  after 1800, **2:441–445**
  before 1500, **2:437–439**

government borrowing, *cont.*
  capital markets and, **1:**326–333
  from 1500 to 1800, **2:439–441**
  to finance wars, **5:**67
  and financing of war, **5:**218
  as origins of stock markets, **5:**23
  Pakistan, **4:**156
  perpetual annuities in England, **5:**67
  war and, **5:**215
  and war finance, **5:**219
Government Habit, The (Hughes),
  2:549
Government of India Act (1935), **3:**30
Government Rubber-Styrene (GR-S),
  4:408–409
Goyen, Jan van, **1:**168
Grabbing Hand, The (Shleifer and
  Vishny), **4:**294
Grabski, Władysław, **4:**205
Graham, George, **1:**451
Graham, Sylvester, **2:**343
Grain Office (Venice), **2:**108–109
grain storage, **2:**340. *See* granaries
  China, ancient, **1:**423
  grain banks in Anuradhapura, **5:**9
  state storage discouraging private
    storage, **1:**55
Gramme, Zénobe Théophile, **2:**180, 181
Gramm-Leach-Bliley Act (1999, U.S.),
  1:233
Gramophone, **3:**75
Gramsci, Antonio, **2:445–446; 3:**464
Granada, **2:446–447**
granaries. *See* grain storage
  antiquity, **1:**51, 55
  China, **1:**51
    Han dynasty, **1:**58
    Qing dynasty, **1:**54, 55
  salt purchased at, **4:**439
Gran Chaco region, **1:**378–379
Grandes Chroniques de France, **2:**254
Grand National Consolidated Trades
  Union, **4:**150
The Grandsons of François de
  Wendel, **5:**263
Grand Tour, **1:**138; **3:**293
Grand Trunk Railway, **1:**315–316
Granger Laws (U.S.), railroad
  regulation and, **4:**346
Granger movement cooperatives, **2:**2
Grantham, George, **4:**240
  consumption data, **1:**527
  on peasantry, **4:**176

Gras, N. S. B., **3:**278
grassland farming, **2:447**
Graunt, John, **3:**85
Gray, **3:**413
Gray, Elisha, **1:**253; **3:**73; **5:**92
Gray, John, **4:**150
grazing and ranch farming, **1:**87;
  2:447–449
  Canada, **1:**317
  cattle, **1:**355–356
  Central South America, **1:**378, 379
  conflicts with homesteaders in
    United States, **2:**528
  Honduras, **2:***448*
Great Britain, **2:449–459**. *See also*
    British Empire; England;
    Scotland; Wales
  actors, **5:**109
  advertising agencies, **1:**10
  aggregate economic growth,
    1700–1860, **5:***130tab1*
  agriculture (*see also* enclosures)
    cattle, **1:**355
    combine harvesters, **1:**84
    cooperative, **2:**2
    crop yields, **2:**49–51
    dairy farming, **2:**62–63
    early agriculture, **1:**77
    and EEC policy, **1:**36
    intensive mixed farming, **3:**528
    productivity of labor in farming,
      1:79–80
    protectionism, **1:**30
    tenant farming, **4:**52–53
    tractors, **1:**84
    wages, **1:**59
    wheat, **1:**383–384
  aircraft industry, **1:**98, 101
  air transportation, **1:**104
  alkali industry, **1:**403
  antitrust policy, **1:**139, 142
  arms industry, **1:**161, 163
  art market, **1:**171–172
  automobile industry, **1:**192
  Babbage and, **1:**201
  Baltic states and, **1:**213
  banking, **1:**229–230
    Barings, **1:**241–242
    commercial (deposit) banks,
      3:134–135
    interest rates, **3:**115
    investment banks, **3:**135–136
    Peel Act on, **1:**233

Native Americans. *See* American
Indian economies
Natives Land Act (1913, South Africa),
4:535
natural disasters. *See also* volcanic
activities and earthquakes
Central America, **1:**368
crop failures, **2:**45–47
and famine, **2:**269
hurricanes in the Caribbean region,
1:337
Korea, **3:**224
and price differentials for
agricultural products, **1:**29
natural gas, **2:**356, 360, 392, 394;
4:310. *See also* gas industry;
public utilities: gas supply and
network
liquefied for transportation, **4:**310
produced in the United States, **5:**168
Natural Gas Act (1938, U.S.), **2:**198
Natural Gas Policy Act (1978, U.S.),
2:198
natural monopolies, **3:**445
economies of scale and, **2:**156
environmental issues and, **4:**56–57
nationalization and privatization
and, **4:**55–56
price controls and, **4:**353
public utilities as, **4:**304–305
natural rate of unemployment, **5:**146
natural resources, **4:**58–67
historical overview, **4:**58–61
Britain, **2:**204
Central Africa, **1:**362
Chile, **1:**419, 420
as common goods, **1:**492–493
environmental regulation and, **2:**221
German shortage of and search for
synthetic resources, **5:**88
Iraq, **3:**147
labor mobility and, **3:**248
Ming and Qing dynasties (China),
1:431
New Zealand, **4:**87–88
nonrenewable, United States as
world's leading producer, **5:**168
North Africa, **4:**115–116
Norway, **4:**103
property rights, **4:61–64**
common property, **2:**330
railroads and, **4:**331
regulation, **4:64–67**

natural resources, *cont.*
Russia, **4:**426
U.S. use of, **2:**223
Nature of Capital and Income, The
(Fisher), **1:**529
"Nature of the Firm, The" (Coase),
3:427
Naucratis, **2:**469
Nauplia, **2:**473
naval industry
and American System, **2:**250
Hanseatic League and, **2:**497
and hemp, **2:**499
Ottoman Empire, **4:**147
Navarrus. *See* Azpilcueta, Martín de
navigation
advances in, **5:**244
celestial, **5:**244
charts, **5:**244
clock making and, **1:**449–450, 451
contracts and, **1:**534
instruments, **5:**244
long-distance trade, **3:**362–363, 364
techniques in Spanish Empire, **4:**541
Navigation Acts (Britain), **2:**450;
4:67–68; 5:15, 255, 256
balance of trade, **1:**486
beggar-my-neighbor policies and,
1:250
cliometrics on, **1:**446–447
Ireland and, **3:**158
and mercantilism, **3:**485
Naylor, George, **5:**196
Naylor, Hutchinson, Vickers and
Company, **5:**195–196
Nazis. *See* national socialism
Near East Development Corporation,
4:132
necatoriasis, **2:**91*tab1*, 93
Necker, Jacques, **5:**68
NEC (Northeast Center) model of
development in Italy, **3:**184
Nedham, Marchamont, **4:**75
needles
in Germany, **2:**408
mass production, **3:**409
Negropont, **2:**473
Nehru, Jawaharlal, **3:**34
Neilson, James B., **3:**495
blast furnace, **3:**51
*Neither Man nor Animal is Immune to
the Plague* (Weiditz), **2:***86*
Nelson, Horatio, **3:**72

Nelson, Ralph L., **3:**107
Nelson, Richard, **2:**129
neoclassical economics
analysis of female labor supply,
5:273–274
cliometrics, **1:**447
growth theory and national
accounts, **4:**33
institutional models of wages, **5:**204
labor markets in, **3:**238–239
and peasantry, **4:**174
theory of marriage, **3:**455
unemployment, **3:**238
on wages, **3:**238; **5:**203
Neo-Malthusians, **1:**60; **3:**425–426
neopopulism and peasantry, **4:**174
neoprene. *See* synthetic rubber
Nepal, **4:68–70**
nepotism of early companies, **2:**317
Ness, Eliot, **4:**143
Nestlé, **2:**339
coffee, **1:**463
oligopoly, **3:**446
Nestlé, Henri, **5:**45
Nestlé, Karl, **4:**179
Nestorians, **3:**308
Net Book Agreement, **1:**278, 282
Netherland Bank, **3:**545
Netherlands. *See also* Dutch empire;
Low Countries
agriculture
capital-intensive, **2:**274
integrated pest management
(IPM), **4:**181–182
output, **1:**42, *43fig1*
polders, **1:**35, 79
potato cultivation, **4:**242
bonds and, **1:**271
canals, **5:**252–253
cheese making, **2:***63*
chemical industry, **1:**401
consumer credit, **1:***520tab2*
corporatism, **2:**9
cotton industry, **2:**29
distilleries and spirits, **2:**95
early open trade of, **2:**380–381
education, **2:**160
enrollment statistics, **2:***162tab1,
163tab2*
European Monetary System and,
2:240–241
gambling, **2:**390
gold standard, **2:**430